# NOTES OF A SON AND BROTHER

# *and* THE MIDDLE YEARS

# Notes of a Son and Brother *and* The Middle Years A CRITICAL EDITION

## Henry James

*Edited by* PETER COLLISTER

UNIVERSITY OF VIRGINIA PRESS

*Charlottesville and London*

University of Virginia Press

© 2011 by the Rector and Visitors of the University of Virginia

All rights reserved

Printed in the United States of America on acid-free paper

*First published 2011*

9  8  7  6  5  4  3  2  1

Library of Congress Cataloging-in-Publication Data

James, Henry, 1843–1916.

Notes of a son and brother : and The middle years /
Henry James ; edited by Peter Collister.

p. cm.

Includes bibliographical references and index.

ISBN 978-0-8139-3083-1 (cloth : alk. paper)

ISBN 978-0-8139-3084-8 (pbk. : alk. paper)

ISBN 978-0-8139-3090-9 (e-book)

1. James, Henry, 1843–1916. I. Collister, Peter. II. James, Henry,
1843–1916. Middle years. III. Title.

PS2120.N6    2011

813′.4—dc22

2010038522

# CONTENTS

# ACKNOWLEDGMENTS

The many biographical works on Henry James and the James family have proved an excellent initial resource in preparing this edition of the novelist's autobiographical writings, as the references in my notes will indicate. For facts about the family background and relationships, Katherine Hastings's genealogical study, "William James (1771–1832) of Albany, N.Y., and His Descendants," offers absolutely accurate detail. Though he has suffered some posthumous disfavor, Leon Edel remains an influential and persuasive voice by means of the broad scope of his endeavors, biographical and editorial. F. O. Matthiessen's *The James Family* contains useful material and commentary relating both to Henry James Sr. and to William James. Robert C. Le Clair's *Young Henry James* offers especially interesting detail on the novelist's playgoing experiences in New York, London, and Paris, and R. W. B. Lewis in *The Jameses* provides insights into the dynamics of family life and the Civil War period.

More recently, Sheldon Novick has constructed a revised and imaginative (if sometimes unreliable) portrait of the novelist's earlier years in *Henry James: The Young Master.* Especially useful for the chapters relating to James's cousin, Mary (Minny) Temple, has been Lyndall Gordon's *A Private Life of Henry James: Two Women and His Art,* while the multivolume edition of the *Correspondence of William James,* edited by Ignas Skrupskelis and Elizabeth M. Berkeley, has been indispensable, especially when considering the Jameses' Cambridge years. Jane Maher's *Biography of Broken Fortunes* was particularly informative about the Civil War years and the lives of Wilky and Bob James.

Because of the wealth of its meticulously researched detail and depth of insight I have been very reliant (as my notes will testify) on Alfred Habegger's *The Father: A Life of Henry James Sr.,* a model of biographical method. Like many others working on the James family, I have received help and encouragement from Professor Habegger, who has been kind enough to read through some of my work and to share his extensive knowledge. Pierre A. Walker has been similarly generous, offering consistently thoughtful and practical advice.

For generously allowing me to quote from previously unpublished James MS materials I am indebted to Bay James, on behalf of the James family, and to Leslie A. Morris, curator of modern books and manuscripts in the Harvard College Library, on behalf of the president and fellows of Harvard College.

During the preparation of this edition I was fortunate to be awarded the Stanley J. Kahrl Fellowship in Literary Manuscripts, Houghton Library, Harvard University. I was grateful for such an endorsement of my project and for the financial support it provided. It was a pleasure to work in such an inspirational environment. All the staff at Houghton were uniformly kind and helpful, and I must mention by name Leslie A. Morris, Peter Accardo, Susan Halpert, and Mary Haegert, who have continued to support my work.

I have also benefited from the excellent resources and the support of the expert staff at the British Library (where I have been helped especially by Jenny Grimshaw, Dorian Hayes, Lyn Norvell, Lisa Oladeinde, Tim Pye, and Matthew Shaw). The staff of the London Library (from where my cycle ride home necessarily involved passing one of James's earliest London addresses, in Half Moon Street) have been characteristically helpful—especially so, in light of the Library's major building project currently in progress. I also used the resources of The Bodleian Library, Oxford, and was made welcome at the Vere Harmsworth Library, Rothermere American Institute, Oxford, where Isabel Holowaty proved very generous in offering me both time and advice. Carroll Odhner, Director of the Swedenborg Library, Bryn Athyn College, Pennsylvania, was very helpful with my queries about Swedenborg. The New England Historic Genealogical Society and the Massachusetts Historical Society also provided me with information.

Many individuals—on both sides of the Atlantic—have offered information and advice and I am grateful to the following: Peter C. Caldwell, Charles Capper, Jack Furniss, Joseph E. Glatthaar, Elaine Grublin, Charles J. Hayes, Celia Heath, Eric Homberger, Park Honan, Steven C. Jobe, Richard Kaufman, Jack Lucy, James M. McPherson, Adeline Morris, William S. Peterson, Jeanne Ritchie, Letha Clair Robertson, Frida Robinson, David J. Rothman, Roberta Sheehan, Richard Sheldon, Alan Steel, Christopher A. Strong, Hannah Sullivan, Kathryn Summerwill, James L. Yarnall, and Greg Zacharias. Any remaining errors are undoubtedly my own.

A very kind woman in Newport, Rhode Island, whose name I didn't get, when asked for directions, insisted on driving me to the stone house on the corner of Spring and Lee streets inhabited by the Jameses in the early 1860s. Its current owner, Charles J. Hayes, welcomed an unannounced stranger and insisted on my viewing the whole place. Nearer home, my string quartet–playing friends have consistently shown more-than-polite interest in my work.

The anonymous readers of my original proposal for the University of Virginia Press made useful suggestions, and Cathie Brettschneider, the Press's Humanities Editor, has been a constant and very supportive presence; I have deeply appreciated her kindness and intelligence. In recent months, Ruth Melville has proved to be an exemplary copy editor of the manuscript, and I have valued her expert advice. Morgan Myers has also been a helpful and responsive project editor. Finally, John Aplin has spared me much time from his own large-scale biographical studies of the Thackeray family and has helped me with many of the challenges—often technological—that have inevitably arisen over the years.

# INTRODUCTION

The sustained prose of *Notes of a Son and Brother* frequently laments the abject state of its author, beset by supplicating ghosts, the presences of remembered figures requesting some memorial. Such powerfully eloquent voices caused him, so he confesses, to sink into "depths of concession" as he scanned despairingly the piles of letters and documents that constituted the matter of family history. This is the version of the composing condition projected by the text, a mood also familiar from the asides and interjections of *The American Scene;* but another exercise of power is also evident. Behind the helpless rhetorical front, James was promoting a magisterial control not only at a lexical level— every document assimilated into these volumes has been edited and revised by him—but also at a level encompassing scale and even time, as he attempted to shape the form, content, tone, of the biographical interest that he foresaw would pursue his name. Of course the gap between the artist as represented through his work and his more mundane, domestic operation, dramatized in a variety of sequences, constitutes the sometimes conflicted thematics of many of James's narratives (invariably applied to a male rather than female artist). Perhaps for more than any other writer, his fiction offers a reflexive commentary on art and creativity, those anomalies between the conditions of the imperturbable art object and its human, more vulnerable creator. They have provided inviting metonymic parallels for many versions of James interpreted across a range of identities defined broadly by culture, class, gender, sexuality, and race.

On the question of his own biographical self, James exercised over the long term an enduring form of control through the systematic destruction of his manuscript material and of letters received, thus closing off two sources of inquiry. The plentiful and often voluminous letters he sent strictly compartmentalize his daily experience, thus ensuring a form of confidentiality to the circles in which he moved. Ironically, his injunction that his letters should be destroyed was ignored (understandably) by many of their recipients. Indeed some of the fiction foresaw the disquieting powerlessness of the individual, the dangers that might threaten his or her privacy, human impotence in the face of inevitable mortality, and, conversely, the potentially dubious motives of those who later come to seek the truth. The aspiring biographer in "The Real Right Thing," granted access to the rich materials and endorsed by the artist's widow, has a momentarily simple reminder that the "artist was what he *did*—he was nothing else" before he finally repents. The spirit of the subject has suddenly withdrawn his blessing and his biographer is compelled to realize the intrusive, objectifying nature of his trade: "We lay him bare. We serve him up. What is it called? We give him to the world."[1] Only in a supernatural dimension can such a deal be enacted between the alert living and the petitioning dead. The result is, of course, that the dead rest in peace and the biographical act is abandoned. In more complicated circumstances, the posthumous privacy of Jeffrey Aspern is maintained only by the defeat of the admirer, frightened off by the bargain offered to him at the end of *The Aspern Papers* and by his own sexual anxiety at the unpalatable prospect of marriage—his life and body in exchange for those unique and long-desired papers.

*Notes of a Son and Brother* lays down the conditions—as James came to decide them—of the stage of life that succeeded the illness and end of boyhood in *A Small Boy and Others*. The narrative, which opens in Europe but quickly shifts to New England, once again predicates and evaluates its insights upon the cumulative experience of the growing artist: anecdotal detail, selections from letters, moments of national significance —all are allocated a place and a weight as the subject plots (in two senses) his own emergence from his contingent, family-bound self. Every item— even the written words of other speakers—is subjected to the author's revisionary approval. Though the degree of self-reflexiveness and under-mining of the genre betoken postmodern directives, the extent of authorial mastery within the text and in extratextual matters may remind us of more traditional, Victorian strategies. Henry James's can be seen as a form of monologic text, monologism described by Martin A. Danahay, following the theory of Bakhtin, as "a denial of alterity, as the writing subject represses the role of the social in the construction of his or her subjectivity. Monologic texts therefore involve a repression of other voices, as the writer seeks mastery over the unsettling forces of the contingent."[2] James's investment is pointedly in the self, the accumulation of experience that might explain the mature artist. Other voices are to be heard in *Notes of a Son and Brother,* but they have been subjected to initial screening and preparation so as to conform with the narrative decided upon. The seeming freestanding independence of a signed letter and its apparent oppor-tunity to introduce a form of alterity of experience or reference is, in reality, much compromised. It is this highly interventionist rationale that would antagonize the author's immediate family, as we shall see later.

*Notes of a Son and Brother* covers the years of James's adolescence and young manhood. After spells in Switzerland and Germany the James family have returned to the United States, spending the years of James's young manhood in Newport, Rhode Island, and in Cambridge. The influential and Europeanized figures of the artists William Morris Hunt and John La Farge give way to his realization of the native moment, an apprehension of "Americanism" (a term he will return to), felt first during his abortive year of study at Harvard Law School and his introduction to the locations and inhabitants of New England. Without direct experience of the Civil War, James turns to the in-the-field observations of his younger brother Wilky, while recalling affectionately the physical presence of the young Union soldiers he encountered far from the arena of battle. The volume concludes with the sequence of letters of the dying young woman Mary Temple (traditionally known as Minny), a remarkably original and free-spirited cousin of the Jameses, whose memory was invoked by the novelist in the sequence of heroines of his mature fiction.

The whole project of recording the recollected figures and events of his earliest family years had been prompted by William James's widow, Alice Howe Gibbens James, and there is ample evidence that his impromptu, conversational reminiscences could be mesmerizing.[3] The initial premise —a selection of William's letters embedded in accompanying material from his younger brother—had soon to be adjusted as the latter's memories themselves took over the first volume. Letters began to cross the Atlantic as James extended his interest: he requested more of his brother's early letters, more of his father's slender correspondence, ironically oblivious to his own long-term policy of destroying letters. The narrative of *Notes of a Son and Brother* terminates in 1870, and a good selection of William's letters covers these years. But the inclusion of the letters of their father, Henry James Sr., introduces a broader perspective as the great names of New England intellectual life and the transcendentalist movement of the midcentury emerge. James Sr.'s developing relationship with Emerson, his philosophical interchanges with Charles Elliot Cabot, help illustrate an aspect of the older man's personality admired by his son, while, in contrast, his letters to women friends in the literary circles of Boston and Cambridge reveal a more mannered, even flirtatious and familiar side.

With their precise detail of names and places and the ongoing events of the Civil War in the Southern states, Wilky James's letters report a range of experience from which Henry himself was excluded. In their recounting of everyday army life, harsh conditions, and physical privations, they supplement the eroticized, lyrical impressions of recuperating or training soldiers by means of which the novelist himself addresses the question of the war earlier in the volume. He is himself aware of the Whitmanesque tenderness of these brief episodes, the "brothering conditions" that he finds so novel, the "common Americanism" of their situation. His own mysterious injury, the "obscure hurt" (*NSB,* 254, 253, 240) sustained in a recent Newport fire which may partly explain his noncombatant status, is translated in typically challenging late Jamesian style into a more abstract historical trauma, fusing national suffering with individual anguish, his own body a self-designated site of the general rebellion. Cousins and other young men of the Jameses' privileged New England circle did enlist in the Union regiments, however, including Oliver Wendell Holmes Jr. and John Chipman Gray, the recipient of Mary Temple's letters. James never became one of those described in Holmes's published war letters and diaries as "touched with fire," and his letters and autobiographical writings confess to a sense of exclusion, experience missed, even a form of manhood unachieved.

Neither the words of his sister, Alice, nor those of his mother find a place in this autobiographical exercise, and so the only emergent female voice is that of Mary Temple. She had been dear to him, as *Notes of a Son and Brother* testifies, and the dispatch by Alice Howe Gibbens James of the letters written in the last year of her life must have revived for the novelist a tangible, momentous sense of his own youthful years. Mary Temple's manner can be anecdotal and conversational, though she also raises spiritual uncertainties that, in the light of her imminent death from tuberculosis at twenty-four, cast a poignant shadow across the domestic detail and plans. The nature of James's editing of these letters is discussed elsewhere,[4] yet Mary Temple's discourse—like that of other contributors —is identifiably distinct from the text in which it is placed. Most of the original versions of William James's letters can be read in print,[5] but even in his brother's revising hands they retain a directness and concision that contrast with the surrounding prose. Even allowing for youthful spirits, William can be patronizing toward women—especially his sister Alice.[6] The origins of those attitudes, which illustrate masculine behaviors, can be traced to their father's dealings with forbidden or unavailable women—

specific and familial exempla rather than more generally reflective of the culture of the day. Writing to Annie Fields, the young wife of the prominent Boston publisher and center of a circle that welcomed eminent literary visitors, Henry James Sr. coyly incorporates admiring, affectionate sentiments within the safety-inducing framework of his own marriage and family, or of his friendly (if at times tense) relationship with her husband. A letter to Jane Norton, a member of the eminent Cambridge family, written on her departure for Europe, relishes the intimate pleasures of speaking tête-à-tête and in confidence, as if decorously testing the boundaries of friendship. Writing to another married friend in the circle of transcendentalists, Caroline Sturgis Tappan, he invites a mood of intimacy, making affectionate and flattering play with her name.

In a spirit of eulogy, James allows these letters to represent his father's relaxed and most charming side (though he had difficulty in selecting material that was not too domestic or private), while his father's letters to Ralph Waldo Emerson (whom he met in 1842) and to Charles Elliot Cabot (later Emerson's editor and the author of a memoir) illustrate the more serious, philosophical thinker. James's text makes no attempt to analyze the content of James Sr.'s theorizing, which in any case was more temperamentally congenial to William James, who edited their father's posthumous *Literary Remains*. Instead, he recounts scenes from his father's life—working all morning at home—while asserting the admirable unity between his writing and his temperament, or the quality of mind or spirit in a recalled tone of voice. Despite being aware of the public neglect accorded his father's work and ideas, James was probably in no position to offer any form of summary that might tempt new readers. When recalling Henry James Sr.'s breakdown or "vastation" in 1844, the novelist, rather than charting its emotional or spiritual motives, speculates on the conversation he might have had with Mrs. Chichester, the person who offered a form of long-term redemption by means of the ideas of Emanuel Swedenborg, admitting his preference for the dramatic appeal of the episode. The novelist appears particularly reluctant to address the minutiae or even the broader outlines of his father's philosophical or religious opinions, or indeed to speculate on his psychological health at certain periods of his life. Other facets of his father's life seem to have been modified in these recollections. The impact of James Sr's meeting with Emerson ranged beyond shared intellectual sympathies into a highly emotional, demanding relationship in which he sought the other man's approval and affection. The sometimes abject tone of the letters (he was invariably frank in expressing emotion) disregards the conventional codes of behavior between men as, from the center of a young, growing family, he longs for a deeper intimacy.[7] At other times, as if perhaps to normalize the emotional excesses of his father's language, James names his sister rather than himself as the recipient of certain letters, though he may have intended to render himself more independent or masculine by this change.

The editing and revising of this material around which the volume is composed was, by current (and even contemporary) standards, cavalier. James's changes ranged from the single-word level to larger-scale recasting of material, and even the invention of fresh matter. But, from the beginning, its initial intention to present a number of William James's letters and its later development into a "Family Book" reflect an uncertainty of genre. What is clear, though, is the novelist's conviction—he is, after all, the final surviving and thus autonomous member of this group—that the material belongs to him and will be subject to what he modestly refers to as his "own weaving hand" (*NSB*, 235). In all tenderness he confidently invokes his credentials as an artist when he writes to Alice Howe Gibbens James to thank his nephew for forwarding typed copies of William James's letters. He will write to him directly,

> & will then tell him how I am entirely at one with him about the *kind* of use to be made by me of all these early things, the kind of setting they must have, the kind of encompassment that the book, as *my* book, my play of reminiscence & almost of brotherly autobiography & filial autobiography not less, must enshrine them in. The book I see & feel will be difficult & unprecedented & perillous [*sic*]—but if I bring it off it will be exquisite & unique; bring it off as I inwardly project it & oh so devoutly desire it.[8]

The stresses and underlinings, the emphases, the centrality of "I," the breathless rhythms, could not more fully express this son and brother's aspiring possession of the past and his faith in the text he will achieve.

The process of "setting," "encompassment," and enshrining of these past documents has clear epistemological weight for James, the context decisive in establishing each voice's message. An incident of 1908, occurring before William James's death, casts additional and more equivocal light on the younger brother's assumed guardianship of the family reputation. He had known that his sister Alice kept a diary up to the time of her death in 1892, and when her partner and carer Kathleen Loring brought out four privately printed unexpurgated copies in 1894, his response was immediate and decisive. He destroyed his copy and hoped she would do the same. The question of the diary seems to have arisen again in 1908, as emerges in a letter to his nephew Harry. Its existence constitutes an affront to his lifelong commitment to propriety and privacy. He argued that without "collateral light"—the perspective available only to her contemporaries—the document in the hands of posterity could be no more than a "profanation." Miss Loring eventually ensured that he failed in this attempt to silence his sister, but the gesture marks his conviction both that such records needed to be placed within an informed framework and that personal privacy must be protected:

> I have always been very nervous about the little volume in question
> and about its perpetuation now that the immediate family to whom the
> writer was known (and who will be the last to have thereby the right
> and indispensable and only aid to appreciation or understanding of it)
> have thoroughly assimilated and possessed themselves of it, got all the
> "good" of it that it concerns, or can concern, anyone to get. Its
> survival of *us,* to generations without collateral light about it, strikes
> me as so sad a profanation, absolutely, that I mean to propose to your
> Dad and to the possessor of the other copy (on my next best
> opportunity) that we agree to destroy it, each our own copy,—feeling
> that it will by then have lived all its life. This is at least the way I feel
> about the matter now; and there is a good deal more to be said from
> the point of view of my own connection with the period during which
> it was kept, and my responsibility, showing everywhere, for so many of
> the "indiscretions" contained in it. That is all for the present.[9]

With its bold assertions that readers beyond the immediate family will be unable to appreciate the journal, and that those members are now somehow—and questionably—in possession of all that needs to survive of its contents, and with its appeal to family loyalty, James evidently hopes to win over his nephew. But his final added point reveals his most pressing motive: he may himself be compromised and revealed as indiscreet in what he had confided—perhaps as a diversion—to his bedridden sister (he had, after all, always enjoyed gossip). It could result—as he had pointed out years earlier—in "some catastrophe of publicity."[10] Most damning of all, of course, is the silence, not of the brother, but of the major critic: the document preserved by Miss Loring reveals the original and courageous spirit of someone who enjoyed hardly any public or social life and whose only memorial is, indeed, her diary, which survived despite her brother's efforts.

In relation to family, then, James proves to be a highly controlling influence, determining the terms on which information is to be disclosed, vetoing certain initiatives, benignly, if self-interestedly, while guarding others. Within the narrative of *Notes of a Son and Brother* only some of the unresolved conflict between close family members emerges. He allows Minny Temple's critical comment about his father—during her illness she found his words "neither reasonable nor consoling"—to remain. According to Habegger, as a person "restless, intellectual, female,"[11] she could not have failed to antagonize Henry James Sr., whose views on women (despite his liberality of religious attitudes) were predominantly retrogressive and whose behavior was patronizing. Questioning or contradicting her uncle's opinions, Mary—whether or not defying the gender conventions of the time—had clearly challenged the behavioral code assented to within the James family. But as an orphaned niece, she was free of a direct, emotionally powerful influence. It is generally agreed, though, that the debilitating ill health suffered by William, Henry, and Alice James in their late adolescence and lasting through their twenties was psychosomatic in origin. Both brothers endured back problems and chronic constipation which may have been exacerbated by bad diet and the exigencies of long-distance travel; William was also troubled by his eyes (possibly relating to his trip to Brazil) and by depressive illness; Alice had suicidal phases and a form of hysteria and nervous affliction described as neurasthenia. Howard M. Feinstein has interpreted illness, its treatment strategies and the discourses surrounding it, within the historical context of New England society,[12] but the tensions within the James family—William, for instance, came to find life at Quincy Street "loathsome," Henry found it "about as lively as the inner sepulchre"[13]—resulted in repressed rage seeking to find an outlet.[14] In this setting, as Carol Holly has proposed, "negative affect will be repressed, shameful secrets suppressed, conflict avoided, and intense loyalty and dependency fostered for the sake of family harmony and order."[15]

Though the difficult later lives of Wilky and Bob James are sensitively referred to in *Notes of a Son and Brother,* James is understandably silent on the damaging familial tensions of the children's formative years, and indeed, he eulogizes both parents. His fiction, as has been pointed out, is, on the other hand, rich in ill-functioning families. A degree of mystery hangs about Henry James Sr.'s early years, but the evidence of a successful, overbearing father (William James of Albany), youthful rebellion, alcohol dependency,[16] and a rift that threatened to slash his inheritance suggests that the experience helped determine the dynamics of his new family. James Sr.'s siblings were also compelled (with only partial success) to accommodate over the long term the effects of their childhoods, and Henry James discreetly mentions some of these uncles in his recollections. Some died young, while others, as if fulfilling their autocratic father's worst fears, and despite their charms, lived in a piecemeal way, sometimes on the verges of society. In the next generation, of Mary Temple's two brothers, one became a Civil War hero and victim, while the other drifted into criminal fraud and jail. James Sr., eventually in receipt of a substantial bequest that left him "leisured for life,"[17] did little to develop such an advantage, spending freely when he chose, justifying expensive European trips (skimmed over by his son), yet failing to support his children equally, and discouraging his sons from cultivating specific career ambitions.[18]

Henry James's position within the family is most revealingly clarified in the context of the Civil War. He was eighteen when it began. The two older brothers were regarded as unfit for service while the two younger boys both enlisted, with their father's compliance. While Wilky and Bob (in their brother's representation) are initiated into lives conventionally designated masculine—actively engaged in warfare, enduring physical deprivation, free of parental influence, witnessing new and sometimes terrible sights, struggling to set themselves up in a new postbellum business enterprise in the defeated South—James regards himself as passive and recumbent, an invalid confined to a couch and reading books, occasionally vibrating to the physical presence of a Union soldier but regretting the opportunity for life-changing experience. Within the family he had been known as "Angel," a benign, gender-neutral familiar whose function, according to Jean Strouse, in taking "the place that might have been filled by the only girl in another family," may well have compounded Alice James's difficulties and their increasingly dramatic expression in nervous-physical illness. Strouse goes on to invoke the suggestion of Henry's most influential biographer; Edel summarizes the novelist's innermost creative impulse as assuming "the spirit of a young adult female, worldly-wise and curious, possessing a treasure of unassailable virginity and innocence and able to yield to the masculine active world-searching side of James an ever-fresh and exquisite vision of feminine youth and innocence."[19] By contrast, the beloved Mary Temple, in her noncompliant, assertive manner, an envied orphan, defiant of age, gender, the decorum of her time, offered not only a conceivably masculine pattern of behavior but a heroism to inspire later tragic protagonists.

The template for such querying of roles and functions is introduced by the aging, recollecting author, and the location for his own field of battle (metaphorical, at least) is the expanse of Harvard Yard.[20] James spent 1862–63 studying law before conceding defeat. Having discovered a common "Americanism" in his interchanges with the young soldiers he visited far from the field of battle, "the soldier single and salient" in his romantic otherness, the author develops in this less familiar New England setting a further sense of nation. Despite his childhood years passed in Albany and New York City and, more recently, Newport, a place filled with nostalgia for Europe, James finds in Cambridge and Boston ("the city by the Charles") a further, authentic national identity. Removed for the time from family, he observes its characteristics by means of some dull law professors and their young students, appreciated as products, "unabsorbed and unreconciled" (*NSB*, 249, 275), of New England. He asserts rather than illustrates such insights, though the remembered death of Hawthorne inspires a more precise and deliberate defining of national moment. He shed tears at the loss of this local, persuasive voice, though it is clear that such a model of creative life, affirming a national culture, failed to prevent what he characterizes as an inevitable and permanent return to Europe.

Leaving Cambridge in 1869, the young James could have imagined no romantic possibilities to be accessed by the aspiring artist, and indeed it wasn't until his final two return trips, of 1904–5 and 1910–11, that he seems to have engaged with the promise as well as the vulgarity of American culture, as *The American Scene* and the unfinished novel *The Ivory Tower* testify. In a letter of 1913, written to his Cambridge-based sister-in-law when he felt lonely and ill and only slowly "wriggling up" again, he confessed his inability ever to consider returning to America. His repugnance relates less to the circumstances of contemporary life than to a fear of being subsumed within the past, a fear lightly but powerfully related to location, but also (the grammatical referents remain loose) to the dynamics of the James family. The conviction of dark and fatally enduring consequences might have been recognized by both his sister Alice and William, in the light of their own suicidal anxieties and psychosomatic afflictions:

> Dearest Alice, I could come back to America (could be carried back on a stretcher) to *die*—but never, never to live. To say how the question affects me is dreadfully difficult because of its appearing

so to make light of you and the children—but when I think of how little Boston and Cambridge were of old ever *my* affair, or anything but an accident, for me, of the parental life there to which I occasionally and painfully and losingly sacrificed, I have a superstitious terror of seeing them at the end of time again stretch out strange inevitable tentacles to draw me back and destroy me.[21]

Such lasting dread and remembered sacrifice (his parents had been dead for more than a generation) remain within the private sphere of the aging novelist's letters. Yet the anguish he feels—however excessive it may now appear—may derive its force from some unresolved, unspecified familial trauma of adolescence, aside from the recorded unhappy experiences as a law student and the later disappointment with Cambridge society and culture as he yearned nostalgically for Europe. Those years spent in New England are sloughed off—an insignificant time as he viewed it from late in life, and clearly containing little of the vividness that characterized earlier childhood experiences (typically represented in the New York City scenes of *A Small Boy and Others*). In the more public domain of *Notes of a Son and Brother*, the richly variegated prose and imaginative energy rarely flag, a feat all the more striking when one recalls the author's increasing infirmities at this time of his life and his involvement in charitable work for the soldiers of the Great War, "a nightmare from which there is no waking save by sleep."[22] He had been overwhelmed by nervous depression in 1910, further saddened by the death of William in August of that year, and becoming increasingly aware of his own loneliness and age; while in Boston he had undergone a course of Freudian therapy. He suffered too a number of debilitating illnesses: a severe bout of shingles, digestive complaints, and cardiac problems. Only in the final chapter (containing Mary Temple's letters) does he link his salvaging of events from memory and the "time-smothered consciousness" with the "dark gulf" of mortality, thereby conceding the question of death itself—what he would greet finally as "the Distinguished Thing."[23] Near the opening of *The Middle Years*, James, in more apocalyptic mode, wonders at the excess of available memories, resolving to rescue a selection from the "welter of death and darkness and ruins" (*TMY*, 414). His amanuensis, Theodora Bosanquet, regretted, incidentally, his failure to complete this volume, considering it "a most remarkable and characteristic gallery of Victorian portraits, quite one of the most arresting ever exhibited," and wondering why he should give time instead to *The Sense of the Past:* "One can be grateful, however, that he did Tennyson and George Eliot and did them beautifully!"[24] However, it is clear from what he writes to his nephew that he regarded *The Middle Years* as reflecting a phase of his life quite distinct from the experiences recounted in *A Small Boy and Others* and *Notes of a Son and Brother:*

> I probably *shall* perpetrate a certain number more passages of retrospect & reminiscences—though quite disconnectedly from these 2 recent volumes, which are complete in themselves & of which the original intention is now a performed & discharged thing. . . . I confess that something of the appeal of the period from 1869 to the beginning of my life in London (the rest of *that* making a history by itself altogether,) *does* a good deal hang about me.[25]

The completed part of *The Middle Years* is set in London, charts the writer's professional rise, and names many of the great Victorians he met. On the more troubled themes of family and America, however, he is largely silent. Unexpectedly perhaps, the fantastical novel *The Sense of the Past,* whose young hero is transported into the past, offers a more revealing reflection on the tension between public and private selves, opportunities for intimate revelations between men, the fear of public exposure —themes that could serve to characterize James's own life in his later years.

Theodora Bosanquet observed the intensity of James's absorption in the impressions and events of his life of sixty years earlier, his pacing up and down, "sounding out the periods in tones of free resonant assurance. At such times he was beyond reach of irrelevant sounds or sights" as he recorded his memories.[26] When the volumes were published they met with the success for which he had long hoped for his fiction; *Notes of a Son and Brother* was especially admired.[27] That other great autobiographer, Henry Adams, commented that *Notes of a Son and Brother* "reduced me to a pulp," though he also wrote more dismissively to another friend that "poor Henry James thinks it all real and actually still lives in that dreary, stuffy Newport and Cambridge with papa James and Charles Eliot Norton."[28] Adams misrepresents James here, of course: the Newport scenes peopled by beloved cousins, by John La Farge and Thomas Sergeant Perry, undeniably evoke the pleasures of distant youth, while the novelist himself shows no indulgence toward his remembered dull years in Cambridge. The comment is perhaps more revealing of Adams's own dissatisfied condition in older age, in sharpest contrast to James's continuing resilience and openness of spirit. In a letter to Adams, James acknowledged that they are both "*of course* . . . lone survivors, of course the past that was our lives is at the bottom of an abyss—if the abyss *has* any bottom; of course too there's no use talking unless one particularly wants to." Yet despite the emphasized inevitability of a kind of obsolescence, the consequence of having been formed within a culture now regarded as irrelevant, the individual still has the choice of salvaging meaning from the distant past through the cultivation of consciousness, even if "with a ghastly grin"—signifying anything from aggression to desperation. Thinking of *Notes of a Son and Brother* and the multiplicity, "in presence of life," of its "reactions," James is led to deliver one of his most famous pronouncements: "It's, I suppose, because I am that queer monster the artist, an obstinate finality, an inexhaustible sensibility . . . it is still an act of life."[29]

The act of commitment to the past, or of self-writing, is founded, therefore, on the enduring energy of the imagination and the capacity to acquire and develop "impressions," a credo that resounds in the late prose of James. Ranging beyond vocation and inhabiting, essentially, an area of selfhood or identity, recounting one's life in the light of a purposeful acquiring of the means of registering experience becomes, it seems, a form of procreation, or, following the alternative trope, a lifeline cast from the abyss. With such an investment of self in this autobiographical project, it is perhaps not surprising that he should exercise what has been judged excessive control over the materials (such as letters) that he included in the volume.

Despite the tangible affection between the novelist and his nephew, the tensions between the two on opposite sides of the Atlantic emerge as work on *Notes of a Son and Brother* progressed. The family letters had never been reached in *A Small Boy and Others,* but Henry's selecting and editing of William's letters for the current volume disturbed his nephew, who himself intended to issue a collection of his father's correspondence. James is never less than sympathetic, even penitent, in his responses to Harry's queries, but, far from wishing to preserve the integrity of the original texts, he argues his role in protecting and presenting his late brother at his best. Over many leaves he painfully and laboriously rehearses his motives, the benevolence and wisdom of his choices, the authority of his position—his possession, indeed, as an artist, of the volume's entirety. In publicly presenting these "relics of our common youth," Henry can hear his brother's voice, reduced to abject pleading and powerless in death: "Oh but you're not going to give me away, to hand me over, in my raggedness and my poor accidents, quite unhelped, unfriended, you're going to do the very best for me you *can*, aren't you, and since you appear to be making such claims for me you're going to let me seem to justify them as much as I possibly may!"[30] Those imagined words, spoken by the dead to the living, represent fraternal loyalty, intense and unbreakable, motivated too, perhaps, by a desire to maintain long-preserved confidentiality, even secrets.

The great acknowledged success of the final chapter of *Notes of a Son and Brother,* in which Mary Temple emerges with a distinct voice—a voice that James heard again only with the arrival of her letters written to John Chipman Gray as he was completing the volume—raises other questions and mysteries. The autobiographer himself remains offstage in this correspondence, offering few evaluative glosses on much of Mary Temple's recorded life. Her passionate admiration for William James attracts no comment, and yet she was one of the most important women in the lives of both these two emotionally and physically ill-adjusted young brothers, part of a family whose functioning seems to have caused the children such suffering. Examining fragments of two letters written by Mary to William in her final weeks of life, Habegger has persuasively suggested that "their longstanding acquaintance underwent an intense transformation just before her death. The evidence is not conclusive, but it appears that Minny helped shape the course of William's breakdown of 1869–70 and that what she said and wrote to him left deep traces on his mature thought." One of the fragments, folded and, from its condition, long left untouched, had been placed behind a portrait of Mary, the rest of its contents having been destroyed at some stage. "He was on the verge of a dive into some abyss in the winter of 1869/70; Minny *had* to keep him at arm's length. When she said no to some proposal of his and also undid her recent conversion to Christianity . . . she bequeathed to William an image of heroic independence that only aggravated his already incurable self-loathing."[31]

Henry was in Europe at this time but, given the level of intimacy in his relationship with his older brother, must have known something of his disturbed state. But now, as the sole survivor (without forgetting, however, William's widow and children), whatever the private anguish aroused on his own and his brother's behalf, the episode represented some trauma not to be revised or revisited. Much simpler, therefore, for James to invoke history and judgment, to dramatize the woman's death in some all-inclusive statement inviting no questions as "the end of our youth." Such a conclusion representing the author's controlling presence as well as some intended declaration of fidelity to the dead reduces his well-documented tinkering with letters to some minor role. And at the level of the book's physical appearance, James's loyalty is tangibly evident. The choice of illustrations, a selection of William's drawings and sketches (some recently and delightedly discovered), as well as a portrait in oils, mark his brother's desire to celebrate that youthful talent which had been long laid aside.[32]

Harry's penciled marginal notes on his uncle's letters betray some of his frustration with the older man, yet James's relationship with the family—including Alice Howe Gibbens James—which had initially urged the project on him, remained affectionate. The publication of *A Small Boy and Others* and *Notes of a Son and Brother* marks the completion of that account of family which attempts to honor both father and brother as well as the novelist's own vocation. It is ironic perhaps that, with the numerous references to William's primacy in those early years, derived only in part from his seniority, the final word should be the "small boy's," not the elder but the second brother's, who has briefly triumphed in time.

The years of the book's appearance were, however, far from triumphant. He was devastated by the ongoing world war—his assumption of British nationality an expression of devotion to the country which had become his home—and moved by the heroism of the young soldiers he met in the London society circles in which he moved: "They kill me!" he confided to his pocket diary in the contemporary vernacular.[33] Events in mainland Europe must have made his memories of Newport and Cambridge and the "conquest" of London seem all the more remote, yet at the same time more living. A late essay on the soldiers of World War I, "The Long Wards,"[34] begins by marveling at "the quite abysmal softness, the exemplary genius for accommodation . . . of the fighting man"—qualities observed first in a Rhode Island recuperation camp of the American Civil War. James did not live to see the end of war, but his advice to an old friend, Edmund Gosse, was characteristic and generously long-term: "Put my volume . . . away on a high shelf—to be taken down again only in the better and straighter light that I invincibly believe in the dawning of."[35]

NOTES

For reading and commenting on this essay, I am indebted to Alfred Habegger.

1. *CT*, 10:475, 483.

2. Martin A. Danahay, *A Community of One: Masculine Autobiography and Autonomy in Nineteenth-Century Britain* (Albany: State University of New York Press, 1993), 5.

3. Edith Wharton, for instance, provides an effusive account of James's recollecting family history: " 'Ah, my dear, the Emmets—ah, the Emmets!' Then he began . . . forgetting everything but the vision of his lost youth . . . the long train of ghosts flung with his

enchanter's wand across the wide stage of the summer night. Ghostlike indeed at first, wavering and indistinct, they glimmered at us through a series of disconnected ejaculations, epithets, allusions, parenthetical rectifications and restatements, till not only our brains but the clear night itself seemed filled with a palpable fog; and then, suddenly, by some miracle of shifted lights and accumulated strokes, there they stood before us as they lived, drawn with a million filament-like lines, yet sharp as an Ingres, dense as a Rembrandt" (*A Backward Glance* [New York: Appleton-Century, 1934], 193-94). Wharton surmises, incorrectly, that this occasion was the stimulus for James's decision to begin work on an autobiography.

4. See, e.g., Alfred Habegger, "Henry James's Re-Writing of Minny Temple's Letters," *American Literature* 58 (May 1986): 159-80, as well as the collection of Mary Temple's letters included in this volume.

5. Most comprehensively in *CWJ*.

6. For William's teasing and sometimes inappropriate gallantry, see Jean Strouse, *Alice James* (London: Harvill, 1980, 1992), 52-55.

7. For a detailed analysis of the James Sr.–Emerson relationship, see Alfred Habegger, *The Father: A Life of Henry James, Sr.* (New York: Farrar, Straus and Giroux, 1994), 186-210.

8. Letter of 13-19 November 1911, in *Dear Munificent Friends: Henry James's Letters to Four Women,* ed. Susan E. Gunter (Ann Arbor: University of Michigan Press, 1999), 83. The more literal-minded Harry James's published thoughts on his uncle's reminiscences combine admiration with some misgivings: "In 'A Small Boy and Others' and 'Notes of a Son and Brother' he reproduced the atmosphere of a household of which he was the last survivor, and adumbrated the figures of Henry James, Senior, and of certain other members of his family with infinite subtlety at every turn of the page. But he too wrote without much attention to particular facts or the sequence of events, and his two volumes were incomplete and occasionally inaccurate with respect to such details" (preface to *The Letters of William James* [London: Longmans, Green, 1926], viii-ix).

9. Letter to Harry James, 5 April 1908 (bMS Am 1094 [1369], Houghton). See *The Diary of Alice James,* ed. Leon Edel (Harmondsworth: Penguin, 1964).

10. Letter to William and Alice Howe Gibbens James, 25 May 1894, in *Henry James: A Life in Letters,* ed. Philip Horne (London: Allen Lane, Penguin Press, 1999), 270 n. 3. When he first saw the Diary, James was in no doubt as to its quality, as he later confessed to William: "I have been immensely impressed with the thing as a revelation & a moral & personal picture. It is heroic in its individuality, its independence—its face-to-face with the universe for-&-by herself—& the beauty & eloquence with which she often expresses this, let alone the rich irony & humour, constitute (I wholly agree with you,) a new claim for the family renown" (ibid.; *CWJ*, 2:311). For further, unflattering detail about the reaction of the James family, see Lyndall Gordon, *A Private Life of Henry James: Two Women and His Art* (New York: Norton, 1999), 368-69.

11. Alfred Habegger, *Henry James and the "Woman Business"* (Cambridge: Cambridge University Press, 1989), 142.

12. Howard M. Feinstein, "The Use and Abuse of Illness in the James Family Circle: A View of Neurasthenia as a Social Phenomenon," in *Our Selves/Our Past: Psychological Approaches to American History*, ed. Robert J. Brugger (Baltimore: Johns Hopkins University Press, 1981), 228–43.

13. Letter to William James, 22 November 1867, *The Complete Letters of Henry James, 1855–1872*, 2 vols., ed. Pierre A. Walker and Greg W. Zacharias (Lincoln: University of Nebraska Press, 2006), 1:188–89.

14. Howard M. Feinstein, *Becoming William James* (Ithaca: Cornell University Press, 1984), 207.

15. Carol Holly, *Intensely Family: The Inheritance of Family Shame and the Autobiographies of Henry James* (Madison: University of Wisconsin Press, 1995), 8. For an interesting discussion of individual malady (especially Bob James's alcoholism) as expressive of a history of family dysfunction, see also her "Understanding the Family: Jane Maher's Biography of Broken Fortunes," *Henry James Review* 8 (Spring 1987): 209–20.

16. See, e.g., Paul Fisher, *House of Wits: An Intimate History of the James Family* (London: Little, Brown, 2008), 13 and 31.

17. James Sr. is said to have muttered this phrase when he discovered the outcome of the case concerning his father's contested will (R. W. B. Lewis, *The Jameses: A Family Narrative* [New York: Farrar, Straus and Giroux, 1991], 30).

18. For further detail on the James ancestry and the "belief in 'tainted inheritance' . . . in nineteenth-century psychiatry," see Feinstein, *Becoming William James*, 304–7, 304n.

19. Strouse, *Alice James*, 49, 50n.

20. Two contrasting versions of male identity, both fictional products of Harvard, are represented by Caspar Goodwood and Ralph Touchett in *The Portrait of a Lady*. See Kim Townsend, *Manhood at Harvard: William James and Others* (New York: Norton, 1996), 148–49.

21. Letter to Alice Howe Gibbens James, 1 April 1913, *HJL*, 4:657–58.

22. Ibid., 570.

23. Quoted in Leon Edel, *Henry James: The Master, 1901–1916* (London: Rupert Hart-Davis, 1972), 546.

24. 31 March [1916], Theodora Bosanquet, Diary Notes (bMS Eng 1213.2, Houghton).

25. MS letter to Harry James, 7 April 1914 (bMS Am 1094 [1408], Houghton). This version of Henry James—removed from his youth and the United States, the more worldly, London-based man of letters—is encapsulated in the original frontispiece for *The Middle Years*. Taken from a lithograph by William Rothenstein (1872–1945), the illustration also appears in *Men and Memories: Recollections of William Rothenstein 1872–1900* (London: Faber, 1931), opposite 304. It is dated 1897. Rothenstein had also asked him to provide some text to accompany a sketch he had made of John Singer Sargent, but the novelist declined the latter request, having already written a number of pieces on the American painter: "After this, how shall I dare to say Yes to your still more flattering proposal that I shall lay my own head on the block? You can so easily chop it off to vent any little irritation my impracticability may have caused you. However, please take it as a proof of my complete trust in

your magnanimity if I answer: With pleasure—do with me whatever you think I now deserve" (HJ to William Rothenstein, 13 July 1897, *HJL*, 4:51). In the right-hand bottom corner of the drawing in the first edition of *TMY* appears in very small print "Annan PhSo." It seems likely that this refers to James Craig Annan (1864–1946) of the Photographic Society, an eminent photographer who produced portraits of many artists and writers of the era.

26. Theodora Bosanquet, *Henry James at Work*, one of the "Hogarth Essays" (London: Hogarth Press, 1924), 11.

27. See, e.g., Carol Holly, "The British Reception of Henry James's Autobiographies," *American Literature* 57 (December 1985): 570–87.

28. Quoted in *HJL*, 4:706.

29. Letter to Henry Adams, 21 March 1914, ibid., 706.

30. Letter to Harry James, 15–18 November 1913 (ibid., 802). Such modifying of tone and language reflects, Tamara Follini argues, James's "desire to use these letters as an entry into the past without becoming implicated in the past" ("Pandora's Box: The Family Correspondence in *Notes of a Son and Brother*," *Cambridge Quarterly* 25, no. 1 [1996]: 36).

31. Alfred Habegger, "New Light on William James and Minny Temple," *New England Quarterly* 60 (March 1987): 30, 52–53.

32. E.g., HJ had recently received the pencil sketch that served as the frontispiece for *NSB* from Katherine Loring, which he then sent on to his nephew Harry. He wrote to his sister-in-law on 18 January 1914, "I sent Harry some time since a strange & precious little windfall of a small drawing received from Katherine Loring as having unexpectedly fallen out of an old book that had belonged to Alice—& which I at once recognized as a *head of himself* (before a looking glass,) done by William upwards of 50 years ago—that is it must belong, at the latest, to about 1866 (& *may* have been as early as '63.) Harry was to take it to the Scribners to be reproduced as a frontispiece to Notes of a Son & Brother, but I have heard nothing about it since from him, & as you don't mention having had a photograph of it from him (or mention it otherwise) I suppose you all know nothing about it. I earnestly hope it will have been found reproducible in N.Y.—it is so interesting & admirable & exhibits so William's 'masterly' young sense of drawing. I had it immediately photographed in facsimile & one of my 2 copies hangs, framed, beside my mantel-shelf in this room. . . . Strange its having lurked ½ a century in such an invisible crevice & been preserved & restored by the rarest of chances. It was evidently most casually done—offhand, on a piece of ruled paper & with another leaf attached to the piece covered with odd old pencil cipherings. The solid lines have fortunately in the photograph been quite conjured away" (*Dear Munificent Friends*, 107–8).

33. "31 August 1915 Tuesday," *CN*, 430.

34. First published in *The Book of the Homeless* (1916), ed. Edith Wharton, rpt. in *Henry James on Culture: Collected Essays on Politics and the American Social Scene*, ed. Pierre A. Walker (Lincoln: University of Nebraska Press, 1999), 170.

35. *HJL*, 4:721.

# A NOTE ON THIS EDITION

This second volume of Henry James's autobiographical writings forms a sequel to *A Small Boy and Others* and contains two texts, originally published separately, *Notes of a Son and Brother* and *The Middle Years*. The text for this new edition, which combines both volumes, is based on the first published book editions. *Notes of a Son and Brother,* published by Charles Scribner's Sons, New York, appeared on 7 March 1914. In addition to a frontispiece, the volume contained five illustrations, all of which are reproduced here, with captions as worded in the first edition. A British edition, published by Macmillan, appeared on 13 March 1914. The rare few textual differences between the two relate to a choice of word, the spelling of a word, or the use of an abbreviation. However, while in the American edition of *NSB* names of books and plays are indicated only by initial capitals, the British edition places them in italics. On the few occasions when James himself includes a note, it is indicated, not by a number—as in the first edition—but by an asterisk.

*The Middle Years,* unfinished when James died on 28 February 1916, was prepared for publication by Percy Lubbock and published in London by Collins as a separate volume, with a frontispiece, on 18 October 1917. It forms the basis for this new edition. Before being published in New York by Charles Scribner's Sons on 23 November 1917, it also appeared in America in *Scribner's Magazine,* in two parts: 62, no. 4 (October 1917): 465-76; 62, no. 5 (November 1917): 608-15. The text (in dense double-column format like the rest of the magazine, and utilizing American spelling) has been heavily cut and modified. There are no breaks reflecting the chapters of the book version. In part 1, which covers the first five chapters, breaks between paragraphs have been changed so that some become shorter, others longer. Many substantial cuts are made, especially of the more diffuse, less circumstantial detail. The shorter part 2 covers chapters 6 and 7. These chapters, describing meetings with Tennyson and HJ's friend Mrs. Greville, are reproduced in full, though the material is contained in one long paragraph, with one brief paragraph at the end. Given James's enduring need to revise and to control his texts, it is unlikely that he would have approved such changes. Scribners, it seems, had been interested in serialization from the earliest stages—when HJ was planning just one volume of WJ's letters with commentary. The novelist wrote to Alice Howe Gibbens James on 26 August 1912, "Charles Scribner, who is in England, is keenly interested & eager, & it's pretty clear that I shall be able to make highly advantageous terms. But the book as such, as a whole, will not be serializable—I entirely understand Scribner's view that it is more of a thing, in every way, than a magazine can 'carry.' . . . What he wants is *two* instalments, for Scribner, 2 only, of the Letters—the Letters *and* the Notes; as illustrative & annunciatory, as it were, before the publication of the book—to be followed *by* the book. This will be very manageable—I shall be perfectly able to lift the 2 instalments, for that use, artfully, out of the mass" (*Dear Munificent Friends,* 94–95).

The surviving typescript for *The Middle Years* (held at the Houghton Library, Harvard University, bMS Am 1237.9) reveals a number of small changes and divisions of paragraphs made by Lubbock as well as a few emendations in James's hand. The most obvious discrepancy between typescript and published version is the disposition of chapters. In the typescript, which is divided between two folders, the original first chapter becomes chapters 1–3 in the published version. The second becomes chapters 4–5; the third, chapter 6; and the fourth, chapter 7. It isn't clear why these divisions were made, for although the twenty-nine chapters of *Small Boy and Others* are similarly short, the thirteen chapters of *Notes of a Son and Brother* are proportionately longer. Paragraphs too are generally shorter in *The Middle Years* (in his editor's note, included here, Lubbock mentions James's unusual practice of leaving such decisions as divisions of paragraphs till late in the process).

This new edition of *The Middle Years* represents the text as mediated by Percy Lubbock, the young critic who, knowing James well, had been entrusted with the job of preparing it by the James family. He also edited two of James's unfinished novels for publication and (influenced by the novelist's nephew Harry) the first edition of two volumes of the novelist's letters in 1920. In preparing the typescript, Lubbock was aided by someone long familiar with James's working methods, his amanuensis Theodora Bosanquet. She was also involved with other posthumous works, recording her copying of *The Ivory Tower* and *The Middle Years* in March 1916, the month after James's death, though it is impossible now to gauge to what extent (if any) her role ranged beyond that of copy-typist (Theodora Bosanquet Diary Notes, 1912–1916, "Transcribed diaries of Theodora Bosanquet" [bMS Eng 1213.2], Houghton).

Had the decision rested entirely with Alice Howe Gibbens James, William James's widow, who had traveled to wartime Britain from America to care for her dying brother-in-law, *The Middle Years* might never have been published. Bosanquet notes how important James B. Pinker, James's literary agent, was in promoting the publication of the work. Her disparaging comment on Alice James must be read in the light of the uneasy relations between the two women (and with Alice's daughter, Mary Margaret) which deteriorated during the final weeks of the novelist's life: "Pinker's theory is that Mrs. James will always be accessible to the argument of pecuniary profit and that perhaps by means of it he can deal with Mr. James's things in the way most in accordance with his wishes. As a sample of her utter lack of literary understanding—she told Pinker that in her opinion 'The Middle Years' wasn't worth publishing!" (entry for 4 May 1916, ibid.; for further detail on this division and on Bosanquet's suspected alliance with Edith Wharton, of whom Alice disapproved, see Susan E. Gunter, *Alice in Jamesland: The Story of Alice Howe Gibbens James* [Lincoln: University of Nebraska Press, 2009], 293–94).

Spelling for both American and British editions invariably follows British conventions. All through *A Small and Boy and Others,* and *Notes of a Son and Brother* as far as chapter 3, James's spelling of "aesthetic" is consistently "æsthetic"; however, from chapter 4 onward it varies between "aesthetic" and "esthetic" (chap. 10, e.g., has both versions). This may reflect a change of compositors. When *The Middle Years* was published (this time with the British publishing house Collins), the spelling remained "aesthetic." Punctuation is habitually placed within quotation marks, although *The Middle Years* breaks with this convention. Any questions relating to possible slips in proofreading or possible mistakes and inconsistencies have been addressed in the editorial notes. One inadvertent repetition of a phrase in *Notes of a Son and Brother,* chapter 5, has been corrected in the text and an explanatory note provided. I have silently amended a first-edition misprint ("dont" for "don't"—the MS also has "don't") near the end of Mary Temple's first letter in chapter 13. Three of the seven chapters (2, 3, and 5) of *The Middle Years* open with an indented paragraph: I have not retained these inconsistencies. I have also corrected a misprint ("it" replacing "i") in chapter 3.

James includes in chapter 5 of *Notes of a Son and Brother* a paragraph of one of William James's letters, written to his parents from Cambridge on 16 September 1861 (*CWJ,* 4:42–45; neither of HJ's versions completely accords with the text given there). There are uncharacteristic anomalies between the Scribner's and Macmillan's texts, the only substantial example of significant differences between American and British editions:

SCRIBNER'S EDITION

The first few days, the first week here, I really didn't know what to do with myself or how to fill my time. I felt as if turned out of doors. I then received H's and Mother's letters. Never before did I know what mystic depths of rapture lay concealed within that familiar word. Never before did the same being look so like two different ones as I going in and out of the P. O. if I bring a letter with me. Gloomily, with despair written on my leaden brow I stalk the street along towards the P.O., women, children and students involuntarily shrinking against the wall as I pass—thus,* as if the curse of Cain were stamped upon my front. But when I come out with a letter an immense concourse of people generally attends me to my lodging, attracted by my excited wild gestures and look.

*Expressive drawing alas irreproducible.

MACMILLAN'S EDITION

The first few days, the first week here, I really didn't know what to do with myself or how to fill my time. I felt as if turned out of doors. I then received H's and Mother's letters. Never before did I know what mystic depths of rapture lay concealed in that familiar word. Never did the same being look so like different ones as I going in and out of the post-office if I bring a letter with me. Gloomily, with despair written on my leaden brow, I stalk the street to the place, women, children and students instinctively shrinking against the wall as I pass—thus,* as if the curse of Cain were stamped upon my front. But when I come out with a letter an immense concourse of people generally attends me to my lodging, attracted by my excited wild gestures and look.

*Expressive drawing alas irreproducible.

The reasons for the discrepancies are not clear. In general, James's narrative and the texts for the letters in both editions are uniform. It is conceivable that he thought British readers' needs might be different in cultural terms from those of their American counterparts and decided to distinguish between the two texts, and then later on (this passage occurs quite early in the extracts from William James's letters) decided that the idea wasn't practicable.

James has been attacked for his revising and rewriting of others' letters (e.g., by Michael Millgate, who demonizes him as "a monster of egotistical voracity" in *Testamentary Acts: Browning, Tennyson, James, Hardy* [Oxford: Oxford University Press, 1992], 93), and where possible, I have pointed out any interesting divergences between surviving MS and published versions. Some changes may have been made inadvertently through mishearings by Theodora Bosanquet and never later picked up—for instance, with reference to Emerson, "the Concord sage" becomes (less appropriately) "the conquered sage" (*NSB*, 203)—the remnants of an American accent heard by English ears. All such anomalies are also noted in the text.

James includes two brief footnotes relating to illustrations. One, referring to the reproduction of a page from one of William James's letters in chapter 5 (quoted above), apologizes, "Expressive drawing alas irreproducible," though in fact the page does appear. At the end of the same chapter he adds a note to a letter reference to "this heavenly group below": "A drawing of figures in evening lamplight." This time the note correctly implies that the illustration was not included.

### EDITORIAL APPROACH

As well as explaining contemporary references and translating most foreign phrases, I have also occasionally provided brief summaries of what seem to me difficult passages. Parts of the text that raise characteristic or important Jamesian themes, or have some history in James studies, have also been given some interpretive support.

One of the first readers of my proposal for this new edition pointed out that—aside from their intrinsic interest and importance—James's autobiographical volumes cast an interesting light on contemporary culture, historic events, and the people who participated in them, and they will therefore be of interest to a range of other readers whose primary interest may not be in James himself. As a consequence, my notes have tried to take some account of this broader context, a perspective in which James's narrative functions as a commentary on the period in which he lived.

When referring to other works by James and to those of other authors I have generally tried to use accessible Penguin paperback editions rather than, say, first editions or, in the case of James, the New York Edition—copies of which can be hard to come by. The fact that a series like Penguin Classics uses different versions of texts (sometimes a first edition, sometimes a later revision) means that I have had to compromise on whether the reader is provided with the original James or with an original later version of James. The question of his texts is famously complex, and differences between the various revisions can be major (see, e.g., Philip

Horne, "The Question of Our Texts," in *The Cambridge Companion to Henry James,* ed. Jonathan Freedman [Cambridge: Cambridge University Press, 1998], 63–78). However, in justifying this choice, I would argue that the quotations I include seldom exceed the length of one sentence and that a reader would have at least a good chance of locating the passage fairly conveniently in a readily available cheap edition.

# ABBREVIATIONS

| | |
|---|---|
| HJ | Henry James |
| HJ Sr. | Henry James (father of the novelist) |
| WJ | William James (brother of the novelist) |

| | |
|---|---|
| *AS* | Henry James, *The American Scene,* ed. Leon Edel (Bloomington: Indiana University Press, 1968) |
| *CN* | *The Complete Notebooks of Henry James,* ed. Leon Edel and Lyall H. Powers (London: Oxford University Press, 1987) |
| *CT* | *The Complete Tales of Henry James,* ed. Leon Edel, 12 vols. (London: Rupert Hart-Davis, 1962–64) |
| *CWJ* | *The Correspondence of William James,* ed. Ignas K. Skrupskelis and Elizabeth M. Berkeley, 12 vols. (Charlottesville: University Press of Virginia, 1992–2004) |
| *HJL* | *Henry James: Letters,* ed. Leon Edel, 4 vols. (Cambridge, Mass.: Belknap Press of Harvard University Press, 1974–84), vol. 1: 1843–75; vol. 2: 1875–83; vol. 3: 1883–95; vol. 4: 1895–1916 |
| Houghton | Houghton Library, Harvard University, Cambridge, Mass. |
| *LC 1* | *Henry James, Literary Criticism: Essays on Literature, American Writers, English Writers,* ed. Leon Edel and Mark Wilson (New York: Library of America, 1984) |
| *LC 2* | *Henry James, Literary Criticism: French Writers, Other European Writers, the Prefaces to the New York Edition,* ed. Leon Edel and Mark Wilson (New York: Library of America, 1984) |
| *NSB* | Henry James, *"Notes of a Son and Brother" and "The Middle Years"* (Charlottesville: University of Virginia Press, 2011) |
| *SBO* | Henry James, *A Small Boy and Others* (Charlottesville: University of Virginia Press, 2011) |
| *TMY* | Henry James, *"Notes of a Son and Brother" and "The Middle Years"* (Charlottesville: University of Virginia Press, 2011) |

# NOTES OF A SON AND BROTHER

*Pencil-drawn portrait of William James by himself about 1866.*
(Houghton Library, Harvard University)

# CHAPTER SUMMARIES

In reminiscing, Henry James can range freely and be highly allusive, so these brief notes may help the reader locate specific subjects and events. Where possible, approximate dates have been provided.

Chapter 1: October 1859: Arrival and schooling in Geneva; trip with WJ; reading pleasures.

Chapter 2: Summer 1860 in Bonn; their lodgings and trips; letters of Wilky and WJ.

Chapter 3: Summer and fall 1860: WJ and study of art; brothers leave Bonn for Paris; return to the United States.

Chapter 4: September 1860: Arrival in Newport, Rhode Island; American cousins; influence of artists William Morris Hunt and John La Farge.

Chapter 5: 1861–63: WJ's and HJ's educational choices; WJ attends Harvard's Lawrence Scientific School; selection of his student letters.

Chapter 6: HJ Sr.'s philosophy and influence of Swedenborg; his letters to Emerson (1848–61) and relationship with Carlyle and James John Garth Wilkinson.

Chapter 7: Fall 1860: Wilky and Bob James enrolled at Franklin B. Sanborn's school at Concord, Massachusetts; HJ Sr.'s letters to Mrs. Caroline Sturgis Tappan (1859–63).

Chapter 8: HJ Sr.'s correspondence with Mrs. Annie Fields (c. 1866–70); Cambridge friends the Nortons; Dickens's visit, 1867; HJ Sr.'s letters to daughter Alice and HJ in Europe (c. 1869–73).

Chapter 9: 1862–63: HJ at Harvard Law School; sense of America; the Civil War and its soldiers; his injury, the "obscure hurt"; visits to army camps.

Chapter 10: 1862–63: Cambridge life, Professor F. J. Child and fellow students; insight into New England and America.

Chapter 11: 1861–65: Civil War; letters from Wilky serving with the Massachusetts 44th and 54th Infantry Regiments, principally in South Carolina.

Chapter 12: 1864, family move to Boston, and in 1866 to Cambridge; HJ's early writing; WJ's letters from Europe, 1867–68.

Chapter 13: 1869–70: Selection of letters from mortally-ill cousin Mary (Minny) Temple to John Chipman Gray.

I It may again perhaps betray something of that incorrigible vagueness of current in our educational drift which I have elsewhere* so
unreservedly suffered to reflect itself that, though we had come
abroad in 1855 with an eye to the then supposedly supreme benefits of
Swiss schooling, our most resolute attempt to tap that supply, after twenty
distractions, waited over to the autumn of the fourth year later on, when we
in renewed good faith retraced our steps to Geneva.[1] Our parents began at

* *A Small Boy and Others.* New York, 1913.

1. At this point HJ omits reference to the second stay in Boulogne-sur-Mer as well as
(more importantly) the family's return to Newport in 1858–59. HJ explained the reason for
the latter omission to his nephew Harry, as Leon Edel records: " 'I've covered over the
fact—so overcome am I by the sense of our poor father's impulsive journeyings to and fro
and of the impression of aimless vacillation which the record might make upon the
reader—that we didn't go to Europe twice, but once.' . . . In a letter written to T. S. Perry, at
the time of the publication of *Notes of a Son and Brother,* the novelist confessed that he
suppressed the 1859 journey to Europe to avoid giving the impression that his father was
'*too* irresponsible and too *saccadé* [jerky] in his generous absence of plan and continuity' "
(*Henry James: The Untried Years, 1843–1870* [London: Rupert Hart-Davis, 1953], 141–
42). HJ may also have been concerned about the work's form, as R. W. B. Lewis points
out: "Literary as well as filial piety was at work in these omissions. He . . . told Tom Perry
(1914) that the reminiscences already contained 'so many choppings and changes and
interruptions and volatilities (on our parents' part, dear people)' that his treatment of it all
was becoming literarily foolish. We have here a fine example of Henry James's fictive
arrangement, as it were, of actual facts: the skippings are made in the interest of dramatic
effect—the lapse into unconsciousness which brings the first volume to a close, the curtain
rising on a large change of European scene in the second" (*The Jameses: A Family
Narrative* [New York: Farrar, Straus and Giroux, 1991], 93n). The family left New York on
8 October 1859 aboard the SS *Vanderbilt* and arrived after a rough passage at Le Havre on
20 October. As Edel also points out (*Untried Years,* 148), Geneva was the "city of Calvin
and of Rousseau . . . of Gibbon and Madame de Staël and even Voltaire" and, under
Calvin's influence, became a center of the Protestant Reformation of the sixteenth century.
Frederick Winterbourne, the young American lover in *Daisy Miller,* had been educated in
"the little metropolis of Calvinism," as well as attending, in the revised versions, as Edel
indicates, "the grey old 'Academy' on the steep and stony hillside" (ibid., 152–53). HJ was
sorry to be leaving Newport, as he wrote to Perry on the day of sailing: "I can scarcely sit
still to write this and feel myself thinking much more of what I leave behind than what I
expect to find. Newport and the Newporters are surrounded with a halo, in my mind
which grows brighter & brighter as two o'clock draws near." In a letter of 18 July 1860 he
described the town on the Atlantic coast as "the place in America we all most care to live
in. . . . I think that if we are to live in America it is about time we boys should take up our
abode there; the more I see of this estrangement of American youngsters from the land of

that season a long sojourn at the old Hôtel de l'Écu,[2] which now erects a somewhat diminished head on the edge of the rushing Rhone—its only rival then was the Hôtel des Bergues opposite, considerably larger and commanding more or less the view of that profiled crest of Mont-Blanc which used to be so oddly likened to the head and face of a singularly supine Napoleon.[3] But on that side the shooting blue flood was less directly and familiarly under the windows; in our position we lived with it and hung over it, and its beauty, just where we mainly congregated, was, I fear, my own sole happy impression during several of those months. It was of a Sunday that we congregated most; my two younger brothers had, in general, on that day their *sortie* from the Pensionnat Maquelin, a couple of miles out of town, where they were then established,[4] and W. J., following courses at the Academy, in its present enriched and amplified form the University, mingled, failing livelier recreation, in the family circle at the hotel. Livelier recreation, during the hours of completest ease, consisted

---

their birth, the less I believe in it. It should also be the land of their breeding" (Virginia Harlow, *Thomas Sergeant Perry: A Biography* [Durham: Duke University Press, 1950], 239, 252). Further detail of the family's stay in Geneva is contained in HJ's letters to Perry in this volume (239–52); *HJL,* 1:6–33, includes a selection of these letters.

2. The Jameses, unable to find a suitable apartment, rented a suite of rooms at the Hôtel de l'Écu de Genève, in the place du Rhône on the south bank of the Rhône, from 25 October. It was popular with Americans and offered views of Lake Geneva and the Bergues Quarter (*Nouveau guide de l'étranger à Genève et dans ses environs en 1854* [Geneva: Jullien, n.d.], 5). In later years HJ confessed to feeling "an old-time kindness . . . for Geneva, to which I was introduced years ago in my school-days, when I was as good an idler as the best." Even then, it seems, he noticed "the want of humor in the local atmosphere, and the absence, as well, of that æsthetic character which is begotten of a generous view of life" ("Swiss Notes" [*Nation,* 1872], rpt. in *Henry James: Collected Travel Writings: The Continent,* ed. Richard Howard [New York: Library of America, 1993], 626–27).

3. Mont Blanc, 4,808 meters high, is in the French-Italian Alps, about fifty miles southeast of Geneva.

4. Wilky and Bob James boarded at the school and, as Alfred Habegger comments, "now irrevocably grouped together, were (as William put it) 'destined for commerce'" (*The Father: A Life of Henry James, Sr.* [New York: Farrar, Straus and Giroux, 1994], 413). "The school was founded at Orbe, Switzerland, in 1822 by Jean François Henri Venel who moved it to Champel in 1831, continuing as director until his death in 1855. The school prospered, having among its pupils at one time Prince Louis Napoleon, later Napoleon III. Upon the death of M. Venel, it was directed by Paul Louis Maquelin, senior professor of the faculty" (Robert C. Le Clair, *Young Henry James 1843–70* [New York: Bookman Associates, 1955], 329 n. 1). The name is given as "Moquelin" in Harlow, *Perry: A Biography,* 240, but this may be a slip in transcription. *Sortie:* release from school.

mostly, as the period drew itself out, of those *courses*,[5] along the lake and along the hills, which offer to student-life in whatever phase, throughout that blest country, the most romantic of all forms of "a little change"; enjoyed too in some degree, but much more restrictedly, by myself—this an effect, as I remember feeling it, of my considerably greater servitude. I had been placed, separately, at still another Institution, that of M. Rochette,[6] who carried on an École Préparatoire aux Écoles Spéciales, by which was meant in particular the Polytechnic School at Zurich, with whatever other like curricula, always "scientific," might elsewhere be aimed at; and I had been so disposed of under a flattering misconception of my aptitudes that leaves me to-day even more wonderstruck than at that immediate season of my distress.

I so feared and abhorred mathematics that the simplest arithmetical operation had always found and kept me helpless and blank—the dire discipline of the years bringing no relief whatever to my state; and mathematics unmitigated were at the Institution Rochette the air we breathed, building us up as they most officiously did for those other grim ordeals and pursuits, those of the mining and the civil engineer, those of the architectural aspirant and the technician in still other fields, to which we were supposed to be addressed. Nothing of the sort was indeed supposed of me—which is in particular my present mystification; so that my assault of the preliminaries disclosed, feeble as it strikingly remained, was mere darkness, waste and anguish. I found myself able to bite, as the phrase was, into no subject there deemed savoury; it was hard and bitter fruit all and turned to ashes in my mouth. More extraordinary however than my good parents' belief—eccentric on their part too, in the light of their usual

5. Excursions or trips.

6. The school, run by Gustave Rochette at number 105 (now number 7; see Le Clair, *Young Henry James,* 300), rue de l'Evéché, prepared students for further, specialized study in engineering and architecture. HJ wrote to Perry, "I have to work harder than I have ever done before, the school-hours being from eight A.M. to 5 P.M. with but an hour's intermission" (Harlow, *Perry: A Biography,* 240). Sheldon Novick has him studying from six in the morning (*Henry James: The Young Master* [New York: Random House, 1996], 64). Edel records (*Untried Years,* 151) that he rose at 6:30 and breakfasted alone. "Perhaps you would like to know about my school," he writes to Perry, contrasting it with the Berkeley Institute, where they both studied in Newport: "It is a dilapidated old stone house in the most triste quarter of the town. Scarcely a soul passes by it all day. . . . Beside it is the prison and opposite the Cathedral of St. Peter, in which Calvin used to preach" (Harlow, *Perry: A Biography,* 242). Zurich, incidentally, was the foremost manufacturing town of Switzerland.

practice and disposition, their habit, for the most part, of liking for us after a gasp or two whatever we seemed to like—was my own failure to protest with a frankness proportioned to my horror. The stiffer intellectual discipline, the discipline of physics and of algebra, invoked for the benefit of an understanding undisputedly weak and shy, had been accepted on my side as a blessing perhaps in disguise. It had come to me by I know not what perversity that if I couldn't tackle the smallest problem in mechanics or face without dismay at the blackboard the simplest geometric challenge I ought somehow in decency to make myself over, oughtn't really to be so inferior to almost everyone else. That was the pang, as it was also the marvel—that the meanest minds and the vulgarest types approached these matters without a sign of trepidation even when they approached them, at the worst, without positive appetite. My attempt not therefore to remain abnormal wholly broke down, however, and when I at last withdrew from the scene it was not even as a conspicuous, it was only as an obscure, a deeply hushed failure. I joined William, after what had seemed to me an eternity of woe, at the Academy, where I followed, for too short a time but with a comparative recovery of confidence, such literary *cours*[7] as I might.

I puzzle it out to-day that my parents had simply said to themselves, in serious concern, that I read too many novels, or at least read them too attentively—*that* was the vice; as also that they had by the contagion of their good faith got me in a manner to agree with them; since I could almost always enter, to the gain of "horizon" but too often to the perversion of experience, into any view of my real interests, so-called, that was presented to me with a dazzling assurance. I didn't consider certainly that I was so forming my mind, and was doubtless curious to see whether it mightn't, by a process flourishing in other applications, get to some extent formed. It wasn't, I think, till I felt the rapture of that method's arrest that I knew how grotesquely little it had done for me. And yet I bore it afterwards no malice—resorting again to that early fatalistic philosophy of which the general sense was that almost anything, however disagreeable, had been worth while; so unable was I to claim that it hadn't involved impressions. I positively felt the impressional harvest rather rich, little as any item of it might have passed at the time for the sort of thing one exhibits as a trophy of learning. My small exhibition was all for myself and

7. Studies, classes. The Académie de Genève in the Bâtiment du Musée Académique in the Grand' Rue was founded in 1559 and became the University of Geneva in 1871 (*Petit guide à Genève* [Geneva: Soullier, 1902], 16).

consisted on the whole but of a dusty, spotty, ugly picture—I took it for ugly well-nigh to the pitch of the sinister. Its being a picture at all—and I clung to that—came from the personal and material facts of the place, where I was the only scholar of English speech, since my companions, with a Genevese predominance, were variously polyglot. They wondered, I couldn't doubt, what I was doing among them, and what lost lamb, almost audibly bleating, I had been charged to figure. Yet I remember no crude chaff, no very free relation of any one with any one, no high pitch, still less any low descent, of young pleasantry or irony; our manners must have been remarkably formed, and our general tone was that of a man-of-the-world discretion, or at the worst of a certain small bourgeois circumspection. The dread in the Genevese of having definitely to "know" strangers and thereby be at costs for any sort of hospitality to them comes back to me as written clear; not less than their being of two sorts or societies, sons of the townspeople pure and simple and sons of the local aristocracy perched in certain of the fine old houses of the Cité and enjoying a background of sturdily-seated lakeside villas and deeply umbrageous campagnes.[8] I remember thinking the difference of type, complexion and general *allure*[9] between these groups more marked, to all the senses, than any "social distinction" I had yet encountered. But the great thing was that I could so simplify our enclosing scene itself, round it in and make it compose—the dark, the dreary Institution, squeezed into a tall, dim, stony-faced and stony-hearted house at the very top of the Cité and directly in the rear of the Cathedral, portions of the apse of which seem to me to have straggled above or protruded toward it, with other odd extraneous masses than itself pressing still nearer. This simplification, quite luxuriously for my young mind, was to mere mean blackness of an old-world sordid order. I recognised *rich* blackness in other connections, but this was somehow of a harsh tradition and a tragic economy; sordid and strong was what I had from the first felt the place, though urging myself always to rub off history from its stones, and suffering thus, after a fashion, by the fact that with history it ought to be interesting and that I ought to know just how and why it was. For that, I think, was ever both the burden and the joy—the complication, I mean, of interest, and the sense, in the midst of the ugly and the melancholy, that queer crooked silent corners behind cathedrals wrought in their way for one, did something, while

8. *Campagnes:* villas.
9. Bearing.

one haunted them, to the imagination and the taste; and that so, once more, since the generalisation had become a habit with me, I couldn't, seeing and feeling these things, really believe I had picked up nothing.

When I sat in a dusky upper chamber and read "French literature" with blighted M. Toeppfer, son of a happier sire, as I was sure the charming writer and caricaturist, in spite of cumbrous cares, must have been;[10] or when, a couple of times a week and in the same eternal twilight (we groped almost lampless through the winter days, and our glimmering tapers, when they sparsely appeared, smelt of a past age), I worried out Virgil and Tite-Live with M. Verchère, or Schiller and Lessing with the ruddy noisy little professor of German,[11] who sat always, the lesson long, in a light brown talma, the sides of which he caused violently to flap for emphasis like agitated wings, I was almost conscious of the breath of culture as I modestly aspired to culture, and was at any rate safe for the time from a summons to the blackboard at the hands of awful little M. Galopin, that dispenser of the paralysing chalk who most affected me. Extremely diminutive and wearing for the most part a thin inscrutable smile, the ghost of a tribute to awkwardness happily carried off, he found in our barren interviews, I believed, a charm to curiosity, bending afresh each time as over the handful of specimen dust, unprecedented product at its finest, extracted from the scratched soil of my intelligence. With M. Toeppfer I was almost happy; with each of these instructors my hour was unshared, my exploits unwitnessed, by others; but M. Toeppfer became a friend, shewed himself a *causeur*,[12] brightened our lesson with memories of his time in Paris, where, if I am not mistaken, he had made, with great animation, his baccalauréat, and whence it was my possibly presumptuous impression he had brought back a state of health, apparently much impaired, which represented contrition for youthful spirits. He had haunted the parterre of the Théâtre Français, and when we read Racine his vision of Rachel, whom he had seen there as often as possible,

10. Charles was the son of the author and teacher Rodolphe Töpffer, whose children's stories (such as *Voyages en zigzag* or *Nouveaux voyages en zigzag*) the James family enjoyed (see *SBO,* n. 470). Twenty-seven years old in 1859, Töpffer had studied sculpture in Paris and executed a bust of his father for Töpffer Square (Le Clair, *Young Henry James*, 302).

11. Publius Vergilius Maro (70–19 BCE), Roman poet, author of the *Aeneid;* Tite-Live, the French version of Titus Livius, or Livy (59 BCE–17 CE), Roman historian; Johann Christoph Friedrich von Schiller (1759–1805), German poet, dramatist, and philosopher; Gotthold Ephraim Lessing (1729–81), German critic and dramatist.

12. Talker.

revived; he was able to say at moments how she had spoken and moved, and I recall in particular his telling me that on her entrance as Phèdre, borne down, in her languorous passion, by the weight of her royal robes— "Que ces vains ornemens, que ces voiles me pèsent!"—the long lapse of time before she spoke and while she sank upon a seat filled itself extraordinarily with her visible woe.[13] But where he most gave me comfort was in bringing home to me that the house commemorated, immortalised, as we call it, in the first of his father's Nouvelles Genevoises, La Bibliothèque de mon Oncle,[14] was none other than the structure facing us where we sat and which so impinged and leaned on the cathedral walls that he had but to indicate to me certain points from the window of our room to reconstitute thrillingly the scenery, the drollery, the whimsical action of the tale. *There* was a demonstration I could feel important, votary and victim of the "scene," the scene and the "atmosphere" only, that I had been formed to be. That I called interesting lore—called it so at least to myself, though feeling it at the same time of course so little *directly* producible that I could perhaps even then have fronted this actually remote circumstance of my never having produced it till this moment. There abode in me, I may add, a sense that on any subject that did appeal and that so found me ready— such subjects being indeed as yet vague, but immensely suggestive of number—I should have grasped the confident chalk, welcomed the very biggest piece, not in the least have feared the blackboard. They were inscribed, alas for me, in no recognised course. I put my hand straight on another of them, none the less, if not on a whole group of others, in my

13. The Théâtre Français in Paris represented the best of artistic values in HJ's eyes; the aesthetic Gabriel Nash in *The Tragic Muse* (1890) provocatively considers "the Théâtre Français a greater institution than the House of Commons" ([London: Penguin, 1995], 48). Rachel (Elizabeth Félix, 1821–58), who had been raised in poverty, became one of the most celebrated of French actors of the nineteenth century; though HJ frequently refers to her, he never saw her perform. *Phèdre* by Jean Racine (1639–99) was first staged on 1 January 1677. Rachel played Phèdre, a role for which she became famous, for the first time on 21 January 1843. The wife of Theseus, Phaedra fell in love with her stepson Hippolytus, who spurned her. HJ quotes from one of her early speeches in the play: "Que ces vains ornements, que ces voiles me pèsent! . . . Tout m'afflige et me nuit, et conspire à me nuire" (How these futile ornaments, these veils weigh me down! . . . Everything overwhelms and harms me, and conspires to harm me).

14. *Nouvelles genevoises* (1841) was a collection of Töpffer's Geneva tales. In the opening pages of "La bibliothèque de mon oncle" (1832), "My Uncle's Library," one of his most successful stories, the young narrator gazes down from his window on the scene before him very much as HJ will observe the city street.

ascent, each morning of the spring or the early summer sémestre,[15] of the admirable old Rue de la Tour de Boël, pronounced Boisl, which, dusky, steep and tortuous, formed a short cut to that part of the Grand' Rue in which the Academy was then seated.

It was a foul and malodorous way—I sniff again, during the tepid weeks, its warm close air and that near presence of rank cheese which was in those days almost everywhere, for the nostril, the note of urban Switzerland; these things blessed me as I passed, for I passed straight to freedom and away from M. Galopin; they mixed with the benediction of the exquisite spring and the rapture, constantly renewed, though for too short a period, of my now substituting literary, or in other words romantic, studies for the pursuits of the Institution Rochette. I viewed them as literary, these new branches of research, though in truth they were loose enough and followed on loose terms. My dear parents, as if to make up to me, characteristically, for my recent absurd strain to no purpose, allowed me now the happiest freedom, left me to attend such lectures as I preferred, only desiring that I should attend several a week, and content—cherished memory that it makes of their forms with me—that these should involve neither examinations nor reports. The Academic authorities, good-natured in the extreme and accustomed to the alien amateur, appear to have been equally content, and I was but too delighted, on such lines, to attend anything or everything. My whole impression now, with my self-respect re-established, was of something exquisite: I was put to the proof about nothing; I deeply enjoyed the confidence shown in my taste, not to say in my honour, and I sat out lecture after lecture as I might have sat out drama, alternate tragedy and comedy, beautifully performed—the professor in each case figuring the hero, and the undergraduates, much more numerous, though not in general maturer than those of the Institution, where I had been, to my perception, every one's junior, partaking in an odd fashion of the nature at once of troupe and spectators. The scientific subjects, in a large suggestive way, figured tragedy, I seemed to feel, and I pushed this form to the point of my following, for conscience' sake, though not with the last regularity, lurid demonstrations, as they affected me, on anatomy and physiology; these in turn leading to my earnest view, at the Medical School, of the dissection of a *magnifique gendarme*—which ordeal brought me to a stand. It was by the literary and even by the

15. HJ attended the Academy from April to July 1860.

philosophic *leçons* that the office of bright comedy was discharged, on the same liberal lines;[16] at the same time that I blush to remember with how base a blankness I must have several times listened to H. F. Amiel, admirable writer, analyst, moralist.[17] His name and the fact of his having been then a mild grave oracle of the shrine are all that remain with me (I was fit to be coupled with my cousin Anne King, named in another place, who, on the same Genevese scene, had had early lessons from the young Victor Cherbuliez, then with all his music in him, and was to live to mention to me that he had been for her "like any one else");[18] the shrine, not to say the temple itself, shining for me truly, all that season, with a mere confounding blur of light. Was it an effect of my intensity of reaction from what I had hated? was it to a great extent the beguiling beauty of a wonderful Swiss spring, into which all things else soothingly melted, becoming together a harmony without parts?—whatever the cause, I owed it to some accident only to be described, I think, as happy, that I moved, those three months, in an acutely enjoying and yet, as would at present appear, a but scantly comparing or distinguishing maze of the senses and the fancy. So at least, to cover this so thin report of my intelligence and my sum of acquisition and retention, I am reduced to supposing.

What essentially most operated, I make out, however, was that force of a renewed sense of William's major activity which always made the presumption of any degree of importance or success fall, with a sort of ecstasy

16. *Magnifique gendarme:* magnificent gendarme, soldier of the police militia; *leçons:* lessons. HJ wrote to Perry on 13 May 1860, "I went the other day in company with half a dozen other students to see a dissection at the Hospital. It was a most unlovely sight. The subject was a strapping big gendarme who had died of inflammation of the lungs. The smell was pretty bad, but I am glad to say that I was not in any way affected by the thing" (Harlow, *Perry: A Biography,* 247).

17. Henri-Frédéric Amiel (1821–81) spent much of his life teaching at the University of Geneva, eventually becoming professor of moral philosophy, though he had traveled and studied across Europe, most significantly in Berlin. His *Journal intime* (1882–84, in 2 vols.), translated into English in 1885 by HJ's long-standing friend Mrs. Humphry Ward, belongs to what she termed "the literature of introspection," and was much admired by her paternal uncle, Matthew Arnold.

18. HJ's cousin Anne was a daughter of Mary James's cousin Charlotte and sister of the much admired Vernon King, who died in the Civil War in 1864; HJ gives an account of both cousins and their mother in *SBO,* chaps. 20 and 28. Charles Victor Cherbuliez (1829–99) was a French novelist and writer born in Geneva, referred to in a letter from HJ to W. E. Henley as "that pitiful prostitute" (*HJL,* 2:183).

of resignation, from my own so minor. Whatever he might happen to be doing made him so interesting about it, and indeed, with the quickest concomitance, about everything else, that what I probably most did, all the while, was but to pick up, and to the effect not a bit of starving but quite of filling myself, the crumbs of his feast and the echoes of his life. His life, all this Geneva period, had been more of a feast than mine, and I recall the sense of this that I had got on the occasion of my accompanying him, by his invitation, toward the end of our stay, to a students' celebration or carouse, which was held at such a distance from the town, at a village or small bourg, up in the Vaud back-country,[19] that we had, after a considerable journey by boat and in heterogeneous and primitive conveyances, tightly packed, to spend two nights there. The Genevese section of the Société de Zoffingue, the great Swiss students' organisation for brotherhood and beer, as it might summarily be defined, of which my brother had become a member, was to meet there certain other sections, now vague to me, but predominantly from the German-speaking Cantons, and, holding a Commerce,[20] to toast their reunion in brimming bowls. It had been thought the impression might amuse, might even interest me—for it was not denied that there were directions, after all, in which I *could* perhaps take notice; and this was doubtless what after a fashion happened, though I felt out in the cold (and all the more that the cold at the moment happened to be cruel), as the only participant in view not crowned with the charming white cap of the society, becoming to most young heads, and still less girt with the parti-coloured ribbon or complementary scarf, which set off even the shabby—for shabbiness considerably figured. I participated vaguely but not too excludedly; I suffered from cold, from

19. *Bourg:* a small market town. The Vaud is a canton of southwest Switzerland between the Lake of Neuchâtel and Lake Geneva. In his letter of 13 May 1860, HJ identifies the village as Moudon, about forty-five miles northeast of Geneva, and gives a full account of this three-day session of "Drinking, smoking big German pipes and singing," which took place in "fearful" weather (Harlow, *Perry: A Biography,* 247–48). The usual spelling for this student group (which still exists) is Société de Zofingue. It meets for study and discussion as well as drinking. Created in 1819, it was intended to foster Swiss unity, numbering among its later members H.-F. Amiel.

20. HJ offers an explanation of the German version of the term in a letter to Sarge Perry: "On the boat were a lot of students from University here, who were going down the river to hold what they call a *Commerz* i.e. to go into a room and swill beer and wine with certain formalities and with emulative vigour till an advanced hour in the morning" (Harlow, *Perry: A Biography,* 259).

hunger and from scant sleeping-space;[21] I found the Bernese and the Bâlois[22] strange representatives of the joy of life, some of them the finest gothic grotesques—but the time none the less very long; all of which, however, was in the day's work if I might live, by the imagination, in William's so adaptive skin. To see that he was adaptive, was initiated, and to what a happy and fruitful effect, that, I recollect, was my measure of content; which was filled again to overflowing, as I have hinted, on my finding him so launched at the Academy after our stretch of virtual separation, and just fancying, with a freedom of fancy, even if with a great reserve of expression, how much he might be living and learning, enjoying and feeling, amid work that was the right work for him and comrades, consecrated comrades, that at the worst weren't the wrong. What was not indeed, I always asked myself, the right work for him, or the right thing of any kind, that he took up or looked at or played with?—failing, as I did more than ever at the time I speak of, of the least glimpse of his being below an occasion. Whatever he played with or worked at entered at once into his intelligence, his talk, his humour, as with the action of colouring-matter dropped into water or that of the turning-on of a light within a window. Occasions waited on him, had always done so, to my view; and there he was, that springtime, on a level with them all: the effect of which recognition had much, had more than aught else, to say to the charming silver haze just then wrapped about everything of which I was conscious. He had formed two or three young friendships that were to continue and to which even the correspondence of his later years testifies; with which it may have had something to do that the Swiss *jeunesse*[23] of the day was, thanks to the political temperature then prevailing, in a highly inflamed and exalted state, and particularly sensitive to foreign sympathy, however platonic, with the national fever. It was the hour at which the French Emperor was to be paid by Victor Emmanuel the price of the liberation of Lombardy; the cession of Nice and Savoie were in the air—with the consequence, in the Genevese breast, of the new immediate neighbourhood thus constituted for its territory. Small Savoie was to be replaced, close against it, by enormous and triumphant France, whose power to

21. "Willie, a German fellow, and I myself did not get scarcely a wink of sleep till near morning because of the constant attacks upon the door of the bed room which we shared together" (ibid., 248).

22. Inhabitants of Bern and Basel.

23. Youth, young people.

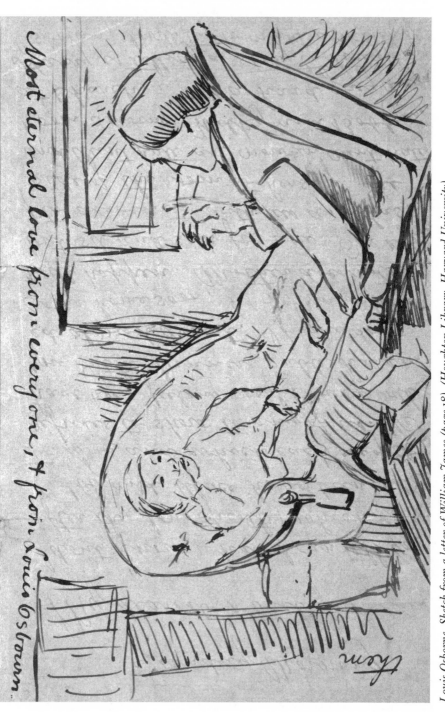

*Louis Osborne. Sketch from a letter of William James (page 18). (Houghton Library, Harvard University)*

absorb great mouthfuls was being so strikingly exhibited.[24] Hence came much hurrying to and fro, much springing to arms, in the way of exercise, and much flocking to the standard—"demonstrations," in other words, of the liveliest; one of which I recall as a huge tented banquet, largely of the white caps, where I was present under my brother's wing, and, out of a sea of agitated and vociferous young heads, sprang passionate protests and toasts and vows and declaimed verses, a storm of local patriotism, though a flurry happily short-lived.

All this was thrilling, but the term of it, by our consecrated custom, already in view; we were transferred at a bound, for the rest of that summer of 1860, to the care, respectively, of a pair of kindly pedagogues at Bonn-am-Rhein;[25] as to which rapid phase I find remembrance again lively, with a letter or two of William's to reinforce it. Yet I first pick up as I pass several young lines from Geneva, and would fain pick up too the drawing that accompanied them—this by reason of the interest of everything of the sort, without exception, that remains to us from his hand. He at a given moment, which came quite early, as completely ceased to ply his pencil as he had in his younger time earnestly and curiously exercised it; and this constitutes exactly the interest of his case. No stroke of it that I have recovered but illustrates his aptitude for drawing, his possible real mastery of the art that was yet, in the light of other interests, so utterly to drop from him; and the example is rare of being so finely capable only to become so indifferent.[26] It was thanks to his later indifference that he

24. In 1859 the Austrians had been defeated by the French in Lombardy. The following year Napoleon III allowed the kingdom of Sardinia, ruled by Victor Emmanuel II (1820–78) to annex Parma, Modena, Tuscany, and the Romagna in return for the shabby cession to France of Nice and Savoy by Count Camillo Cavour (1810–61) of Piedmont, a leading figure in Italy's unification movement. In a letter of 26 March 1860 to Perry, HJ comments, "I suppose you have heard even in your uncivilized parts about the annexation of Savoy to France. It has just taken place and the Swiss are in an 'awful wax' about it, as there is danger of their being compromised by it. I don't suppose there will be any fighting on the subject although Switzerland *has* begun to marshall her troops. During yesterday and to day these streets have filled with soldiers" (Harlow, *Perry: A Biography*, 246).

25. The summer in Bonn is detailed in *NSB*, chap. 2.

26. WJ was a serious student of art in these years and the family returned to Newport ostensibly so that he could work under one of the foremost American painters, William Morris Hunt. The irony of returning from Paris to study in Newport was not lost on HJ. None of the James children were offered much guidance about careers by their parents, though the eldest, WJ and HJ, were provided with considerable financial support when they finally found a vocation. When he took up the study of science, WJ abandoned all

made no point of preserving what he had done—a neglect that, still more lucklessly, communicated itself to his circle; so that we also let things go, let them again and again stray into the desert, and that what might be reproducible is but the handful of scraps that have happened not to perish. "Mother," he writes to his father in absence, "does nothing but sit and cry for you. She refuses to associate with us and has one side of the room to herself. She and the Aunt are now in the Aunt's room. Wilky and Bobby, at home for the day, are at church. It is a hard grey day. H. is telling a story to Louis Osborne, and I will try to make a sketch of them. There has been a terrible bise; the two Cornhill Magazines have come; Mrs. Thomas has been too sick to be at dinner, and we have seen something of some most extraordinary English people."[27] Mrs. Thomas, of New York, was a handsome American widow with handsome children, all from the Avenue Gabriel in Paris, and with the boys enjoying life, among many little compatriots, at the admired establishment of M. Haccius, even as our

---

artistic aspirations, though some of his drawings and illustrations from letters have survived. His change of direction may have been engineered by his father: Howard M. Feinstein believes that HJ Sr., "after reluctantly approving William's painting experiment . . . aborted it covertly by threatening suicide—a threat that a dutiful son could not ignore." In a chapter titled "The Murdered Self," Feinstein analyzes some of WJ's early sketches and drawings to reveal an underlying rage and rebellion that hardly emerge in his letters (*Becoming William James* [Ithaca: Cornell University Press, 1984], 103, 123–35).

27. This letter, dated "Sunday morning [Geneva 1860]," is included in *CWJ*, 4:27–29. "The Aunt" is Aunt Kate, Mary James's sister, who lived semipermanently with the family and traveled with them; *bise* is a seasonal cold north wind. The *Cornhill Magazine*, edited by William Makepeace Thackeray (1811–63), first appeared in 1860 and HJ was enthusiastic: "I have seen the three numbers that are out and find it very good, and what is best of all and indicative of Thackeray setting up to be no more than it is and intends to be" (Harlow, *Perry: A Biography*, 245). He was just one of many happy readers: "The magazine's success was immense. The first number sold 120,000 copies, a record total for an English periodical, and was read by half a million readers" (Gordon N. Ray, *Thackeray: The Age of Wisdom, 1847–63* [London: Oxford University Press, 1958], 296). For a further illustration of warm family feeling, see Wilky's December 1859 letter to his father, written from Geneva: "We arrived a little while ago from School and have already read your welcome letters that have made me feel very sympathetic for you, but still I cannot help smiling, at the easy graceful & homesick style in which they flow. I can sympathise readily with you, & I know if I was in your trying situation I should soon want to come back. How do you find Paris & London? I would give a great deal to be there with you, to be arm in arm with you in Regents Street or St Johns Wood. But I suppose those sweet days have passed" (bMS Am 1095 [2], Houghton).

small brothers were doing at that of M. Maquelin;[28] yet with their destiny of ultimate Europeanisation, of finally complete absorption into the French system, already rather written for them—as a like history, for like foredoomed young subjects, was in those years beginning to be pre-figured, through marriages of daughters and other such beguilements, almost wherever one looked. The extraordinary English people were perhaps an amiable family of whom I retain an image as conversing with our parents at the season when the latter were in their prompt flush of admiration for George Eliot's first novel, Adam Bede, then just given to the world and their copy of which they had rejoicingly lent to their fellow Anglo-Saxons.[29] I catch again the echo of their consternation on receiving it back with the remark that all attempt at an interest in such people, village carpenters and Methodists, had proved vain—for that style of Anglo-Saxon; together with that of my own excited wonder about such other people, those of the style in question, those somehow prodigiously pre-sented by so rare a delicacy, so proud a taste, and made thus to irradiate a strange historic light. It *referred* them, and to a social order, making life more interesting and more various; even while our clear democratic air, that of our little family circle, quivered as with the monstrosity.[30] It might,

28. HJ Sr. had originally considered sending his two younger sons, Wilky and Bob, to Dr. Haccius's school at the Château de Lancy outside the city. It had "already established a wide reputation. Though founded only two years earlier, it numbered among its students Baron de Malorne, nephew of Bismarck, and Samuel Vanderpool, son of Judge Vander-pool of New York." Dr. Haccius permitted only music and no dancing on a Sunday evening (Le Clair, *Young Henry James*, 156, 166). Le Clair points out (175 n. 6) that Edel is wrong in asserting that any of the James boys attended Haccius's school.

29. George Eliot (born Mary Ann Evans, 1819–80) published *Adam Bede* in 1859 and the novel met with great success. In an early essay, HJ concludes that George Eliot's "sympathies are with common people," that she is "unmistakably a painter of *bourgeois* life" ("The Novels of George Eliot" [1866], *LC* 1, 913).

30. Compare HJ Sr.'s sentiments in "The Social Significance of Our Institutions" (1861), in which he compares European with American society (with much emphasis on male as opposed to female values) and concludes, "Our very Constitution binds us . . . the very breath of our political nostrils binds us, to disown all distinctions among men, to disregard persons, to disallow privilege the most established and sacred, to legislate only for the common good, no longer for those accidents of birth or wealth or culture which spiritually individualize man from his kind" (F. O. Matthiessen, *The James Family* [New York: Knopf, 1947], 66). Years later HJ's sister, Alice, scorns the fawning ways of her landlady at Leamington Spa on comparable grounds: "It's this vast class in England, the only nation where it exists, which like the cringing dog is ready to lick the hand that

this note that made us, in the parlance of to-day, sit up, fairly have opened to me that great and up to then unsuspected door of the world from which the general collection of monstrosities, its existence suddenly brought home to us, would doubtless stretch grandly away. The story I told Louis Osborne has quite passed from me, but not little Louis himself, an American child of the most charming and appealing intelligence, marked by some malady that was more or less permanently to cripple, or was even cruelly to destroy him, and whom it was a constant joy to aspire to amuse.[31] His mother was schooling her elder son in the company of our own brothers, his father having established them all at Geneva that he might go for a tour in the East. Vivid to me still is the glimpse I happened to get one Sunday betimes of the good Maquelin couple, husband and wife, in deep mourning[32]—a touch of the highest decency—who had come, with faces a yard long, to announce to Mrs. Osborne the death of her husband in the Holy Land, communicated to them, by slow letter, in the first instance. With little Louis on one's knee one didn't at all envy M. and Madame Maquelin; and than this small faint phantom of sociable helpless little listening Louis none more exquisite hovers before me.

With which mild memories thus stands out for me too the lively importance, that winter, of the arrival, from the first number, of the orange-covered earlier Cornhill—the thrill of each composing item of that first number especially recoverable in its intensity. Is anything like that thrill possible to-day—for a submerged and blinded and deafened generation, a generation so smothered in quantity and number that discrimination, under the gasp, has neither air to breathe nor room to turn round? Has any like circumstance now conceivably the value, to the charmed attention, so far as anything worth naming attention, or any charm for it, is anywhere left, of the fact that Trollope's Framley Parsonage there began?—let alone the still other fact that the Roundabout Papers did and that Thackeray thus appeared to us to guarantee personally, intimately, with a present audibility that was as the accent of good company, the new relation with him and with others of company not much worse, as they then seemed, that such a

<hr>

chastises, that gives you in time what you expect so little at first, a sense of unmanliness" (*The Diary of Alice James,* ed. Leon Edel [London: Rupert Hart-Davis, 1965], 157).

31. WJ's letter to his father of 1860 (see n. 27 above) comments (with a different spelling of the surname) that "Harry is telling a story to Louis Osbourn" and later records that "Louis Osbourn has just blotted my writing with the paper cutter" (*CWJ,* 4:27).

32. M. Maquelin was the director of the school attended by Louis's brother and two of HJ's brothers (see above, n. 4).

medium could establish.[33] To speak of these things, in truth, however, is to feel the advantage of being able to live back into the time of the more sovereign periodical appearances much of a compensation for any reduced prospect of living forward. For these appearances, these strong time-marks in such stretches of production as that of Dickens, that of Thackeray, that of George Eliot, had in the first place simply a genial weight and force, a direct importance, and in the second a command of the permeable air and the collective sensibility, with which nothing since has begun to deserve comparison. They were enrichments of life, they were *large* arrivals, these particular renewals of supply—to which, frankly, I am moved to add, the early Cornhill giving me a pretext, even the frequent examples of Anthony Trollope's fine middle period, looked at in the light of old affection and that of his great heavy shovelfuls of testimony to constituted English matters; a testimony of course looser and thinner than Balzac's to *his* range of facts, but charged with something of the big Balzac authority.[34] These various, let alone numerous, deeper-toned strokes of the great Victorian clock were so many steps in the march of our age, besides being so many notes, full and far-reverberating, of our having high company to keep— high, I mean, to cover all the ground, in the sense of the genial pitch of it. So it was, I remember too, that our parents spoke of their memory of the successive surpassing attestations of the contemporary presence of Scott;[35] to which we might have replied, and doubtless after no great space began to reply, that our state, and even their later one, allowing for a certain gap, had nothing to envy any other. I witnessed, for that matter, with all my senses, young as I was, the never-to-be-equalled degree of difference made, for what may really be called the world-consciousness happily exposed to it, by the prolonged "coming-out" of The Newcomes, yellow number by number, and could take the general civilised participation in

33. *Framley Parsonage,* by Anthony Trollope (1815–82), first serialized in the *Cornhill Magazine,* was published in 1861. HJ's essay on Trollope in *Partial Portraits* (1883) was originally published in the *Century Magazine,* July 1883 (*LC* 1, 1330–54). Thackeray's series of familiar essays in the manner of Charles Lamb, *Roundabout Papers,* first appeared in the *Cornhill.*

34. Charles Dickens (1812–70), Thackeray, and George Eliot represent the mid-Victorian novel at its best and most diverse, and they exercised a powerful influence on HJ. He makes numerous allusions to their works in his critical writing, though he most enduringly admired Honoré de Balzac (1799–1850), for his depiction of nineteenth-century provincial and urban society in France.

35. During his career, the novels of Sir Walter Scott (1771–1832) enjoyed unparalleled success.

the process for a sort of basking in the light of distinction.[36] The process repeated itself for some years under other forms and stimuli, but the merciless change was to come—so that through whatever bristling mazes we may now pick our way it is not to find them open into any such vales of Arcady.[37] My claim for our old privilege is that we did then, with our pace of dignity, proceed from vale to vale.

II My point at any rate, such as it is, would be that even at the age I had reached in 1860[38] something of the happier time still lingered—the time in which a given product of the press might have a situation and an aspect, a considerability, so to speak, a circumscription and an *aura;* room to breathe and to show in, margin for the casting of its nets. The occasion at large was doubtless shrinking, one could note—shrinking like the unlet "house" on a night of grandest opera, but "standing room only" was not yet everywhere the sign, and the fine deliberate thing could here and there find its seat. I really indeed might have held it the golden age of letters still, and of their fond sister leisure, with that quiet swim into our ken on its appointed day, during our Bonn summer,[39] of the charming Once a Week of the prime, the prime of George

36. Thackeray completed some numbers, or installments, of *The Newcomes* during the summer of 1854 when he was staying near Boulogne-sur-Mer (just a few years ahead of the James family); the Dickens family was also holidaying in the town. The novel was first published serially before its complete appearance in 1855. Gordon Ray points out that, in "The Younger Generation" (*Times Literary Supplement,* 19 March and 2 April 1914; rpt. as "The New Novel," *LC* 1, 124–59), HJ "found the characteristic note of the Edwardian novel to be the degree of 'saturation' that its writers achieved, their 'state of inordinate possession.' Yet *Clayhanger, Tono-Bungay,* and *The Man of Property* . . . seem the work of frivolous impressionists when placed beside *The Newcomes*" (*The Age of Wisdom,* 237).

37. Arcadia, a central district of the Greek Peloponnesus, becomes in the poetry of Virgil an idyllic pastoral scene.

38. HJ reached seventeen in April 1860. The opening of this chapter continues to recall the great literature of his youth.

39. The Jameses left Switzerland in early July 1860. HJ and WJ hiked for a week in the Alps, traveling over the St. Bernard Pass, before they met the rest of the family at Interlaken. Youngest brother Bob remained in Geneva at the Pensionnat Maquelin (*CWJ,* 4:30) before going on a school trip to the Italian lakes and Genoa. HJ offered a colorful account of his Alpine week in a letter to Perry (Harlow, *Perry: A Biography,* 252–56). Writing in French, WJ also records the journey in a letter to his Genevan friend Charles Ritter (*CWJ,* 4:29–32). The original plan was that the family should stay in Germany for the coming year.

Meredith and Charles Reade and J. E. Millais and George du Maurier;[40] which our father, to bridge our separation from him, sent us, from Paris and elsewhere, in prompt and characteristic relief of our plotted, our determined strict servitude to German,[41] and to the embrace of the sweet slim essence of which the strain of one's muscles round a circular ton of advertisement was not a condition attached. I should like to say that I rioted, all that season, on the supreme German classics *and* on Evan Harrington, with Charles Reade's A Good Fight, the assured little prelude to The Cloister and the Hearth, thrown in;[42] and I should indeed be ready to say it, were not the expression gross for the really hushed piety of my attitude during those weeks. It was perhaps not quite till then that I fully emerged from the black shadow of the École Préparatoire aux Écoles Spéciales, not quite till we had got off beyond the blest Rhine at Basle that I ceased to hear and feel all but just behind me, portentous perhaps of another spring, the cold breath of the monster. The guttery Bonn-Gasse was during those weeks of the year close and stale, and the house of our good Herr Doctor Humpert, professor at the Bonn Gymnasium, in which

40. The magazine *Once a Week: An Illustrated Miscellany of Literature, Art, Science, & Popular Information* (1859–80), edited by Samuel Lucas, employed many writers and illustrators from *Punch* and was aimed at a young readership. George Meredith (1828–1909) was a novelist and poet; Charles Reade (1814–84) was a dramatist and novelist. As well as being an important Pre-Raphaelite painter (see *SBO*, n. 479), John Everett Millais (1829–96) provided illustrations for fiction (including *Framley Parsonage*, mentioned in *NSB*, chap. 1). George du Maurier (1834–96) was both a cartoonist and writer; he had a great success with the novel *Trilby*, and was to become a friend of HJ's in later years (recorded in fictionalized form in David Lodge's *Author, Author* [London: Secker and Warburg, 2004]). HJ's May 1883 essay "George du Maurier" for the *Century Magazine* was reprinted in *Partial Portraits* (1888), and he provided notes on du Maurier's drawings for a catalogue of the Fine Art Society in 1884. HJ discussed his friend as a novelist in *Harper's Weekly* in 1894, and a longer essay, also titled "George du Maurier," appeared in *Harper's New Monthly Magazine* in 1897 (*LC* 1, 870–76; 876–906).

41. With recently improved rail links, HJ Sr. could relatively easily visit both Paris and London; he made several quite lengthy trips from Geneva, though "what he did can only be conjectured" (Habegger, *The Father*, 414)! With the three oldest boys settled in Bonn, the adults moved on 6 August to Paris to stay at the Hôtel des Trois Empereurs on the rue de Rivoli. HJ records that his mother's Bonn lodgings "are in a huge brick mansion built to imitate a feudal castle, situated immediately on the flat shore of the Rhine, so that the water, I am told, sweeps in winter round its base" (Harlow, *Perry: A Biography*, 259).

42. Meredith's comic novel *Evan Harrington*, was published in *Once a Week* in 1860, while *A Good Fight* and *The Cloister and the Hearth* appeared in the same magazine in 1859 and 1861, respectively.

I shared a room with my brother Wilky, contracted and dim, as well as fragrant through a range of assaults that differed only in kind and not at all in number from those of the street itself;[43] and yet I held the period and the whole situation idyllic—the slightly odd sense of which was one's being to that extent attuned to the life of letters and of (oh the great thing!) impressions "gone in for." To feel a unity, a character and a tone in one's impressions, to feel them related and all harmoniously coloured, that *was* positively to face the æsthetic, the creative, even, quite wondrously, the critical life and almost on the spot to commence author.[44] They had begun, the impressions—that was what was the matter with them—to scratch quite audibly at the door of liberation, of extension, of projection; what they were *of* one more or less knew, but what they were *for* was the question that began to stir, though one was still to be a long time at a loss directly to answer it.

There, for the present, was the rub,[45] the dark difficulty at which one could but secretly stare—secretly because one was somehow ashamed of its being there and would have quickly removed one's eyes, or tried to clear them, if caught in the act of watching. Impressions were not merely all right but were the dearest things in the world; only one would have gone to the stake rather than in the first place confessed to some of them, or in the second announced that one really lived by them and built on them. This failure then to take one's stand in the connection could but come from the troubled view that they were naught without a backing, a stout stiff hard-grained underside that would hold them together and of which the terrible name was simply science, otherwise learning, and learning exclusively by books, which were at once the most beautiful and the most dreadful things in the world, some of them right, strikingly, showily right, some of them disgracefully and almost unmentionably wrong, that is

43. Wilky and HJ stayed with Dr. Humpert and his family, a Gymnasium professor of Latin and Greek at 190, Bonngasse, not far from Beethoven's birthplace, in the center of Bonn (Edel, *Untried Years,* 156). "Philippus Humpert (b. 1814) defended a thesis on Homer at Bonn in 1839" (*CWJ,* 4:39 n. 2), presumably the same man. WJ lodged close by with a university professor, Theodor Stromberg, and his family.

44. Compare Wilky's light-hearted comment made during the stay in Geneva: "Harry has become an author I believe, for he keeps his door locked all day, & a little while ago, I got a peep in his room, and saw some poetical looking manuscripts lying on the table, & himself looking in a most authorlike way" (Harlow, *Perry: A Biography,* 249).

45. HJ perhaps recollects some famous lines from *Hamlet:* "To die, to sleep; / To sleep, perchance to dream—ay, there's the rub: / For in that sleep of death what dreams may come, / When we have shuffled off this mortal coil" (3.1.64–68).

grossly irrelevant, as for instance a bound volume of Once a Week would be, but remarkable above all for overwhelming number and in general for defiance of comprehension. It was true that one had from time to time the rare adventure of one's surprise at understanding parts of them none the less—understanding more than a very little, more than much too little; but there was no practical support to speak of in that, even the most one could ever hope to understand being a mere drop in the bucket. Never did I quite strike it off, I think, that impressions might themselves *be* science— and this probably because I didn't then know them, when it came to the point, as anything but life. I knew them but by that collective and unpractical—many persons would have said that frivolous—name; which saw me little further. I was under the impression—this in fact the very liveliest of what might have been called the lot—that life and knowledge were simply mutual opposites, one inconsistent with the other; though hovered about, together, at the same time, by the anomaly that when knowledge impinged upon life, pushed against her, as it were, and drove her to the wall, it was all right, and such was knowledge's way and title; whereas when life played the like tricks with knowledge nothing but shame for the ruder, even if lighter, party could accrue. There was to come to me of course in time the due perception that neither was of the least use—use to myself—without the other;[46] but meanwhile, and even for much after, the extreme embarrassment continued: to whichever of the opposites one gave one's self it was with a sense of all but basely sacri-ficing the other. However, the conflict and the drama involved in the question at large was doubtless what was to make consciousness—under whichever of the two names one preferred to entertain it—supremely intense and interesting.

This then is by way of saying that the idyll, as I have called it, of the happy juncture I glanced at a moment back came from the fact that I didn't at all know how much I was living, and meanwhile quite supposed I was considerably learning. When, rising at some extraordinary hour of the

46. Le Clair (*Young Henry James*, 317) notes the links between HJ's evaluation of the cumulative power of impressions and a similar idea expressed in "The Art of Fiction" (1884): "The power to guess the unseen from the seen, to trace the implication of things, to judge the whole piece by the pattern, the condition of feeling life in general so completely that you are well on your way to knowing any particular corner of it—this cluster of gifts may almost be said to constitute experience. . . . If experience consists of impressions, it may be said that impressions *are* experience, just as (have we not seen it?) they are the very air we breathe" (*LC* 1, 53).

morning, I went forth through the unawakened town (and the Germans, at that time, heaven knows, were early afoot too), and made for the open country and the hill, in particular, of the neighbouring Venusberg,[47] long, low and bosky, where the dews were still fresh and ancient mummies of an old cloister, as I remember it, somewhere perched and exposed, I was doing, to my sense, an attuned thing; attuned, that is, to my coming home to bend double over Schiller's Thirty Years' War in the strenuous spirit that would keep me at it, or that would vary it with Goethe's Wahlver-wandtschaften, till late in the warm afternoon.[48] I found German prose much tougher than the verse, and thereby more opposed to "life," as to which I of course couldn't really shake off the sense that it might be worked as infinitely comprehensive, comprehensive even of the finest discriminations against it. The felicity, present but naturally unanalysed, was that the whole thing, our current episode, *was* exactly comprehensive of life, presenting it in particular as characteristically German, and therein freshly vivid—with the great vividness that, by our parents' vague wish, we were all three after or out for; in spite of our comparatively restricted use, in those days, of these verbal graces. Such therefore was the bright unity of our experience, or at least of my own share in it—this luck that, through the intensity of my wanting it to, all consciousness, all my own immediate, *tasted* German, to the great and delightful quickening of my imagination.[49] The quickening was of course no such matter as I was to know nearly ten years later on plunging for the first time over the Alps into Italy; but,

47. The Venusberg is in the southern quarters of Bonn, on the east side of the Melb Valley (*Cologne and Bonn with Environs: Handbook for Travellers by Karl Baedeker* [Frei-berg: Karl Baedeker, 1961], 164).

48. *The History of the Thirty Years' War,* by Johann Christoph Friedrich von Schiller (1759-1805), was published in 1791-93. A novel by the great polymath Johann Wolfgang von Goethe (1749-1832), *Wahlverwandtschaften,* or *Elective Affinities,* came out in 1809. Goethe uses the term (scientific in source) to indicate the adulterous attraction felt between the couple at the center of the novel. HJ's unsigned review of Thomas Carlyle's translation of Goethe's *Wilhelm Meister's Apprenticeship and Travels* appeared in the *North American Review* (July 1865) (*LC* 2, 944-49).

49. HJ, unlike WJ, never became involved in German language and culture and, as Edel points out, "satirizes the Germans in a number of his tales" (*Untried Years,* 157). When he went to stay near Naples in 1880 with his friend Paul Zhukovski, then "living in great intimacy with Richard Wagner," HJ was invited to meet the composer, but he re-fused: "I kept away because Wagner speaks no French and I no German" (*HJL,* 2:287)—which couldn't have been entirely true. The Rhineland landscape is the setting for Wag-ner's *Ring* cycle.

letting alone that I was then so much older, I had wondered about Italy, to put it embracingly, far more than I was constitutionally capable of wondering about Germany. It was enough for me at Bonn that I felt no lack of appetite—had for the time all the illusion of being on the way to something; to something, I mean, with which the taste of German might somehow *directly* mix itself. Every aspect and object round about was a part, at all events, of the actual mixture; and when on drowsy afternoons, not a little interspaced indeed, I attempted the articulate perusal of Hermann und Dorothea with our good Professor, it was like dreaming, to the hum of bees, if not to the aftertaste of "good old Rhenish," in some homely fruity eighteenth-century garden.[50]

The good old Rhenish is no such false note in this reconstitution; I seem to see the Frau Doctorin and her ancient mildly-scowling sister Fräulein Stamm, who reminded me of Hepzibah Pyncheon in The House of the Seven Gables,[51] perpetually wiping green hock-glasses and holding them up to our meagre light, as well as setting out long-necked bottles, with rather chalky cakes, in that forward section of our general eating-and-living-room which formed our precinct of reception and conversation. The unbroken space was lighted at either end, from street and court, and its various effects of tempered shade or, frankly speaking, of rather greasy gloom, amid which the light touch of elegance gleamed but from the polish of the glasses and the sloping shoulders of their bottle, comes back to me as the view of an intensely internal interior. I recall how oppressively in that apartment, how congestedly, as in some cage of which the wires had been papered over, I felt housed and disconnected; I scarce then, I

50. *Hermann und Dorothea* is Goethe's epic poem of 1798. "Rhenish," or hock, is the white wine of the Rhine valley.

51. Mrs. Humpert and her sister Miss Stamm are discussed scathingly in HJ's letter of 18 July 1860: it was intended they should help "in the task of conversing ceaselessly with us (a task for which they might seem to be but ill-qualified as I don't believe that between them they can muster, Germanlike, more than half a dozen teeth)." He goes on to say, more generally, "The women stop at home all day, doing the house-work, drudging, and leading the most homely and I should say joyless lives. I fancy they never look at a book, and all their conversation is about their pots and pans. The sister asked me the other day if we hadn't a king in the United States!" (Harlow, *Perry: A Biography*, 255). WJ seems to have shared HJ's view: "They have been so shut out from the world and have been melting together so long by the kitchen fire that the minds of both have become confounded into one, and they seem to constitute a sort of two bodied individual" (*CWJ*, 4:37). Hepzibah Pyncheon is the aged and reclusive inmate of the House of the Seven Gables in Hawthorne's novel of 1851.

think, knew what the matter was, but it could only have been that in all those summer weeks, to the best of my belief, no window was ever once opened.[52] Still, there was the scene, the thick, the much-mixed chiaroscuro through which the two ladies of the family emerged from an exiguous retreat just off the back end of the place with ample platters of food; the almost impenetrable dusk of the middle zone, where the four or five of us, seated with our nutcracker-faced pastor, conveyed the food to our mouths with a confidence mainly borrowed from the play of his own deep-plunging knife; and then the forward, the festal extension, the privilege of occasionally lingering in which, or of returning to it for renewed refreshment, was a recognition both of our general minding of our business upstairs—left as we were to thumb our Flügel's Dictionary[53] by the hour so long as we invoked no other oracle. Our drowsy Doctor invited no such approach; he smiled upon us as if unseen forefingers of great force had been inserted for the widening of his mouth at the corners, and I had the sense of his not quite knowing what to make of our being so very gently barbaric, or rather so informally civilised; he safely housed and quite rankly fed us, guided us to country walks and to the swimming-baths by the Rhineside, introduced us to fruit-gardens where, on payment of the scantest tribute, we were suffered to consume off-hand bushels of cherries, plums and pears; suffered us to ascend the Drachenfels and to partake of coffee at Rolandseck and in other friendly open-air situations;[54] but

52. HJ perhaps reveals here his American credentials in his distaste for such European airlessness. When he hears of Hawthorne's death in chap. 12 below, the shutters are "drawn to against openest windows" (it was May). And when Gray Fielding, after years spent in Europe, arrives at his uncle's Newport home, the narrator comments, "There was an American way for a room to be a room, a table a table, a chair a chair and a book a book—let alone a picture on a wall a picture, and a cold gush of water in a bath of a hot morning a promise of purification; and of this license all about him, in fine, he beheld the refreshing riot" (*The Ivory Tower,* ed. Percy Lubbock [London: Collins, 1917], 74).

53. Flügel's German and English dictionary had a first edition in 1841 and a second ("new") edition in 1842. Some controversy arose in the 1840s around the editorship of the German-English volume (not by Dr. Flügel), but the dictionary in its several editions continued to be popular with British and American students (C. A. Feiling, A. Heimann, and John Oxenford, *Flügel's Complete Dictionary of the German and English Languages in two parts* [London: Whittaker, 1857], iii–v). It is not clear which edition the James brothers consulted.

54. As HJ points out in a letter to Perry, the Drachenfels (or Dragon Rock) is "a mountain on the other side of the Rhine," which they walked up: "On the top of the mountain, there stands a high crag with a ruined castle on the top of *it,* in truly Rhenish fashion" (Harlow, *Perry: a Biography,* 259). HJ provided an illustration, described in

flung his gothic shadow as little as possible over my so passive page at least, and took our rate of acquisition savingly for granted.

This, in the optimism of the hour, I have no memory of resenting; the page, though slow, managed at the same time to be stirring, and I asked no more of any one or anything but that they should be with all due gothicism whatever they most easily might. The long vistas of the beeches and poplars on the other side of the Rhine, after we had crossed by the funicular ferry, gothically rustled and murmured: I fancied their saying perpetually "We are German woods, we are German woods—which makes us very wonderful, do you know? and unlike any others: don't you feel the spell of the very sound of us and of the beautiful words, 'Old German woods, old German woods,' even if you can't tell why?" I couldn't altogether tell why, but took everything on trust as mystically and valuably gothic—valuably because ministering with peculiar directness, as I gathered, to culture. I was in, or again I was "out," in my small way, for culture; which seemed quite to come, come from everywhere at once, with the most absurd conciliatory rush, pitifully small as would have been any list of the sources I tapped. The beauty was in truth that everything was a source, giving me, by the charmingest breach of logic, more than it at all appeared to hold; which was exactly what had not been the case at the Institution Rochette, where things had appeared, or at least had pretended, to hold so much more than they gave. The oddity was that about us now everything—everything but the murmur of the German woods and the great flow and magic name of the Rhine—was more ugly than beautiful, tended in fact to say at every turn: "You shall suffer, yes, indeed you *are* doing so (stick up for your right to!) in your sense of form; which however is quite compatible with culture, is really one of the finest parts of it, and may decidedly prove to you that you're getting it." I hadn't, in rubbing, with whatever weakness, against French and, so far as might be, against France, and in sinking, very sensibly, more and more into them, particularly felt that I was getting it *as* such; what I was getting as such was decidedly rather my famous "life," and without so much as thinking of the degree, with it all, of the valuable and the helpful.

Life meanwhile I had a good deal of at my side in the person of my

_____

Edel's edition as a "drawing of river bordered on each side by many mountains of equal size, each topped with a castle" (*HJL,* 1:31). The Drachenfels, overlooking the Rhine, is the most popular of the Seven Mountains, or Siebengebirge. Rolandseck is a village on the left bank of the Rhine, a popular summer resort eight miles above Bonn.

brother Wilky, who, as I have had occasion elsewhere to say, contrived in those years to live, or to have every appearance of so doing, with an immediacy that left me far in the lurch. I was always still wondering how, while he had solved the question simply *ambulando*,[55] which was for him but by the merest sociable stroll. This represented to me success—success of a kind, but such an assured kind—in a degree that was my despair; and I have never forgotten how, that summer, when the Herr Doctor did look in, did settle down a little to have the bristling page out with us, Wilky's share of the hour took on the spot the form of his turning at once upon our visitor the tables of earnest inquiry. He delighted, after this tribute of eagerness, to meet the Doctor's interrogative advance; but the communication so made was of anything and everything except the fruit of his reading (the act of reading was inhuman and repugnant to him), and I amazedly noted while I nursed my small hoard that anything he offered did in the event quite as well: he could talk with such charm, such drollery of candour, such unexpectedness of figure, about what he had done and what he hadn't—or talk at least before it, behind it and beside it. We had three or four house-companions, youths from other places attending the Gymnasium[56] and committed to our Professor's care, as to whom I could somehow but infer that they were, each in his personal way, inordinately gothic—which they had to be to supply to my mind a relation, or a substitute for a relation, with them; whereas my younger brother, without a scrap of a view of them, a grain of theory or formula, tumbled straight into their confidence all round. Our air for *him* was by just so much life as it couldn't have dreamed of being culture, and he was so far right that when the son of the house and its only child, the slim and ardent Theodor, who figured to me but as a case of such classic sensibility, of the Lieder or the Werther sort,[57] as might have made, with the toss of a yellow lock or the gleam of a green blouse, the image for an Uhland or a Heine

55. By walking (Lat.).

56. The Gymnasium in Germany and other European countries provides the final stage of education before university.

57. HJ suggests that Theodor appeared to him as a figure from a Romantic poem or art song (the lied was one of the greatest musical forms of nineteenth-century Romanticism) or the hero of Goethe's loosely autobiographical *Die Leiden des jungen Werthers*, or *The Sorrows of Young Werther* (1774); Werther, in his unhappy love and consequent suicide, became a quintessential embodiment of the mood of the Romantic Sturm und Drang period.

stanza,[58] had imparted to him an intention of instant suicide under some resentment of parental misconception, he had been able to use dissuasion, or otherwise the instinct of then most freely fraternising, with a success to which my relish for so romantic a stroke as charmingly in Theodor's character and setting mightn't at all have attained. There is a small something of each of us in a passage of an ingenuous letter addressed by him from the midst of these conditions to his parents. I fondly catch, I confess, at any of these recoverable lights; finding them at the best too scant for my commemorative purpose.[59]

Willy got his photograph this morning after three hours' hard work. From the post-office he was sent to the custom-house, and there was obliged to sign his name and to go to some neighbouring bookstore to buy a seal. On returning to the custom-house he was sent back to the post-office to get some document or other. After obtaining this article he turned his steps once more to the custom-house, where an insolent officer told him he must wait an hour. W. informed him that he would return at the end of the hour, and accordingly for the third time went to the C.H., and was conducted by the clerk to a cellar where the packages were kept, and there told to take off his hat. He obeyed, raging, and then was a fourth time sent to the P.O.—this time to pay money. Happily he is now in possession of his property. H. and he took a walk this afternoon to a fruit–garden, where plums, cherries, gooseberries and currants were abundant. After half an hour's good work H. left W. finishing merely the plums—the cherry and gooseberry course to come later. He was so enchanted that he thought H. a great fool to leave so soon. How does Paris now strike you? It can't be as nice as Bonn. You had better write to Bob.

Bob, our youngest brother, had been left at Geneva with excellent M. Maquelin and was at that time *en course,* over the Alps, with this gentleman and their young companions; a most desirable, delicious excursion, which I remember following in envious fancy, as it included a descent to the Italian Lakes and a push on as far as Genoa. In reference to which excursion I cull a line or two from a faded scrap of a letter ad-

58. Ludwig Uhland (1787–1862) and Heinrich Heine (1797–1856) were lyrical poets of the German Romantic movement.

59. The original of this letter, written in the summer of 1860, is held at the Houghton library (bMS Am 1095 [3]).

dressed a little later by this youngest of us to his "Beloved Brother" William. "This is about our Grande Course. We started at 5 o'clock in the morning with our faces and hands all nicely washed and our nails clean. The morning was superb, and as we waited in the court the soft balmy air of the mountains came in bringing with it the melodious sound of the rappel for breakfast. This finished we bade adieu, and I could see the emotions of the kind and ever-watchful Madame Maquelin as a few silent drops trickled down her fair cheeks. We at last arrived at the boat, where we met Mr. Peters, a portly gentleman from the city of Philadelphia, with his two sweet sons, one twelve, the other seven years old, the eldest coming from Mr. E.'s school with no very good opinion of the principal— saying he had seen him in a state of tightness several times during his stay there." Mr. Peters appears to have been something of a pessimist, for, when at a later stage "it began to rain hard, and half the road was a foot deep in water, and the cocher[60] had stopped somewhere to get lanterns and had at the same time indulged in certain potations which didn't make him drive any the straighter," this gentleman "insinuated that we had all better have been with our mothers." The letter records at some length the early phases of the affair, but under the weight of the vision of Italy it rather breaks down and artlessly simplifies. "Genoa is a most lively town, and there is a continual swarm of sailors in the street. We visited several palaces, among others that of Victor Emanuel, which is very fine, and the fruit is very cheap. We stayed there several days, but at last started for Turin, where we spent a Sunday—a place I didn't much like, I suppose because of that reason. We left Turin the next day on foot, but lost our road and had to come back." I recover even in presence of these light accents my shade of wonder at this odd chance that made the least developed of us the subject of what seemed to me even then a privilege of the highest intensity; and there again keeps it company my sense, through all the after years, that this early glimpse of the blest old Italy, almost too early though it appears to have but just missed being, might have done something towards preparing or enriching for Bob the one little plot of consciousness in which his deeply troubled life was to find rest.[61] He was

60. *Cocher:* coachman.

61. Whatever Italy's potential for redeeming the life of the troubled Bob James might have been, HJ here recalls it in the light of his own lifelong devotion. The country, of course, became unified only in 1870. *Italian Hours* includes essays written between 1870 and 1909, a record of his fourteen visits to the country. His fiction also includes many scenes set in Italy. HJ—as well as Bob—was enthusiastic about the sailors in the streets of

in the event also fondly to aim at painting, like two of his brothers;[62] but whereas they were to fumble with the lock, in their very differing degree, only in those young years, he was to keep at it most as he grew older, though always with a perfect intelligence of the inevitable limits of the relation, the same intelligence that was so sharp and sad, so extraordinarily free and fine and detached in fact, as play of mind, play of independent talk and of pen, for the limits of his relation to many other matters.[63] Singularly intelligent all round, yet with faculties that had early declined any consummation of acquaintance with such training as under a different sort of pressure he might have enjoyed, he had an admirable hand and eye, and I have known no other such capacity for absorbing or storing up the minutest truths and shades of landscape fact and giving them out afterward, in separation from the scene, with full assurance and felicity. He could do this still better even than he cared to do; I for my part cared much more that he should than he ever did himself, and then it was, I dare say, that I made the reflection: "He took in the picture of Italy, with his firm hard gift, having the chance while William and I were still, comparatively, small untouched and gaping barbarians; and it should always be in him to do at some odd fine moment a certain honour to that." I held to it that that sensibility had played in him more than by any outward measure at the time; which was perhaps indeed one of the signs within me of the wasteful habit or trick of a greater feeling for people's potential propriety or felicity or full expression than they seemed able to have themselves. At all events I was absolutely never to cease to remember for Bob, through everything—and there was much and of the most agitated and agitating—that he had been dipped as a boy into the sacred

Genoa, "magnificently sunburnt . . . mahogany-coloured, bare-chested mariners with earrings and crimson girdles" (*Italian Hours,* ed. John Auchard [Harmondsworth: Penguin, 1995], 107–8). HJ shared Bob's disappointment in Turin, considering it "no city of a name to conjure with" (ibid., 100). Bob James's memories of school days in Boulogne were of more successful boys than he or Wilky who would ascend the mayor's throne, "kneel at his feet, and receive crown or rosettes, or some symbol of merit which *we* did not get. The luck had begun to break early" (quoted in Jane Maher, *Biography of Broken Fortunes: Wilkie and Bob, Brothers of William, Henry, and Alice James* [Hamden, CT: Archon, 1986], 6). Having failed to sustain his marriage, and beset by alcohol problems, Bob died in 1910. See also Lewis, *The Jameses,* 567–72.

62. HJ describes the classes of William Morris Hunt he attended in Newport with WJ in chap. 4 below.

63. Two of Bob's drawings and sketches are reproduced in Maher, *Biography of Broken Fortunes,* as well as a portrait by John La Farge of Bob as a boy playing the flute.

stream; to some effect which, thanks to two or three of his most saving and often so amusing sensibilities, the turbid sea of his life might never quite wash away.[64]

William had meanwhile come to Bonn with us, but was domiciled with another tutor, younger and fairer and more of the world, above all more ventilated and ventilating, Herr Stromberg,[65] whose defect might in fact have seemed that, with his constant exhibition of the stamp received by him from the writings of Lord Macaulay,[66] passages of which he could recite by heart, and the circumstance that his other pupil, William's comrade for a time, was of unmitigatedly English, that is of quasi-Byronic association, he didn't quite rise to the full gothic standard. Otherwise indeed our brother moved on the higher plane of light and air and ease, and above all of enjoyed society, that we felt he naturally must. Present to me yet is the thrill of learning from him that his English fellow-pupil was the grandson, if I remember rightly the degree of descent, of Mary Chaworth, Byron's "first love," and my sense afterwards, in gaping at young Mr. Musters himself, that this independently romantic contact would have been more to my own private purpose at least than the most emphasised gothicism.[67] None the less do I regain it as a part of my current vision that Frau Stromberg, who was young and fair, wrote tragedies as well as made

64. In this finely judged elegy on the life of his troubled brother, HJ links his ironically unrealized potential with those early opportunities offered by Italy, a country the novelist would not visit himself until 1869 and which, when writing these recollections, he knew he would never return to again. William's wife, Alice Howe Gibbens James, was pleased that HJ had dealt with both younger brothers so justly, writing "how tenderly you have interpreted Bob and Wilky and done honor to each as faithfully as to William" (MS Letter, 14 March 1914, bMS Am 1092.11 [54], Houghton).

65. Theodor Stromberg (b. 1827) is described by WJ as *"un grand blondin,"* a fair-haired person, while, in another letter, WJ complains (presumably thinking of Stromberg) that "an old white bear of a fellow literally dances attendance on me from morning till night. He is the best natured most innocent fellow *I ever knew*" (*CWJ*, 4:31, 33). "In 1859–60 he was a privatdocent at Bonn and resided at 57 Kleinhöfchen" (ibid., 618).

66. Thomas Babington Macaulay, 1st Baron Macaulay (1800–59), was an influential historian and politician who also wrote essays and poetry (most famously *The Lays of Ancient Rome*) that were highly popular in the Victorian period.

67. Mary Chaworth (1785–1832), of Annesley Hall, Nottinghamshire, had been a neighbor of George, Lord Byron (1788–1824). Having captivated him, she went on to marry John (Jack) Musters in 1805. It was an anecdote concerning Byron and his lover Mary Jane Clairmont, mother of his daughter, Allegra, which inspired the novella *The Aspern Papers* (1888) (see *CN*, 33–34).

pancakes[68]—which were served to each consumer double, a thick confi-
ture within being the reason of this luxuriance, and being also a note
beyond our experience in the Bonn-Gasse; and that with the printed five
acts of a certain "Cleopatra" before me, read aloud in the first instance to
her young inmates and by my brother passed on to me, I lost myself in the
view of I scarce knew what old-world Germanic grace, positively, or
little court-city practice of the theatre: these things so lived in the small
thick pamphlet, "grey paper with blunt type" and bristling, to my discomfiture, with descriptive stage directions, vast dense bracketed tracts, gothic
enough in all conscience, as to which I could already begin to wonder
whether such reinforcements of presentation proved more for or against
the true expressional essence of the matter;[69] for or against, that is, there
being nothing at all so dramatic, so chargeable with meaning and picture,
as speech, of whatever sort, made perfect. Such speculations, I may parenthesise, might well have been fostered, and doubtless were, by an impression that I find commemorated in a few lines of a letter of my father's to a
friend in America—he having brought us on to Bonn, introduced us to
our respective caretakers and remained long enough to have had an eve-

68. WJ refers to Frau Stromberg as "la premiére [sic] cuisinière de Bonn" (Bonn's
premier cook) (CWJ, 4:31), but the James family clearly had little idea of her significance in
the history of ideas. It seems that she had only recently married, in 1857. Mathilde
Reichardt-Stromberg (b. 1823), initially heavily influenced by Jacob Moleschott, promoted
radical, atheistic ideas that placed nature in its diversity at the center of human life, giving
minimal weight to the exercise of morality or the conflict of good and evil. In later years she
adopted a strongly antifeminist stance, locating women's power in the home, more specifically in the kitchen, elevating her to the role of priestess representing civilization, the family
occupying a crucial position within society. There seems to be no record of a play called
*Cleopatra,* though she did publish a five-act drama, *Aspasia,* in 1852 (Sophie Pataky,
*Lexikon deutscher Frauen der Feder* [Berlin: Pataky, 1898], 2:174). I am indebted to
Peter C. Caldwell for offering me this information.

69. HJ was fond of the phrase "grey paper with blunt type": he also uses it in a
figurative passage describing the old State House at Richmond, Virginia, as reading like "a
page of some dishonoured author" (*AS,* 379). The line comes from Browning's "Soliloquy
of the Spanish Cloister," in which he characteristically attacks excessive or unwholesome
religious devotion. If in the monastery you stray by reading some "woeful sixteenth
print" of a licentious volume, you may be overwhelmed by lust: "my scrofulous French
novel / On grey paper with blunt type! / Simply glance at it, you grovel / Hand and foot in
Belial's gripe" (*The Poems of Browning,* vol. 2: *1841–1846,* ed. John Woolford and Daniel
Karlin [New York: Longman, 1991], 170). HJ published three essays on Browning (*LC* 1,
782–811), and the poet also appears in his biography of the sculptor William Wetmore
Story (see also n. 141 below).

ning at the theatre, to which we accompanied him. "We had Ristori to play Mary Stuart for us last night—which was the vulture counterfeiting Jenny Wren. Every little while the hoarse exulting voice, the sanguinary beak, the lurid leer of menace, and the relentless talons looked forth from the feathery mass and sickened you with disgust. She would do Elizabeth better."[70] I recall the performance in every feature, as well as my absence of such reserves, though quite also the point to which I was impressed by the utterance of them; not that it didn't leave me at the same time free to feel that the heroine of history represented could scarce have been at all a dove-like, much less a wren-like person. She had indeed on Madame Ristori's showing prodigious resources of militant mobility—of what in fact would be called to-day mobilisation. Several years later on I was to see the actress play the same part in America; and then, if I am not mistaken, was to note scarce more than one point; the awful effect on *any* histrionic case, even on one so guardedly artful as hers, of having been dragged round the globe and forced home, so far as might be, to imperfect comprehensions. The big brush had come fairly to daub the canvas. Let the above, however, serve in particular to lead in as many examples of my father's singularly striking and personal habit of expression and weight of thought as these pages may find room for.

The one difficulty is that to open that general door into the limbo of old letters, charged with their exquisite ghostly appeal, is almost to sink into depths of concession. I yield here for instance to the claim of a page or two from William, just contemporary and addressed to our parents in Paris— and yield perhaps but for no better reason than that of the small historic value or recoverable charm that I am moved to find in its illustrative items.

70. This paragraph ends a letter to Edmund, or "dear old" or "darling" "Tweedius," as HJ Sr. often called him, written from Bonn on 24 July 1860 (bMS Am 1092.9 [4286], Houghton). HJ saw Adelaide Ristori (1822–1906) perform in New York City in the mid-seventies (see *SBO*, n. 259), and she became popular in America. He also devoted an essay to her, published in the *Nation*, 18 March 1875 (rpt. in *The Scenic Art: Notes on Acting and the Drama, 1872–1901*, ed. Allan Wade [London: Hart-Davis, 1949], 28–32). Schiller's *Mary Stuart* (1800) dramatizes the tragic conflict between Mary and Elizabeth, daughter of Henry VIII. In November 1880 HJ saw Helen Modjeska perform the role of Mary, and in *The Tragic Muse* when the aspiring actor Miriam Rooth sadly shakes her head, the narrator comments that "she might have been trying some effect for Mary Stuart in Schiller's play" (361). Ralph Barton Perry comments that Ristori "began playing the title rôle of *Marie Stuart* when she was eighteen. She later did take the part of Elizabeth in Giacometti's play by the same name" (*The Thought and Character of William James*, 2 vols. [Boston: Little, Brown, 1935], 1:193 n. 3).

The reference of its later lines is to a contemporary cousin,[71] young and blooming, by whom I have already ever so lightly brushed* and who figured quite with the grand air on our young horizon; the only daughter of the brightest of the Albany uncles (by that time lost and mourned) now on the tour of Europe with a pair of protective elders for her entrance upon life and at that hour surrounding our parents, her uncle and aunt, with a notably voluminous rustle of fresh Paris clothes, the far-spreading drapery of the more and more draped and flounced and "sloped" second Empire. This friendly frou-frou almost reached our ears, so sociable for us was every sound of her, in our far-off Rhineland. She was with her stature and shape the finest possible person to carry clothes, and I thought of her, with a revival of the old yearning envy, as now quite transcendently or-phaned and bereft, dowered, directed and equipped.[72]

> Your hearts, I know, would have been melted if you had had a view of us this Sunday morning.[73] I went directly after breakfast for the boys, and though H. had an "iron stomach-ache," as he called it, we went off together to that low wooded hill which the Aunt could see from her window when you were here, and walked about till dinner-time, H. being all the while in great pain.[74] In one part we found a platform with a stone bench commanding a view of the whole valley, and, as we were rather tired, sat down on it, H. and Wilky each with a Once a Week, while I tried to draw the view in my pocket-book. We wondered what our beloved parents were doing at that moment, 11.30, and thought you must all have been in your salon, Alice at the window with her eyes fixed on her novel, but eating some rich fruit that Father has just brought in for her from the Palais Royal, and the lovely Mother and Aunt in armchairs, their hands crossed in front of them,

*A Small Boy and Others, 1913.

71. This is Mary Helen James, the daughter of John Barber James and Mary Helen Vanderburgh; her troubled brother, John Vanderburgh, had died in 1858. In 1868 she became the second wife of Charles Alfred Grymes (1820–1905). She appears in SBO, chap. 14 (see also nn. 335 and 340 in that chap.).

72. It is likely that HJ is referring to SBO and the close of chap. 1 where, as a child, he had felt that to be "parentally bereft" was "more thrilling."

73. The full text of this letter, written on Sunday, 12 August 1860, by WJ to his parents, is included in CWJ, 4:34–36, where the editors refer to changes made by HJ; some may have been a late response to his brothers' teasing.

74. "Aunt" is Aunt Kate. In his young adult years HJ would suffer from chronic constipation, for which, with WJ's advice, he sought a range of remedies.

listening to Father, who walks up and down talking of the superiority of America to these countries after all, and how much better it is we should have done with them.[75] We wished, oh we wished we could have been with you to join in the conversation and partake of the fruit. We got up from the seat and went on with a heavy sigh, but in a way so fraternal, presenting such a sweet picture of brotherly unitedness and affection, that it would have done you good to see us.

And so it is every day that we meet for our shorter walks and talks. The German gets on slowly, but I notice a very marked improvement in talking. I have not kept at it so hard this last week as before, and I prevent H. from working his eyes out, which he seems on the whole rather less inclined to do. I am going to read as much as I can the rest of the time we are here. It seems a mere process of soaking, requiring no mental effort, but only time and steady patience. My room is very comfortable now I've got used to it, and I have a pair of slippers of green plush heavy and strong enough to last all my life and then be worn by my children. The photograph of our Zoffingen group has come, which gives me a moustache big enough for three lifeguardsmen. Tell us something more about Mary Helen. How long does she expect to stay in Europe, and who is this Dr. Adams—the man she is engaged to? She directs me to write to her in his care—so that I wish you would ask her, as she says she hopes to meet me, whether I shall still address her as Miss James? Of course it would be painful, but I think I could do it if Adams weren't there. Let the delicious little grey-eyed Alice be locked up alone on the day after the receipt of this with paper and envelopes to write a letter unassisted, uncorrected and unpunctuated to her loving brothers, who

75. This imagined scene, however tongue-in-cheek, must mirror HJ Sr.'s opinions at this time. Having experimented with the educational practices of a number of European countries—chiefly, it seems, in attempting to find the best opportunities for WJ—he may well have rationalized what are generally agreed to be erratic decisions, and based the family's return to America on a rejection of Europe and a need (despite paternal efforts to move him toward science) to provide WJ with further sound art teaching. Father and son clearly discussed the matter in letters, but, as HJ points out in the next chapter, these documents are lost. The needs of the other children were not a priority. Alice's education had been consigned to a governess, and the younger three boys HJ Sr. regarded as not "cut out for intellectual labours" (letter of 18 July [1860] to Edmund Tweedy, given in Perry, *Thought and Character of William James*, 1:191). Habegger interestingly suggests that HJ, having read that line, then went on to amend a phrase in a letter of WJ's with uncharacteristic harshness so that his father's "faults" become "striking defects": "In general, the aged novelist tried to present an ennobling portrait of his crazed old man" (*The Father*, 418).

would send her novels and peaches if they could. What a blessing it is to have such parents, such a perfect Mother and magnificent Father and dear good Aunt and splendid little Sister!

I may mention that Mary Helen was not "engaged" to the gentleman above-mentioned, and was eventually to marry the late Alfred Grymes, originally of Louisiana.[76] Also that a letter subsequent to this, apparently of the first days in September, sounds to his father the first note of my brother's definite personal preference, as he seemed lately and increasingly, though not in conditions markedly propitious, to have become aware of it, for an adoption of the "artistic career."[77] It was an odd enough circumstance, in respect to the attested blood in our veins, that no less than three of our father's children, with two of his grandsons to add to these, and with a collateral addendum representing seven, in all, of our grandfather's, William James's, descendants in three generations, should have found the artistic career in general and the painter's trade in particular irresistibly solicit them.[78]

I wish you would as you promised set down as clearly as you can on paper what your idea of the nature of Art *is,* because I do not, probably, understand it fully, and should like to have it presented in a form that I might think over at my leisure. I wish you would do so as fully as you conveniently can, so that I may ruminate it—and I won't say more about it till I have heard from you again.[79] As for what your

76. Dr. Grymes was born in New Orleans; the couple had no children.

77. WJ studied for a year (alongside the artist John La Farge) in William Morris Hunt's studio in Newport before suddenly—and irrevocably—giving up art for science in 1861. That this year saw the outbreak of Civil War may be a significant factor in his change of course. On WJ's death, La Farge spoke highly of his artistic potential, saying he might have been "a remarkable, perhaps a great painter" (quoted in *CWJ,* 1:402).

78. HJ refers to WJ, Bob, and himself, and to two of WJ's sons, William (Billy) and Alexander (Aleck). "Collateral addendum" is a loose term, but HJ had great affection for the niece of his cousin Minny Temple, Ellen, known as Bay Emmet, who worked as an illustrator and became "one of the first women in America to become a professional portraitist." He commissioned from her a portrait of himself in 1900 (Lyndall Gordon, *A Private Life of Henry James: Two Women and His Art* [New York: Norton, 1999], 299, 304–5; illus. opposite 309). This adds up to six, not seven artists.

79. The full text of this letter written by WJ to his father on 19 August 1860 is given in *CWJ,* 4:36–39. The desire for some elaboration on the nature of "Art" is perhaps characteristic of WJ's systematic, highly analytical mind, which would lead him to the study of psychology and philosophy. It is clear too that even at sixteen he was concerned about a

last letter did contain, what can I do but thank you for every word of it and assure you that they went to the right spot. Having such a Father with us, how can we be other than in some measure worthy of him?— if not perhaps as eminently so as the distance leads his fond heart to imagine. I never value him so much as when I am away from him. At home I see only his striking defects, but here he seems all perfection, and I wonder as I write why I didn't cherish him more when he was beside me. I beg darling old Mother's forgiveness too for the rude and dastardly way in which I snub her, and the Aunt for the impatience and violence I have always shown her. I shall be a perfect sherry-cobbler to both of them,[80] and to the small Alice too, young as she may be for such treats.

I have just got home from dining with the boys and their Humperts; where I found the Doctor as genial as ever and the two old ladies perfect characters for Dickens. They have been so shut out from the world and melting together so long by the kitchen fire that the minds of both have become fused into one, and then seem to constitute a sort of two-bodied individual. I never saw anything more curious than the way they sit mumbling together at the end of the table, each using simultaneously the same comment if anything said at our end strikes their ear. H. pegs away pretty stoutly, but I don't think you need worry about him. He and Wilky appear to get on in great harmony and enliven themselves occasionally by brotherly trials of strength, quite good-natured, in their room, when excess of labour has made them sleepy or heavy. In these sometimes one, sometimes the other is victorious. They often pay me a visit here while I am dressing, which of course is highly convenient—and I have more than once been with *them* early enough to be present at Wilky's tumble out of bed and consequent awakening, with the call on the already-at-work H.: "Why the mischief didn't you stop me?" Wilky and I walked to Rolandseck

---

choice of career, as two letters to his friend Edgar Beach Van Winkle, reveal (*CWJ*, 4:8–9, 11–14). He also had a more developed appreciation of his father's published writings than HJ. For his father's reaction to WJ's change of career plan during the summer, see HJ Sr.'s letters to Edmund Tweedy in Le Clair, *Young Henry James*, 322–24. Quoting from this letter, Feinstein regards WJ's tone as challenging: "What depth of indictment hides behind the apparently deferential phrase 'as clearly as you can'! This was a son who had virtually teethed on philosophic discussion with his utopian father, and he knew all too well by then that clarity was not one of the elder Henry's virtues" (*Becoming William James*, 136).

80. A sherry cobbler is a cocktail of sherry, raspberries, and ice.

yesterday afternoon, and after a furious race back to the station found ourselves too late for the train by a second. So we took a boat and rowed down here, which was delightful. We are going to put H. through a splashing good walk daily. A thousand thanks to the cherry-lipped, apricot-nosed, double-chinned little Sister for her strongly dashed-off letter, which inflamed the hearts of her lonely brothers with an intense longing to smack her celestial cheeks.

III I have before me another communication of about the same moment, a letter addressed to his father in Paris within that month; from which, in spite of its lively interest as I hold, I cull nothing—and precisely because of that interest, which prescribes for it a later appearance in conditions in which it may be given entire. William is from this season on, to my sense, so livingly and admirably reflected in his letters, which were happily through much of his career both numerous and highly characteristic, that I feel them particularly plead, in those cases in which they most testify to his personal history, for the separate gathered presentation that happily awaits them.[81] *There* best may figure the serious and reasoned reply drawn from him by some assuredly characteristic enough communication of our parent's own in respect to his declared preference for a painter's life over any other. Lost is this original and, in the light of later matters, sufficiently quaint declaration, and lost the paternal protest answered by my brother from Bonn and anything *but* infelicitous, on its side, so far as the truer apprehension went, under the showing of the time to come. The only thing was that our father had a wonderful way of being essentially right without being practically or, as it were, vulgarly, determinant, and that this relegation of his grounds of contention to the sphere of the non-immediate, the but indirectly urgent, from the point of view of the thing really to *do*, couldn't but often cause impatience in young breasts conscious of gifts or desires or ideals of which

81. HJ here acknowledges in the text that the original plan to produce a collection of WJ's letters no longer applies; the discourse itself reflects the evolving composition of the volumes and, by this stage, the letters seem destined for another book entirely. Eventually HJ's nephew Harry, who had been concerned about his uncle's use of WJ's correspondence, would complete the task in *The Letters of William James Edited by His Son Henry James*, 2 vols. (London: Longmans, Green, 1920); note the clearly worded title. Meanwhile HJ will offer, as part of some family correspondence written before and during the Civil War, a selection of his brother's early letters.

the very sign and warrant, the truth they were known by, was that they were susceptible of application. It was in no world of close application that our wondrous parent moved, and his indifference at the first blush to the manifestation of special and marketable talents and faculties, restlessly outward purposes of whatever would-be "successful" sort, was apt to be surpassable only by his delight subsequently taken in our attested and visible results, the very fruits of application; as to which the possibility, perhaps even the virtual guarantee, hadn't so much left him cold in advance as made him adversely and "spiritually" hot. The sense of that word was the most living thing in the world for him—to the point that the spiritual simply meant to him the practical and the successful, so far as he could get into touch with such denominations, or so far, that is, as he could face them or care for them *a priori*.[82] Fortunately, as he had observational powers of the happiest, perceptions—perceptions of character and value, perceptions of relation and effect, perceptions in short of the whole—turned to the ground sensibly beneath our feet, as well as a splendid, an extraordinarily animated and, so far as he himself at least was concerned, guiding and governing soul, justice and generosity always eventually played up, the case worked itself happily out, and before we knew it he had found it quite the rightest of all cases, while we on our side had had the liveliest, and certainly the most amusing and civilising, moral or, as he would have insisted, spiritual recreation by the way.

My brother challenges him, with a beautiful deference, on the imputed damage to what might be best in a man by the professional pursuit of "art"—which he appears to have set forth with characteristic emphasis;

82. HJ seems intent in these pages on stressing his father's far from dogmatic influence on WJ's plans, his characteristically original perception of the spiritual as promoting useful action in the world, and his never questioning the choice of art as a career for fear of its impracticality. It is clear, however, that HJ Sr. was keen that WJ should pursue the study of science and that the other children's needs occupied much less attention. He might be regarded as casual, even irresponsible, or just opposed to any "narrowing" of his children's interests. The European visits, presented as part of the plan for his children's education, may well have been fulfilling his own personal preferences. In a letter to his mother of 25 September 1855, he concludes that "home tuition will be the best for all of them; that while it will be much the least expensive, it will also be greatly to the interest of the children both in moral and intellectual regards" (Le Clair, *Young Henry James*, 171), yet the children attended a number of schools in Europe, as well as at times having private tutors. Two years later (10 September 1857), near the end of this first stay in Europe, he wrote, "I have no doubt for all I can gather, that our own schools are . . . much superior to the European schools" (bMS Am 1092.9 [4187], Houghton).

and I take the example for probably one of the rarest in all the so copious annals of parental opposition to the æsthetic as distinguished from some other more respectable course. What was marked in our father's prime uneasiness in presence of any particular form of success we might, according to our lights as then glimmering, propose to invoke was that it bravely, or with such inward assurance, dispensed with any suggestion of an alternative. What we were to do instead was just to *be* something, something unconnected with specific doing, something free and uncommitted, something finer in short than being *that,* whatever it was, might consist of. The "career of art" has again and again been deprecated and denounced, on the lips of anxiety or authority, as a departure from the career of business, of industry and respectability, the so-called regular life, but it was perhaps never elsewhere to know dissuasion on the very ground of its failing to uplift the spirit in the ways it most pretends to. I must in fairness add, however, that if the uneasiness I here refer to continued, and quite by exception as compared with the development of other like episodes, during the whole of my brother's fortunately but little prolonged studio season, it was really because more alternatives swarmed before our parent's eyes, in the cause, than he could bring himself to simplify it by naming. He apprehended ever so deeply and tenderly his eldest son's other genius—as to which he was to be so justified; though this indeed was not to alter the fact that when afterwards that subject went in, by a wondrous reaction, for the pursuit of science, first of chemistry and then of anatomy and physiology and medicine, with psychology and philosophy at last piling up the record,[83] the rich *malaise* at every turn characteristically betrayed itself, each of these surrenders being, by the measure of them in the parental imagination, so comparatively narrowing. That was the nearest approach to any plea for some other application of the spirit— that they *were* narrowing. When I myself, later on, began to "write" it was breathed upon me with the finest bewildering eloquence, with a power of suggestion in truth which I fairly now count it a gain to have felt play over me, that this too was narrowing. On the subsequent history of which high

83. WJ enrolled at the Lawrence Scientific School at Harvard in autumn 1861; after a period of illness he switched in the fall of 1863 from the study of chemistry to comparative anatomy and was taught by Professor Jeffries Wyman, a man he much admired (Lewis, *The Jameses,* 168). "This change in his field of concentration was the first in a series of adjustments in his scientific education that would carry him from anatomy to physiology and then, some thirteen years later, to psychology" (Giles Gunn, "Introduction," *CWJ,* 4:xxix).

paradox no better comment could occur to me than my find of a passage in a letter long subsequently addressed to Mr. James T. Fields, then proprietor and editor of the Atlantic Monthly magazine[84]—a letter under date of May 1868 and referring clearly to some published remarks on a certain young writer which did violence to the blessedly quick paternal prejudice.

I had no sooner left your sanctum yesterday than I was afflicted to remember how I had profaned it by my unmeasured talk about poor H. Please forget it utterly. I don't know how it is with better men, but the parental sentiment is so fiendish a thing with me that if anyone attempt to slay my young, especially in a clandestine way, or out of a pious regard (*e.g.*) to the welfare of the souls comprised in the diocese of the Atlantic, I can't help devoting him bag and baggage to the infernal gods. I am not aware of my animus until I catch, as yesterday, a courteous ear; then the unholy fire flames forth at such a rate as to leave me no doubt on reflection where it was originally lighted.[85]

84. James Thomas Fields (1817–81) succeeded J. R. Lowell as editor of the *Atlantic Monthly* (1861–71). With his young wife, Annie (1834–1915), he provided at his home on Charles Street an important meeting place for the writers of Boston and neighboring Cambridge as well as for visiting literary figures. Founded in 1857, the *Atlantic Monthly* became "an institution that represented a significant voice in American 'high' literary or intellectual culture" (Ellery Sedgwick, *The Atlantic Monthly, 1857–1909: Yankee Humanism at High Tide and Ebb* [Amherst: University of Massachusetts Press, 1994], 3). Fields encouraged HJ from the earliest days, publishing reviews and many stories and novels. One of HJ's last essays, "Mr. and Mrs. James T. Fields," was published in the *Atlantic* in 1915 (*LC* 1, 160–76); he also makes oblique reference to the couple and their "long drawing-room that looks over the water and toward the sunset, with a seat for every visiting shade from Thackeray down . . . the votive temple to memory" in *AS* (244–45). See also Novick, *Young Master* (101–3); and Sedgwick: "Howells has generally been credited with giving James the exposure afforded by the *Atlantic,* and certainly as assistant editor he consistently supported the publication of James's work. But Fields had accepted the first stories before Howells came to the magazine" (*The Atlantic Monthly,* 97).

85. This letter of 2 May 1868 is signed off penitently by HJ Sr. as "your sinful & suffering but cordial friend" (bMS Am 1092.9 [4139], Houghton). Up to May 1868 the *Atlantic Monthly* had published the following stories by HJ: "The Story of a Year" (March 1865), "A Landscape Painter" (February 1866), "My Friend Bingham" (March 1867), "Poor Richard" (June–August 1867), "The Romance of Certain Old Clothes" (February 1868), and "A Most Extraordinary Case" (April 1868); as well as a review, "The Novels of George Eliot" (October 1866). The magazine would go on to publish much more of his fiction (including *Roderick Hudson, The Portrait of a Lady,* and *The Aspern Papers*) and also reviews and travel writing. Edel mentions "an adverse notice" of "Poor Richard" in the *Nation* in summer 1867, though "the notice seems not as sharp today as it may have

Almost all my dear father is there, making the faded page to-day inexpressibly touching to me; his passionate tenderness, his infinite capacity for reaction on reaction, a force in him fruitful in so many more directions than any high smoothness of *parti-pris*[86] could be, and his beautiful fresh individual utterance, always so stamped with the very whole of him. The few lines make for me, after all the years, a sort of silver key, so exquisitely fitting, to the treasure of living intercourse, of a domestic air quickened and infinitely coloured, comprised in all our younger time. The renewed sense of which, however, has carried me for the moment too far from the straighter line of my narrative.

The author of the young letter of which I have deferred presentation met in Paris, shortly after that date, the other party to the discussion; and the impression of the endless day of our journey, my elder and my younger brothers' and mine, from Bonn to that city, has scarcely faded from me. The railway service was so little then what it has become that I even marvel at our having made our connections between our early rise in the Bonn-Gasse and our midnight tumble into bed at the Hôtel des Trois Empereurs in the Place du Palais Royal; a still-felt rapture, a revelation of the Parisian idea of bed after the rude German conception, our sore discipline for so many weeks. I remember Cologne and its cathedral almost in the bland dawn, and our fresh start thence for Strasbourg, now clearly recog-

---

appeared then to the young aspirant in letters and his editor" (*Untried Years*, 276). This review may have antagonized HJ Sr., though it was a year earlier. The *Nation* carried brief comments on HJ's earliest pieces on 1 February 1866, 28 February 1867, 30 January 1868, and 28 May 1868 (Linda J. Taylor, *Henry James, 1866–1916: A Reference Guide* [Boston: Hall, 1982], 1–2), but these are predominantly positive. More critical points are raised in the short-lived magazine *Round Table*, of 27 June 1869 (after HJ Sr.'s chat with James Fields, of course, but indicating some contemporary misgivings), which referred to "an air of unreality," especially in relation to HJ's female characters (quoted in Richard Nicholas Foley, *Criticism in American Periodicals of the Works of Henry James from 1866 to 1916* [Washington, D.C.: Catholic University of America Press, 1944], 5–6). It is easy now, of course, to underplay the originality or potential for controversy in these early works: "With Fields's endorsement, James's form of realism . . . was to challenge the moral and literary assumptions of the *Atlantic* audience" (Sedgwick, *The Atlantic Monthly*, 97). Certainly HJ Sr. could be strongly defensive of his son's writing and reputation. Anna Robeson Burr records that James T. Fields, "having refused a story by Henry James Junior had received a blast of indignation from the boy's father" (*Alice James: Her Brothers—Her Journal*, ed. Burr [London: Macmillan, 1934], 6). LeClair suggests that "poor H." may refer to Thomas Wentworth Higginson (*Young Henry James*, n. 449), who made some negative comments on HJ's stories that Mary Temple mentioned to her cousin (letter 3 of June 1869).

86. Taking sides, prejudice.

nised, alas, as a start back to America, to which it had been of a sudden settled that we were, still with a fine inconsequence, to return. We had seen Cologne cathedral by excursion from Bonn, but we saw Strasbourg, to my sorrow until a far later occasion soothed it, only as a mild monster behind bars, that is above chimneys, housetops and fortifications; a loss not made up to me by other impressions or particulars, vivid and significant as I found myself none the less supposing several of these. Those were the September days in which French society, so far as it was of the Empire at least, moved more or less in its mass upon Homburg and Baden-Baden;[87] and we met it in expressive samples, and in advance and retreat, during our incessant stops, those long-time old stops, unknown to the modern age, when everyone appeared to alight and walk about with the animation of prisoners suddenly pardoned, and ask for conveniences, and clamour for food, and get mixed with the always apparently still dustier people of opposite trains drawn up for the same purposes. We appeared to be concerned with none but first-class carriages, as an effect of which our own was partly occupied, the livelong day, by the *gens*[88] of a noble French house as to which we thus had frequent revelations—a pair of footmen and a lady's maid, types of servile impudence taking its ease, who chattered by the hour for our wonderstruck ears, treating them to their first echo of the strange underworld, the sustaining vulgarity, of existences classified as "great." They opened vistas, and I remember how when, much later, I came to consider the designed picture, first in Edmond About and then in Alphonse Daudet, of fifty features symptomatic of the social pace at which the glittering régime hurried to its end, there came back to me the breath of this sidewind of the frenzied dance that we had caught during those numerous and so far from edifying hours in our fine old deep-seated compartment.[89] The impression, I now at any rate

87. Homburg, in Hesse, was famous for its mineral waters, spa, and casino; Baden-Baden, in the foothills of the Black Forest, was also a fashionable health resort for summer visitors. These locations appear in HJ's fiction, e.g., "Eugene Pickering" (1874), *Confidence* (1879–80), and "Louisa Pallant" (1888). He published an essay "Homburg Reformed" in the *Nation* on 28 August 1873 (*Henry James: Collected Travel Writings: The Continent*, 635–43).

88. Servants or domestics.

89. Edmond François Valentin About (1828–85) was an anticlerical novelist and journalist. Novick (*Young Master,* 56) records that HJ was given by his mother a copy of his popular novel *Tolla* (1855), and contends that it was "to become for Harry a kind of legend of Europe, with the truth of a fable," adding "its note of enchantment to Rome when he came to live there; he would rework its plot in his own novels and plays." HJ had some

perfectly recover, was one that could feed full enough any optimism of the appointedly modest condition. It was true that Madame la Marquise, who was young and good-natured and pretty without beauty, and unmistakably "great," exhaling from afar, as I encouraged myself to imagine, the scented air of the Tuileries, came on occasion and looked in on us and smiled, and even pouted, through her elegant patience; so that she at least, I recollect, caused to swim before me somehow such a view of happy privilege at the highest pitch as made me sigh the more sharply, even if the less professedly, for our turning our backs on the complex order, the European, fresh to me still, in which contrasts flared and flourished and through which discrimination could unexhaustedly riot—pointing so many more morals, withal, if that was the benefit it was supposed to be, than we should find pretexts for "on the other side." We were to fall as soon as we were at home again to reading the Revue des Deux Mondes—though doubtless again I should speak here, with any emphasis, but for myself;[90] my chin, in Europe, had scarce risen to the level of that publication; but at Newport in Rhode Island, our next following place of sojourn, I speedily shot up so as quite to bend down to it: it took its place therewith as the very headspring of culture, a mainstay in exile, and as opening wide in especial the doors of that fictive portrayal of a society which put a price, for the brooding young reader, on cases, on *cadres,* in the Revue parlance,[91] already constituted

admiration for the work of Alphonse Daudet (1840–97) and acknowledged that his own story "The Liar" (1888) was, to a degree, influenced by Daudet's novel *Numa Roumestan* (*CN,* 28). HJ wrote a number of essays on Daudet, of which the most substantial was included in *Partial Portraits* (1888) (*LC* 2, 223–49). He refers to Daudet's *Jack* in *SBO,* p. 352. As for the "glittering régime" of France's Second Empire in these years, "International showmanship, both commercial and political, was a constant feature. . . . Down their bright new boulevards the inhabitants of the scientific, gas-lit Empire danced their way to the tinkling tunes of Offenbach—their way to the national disaster of Sedan and to the horrors of the Paris Commune of 1871" (David Thomson, *Europe since Napoleon* [Harmondsworth: Penguin, 1966], 270).

90. For HJ, especially on his return to the United States, the *Revue des deux mondes* represented the best in French, even European, culture of the time, publishing many of the leading French authors. Translations by Lucien Biart of five of HJ's tales appeared in the journal in the 1870s, though they "were nearly all ruthlessly edited" (Leon Edel and Dan H. Laurence, *A Bibliography of Henry James,* 3rd ed., rev. with assistance of James Rambeau [Winchester, U.K.: St. Paul's Bibliographies; New Castle, Del.: Oak Knoll Press, 1999], 364, 359). In 1883 the *Revue* published an essay of forty pages by "Madame Bentzon" devoted to HJ. In *AS* the European credentials of the remembered inhabitants of Newport are endorsed by "their loan and their return of the *Revue des Deux Mondes*" (223).

91. Literally, "frames"; here, outlines or plans for fiction.

and propitiously lighted. Then it was that the special tension of the dragged-out day from Cologne to Paris proved, on the absurdest scale, a preparation, justified itself as a vivid point of reference: I was to know what the high periodical meant when I encountered in its *études de mœurs* the blue-chinned corruptible, not to say corrupt, *larbin* and the smart soubrette;[92] it was above all a blessing to feel myself, in the perusal of M. Octave Feuillet, an education, as I supposed, of the taste, not at a marked disadvantage;[93] since who but the Petite Comtesse herself had swung her crinoline in and out of my prospect, or, to put it better, of my preserved past, on one of my occasions of acutest receptivity?

The truth was that acute, that quite desperate receptivity set in for me, under a law of its own—may really be described as having quite raged for me—from the moment our general face, by the restless parental decree (born not a little of parental homesickness and reinforced by a theory of that complaint on our own part, we having somehow in Europe "no companions," none but mere parents themselves), had been turned again to the quarter in which there would assuredly be welcomes and freedoms and unchecked appropriations, not to say also cousins, of both sexes and of a more and more engaging time of life, cousins kept and tended and adorned for us in our absence, together with the solicitation for our favour of possible, though oh so just barely possible, habitats before which the range of Europe paled; but which, nevertheless, to my aching fancy, meant premature abdication, sacrifice and, in one dreadful word, failure.[94] I had had cousins, naturally, in the countries we were quitting, but to a limited

92. *Études de mœurs:* studies of manners or morals; *larbin:* flunkey. In this context, the phrase "blue-chinned corruptible" may well be intended to invoke Maximilien de Robespierre, known as the sea-green Incorruptible, and leader of the Terror of the French Revolution.

93. Much of the fiction of the novelist and dramatist Octave Feuillet (1821–90) was published in the *Revue des deux mondes.* HJ reviewed two of his novels, *Camors; or, Life under the New Empire* and *Les amours de Philippe* for the *Nation* (*LC* 2, 281–88). See also Adeline Tintner, *The Cosmopolitan World of Henry James: An Intertexual Study* (Baton Rouge: Louisiana State University Press, 1991), 61–79, and Angus Wren, *Henry James and the Second Empire* (London: Legenda, 2009), 99–123. For a discussion of allusions to Feuillet in *The Princess Casamassima,* see Pierre A. Walker, *Reading Henry James in French Cultural Contexts* (DeKalb: North Illinois University Press, 1995), 18–41.

94. HJ's thoughts here seem to rationalize, so far as possible, his father's decision to return to America, though he also goes on to record (with knowledge of his own future) his sense of these days as a private farewell to Europe. The remainder of this volume has a New England setting.

degree; yet I think I already knew I had had companions in as full a measure as any I was still to know—inasmuch as my imagination made out one, in the complex order and the coloured air, almost wherever I turned; and, inasmuch as, further, to live by the imagination was to live almost only in that way, so to foresee the comparative, not to say the absolute, absence of tonic accent in the appearances complacently awaiting me, as well as to forecast in these appearances, at the best, a greater paucity, was really to enjoy a sharp prevision of dearth. Certain it is that those supreme moments of Paris, those after-days at the Trois Empereurs, were to flush for me, as they ebbed, with images and visions; judged by any achieved act of possession I hadn't assuredly much to give up, but intensity of sentiment, resting on a good disposition, makes for its own sake the most of opportunity, and I buried my associations, which had been in a manner till lately my hopes as well, with all decent dignity and tenderness. These more or less secret obsequies lent to our further brief delay a quality of suppressed excitement; the "old-world" hours were numbered too dreadfully—had shrunk but to a handful: I had waked up to that, as with a passionate even if private need for gathering in and saving, on the mor-row of our reaching our final sticking-place: I had slipped from my so cushioned sleep, my canopied couch, to hang, from the balcony of our quatrième,[95] my brothers' and mine, over that Place du Palais Royal and up against that sculptured and storied façade of the new Louvre which seemed to me then to represent, in its strength, the capacity and chiselled rim of some such potent vivifying cup as it might have been given us, under a happier arrangement, to taste now in its fulness and with a braver sense for it.[96] Over against us on the great palace wall, as I make out—if not for that occasion then for some other—were statues of heroes, Napo-leon's young generals, Hoche, Marceau, Desaix or whoever, such a galaxy as never was or should ever be again for splendid monumental reference;[97] and what it somehow came to was that here massed itself the shining

95. *Quatrième:* fourth floor.

96. Napoleon III oversaw the completion of the north wing, linking the palace of the Louvre and the Tuileries; this entailed new building work along the rue de Rivoli and two new wings with interior courtyards. The "Cour Napoléon" was completed in 1857. HJ's position, hanging over a Parisian balcony, would be a scene enacted by some of his fictional observers.

97. The Napoleonic heroes were General Lazare Hoche (1768–97), General François-Séverin Marceau-Desgraviers (1769–96), and General Louis-Charles-Antoine Desaix de Veygoux (1768–1800).

second Empire, over which they stood straight aloft and on guard, like archangels of the sword, and that the whole thing was a high-pitched wonder and splendour, which we had already, in our small gaping way, got into a sort of relation with and which would have ever so much more ever so thrillingly to give us. What it would give us loomed but vaguely enough out of the great hum and the great toned perspective, and withal the great noble expense, of which we had constant reminder; but that we were present at something it would be always after accounted a privilege to have been concerned with, and that we were perversely and inconsiderately dropping out of it, and for a reason, so far as there might be a reason, that was scarcely less than strange—all this loomed large to me as our interval shrank, and I even ask myself before the memory of it whether I was ever again in the later and more encompassing and accommodating years to have in those places so rich a weight of consciousness to carry or so grand a presumption of joy. The presumption so boldly entertained was, if you please, of what the whole thing meant. It meant, immensely, the glittering régime, and *that* meant in turn, prodigiously, something that would probably never be meant quite to any such tune again: so much one positively and however absurdly said to one's self as one stood up on the high balcony to the great insolence of the Louvre and to all the history, all the glory again and all the imposed applause, not to say worship, and not to speak of the implied inferiority, on the part of everything else, that it represented.[98] And the sense was of course not less while one haunted at odd hours the arcades and glass galleries of the Palais Royal close at hand—as if to store up, for all the world, treasures of impression that might be gnawed, in seasons or places of want, like winter pears or a squirrel's hoard of nuts, and so perhaps keep one alive, as to one's most vital faculty above-mentioned, till one should somehow or other be able to scramble back.

The particular ground for our defection, which I obscurely pronounced mistaken, was that since William was to embrace the artistic career—and freedom for this experiment had been after all, as I repeat that it was always

98. The terms of HJ's pleasure in Second Empire Paris, the rhythms of his prose, the invocation of time and history, the recognition of the experience as a source of future sustenance, may remind us of the climactic moment in the Galerie d'Apollon when he foresaw his vocation and recognized the redeeming potential of Style (*SBO*, 275–76). Paris, more precisely the place Vendôme, with its Napoleonic associations, was also, of course, the site of what he held to be his earliest memory (related in *SBO*, chap. 5), suggesting perhaps that his consciousness became engaged in the city.

in like cases to be, not in the least grudgingly granted him—our return to America would place him in prompt and happy relation to William Hunt, then the most distinguished of our painters as well as one of the most original and delightful of men, and who had cordially assured us that he would welcome such a pupil.[99] This was judged among us at large, other considerations aiding, a sound basis for action; but never surely had so odd a motive operated for a break with the spell of Paris. We named the motive generally, I think, and to the credit of our earnest good faith, with confidence—and I am of course not sure how often our dear father may not explicatively have mentioned the shy fact that he himself in any case had gradually ceased to "like" Europe.[100] This affects me at present as in the highest degree natural: it was to be his fortune for the rest of his life to find himself, as a worker in his own field and as to what he held most dear, scantly enough heeded, reported or assimilated even in his own air, no brisk conductor at any time of his remarkable voice; but in Europe his isolation had been utter—he had there had the sense of playing his mature and ardent thought over great dense constituted presences and opaque surfaces that could by their very nature scarce give back so much as a shudder. No more admirable case of apostolic energy combined with philosophic patience, of constancy of conviction and solitary singleness of production unperturbed, can I well conceive; and I certainly came later on to rejoice in his having had after a certain date to walk, if there was a preference, rather in the thin wilderness than in the thick. I dare say that when we returned to America toward the end of 1860, some five years and a half after our departure, it may have been with illusions not a few for him about the nature of the desert, or in other words about the degree of sensibility of the public, there awaiting him;[101] but the pretext given him by

99. The painter and teacher William Morris Hunt (1824–79) had a studio in Newport in 1856 before he moved to Boston in 1862. Born in Brattleboro, Vermont, the artist studied sculpture at Harvard before moving to Germany and France for further study. He returned from Europe in 1855, deeply influenced by the French Barbizon school of painters, especially Millet. Hunt was instrumental in introducing the ideals of contemporary French art and in promoting French painters in New England.

100. Ten years later HJ Sr. continued to endorse the values of the New World: "The historical consciousness rules to such a distorted excess in Europe that I have always been restless there and ended by pining for the land of the future exclusively" (quoted in Habegger, *The Father*, 416).

101. The neglect of HJ Sr.'s writings in his own lifetime has continued, but his ideas certainly influenced the thinking of WJ. Though W. D. Howells admired HJ Sr.'s writing at sentence level, his familiar comment that in *The Secret of Swedenborg* he had effectively

his so prized and admired eldest son was at the worst, and however eccentric our action, inspiring: I alone of the family perhaps made bold not to say quite directly or literally that we went home to learn to paint. People stared or laughed when we said it, and I disliked their thinking us so simple—though dreaming too a little perhaps that they might have been struck with our patriotism. This however conveyed but a chill the more— since we didn't in the least go to our friend, who had been Couture's and Frère's pupil,[102] who had spent years in France and of whom it was the common belief that you couldn't for the life of you tell him from a French painter, because he was patriotic; but because he was distinguished and accomplished, charming and kind, and above all known to us and thereby in a manner guaranteed. He looked, as people get to look under such enjoyed or even suffered exposures, extremely like a Frenchman, and, what was noteworthy, still more like a sculptor of the race than a painter; which doubtless had to do with my personally, though I hope, in present culti- vated anxiety, not too officiously, sighing at all the explanation the whole thing took. I am bound to add none the less that later on, repatriated and, as to my few contacts, reassured, I found this amount, the apprehension of which had haunted me, no great charge; and seem even to make out that for the first six months of our Newport phase at least we might have passed for strikingly wise. For here *was,* beyond doubt, a genial, an admirable master; and here also—at such a rate did sparse individuals, scattered notches in the long plain stick, count—was John La Farge.[103] Here moreover—here

---

succeeded in keeping the philosopher's secret perhaps sums up the difficulty (pointed out even in journals of the time devoted to the ideas of Swedenborg) of reading the older James's works. Of course HJ offers an enlightening summary of his father's cast of mind at the opening of this chapter. But whereas WJ shows, in his introduction to his father's *Literary Remains* (1885), a depth of understanding and intellectual sympathy, HJ felt compelled to confess "I can't enter into it (much) myself—I can't be so theological, nor grant his extraordinary premises. . . . But I can enjoy greatly the spirit, the feeling & the manner of the whole thing (full as this last is of things that *dis*please me too,)" (*CWJ,* 2:1).

102. Thomas Couture (1815–79), who painted in a traditional, classically influenced style, was a respected teacher of both French and American painters. HJ considered his effect on Lizzy Boott, an old friend, to be negative and, meeting him, described him as "a vulgar little fat and dirty old man" (Leon Edel, *Henry James: The Conquest of London, 1870–1883* [London: Rupert Hart-Davis, 1962], 262; see also *SBO,* n. 572). Pierre Edouard Frère (1819–86), a pupil of Delaroche and admired by John Ruskin, was a popular domestic genre painter.

103. John La Farge (1835–1910), the eminent American painter, designer in stained glass, and writer, with his European background and breadth of reading, became one of

and everywhere about me, before we could quite turn round—was the War, with its infinite, its truly quite humiliating correction of my (as I now can but so far call it) fatuous little confidence that "appearances," on the native scene, would run short. They were in the event, taking one thing with another, never to hold out for me as they held during those four years. Wondrous this force in them as I at present look back—wondrous I mean in view of that indirectness of its play which my conditions confined me, with such private, though I must add, alas, such helplessly unapplied resentment, to knowing it by.[104] If the force was great the attenuation of its reach was none the less preappointed and constant; so that the case must have come back again but to the degree—call *it* too, frankly, the force—of one's sensibility, or in other words the blest resource, the supremely breatheable and thereby nourishing and favouring air of one's imaginative life. There were of a truth during that time probably more appearances at one's command in the way of felt aspects, images, apprehended living relations and impressions of the stress of life, than during any other season one was to know; only doubtless with more of the work of their figuring to their utmost, their giving all they could, to do by one's self and, in the last resort, deep within one's breast. The point to be made just here, in any case, is that if we had not recrossed the sea, by way, rather, of such an anticlimax, to

---

the most formative influences for HJ, as he explains in the pages to follow. Having lived in Paris, La Farge studied with William Morris Hunt in Newport, as HJ relates in chap. 4 below. He provided the illustrations for *The Turn of the Screw* (1898) on its original appearance in *Collier's Weekly*, and, according to *NSB*, chap. 12, painted HJ on a number of occasions (see also *CWJ*, 1:376–77). A very fine portrait, the only one that survives, is reproduced in Lewis's *The Jameses*, after 74, and "hangs in the Century Club on West Forty-third Street, New York City" (644). WJ also completed a portrait of La Farge (Gerald E. Myers, "Introduction," *CWJ*, 1:xxii). In a period when the Hudson River school of painters was dominant, La Farge's work appeared distinctively modern. In a piece for the *Galaxy* magazine (1875) HJ commented of him, "There is one artist—a complex and suggestive one if there ever was . . . whose pictures are always a challenge to the imagination and the culture of the critic" ("On Some Pictures Lately Exhibited," in *The Painter's Eye: Notes and Essays on the Pictorial Arts by Henry James*, ed. John L. Sweeney [Madison: University of Wisconsin Press, 1956, 1989], 91).

104. HJ refers to the American Civil War, invariably for him "the War." He also hints at some of the tensions upon which he elaborates in later pages: his "obscure hurt" sustained at a Newport fire which may have prevented his enlisting for military service (described in chap. 9 below), and the sense of an important, enriching experience that decisively changed the lives of Wilky and Bob. He goes on, too, to register the ironic insignificance of the issues surrounding the family's return to the United States in the light of the national tragedy that was about to begin and that would, in any case, have brought them home.

William Hunt, we should certainly with brief delay have found ourselves doing it, on the first alarm of War, for the experience I thus too summarily glance at and which I don't pretend to speak of as all my own.

IV    Newport, with repatriation accepted, would have been on many grounds inevitable, I think—as it was to remain inevitable for several years, and this quite apart from William's having to paint; since if I spoke just now of the sweep of our view, from over the water, of a continent, or well-nigh, waiting to receive us, the eligibility of its innumerable sites was a matter much more of our simplified, our almost distressfully uninvolved and unconnected state than of the inherent virtue of this, that or the other particular group of local conditions.[105] Our parents had for us no definite project but to be liberally "good"—in other words so good that the presumption of our being so would literally operate anywhere and anyhow, would really amount in itself to a sort of situated state, a sufficient prime position, and leave other circumstances comparatively irrelevant. What would infallibly have occurred at the best, however, was what did punctually happen—its having to be definitely gathered that, though we might apparently be good, as I say, almost on any ground, there was but one place in which we should even at a restricted pitch be well: Newport imposed itself at that period to so remarkable a degree as the one right residence, in all our great country, for those tainted, under whatever attenuations, with the quality and the effect of detachment. The effect of detachment was the fact of the experience of Europe.[106] Detachment might of course have come from many

105. After an unpleasant crossing of the Atlantic aboard the *Adriatic*, the Jameses arrived in New York City on 24 September 1860. Reaching Newport a week later, they rented 13 Kay Street, where they lived until spring 1862. They then moved to a fine stone house on the corner of Spring Street and Lee Avenue which still survives, purchased from a Captain Breeze (Lewis, *The Jameses*, 145). Newport, founded in the 1640s, traditionally had a strong agricultural and fishing economy. When the Jameses lived there, it was becoming a fashionable coastal resort both for the wealthy of New York City and for Southern landlowners and merchants. Most of the luxurious mansions of Bellevue Avenue, funded by wealth accrued from industry and business, were yet to be built, but HJ's unfinished novel *The Ivory Tower* confronts both the grandeur and the vulgarity of the developments, "a mere breeding ground for white elephants," as he comments in *AS* (224).

106. In his nostalgic evocation of Newport in *AS* HJ recollects its "densely shrubbed and perfectly finished little headlands" and its inhabitants, all of them with the "sharp outland dart" of Europe in their sides (223). Yet, to his twentieth-century eyes, these

causes, but it truly came in most cases but from one, though that a fairly merciless: it came from the experience of Europe, and I think was on the whole regarded as—what it could only have been in the sphere of intimacy and secrecy felt to be—without an absolute remedy. As comparatively remedial Newport none the less figured, and this for sundry reasons into the detail of which I needn't go. Its rare distinction and precious attribute was that, being a watering-place, a refuge from summer heats, it had also, were the measure considerably stretched, possibilities of hibernation. We could, under stress, brave there the period from November to June; and it was to be under stress not to know what else to do. That was the pinch to which Europe reduced you; insidiously, fatally disconnected, you could but make the best, as a penalty, of the one marked point of reattachment. The philosophy of all of which was that to confess to disconnection was to confess by the same stroke to leisure—which involved also an admission, however rueful at once and deprecatory, of what might still at that time pass in our unregenerate country for something in the nature of "means." You had had the means, that is, to *become,* so awkwardly, detached—for you might then do that cheaply; but the whole basis of the winter life there, of that spare semblance of the Brighton life, the Folkestone life, the Bath or the Cheltenham or the Leamington life, was that your occupation or avocation should be vague enough;[107] or that you shouldn't in other

---

people are marginalized "excrescences on the American surface," and they carry some beautiful but ineradicable element of death, "embalmed . . . in that scented, somewhat tattered, but faintly spiced, wrapper of their various 'European' antecedents" (222). In 1883 HJ had written to Perry, "Newport is always Newport, & the dead past lives again— just a little—in the interstices of its modern excrescences. It is lost, forever, nevertheless, to the truly romantic soul" (Harlow, *Perry: A Biography,* 313). HJ's early essay on Newport appeared in the *Nation,* 15 September 1870 (*Henry James: Travel Writings: Great Britain and America,* ed. Richard Howard [New York: Library of America, 1993], 759-66).

107. Brighton, on the Channel coast of Sussex, had become popular and fashionable after being frequented by the Prince of Wales toward the end of the eighteenth century. Folkestone was another favored resort and watering place from which ferries departed for Boulogne-sur-Mer (as recorded in *What Maisie Knew*). In an 1896 note to a niece, how-ever, he reveals some misgivings about the town (laced with the standard racial prejudice of the time): "I doubt if you would find any comfortable accommodation there at all. It is fashionable (for Jews, etc.) in Aug & September" (quoted in Sheldon Novick, *Henry James: The Mature Master* [New York: Random House, 2007], 261). Bath (Somerset-shire), Cheltenham (Gloucestershire), and Leamington (Warwickshire) were spa towns close to the Cotswold Hills, familiar locations in Jane Austen's novels. In her last years spent in England, Alice James, beset by ill health, enjoyed staying in Leamington with her companion, Katherine Loring.

words be, like everyone you might know save a dozen or so at the most, in business. I remember well how when we were all young together we had, under pressure of the American ideal in that matter, then so rigid, felt it tasteless and even humiliating that the head of our little family was *not* in business, and that even among our relatives on each side we couldn't so much as name proudly anyone who was—with the sole exception of our maternal uncle Robertson Walsh, who looked, ever so benevolently, after our father's "affairs," happily for us.[108] Such had never been the case with the father of any boy of our acquaintance; the business in which the boy's father gloriously *was* stood forth inveterately as the very first note of our comrade's impressiveness. *We* had no note of that sort to produce, and I perfectly recover the effect of my own repeated appeal to our parent for some presentable account of him that would prove us respectable. Business alone was respectable—if one meant by it, that is, the calling of a lawyer, a doctor or a minister (we never spoke of clergymen) as well; I think that if we had had the Pope among us we should have supposed the Pope in business, just as I remember my friend Simpson's telling me crushingly, at one of our New York schools, on my hanging back with the fatal truth about our credentials, that the author of *his* being (we spoke no more of "governors" than we did of "parsons") was in the business of a stevedore. That struck me as a great card to play—the word was fine and mysterious; so that "What shall we tell them you *are*, don't you see?" could but become on our lips at home a more constant appeal. It seemed wantonly to be prompted for our father, and indeed greatly to amuse him, that he should put us off with strange unheard-of attributions, such as would have made us ridiculous in our special circles; his "Say I'm a philosopher, say I'm a seeker for truth, say I'm a lover of my kind, say I'm an author of books if you like; or, best of all, just say I'm a Student," saw us so very little further. Abject it certainly appeared to be reduced to the "student" plea; and I must have lacked even the confidence of my brother Bob, who, challenged, in my hearing and the usual way, was ready not only with the fact that our parent "wrote," but with the further fact that he had written *Lectures and Miscellanies James.*[109] I think that when we settled awhile at Newport there was no one there who had written but Mr.

108. Alexander Robertson Walsh was Mary James's oldest brother. "His line was hardware and lumber, and he and his partner operated out of 211 Pearl Street, in the financial and mercantile section of lower Manhattan" (Habegger, *The Father*, 235).

109. Henry James [Sr.], *Lectures and Miscellanies* (New York: Redfield, 1852).

Henry T. Tuckerman, a genial and graceful poet of the Artless Age, as it might still be called in spite of Poe and Hawthorne and Longfellow and Lowell, the most characteristic works of the first and the two last of whom had already appeared;[110] especially as those most characteristic of Mr. Tuckerman referred themselves to a past sufficiently ample to have left that gentleman with a certain deafness and a glossy wig and a portly presence and the reputation, positively, of the most practised and desired of diners-out. He was to be recognised at once as a social value on a scene not under that rubric densely peopled; he constituted indeed such a note as would help to keep others of the vague definability in countenance. Clearly indeed it might happen that an association of vaguenesses would arrive in time, by fondly cleaving together, at the semblance of a common identity; the nature of the case then demanding, however, that they should be methodically vague, take their stand on it and work it for all it was worth. That in truth was made easy by the fact that what I have called our common disconnectedness positively projected and proclaimed a void; disconnected from business we could only be connected with the negation of it, which had as yet no affirmative, no figurative side. This probably would come; figures, in the void, would one by one spring up; but what

110. Henry Theodore Tuckerman (1813–71) was a critic and poet whose earlier works include *The Italian Sketchbook* (1835), *Isabel of Sicily: A Pilgrimage* (1839), *Artist Life; or, Sketches of American Painters* (1847), as well as volumes of literary criticism, a book of poems, and two volumes of familiar essays. James Thomas Flexner writes that "the books he threw off almost carelessly in such profusion earned him a tremendous reputation. Literary standards were not high in the United States in those days and he was considered somewhat of a genius. Praised for exhibiting 'a pleasant discursive vein of thought,' he was encouraged to put down, without any strong effort at conscious control, whatever ideas came to mind. As a result, his prose rambled, subjects being picked up and dropped and then picked up again in a slightly different context" ("Tuckerman's 'Book of the Artists,'" *American Art Journal* 1 [Autumn 1969]: 55). By the "Artless Age" HJ means the era mentioned by Flexner before the greatest works of Hawthorne, Longfellow, and Lowell had appeared. In his biography of Hawthorne he comments, "There was but little literary criticism in the United States at the time Hawthorne's earlier works were published" (*Hawthorne* [1879], LC 1, 367). Edgar Allan Poe (1809–49) was an influential writer of often uncanny tales and poetry (see also *SBO*, n. 93); Nathaniel Hawthorne (1804–64) is most famous for his novels *The Scarlet Letter* and *The House of the Seven Gables* (see also *SBO*, n. 136). Henry Wadsworth Longfellow (1807–82), best remembered for his narrative poem *The Song of Hiawatha* had been a celebrity in Cambridge for many years and taught at Harvard until 1854. HJ became close to James Russell Lowell (1819–91), poet, diplomat, and Harvard professor, when the older man served in England. Lowell was a model for the ambassador in *The Sense of the Past*.

would be thus required for them was that the void should be ample and, as it were, established. Not to be afraid of it they would have to feel it clear of everything and everyone they knew in the air actually peopled.

William Hunt, for that matter, was already a figure unmistakable, superficially speaking unsurpassable, just as John La Farge, already mentioned, was so soon to prove to be.[111] They were only two indeed, but they argued the possibility; and so the great thing, as I say, was that, to stand out, they should have margin and light. We couldn't all be figures—on a mere margin, the margin of business, and in the light of the general wonder of our being anything, anything *there;* but we could at least understand the situation and cultivate the possibilities, watch and protect the germs. This consciousness, this aim or ideal, had after all its own intensity—it burned with a pure flame:[112] there is a special joy, clearly, in the hopeful conversion of the desert into the garden, of thinness into thickness, a joy to which the conversion of the thick into the mere dense, of the free into the rank or the close, perhaps gives no clue. The great need

111. It is significant that both men (Hunt looked like a French sculptor, La Farge was a Franco-American) became congenial figures for HJ after the family's break with Europe. For both painters, see also nn. 99 and 103 above. Henry Tuckerman was enthusiastic about Hunt, incidentally, in his *Book of the Artists, American Artist Life* (New York: Putnam, 1867), 449–50.

112. With his recollected private devotion to the acquisition of impressions and his acknowledgment of the rich possibilities of artistic enterprise even in unpromising circumstances, HJ echoes the famous lines from the controversial Conclusion to Walter Pater's *Studies in the History of the Renaissance* (1873), which the author had had originally to withdraw from publication: "Not the fruit of experience, but experience itself, is the end. A counted number of impulses only is given to us of a variegated, dramatic life. . . . To burn always with this hard, gem-like flame, to maintain this ecstasy, is success in life" (*The Renaissance: Studies in Art and Poetry: The 1893 Text,* ed. Donald L. Hill [Berkeley: University of California Press, 1980], 188–89). The Conclusion, with what some regarded as its neo-pagan moral implications, marked a key moment in the development of the aesthetic movement in Britain to which HJ refers later in this chapter. Tintner contends that the phrase "a cold still flame," linked to Adam Verver and his dedication to "the aesthetic principle" in chap. 9 of *The Golden Bowl* (1904), relates to the same passage in Pater. She offers a range of Paterian echoes and insights in HJ's fiction (*The Book World of Henry James: Appropriating the Classics* [Ann Arbor: UMI Research Press, 1987], 143–63). HJ records writing a review of *Studies in the History of the Renaissance,* though it was never published; however, "some of the fruits of that unpublished review might have found their way into or have been published as 'Old Italian Art' and reprinted as part four of 'Florentine Notes' in *Transatlantic Sketches* (296–301)" (*The Complete Letters of Henry James, 1872–1876,* ed. Pierre A. Walker and Greg W. Zacharias [Lincoln: University of Nebraska Press, 2009], 2:73n).

that Newport met was that of a basis of reconciliation to "America" when the habit, the taking for granted, of America had been broken or intermitted: it would be hard to say of what subtle secret or magic the place was possessed toward this end, and by a common instinct, I think, we didn't attempt to formulate it—we let it alone, only looking at each other hard, only moving gently, on the brave hypothesis, only in fine deprecating too rude and impatient, too precipitate a doubt of the spell that perhaps might work if we waited and prayed. We did wait and pray, accordingly, scantly-served though the board we might often have felt we had sat down to, and there was a fair company of us to do so, friendliest among whom to our particular effort was my father's excellent friend of many years Edmund Tweedy, already named in pages preparatory to these and who, with his admirable wife, presented himself as our main introducer and initiator. He had married, while we were all young in New York together, a manner of Albany cousin, Mary Temple the elder, aunt of the younger,* and had by this time "been through" more than anything, more than everything, of which there could be question for ourselves. The pair had on their marriage gone at once to Europe to live, had put in several years of Italy and yet had at last, particular reasons operating, returned to their native, that is to sterner, realities;[113] those as to which it was our general theory, of so touching a candour as I look back to it, that they offered themselves at Newport in a muffling mitigating air. The air, material, moral, social, was in fact clear and clean to a degree that might well have left us but dazed at the circumjacent blankness; yet as to that I hasten to add too that the blowing out of our bubble, the planting of our garden, the correction of our thinness, the discovery, under stress, of such scraps of colour and conversation, such saving echoes and redeeming references as might lurk for us in each other, all formed in themselves an active, and might at last even grow to suggest an absolutely bustling, process.

I come back with a real tenderness of memory for instance to that

---

* *A Small Boy and Others*, 1913.

113. Edmund Tweedy, an affluent New York banker, had met HJ Sr. in the winter of 1845–46 and married Mary Temple in 1848, whereupon they left for Lucca in Tuscany. HJ's Aunt Catharine had married Colonel Robert Emmet Temple; Mary was his sister. "According to his obituary, Edmund Tweedy, an intimate friend of Nathaniel Hawthorne, was eighty-nine years old when he died. The Tweedys lived in Pelham, N.Y., and owned a villa at Bellevue Court, Newport" (*CWJ*, 4:619). See also *SBO*, n. 444. Without naming them, HJ refers to the Tweedys' Roman apartment and its "little crimson drawing-room" at 33 Via Gregoriana in his 1872 essay "From a Roman Note-book" (*Italian Hours*, 176–77).

felicity of the personal, the social, the "literary and artistic," almost really the romantic, identity responding, after a fashion quite to bring tears to the eyes, in proportion as it might have seemed to feel by some divine insufflation what it practically could stand for. What should one call this but the brave triumph of values conscious of having to be almost missionary? There were many such that in "Europe" hadn't had to be missionary at all; in Europe, as it were, one hadn't—comparatively—seen, if not the forest for the trees, then the trees for the forest; whereas on this other great vacuous level every single stem seemed to enjoy for its distinction quite the totality of the daylight and to rise into the air with a gladness that was itself a grace. Of some of the personal importances that acted in that way I should with easier occasion have more to say—I shall as it is have something; but there could perhaps be no better sample of the effect of sharpness with which the forces of culture might emerge than, say, the fairly golden glow of romance investing the mere act of perusal of the Revue des Deux Mondes.[114] There was the charm—though I grant of course that I speak here all for myself, constitutionally and, face to face *with* myself, quite shamelessly an inquirer, a hunter, for charm—that whereas the spell cast had more or less inevitable limits in the world to which such a quality as the best things of the Revue, such a performance of the intellectual and expressional engagement as these suggested, was native and was thereby relative to other generally like phenomena, so it represented among *us*, where it had to take upon itself what I have already alluded to as all the work, far more than its face value. Few of the forces about us reached as yet the level of representation (even if here and there some might have been felt as trying for it); and this made all the difference. Anything suggestive or significant, anything promising or interesting, anything in the least finely charming above all, immensely counted, claimed tendance and protection, almost claimed, or at any rate enjoyed, worship; as for that matter anything finely charming does, quite rightly, anywhere. But our care, our privilege, on occasion our felt felicity, was to foster every symptom and breathe encouragement to every success; to hang over the tenderest shoots that betrayed the principle of growth—or in other words to read devoutly into everything, and as straight as possible, the very fullest mean-

114. The *Revue des deux mondes* was founded in 1829 by François Buloz, who became its long-serving editor. Its title suggests an intention to relate to the world beyond Europe, including, of course, the United States. The journal (which continues to thrive) was especially influential in the nineteenth century, when it published many of France's leading authors. See also above, n. 90.

ing we might hope it would learn to have. So at least quite at first—and so again very considerably after the large interval and grim intermission represented by the War; during which interest and quality, to say nothing of quantity, at the highest pitch, ceased in any degree to fail us, and what might be "read into" almost any aspect without exception paled in the light of what was inevitably read out from it. It must be added at the same time that with its long duration the War fell into its place as part of life at large, and that when it was over various other things still than the love of peace were found to have grown.

Immediately, at any rate, the Albany cousins, or a particular group of them, began again to be intensely in question for us; coloured in due course with reflections of the War as their lives, not less than our own, were to become—and coloured as well too, for all sorts of notation and appreciation, from irrepressible private founts. Mrs. Edmund Tweedy, bereft of her own young children, had at the time I speak of opened her existence, with the amplest hospitality, to her four orphaned nieces, who were also our father's and among whom the second in age, Mary Temple the younger, about in her seventeenth year when she thus renewed her appearance to our view, shone with vividest lustre, an essence that preserves her still, more than half a century from the date of her death, in a memory or two where many a relic once sacred has comparatively yielded to time.[115] Most of those who knew and loved, I was going to say adored, her have also yielded—which is a reason the more why thus much of her, faint echo from too far off though it prove, should be tenderly saved. If I have spoken of the elements and presences round about us that "counted," Mary Temple was to count, and in more lives than can now be

115. During the 1850s in Europe, Edmund and Mary Tweedy lost their three children to diphtheria and then, back in America, took into their home for eight years the four Temple girls, the orphaned children of Robert and Catharine Temple, who both died in 1854 (see also *SBO*, n. 21). Minny Temple exercised a powerful influence over HJ (as well as WJ) and, following her death at the age of twenty-four from consumption, she seems to have inspired some of his greatest fictional portrayals of women, including, most notably, Isabel Archer in *The Portrait of a Lady* and Milly Theale in the *Wings of the Dove*. Minny Temple's independence of mind was less popular with other members of the James family, including HJ Sr., as Habegger has concluded: "Not only was she a sterling example of the earnest, restless young woman, a much publicized type in the late 1860s that the Jameses and many other Brahmins tended to frown on, but she denounced the philosopher's ideas to his face" (*Henry James and the "Woman Business"* [Cambridge: Cambridge University Press, 1989], 11–12). Gordon's *A Private Life of Henry James* offers a detailed account of the novelist's relationship with his cousin.

named, to an extraordinary degree; count as a young and shining apparition, a creature who owed to the charm of her every aspect (her aspects were so many!) and the originality, vivacity, audacity, generosity, of her spirit, an indescribable grace and weight—if one might impute weight to a being so imponderable in common scales. Whatever other values on our scene might, as I have hinted, appear to fail, she was one of the first order, in the sense of the immediacy of the impression she produced, and produced altogether as by the play of her own light spontaneity and curiosity —not, that is, as through a sense of such a pressure and such a motive, or through a care for them, in others. "Natural" to an effect of perfect felicity that we were never to see surpassed is what I have already praised all the Albany *cousinage* of those years for being;[116] but in none of the company was the note so clear as in this rarest, though at the same time symptomatically or ominously palest, flower of the stem; who was natural at more points and about more things, with a greater range of freedom and ease and reach of horizon than any of the others dreamed of. They had that way, delightfully, with the small, after all, and the common matters—while she had it with those too, but with the great and rare ones over and above; so that she was to remain for us the very figure and image of a felt interest in life, an interest as magnanimously far-spread, or as familiarly and exquisitely fixed, as her splendid shifting sensibility, moral, personal, ner-

116. HJ voices a similar admiration for such naturalness in his female cousins at the opening of chap. 4 of *SBO*. The Temple *"cousinage,"* or cousinhood, met with mixed fortunes. Robert, the eldest of the six surviving Temple children (three died in infancy), joined the army. Overly dependent on alcohol, he was referred to by WJ in 1869 as a "lout positive & absolute" (*CWJ*, 1:101): WJ speaks of him in more positive terms in chap. 5 below. William was killed during the Civil War at Chancellorsville, as HJ recalls in chap. 5. As another beloved cousin, Gus Barker (himself soon to die), wrote, "A brother's death could not have had a more melancholy effect upon me, as I had known him so intimately, both at home and at school, and lastly at college" (quoted in Rufus W. Clark, *The Heroes of Albany: A Memorial of the Patriot-Martyrs of the City and County of Albany* [Albany: S.R. Gray, 1866], 411). Katharine, or Kitty, shocked the Jameses by marrying Richard Stockton Emmet (1821–1902), a wealthy man twenty-two years her senior, though this may have been to provide a home for her younger sisters (Gordon, *A Private Life,* 89). Ellen, or Elly, perhaps for similar reasons, became engaged at the age of nineteen to his brother, Christopher Temple Emmet, a railroad magnate. HJ commented in 1869, "Elly's marriage strikes me as absolutely *sad.* I care not how good a fellow T. Emmet may be: Elly deserved a younger man" (*HJL,* 1:144). Each sister had six children. The youngest, Henrietta (b. 1853), married Leslie Pell-Clarke, known to the James family since their first arrival in Newport. Gordon comments that "James found Henrietta informed and 'superb' when she breakfasted with him in Bolton Street on her wedding tour in 1878" (*A Private Life of Henry James,* 132).

vous, and having at once such noble flights and such touchingly discouraged drops, such graces of indifference and inconsequence, might at any moment determine. She was really to remain, for our appreciation, the supreme case of a taste for life as life, as personal living; of an endlessly active and yet somehow a careless, an illusionless, a sublimely forewarned curiosity about it: something that made her, slim and fair and quick, all straightness and charming tossed head, with long light and yet almost sliding steps and a large light postponing, renouncing laugh, the very muse or amateur priestess of rash speculation. To express her in the mere terms of her restless young mind, one felt from the first, was to place her, by a perversion of the truth, under the shadow of female "earnestness"—for which she was much too unliteral and too ironic; so that, superlatively personal and yet as independent, as "off" into higher spaces, at a touch, as all the breadth of her sympathy and her courage could send her, she made it impossible to say whether she was just the most moving of maidens or a disengaged and dancing flame of thought. No one to come after her could easily seem to show either a quick inward life or a brave, or even a bright, outward, either a consistent contempt for social squalors or a very marked genius for moral reactions. She had in her brief passage the enthusiasm of humanity—more, assuredly, than any charming girl who ever circled, and would fain have continued to circle, round a ballroom. This kept her indeed for a time more interested in the individual, the immediate human, than in the race or the social order at large; but that, on the other hand, made her ever so restlessly, or quite inappeasably, "psychologic." The psychology of others, in her shadow—I mean their general resort to it—could only for a long time seem weak and flat and dim, above all not at all amusing.[117] She burned herself out; she died at twenty-four.

At the risk perhaps of appearing to make my own scant adventure the pivot of that early Newport phase I find my reference to William Hunt and his truly fertilising action on our common life much conditioned by the fact that, since W. J., for the first six months or so after our return, daily and devotedly haunted his studio, I myself did no less, for a shorter

117. Minny must have subscribed, according to HJ's recollection, to the processes and observations of what he termed in 1888 "the new psychology" ("The Middle Years," *CT*, 9:62), and was thus distinguished from the less inquiring New England society of her time. The noticeable quotation marks for a term so closely associated with one of psychology's most eminent theorists—WJ—perhaps enlists HJ's brother in the commemoration of this rare individual. The final chapter of *NSB* is given over to a selection of Minny Temple's letters.

stretch, under the irresistible contagion.[118] The clearness of the whole passage for me, the clearest impression, above all, of the vivid and whimsical master, an inspirer, during a period that began a little later on, of numberless devotions and loyalties, is what this fond memory of my permitted contact and endeavour still has to give me. Pupils at that time didn't flock to his gates—though they were to do so in Boston, during years, later on;[119] an earnest lady or two, Boston precursors, hovered and flitted,[120] but I remember for the rest (and I speak of a short period) no thoroughgoing *élèves* save John La Farge and my brother.[121] I remember, for that matter, sitting quite in solitude in one of the grey cool rooms of the studio, which thus comes back to me as having several, and thinking that I really might get to copy casts rather well, and might in particular see myself congratulated on my sympathetic rendering of the sublime uplifted face of Michael Angelo's "Captive" in the Louvre.[122] I sat over this effort and a few others for long quiet hours, and seem to feel myself again aware, just to that tune, of how happy I ought to be. No one disturbed me; the

118. "The studio which he occupied in Church Street was large and commodious. The building was of two stories and had a carriage house and stalls for horses. It is still standing and occupied in the summer by New York artists" (Martha A. S. Shannon, *Boston Days of William Morris Hunt* [Boston: Marshall Jones, 1923], 44).

119. Hunt "functioned as an unofficial arbiter of Boston taste in matters artistic. . . . Boston's leading citizens unfailingly turned to Hunt for advice, and his word was law" (Christopher Riopelle, "American Artists in France / French Art in America," in Kathleen Adler, Erica E. Hirshler, and H. Barbara Weinberg, *Americans in Paris, 1860–1900* (London: National Gallery, 2006), 211. In 1868 Hunt opened a class for female students, numbering about forty, in the Mercantile Building, Summer Street, and was "severely criticized for spending his time 'teaching a lot of women'" (Shannon, *Boston Days of William Morris Hunt*, 99). It was because of his influence that the Boston Museum of Fine Arts acquired an unparalleled collection of Millet's paintings.

120. One of these was a "Miss Gibbs," and another, Miss Theodora Watson, who in 1913 recalled, "My easel stood here, and John La Farge's there, Henry and William James were on the other side" (Shannon, *Boston Days of William Morris Hunt*, 45, 47).

121. In his memoir of John La Farge, Royal Cortissoz records the painter's admiration for WJ, who he considered "drew 'beautifully' . . . repeating the word three or four times." La Farge considered that HJ had "the painter's eye, adding that few writers possessed it. . . . In those old days he advised Henry James to turn writer, but, he said, he did not offer his counsel dogmatically" (*John La Farge: A Memoir and a Study* [Boston: Houghton Mifflin, 1911], 117).

122. *The Dying Captive* (1513–16), intended for the tomb of Pope Julius II, is one of Michelangelo's most famous sculptures. Novick, referring to Theodora Watson's recollections above, believes that HJ is here being "partial and self-effacing" (*Young Master,* 464 n. 23). The copying of great works of art was, of course, part of the curriculum for aspiring atists.

earnest workers were elsewhere; I had a chamber of the temple all to myself, with immortal forms and curves, with shadows beautiful and right, waiting there on blank-eyed faces for me to prove myself not helpless; and with two or three of Hunt's own fine things, examples of his work in France, transporting me at once and defying. I believed them great productions—thought in especial endless good of the large canvas of the girl with her back presented while she fills her bucket at the spout in the wall, against which she leans with a tension of young muscle, a general expression of back, beneath her dress, and with the pressure of her raised and extended bare arm and flattened hand: this, to my imagination, could only become the prize of some famous collection, the light of some museum, for all the odd circumstance that it was company just then for muddled *me* and for the queer figures projected by my crayon.[123] Frankly, intensely—that was the great thing—these were hours of Art, art definitely named, looking me full in the face and accepting my stare in return—no longer a tacit implication or a shy subterfuge, but a flagrant unattenuated aim. I had somehow come into the temple by the back door, the *porte d'honneur*[124] opened on another side, and I could never have believed much at best in the length of my stay; but I was there, day by day, as much as any one had ever been, and with a sense of what it "meant" to be there that the most accredited of pupils couldn't have surpassed; so that the situation to this extent really hummed with promise. I fail, I confess, to reconstitute the relation borne by my privilege to that of tuition "in the higher branches," to which it was quite time I should have mounted, enjoyed at the hands of the Reverend William C. Leverett, curate to the then "rector," Doctor Mercer, of that fine old high-spired Trinity Church in which had throbbed, from long before the Revolution as they used to say, the proud episcopal heart of Newport;[125] and feel indeed that I must

123. Hunt's *Girl at the Fountain* (1852–54) is now in the Metropolitan Museum of Art, New York. In an 1872 review entitled "Pictures by William Morris Hunt, Gérôme and Others" for the *Atlantic Monthly,* HJ praised the painting for reflecting "the artist's best powers" (*Painter's Eye,* 50).

124. Literally, "gate of honor," or main entrance.

125. The Reverend Leverett ran the Berkeley Institute, the school attended by HJ, at 10 Washington Square in Newport. With his five assistants, Leverett offered a fairly narrow curriculum featuring "English, Classical, French, German, Spanish, Drawing and Music" (Harlow, *Perry: A Biography,* 8). HJ had limited respect, it seems, for the clergyman as a teacher. Trinity Church on Queen Anne Square, modeled on Boston's Old North Church and the designs of Christopher Wren, has a spire of almost forty-six metres which came to serve as a beacon for ships. HJ refers, of course, to the American Revolution of 1763–83.

pretty well have shaken off, as a proved absurd predicament, all submission to my dilemma: all submission of the mind, that is, for if my share of Mr. Leverett's attention was less stinted than my share of William Hunt's (and neither had much duration) it failed to give me the impression that anything worth naming had opened out to me, whereas in the studio I was at the threshold of a world.

It became itself indeed on the spot a rounded satisfying world, the place did; enclosed within the grounds, as we then regarded them, of the master's house, circled about with numerous trees, as we then counted them, and representing a more direct exclusion of vulgar sounds, false notes and harsh reminders than I had ever known. I fail in the least to make out where the real work of the studio went forward; it took somewhere else its earnest course, and our separation—mine from the real workers, my indulged yet ignored state—kept me somehow the safer, as if I had taken some mild and quite harmless drug through which external rubs would reach me from a distance, but which left my own rubbing power, not to say my own smearing or smutching, quite free. Into the world so beautifully valid the master would occasionally walk, inquiring as to what I had done or would do, but bearing on the question with an easy lightness, a friendliness of tact, a neglect of conclusion, which it touches me still to remember. It was impossible to me at that time not so to admire him that his just being to such an extent, as from top to toe and in every accent and motion, the living and communicating Artist, made the issue, with his presence, quite cease to be of how one got on or fell short, and become instead a mere self-sacrificing vision of the picturesque itself, the constituted picturesque or treated "subject," in efficient figure, personal form, vivid human style. I then felt the man the great mystery could mark with its stamp, when wishing the mark unmistakable, teach me just in himself the most and best about any art that I should come to find benignantly concerned with me, for moments however smilingly scant. William Hunt, all muscular spareness and brownness and absence of waste, all flagrant physiognomy, brave bony arch of handsome nose, upwardness of strong eyebrow and glare, almost, of eyes that both recognised and wondered, strained eyes that played over questions as if they were objects and objects as if they were questions, might have stood, to

---

Having signed the Declaration of Independence, Rhode Island (along with North Carolina) notably held out against the Constitution until the addition of the Bill of Rights, ratified in 1791.

the life, for Don Quixote, if we could associate with that hero a far-spreading beard already a little grizzled, a manner and range of gesture and broken form of discourse that was like a restless reference to a palette and that seemed to take for granted, all about, canvases and models and charming, amusing things, the "tremendously interesting" in the seen bit or caught moment, and the general unsayability, in comparison, of anything else. He never would have perched, it must be added, on Rosinante —he was fonder of horses even than of the method of Couture, and though with a shade of resemblance, as all simple and imaginative men have, to the knight of La Mancha, he least suggested that analogy as he passed in a spinning buggy, his beard flying, behind a favourite trotter.[126] But what he perhaps most puts before me to-day is the grim truth of the merciless manner in which a living and hurrying public educates itself, making and devouring in a day reputations and values which represent something of the belief in it that it has had in *them,* but at the memory of which we wince, almost to horror, as at the legend of victims who have been buried alive. Oh the cold grey luminaries hung about in odd corners and back passages, and that we have known shining and warm! They serve at the most now as beacons warning any step not to come *that* way, whatever it does; the various attested ways it may not with felicity come growing thus all the while in number.[127]

John La Farge became at once, in breaking on our view, quite the most interesting person we knew, and for a time remained so; he became a great many other things beside—a character, above all, if there ever was one; but he opened up to us, though perhaps to me in particular, who could absorb all that was given me on those suggestive lines, prospects and possibilities that made the future flush and swarm. His foreignness, which seemed great at that time, had gained a sharper accent from a long stay made in France, where both on his father's and his mother's side he had relations, and had found, to our hovering envy, all sorts of charming occasions. He had spent much time in Brittany, among kindred the most romantically interesting, people and places whose very names, the De Nanteuils of

126. HJ refers to the picaresque novel *Don Quixote* (1605), by Miguel de Cervantes Saavedra (1547–1616); William Morris Hunt is similar to the eponymous knight of La Mancha only in physical terms. Rosinante was the name of Don Quixote's horse.

127. HJ's lament at the fickle public and its power to consign artists to obscurity may well reflect his own sense of neglect. The unexpected success of these autobiographical writings, so late in his life, came as a surprise. It is typical of HJ's insouciance that his language here seems deliberately intent on the double entendre.

Saint-Pol-de-Léon, I seem to remember for instance, cast a spell across comparatively blank Newport sands;[128] he had brought home with him innumerable water-colour sketches, Breton peasants, costumes, interiors, bits of villages and landscape;[129] and I supposed him to have had on such ground the most delightful adventure in the world. How was one not to suppose it at a time when the best of one's education, such as that was, had begun to proceed almost altogether by the aid of the Revue des Deux Mondes, a periodical that supplied to us then and for several years after (or again I can but speak for myself) all that was finest in the furniture and the fittings of romance? Those beginnings of Newport were our first contact with New England—a New England already comparatively sub-dued and sophisticated, a Samson shorn of his strength by the shears of the Southern, and more particularly of the New York, Delilah; the result of which, still speaking for myself, was a prompt yearning and reaching out, on the part of the spirit, for some corrective or antidote to whatever it was that might be going, in the season to come, least charmingly or infor-mingly or inspiringly to press upon us.[130] I well recall my small anxious foresight as to a required, an indispensable provision against either assault or dearth, as if the question might be of standing an indefinite siege; and how a certain particular capacious closet in a house we were presently to occupy took on to my fond fancy the likeness at once of a store of edibles, both substantial and succulent, and of a hoard of ammunition for the

---

128. Saint-Pol-de-Léon is on Brittany's north coast, just south of Roscoff in the depart-ment of Finistère. In late May 1856 La Farge took his two younger brothers to this northwest edge of Brittany where they visited their maternal aunt, Angèle-Adelaide, who was married to the wealthy Pierre-Antoine-Auguste, comte de la Barre de Nanteuil. Their summer home was at Saint-Pol-de-Léon. See James L. Yarnall, "Adventures of a Young Antiquarian: John La Farge's *Wanderjahr* in Europe," *American Art Journal* 30, no. 1/2 (1999): 102–32, who also reproduces some of La Farge's scenes of Breton life to which HJ refers. Yarnall points out, however, that there are "few surviving watercolors from the trip" (107), though the Yale University Art Gallery possesses a sketchbook.

129. Scenes of the countryside and seaside life of Normandy and Brittany were, of course, popular with painters both French and American, especially between 1870 and 1910, a period when a variety of artists' colonies grew up in northwest France (H. Barbara Weinberg, "Summers in the Country," in Adler et al., *Americans in Paris*, 114–74).

130. In this trope, derived from the Old Testament's book of Judges, HJ is most likely referring to the midcentury gentrification of the traditional fishing port by newly rich inhabitants or summer residents who escaped from the heat of the southern states or from the rapidly expanding city of New York.

defence of any breach—the Revue accumulating on its shelves at last in serried rows and really building up beneath us with its slender firm salmon-coloured blocks an alternative sphere of habitation.[131] There will be more to say of this, bristling or rather flowering with precious particulars, if I stray so far; but the point for the moment was that one would have pushed into that world of the closet, one would have wandered or stumbled about in it quite alone if it hadn't been that La Farge was somehow always in it with us. That was in those years his admirable function and touch—that he affected me as knowing his way there as absolutely no one else did, and even as having risen of a sudden before us to bear us this quickening company. Nobody else, not another creature, was free of it to that tune; the whole mid-century New England—as a rough expression of what the *general* consciousness most signified—was utterly out of it; which made, you see, a most unequal division of our little working, or our totally cogitative, universe into the wondrous esoteric quarter peopled just by us and our friend and our common references, and the vast remainder of the public at large, the public of the innumerably uninitiated even when apparently of the most associated.

All of which is but a manner of expressing the intensity, as I felt it, of our Franco-American, our most completely accomplished friend's presence among us. Out of the safe rich home of the Revue, which opened away into the vastness of visions, he practically stepped, and into it, with all his ease, he mysteriously returned again: he came nearer to being what might have been meant concretely throughout it all—though meant most of course in its full-charged stream of fiction—than any other visiting figure. The stream of fiction was so constant an appeal to the charmed, by which I mean of course the predisposed, mind that it fairly seemed at moments to overflow its banks and take to its bosom any recognised, any congruous creature or thing that might happen to be within reach. La Farge was of the type—the "European," and this gave him an authority for me that it verily took the length of years to undermine; so that as the sense of those first of them in especial comes back to me I find it difficult, even under the appeal to me of the attempt, to tell how he was to count in my earliest culture. If culture, as I hold, is a matter of attitude quite as much as

131. The covers of the magazine were salmon colored. As in *SBO*, HJ temporaarily resorts to American usage in referring to this storage space as a "closet" rather than using the British term "cupboard."

of opportunity, and of the form and substance of the vessel carried to the fountain no less than of the water-supply itself, there couldn't have been better conditions for its operating drop by drop.[132] It operates ever much more, I think, by one's getting whatever there may happen to be out for one's use than by its conforming to any abstract standard of quantity or lustre. It may work, as between dispenser and subject, in so incalculably personal a manner that no chemical analysis shall recover it, no common estimate of forces or amounts find itself in the least apply. The case was that La Farge swam into our ingenuous ken as the figure of figures, and that such an agent, on a stage so unpeopled and before a scene so unpainted, became salient and vivid almost in spite of itself.[133] The figure was at a premium, and fit for any glass case that its vivacity should allow to enclose it—wherein it might be surrounded by wondering, admiring and often quite inevitably misconceiving observers. It was not that these too weren't agents in their way, agents in some especial good cause without the furtherance of which we never should have done at all; but they were by that very fact specialised and stiffened, committed to their one attitude, the immediately profitable, and incapable of that play of gesture in which we recognise representation. A representative, a rounded figure, however, is as to none of its relations definable or announceable beforehand; we only know it, for good or for ill, but with something of the throb of elation always, when we see it, and then it in general sufficiently accounts for itself. We often for that matter insist on its *being* a figure, we positively make it one, in proportion as we seem to need it—or as in other words we too acutely miss the active virtue of representation. It takes some extraordinary set of circumstances or time of life, I think, either to beguile or to

132. HJ suggests here that the workings of culture (in the development, perhaps, of the young artist) relate more powerfully to the individuals involved in its pursuit than to any more defining idea of culture itself as some kind of recognizable entity.

133. The language in HJ's late essay on the poet Rupert Brooke is more erotically charged, but his terms there are reminiscent of this passage, as if he perceives creativeness, specifically in the male, in a figuratively unified light. He sees the poet moving in his own "poetic consciousness . . . as a stripped young swimmer might have kept splashing through blue water and coming up at any point that friendliness and fancy, with every prejudice shed, might determine. . . . so much fuller a report would surely proceed, could we appeal to their memory, their sense of poetry, from those into whose ken he floated" (*LC* 1, 749–50, 763). See also Hazel Hutchison, "The Art of Living Inward: Henry James on Rupert Brooke," *Henry James Review* 29 (Spring 2008): 132–43. La Farge himself becomes an exhibit for examination by other figures (including HJ), themselves influential participants in this transmission of culture, his appearance unexpected yet inevitable.

hustle us into indifference to some larger felt extension roundabout us of "the world"—a sphere the confines of which move on even as we ourselves move and which is always there, just beyond us, to twit us with the more it should have to show if we were a little more "of" it. Sufficiency shuts us in but till the man of the world—never prefigured, as I say, only welcomed on the spot—appears; when we see at once how much we have wanted him. When we fail of that acknowledgment, that sense as of a tension, an anxiety or an indigence relieved, it is of course but that the extraordinary set of circumstances, or above all the extraordinary time of life I speak of, has indeed intervened.

It was as a man of the world that, for all his youth, La Farge rose or, still better, bowed, before us, his inclinations of obeisance, his considerations of address being such as we had never seen and now almost publicly celebrated. This was what most immediately and most iridescently showed, the truth being all the while that the character took on in him particular values without which it often enough, though then much more grossly, flourishes. It was by these enrichments of curiosity, of taste and genius, that he became the personality, as we nowadays say, that I have noted—the full freshness of all of which was to play but through his younger time, or at least through our younger apprehension. He was so "intellectual"—that was the flower; it crowned his being personally so finished and launched. The wealth of his cultivation, the variety of his initiations, the inveteracy of his forms, the degree of his *empressement*[134] (this in itself, I repeat, a revelation) made him, with those elements of the dandy and the cavalier to which he struck us as so picturesquely sacrificing, a cluster of bright promises, a rare original and, though not at all a direct model for simpler folk, as we then could but feel ourselves, an embodiment of the gospel of esthetics.[135] Those more resounding forms

134. Eagerness, readiness.

135. The youthful self-portrait (1859) of the artist standing ready to set out for a day's sketching and painting may have influenced HJ's characterization here. La Farge, incidentally, "became the protagonist in one of James's earliest published stories, an entertaining spoof of Newport's artistic life titled 'A Landscape Painter' " (Henry Adams, "The Mind of John La Farge," in *John La Farge: Essays,* by Henry Adams et al. [New York: Abbeville Press, 1987], 17). The nineteenth-century dandy was a type characterized most influentially by Baudelaire in *The Painter of Modern Life* (1859–60): "He used the term to describe a new kind of aristocrat whose superiority depended not upon birth but upon the cultivation of a personal originality and a dedicated opposition to triviality and vulgarity" (Alexander Sturgis et al., *Rebels and Martyrs: The Image of the Artist in the Nineteenth Century* [London: National Gallery Company, 2006], 119).

that our age was to see this gospel take on were then still to come,[136] but I was to owe them in the later time not half the thrill that the La Farge of the prime could set in motion. He was really an artistic, an esthetic nature of wondrous homogeneity; one was to have known in the future many an unfolding that went with a larger ease and a shrewder economy, but never to have seen a subtler mind or a more generously wasteful passion, in other words a sincerer one, addressed to the problems of the designer and painter. Of his long later history, full of flights and drops, advances and retreats, experiment and performance, of the endless complications of curiosity and perversity, I say nothing here save that if it was to contradict none of our first impressions it was to qualify them all by others still more lively; these things belonging quite to some other record. Yet I may just note that they were to represent in some degree an eclipse of the so essentially harmonious person round whom a positive grace of legend had originally formed itself. I see him at this hour again as that bright apparition; see him, jacketed in black velvet or clad from top to toe in old-time elegances of cool white and leaning much forward with his protuberant and overglazed, his doubting yet all-seizing vision,[137] dandle[138] along the shining Newport sands in far-away summer sunsets on a charming chestnut mare whose light legs and fine head and great sweep of tail showed the

136. The idea (or, more devoutly, the "gospel") of art for art's sake (*l'art pour l'art*) was derived from the writing of Théophile Gautier (1811–72). Rejecting the prevailing assumption that art should be morally improving, the aesthetes (following the musings of Walter Pater) argued controversially that it must simply pursue beauty and represent the sometimes unorthodox vision of the artist. In the decadent 1890s HJ contributed a number of his short stories to *The Yellow Book*, a magazine notorious not least for its illustrations provided by Aubrey Beardsley (1872–98). HJ later came to see the movement, which embraced "the conception of the 'esthetic' law of life," as indigestible—something imported from foreign climes which could not prosper in Anglo-Saxon culture, "a queer high-flavoured fruit from overseas, grown under another sun than ours" ("Gabriele D'Annunzio," *Quarterly Review* [1904], *LC* 2, 908).

137. La Farge had weak eyesight and wore spectacles.

138. "Dandle" appears in the first edition of the work and has been repeated since, though "dawdle" might be more appropriate—unless HJ intended to suggest something of La Farge's dandified appearance. The *OED* offers little beyond the primary meaning of bouncing a child on the knee. Interestingly, HJ uses the term in a similar sense in *The Princess Casamassima* (1886) when Hyacinth Robinson observes the careless crowds of London, among them "the young man in a white tie and a crush-hat who dandled by on his way to a dinner-party in a hansom that nearly ran one over" ([Harmondsworth: Penguin, 1977], 132).

Arab strain—quite as if (what would have been characteristic of him) he had borrowed his mount from the adorable Fromentin, whom we already knew as a painter, but whose acquaintance as a writer we were of course so promptly to owe him that when "Dominique" broke upon us out of the Revue as one of the most exquisite literary events of our time it found us doubly responsive.[139]

So, at any rate, he was there, and there to stay—intensely among us but somehow not withal *of* us; his being a Catholic, and apparently a "real" one in spite of so many other omnisciences, making perhaps by itself the greatest difference. He had been through a Catholic college in Maryland, the name of which, though I am not assured of it now, exhaled a sort of educational elegance;[140] but where and when he had so miraculously laid up his stores of reading and achieved his universal saturation was what we longest kept asking ourselves. Many of these depths I couldn't pretend to sound, but it was immediate and appreciable that he revealed to us Browning for instance; and this, oddly enough, long after Men and

139. Eugène Fromentin (1820–76) is noted as a painter for his depictions of North African scenes and for wild animals, many showing the influence of Delacroix (see *The Orientalists: Delacroix to Matisse: European Painters in North Africa and the Near East*, ed. MaryAnne Stevens [London: Royal Academy of Arts, in association with Weidenfeld and Nicolson, 1984], 132–36). He also became a successful writer, and the novel *Dominique* (dedicated to George Sand) appeared in the *Revue des deux mondes* in 1862. Fromentin later completed a study of Dutch and Flemish Old Masters, *Les maîtres d'autrefois*, which HJ reviewed in 1876 for the *Nation*. In this essay he praises "the charming novel of *Dominique*" for its "art of analysing delicate moral and intellectual phenomena" (*Painter's Eye*, 116). Ironically, HJ's criticism of *Les maîtres d'autrefois* anticipates some of the negative responses to his own late style: "his whole dissertation is a good example of the vanity of much of the criticism in the super-subtle style. We lay it down perplexed and bewildered, with a wearied sense of having strained our attention in a profitless cause" (ibid., 118).

140. Before his 1856 European tour, La Farge had attended Columbia Grammar School and received a conventional Catholic education at St. John's College, New York (which became Fordham University) and Mt. St. Mary's College at Emmitsburg, Maryland, from which he graduated in 1853 (see Cortissoz, *La Farge*, 68 n. 1). In fact, his was "a checkered college career. Always a rebellious student, he was expelled in his junior year of college for fighting with a classmate. An uncle intervened to get him readmitted" (Linda Simon, *Genuine Reality: A Life of William James* [New York: Harcourt Brace, 1998], 78). Originally, HJ had thought La Farge's early Maryland college might have been "the *William and Mary*??" (*HJL*, 4:685), but the College of William and Mary is, of course, in Williamsburg, Virginia, and its earliest links were with the Church of England.

Women had begun (from our Paris time on, if I remember) to lie upon our parents' book-table.[141] *They* had not divined in us as yet an aptitude for that author; whose appeal indeed John reinforced to our eyes by the reproduction of a beautiful series of illustrative drawings, two or three of which he was never to surpass—any more than he was to complete his highly distinguished plan for the full set, not the least faded of his hundred dreams.[142] Most of all he revealed to us Balzac; having so much to tell me of what was within that formidably-plated door, in which he all expertly and insidiously played the key, that to re-read even after long years the introductory pages of Eugénie Grandet, breathlessly seized and earnestly absorbed under his instruction, is to see my initiator's youthful face, so irregular but so refined, look out at me between the lines as through blurred prison bars.[143] In Mérimée, after the same fashion, I meet his expository ghost—hovering to remind me of how he started me on La Vénus d'Ille;[144] so that nothing would do but that I should translate it, try

141. The two volumes of *Men and Women* (London: Chapman and Hall) by Robert Browning (1812–89), containing some of his most famous poetry (e.g., "Fra Lippo Lippi," "A Toccata of Galuppi's," "Childe Roland," "Bishop Blougram's Apology," "Andrea del Sarto"), came out in 1855. Robert and Elizabeth Barrett Browning (1806–61) were friends of William Wetmore Story's in Italy; HJ's biography of the sculptor contains letters and other material relating to the Brownings. Aside from his review of Barrett Browning's letters (*LC* 1, 776–81), HJ wrote three essays on Browning, most notably, "The Novel in *The Ring and the Book*," included in *Notes on Novelists* (1914) (*LC* 1, 791–811). When, in *AS,* HJ recalls the Newport of the "middle years" of the nineteenth century and the "fortunate folk" of what must be assumed to be his social circle, the mood seems reminiscent of a Browning lyric: "on the old lawns and verandahs I saw them gather, on the old shining sands I saw them gallop, past the low headlands I saw their white sails verily flash, and through the dusky old shrubberies came the light and sound of their feasts" (219–20).

142. With a number of other artists, La Farge contributed some illustrations to an edition of Tennyson's *Enoch Arden,* published in 1864. Cortissoz records (*La Farge,* 138, 139) that La Farge "contemplated producing over three hundred drawings" for *Men and Women,* but "comparatively few of these illustrations were actually engraved, and printed at the time"—and they were never published (see James L. Yarnall with Mary La Farge, "Chronology," in Adams et al., *La Farge: Essays,* 240). On a trip to Louisiana in spring 1860, La Farge records "keeping secret to myself some of the drawings . . . which were made to illustrate Browning's poems" (Cortissoz, *La Farge,* 120).

143. HJ had a lifelong admiration for Honoré de Balzac and wrote five substantial essays on the novelist between 1875 and 1913. *Eugénie Grandet* (1833) forms one of the Comédie Humaine sequence of novels, Balzac's detailed documentation of provincial French life.

144. *La Vénus d'Ille* by novelist and poet Prosper Mérimée (1803–70)—also author of the original novella of *Carmen*—is a horror story in which a bronze statue of Venus is dug up and seemingly comes to life, as HJ comments in 1874, "a version of the old legend of a

to render it as lovingly as if it were a classic and old (both of which things it now indeed is) and send it off to the New York weekly periodical of that age of crudest categories which was to do me the honour neither of acknowledging nor printing nor, clearly, since translations did savingly appear there, in the least understanding it. These again are mild memories —though not differing in that respect from most of their associates; yet I cherish them as ineffaceable dates, sudden milestones, the first distinctly noted, on the road of so much inward or apprehensive life. Our guest—I call him our guest because he was so lingeringly, so abidingly and super-sedingly present—began meanwhile to paint, under our eyes, with devo-tion, with exquisite perception, and above all as with the implication, a hundred times beneficent and fertilising, that if one didn't in these con-nections consistently take one's stand on supersubtlety of taste one was a helpless outsider and at the best the basest of vulgarians or flattest of frauds—a doctrine more salutary at that time in our world at large than any other that might be sounded. Of all of which ingenuous intensity and activity I should have been a much scanter witness than his then close condisciple, my brother, had not his personal kindness, that of the good-natured and amused elder youth to the enslaved, the yearningly gullible younger, charmed me often into a degree of participation. Occasions and accidents come back to me under their wash of that distilled old Newport light as to which we more and more agreed that it made altogether excep-tionally, on our side of the world, for possibility of the *nuance,* or in other words for picture and story;[145] such for example as my felt sense of how unutterably it was the real thing, the gage of a great future, when I one morning found my companions of the larger, the serious studio inspired to splendid performance by the beautiful young manly form of our cousin

---

love-pledge between a mortal and an effigy of the goddess. . . . Mérimée, making his heroine an antique bronze statue, disinterred in the garden of a little château in Gascony, and her victim the son of the old provincial antiquarian who discovered her, almost makes us believe in her actuality. This was the first known to us of Mérimée's tales, and we shall never forget our impression of its admirable art" (review of *Dernières nouvelles,* in *LC* 2, 564). The bronze is seen by Novick as "an embodiment of disconcerting female lust" (*Young Master,* 78), and HJ's short story "The Last of the Valerii" was perhaps indebted to the earlier piece. HJ wrote four essays on the French author, one of which, on Mérimée's letters, was republished in *French Poets and Novelists* (1878).

145. The chapter devoted to Newport in *AS* also elaborates upon the unique light effects. HJ wrote to Edith Wharton in November 1904, "I found Newport quite exquisite, like a large softly-lighted pearl (and with the light partly of far-away associations)" (*HJL,* 4:334).

Gus Barker, then on a vivid little dash of a visit to us and who, perched on a pedestal and divested of every garment, was the gayest as well as the neatest of models. This was my first personal vision of the "life," on a pedestal and in a pose, that had half gleamed and half gloomed through the chiaroscuro of our old friend Haydon; and I well recall the crash, at the sight, of all my inward emulation—so forced was I to recognise on the spot that I might niggle for months over plaster casts and not come within miles of any such point of attack. The bravery of my brother's own in especial dazzled me out of every presumption; since nothing less than that meant drawing (they were not using colour) and since our genial kinsman's perfect gymnastic figure meant living truth, I should certainly best testify to the whole mystery by pocketing my pencil.[146]

146. HJ had seen the expansive paintings of the British painter Benjamin Haydon (1786–1846) in London as a child (see *SBO*, n. 432). HJ much admired his cousin Gus Barker (1842–63), who was killed in the Civil War and whom he recalls in *SBO*, chap. 13. In the artist's studio HJ is not merely permitted but required in his trainee role to gaze upon the unclothed male form. The moment powerfully dramatizes his realization that the task is beyond him while asserting the unquestionable beauty of the male torso. The contented security of copying plaster casts is banished. The autobiographical James, having charted the physical and personal charms of cousin Gus in earlier pages, allows this unveiling of the young man to form the climax of his portrait (his last, valedictory sight of him is in the next chapter), a moment when the aesthetic and the erotic seem united, whatever his technical limitations with a pencil. At this private (or unspeakable, as he might have said) revelation, sexual panic seems contained only by the more serene sensibility of the older man recollecting. His division from the others present is complete. The young James becomes passively abject, unable to consummate the insight in any medium, having to be content with WJ's sketch, which he requested afterward and kept. HJ offers a comparable crisis in his short story "The Liar" (1888), in which a professional artist, through several sessions with his handsome (clothed) subject, so excites and stimulates the sitter that the finished portrait discloses the latter's inner, concealed self, a moral delinquency that divides him from the civilized values of his circle—an uncontrollable urge to lie.

As occurs frequently in HJ's late writing, the narrative pursues a homoerotic line, expressive and expansive (in the manner of his letters to his younger male friends of the time), yet, as here, within a medium of allusion discreetly established. The observed living body of the heroic Gus Barker can be regarded as a foil to the other naked, sculpted form of a young man mentioned by HJ, Michelangelo's *Dying Slave* in the Louvre, posed with one hand voluptuously placed behind his head, a more strikingly physical than allegorical presence. The presence of Walter Pater, implicit in the mention of the aesthetic movement, has a bearing too on the Michelangelo allusion. Referring to the Louvre pair of sculptures, the dying and the heroic slave, Pater bewails their physical discomfort in one of the essays of *The Renaissance*, "The Poetry of Michelangelo": "What a sense of wrong in those two captive youths, who feel the chains like scalding water on their proud and delicate flesh!"

I secured and preserved for long William's finished rendering of the happy figure—which was to speak for the original, after his gallant death, in sharper and finer accents perhaps than aught else that remained of him; and it wanted but another occasion somewhat later on, that of the sitting to the pair of pupils under Hunt's direction of a subject presented as a still larger challenge, to feel that I had irrecoverably renounced. Very handsome were the head and shoulders of Katherine Temple, the eldest of those Albany cousins then gathered at Newport under their, and derivatively our, Aunt Mary's wing, who afterwards was to become Mrs. Richard Emmet—the Temples and the Emmets being so much addicted to alliances that a still later generation was to bristle for us with a delightful Emmetry, each member of it a different blessing;[147] she sat with endless patience, the serenest of models, and W. J.'s portrait of her in oils survives (as well as La Farge's, dealing with her in another view) as a really mature, an almost masterly, piece of painting, having, as has been happily suggested to me, much the air of a characteristic Manet. Such demonstrations would throw one back on regret, so far as my brother was concerned, if subsequent counter-demonstrations hadn't had it in them so much to check the train. For myself at the hour, in any case, the beautiful success with Kitty Temple did nothing but hurry on the future, just as the sight of the charming thing to-day, not less than that of La Farge's *profil perdu*, or presented ear and neck and gathered braids of hair, quite as charming and

(*The Renaissance,* 63). Arthur Benson, one of the young men who became a close friend of HJ's, brought out early in 1906 a monograph on Walter Pater in the English Men of Letters series (to which HJ had himself contributed a volume on Hawthorne). In his congratulatory letter of 31 May 1906, HJ's terms (he confirms Pater as a "figure" who counts) are similar to those used of Minny Temple and John La Farge in this chapter: "You have done in especial *this* delightful and interesting thing—that you have ministered to that strange, touching, edifying (to me quite thrilling) operation of the whirligig of time, through which Pater has already, in these few years, and little as he seemed marked out for it, become in our literature that very rare and sovereign thing, a Figure: a figure in the sense in which there are so few!" (quoted in Tintner, *The Book World of Henry James,* 144). Many of HJ's earlier comments on Pater are more disparaging; for a discussion of the two as "fellow travelers" in (sub)merging the erotic in the aesthetic, see Wendy Graham, *Henry James's Thwarted Love* [Stanford: Stanford University Press, 1999], 125–27).

147. As indicated in n. 116 above, Katharine (not "Katherine") Temple married Richard Emmet, while her sister Ellen married his brother, Christopher Temple Emmet. In later life, HJ became particularly fond of Ellen's daughter Bay, who was a professional artist.

*Portrait in oils of Miss Katherine Temple, 1861.*

quite as painted, touchingly reanimates the past.[148] I say touchingly because of the remembered pang of my acceptance of an admonition so
sharply conveyed. Therefore if somewhat later on I could still so fondly
hang about in that air of production—so far at least as it enveloped our
friend, and particularly after his marriage and his setting up of his house at
Newport, vivid proofs alike, as seemed to us all, of his consummate, his
*raffiné* taste, even if we hadn't yet, I think, that epithet for this—it was
altogether in the form of mere helpless admirer and inhaler, led captive in
part by the dawning perception that the arts were after all essentially one
and that even with canvas and brush whisked out of my grasp I still
needn't feel disinherited.[149] That was the luxury of the friend and senior
with a literary side—that if there were futilities that he didn't bring home
to me he nevertheless opened more windows than he closed; since he
couldn't have meant nothing by causing my eyes to plunge so straight into

148. WJ's portrait of Kitty Temple, originally passed to her son William Temple Emmet
(1869-1918), and now in a private collection, is executed in profile as she sits in a chair
sewing (HJ's misspelling of her name has been retained in the picture caption, incidentally). It is "remarkably similar to a study of the same model by La Farge (1860, Mrs. Mott
Schmidt, New York)" (Sally Webster, *William Morris Hunt, 1824-1879* [Cambridge:
Cambridge University Press, 1991], 57). Both are similar, too, to William Morris Hunt's
*The Lost Profile* (Ruthmere Museum, Elkart, Ind.), or, as HJ calls the pose, *profil perdu*
(ibid., 57). The term describes the way in which the sitter's head is turned away from the
viewer, leaving only a side of the face and the back of the neck in view. The subject for *The
Lost Profile* "has been identified as Hunt's wife, Louisa, but given the similarity of hairdo
and dress, it may well be a portrait of Miss Temple that Hunt painted as a demonstration
piece (a practice he often followed for his classes in the 1870s) for his students in Newport. . . . Both La Farge and James ably record the profiled figure in full light, although the
one by James, with details of the young woman's task, is more engaging" (ibid., 59-60).
HJ's explanatory note for WJ's picture of Kitty Temple gives a date of 1861. However, the
other two portraits are dated 1860, as Novick (*Young Master,* 464 n. 32) points out, though
(presumably following Webster) he gives the date of WJ's picture as 1859. WJ had, of
course, met Hunt in Newport in 1858-59 (Edel, *Untried Years,* 158) before the family
returned to Europe for a year in October 1859, but in their mood and detail the three
paintings give every impression of contemporaneity. Édouard Manet (1832-83) was one of
the most influential of the French impressionist painters.

149. John La Farge married Margaret Mason Perry (1840-1925), the older sister of HJ's
friend T. S. Perry, on 15 October 1860. *Raffiné* (subtle, delicate) signifies, as HJ points out
in his 1874 review of Mérimée's *Letters,* "something more than our 'refined'" (*LC* 2, 567).
Baudelaire, in his *The Painter of Modern Life,* included the term in a list of those dissident
social types motivated by a spirit of opposition and revolt (D. J. Gordon and John Stokes,
"The Reference of *The Tragic Muse,*" in *The Air of Reality: New Essays on Henry James,*
ed. John Goode [London: Methuen, 1972], 148).

the square and dense little formal garden of Mérimée. I might occasionally serve for an abundantly idle young out-of-doors model—as in fact I frequently did, the best perhaps of his early exhibitions of a rare colour-sense even now attesting it;[150] but mightn't it become possible that Mérimée would meanwhile serve for *me*? Didn't I already see, as I fumbled with a pen, of what the small dense formal garden might be inspiringly symbolic? It was above all wonderful in the La Farge of those years that even as he painted and painted, very slowly and intently and belatedly—his habit of putting back the clock and ignoring every time-scheme but his own was matched only by his view of the constant timeliness of talk, talk as talk, for which no moment, no suspended step, was too odd or too fleeting—he remained as referentially and unexhaustedly bookish, he turned his back by the act as little on our theory of his omniscience as he ceased to disown his job, whatever it might be, while endlessly burying his salient and reinforced eyes and his visibly active organ of scent in some minutest rarity of print, some precious ancientry of binding, mechanically plucked, by the hazard of a touch, from one of the shelves of a stored collection that easily passed with us for unapproached.

He lost himself on these occasions both by a natural ease and by his early adoption and application of the principle of the imperturbable, which promised even from those days to govern his conduct well-nigh to the exclusion of every other. We were to know surely as time went on no comparable case of consistency of attitude—no other such prompt grasp by a nature essentially entire, a settled sovereign self, of the truth of what would work for it most favourably should it but succeed in never yielding the first inch of any ground. Immense every ground thus became by its covering itself from edge to edge with the defence of his serenity, which, whatever his fathomless private dealings with it, was never consentingly, I

150. La Farge's 1862 portrait of HJ, oil on canvas, owned by the Century Association; see above, n. 103. It is in profile and "with its vibrant halation of pinks and greens, takes on special interest as a characterization by the first person to foresee the youthful writer's greatness. Through the slightly parted lips La Farge suggested James's perpetual appearance of incipient speech; through the priestly dark costume, with its thin white collar, he effectively evoked James's celibate pursuit of his art" (Henry Adams, "The Mind of John La Farge," 17). This last point does, of course, credit La Farge with a degree of prescience. Less well known is his beautifully executed oil painting (c. 1859–60) of Wilky, who was fourteen at the time (*Portrait of a Seated Boy*, Helen Dill Collection, Denver Art Museum). An unfinished 1865 pencil sketch of T. S. Perry "talking with John Bancroft" also survives from this period, in the collection of Frances S. Childs (see Adams et al., *La Farge: Essays*, 260–61).

mean publicly, to suffer a grain of abatement. The artist's serenity, by this conception, was an intellectual and spiritual capital that must never brook defeat—which it so easily might incur by a single act of abdication. That was at any rate the case for the particular artist and the particular nature he felt himself, armour-proof as they became against the appeal of sacrifice. Sacrifice was fallibility, and one could only of course be consistent if one inveterately *had* hold of the truth. There was no safety or, otherwise, no inward serenity or even outward—though the outward came secondly— unless there was no deflection; none into the question, that is, of what might make for the serenity of others, which was their own affair and which above all seemed not urgent in comparison with the supreme artistic. It wasn't that the artist hadn't to pay, to pay for the general stupidity, perversity and perfidy, from the moment he might have to deal with these things; that was the inevitable suffering, and it was always there; but it could be more or less borne if one was systematically, or rather if one was naturally, or even, better still, preternaturally, in the right; since this meant the larger, the largest serenity. That account of so fine a case of inward confidence would indeed during those very first years have sinned somewhat by anticipation; yet something of the beauty—that is of the unmatched virtuosity—of the attitude finally achieved did even at the early time colour the air of intercourse with him for those who had either few enough or many enough of their own reserves.[151] The second of these conditions sprang from a due anxiety for one's own interests, more or less defined in advance and therefore, as might be, more or less menaced; the other proviso easily went with vagueness—vagueness as to what things *were* one's interests, seeing that the exhibited working of an esthetic and a moral confidence conjoined on that scale and at play together unham- pered would perhaps prove for the time an attraction beyond any other.

151. It is difficult to read this extended consideration of La Farge's hard-won and always receptive artistic integrity without thinking of HJ's own position at the end of his life. Always hoping for popularity and large sales, he nevertheless remained true to his own development (as expressed in the corpus of New York Edition Prefaces), in effect moving the novel on, both technically and formally, from its late-Victorian achievement. It has been suggested too that in these earliest days of HJ's aspiring to be an artist, he was much influenced by his older mentor: "It seems likely that James's distinctive and tortuous ver- bal style—with its long digressions and parentheses, its ambiguity, its tireless pursuit of nuance—was modeled to some degree on La Farge's famously elaborate conversation" (Henry Adams, "The Mind of John La Farge," 17). The style as characterized here, of course, only really finds a voice in HJ's writing in the final years of the nineteenth century.

This reflection must verily, in our relation, have brought about my own quietus—so far as that mild ecstasy could be divorced from agitation.[152] I recall at all events less of the agitation than of the ecstasy; the primary months, certain aspects even of the few following years, look out at me as from fine accommodations, acceptances, submissions, emotions, all melted together, that one must have taken for joys of the mind and gains of the imagination so clear as to cost one practically nothing. They are what I see, and are all I want to see, as I look back; there hangs about them a charm of thrilled good faith, the flush and throb of crowding apprehensions, that has scarce faded and of which I can only wish to give the whole picture the benefit. I bottle this imponderable extract of the loitering summers of youth, when every occasion really seemed to stay to be gathered and tasted, just for the sake of its faint sweetness.

Some time since, in Boston, I spent an hour before a commemorative cluster of La Farge's earlier productions, gathered in on the occasion of his death, with the effect as of a plummet suddenly dropped into obscure depths long unstirred, that of a remembered participation, it didn't seem too much to say, in the far-away difficult business of their getting themselves born.[153] These things, almost all finished studies of landscape, small and fond celebrations of the modest little Newport harmonies, the spare felicities and delicacies of a range of aspects that have ceased to appeal or to "count," called back into life a hundred memories, laid bare the very footsteps of time, light and uncertain though so often the imprint.[154] I seemed so to have been there by the projection of curiosity and

152. By "quietus," which can have associations of being released into death (as in *Hamlet:* "When he himself might his quietus make / With a bare bodkin"), HJ suggests a receipt for a balancing of accounts, or a reconciliation between anxiety and excitement in the challenges of creativeness.

153. The La Farge Memorial Exhibition was held at the Museum of Fine Arts, Boston, 1–31 January 1911. More than 175 works were exhibited, including 39 oils, 123 watercolors, 13 drawings, and a stained glass window. No catalog was published (James L. Yarnall with Amy B. Werbel, "Major Exhibitions and Sales," in Adams et al., *La Farge: Essays,* 247). HJ had returned to the United States in August 1910, accompanying the mortally ill WJ and his wife, Alice, back to Chocorua, New Hampshire. WJ died on 26 August 1910. HJ stayed in Cambridge with Alice and her family (with occasional trips to New York) for almost a year, leaving for the United Kingdom on 30 July 1911. John La Farge died at Providence, Rhode Island, on 14 November 1910.

154. In the late 1850s and early '60s the grand panoramas of the Hudson River school were at their most popular; in contrast, La Farge's Newport watercolors were considered revolutionary, showing a strongly marked French influence. Henry Adams notes of these

sympathy, if not by having literally looked in, when the greater number of such effects worked themselves out, that they spoke to me of my own history—through the felt intensity of my commission, as it were, to speak for my old friend. The terms on which he was ever ready to draw out for us the interesting hours, terms of patience as they essentially were for the edified party, lived again in this record, but with the old supposition of profit, or in other words the old sense of pleasure, of precious acquisition and intenser experience, more vivid than anything else. There recurs to me for instance one of the smallest of adventures, as tiny a thing as could incur the name and which was of the early stage of our acquaintance, when he proposed to me that we should drive out to the Glen, some six miles off, to breakfast, and should afterwards paint—*we* paint!—in the bosky open air. It looks at this distance a mythic time, that of felt inducements to travel so far at such an hour and in a backless buggy on the supposition of rustic fare. But different ages have different measures, and I quite remember how ours, that morning, at the neat hostel in the umbrageous valley, overflowed with coffee and griddle-cakes that were not as other earthly refreshment, and how a spell of romance rested for several hours on our invocation of the genius of the scene: of such material, with the help of the attuned spirit, may great events consent to be composed. My companion, his easel and canvas, his palette and stool and other accessories happily placed, settled to his subject, while I, at a respectful distance, settled to mine and to the preparation of this strange fruit of time, my having kept the impression as if it really mattered. It did indeed matter, it was to continue to have done so, and when I ask myself the reason I find this in something as rare and deep and beautiful as a passage of old poetry, a scrap of old legend, in the vagueness of rustling murmuring green and plashing water and woodland voices and images, flitting hovering possibilities; the most retained of these last of course being the chance that one's small daub (for I too had my easel and panel and palette) might incur appreciation by the eye of friendship. This indeed was the true source of the spell, that it was in the eye of friendship, friendship full of character

---

paintings "the free brushwork, the Romantic mood, the interest in 'the sketch,' and even the long descriptive titles" ("The Mind of John La Farge," 69). HJ had always admired these Newport watercolors, referring in an 1872 *Atlantic Monthly* review, "French Pictures in Boston" (which included "three or four American pictures" as well), to "the view of a deep seaward-facing gorge, seen from above, at Newport. . . . in every way a remarkable picture, full of the most refined intentions and the most beautiful results, of light and atmosphere and of the very poetry of the situation" (*Painter's Eye*, 49).

and colour, and full of amusement of its own, that I lived on any such occasion, and that I had come forth in the morning cool and had found our breakfast at the inn a thing of ineffable savour, and that I now sat and flurriedly and fearfully aspired. Yes, the interesting ineffectual and exquisite array of the Boston "show" smote for me most the chord of the prime questions, the admirations and expectations at first so confident, even that of those refinements of loyalty out of which the last and highest tribute was to spring; the consideration, I mean, of whether our extraordinary associate, neither promptly understood nor inveterately accepted, might not eventually be judged such a colourist and such a poet that owners of his first felicities, those very ones over which he was actually bending, and with a touch so inscrutable, such "tonalities" of his own, would find themselves envied and rich. I remember positively liking to see most people stupid about him, and to make them out, I dare say, more numerously stupid than they really were: this perhaps in some degree as a bright communication of his own spirit—which discerned from so far off that of the bitterest-sweet cup it was abundantly to taste; and partly because the case would after that fashion only have its highest interest.[155] The highest interest, the very highest, it certainly couldn't fail to have; and the beauty of a final poetic justice, with exquisite delays, the whole romance of conscious delicacy and heroic patience intervening, was just what we seemed to see meanwhile stow itself expectantly away.

This view of the inevitable fate of distinguished work was thus, on my part, as it comes before me again, of early development, and I admit that I should appear to antedate it hadn't I in renewed presence of each of the particular predestined objects of sacrifice I have glanced at caught myself in the very act of that invidious apprehension, that fondest contemporaneity. There were the charming individual things round the production of which I had so at once elatedly and resignedly circled; and nothing remained at the end of time but to test the historic question. *Was* the quiet chamber of the Boston museum a constitution of poetic justice long awaited and at last fully cognisant?—or did the event perhaps fail to give out, after all, the essence of our far-away forecast? I think that what showed clearest, or what I, at any rate, most sharply felt, was the very

155. "During the 1860s viewers found his Newport paintings experimental and somewhat outlandish, although imbued with an intensely personal flavor" (Adams, "The Mind of John La Farge," 70). Typically, HJ goes on to consider the "interest" of La Farge's work in artistic as well as financial terms.

difficulty of saying; which fact meant of course, I recognise, that the story fell a little short, alas, of rounding itself off. Poetic justice, when it comes, I gather, comes ever with a great shining; so that if there is any doubt about it the source of the doubt is in the very depths of the case and has been from the first at work there. It literally seems to me, besides, that there was more history and thereby more interest recoverable as the matter stood than if every answer to every question about it hadn't had a fine ambiguity. I like ambiguities and detest great glares; preferring thus for my critical no less than for my pedestrian progress the cool and the shade to the sun and dust of the way.[156] There was an exquisite effort of which I had been peculiarly sure; the large canvas of the view of the Paradise Rocks over against Newport, but within the island and beyond the "second beach"— such were our thin designations! On the high style and the grand manner of this thing, even though a little uneasy before the absence from it of a certain *crânerie* of touch, I would have staked every grain of my grounded sensibility—in spite of which, on second thoughts, I shall let that faded fact, and no other contention at all, be my last word about it.[157] For the prevailing force, within the Boston walls, the supreme magic anything was to distil, just melted into another connection which flung a soft mantle as over the whole show. It became, from the question of how even a man of

156. In questioning whether justice had been done in recognizing La Farge's achievement—and the need to ask the question implies a degree of doubt—HJ may once more be motivated by feelings about his own position as an artist with predominantly high critical acclaim and some public neglect. Boston's Museum of Fine Arts moved west down Huntington Avenue from its earlier location in Copley Square in 1909.

157. *Crânerie:* jauntiness, swagger. La Farge's Newport paintings in oils of the 1860s show significant French influences, as well as anticipating works such as Whistler's *Nocturnes,* though they were given "a lukewarm reception" (Kathleen A. Foster, "John La Farge and the American Watercolor Movement: Art for the 'Decorative Age,' " in Adams et al., *La Farge: Essays,* 133). A number of the most important pieces have as their location the coastal area around Middletown, known as Paradise, about five miles north of Newport; La Farge was renting a cottage at Howard Farm on Paradise Road. Aside from pencil sketches, they include *Clouds over Sea; from Paradise Rocks* (1863) and *Paradise Valley* (1866–68), his first important landscape and, according to Cortissoz, "a picture of peculiar significance in the history of American art" (*La Farge: A Memoir,* 127–28), as well as *The Last Valley—Paradise Rocks* (1867–68). The latter work was, as La Farge said, "painted from nature, in the same way as the other [*Paradise Valley*], and took a very long time to paint, so as to get the same light as possible. By going very frequently,—if necessary, everyday, and watching for a few minutes, I could occasionally get what I wanted" (quoted in James L. Yarnall, "Nature and Art in the Painting of John La Farge," in Adams et al, *La Farge: Essays,* 92).

perceptive genius had painted what we then locally regarded as our scenery, a question of how we ourselves had felt and cherished that scenery; which latter of these two memories swept for me everything before it. The scenery we cherished—by which I really mean, I fear, but four or five of us—has now been grossly and utterly sacrificed; in the sense that its range was all for the pedestrian measure, that to overwalk it was to love it and to love it to overwalk it, and that no such relation with it as either of these appears possible or thinkable to-day.[158] We had, the four or five of us, the instinct—the very finest this must have been—of its scale and constitution, the adorable wise economy with which nature had handled it and in the light of which the whole seaward and insular extension of the comparatively futile town, untrodden, unsuspected, practically all inviolate, offered a course for the long afternoon ramble more in harmony with the invocations, or for that matter the evocations, of youth than we most of us, with appreciation so rooted, were perhaps ever to know. We knew already, we knew then, that no such range of airs would ever again be played for us on but two or three silver strings. They were but two or three—the sea so often as of the isles of Greece, the mildly but perpetually embayed promontories of mossy rock and wasted thankless pasture, bathed in a refinement of radiance and a sweetness of solitude which amounted in themselves to the highest "finish";[159] and little more than the feeling, with all this, or rather with no more than this, that possession, discrimination, far frequentation, were ours alone, and that a grassy rocky tide-washed, just a bare, though ever so fine-grained, toned and tinted breast of nature and field of fancy stretched for us to the low horizon's furthest rim. The vast region—it struck us then as vast—was practically roadless, but this, far

158. HJ refers to the expansion of Newport toward the end of the nineteenth century and to the grandiose mansions of the wealthy families which transformed the place. Rosanna Gaw in *The Ivory Tower* observes "the big bright picture of the villas, the palaces, the lawns and the luxuries," hearing "something like the chink of money itself in the murmur of the breezy little waves at the foot of the cliff" (22). Modeled as they are on largely European architectural traditions, the Newport mansions symbolize (ironically) another facet of the town's nostalgia for Europe, elsewhere celebrated by HJ.

159. Compare a moment in *AS* when HJ revives some Arcadian sense of Newport as it existed in his earlier days. He recalls a mild November drive along the coast: "The place itself . . . had taken it over, was more than ever, to the fancy, like some dim, simplified ghost of a small Greek island, where the clear walls of some pillared portico or pavilion, perched afar, looked like those of temples of the gods, and where Nature . . . might have shown a piping shepherd on any hillside or attached a mythic image to any point of rocks" (224).

from making it a desert, made it a kind of boundless empty carpeted saloon. It comes back to me that nobody in those days walked, nobody but the three or four of us—or indeed I should say, if pushed, the single pair in particular of whom I was one and the other Thomas Sargeant Perry, superexcellent and all-reading, all-engulfing friend of those days and still, sole survivor, of these,[160] I thus found deeply consecrated that love of the long, again and again of the very longest possible, walk which was to see me, year after year, through so many of the twists and past so many of the threatened blocks of life's road, and which, during the early and American period, was to make me lone and perverse even in my own sight: so little was it ever given me then, wherever I scanned the view, to descry a fellow-pedestrian. The pedestrians came to succumb altogether, at Newport, to this virtual challenge of their strange agitation—by the circumstance, that is, of their being offered at last, to importunity, the vulgar road, under the invasion of which the old rich alternative miserably dwindled.[161]

160. For some reason Perry's name is spelled "Sargeant" rather than "Sergeant"; indeed, HJ had often referred to him as "Sarge" in youth. HJ met Perry in Newport in the summer of 1858, and they remained lifelong friends. Perry was to work as a scholar, translator, and editor, and, as HJ hints in *AS* (217), came from distinguished stock: his mother was a descendant of Benjamin Franklin; his grandfather, Commodore Oliver Hazard Perry, became a national hero by leading the defeat of a British naval force on Lake Erie during the War of 1812; and his great uncle, Commodore Matthew Calbraith Perry, was instrumental in opening up Japan to the outside world in the 1850s.

T. S. Perry married Lilla Cabot, who became an eminent American impressionist painter, much influenced by Monet. HJ checked some of the detail of his recollections with Perry, and wrote poignantly to him afterward that he found "strange and moving our survivorship of that golden haze of all the ancient history" (*HJL,* 4:685). After the publication of *NSB* and the "acclamation of welcome" it received, he wrote to Perry, "its intelligent reader of all readers": "I felt again & again that you would be the only person alive who would understand what I meant *there,* & that though others might think they did it wouldn't be so true of any of them as of you" (Harlow, *Perry: A Biography,* 345). To Perry's sister, Margaret, now the widow of John La Farge, HJ wrote: "That I have made the unspeakable Past live again a little for you is delightful to me. . . . There are passages and pages in the book which Tom and you are the sole persons living who will have understood" (John LaFarge, "Henry James's Letters to the Lafarges," *New England Quarterly* 22 [June 1949]: 192).

161. HJ refers to the vulgar forces of money that had transformed Newport, but he also recalls his earlier years as an aspiring writer before eventually and permanently migrating to Europe in 1875, aged thirty-two, to "take possession of the old world—I inhale it—I appropriate it!" (*HJL,* 1:484).

V Nothing meanwhile could have been less logical, yet at the same time more natural, than that William's interest in the practice of painting should have suddenly and abruptly ceased; a turn of our affair attended, however, with no shade of commotion, no repining at proved waste; with as little of any confessed ruefulness of mistake on one side as of any elation of wisdom, any resonance of the ready "I told you so" on the other. The one side would have been, with a different tone about the matter and a different domestic habit than ours, that of my brother's awkwardness, accompanying whatever intelligence, of disavowal, and the other been our father's not unemphatic return to the point that his doubts, those originally and confidently intimated, had been justified by the fact. Tempting doubtless in a heavier household air the opportunity on the latter's part to recall that if he had perfectly recognised his son's probable progress to a pitch of excellence he had exactly not granted that an attainment of this pitch was likely in the least, however uncontested, to satisfy the nature concerned; the foregone conclusion having all the while been that such a spirit was competent to something larger and less superficially calculable, something more expressive of its true inwardness. This was not the way in which things happened among us, for I really think the committed mistake was ever discriminated against—certainly by the head of the family—only to the extent of its acquiring, even if but speedily again to fade, an interest greater than was obtainable by the too obvious success. I am not sure indeed that the kind of personal history most appealing to my father would not have been some kind that should fairly proceed by mistakes, mistakes more human, more associational, less angular, less hard for others, that is less exemplary for them (since righteousness, as mostly understood, was in our parent's view, I think, the cruellest thing in the world) than straight and smug and declared felicities. The qualification here, I allow, would be in his scant measure of the difference, after all, for the life of the soul, between the marked achievement and the marked shortcoming. He had a manner of his own of appreciating failure, or of not at least piously rejoicing in displayed moral, intellectual, or even material, economies, which, had it not been that his humanity, his generosity and, for the most part, his gaiety, were always, at the worst, consistent, might sometimes have left us with our small savings, our little exhibitions and complacencies, rather on our hands. As the case stood I find myself thinking of our life in those years as profiting greatly for animation and curiosity by the interest he shed for us on the whole side of the human scene usually held least interesting—the element, the appearance, of *waste* which plays there such a part and into which he could read under provocation so much character and colour and charm, so many implications of the fine and the worthy, that, since the art of missing or of failing, or of otherwise going astray, did after all in his hands escape becoming either a matter of real example or of absolute precept, enlarged not a little our field and our categories of appreciation and perception. I recover as I look back on all this the sense as of an extraordinary young confidence, our common support, in our coming round together, through the immense lubrication of his expressed thought, often perhaps extravagantly working and playing, to plenty of unbewildered rightness, a state of comfort that would always serve—whether after strange openings into a sphere where nothing practical mattered, or after even still quainter closings in upon us of unexpected importances and values. Which means, to my memory, that we breathed somehow an air in which waste, for us at least, couldn't and didn't live, so certain were aberrations and discussions, adventures, excursions and alarms of whatever sort, to wind up in a "transformation scene" or, if the term be not profane, happy harlequinade; a figuration of each involved issue and item before the footlights of a familiar idealism, the most socialised and ironised, the most amusedly generalised, that possibly could be.

Such an atmosphere was, taking one of its elements with another, doubtless delightful; yet if it was friendly to the suggested or imagined thing it promoted among us much less directly, as I have already hinted, the act of choice—choice as to the "career" for example, with a view of the usual proceedings thereupon consequent. I marvel at the manner in which the door appears to have been held or at least left open to us for experiment, though with a tendency to close, the oddest yet most inveterately perceptible movement in that sense, before any very earnest proposition in particular.[162] I have no remembrance at all of marked prejudices on our father's

162. HJ's assertions about HJ Sr.'s hands-off treatment of his sons and their choice of career (clearly their mother played no role in this account) have been repeated and also questioned in much of the later biographical writing on the family. Feinstein regards HJ Sr.'s influence on WJ as replicating William James of Albany's oppressive attempts to control HJ Sr.'s behavior and choices. He even deployed his own health (he suffered at the time from fainting fits) in the process: "The picture of Henry upsetting the household with death threats is peculiar to the second Newport winter, when William was painting." Feinstein also provides a useful summary of the varying interpretations of the sudden change in WJ's vocation (*Becoming William James*, 140–41). Charles Hoffmann and Tessa Hoffmann ("Henry James and the Civil War," *New England Quarterly* 62 [December 1989]: 529–52), suggest that WJ may have given up art from a sense of duty to country (535).

part, but I recall repeated cases, in his attitude to our young affairs, of a disparagement suggested as by stirred memories of his own; the instance most present to me being his extreme tepidity in the matter of William's, or in fact of my, going, on our then American basis, to college. I make out in him, and at the time made out, a great revulsion of spirit from that incurred experience in his own history, a revulsion I think moreover quite independent of any particular or intrinsic attributes of the seat of learning involved in it. Union College, Schenectady, New York, the scene of his personal experiment and the natural resort, in his youth, of comparatively adjacent Albanians, might easily have offered at that time no very rare opportunities—few were the American country colleges that then had such to offer; but when, after years, the question arose for his sons he saw it in I scarce know what light of associational or "subjective" dislike.[163] He had the disadvantage—unless indeed it was much more we who had it—of his having, after many changes and detachments, ceased to believe in the Schenectady resource, or to revert to it sentimentally, without his forming on the other hand, with his boys to place, any fonder presumption or preference. There comes out to me, much bedimmed but recognisable, the image of a day of extreme youth on which, during a stay with our grandmother at Albany, we achieved, William and I, with some confused and heated railway effort, a pious pilgrimage to the small scholastic city—pious by reason, I clearly remember, of a lively persuasion on my brother's part that to Union College, at some indefinite future time, we should both most naturally and delightedly repair. We invoked, I gather, among its scattered shades, fairly vague to me now, the loyalty that our parent appeared to have dropped by the way—even though our attitude about it can scarce have been prematurely contentious; the whole vision is at any rate to-day bathed and blurred for me in the air of some charmed and beguiled dream, that of the flushed good faith of an hour of crude castle-building. We were helped

163. Union College, founded in 1795 and overlooking the Mohawk River, was a fifteen-mile rail journey from Albany. For the detail of HJ Sr.'s unhappy student experience, see Habegger, *The Father,* 83–100. He seems to have been an uncommitted student achieving poor grades as well as a heavy drinker and gambler; he also found himself in religious conflict with his overbearing father. William James of Albany had been an important financial backer of this relatively new college, which quickly expanded in size under the long presidency of Eliphalet Nott. Lewis notes a pleasing comic moment with a James family relevance in "Daisy Miller": When the heroine's brother points out that his father is "in a better place than Europe," it isn't—as the listener supposes—a pious reference to premature death: "My father's in Schenectady. He's got a big business. My father's rich, you bet" (*The Jameses,* 23–24).

to build, on the spot, by an older friend, much older, as I remember him, even than my brother, already a member of the college and, as it seemed, greatly enjoying his life and those "society" badges and trinkets with which he reappears to me as bristling and twinkling quite to the extinction of his particular identity.[164] This is lost, like everything else, in the mere golden haze of the little old-time autumn adventure. Wondrous to our sensibility may well have been the October glamour—if October it was, and if it was not it ought to have been!—of that big brave region of the great State over which the shade of Fenimore Cooper's Mohawks and Mohicans (if this be not a pleonasm) might still have been felt to hang.[165] The castle we had built, however, crumbled—there were plenty of others awaiting erection; these too successively had their hour, but I needn't at this time stoop to pick up their pieces. I see moreover vividly enough how it might have been that, at this stage, our parents were left cold by the various appeal, in our interest, of Columbia, Harvard and Yale. Hard by, at Providence, in the Newport time, was also "Brown";[166] but I recover no connection in which that mystic syllable swept our sky as a name to conjure with. Our largest licence somehow didn't stray toward Brown. It was to the same tune not conceivable that we should have been restored for educational purposes to the swollen city, the New York of our childhood, where we had then so tumbled in and out of school as to exhaust the measure, or as at least greatly to deflower the image, of our teachability on that ground. Yale, off our beat from every point of view, was as little to be thought of, and there was moreover in our father's imagination no grain of susceptibility to what might have been, on the general ground, "socially expected." Even Harvard, clearly—and it was perhaps a trifle odd—moved him in our interest as little as Schenectady could do; so that, for authority, the voice of social expectation would have had to sound with an art or an accent of which it had by no means up to that time learned roundabout us the trick. This

164. The likeliest person is Edgar Beach Van Winkle, a friend of the James boys from their New York City days (see *CWJ*, 4:8–9).

165. HJ refers to the Leatherstocking Tales of James Fenimore Cooper (1789–1851), called by Leslie A. Fiedler "the greatest of American mythographers" (*Waiting for the End* [Harmondsworth: Penguin, 1967], 79). The most famous is *The Last of the Mohicans* (1826), a heroic story of the frontier, portraying native American life and the British and French conflicts of the eighteenth century. HJ's friend in his middle years, Constance Fenimore Woolson (1840–94), was Cooper's great-niece.

166. All of these Ivy League institutions—Columbia in New York City, Harvard in Cambridge, Yale in New Haven, and Brown in Providence—were within familiar territory (Yale less so, as HJ points out later) for the James family.

indeed (it comes to saying) is something that, so far as our parents were concerned, it would never have learned. They were, from other preoccupations, unaware of any such pressure; and to become aware would, I think, primarily have been for them to find it out of all proportion to the general pitch of prescription. We were not at that time, when it came to such claims, in presence of persuasive, much less of impressive, social forms and precedents—at least those of us of the liberated mind and the really more curious culture were not; the more curious culture, only to be known by the positive taste of it, was nowhere in the air, nowhere seated or embodied.[167]

Which reflections, as I perhaps too loosely gather them in, refresh at any rate my sense of how we in particular of our father's house actually profited more than we lost, if the more curious culture was in question, by the degree to which we were afloat and disconnected; since there were at least luxuries of the spirit in this quite as much as drawbacks—given a social order (so far as it *was* an order) that found its main ideal in a "strict attention to business," that is to buying and selling over a counter or a desk, and in such an intensity of the traffic as made, on the part of all involved, for close localisation. To attend strictly to business was to be invariably *there*, on a certain spot in a certain place; just as to be nowhere in particular, to *have* to be nowhere, told the queer tale of a lack or of a forfeiture, or possibly even of a state of intrinsic unworthiness. I have already expressed how few of these elements of the background we ourselves had ever had either to add to or to subtract from, and how this of itself did after a fashion "place" us in the small Newport colony of the despoiled and disillusioned, the mildly, the reminiscentially desperate.[168]

167. Strangely, HJ seems blind to the complacencies induced by privilege and considerable inherited wealth evident in the recalled attitudes of his parents. A significant amount of the fortune (though not all the real estate) originally inherited by HJ Sr. seems to have gone by the time of his death. The lackadaisical attitude toward possible careers or training for his children had long-term damaging effects. Typically for her time, Alice was never expected to work for a living, but it took WJ years to settle into what would be a distinguished career. HJ quickly and independently taught himself the craft of professional writing. Neither Wilky nor Robertson received any comparable attention or sustained financial support (though Wilky was backed in his failing postwar Florida enterprise). After the Civil War, both tried a number of jobs with limited degrees of success.

168. This might be regarded as the "desperation" of the moneyed classes, those Americans who in *AS* have been displaced and infected by their exposure to the cultural and historical riches of Europe. They have experienced both exile and return, a sequence familiar from HJ's novels as well, of course, as from much American fiction to come in the twentieth century.

As easy as might be, for the time, I have also noted, was our footing there; but I have not, for myself, forgotten, or even now outlived, the particular shade of satisfaction to be taken in one's thus being in New England without being of it. To have originally been of it, or still to have to be, affected me, I recall, as a case I should have regretted—unless it be more exact to say that I thought of the condition as a danger after all escaped. Long would it take to tell why it figured as a danger, and why that impression was during the several following years much more to gain than to lose intensity.[169] The question was to fall into the rear indeed, with ever so many such secondary others, during the War, and for reasons effective enough; but it was afterwards to know a luxury of emergence—this, I mean, while one still "cared," in general, as one was sooner or later to stop caring. Infinitely interesting to recover, in the history of a mind, for those concerned, these movements of the spirit, these tides and currents of growth—though under the inconvenience for the historian of such ramifications of research that here at any rate I feel myself warned off. There appeared to us at Newport the most interesting, much, of the Albany male cousins, William James Temple—coming, oddly enough, first from Yale and then from Harvard; so that by contact and example the practicability of a like experience might have been, and doubtless was, put well before us. "Will" Temple, as we were in his short life too scantly to know him, had made so luckless, even if so lively a start under one alma mater that the appeal to a fresh parentship altogether appears to have been judged the best remedy for his case: he entered Harvard jumping, if I mistake not, a couple of years of the undergraduate curriculum, and my personal memory of these reappearances is a mere recapture of admiration, of prostration, before him. The dazzled state, under his striking good looks and his manly charm, was the common state; so that I disengage from it no presumption of a particular plea playing in our own domestic air for his temporary Cambridge setting; he was so much too radiant and gallant and

169. The question concerning what are characterized as the dangers of residency in New England is not resolved, though elsewhere HJ sometimes regards the region as quaint and provincial (see also n. 515 below). More concretely, Edel comments that HJ "could never reconcile himself to the gentility of the Brahmins and the frugality of Concord, or the manner in which New England considered culture to be an arduous duty rather than a joy of life and of civilization" (*Untried Years*, 195). Yet HJ also asserts that Concord, aside from the "three or four biggest cities," "had an identity more palpable to the mind, had nestled in other words more successfully beneath her narrow fold of the mantle of history, than any other American town" (*AS*, 256).

personal, too much a character and a figure, a splendid importance in himself, to owe the least glamour to settings; an advantage that might have seemed rather to be shed on whatever scene by himself in consenting to light it up. He made all life for the hour a foreground, and one that we none of us would have quitted for a moment while he was there.[170]

In that form at least I see him, and no revival of those years so puts to me the interesting question, so often aimlessly returned upon in later life, of the amount of truth in this or that case of young confidence in a glory to come—for another than one's self; of the likelihood of the wonders so flatteringly forecast. Many of our estimates were monstrous magnifications—though doing us even at that more good than harm; so that one isn't even sure that the happiest histories were to have been those of the least liberal mistakes. I like at any rate to think of our easy overstrainings—the possible flaw in many of which was not indeed to be put to the proof. That was the case for the general, and for every particular, impression of Will Temple, thanks to his early death in battle—at Chancellorsville, 1863; he having, among the quickened forces of the time, and his father's record helping him, leaped to a captaincy in the regular Army;[171] but I cling to the idea that the siftings

170. William James Temple was the second eldest of the orphaned Temple children. According to Clark (*Heroes of Albany*, 410, 412–13), he attended school with Mr. Watson of Kinderhook, New York, Dr. Thomas Read of Geneva, and Mr. A. N. Skinner of New Haven. Having entered Yale College, he left after one year in 1858 and was attending Harvard College at the outbreak of war. A correspondent, under the signature T.W., recalls meeting the young man just three weeks before his death, "the same quiet, modest, gentlemanly person I first met two years ago. . . . Yesterday, upon entering the Hudson river baggage car, at New York, my eyes rested upon a square, ominously proportioned box, with 'Capt. WILLIAM J. TEMPLE, 17th U.S. Infantry, Albany.' inscribed upon its lid. And there, cold, inanimate and disfigured, lay all that remains of the gallant young officer who, with beaming eye, elastic step and buoyant spirit, I had so recently conversed with." He seems to have been a strong-willed figure; while at Harvard (still only in his teens and popular with his fellow students), "the strict discipline of the University made it necessary that for a while he should pursue his studies elsewhere, and he was sent for a few months to Stockbridge." He fought at Second Bull Run but was "a mere spectator" at Antietam. Suffering from fever, William spent three months' sick leave with his sisters in Newport in the winter of 1862–63; he was killed on 1 May 1863 (*Harvard Memorial Biographies* (Cambridge, Mass.: Sever and Francis, 1867), 2:335, 339–40, 342). Though HJ had left Newport to attend Harvard by this time, his family lived in the town until 1864, and so it is possible that HJ saw him in this three-month period.

171. Will's father, Colonel Robert Temple, trained at the U.S. Military Academy at West Point, serving in the army till 1839. He then became a lawyer, but was appointed a colonel in the U.S. Army in 1847, serving for one year and seeing action in the Mexican War. He

and sortings of life, had he remained subject to them, would still have left him the lustre that blinds and subdues. I even do more, at this hour; I ask myself, while his appearance and my personal feeling about it live for me again, what possible aftertime could have kept up the pitch of my sentiment —aftertime either of his or of mine.[172] Blest beyond others, I think as we look back, the admirations, even the fondest (and which indeed were not of their nature fond?) that were not to know to their cost the inevitable test or strain; they are almost the only ones, of the true high pitch, that, without broken edges or other tatters to show, fold themselves away entire and secure, even as rare lengths of precious old stuff, in the scented chest of our savings. So great misadventure have too often known at all events certain of those that were to come to trial. The others are the *residual,* those we must keep when we can, so to be sure at least of a few, sacrificing as many possible mistakes and misproportions as need be to pay but for two or three of them. There could be no mistake about Gus Barker, who threw himself into the fray, that is into the cavalry saddle, as he might into a match at baseball (football being then undreamt of ),[173] and my last reminiscence of whom is the sight of him on a brief leave for a farewell to his Harvard classmates after

---

went on to practice law in Albany. See Katharine Hastings, "William James (1771–1832) of Albany, N.Y., and His Descendants," *New York Genealogical and Biographical Record* 55, no. 2 (April 1924): 101–19, on 116; genealogy continued in no. 3 (July 1924): 222–36, with a final section in no. 4 (October 1924): 301–13. Lewis elaborates some of this information: "A darkly romantic aura hung over the Temples; there was a bad streak in them, according to one family source. Colonel Temple, a West Point graduate in the class of 1828, was briefly Adjutant General of the United States Army until, as it seems, he was implicated in an army scandal and was removed" (*The Jameses,* 107). He married (as his second wife) Catharine Margaret James, HJ's paternal aunt, in 1839.

172. HJ's hyperbole, his inability to imagine any later less youthfully ideal life for William Temple that might measure up to this early promise, may be a recollection of HJ Sr.'s reaction to his nephew's death. As William's sister Minny records, "Uncle Henry says that no human-being can stand for a life time without almost superhuman strength the spontaneous *worship* almost that everyone gave him," and her own letter of 12 May 1863 is a moving tribute to the young man (Gordon, *A Private Life of Henry James,* 56–57). Indeed HJ's sentiments on the death of Minny herself in 1870 invoke a comparable perspective, her life defined as a form of completion, "a steady unfaltering luminary in the mind rather than as a flickering wasting earth-stifled lamp. . . . a sort of measure and standard of brightness and repose" (*HJL,* 1:227). The way in which HJ's discourse continues, returning to the memory of Gus Barker, another cousin killed in the Civil War, suggests William Temple's status as an exemplar of heroic masculinity for the aging novelist.

173. Intercollegiate football developed in codified form among the Ivy League universities only in the 1870s.

he had got his commission, crossing with two or three companions the expanse of Harvard Square that faced the old Law School, of which I found myself for that year (1862–63) a singularly alien member.[174] I was afterwards sharply to regret the accident by which I on that occasion missed speech of him; but my present vision of his charming latent agility, which any motion showed, of his bright-coloured wagging head and of the large gaiety of the young smile that made his handsome teeth shine out, is after all the years but the more happily uneffaced. The point of all which connections, however, is that they somehow managed to make in the parental view no straight links for us with the matter-of-course of college. There were accidents too by the aid of which they failed of this the more easily. It comes to me that, for my own part, I thought of William at the time as having, or rather as so much more than having, already graduated; the effect of contact with his mind and talk, with the free play of his spirit and the irrepressible brush of his humour, couldn't have been greater had he carried off fifty honours. I felt in him such authority, so perpetually quickened a state of intellect and character, that the detail or the literal side of the question never so much as came up for me: I must have made out that to plenty of graduates, or of the graduating, nothing in the nature of such appearances attached. I think of our father moreover as no less affected by a like impression; so extremely, so immensely disposed do I see him to generalise his eldest son's gifts as by the largest, fondest synthesis, and not so much proceed upon them in any one direction as proceed *from* them, as it were, in all.[175]

Little as such a view might have lent itself to application, my brother's searching discovery during the summer of 1861 that his vocation was not "after all" in the least satisfyingly for Art, took on as a prompt sequel the recognition that it was quite positively and before everything for Science, physical Science, strenuous Science in all its exactitude; with the oppor-

174. Harvard Law School, where HJ attended morning lectures, was housed at this time in Dane Hall, "a modest, new building designed in the Greek Revival style, its portico ornamented by four wooden pillars, on a corner of the College Yard just off the street" (Novick, *Young Master*, 83). It was completed in 1832 and occupied by the law school until 1882.

175. One needs to remember that the life of WJ was, of course, the originating cause of HJ's reminiscences: that they invariably grant priority to the older brother, and tend to endorse HJ Sr.'s evaluation of his children's potential. WJ's educational needs—however disruptive to the family's general stability—frequently came first; he alone, in the father's view, was "cut out for intellectual labours" (see above, n. 75).

tunity again forthcoming to put his freshness of faith to the test. I had presumed to rejoice before at his adoption of the studio life, that offering as well possible contacts for myself; and yet I recall no pang for his tergiversation, there being nothing he mightn't have done at this or at any other moment that I shouldn't have felt as inevitable and found in my sense of his previous age some happy and striking symptom or pledge of. As certain as that he had been all the while "artistic" did it thus appear that he had been at the same time quite otherwise inquiring too—addicted to "experiments" and the consumption of chemicals, the transfusion of mysterious liquids from glass to glass under exposure to lambent flame, the cultivation of stained fingers, the establishment and the transport, in our wanderings, of galvanic batteries, the administration to all he could persuade of electric shocks, the maintenance of marine animals in splashy aquaria, the practice of photography in the room I for a while shared with him at Boulogne,[176] with every stern reality of big cumbrous camera, prolonged exposure, exposure mostly of myself, darkened development, also interminable, and ubiquitous brown blot. Then there had been also the constant, as I fearfully felt it, the finely speculative and boldly disinterested absorption of curious drugs. No livelier remembrance have I of our early years together than this inveteracy, often appalling to a nature so incurious as mine in *that* direction, of his interest in the "queer" or the incalculable effects of things. There was apparently for him no possible effect whatever that mightn't be more or less rejoiced in as such—all exclusive of its relation to other things than merely knowing. There recurs to me withal the shamelessness of my own indifference—at which I also, none the less, I think, wondered a little; as if by so much as it hadn't been given me to care for visibly provoked or engineered phenomena, by that same amount was I open to those of the mysteriously or insidiously aggressive, the ambushed or suffered sort. Vivid to me in any case is still the sense of how quite shiningly light, as an activity and an appeal, he had seemed to make everything he gave himself to; so that at first, until the freshness of it failed, he flung this iridescent mantle of interest over the then so grey and scant little scene of the Harvard (the Lawrence) Scientific School, where in the course of the months I had had a glimpse or two of

176. The James family stayed in Boulogne-sur-Mer on the northern coast of France twice during their European trip, in 1857 and 1858 (see *SBO*, chap. 29 and nn. 558, 643).

him at work.[177] Early in the autumn of 1861 he went up from Newport to Cambridge to enter that institution; in which thin current rather than in the ostensibly more ample began to flow his long connection with Harvard, gathering in time so many affluents.[178] His letters from Cambridge during the next couple of years, many of them before me now, breathe, I think, all the experience the conditions could have begotten at the best; they mark the beginning of those vivacities and varieties of intellectual and moral reaction which were for the rest of his life to be the more immeasurably candid and vivid, the more numerous above all, and the more interesting and amusing, the closer view one had of him. That of a certainty; yet these familiar pages of youth testify most of all for me perhaps to the forces of amenity and spontaneity, the happy working of all relations, in our family life. In such parts of them as I may cite this will shine sufficiently through—and I shall take for granted thus the interest of small matters that have perhaps but that reflected light to show. It is in a letter to myself, of that September, dated "Drear and Chill Abode," that he appears to have celebrated the first steps of his initiation.[179]

Sweet was your letter and grateful to my eyes. I had gone in a mechanical way to the P.O. not hoping for anything (though "on espère alors qu'on désespère toujours,")[180] and, finding nothing, was

177. The school opened in 1847 to provide teaching in engineering and the physical sciences and was intended to counterbalance Harvard's humanities emphasis. In 1857 Abbott Lawrence, owner of profitable textile factories, donated $50,000. Arriving at this propitious time, WJ initially studied chemistry, moving across to the medical school in 1863. "The Scientific School did not have the demanding social traditions typical of American colleges at the time" (*CWJ*, 4:20 n. 2).

178. Despite his desire for freedom in later years and the odd job possibility at other institutions, such as, in 1878, the newly established and innovative Johns Hopkins in Baltimore, WJ spent virtually all his working life at Harvard during a period when it was undergoing great expansion. Appointed initially as an instructor in physiology in 1873, he retired at the end of 1906 (just three and a half years before he died) having taught physiology, anatomy, psychology, and philosophy. The two eldest James brothers attended Harvard as it was emerging from one of its least distinguished periods; it lacked academic direction and continued to embrace the most conservative political beliefs, notably on the question of slavery (see, e.g., Carol Bundy, *The Nature of Sacrifice: A Biography of Charles Russell Lowell, Jr., 1835–64* [New York: Farrar, Straus and Giroux, 2005], 78).

179. This letter was written on 7 September 1861 (*CWJ*, 1:1).

180. "One always hopes even as one despairs." At this time mail was delivered between post offices, to be collected by the recipient, though some cities made personal deliveries for an extra two cents. By 1863 Congress had introduced procedures for house deliveries.

turning heavily away when a youth modestly tapped me and, holding out an envelope inscribed in your well-known character, said, "Mr. J., this was in our box!" 'Twas the young Pascoe, the joy of his mother[181] —but the graphic account I read in the letter he gave me of the sorrow of *my* mother almost made me shed tears on the floor of the P.O. Not that on reflection I should dream—! for reflection shows me a future in which she shall regard my vacation visits as "on the whole" rather troublesome than otherwise; or at least when she shall feel herself as blest in the trouble I spare her when absent as in the glow of pride and happiness she feels at the sight of me when present. But she needn't fear I can ever think of *her* when absent with such equanimity. I oughtn't to "joke on such a serious subject," as Bobby would say though;[182] for I have had several pangs since being here at the thought of all I have left behind at Newport—especially gushes of feeling about the *place*. I haven't for one minute had the feeling of being at home here. Something in my quarters precludes the possibility of it, though what this is I don't suppose I can describe to you.

As I write now even, writing itself being a cosy cheerful-looking amusement, and an argand gas-burner[183] with a neat green shade merrily singing beside me, I still feel unsettled. I write on a round table in the middle of the room, with a fearful red and black cloth. Before me I see another such-covered table of oblong shape against the wall, capped by a cheap looking-glass and flanked by two windows, curtainless and bleak, whose shades of linen flout the air as the sportive wind impels them. To the left are two other such windows, with a horse-hair sofa between them, and at my back a fifth window and a vast wooden mantel-piece with nothing to relieve its nakedness but a large cast, much plumbago'd, of a bust of Franklin.[184] On my right the Bookcase, imposing and respectable with its empty drawers and with my little array of printed wisdom covering nearly *one* of the shelves. I hear the people breathe as they go past in the street, and the

181. He was the son of Mrs. Pasco (WJ's landlady) (*CWJ*, 1:3 n. 2).
182. Though acknowledged within his family for his seriousness and earnestness, Bob was a popular schoolmate, as Julian Hawthorne (the novelist's son) recalled: "Bob . . . was robust and hilarious, tough, tireless as hickory, great in the playground, not much of a scholar" (quoted in Maher, *Biography of Broken Fortunes*, 19).
183. A ring-shaped gas burner invented by Aimé Argand (1755–1803).
184. "Plumbago" relates to lead ore; presumably the decorative cast of Benjamin Franklin had been black-leaded.

roll and jar of the horse-cars is terrific.[185] I have accordingly engaged the other room from Mrs. Pascoe, with the little sleeping-room upstairs. It looks infinitely more cheerful than this, and if I don't find the grate sufficient I can easily have a Franklin stove put up.[186] But she says the grate will make an oven of it. . . . John Ropes I met the other day at Harry Quincy's room, and was very much pleased with him.[187] Don't fail to send on Will Temple's letters to him and to Herbert Mason, which I left in one of the library's mantelpiece jars, to use the Portuguese idiom.[188] Storrow Higginson has been very kind to me, making inquiries about tables etc.[189] We went together this morning to the house of the Curator of the Gray collection of Engravings, which is solemnly to unfold its glories to me to-morrow. He is a most serious stately German gentleman, Mr. Thies by name, fully sensible of the deep vital importance of his treasures and evidently thinking a visit to them a great affair—to *me*. Had I known how great, how tremendous and formal, I hardly think I should have ventured to call.[190] Tom Ward

185. Horsecars constituted the chief form of public transport in Cambridge at the time, offering a regular service crossing the Charles River into Boston.

186. The Franklin, or circulating stove, was reputed to have been invented by Benjamin Franklin. With an open front and vents for effective airflow, the metal-lined fireplace was a highly efficient heater.

187. John Codman Ropes (1836–99), who lived in Cambridge, was the son of the Boston merchant William Ropes (d. 1869) and Mary Anne Codman Ropes (d. 1873) (*CWJ*, 4:58–59 n. 10). He became a military historian and lawyer, establishing a legal firm with John Chipman Gray, a friend of Minny Temple's (see p. 759 below). Henry Parker Quincy (1838–99) graduated from Harvard in 1862, worked as a physician, and was later a professor at the Harvard Medical School (*CWJ*, 1:3 n. 5).

188. Herbert Cowpland Mason (1840–1884) became a captain in the Union army and was wounded at Gettysburg on 3 July 1863 (*CWJ*, 1:3 n. 7). In the first American and English editions there is a proofreading error in this sentence which reads, "which I left in one of the of the library's mantel-piece jars."

189. Samuel Storrow Higginson (1842–1907) had attended Frank Sanborn's school in Concord, Massachusetts, with Wilky and Bob James. Having been a student at Harvard, he became a chaplain in a black regiment before going into business (*CWJ*, 1:3 n. 8). The coeducational school of the educator and writer Franklin Benjamin Sanborn (1831–1917), sponsored by Emerson, was popular with many New England writers and intellectuals of the time. Sanborn had been a prominent abolitionist and admirer of the fanatical John Brown, hanged in 1859. He had recently been sought by the law for failing to testify (having known of Brown's raid on Harper's Ferry in advance). Two of Brown's daughters boarded at the school; the children of Emerson, Hawthorne, Judge Hoar, and the abolitionist George Stearns were also on the roll; the Alcott girls attended some activities.

190. The collection of engravings belonging to Francis Calley Gray (1790–1856) had

pays me a visit almost every evening. Poor Tom seems a-cold too.[191] His deafness keeps him from making acquaintances. Professor Eliot, at the School, is a fine fellow, I suspect; a man who if he resolves to do a thing won't be prevented.[192] I find analysis very interesting *so far!* The Library has a reading-room, where they take all the magazines; so I shan't want for the Rev. des 2 M.[193] I remain with unalterable sentiments of devotion ever, my dear H., your Big Brother Bill.

This record of further impressions closely and copiously followed.[194]

Your letter this morning was such a godsend that I hasten to respond a line or two, though I have no business to—for I have a fearful lesson to-morrow and am going to Boston to-night to hear Agassiz lecture (12 lectures on "Methods in Nat. Hist."), so that I will only tell you that I am very well and my spirits just getting good.[195]

---

been donated to Harvard in 1857 and was located in Gore Hall; it is now part of the William Hayes Fogg Art Museum. Access to the collection was limited, and its curator was Louis Thies (d. 1871), a German pharmacist. When the Thies family visited Europe in 1866, the Jameses rented their house at 20 Quincy Street in Cambridge (*CWJ*, 1:3 n. 9, and 410).

191. Thomas Wren Ward (1844–1940) graduated from Harvard in 1866. His father was Samuel Gray Ward, a Boston banker who also looked after the finances of his friend HJ Sr. Tom's mother, Anna Hazard Barker, was a sister to William H. Barker, who had married Jeannette James, and was thus an aunt to Gus Barker, as HJ mentions below (see also n. 393 below). Tom Ward took part in the 1865–66 expedition to Brazil led by Professor Louis Agassiz (see n. 195 below) of which WJ was also a member. The "poor Tom seems a-cold" quotation is from *King Lear*. In act 3, scene 4, the faithful Edmund, "disguised as a madman," tells his disturbed father, referring to himself, that "Poor Tom's a-cold."

192. At this time Charles William Eliot (1834–1926) was running the chemistry department (1861–63), but from 1869 to 1909 he was president of Harvard, much admired for his administrative and organizational skills, and instrumental in fostering WJ's academic career. Lewis quotes a line from the philosopher Alfred North Whitehead, lamenting James Bryant Conant's appointment as president of Harvard to a reporter: " 'A chemist! Imagine a *chemist* the president of Harvard!' 'But, sir,' the reporter said, 'President Eliot was a chemist.' 'Yes,' said Whitehead sadly, 'but he was a very *bad* chemist' " (*The Jameses*, 120n).

193. *Revue des deux mondes.*

194. This letter combines two written by WJ; the first paragraph is most of a letter written to his mother on 10 September 1861; the succeeding paragraphs come from a letter to the family, written on 16 September, of which HJ omits the final part (*CWJ*, 4:41–42, 42–45).

195. The Swiss-born naturalist Jean Louis Rodolphe Agassiz (1807–73), after a brilliant career in Europe, was appointed to a chair of zoology and geology at Harvard in 1847 and became celebrated for his scientific writings. *Methods of Study in Natural History* came out in 1863. "The text consists of lectures given at the Lowell Institute in Boston during 1861–62" (*CWJ*, 4:42 n. 2).

Miss Upham's table is much pleasanter than the other.[196] Professor F. J. Child is a great joker—he's a little flaxen-headed boy of about 40.[197] There is a nice old lady boarder, another man of about 50, of aristocratic bearing, who interests me much, and 3 intelligent students. At the other table was no conversation at all; the fellows had that American solemnity, called each other Sir, etc. I cannot tell you, dearest Mother, how your account of your Sunday dinner and of your feelings thereat brought tears to my eyes. Give Father my ardent love and cover with kisses the round fair face of the most kissworthy Alice. Then kiss the Aunt till you get tired, and get all the rest of them to kiss *you* till you cry hold enough!

This morning as I was busy over the 10th page of a letter to Wilky in he popped and made my labour of no account. I had intended to go and see him yesterday, but found Edward Emerson and Tom Ward were going, and so thought he would have too much of a good thing. But he walked over this morning with, or rather without them, for he went astray and arrived very hot and dusty.[198] I gave him a bath and took him to dinner, and he is now gone to see Andrew Robeson and

196. WJ ate his meals at Miss Catharine Upham's house in Cambridge at the junction of Kirkland and Oxford streets, just north of Harvard Yard, while lodging at Mrs. Pasco's. Hers was a yellow house on the corner of Linden and Harvard streets, "about 12 paces" from the horsecar stop; WJ's room was at the head of the stairs, on the right (*CWJ*, 4:60). Miss Upham, it seems, entertained a range of eminent guests: Charles Francis Adams recalls visiting, early in 1861, "Russell Lowell, then a professor at Harvard and editor of the *Atlantic*. . . . He was then living, with his wife, at Mrs. Upham's lodging-house" (*Charles Francis Adams, 1835–1915: An Autobiography*, prepared for the Massachusetts Historical Society [Boston: Houghton Mifflin, 1916], 41).

197. Frances James Child (1825–96), a Harvard professor of English, published a five-volume edition of Edmund Spenser, *Observations on the Language of Chaucer*, and a celebrated edition of English and Scottish ballads. He remained especially close to WJ, and he and his wife, Elizabeth Ellery Sedgwick, living in Cambridge, became friends of the James family.

198. Edward Waldo Emerson (1844–1930), son of Ralph Waldo Emerson, had been a fellow pupil with Wilky and Bob James at Frank Sanborn's school in Concord. Wilky still attended the school, and so must have completed a fifteen-mile walk into Cambridge (not exceptional at the time). Edward trained in medicine at Harvard and married Annie Shepard Keyes, later to become a writer and teacher of art anatomy. An old friend, George Partridge Bradford, once asked him about Alice James: " 'And what sort of a girl is Alice?' . . . Bradford replied somewhat stiffly: 'She has a highly moral nature'; and at this Emerson, laughing, said: 'How in the world does her father get on with her?' " (quoted in Lewis, *The Jameses*, 106).

E. E.[199] His plump corpusculus looks as always.[200] I write in my new parlour whither I moved yesterday. You have no idea what an improvement it is on the old affair—worth double the cost, and the little bedroom under the roof is perfectly delicious, with a charming outlook on little back yards with trees and pretty old brick walls. The sun is upon *this* room from earliest dawn till late in the afternoon— a capital thing in winter. I like Miss Upham's very much. Dark "aristocratic" dining-room, with royal cheer. "Fish, roast beef, veal cutlets, pigeons!" says the splendid, tall, noble-looking, white-armed, black-eyed Juno of a handmaid as you sit down. And for dessert a choice of three, *three*, darling Mother, of the most succulent, unctuous (no, not unctuous, unless you imagine a celestial unction without the oil) pie-like confections, always 2 platesful—my eye! She has an admirable chemical, not mechanical, combination of cake and jam and cream which I recommend to Mother if she is ever at a loss; though there is no well-stored pantry like that of good old Kay Street, or if there is it exists not for miserable me.[201]

This chemical analysis is so bewildering at first that I am "muddled and bet"[202] and have to employ almost all my time reading up. Agassiz is evidently a great favourite with his Boston audience and feels it himself. But he's an admirable earnest lecturer, clear as day, and his accent is most fascinating. Jeffries Wyman's lectures on Comp. Anatomy of Verts. promise to be very good; prosy perhaps a little and monotonous, but plain and well-arranged and nourris.[203] Eliot I have not seen much more of; I don't believe he is a *very* accomplished

199. Andrew Robeson (b. 1843) is described as a schoolmate of HJ's at the Berkeley Institute in Newport in *The Complete Letters of Henry James, 1855–1872*, ed. Pierre A. Walker and Greg W. Zacharias (Lincoln: University of Nebraska Press, 2006), 1:346, and HJ lists him among his Newport friends in a letter of 1859 (ibid., 19).

200. "Corpusculus" is an affectionate diminutive derived from the Latin "corpus" or body, hence "dear little body." Wilky was inclined to plumpness, as is suggested by his father's jocular reference to "the adipose and affectionate Wilkie" (Edward Waldo Emerson, *The Early Years of the Saturday Club 1855–1870* [1918; Freeport, N.Y.: Books for Libraries, 1967], 328).

201. At this time the Jameses were renting 13 Kay Street in Newport.

202. " 'Bet' is used in some Irish and Scottish dialects for 'beat' " (*CWJ*, 4:45 n. 6). The expression perhaps hints at the Jameses' ancestry.

203. Jeffries Wyman (1814–74) was an anatomist and physician who taught at the Lawrence Scientific School and became the first curator of the Peabody Museum of Archaeology and Ethnology. *Nourris:* full and copious.

letters. Never before did I know what mystic depths of rapture *lay concealed within that familiar word. Never did the same being look so like two different ones, as I going in and coming ob out of the P.O. if I bring a letter with me. Gloomily, with despair written on my leaden brow I stalk the street along towards the P.O. women, children and students inoblentarily shrinking against the wall as I pass, - thus

But when I come out with a letter an immense concourse of people attends me to my lodging attracted by my excited wild gestures and look.

*A leaf from the letter quoted on page 105–6. (Houghton Library, Harvard University)*

chemist, but can't tell yet. We are only about 12 in the Laboratory, so that we have a very cosy time. I expect to have a winter of "crowded life." I can be as independent as I please, and want to live regardless of the good or bad opinion of every one. I shall have a splendid chance to try, I know, and I know too that the native hue of resolution[204] has never been of very great shade in me hitherto. I am sure that that feeling is a right one, and I mean to live according to it if I can. If I do so I think I shall turn out all right.

I stopped this letter before tea, when Wilky the rosy-gilled and Frank Higginson came in.[205] I now resume it by the light of a taper and that of the moon. Wilky read H.'s letter and amused me "metch" by his naive[206] interpretation of Mother's most rational request that I should "keep a memorandum of all moneys I receive from Father." He thought it was that she might know exactly what sums her prodigal philosopher really gives out, and that mistrust of his generosity caused it. The phrase has a little sound that way, as H. subtly framed it, I confess![207]

The first few days, the first week here, I really didn't know what to do with myself or how to fill my time. I felt as if turned out of doors. I then received H.'s and Mother's letters. Never before did I know what mystic depths of rapture lay concealed within that familiar word. Never did the same being look so like two different ones as I going in and out of the P.O. if I bring a letter with me. Gloomily, with despair written on my leaden brow I stalk the street along towards the P.O., women, children and students involuntarily shrinking against the wall as I pass—thus,* [208] as if the curse of Cain were stamped upon my front. But when I come

* Expressive drawing alas irreproducible.

204. WJ echoes Hamlet, when he fears that "conscience does make cowards of us all, / And thus the native hue of resolution / Is sicklied o'er with the pale cast of thought" (*Hamlet*, 3.1.83–85).

205. Francis Lee Higginson (1841–1925) was one of a number of brothers who were friends of the Jameses. He attended the Sanborn School with Wilky and later became a financier.

206. This is the spelling in the first American edition; it was changed to "naïve" in the British edition.

207. Mrs. James does indeed emerge as the parent who expected some financial accountability from her adult sons; she was similarly assiduous over HJ's spending on his European journeys a few years later.

208. Despite HJ's footnote regretting the lack of WJ's illustration, a page of the letter, with drawing, is reproduced in both American and British editions. Perhaps its inclusion was a late change.

out with a letter an immense concourse of people generally attends me to my lodging, attracted by my excited wild gestures and look.

Christmas being sparely kept in the New England of those days,[209] William passed that of 1861, as a Cambridge letter of the afternoon indicates, without opportunity for a seasonable dash to Newport, but with such compensations, nearer at hand as are here exhibited. Our brother Wilky, I should premise, had been placed with the youngest of us, Bob, for companion, at the "co-educational" school then but a short time previously established by Mr. F. B. Sanborn at Concord, Massachusetts—and of which there will be more to say.[210] "Tom" Ward, already mentioned and who, having left the Concord school shortly before, had just entered Harvard, was quickly to become William's intimate, approved and trusted friend; the diversion of whose patient originality, whose intellectual independence, ability and curiosity from science and free inquiry to hereditary banking— consequent on the position of the paternal Samuel Gray Ward as the representative for many years in the United States of the house of Baring Brothers—he from the first much regretted:[211] the more pertinently doubtless that this companion was of a family "connected" with ours through an intermarriage, Gus Barker, as Mrs. S. G. Ward's nephew, being Tom's first cousin as well as ours, and such links still counting, in that age of comparatively less developed ramifications, when sympathy and intercourse kept pace as it was kept between our pairs of parents.

I have been in Boston the whole blest morning, toted round by the Wards, who had as usual asked me to dine with them.[212] I had happily provided myself with an engagement here for all such emergencies, but, as is my sportive wont, I befooled Tom with divers answers, and finally let him believe I would come (having refused several dazzling chances for the purpose) supposing of course I should see him here yesterday at Miss Upham's board and disabuse him. But the young viper went home right after breakfast—so I had to go into Boston this

209. Only Christmas Day itself was a holiday at Harvard.
210. HJ Sr. referred to him as "the famous Mr. Sanborn" and asserts (p. 178 below), "I can't but felicitate our native land that such magnificent experiments in education go on among us." Sanborn took on the running of the academy in 1855.
211. Samuel Gray Ward (1817–1907), financier and patron of the arts, became, in 1869, one of the founders of the Metropolitan Museum of Art in New York. See also n. 191 above.
212. This is part of a letter written on Christmas Day 1861 to the James family (CWJ, 4:61–64).

morning and explain. Wilky had come up from Concord to dine in said Commonwealth Avenue, and I, as it turned out, found myself in for following the innocent lamb Lily up and down the town for two hours, to hold bundles and ring bells for her; Wilky and Tom having vanished from the scene.[213] Clear sharp cold morning, thermometer 5 degrees at sunrise, and the streets covered with one glare of ice. I had thick smooth shoes and went sliding off like an avalanche every three steps, while she, having india-rubbers and being a Bostonian, went ahead like a swan. I had among other things to keep her bundles from harm, to wipe away every three minutes the trembling jewel with which the cold *would* with persistent kindness ornament my coral nose; to keep a hypocritic watchful eye on her movements lest she fall; to raise my hat gracefully to more and more of her acquaintances every block; to skate round and round embracing lamp-posts and door-scrapers by the score to keep from falling, as well as to avoid serving old lady-promenaders in the same way; to cut capers 4 feet high at the rate of 20 a second, every now and then, for the same purpose; to keep from scooting off down hills and round corners as fast as my able-bodied companion; often to do all these at once and then fall lickety-bang like a chandelier, but *when* so to preserve an expression of placid beatitude or easy nonchalance despite the raging fiend within: oh it beggars description! When finally it was over and I stood alone I shook my companion's dust from my feet and, biting my beard with rage, sware[214] a mighty oath unto high heaven that I would never, while reason held her throne in this distracted orb, *never* NEVER, by word, look or gesture and this without mental reservation, acknowledge a "young lady" as a human being. The false and rotten spawn might die before I would wink to save it. No more Parties now!—at last I am a Man, etc., etc.![215]

213. Commonwealth Avenue is the magnificent street with a central grassy mall in Boston's Back Bay district. Ward had had number 20 built only in 1861. According to Lewis (*The Jameses,* 121), Miss Lily is Elizabeth Hazard Barker (1836–1901), Gus's sister, though the reference could be to one of Tom Ward's sisters, either Elizabeth Ward de Schönberg (listed in *CWJ,* 4:617), or Lydia Gray Ward von Hoffmann (*CWJ,* 4:64 n. 2).

214. Archaic for "swore."

215. WJ's elaborately mock-heroic language seems derived from the poetry of Alexander Pope and, along with the Shakespearean echoes, typifies his sometimes mannered style of letter writing. He signs off a letter to T. S. Perry, written 23 December 1861, with a similar phrase: "Ever Sargy while memory holds a seat in this distracted Orb" (*CWJ,*

My enthusiasm ran very high for a few minutes, but I suddenly saw that I was a great ass and became sobered instantly, so that on the whole I am better for the circumstance, being a sadder and a wiser man. I also went to the Tappans' and gave the children slight presents;[216] then, coming home to my venal board, behaved very considerately and paternally to a young lady who sat next to me, but with a shade of subdued melancholy in my manner which could not have been noticed at the breakfast-table. Many times and bitterly to-day have I thought of home and lamented that I should have to be away at this merry Christmastide from my rare family; wondering, with Wilky, if they were missing us as we miss them. And now as I sit in the light of my kerosene, with the fire quietly consuming in the grate and the twilight on the snow outside and the melancholy old-fashioned strains of the piano dimly rising from below, I see in vision those at home just going in to dinner; my aged, silvered Mother leaning on the arm of her stalwart yet flexible H., merry and garrulous as ever, my blushing Aunt with her old wild beauty still hanging about her, my modest Father with his rippling raven locks, the genial auld Rob and the mysterious Alice, all rise before me, a glorified throng; but two other forms, one tall, intellectual, swarthy, with curved nose and eagle eye, the other having breadth rather than depth, but a

---

4:61). By contrast, he also enjoys the vividness of the vernacular. His more formal, professional writing would remain essentially plain and direct. It is unsurprising, then, that he became increasingly impatient with HJ's style, especially in its later developments. In a letter of 1907 he confesses that his own aim is "to say a thing in one sentence as straight and explicit as it can be made." His brother, however, seems "to avoid naming it straight, but by dint of breathing and sighing all round it and round it, to arouse in the reader . . . the illusion of a solid object, made . . . wholly out of impa[l]pable materials, air, and the prismatic interferences of light, ingeniously focused by mirrors upon empty space" (letter to HJ, 4 May 1907, *CWJ*, 3:337–38).

216. William Aspinwall Tappan, "the shy scion of New York's most prominent evangelical abolitionist family" (Charles Capper, *Margaret Fuller: An American Romantic Life: The Public Years* [New York: Oxford University Press, 2007], 364), and Caroline Sturgis Tappan (1818–88) had two children, Ellen Sturgis (b. 1849) and Mary Aspinwall (1852?–1941). They lived in Boston's Back Bay, "on Beacon Street, looking down Dartmouth" (Perry, *Thought and Character of William James*, 355), but spent summers at their Tanglewood estate in Lenox, in the Berkshires of western Massachusetts (donated by the younger daughter at a later date to the Boston Symphony Orchestra). They were old friends of the James family and they had met up in Paris in 1856.

goodly morsel too, are wanting to complete the harmonious whole.[217] Eftsoons they vanish and I am again alone, *alone*—what pathos in the word! I have two companions though, most all the time—remorse and despair! T. S. Perry took their place for a little, and to-day they have not come back. T. S. seemed to enjoy his visit very much. It was very pleasant for me to have him; his rustic wonder at the commonest sights was most ludicrous, and his conversation most amusing and instructive.

The place here improves to me as I go on living in it, and if I study with Agassiz 4 or 5 years there is nothing I should like better than to have you all with me, regular and comfortable. I enclose another advertisement of a house—but which would be too small for us, I believe, though it might be looked at.[218] I had a long talk with one of A.'s students the other night, and saw for the first time how a naturalist may feel about his trade exactly as an artist does about his. For instance Agassiz would rather take wholly uninstructed people—"for he has to unteach them all they have learnt." He doesn't let them so much as look into a book for a long while; what they learn they must learn for themselves and be *masters* of it all. The consequence is he makes Naturalists of them—doesn't merely cram them; and this student (he had been there 2 years) said he felt ready to go anywhere in the world now with nothing but his notebook and study out anything quite alone. A. must be a great teacher. Chemistry comes on tolerably, but not so fast as I expected. I am pretty slow with my substances, having done but 12 since Thanksgiving and having 38 more to do before the end of the term.

Comment on the abundance, the gaiety and drollery, the generous play of vision and fancy in all this, would seem so needless as to be almost officious, were not the commentator constantly, were he not infinitely, arrested and reminded and solicited; which is at once his advantage and his embarrassment. Such a letter, at all events, read over with the general key,

217. Later in this chapter HJ feels obliged to set the record straight on this comic-romantic version of the James family. Aunt Kate, Catharine Walsh, having been briefly and unhappily married, lived with them for most of her life (see *SBO*, n. 103). The form having more breadth than depth was Wilky.

218. It was always assumed that the family would leave Newport, though this happened only in 1864 with their move into 13 Ashburton Place, Boston.

touches its contemporary scene and hour into an intensity of life for him; making indeed the great sign of that life my brother's signal vivacity and cordiality, his endless spontaneity of mind. Every thing in it is characteristic of the genius and expressive of the mood, and not least, of course, the pleasantry of paradox, the evocation of each familiar image by its vivid opposite. Our mother, *e.g.,* was not at that time, nor for a good while yet, so venerably "silvered"; our handsome-headed father had lost, occipitally, long before, all pretence to raven locks, certainly to the effect of their "rippling"; the beauty of our admirable aunt was as happily alien either to wildness or to the "hanging" air as it could very well be; the "mystery" of our young sister consisted all in the candour of her natural bloom, even if at the same time of her lively intelligence; and H.'s mirth and garrulity appear to have represented for the writer the veriest ironic translation of something in that youth, I judge, not a little mildly—though oh *so* mildly!—morose or anxiously mute.[219] To the same tune the aquiline in his own nose heroically derides the slightly relaxed line of that feature; and our brother Wilky's want of physical "depth" is a glance at a different proportion. Of a like tinge of pleasantry, I may add, is the imputation of the provincial gape to our friend T. S. Perry, of Newport birth and unintermitted breeding,[220] with whom we were to live so much in the years to come, and who was then on the eve of entering Harvard—his face already uninterruptedly turned to that love of letters, that practice of them by dauntless and inordinate, though never at all vulgarly resonant, absorption which was to constitute in itself the most disinterested of careers. I had myself felt him from the first an exemplary, at once, and a discouraging friend; he had let himself loose in the world of books, pressed and roamed through the most various literatures and the most voluminous authors, with a stride that, as it carried him beyond all view, left me dismayed and helpless at the edge of the forest, where I listened wistfully but unemulously to the far-off crash from within of his felled timber, the clearing of

219. HJ is right in pointing out WJ's misleading irony. Compare Perry's account of his first meeting with the family (he makes no mention of Robertson): "I have often thought that the three brothers shewed that evening some of their characteristic qualities. I remember walking with Wilky hanging on my arm, talking to me as if he had found an old friend after long absence. When we got to the house and the rest of us were chattering, HJ sat on the window-seat reading Leslie's Life of Constable with a certain air of remoteness. William was full of merriment and we were soon playing a simple and childish game" (quoted in Matthiessen, *The James Family,* 88).

220. For Perry's distinguished ancestors, see above, n. 160.

whole spaces or periods shelf by shelf or great tree by tree. The brother-in-law of John La Farge, he had for us further, with that reviving consciousness of American annals which the War was at once so rudely and so insidiously to quicken in us, the glamour of his straight descent from the Commodores Perry of the Lake Erie in the war of 1812, respectively, and of the portentous penetration of Japan just after the mid-century, and his longer-drawn but equally direct and so clean and comfortable affiliation to the great Benjamin Franklin: as these things at least seemed to me under my habit (too musing and brooding certainly to have made for light loquacity) of pressing every wind-borne particle of personal history—once the persons were only other enough from myself—into the service of what I would fain have called picture or, less explicitly, less formulatedly, romance.

These, however, are but too fond insistences, and what mainly bears pointing out is my brother's already restless reach forth to some new subject of study. He had but lately addressed himself, not without confidence, to such an investigation of Chemistry as he might become conscious of a warrant for, yet the appeal of Agassiz's great authority, so much in the air of the Cambridge of that time, found him at once responsive; it opened up a world, the world of sentient life, in the light of which Chemistry faded. He had not, however, for the moment done with it; and what I at any rate find most to the point in the pages before me is the charm of their so witnessing to the geniality and harmony of our family life, exquisite as I look back on it and reflected almost as much in any one passage taken at hazard as in any other. He had apparently, at the date of the following, changed his lodging.[221]

President Felton's death has been the great event of the week—two funerals and I don't know how many prayers and sermons.[222] To-day I thought I would go to University chapel for the sake of variety and hear Dr. Peabody's final word on him—and a very long and lugubrious one it was.[223] The prayer was a prolonged moan in which

221. The following letter was written on 9 March 1862 (*CWJ*, 4:66), and HJ makes some omissions. At the end of February WJ moved from the Pascos' house to lodge with the Sweetsers on Trowbridge Street (*CWJ*, 4:65).

222. Cornelius Conway Felton (1807–62) had been a classical scholar before becoming president of Harvard. He died on 26 February 1862.

223. Andrew Preston Peabody (1811–93), Plummer Professor of Christian Morals at Harvard, published *A Sermon Preached in the Appleton Chapel, March 9 1862, Being the Sunday after the Funeral of Cornelius Conway Felton* in 1862.

the death (not in its consequences, but in itself) was treated as a great calamity, and the whole eulogy was almost ridiculously overcharged. What was most disagreeable throughout was the wailing tones, not a bit that of simple pagan grief at the *loss*—which would have been honest; but a whine consciously put on as from a sense of duty, and a whine at nothing definite either, only a purposeless clothing of all his words in tears. The whole style of the performance was such that I have concluded to have nothing more to do with funerals till they improve.

The walking here has been terrible with ice or slush these many weeks, but over head celestial. No new developments in this house. The maniac sometimes chills my very marrow by hoarsely whispering outside the door, "Gulielmo, Gulielmo!"[224] Old Sweetser sits in his dressing-gown smoking his pipe all day in a little uncomfortable old *bathroom* next door to me. He may with truth be called a queer cuss. The young ladies have that very nasty immodest habit of hustling themselves out of sight precipitately whenever I appear. I dined with Mrs. —— yesterday all alone.[225] She was quite sick, very hoarse, and *he* was in the country, so that on the whole it was a great bore. She is very clumsy in her way of doing things, and her invitation to me was for the wife of an artist—not artistic!

I am now studying organic Chemistry. It will probably shock Mother to hear that I yesterday destroyed a pockethandkerchief—but it was an old one and I converted it into some sugar which though rather brown is very good. I believe I forgot to tell you that I am shorn of my brightest ornament. That solitary hirsute jewel which lent such a manly and martial aspect to my visage is gone, and the place thereof is naked. I don't think anyone will know the difference, and moreover it is not dead, it only sleeps and will some day rise phoenix-like from its ashes with tenfold its former beauty. When Father comes will he please bring Ganot's Physique *if H. doesn't want it?*[226]

224. WJ explains the circumstances of the Sweetser family in a letter included later in the chapter. A disturbed woman lodger ("the maniac") is calling to William ("Gulielmo").

225. HJ has omitted the name of Hunt (see *CWJ*, 4:67). Louisa Perkins Hunt was the wife of William Morris Hunt.

226. Adolphe Ganot (1804–87) wrote two physics manuals, *Traité élémentaire de physique expérimentale et appliquée* and *Cours de physique purement expérimentale;* given HJ's well-known distaste for science and mathematics, this question may be sarcastic.

In none of these earlier communications from Cambridge is the element of affectionate pleasantry more at play than in those addressed to his sister.[227]

Charmante jeune fille,[228] I find the Tappans *really* expected me to bring you to them and were much disappointed at my failure. Ellen has grown very fat and big. Mary calls everybody "horrid." Lyly Barker is with the Wards.[229] I haven't seen her yet, but shall do so on Saturday, when I am also to dine with the Hunts. I hope your neuralgia, or whatever you may believe the thing was, has gone and that you are back at school instead of languishing and lolling about the house. I send you herewith a portrait of Prof. Eliot, a very fair likeness, to grace your book withal. Write me whenever you have the slightest or most fleeting inclination to do so. If you have only one sentence to say, don't grudge paper and stamps for it. You don't know how much good you may do me at an appropriate time by a little easy scratching of your graceful nimble pen.

In another apostrophe to the same correspondent, at the same season, his high spirits throw off the bonds of the vernacular.

Est-ce que tu songes jamais à moi comme moi je songe à toi?—oh je crois bien que non! Maintes fois dans la journée l'image d'une espèce d'ange vêtue de blanc avec de longs boucles noirs qui encadrent une figure telle que la plupart des mortels ne font que l'entrevoir dans leur rêves, s'impose à mes sens ravis; créature longue et fluette qui se dispose à se coucher dans une petite chambrette verte où le gaz fait un grand jour. Eh, oua, oua, oua! c'est à faire mourir de douleur. Mais je parie que tout de même pas une étincelle ne vibre pour moi dans les fibres de ton coeur endurci. Hélas, oublié de mes parents et de mes semblables, je ne vois, où que je regarde, qu'un abîme de désespoir, un gouffre noir et peuplé de démons, qui tôt ou tard va m'engloutir. Tu ne m'écris jamais sauf pour me soutirer des objets de luxe. La vaste mère me déteste, il n'y a que le frère qui me reste attaché, et lui par esprit d'opposition plus que par autre chose. Eh mon Dieu, que vais-

227. Letter is headed "Cambridge. Thursday Evening 6 March [1862]" (*CWJ*, 4:593).
228. *Charmante jeune fille:* charming girl.
229. See n. 213 above.

je devenir? En tout cas je vais clore cette lettre, qui s'est allongée malgré moi. Ton frere, James William.[230]

Of the same bright complexion is this report, addressed to his parents, of the change of lodging already noted.[231]

The presence of the Tweedys has been most agreeable and has contributed in no small degree to break the shock of removal to these new rooms, which are not near so cosy as the old; especially with the smoking of my stove, which went on all the first two days. That has been stopped, however, and the only trouble is now to get the fire alight at all. I have generally to start it 3 or 4 times, and the removal of the material of each failure from the grate is a fearful business. I have also to descend to the cellar myself to get my coal, and my "hod," as Ma Sweetser, my landlady, calls it, not being very much bigger than a

230. "Do you ever dream of me as I dream of you?—oh, I don't think so. Many times in the day the image of a kind of angel dressed in white with long black ringlets which frame such a face as most mortals catch only a glimpse of in their dreams, foists itself on my ravished senses; tall slender creature who prepares herself to go to bed in a tiny green room in which gas makes it daylight. Oh, yeah, yeah yeah! it's enough to make you die of grief. But I bet, all the same, that not a single spark vibrates for me in the fibres of your callous heart. Alas, forgotten by my parents and my fellow-creatures, I see only wherever I look an abyss of despair, a black gulf inhabited by demons which will sooner or later swallow me up. You never write except to wheedle out of me luxury items. My vast mother hates me, only my brother remains devoted, and he more in a spirit of opposition than anything else. Oh my God, what is to become of me? In any case I shall close this letter which has grown in spite of me. Your brother, James William." Lewis points out that *oua* was a "Swiss slang perversion of *Oui*"; perhaps it was picked up during the children's stay in Geneva. He also notes that the inappropriate "*vaste mère*" puns romantically on *la vaste mer*" (*The Jameses*, 123n). The letter from which this extract comes is dated 14 September 1861, though the correct date is 14 October 1861, and WJ signs off, more accurately, as "Ton frère" (*CWJ*, 4:47 and n. 1). Its first part explains how WJ has preserved for Alice a pair of pigeon wings as a present. The final third in French (however full of "high spirits") may seem less appealing (or even inappropriate) to modern readers with its mock-gallant tone and romantic abjectness. Alice is frequently addressed flirtatiously by her older brother: for consideration of its implications, see Jean Strouse, *Alice James* (New York: Houghton Mifflin, 1980; London: Harvill, 1992), 52–55; Lewis, *The Jameses* 95–96; and Feinstein, *Becoming William James*, 280–85. Only a few years later WJ would in reality be subject to suicidal tendencies. For consideration of this "partly incestuous rhetoric of lovers," see also Fred Kaplan, *Henry James: The Imagination of Genius: A Biography* (London: Hodder and Stoughton, 1992), 85.

231. The following is extracted from a letter of 2 March 1862 to his parents (*CWJ*, 4:65–66).

milk-pitcher, doesn't add to the charm. The coal is apt to drop on the stairs, and I have to pick it all up. At present the stove fills the room with a nephitic and pestilential gas, so that I have to keep the window open. I went last night with the Tweedys to the concert for which they came up, and with them this morning to hear Wendell Phillips.[232] This Sweetser family is worthy of Dickens. It consists of a Mr. and Miss S., Mr. S.'s three gushing girls, a parrot and a maniac. The maniac is very obstreperous. Her husband left her boarding here 3 months ago and went to Cuba. When she got mad he was written to, but has sent no reply, and they are keeping her. For the Aunt's sake I keep my drawer locked against her at night.[233] Old Sweetser is a riddle I hope to do justice to at some future time, but can't begin on now. His sister shakes like an aspen whenever she is spoken to. Oh I forgot the most important character of all, the black wench who "does" the room. She is about 20 years old and wears short frocks, but talks like Alice Robeson and has an antediluvian face about as large as the top of a flour-barrel.[234]

I can really keep my hand from nothing, of whatever connection, that causes his intensity of animation and spontaneity of expression to revive. On a Sunday evening early in 1862[235] he had

just returned from Milton,[236] and, after removing from my person a beetle, sit down to write you immediately. Ever since 10.30 this A.M. the beetle s'est promené à l'envi sur ma peau.[237] The first feeling I had of his becoming attached to it made me jump so as to scare an old lady opposite me in the car into fits. Finding him too hard to crush I let

232. For the Tweedys, old family friends, see above, n. 113. Wendell Phillips (1811–84) was a celebrated orator and abolitionist. "The concert at the Boston Music Hall on 1 March 1862 was to commemorate recent 'Union Victories.' Wendell Phillips spoke there on 2 March" (*CWJ*, 4:66 n. 2).

233. WJ refers humorously to his Aunt Kate, who would have been concerned about his welfare. The original letter had "door" rather than "drawer" (see *CWJ*, 4:65), which makes better sense; if HJ were dictating portions of this letter to his amanuensis, Theodora Bosanquet, she may have misheard and the slip gone unnoticed. Compare n. 421.

234. Alice Robeson has not been identified (*CWJ*, 4:66 n. 3), though she may well be related to Andrew Robeson, mentioned previously. Even in the more liberal enclaves of the North, racial attitudes still depended on stereotypes.

235. On 18 May (*CWJ*, 4:71).

236. Milton is in Norfolk County, just south of Boston.

237. "The beetle walked on my skin over and over again."

him run, and at last got used to him though at times he tickled me to excruciation. I ache in every limb and every cranny of my mind from my visit. . . . They had the usual number of stories, wonderful and not wonderful, to tell of their friends and relatives (of Stephen somebody, *e.g.*, who had a waggon weighing several tons run over his chest without even bruising him, and so on). They are very nice girls indeed all the same.[238] I then went, near by, to the Forbes's in a state of profuse perspiration, and saw handsome Mrs. F. and her daughters, and a substitute for Governor Andrew in the person of his wife;[239] after which I returned here, being driven back in the car, as I perceived on the front platform, by our old familiar—familiar indeed! —friend William (I mean our Irish ex-coachman) whom age doesn't seem to render more veracious, as he told me several very big stories about himself: how he smashed a car to pieces the other night, how he first gave the alarm of the great fire, etc.[240]

I went to the theatre the other night, and, asking a gentleman to make room for me, found him to be Bob Temple, who had arrived in Boston that day.[241] He looks very well and talks in the most

238. As is clear from the full version of the letter, WJ had been visiting Robert Sedgwick Watson (1809–88) and his family of six daughters (see *CWJ*, 1:5 n. 7; 6:72 n. 2).

239. It is suggested that this probably refers to Sarah Hathaway Forbes (wife of John Murray Forbes) and her daughters, or (less likely) to the wife of Robert Bennett Forbes, who, however, had only one daughter. John Albion Andrew (1818–67) was governor of Massachusetts and his wife was Eliza Jones Hersey; they had two daughters (see *CWJ*, 4:72 nn. 3 and 4).

240. There had been a major conflagration in downtown Boston at Broad and Milk streets on 21 May 1862 (see *CWJ*, 4:73 n. 5). The famous, even greater fire occurred in 1872.

241. Robert Temple was the eldest of the Jameses' six orphaned Temple cousins (see above, n. 116). He "sailed from New York for Liverpool on the *Australasian* on 21 May 1862" (*CWJ*, 4:73 n. 7). WJ would soon become much more critical of his cousin's dissolute life. He had Southern sympathies, which may explain WJ's reference to his views on slavery. See also Gordon, *A Private Life of Henry James*, 108. Bob Temple unappealingly tried to exploit his family connections, hoping for benefits from his new rich brother-in-law Temple Emmet, while otherwise denouncing the unsuitability of the marriage on grounds of the couple's age difference. Mary James writes rather snobbishly of Bob to HJ on 21 September [1869?], "He looks grey and grave beyond his years and is such an image of his father that it is startling. He told Father that he had perfect self control in drinking, and he certainly *looks* perfectly steady—He counts upon Temple Emmet who is largely interested in Rail-roads in Oregon to give him employment. What he would prefer to any other occupation (a high ideal you will think) is to go to Texas and keep a

extraordinary way you ever heard about Slavery and the wickedness of human society, and is apparently very sincere. He sailed for Europe on Wednesday. I exhorted him to stop over at Newport, but he wouldn't. There was something quite peculiar about him—he seemed greatly changed. I can tell you more at home, but wish I might have seen more of him. I have been the last three nights running to hear John Wilkes Booth, the "young American Roscius."[242] Rant, rant, rant of the most fearful kind. The worst parts most applauded, but with any amount of fire and energy in the passionate parts, in some of which he really becomes natural. . . . You don't know what a regular Sévigné you have in Alice.[243] I blush for my delinquencies toward her, but bow my head with meek humility, contented to be her debtor all my life and despairing of ever repaying her the value of her letters. Mother and Aunt I pine to see, and the honest Jack Tar of the family, the rough Bob, with his rude untutored ways!

Traps for remembrance I find set at every turn here, so that I have either to dodge them or patiently to suffer catching. I try in vain for instance merely to brush past the image of our kinsman Robert Temple the younger, who made with his brother Will the eldest pair in that house of cousins: he waylays, he persuades me too much, and to fail of the few right words for him would be to leave a deep debt unrepaid—his fitful hovering presence, repeatedly vivid and repeatedly obscured, so considerably "counted" for us, pointing the sharpest moral, pointing fifty morals, and adorning a perpetual tale. He was for years, first on the nearer and then little by little on the further, the furthest, horizon, quite the most emphasised of all our wastrels, the figure bristling most with every irregular accent that we were to find ourselves in any closeness of relation with. I held him for myself at least, from far back, a pure gift of free-handed

---

grocery store! Something I presume will be provided for him by the blessed Emmets and another chance will be given him" (bMS Am 1093.1 [37], Houghton).

242. John Wilkes Booth (1838–65), son of the Anglo-American actor Junius Brutus Booth, was soon to become notorious for his assassination of Abraham Lincoln. In earlier days HJ had watched his brother Edwin Thomas Booth perform in New York (see *SBO*, p. 95). Quintus Roscius Gallus (c. 126–162 BCE) was a great Roman comic actor whose talent released him from slavery.

243. The letters of Madame de Sévigné (Marie de Rabutin-Chantal, Marquise de Sévigné, 1626–95) provide a classic account of aristocratic life in seventeenth-century France.

chance to the grateful imagination, the utmost limit of whose complaint of it could be but for the difficulty of rendering him the really proper tribute. I regarded him truly, for a long time, as a possession of the mind, the human image swung before us with most of the effect of strong and thick and inimitable colour. If to be orphaned and free of range had affected my young fancy as the happy, that is the romantic, lot, no member of the whole cousinship, favoured in that sense as so many of them were, enjoyed so, by my making out, the highest privilege of the case.[244] Nothing, I could afterwards easily see, had been less inevitable and of a greater awkwardness of accident than his being, soon after the death of his parents, shipped off from Albany, in pursuit of an education, to an unheard-of school in a remote corner of Scotland; which fact it was, however, that played for me exactly the bright part of preparing to show with particular intensity what Europe again, with the opportunity so given, was going to proceed to. It thus shone out when after the lapse of several years he recurred to our more competent view that, quite richly erratic creature as he might appear, and to whatever degree of wonder and suspense, of amusement and amazement, he might wind us up, the rich alien influence, full of special queernesses and mysteries in this special connection, had complacently turned him out for us and had ever so irretrievably and ineffaceably stamped him. He rose before us, tall and goodlooking and easy, as a figure of an oddly *civilised* perversity; his irreverent challenging humour, playing at once, without mercy, over American aspects, seemed somehow not less cultivated than profane—just which note in itself caused the plot beautifully to thicken; for this was to distinguish and almost embellish him throughout a long career in which he was to neglect no occasion, however frankly forbidding, for graceless adventure, that he had the pure derisive, the loose and mocking mind, yet initiated, educated, almost elegantly impudent, in other words successfully impertinent, and which expressed itself, in particular by the pen, with a literary lightness that we used to find inimitable. He had dangled there, further off and nearer, as a character, to my attention, in the sense in which "people in books" were characters, and other people, roundabout us, were somehow not; so that I fairly thought of him (though this more, doubtless, with the lapse of time) very much as if we had owed him to Thackeray or Dickens,

244. HJ's childhood envy of his parentless cousins has been charted from the opening chapter of *SBO,* where he confesses that the charm of his grandmother's Albany home lay partly in its unofficial function as an orphanage.

the creators of superior life to whom we were at that time always owing most, rather than to any set of circumstances by which we had in our own persons felt served; that he was inimitable, inimitably droll, inimitably wasted, wanton, impossible, or whatever else it might be, making him thus one with the rounded and represented creature, shining in the light of art, as distinguished from the vague handful of more or less susceptible material that had in the common air to pass for a true concretion. The promise of this had been, to my original vision, in every wind-borne echo of him, however light; I doubtless put people "into books" by very much the same turn of the hand with which I took them out, but it had tinged itself with the finely free that, proceeding in due course from his school at Fochabers to the University of Aberdeen (each sound and syllable of this general far cry from Albany had in itself an incoherence!) he had encountered while there the oddest of all occasions to embrace the Romish faith.[245] In the same way it ministered to the vivid, even if baffled, view of him that he appeared then to have retreated upon the impenetrable stronghold of Nairn, described by him as a bleak little Scotch watering-place which yet sufficed to his cluster of predicaments:[246] whence he began to address to his bewildered pair of Albany guardians and trustees[247] the earlier of that series of incomparably amusing letters, as we judged them, the arrival of almost any one of which among us, out of the midst of indocilities at once more and more horrific and more and more reported with a desperate drollery, was to constitute an event so supremely beguiling that distressful meanings and expensive remedies found themselves alike salved to consciousness by the fact that such compositions could only be, for people of

245. Fochabers is a village on the River Spey, in Moray, Scotland, about forty-seven miles northwest of Aberdeen. Bob attended a "noted boys' school," Milne's Free School, and then spent two years (1857–59) at the University of Aberdeen (Habegger, *The Father*, 361).

246. Nairn, a popular summer resort, is on the Moray Firth, about thirty miles west of Fochabers.

247. Edmund and Mary Tweedy cared for the four youngest Temple children, all girls, when their parents died in 1854; the oldest child, Bob, was sent off to school in Scotland at this time. Though Mary Tweedy had earlier links with Albany, the couple lived in Pelham, New York, and in Newport. The James grandmother kept an open house in Albany for some of her sons and other members of the family, so it may be this household and "a pair of guardians" to which HJ refers. In a letter written to Edmund Tweedy from Bonn, 24 July 1860, HJ Sr. gives a long extract from one of his nephew's letters, referring to its "irredeemable Bobbishness," adding "how relieved by humour!" (bMS Am 1092.9 [4286], Houghton).

taste, enjoyable. I think of this hapless kinsman throughout as blest with a "form" that appealed to the finer fibres of appreciation; so that, variously misadventurous as he was ever to continue, his genius for expression again and again just saved him—saved him for bare life, left in his hand a broken piece of the effective magic wand, never perhaps waved with anything like that easy grace in an equally compromised interest.[248]

It was at any rate as if I had from the first collected and saved up the echoes—or so at least it seems to me now: echoes of him as all sarcastically and incorrigibly mutinous, somewhat later on, while in nominal charge of a despairing *pasteur* at Neuchâtel—followed by the intensified sense of him, after I scarce remember quite what interval, on his appearing at Newport, where his sisters, as I have mentioned, had been protectively gathered in, during the year, more or less, that followed our own installation there.[249] Then it was that we had the value of his being interesting with less trouble taken to that end—in proportion to the effect achieved— than perhaps ever served such a cause; it would perhaps scarce even be

248. Despite Bob Temple's criminal life—he enlisted in the army under the false name of Robert Travis; was sentenced to a year's hard labor on Bedloe's Island (now Liberty Island); was jailed again in Great Falls, Montana, for forgery—and his frequent begging letters to members of the James family, it is clear that HJ regarded him with affection. Bob mutilated his hand while hunting in 1877, and Gordon points out the parallel with the ghostly "other" presence in the late tale "The Jolly Corner," a similarly disfigured form who is sympathized with by a female protagonist but who almost destroys the hero, his alternative self. Gordon also illustrates the rapport between Bob and HJ, known within the family circle as "the angel": "In 1885, when Temple was imprisoned out west, he penned disconcertingly graceful and amusing letters to members of his family (who, he well knew, would like to disown him). At this time he had appealed for help to his cousin Harry, the angel of the James family, who refused—'Harry has deserted me, and the last prop has gone,' Temple declared in mock-despair" (*A Private Life of Henry James*, 334n). Nevertheless, HJ wrote to WJ's wife in 1892: "P.S. Please say to W. that I *have* sent to B. Temple 10 dollars" (*Dear Munificent Friends: Henry James's Letters to Four Women*, ed. Susan E. Gunter [Ann Arbor: University of Michigan Press, 1999], 30.

249. Bob Temple was in Neuchâtel, in the Jura of western Switzerland in 1860; HJ Sr., resident with his family in Geneva at the time, went to visit him in May. He thought him "shockingly indolent, and his mobile grin suggested that 'vive la bagatelle' was his philosophy of life." HJ heard his father's opinion: "In *Roderick Hudson* . . . (with a number of open-air scenes in Switzerland), he would recount the downfall of a self-indulgent painter who bears a strong resemblance to Bob Temple. This work draws on a number of family stories about the *Hudson* Valley Jameses and seems premised on the great James fear that unfocused energies may provoke a sudden and complete collapse of the will" (Habegger, *The Father*, 414).

too much to say that, as the only trouble he seemed capable of was the trouble of quite positively declining to interest on any terms, his essential Dickensism, as I have called it, or his Thackerayan tint if preferred, his comedy-virtue in fine, which he could neither disown nor, practically speaking, misapply, was stronger even than his particular sardonic cynicism, strongly as that was at last to flower. I won't in the least say he dazzled—that was reserved for his so quite otherwise brilliant, his temporarily triumphant, younger brother, at whom I have already glanced, who was on no possible terms with him, and never could have been, so that the difficulty of their relation glimmers upon me as probably half the good reason for the original queer despatch of the elder to about the remotest, the most separating, point in space at which "educational advantages" could be conceived as awaiting him. I must have had no need by that time to be dazzled, or even to be charmed, in order more or less fondly, often indeed doubtless fearfully, to apprehend; what I apprehended being that here was a creature quite amusedly and perceptively, quite attentively and, after a fashion, profitably, living without a single one of the elements of life (of the inward, I mean, those one would most have missed if deprived of them) that I knew as most conducive to animation. What could have roused more curiosity than this, for the time at least, even if there hadn't been associated with it such a fine redolence, as I then supposed it, of the rich and strange places and things, as I supposed *them*, that had contributed to making him over? He had come back made—unless one was already, and too conveniently or complacently, to call it unmade: *that* was the point (and it certainly wasn't Albany that ever would have made him); he had come back charged, to my vision, with prodigious "English" impressions and awarenesses, each so thoroughly and easily assimilated that they might have played their part as convictions and standards had he pretended to anything that would in that degree have satisfied us. He never spoke of his "faith," as that might have been the thing we could have held him to; and he knew what not too gracelessly to speak of when the sense of the American grotesque in general and the largely-viewed "family" reducibility to the absurd in particular offered him such free light pasture. He had the sign of grace that he ever perfectly considered my father—so far as attitude, distinct from behaviour, went; but most members of our kinship on that side still clung to this habit of consideration even when, as was in certain cases but too visible, they had parted with all sense of any other. I have preserved no happier truth about my father than that the graceless whom, according to their own fond term, he, and he alone of all of us, "understood," returned to him as often and appealed to him as freely as those happier, though indeed scarce less importunate, in their connection, who found attraction and reason enough in their understanding *him*. My brother's impression of this vessel of intimations that evening at the Boston theatre, and of his "sincerity" and his seeming "greatly changed," doesn't at all events, I feel, fail in the least to fit into one of those amplifications upon which my incurable trick of unwillingness wholly to sacrifice any good value compromised by time tends to precipitate me with a force that my reader can scarce fear for me more than I fear it for myself. There was no "extraordinary way" in which our incalculable kinsman *mightn't* talk, and that William should have had for the hour the benefit of this general truth is but a happy note in my record. It was not always the case that one wished one "might have seen more of him," but this was only because one had had on any contact the sense of seeing so much. That produced consequences among which the desire for more might even be uncannily numbered. John Wilkes Booth, of the same evening, was of course President Lincoln's assassin-to-be, of whose crudely extravagant performance of the hero of Schiller's Robbers I recall my brother's imitative description—I never myself saw him; and it simplifies his case, I think, for distracted history, that he must have been quite an abominable actor.[250] I appear meanwhile to have paid William at Cambridge a visit of which I have quite oddly lost remembrance—by reason doubtless of its but losing itself in like, though more prolonged, occasions that were to follow at no great distance and that await my further reference. The manner of his own allusion to it more than suffices.[251]

The radiance of H's visit has not faded yet, and I come upon gleams of it three or four times a day in my farings to and fro, but it has never a bit diminished the lustre of far-off shining Newport, all

250. Booth "performed at the Boston Museum from 12 May to 23 May 1862. On the 'last three nights' [quoting from WJ's letter above of 18 May] WJ would have seen three Shakespeare plays, *Richard III, Hamlet,* and *Romeo and Juliet. . . . The Robbers* was performed on 14 and 21 May in 1862. WJ could have seen *The Robbers* on other occasions since John Wilkes Booth performed in the play in Boston in 1863 and 1864" (*CWJ,* 4:73 n. 8). WJ saw the play again (in German) in May 1867 when he was staying in Dresden (*CWJ,* 4:179). *Die Raüber,* first published in 1781, with its melodramatic style and inclusion of violent action, stands as one of the earliest examples of the romantic Sturm und Drang movement.

251. The following forms part of a letter written on 10 November 1861 (*CWJ,* 4:50).

silver and blue, and of this heavenly group below* [252]—all being
more or less failures, especially the two outside ones. The more so
as the above-mentioned H. could in no wise satisfy my craving for
knowledge of family and friends—he didn't seem to have been on
speaking terms with anyone for some time past, and could tell me
nothing of what they did, said or thought, about any given subject.
Never did I see a so-much uninterested creature in the affairs of those
about him. He is a good soul, though, in his way, too; and less fatal
than the light fantastic and ever-sociable Wilky, who has wrought
little but disaster during his stay with me; breaking down my good
resolutions about food, keeping me from all intellectual exercise,
working havoc on my best hat by wearing it while dressing, while in
his nightgown, while washing his face, and all but going to bed with it.
He occupied my comfortable arm-chair all the morning in the position
represented in the fine plate that accompanies this letter—but one
more night though, and he will have gone, and no thorn shall pierce
the side of the serene and hallowed felicity of expectation in which I
shall revel till the time comes for returning home, home to the hearth
of my infancy and budding youth. As Wilky has submitted to you a
résumé of his future history for the next few years, so will I of mine,
hoping it will meet your approval. Thus: one year Chemistry, then one
term at home. Then one year with Wyman, followed by a medical
education. Then five or six years with Agassiz; after which probably
death, death, death from inflation and plethora of knowledge. This
you had better seriously consider. So farewell till 8.45 some Sunday
evening soon. Your bold, your beautiful, your blossom!

"I lead, as ever," he meanwhile elsewhere records, "the monotonous
life of the scholar, with few variations."[253]

We have very general talk at our table, Miss Upham declaiming
against the vulgarity of President Lincoln and complacently telling of
her own ignorance as to the way the wind blows or as to the political
events going on, and saying she thinks it a great waste of time and of

* A drawing of figures in evening lamplight
252. Though HJ explains the reference to "this heavenly group below" in his footnote,
the illustration was not included in the first edition.
253. From a letter written on 15 December 1861 (*CWJ*, 4:55).

"no practical account" to study natural history.[254] F. J. Child impresses one as very witty and funny, but leaves it impossible to remember what he says. I took a walk with the Divinity student this splendid afternoon. He told me he had been walking yesterday with one of the Jerseymen and they had discussed the doctrine of a future state.[255] The Jerseyman thought that if the easy Unitarian doctrines were to become popular the morals of the community would be most terribly relaxed. "Why," said the other, "here you are in the very thick of Unitarianism; look about you—people are about as good as anywhere." "Yes," replied the Jerseyman, "I confess to you that that is what has *staggered* me, and I don't understand it yet!"[256]

I stretch over to the next year, 1863, for the sake of the following to his sister.[257]

Chérie charmante,[258] I am established in a cosy little room, with a large recess with a window in it containing bed and washstand, and separated from the main apartment by a rich green silk curtain and a large gilt cornice. This gives the whole establishment a splendid look. I found when I got back here that Miss Upham had raised her price; so great efforts were made by two of us to form a club.[259] But too little enthusiasm was shown by any one else, and it fell through. I then with that fine economical instinct which distinguishes me resolved to take breakfast and tea, of my own finding and making, in my room, and

254. Abraham Lincoln (1809–65) was elected president on 6 November 1860 and inaugurated in March 1862.

255. This may be a reference to a group that established itself in New Jersey. In a letter of 6 March 1850 to HJ Sr., Emerson mentions Marcus Spring, "a Quaker philanthropist, who owned the large estate of Eagleswood near Perth Amboy, N.J., and developed there a 'colony.' He was a typical radical and reformer of the times. Henry Thoreau was engaged to survey Eagleswood, and while there made the acquaintance of Walt Whitman. George Inness, Bronson Alcott, Horace Greeley, and Steele MacKaye were other residents or visitors" (Perry, *Thought and Character of William James*, 1:67–68 n. 6).

256. Since its inception in 1816 the Harvard Divinity School had had strongly Unitarian leanings. Unitarians, as the name suggests, followed the Christian system of thought that emphasized the power of God the Father, rather than the Trinity of Father, Son, and Holy Spirit, while valuing the living example of Jesus Christ within human society. The Bostonian Dr. William Ellery Channing (1780–1842) had been the church's leader (see also *SBO*, n. 412).

257. Part of a letter written on 13 September 1863 (*CWJ*, 4:83–85).

258. Charming beloved.

259. Though WJ dined at Miss Upham's, he lodged at this time with Mrs. Sophie H. Appleton at 610 Main Street, Cambridge (*CWJ*, 4:84 n. 1).

only pay Miss Upham for dinners. Miss U. is now holding forth at Swampscott, so I asked to see her sister Mrs. Wood and learn the cost of the 7 dinners a week.[260] She with true motherly instinct said that I should only make a slop with my self-made meals in my room, and that she would rather let me keep on for 4.50, seeing it was me. I said she must first consult Miss Upham. She returned from Swampscott saying that Miss U. had sworn she would rather pay *me* a dollar a week than have me go away. Ablaze with economic passion I cried "Done!"— trying to make it appear that she had made me a formal offer to that effect. But she then wouldn't admit it, and after much recrimination we separated, it being agreed that I should come for 4.50, *but tell no one.* So mind *you* don't either. I now lay my hand on my heart and confidently look to my Mother for that glance of approbation which she *must* bestow. Have I not redeemed any weaknesses of the past? Though part of my conception fails, yet it was boldly planned and would have been a noble stroke.

I have been pretty busy this week. I have a filial feeling toward Wyman already. I work in a vast museum at a table all alone, surrounded by skeletons of mastodons, crocodiles and the like, with the walls hung about with monsters and horrors enough to freeze the blood. But I have no fear, as most of them are tightly bottled up. Occasionally solemn men and women come in to see the museum, and sometimes timid little girls (reminding me of thee, my love, only they are less fashionably dressed), who whisper "Is folks allowed here?" It pains me to remark, however, that not all the little girls are of this pleasing type, many being bold-faced jades. Salter is back here, but morose. One or two new students and Prof. Goodwin, who is very agreeable.[261] Also William Everett, son of the great Edward, very intelligent and a capital scholar, studying law. He took honours at the English Cambridge.[262] I send a photograph of General Sickles for your

260. A summer resort with clapboard houses overlooking Nahant Bay in Essex County, Massachusetts, Swampscott is described by HJ below as a "then rural retreat . . . forty minutes by train northward from Boston" (341).

261. Charles Christie Salter (1839–70) graduated at Harvard in 1861 and was a divinity student in 1863–64. William Watson Goodwin (1831–1912) was a professor of Greek at Harvard (*CWJ*, 4:617, 85 n. 5).

262. William Everett (1839–1910) graduated in 1859 and studied at Harvard Law School in 1863–65; as well as teaching, he ran for the governorship of Massachusetts. His father, Edward Everett (1794–1865), was a statesman and Unitarian clergyman (*CWJ*, 4:85 n. 6).

and Wilky's amusement. It is a part of a great anthropomorphological collection which I am going to make. So take care of it, as well as of all the photographs you will find in the table-drawer in my room. But isn't he a bully boy? Desecrate the room as little as possible. If Wilky wants me as an extra nurse send for me without hesitation.[263]

VI These returns to that first year or two at Newport contribute meanwhile to filling out as nothing in the present pages has yet done for me that vision of our father's unsurpassable patience and independence, in the interest of the convictions he cherished and the expression of them, as richly emphatic as it was scantly heeded, to which he daily gave himself. We took his "writing" infinitely for granted—we had always so taken it, and the sense of him, each long morning, at his study table either with bent considering brow or with a half-spent and checked intensity, a lapse backward in his chair and a musing lift of perhaps troubled and baffled eyes, seems to me the most constant fact, the most closely interwoven and underlying, among all our breaks and variations.[264] He applied himself there with a regularity and a piety as little subject to sighing abatements or betrayed fears as if he had been working under pressure for his bread and ours and the question were too urgent for his daring to doubt. This play of his remarkable genius brought him in fact throughout the long years no ghost of a reward in the form of pence, and could proceed to publicity, as it repeatedly did, not

263. Daniel Edgar Sickles (1819–1914) was a New York congressman who became a Civil War general; a colorful figure, he notoriously shot his wife's lover and escaped jail on the grounds of temporary insanity. He also proved to be an impetuous military leader. Having lost a leg at Gettysburg, he used, after the war, to take visitors to view the bones, which he had donated to the medical museum in Washington (Gary W. Gallagher et al., *The American Civil War: This Mighty Scourge of War* [Oxford: Osprey Publishing, 2003], 176–77). Wilky, having enlisted, went on to serve as an officer with the 54th Massachusetts, the African-American regiment led by Robert Gould Shaw. He was badly wounded in the disastrous attack on Fort Wagner in South Carolina on 18 July 1863 and was still recovering at home in Newport in September. The episode is narrated in chap. 9 below.

264. HJ Sr. published his own works, including *What Constitutes the State* (1846), *Letter to a Swedenborgian* (1847), *Moralism and Christianity* (1850), *Lectures and Miscellanies* (1852), *The Church of Christ not an Ecclesiasticism* (1854), *The Nature of Evil* (1855), *Christianity the Logic of Creation* (1857), *The Social Significance of our Institutions* (1861), *Substance and Shadow* (1866), *The Secret of Swedenborg* (1869), *Society the Redeemed Form of Man* (1879).

only by the copious and resigned sacrifice of such calculations, but by his meeting in every single case all the expenses of the process. The untired impulse to this devotion figured for us, comprehensively and familiarly, as "Father's Ideas," of the force and truth of which in his own view we were always so respectfully, even though at times so bewilderedly and confoundedly persuaded, that we felt there was nothing in his exhibition of life that they didn't or couldn't account for. They pervaded and supported his existence, and very considerably our own; but what comes back to me, to the production of a tenderness and an admiration scarce to be expressed, is the fact that though we thus easily and naturally lived with them and indeed, as to their more general effects, the colour and savour they gave to his talk, breathed them in and enjoyed both their quickening and their embarrassing presence, to say nothing of their almost never less than amusing, we were left as free and unattacked by them as if they had been so many droppings of gold and silver coin on tables and chimney-pieces, to be "taken" or not according to our sense and delicacy, that is our felt need and felt honour. The combination in him of his different vivacities, his living interest in his philosophy, his living interest in us and his living superiority to all greed of authority, all overreaching or ever-emphasising "success," at least in the heated short run, gave his character a magnanimity by which it was impossible to us not to profit in all sorts of responsive and in fact quite luxurious ways. It was a luxury, I to-day see, to have all the benefit of his intellectual and spiritual, his religious, his philosophic and his social passion, without ever feeling the pressure of it to our direct irritation or discomfort. It would perhaps more truly figure the relation in which he left us to these things to have likened our opportunities rather to so many scattered glasses of the liquor of faith, poured-out cups stood about for our either sipping or draining down or leaving alone, in the measure of our thirst, our curiosity or our strength of head and heart. If there was much leaving alone in us—and I freely confess that, so far as the taking any of it all "straight" went, my lips rarely adventured—this was doubtless because we drank so largely at the source itself, the personally overflowing and irrigating. What it then comes to, for my present vision, was that he treated us most of all on the whole, as he in fact treated everything, by his saving imagination—which set us, and the more as we were naturally so inclined, the example of living as much as we might in some such light of our own. If we had been asked in our younger time for instance what *were* our father's ideas, or to give an example of one of them, I think we should promptly have answered (I should myself have hastened to do so) that the principal was a devoted attachment to the writings of Swedenborg; as to whom we were to remember betimes, with intimate appreciation, that in reply to somebody's plea of not finding him credible our parent had pronounced him, on the contrary, fairly "insipid with veracity." We liked that partly, I think, because it disposed in a manner, that is in favour of our detachment, of the great Emanuel, but when I remember the part played, so close beside us, by this latter's copious revelation, I feel almost ashamed for my own incurious conduct.[265] The part played consisted to a large extent in the vast, even though incomplete, array of Swedenborg's works, the old faded covers of which, anciently red, actually apt to be loose, and backed with labels of impressive, though to my sense somewhat sinister London imprint, Arcana Coelestia, Heaven and Hell and other such matters[266]—they all had, as from other days, a sort of black emphasis of dignity—ranged themselves before us wherever, and however briefly, we disposed ourselves, forming even for short journeys the base of our father's travelling library and perhaps at some seasons therewith the accepted strain on our mother's patience. I recall them as inveterately part of our very luggage, requiring proportionate receptacles; I recall them as, in a number considerable even when reduced, part of their proprietor's own most particular dependence on his leaving home, during our more agitated years, for those speculative visits to possible better places (than whatever place of

265. Given that, as he himself recognized, HJ Sr.'s ideas never gained great currency, the range and development of his writing is remarkable. Having escaped the repressions of a severely Calvinistic background embodied in the figure of his father, HJ Sr. embraced a liberal perspective in his considerations of human behavior and motive, valuing spontaneity and believing that mankind's duties were to nature, society, and, finally, God. In his theological writing evil came to be regarded and accepted as an excessive attachment to self. After a mental and spiritual collapse in 1844, which he called a "vastation," a term derived from Emanuel Swedenborg (1688–1772), HJ Sr. permanently embraced the ideas of the Swedish mystic, scientist, and philosopher, who charted his visionary experiences of heaven and hell to reach an understanding of humanity's relationship with God. In a series of revelatory visions Swedenborg "had seen that the material world of the ordinary senses was only a segment of a larger, spiritual reality. Inert and senseless matter was like a line that transected an angle, or an angle that cut a shape from a larger sphere. The world of spirit was not in some distant, future life, after death or in heaven; it was present like a higher dimension of the ordinary world, giving it life and movement" (Novick, Young Master, 13). See also Austin Warren, The Elder Henry James (New York: Macmillan, 1934), 70–72.

266. Arcana Coelestia, or Heavenly Secrets (8 vols., 1749–56), discusses the spiritual meanings of the Old Testament books of Genesis and Exodus. Heaven and Hell (1758) considers the afterlife, its locations and varied inhabitants.

the moment) from which, as I have elsewhere mentioned, he was apt to return under premature, under passionate nostalgic, reaction.[267] The Swedenborgs were promptly out again on their customary shelves or sometimes more improvised perches, and it was somehow not till we had assured ourselves of this that we felt *that* incident closed.

Nothing could have exceeded at the same time our general sense— unless I all discreetly again confine myself to the spare record of my own— for our good fortune in never having been, even when most helpless, dragged by any approach to a faint jerk over the threshold of the inhabited temple. It stood there in the centre of our family life, into which its doors of fine austere bronze opened straight; we passed and repassed them when we didn't more consciously go round and behind; we took for granted vague grand things within, but we never paused to peer or pene- trate, and none the less never had the so natural and wistful, perhaps even the so properly resentful, "Oh I say, do look in a moment for manners if for nothing else!" called after us as we went. Our admirable mother sat on the steps at least and caught reverberations of the inward mystic choir; but there were positive contemporary moments when I well-nigh became aware, I think, of something graceless, something not to the credit of my aspiring "intellectual life," or of whatever small pretensions to seriousness I might have begun to nourish, in the anything but heroic impunity of my inattention. William, later on, made up for this not a little, redeeming so, to a large extent, as he grew older, our filial honour in the matter of a decent sympathy, if not of a noble curiosity: distinct to me even are certain echoes of passages between our father and his eldest son that I assisted at, more or less indirectly and wonderingly, as at intellectual "scenes," gather- ing from them portents of my brother's independent range of speculation, agitations of thought and announcements of difference, which could but have represented, far beyond anything I should ever have to show, a gained and to a considerable degree an enjoyed, confessedly an interested, acquaintance with the paternal philosophic *penetralia*.[268] That particular

267. Alice James recalled in later years HJ Sr.'s "demon homesickness," his "sudden returns at the end of 36 hours, having left to be gone a fortnight, with Mother beside him holding his hand and we five children pressing close around him 'as if he had just been saved from drowning,' and he pouring out, as he alone could, the agonies of desolation thro' which he had come" (*Diary,* 57–58).

268. The inner room (Lat.). WJ was rightly aware of his own intellectual indebtedness to HJ Sr.'s ideas. His long introduction to his father's *Literary Remains* (which includes the unfinished *Spiritual Creation* as well as *Autobiography* and *Recollections of Carlyle*)

impression refers indeed to hours which at the point I have reached had not yet struck; but I am touched even now, after all the years, with something exquisite in my half-grasped premonitory vision of their belonging, these belated discussions that were but the flowering of the first germs of such *other,* doubtless already such opposed, perceptions and conclusions, to that order of thin consolations and broken rewards which long figured as the most and the best of what was to have been waited for on our companion's part without the escape of a plaint. Yet I feel I may claim that our awareness of all that was so serenely dispensed with—to call it missed would have been quite to falsify the story and reflect meanly on the spirit—never in the least brutally lapsed from admiration, however unuttered the sentiment itself, after the fashion of raw youth; it is in fact quite distinct to me that, had there been danger of this, there came to us from our mother's lips at intervals long enough to emphasise the final sincerity and beauty a fairly sacred reminder of that strain of almost solely self-nourished equanimity, or in other words insuperable gaiety, in her life's comrade, which she had never seen give way. This was the very gaiety that kept through the years coming out for us—to the point of inviting free jokes and other light familiarities from us at its expense. The happiest household pleasantry invested our legend of our mother's fond habit of address, "Your father's *ideas,* you know—!" which was always the signal for our embracing her with the last responsive finality (and, for the full pleasure of it, in his presence).[269] Nothing indeed so much as his presence encouraged the licence, as I may truly call it, of the legend—that is of our treatment *en famille*[270] of any reference to the attested public weight of his labours; which, I hasten to add, was much too esoteric a ground of

---

offers a lucid and sympathetic exposition of the older man's thinking, encapsulated in the recurrent theme of the nature of the relationship between humanity and its creator. Matthiessen has suggested that WJ may have derived from his father the saintly qualities described in *The Varieties of Religious Experience,* the "immense elation of freedom, as the outlines of the confining selfhood melt down" (*The James Family,* 11). Habegger goes further, regarding the same work as a remorseful WJ's "ambitious and quasi-scientific interpretation of his father's message to the world" (*The Father,* 161).

269. These lines and a further recollection later in the chapter are among the few references to Mary Walsh James in the autobiography; the context is predictably domestic and her role acquiescent and enabling. "When one of his nephews expressed regret at the omission of a longer characterization, HJ responded: 'Oh! my dear Boy—that memory is too sacred!' " (Matthiessen, *The James Family,* 127).

270. Within the family.

geniality, a dear old family joke, not to be kept, for its value, to ourselves. But there comes back to me the impression of his appearing on occasion quite moved to the exuberance of cheer—as a form of refreshment he could draw on for a stronger and brighter spurt, I mean—by such an apology for resonance of reputation as our harmless, our of course utterly edgeless, profanity represented. It might have been for him, by a happy stretch, a sign that the world *did* know—taking us for the moment, in our selfish young babble, as a part of the noise of the world. Nothing, at the same time, could alter the truth of his case, or can at least alter it to me now: he had, intellectually, convictionally, passionally speaking, a selfless detachment, a lack of what is called the eye for effect—always I mean of the elated and interested order—which I can but marvel at in the light of the rare aptitude of his means to his end, and in that of the beauty of both, though the stamp was doubtless most vivid, for so differing, so gropingly "esthetic" a mind as my own, in his unfailingly personal and admirable style.[271] We knew he had thoroughly his own "unconventional" form, which, by the unspeakable law of youth, we managed to feel the distinction of as not platitudinous even while we a bit sneakingly felt it as quotable, on possible occasions, against our presence of mind; the great thing was at all events that we couldn't live with him without the sense that if his books resembled his talk and his character—as we moreover felt they couldn't help almost violently doing—they might want for this, that or the other which kept the conventional true to its type, but could as little fail to flush with the strong colour, colour so remarkably given and not taken, projected and not reflected, colour of thought and faith and moral and expressional atmosphere, as they could leave us without that felt side-wind of their strong composition which made after all so much of the air we breathed and was in the last resort the gage of something perpetually fine going on.

It is not too much to say, I think, that our religious education, so far as we had any, consisted wholly in that loose yet enlightening impression: I say so far as we had any in spite of my very definitely holding that it would absolutely not have been possible to us, in the measure of our sensibility,

271. "No less exacting a critic than E.L. Godkin, the founder of the *Nation,* though baffled as to the precise nature of James's philosophy, declared: 'He was a writer of extraordinary vigor and picturesqueness, and I suppose there was not in his day a more formidable master of English style.' . . . His style became 'vascular,' as William James said, racily colloquial, satiric, stinging, and tender, in robust and ardent sequence" (Matthiessen, *The James Family,* 14).

to breathe more the air of that reference to an order of goodness and power greater than any this world by itself can show which we understand as the religious spirit. Wondrous to me, as I consider again, that my father's possession of this spirit, in a degree that made it more deeply one with his life than I can conceive another or a different case of its being, should have been unaccompanied with a single one of the outward or formal, the theological, devotional, ritual, or even implicitly pietistic signs by which we usually know it. The fact of course was that his religion was nothing if not a philosophy, extraordinarily complex and worked out and original, intensely personal as an exposition, yet not only susceptible of application, but clamorous for it, to the whole field of consciousness, nature and society, history, knowledge, all human relations and questions, every pulse of the process of our destiny. Of this vast and interesting conception, as striking an expression of the religious spirit surely as ever was put forth, his eldest son has given an account* [272]—so far as this was possible at once with brevity and with full comprehension—that I should have been unable even to dream of aspiring to, and in the masterly clearness and justice of which the opportunity of the son blends with that of the critic, each character acting in perfect felicity, after a fashion of which I know elsewhere no such fine example.[273] It conveys the whole sense of our father's philosophic passion, which was theologic, by my direct impression of it, to a degree fairly outdistancing all theologies; representing its weight, reproducing its utterance, placing it in the eye of the world, and making for it the strong and single claim it suggests, in a manner that

---

*Literary Remains of Henry James, Boston, 1885. The portrait accompanying the volume gave us, alas, but the scantest satisfaction.

272. The frontispiece portrait alluded to in HJ's footnote was engraved by H. B. McLellan of 7 Pemberton Square, Boston. It shows HJ Sr. in comparatively old age with a long white beard, similar in pose and age to the portrait by Frank Duveneck; there is no indication whether the engraving was based on a painting or a photograph.

273. Compare HJ's letter to his brother, 2 January 1885: "I can't enter into it (much) myself—I can't be so theological nor grant his extraordinary premises, nor through [throw] myself into conceptions of heavens and hells, nor be sure that the keynote of nature is humanity etc. But I can enjoy greatly the spirit, the feeling and the manner of the whole thing (full as this last is of things that *dis*please me too,) and feel really that poor Father, struggling so alone all his life, and so destitute of every worldly or literary ambition, was yet a great writer" (*HJL*, 3:62; Edel's square brackets). Later in this chapter HJ goes on to recall his youthful misgivings (which were not modified in later life) concerning the nature of his father's style, its essentially indeterminate generic status—philosophical yet living, literary yet overly functional.

leaves nothing to be added to the subject. I am not concerned with the intrinsic meaning of these things here, and should not be even had they touched me more directly, or more converted me from what I can best call, to my doubtless scant honour, a total otherness of contemplation, during the years when my privilege was greatest and my situation for inquiry and response amplest;[274] but the active, not to say the obvious, moral of them, in all our younger time, was that a life of the most richly consequent flowed straight out of them, that in this life, the most abundantly, and above all naturally, communicated *as* life that it was possible to imagine, we had an absolutely equal share, and that in fine I was to live to go back with wonder and admiration to the quantity of secreted thought in our daily medium, the quality of intellectual passion, the force of cogitation and aspiration, as to the explanation both of a thousand surface incoherences and a thousand felt felicities. A religion that was so systematically a philosophy, a philosophy that was so sweepingly a religion, being together, by their necessity, as I have said, an intensity of relation to the actual, the consciousness so determined was furnished forth in a way that met by itself the whole question of the attitude of "worship" for instance; as I have attempted a little to show that it met, with a beautiful good faith and the easiest sufficiency, every other when such came up: those of education, acquisition, material vindication, what is called success generally. In the beauty of the whole thing, again, I lose myself—by which I mean in the fact that we were all the while partaking, to our most intimate benefit, of an influence of direction and enlargement attended with scarce a single consecrated form and which would have made many of these, had we been exposed to intrusion from them, absurdly irrelevant. My father liked in our quite younger period to read us chapters from the New Testament and the Old, and I hope we liked to listen to them—though I recall their seeming dreary from their association with school practice; but that was the sole approach to a challenge of our complete freedom of inward, not less than our natural ingenuity of outward, experience. No

274. Compare Matthiessen: "When their father was about to publish *Substance and Shadow* . . . WJ amused them all, as T.S. Perry remembered, 'by designing a small cut to be put on the title-page, representing a man beating a dead horse.' Sometimes such freedom struck outsiders as a constraint upon Henry Senior. As Howells remarked, after an evening at the house: 'Now and then he'd break out and say something that each of the others had to modify and explain away, and then he'd be clapped back into durance again.' But Henry Senior no doubt took all such sallies in the spirit of high comedy in which they were meant" (*The James Family*, 136).

other explicit address to us in the name of the Divine could, I see, have been made with any congruity—in face of the fact that invitations issued in all the vividest social terms, terms of living appreciation, of spiritual perception, of "human fellowship," to use the expression that was perhaps oftenest on his lips and his pen alike, were the very substance of the food supplied in the parental nest.

The freedom from pressure that we enjoyed in every direction, all those immunities and exemptions that had been, in protracted childhood, positively embarrassing to us, as I have already noted, before the framework, ecclesiastical and mercantile, squared at us as with reprobation from other households, where it seemed so to conduce to their range of resource[275]— these things consorted with our yet being yearned over or prescribed for, by every implication, after a fashion that was to make the social organisation of such invidious homes, under my subsequent observation of life, affect me as so much bleak penury or domestic desert where these things of the spirit, these genialities of faith were concerned. Well do I remember, none the less, how I was troubled all along just by this particular crookedness of our being so extremely religious without having, as it were, anything in the least classified or striking to show for it; so that the measure of other-worldliness pervading our premises was rather a waste, though at the same time oddly enough a congestion—projecting outwardly as it did no single one of those usual symptoms of propriety any of which, gathered at a venture from the general prospect, might by my sense have served: I shouldn't have been particular, I thought, as to the selection. Religion was a matter, by this imagination, to be worked off much more than to be worked in, and I fear my real vague sentiment to have been but that life would under the common equipment be somehow more amusing; and this even though, as I don't forget, there was not an item of the detail of devotional practice that we had been so much as allowed to divine. I scarce know why I should have wanted anything more amusing, as most of our coevals would have regarded it, than that we had from as far back as I could remember indulged in no shade of an approach to "keeping Sunday"; which is one of the reasons why to speak as if piety could have borne for us any sense but the tender human, or to speak at all of devotion, unction, initiation, even of the vaguest, into the exercises or professions,

275. See, e.g., *SBO*, p. 49, where HJ recollects (with a degree of inverted snobbery) the embarrassment of the family's being "a lamentable case," ignorant of "the actualities of business."

as among our attributes, would falsify altogether our mere fortune of a general liberty of living, of making ourselves as brightly at home as might be, in that "spiritual world" which we were in the habit of hearing as freely alluded to as we heard the prospect of dinner or the call of the postman.[276] The oddity of my own case, as I make it out so far as it involved a confused criticism, was that my small uneasy mind, bulging and tightening in the wrong, or at least in unnatural and unexpected, places, like a little jacket ill cut or ill sewn, attached its gaping view, as I have already more than enough noted, to things and persons, objects and aspects, frivolities all, I dare say I was willing to grant, compared with whatever manifestations of the serious, these being by need, apparently, the abstract; and that in fine I should have been thankful for a state of faith, a conviction of the Divine, an interpretation of the universe—anything one might have made bold to call it—which would have supplied more features or appearances. Feeling myself "after" persons so much more than after anything else—to recur to that side of my earliest and most constant consciousness which might have been judged most deplorable—I take it that I found the sphere of our more nobly supposititious habitation too imperceptibly peopled; whereas the religious life of every other family that could boast of any such (and what family didn't boast?) affected my fancy as with a social and material crowdedness. That faculty alone was affected—this I hasten to add; no directness of experience ever stirred for me; it being the case in the first place that I scarce remember, as to all our young time, the crossing of our threshold by any faint shade of an ecclesiastical presence, or the lightest encounter with any such elsewhere, and equally of the essence, over and above, that the clerical race, the pre-eminently restrictive tribe, as I apprehended them, couldn't very well have agreed less with the general colour of my fondest vision: if it be not indeed more correct to say that I was reduced to *supposing* they couldn't. We knew in truth nothing whatever about them, a fact that, as I recover it, also flushes for me with its fine awkwardness—the social scene in general handsomely bristling with them to the rueful view I sketch, and they yet remaining for us, or at any rate for myself, such creatures of pure hearsay that when late in my teens, and in

276. Before marrying, Mary Walsh James had been a devout member of the Murray Street Presbyterian Church in New York City. Her marriage was a civil ceremony, however, doubtless on HJ Sr.'s recommendation. "The church, James was beginning to believe and to argue, was much rather an *inward* reality; in his later phrasing, 'the actual life of God himself in human nature,' a divine life-in-man which was not other than the spiritual and social welfare of mankind on earth" (Lewis, *The Jameses*, 42).

particular after my twentieth year, I began to see them portrayed by George Eliot and Anthony Trollope the effect was a disclosure of a new and romantic species.[277] Strange beyond my present power to account for it this anomaly that amid a civilisation replete with "ministers"—for we at least knew the word—actively, competitively, indeed as would often appear quite violently, ministering, so little sense of a brush against approved examples was ever to attend me that I had finally to draw my nearest sufficiency of a true image from pictures of a social order largely alien to our own. All of which, at the same time, I allow myself to add, didn't mitigate the simple fact of my felt—my indeed so luxuriously permitted—detachment of sensibility from everything, everything, that is, in the way of great relations, as to which our father's emphasis was richest. *There* was the dim dissociation, there my comparative poverty, or call it even frivolity, of instinct: I gaped imaginatively, as it were, to such a different set of relations. I couldn't have framed stories that would have succeeded in involving the least of the relations that seemed most present to *him;* while those most present to myself, that is more complementary to whatever it was I thought of as humanly most interesting, attaching, inviting, were the ones his schemes of importances seemed virtually to do without. Didn't I discern in this from the first a kind of implied snub to the significance of mine?—so that, in the blest absence of "pressure" which I just sought here passingly to celebrate, I could brood to my heart's content on the so conceivable alternative of a field of exposure crammed with those objective appearances that my faculty seemed alone fitted to grasp.[278] In which there was ever the small torment of the fact—though I don't quite see to-

277. Eliot's "The Sad Fortunes of the Reverend Amos Barton" was the first of her *Scenes from Clerical Life,* which came out in 1858. There are further insights into clerical life (and religious dissent) in *Adam Bede* (1859), *The Mill on the Floss* (1860), and *Silas Marner* (1861). Anthony Trollope's sequence of Barsetshire novels, peopled with a range of provincial cathedral churchmen and their families, began with *The Warden* (1855) and *Barchester Towers* (1857). One of HJ's early reviews was of Eliot's *Felix Holt, the Radical* (1866) and he went on to write a number of other essays on her work. He also reviewed four of Trollope's novels in the 1860s and wrote a more extended essay on the novelist after his death in 1883 which was reprinted in *Partial Portraits* (1888; all in *LC* 1, 1312–54).

278. This divergence of interest and sympathy between the two men—HJ's stated antipathy for the abstract and his intuitive and inexhaustible insight into the more tangible arena of human values and motives—may help explain his father's evidently dismissive estimation of his potential as a boy. At a simple level, HJ Sr.'s conception of the human experience seems to have relegated the temporal and mankind's place in society to an allegorical medium, most readily interpreted in light of the eternal and divine.

day why it should not have been of a purely pleasant irritation—that what our parent most overflowed with was just the brave contradiction or opposition between all his parts, a thing which made for perfect variety, which he carried ever so easily and brightly, and which would have put one no less in the wrong had one accused him of knowing only the abstract (as I was so complacently and invidiously disposed to name it) than if one had foolishly remarked on his living and concluding without it. But I have already made clear his great mixed range—which of course couldn't *not* have been the sign of a mind conceiving our very own breathing humanity in its every fibre the absolute expression of a resident Divinity. No element of character, no spontaneity of life, but instantly seized his attention and incurred his greeting and his comment; which things could never possibly have been so genially alert and expert—as I have, again, before this, superabundantly recorded—if it had not fairly fed on active observation and contact. He could answer one with the radiant when one challenged him with the obscure, just as he could respond with the general when one pulled at the particular; and I needn't repeat that this made for us, during all our time, anything but a starved actuality.

None the less, however, I remember it as savouring of loss to me—which is my present point—that our so thoroughly informal scene of susceptibility seemed to result from a positive excess of familiarity, in his earlier past, with such types of the shepherd and the flock, to say nothing of such forms of the pasture, as might have met in some degree my appetite for the illustrational. This was one of the things that made me often wish, as I remember, that I might have caught him sooner or younger, less developed, as who should say; the matters that appeared, however confusedly, to have started his development being by this measure stranger and livelier than most of those that finally crowned it, marked with their own colour as many of these doubtless were. Three or four strongest pages in the fragment of autobiography gathered by his eldest son into the sheaf of his Literary Remains describe the state of soul undergone by him in England, in '44, just previous to the hour at which Mrs. Chichester, a gentle lady of his acquaintance there, brought to his knowledge, by a wondrous chance, the possibility that the great Swedenborg, from whom she had drawn much light, might have something to say to his case;[279] so

279. This is HJ's low-key reference to the serious breakdown, mental and spiritual, suffered by his father in 1844 when he visited Europe with his young family. His first trip in 1837 had been disappointing, but on this occasion, carrying letters of introduction from

that under the impression of his talk with her he posted at once up to London from the neighbourhood of Windsor, where he was staying, possessed himself of certain volumes of the writings of the eminent mystic (so-called I mean, for to my father this description of him was grotesque), and passed rapidly into that grateful infinitude of recognition and application which he was to inhabit for the rest of his days. I saw him move about there after the fashion of the oldest and easiest native, and this had on some sides its own considerable effect, tinged even on occasion with romance; yet I felt how the *real* right thing for me would have been the hurrying drama of the original rush, the interview with the admirable Mrs.

---

Emerson to John Sterling and Thomas Carlyle, HJ Sr. met some of the foremost thinkers and writers of the time, including John Stuart Mill, Tennyson, and George Henry Lewes. His account of his sudden crisis—or *"vastation"*—his severe psychological depression, and the remedy he found in the writings of Swedenborg is to be found in *Society the Redeemed Form of Man and the Earnest of God's Omnipotence in Human Nature Affirmed in Letters to a Friend* (Boston: Osgood, 1879), a series of twenty-eight letters. HJ Sr.'s recollections of the decisive spring of 1844, "that memorable chilly afternoon in Windsor" when his "faith in selfhood" "had inwardly shrivelled to a cinder" (74), are contained in letters 5 and 6. Feinstein comments that his "description invites belief, but the text owes more to John Bunyan's seventeenth-century *Pilgrim's Progress* and Holy Scripture than it does to material fact." The record of the event was published thirty-five years later: "By then the experience had been refracted by evangelical imagery . . . the tale was intended to illustrate a well-developed theological position. . . . James's story is Bunyan in microcosm" (*Becoming William James,* 68–69). In his introduction to *The Literary Remains of Henry James* (Boston: Osgood, 1885), 58–71, WJ quotes the whole of letter 5 and the first paragraph of letter 6, and HJ is referring to this long introductory essay. In the first volume of his James biography, *The Young Master,* Novick seems to confuse the content of the autobiographical fragment (a fictionalized account, as told by Stephen Dewhurst) with the spiritual explorations of *Society the Redeemed Form of Man* (published under the author's name). Thus the statement that "a famous story of HJ Sr.'s conversion to Swedenborgianism is told in a fictionalized, autobiographical fragment" and the resulting contention that "there is no independent evidence that the story of the conversion experience is anything other than fiction" (*Young Master,* 455 n. 24) are both inaccurate: the narrative of HJ Sr.'s conversion to Swedenborg was published under his own name in 1879, three years before his death. Sophia Chichester helped fund an experimental school at Ham Common, near Petersham, in southwest London, where HJ Sr. had sought a water-cure treatment. He discussed his ailment with her: "Finding it was an overtasked brain, and overtasked too in the pursuit of the highest questions, she said you need Swedenborg, he is your physician, so not a word more till you go up to London, and bring him down in the shape of one or more of his ponderous books" (quoted in Habegger, *The Father,* 227). See also Jacqueline E. M. Latham, "Henry James Senior's Mrs. Chichester," *Henry James Review* 14 (Spring 1993): 132–40.

Chichester, the sweet legend of his and my mother's charmed impression of whom had lingered with us—I admired her very name, there seeming none other among us at all like it; and then the return with the tokens of light, the splendid agitation as the light deepened, and the laying in of that majestic array of volumes which were to form afterward the purplest rim of his library's horizon and which I was thus capable, for my poor part, of finding valuable, in default of other values, as coloured properties in a fine fifth act.[280] It was all a play I hadn't "been to," consciously at least—that was the trouble; the curtain had fallen while I was still tucked in my crib, and I assisted but on a comparatively flat home scene at the echo of a great success. I could still have done, for the worst, with a consciousness of Swedenborg that should have been graced at least with Swedenborgians—aware as I was of the existence of such enrolled disciples, ornaments of a church of their own, yet known to us only as persons rather acidly mystified by the inconvenience, as we even fancied them to feel it, of our father's frankly independent and disturbingly irregular (all the more for its being so expressive) connection with their inspirer. In the light or the dusk of all this it was surely impossible to make out that he professed any faint shade of that clerical character as to his having incurred which we were, "in the world," to our bewilderment, not infrequently questioned. Those of the enrolled order, in the matter of his and their subject of study, might in their way too have raised to my regard a fretted vault or opened a long-drawn aisle, but they were never at all, in the language of a later day, to materialise to me; we neither on a single occasion sat in their circle, nor did one of them, to the best of my belief, ever stray, remonstrantly or invitingly, into ours; where Swedenborg was read not in the least as the Bible scarce more than just escaped being, but even as Shakespeare or Dickens or Macaulay was content to be—which was without our arranging or subscribing for it.[281] I seem to distinguish that if a fugitive or a shy

280. This might serve as an illustration of the distinction between HJ and his father, the novelist drawn by the human or moral interaction rather than by the spiritual significance of Swedenborg's ideas, which served to redeem HJ Sr. "The real right thing" and "The real thing" are, incidentally, the titles of short stories by HJ.

281. Among those influenced by Swedenborg's ideas were the British poet, artist, and mystic William Blake (1757–1827), and Ralph Waldo Emerson, whom HJ Sr. met in 1842. HJ mentions no names of those who conferred with his father, but Habegger points out that "most of Swedenborg's followers in the 1830s and 1840s were well-educated Protestants who were engaged in slipping their orthodox tethers. . . . There was a very long shelf of texts to master, and they required a high degree of cultivated application"

straggler from the pitched camp did turn up it was under cover of night or of curiosity and with much panting and putting off of the mantle, much nervous laughter above all—this safe, however, to become on the shortest order amusement easy and intimate. That *figured* something in a slight way—as at least I suppose I may infer from the faint adumbration I retain; but nothing none the less much attenuated what I suppose I should have denounced as the falsity of our position (meaning thereby of mine) had I been constitutionally at all voluble for such flights. Constructionally we had all the fun of licence, while the truth seemed really to be that fun in the religious connection closely depended on bondage. The fun was of course that I wanted in this line of diversion something of the coarser strain; which came home to me in especial, to cut the matter short, when I was present, as I yielded first and last to many an occasion for being, at my father's reading out to my mother with an appreciation of that modest grasp of somebody's attention, the brief illusion of publicity, which has now for me the exquisite grace of the touching, some series of pages from among his "papers" that were to show her how he had this time at last done it. No touch of the beautiful or the sacred in the disinterested life can have been absent from such scenes—I find every such ideally there; and my memory rejoices above all in their presentation of our mother at her very perfectest of soundless and yet absolutely all-saving service and trust. To have attempted any projection of our father's aspect without an immediate reference to her sovereign care for him and for all of us as the so widely open, yet so softly enclosing, lap of all his liberties and all our securities, all our variety and withal our harmony, the harmony that was for nine-tenths of it our sense of her gathered life in us, and of her having no other—to have so proceeded has been but to defer by instinct and by scruple to the kind of truth and of beauty before which the direct report breaks down. I may well have stopped short with what there would be to say, and yet what account of us all can pretend to have gone the least bit deep without coming to our mother at every penetration? We simply lived by her, in proportion as we lived spontaneously, with an equanimity of confidence, an independence of something that I should now find myself think of as decent compunction if I didn't try to call it instead morbid

(*The Father*, 229-30). As HJ recalls in *SBO*, he was exposed to the work of Shakespeare and Dickens from his earliest years; the historical writings and poetry of Lord Macaulay (1800-1859)—particularly the *Lays of Ancient Rome*—were also popular in the nineteenth-century schoolroom.

delicacy, which left us free for detachments of thought and flights of mind, experiments, so to speak, on the assumption of our genius and our intrinsic interest, that I look back upon as to a luxury of the unworried that is scarce of this world. This was a support on which my father rested with the absolute whole of his weight, and it was when I felt her listen with the whole of her usefulness, which needed no other force, being as it was the whole of her tenderness and amply sufficing by itself, that I understood most what it was so to rest and so to act. When in the fulness of the years she was to die, and he then to give us time, a few months, as with a beatific depth of design, to marvel at the manner of his acceptance of the stroke, a shown triumph of his philosophy, he simply one day consciously ceased, quietly declined to continue, as an offered measure of his loss of interest. Nothing—he had enabled himself to make perfectly sure—was in the least worth while without her; this attested, he passed away or went out, with entire simplicity, promptness and ease, for the definite reason that his support had failed.[282] His philosophy had been not his support but his suspension, and he had never, I am sure, felt so lifted as at that hour, which splendidly crowned his faith. It showed us more intimately still what, in this world of cleft components, one human being can yet be for another, and how a form of vital aid may have operated for years with such perfection as fairly to have made recognition seem at the time a sort of

282. Mary Walsh James died on 29 January 1882; Henry James Sr., having refused most food for two and a half weeks, died on 18 December 1882. Biographers have contrasted such eulogistic accounts of Mary James (dominant too in contemporary letters) with other facts, her impact on members of the family, and the less direct evidence of the imagination as represented in HJ's fiction. Lewis points out that "what she was, in fact, as Edel sees her, was a woman who was in no small degree responsible for the strains and contradictions— in some filial cases (the younger brothers and Alice) destructive ones—that darkened the family life. The main evidence for this view is the series of mothers in Henry James's fiction: 'strong, determined, demanding, grasping women' like Mrs. Touchett, or Mrs. Gereth in *The Spoils of Poynton*, or Mrs. Newsome in *The Ambassadors*. It is in these portraits that Henry's true feelings about his mother get expressed" (*The Jameses*, 337). Lewis offers some caveats, however, listing, in contrast, a number of fictional and equally dubious father figures, and indeed it is probably impossible to reconcile the contradictions between these differing versions of Mary Walsh James. Even here, though, HJ goes on to raise his mother's intense involvement with the workings of her family, a kind of selfless possessiveness that might be problematic. Habegger, referring to some of HJ Sr.'s correspondence, concludes that he found his wife "narrow, technical, and anxious. Henry got a great deal from his marriage, but one thing he clearly missed was equal companionship" (*The Father*, 290). Certainly, her surviving letters seldom stray from the conventional.

excess of reaction, an interference or a pedantry.[283] All which is imaged for me while I see our mother listen, at her work, to the full music of the "papers." She could do that by the mere force of her complete availability, and could do it with a smoothness of surrender that was like an array of all the perceptions. The only thing that I might well have questioned on these occasions was the possibility on the part of a selflessness so consistently and unabatedly active of its having anything ever left *acutely* to offer; to abide so unbrokenly in such inaptness for the personal claim might have seemed to render difficult such a special show of it as any particular pointedness of hospitality would propose to represent. I dare say it was our sense of this that so often made us all, when the explicit or the categoric, the impulse of acclamation, flowered out in her, find our happiest play of filial humour in just embracing her for the sound of it; than which I can imagine no more expressive tribute to our constant depths of indebtedness. She lived in ourselves so exclusively, with such a want of use for anything in her consciousness that was not about us and for us, that I think we almost contested her being separate enough to be proud of us—it was too like our being proud of ourselves. We were delightedly derisive with her even about pride in our father—it was the most domestic of our pastimes; for what really could exceed the tenderness of our fastening on her that she *was* he, *was* each of us, was our pride and our humility, our possibility of *any* relation, and the very canvas itself on which we were floridly embroidered? How can I better express what she seemed to do for her second son in especial than by saying that even with her deepest delicacy of attention present I could still feel, while my father read, why it was that I most of all seemed to wish we might have been either much less religious or much more so? Was not the reason at bottom that I so suffered, I might almost have put it, under the impression of his style, which affected me as somehow too philosophic for life, and at the same time too living, as I made out, for thought?—since I must weirdly have opined that by so much as you were individual, which meant personal, which meant monotonous, which meant limitedly allusive and verbally

283. Compare HJ Sr.'s own words on his wife's role in his life: "She was not to me 'a liberal education,' intellectually speaking . . . but she really did arouse my heart, early in our married life, from its selfish torpor, and so enabled me to become a man. And this she did altogether unconsciously . . . solely by the presentation of her womanly sweetness and purity. . . . I would sooner rejoin her in her modesty, and find my eternal lot in association with her, than have the gift of a noisy delirious world!" (Matthiessen, *The James Family*, 129).

repetitive, by so much you were not literary or, so to speak, *largely* figurative. My father had terms, evidently strong, but in which I presumed to feel, with a shade of irritation, a certain narrowness of exclusion as to images otherwise—and oh, since it was a question of the pen, so multitudinously!—entertainable. Variety, variety—*that* sweet ideal, *that* straight contradiction of any dialectic, hummed for me all the while as a direct, if perverse and most unedified, effect of the parental concentration, with some of its consequent, though heedless, dissociations. I heard it, felt it, saw it, both shamefully enjoyed and shamefully denied it as form, though as form only; and I owed thus supremely to my mother that I could, in whatever obscure levity, muddle out some sense of my own preoccupation under the singular softness of the connection that she kept for me, by the outward graces, with that other and truly much intenser which I was so little framed to share.

If meanwhile my father's tone, so far as that went, was to remain the same, save for a natural growth of assurance, and thereby of amplitude, all his life, I find it already, and his very voice as we were to know them, in a letter to R. W. Emerson of 1842, without more specific date, after the loose fashion of those days, but from 2 Washington Place, New York, the second house in the row between the University building and Broadway, as he was next to note to his correspondent in expressing the hope of a visit from him. (It was the house in which, the following year, his second son was born.)[284]

284. Emerson gave the first of a series of six increasingly popular lectures in New York on 3 March 1842, his first appearance in the city. HJ Sr. attended and was immediately captivated, writing him an impassioned letter and offering "the cordial grasp of a fellow pilgrim" (Matthiessen, *The James Family*, 39). The two men met the next day, and a long friendship began. Habegger comments of HJ Sr.'s surviving letters: "If these documents, the richest emotional outpourings he left behind, are not love letters, it is hard to know what to call them" (*The Father*, 186). It is certainly true that HJ Sr. presses and importunes for a greater intimacy, desiring to know the Emerson who "thinks and feels and lives." He confides in another letter, "I was going to write you yesterday . . . to shape into voice if that were possible an inward yearning which frequently haunts me towards you. . . . I often am inwardly moved to write you and and [*sic*] withheld only by a quiet-growing despair of doing so to any profit. Whether I write or not I shall not cease to think of you nor to lie in wait for a better appreciation of you in that respect wherein you now give me intense pain" (MS letters, the first dated in another hand "1842" but in fact referring to HJ Sr.'s 1843 lectures in New York, and the second, 11 May 1843, bmS Am 1092.9 [4097 and 4098], Houghton). Some of HJ's detail about events in HJ Sr.'s public life is inaccurate. His not very successful series of free lectures at the Stuyvesant Institute (to which HJ Sr. alludes in

I came home to-night from my lecture a little disposed to think, from the smart reduction of my audience, that I had about as well not have prepared my course, especially as I get no tidings of having interested one of the sort (the religious) for whom they are wholly designed. When I next see you I want a half-hour's support from you under this discouragement, and the purpose of this letter is to secure it. When I am *with* you I get no help from you—of the sort you can give me, I feel sure; though you must know what I want before I listen to you next. Usually the temper you show, of perfect repose and candour, free from all sickening partisanship and full of magnanimous tenderness for every creature, makes me forget my wants in your lavish plenty. But I know you have the same as I have, deep down in your breast, and it is by these I would fain know you. I am led, quite without any conscious wilfulness either, to seek the *laws* of these appearances that swim round us in God's great museum, to get hold of some central facts which may make all other facts properly circumferential and orderly; and you continually dishearten me by your apparent indifference to such law and such facts, by the dishonour you seem to cast on our intelligence as if it were what stands in our way. Now my conviction is that my intelligence is the necessary digestive apparatus for my life; that there is nihil in vita— worth anything, that is—quod non prius in intellectu.[285] Now is it not so in truth with you? Can you not report your life to me by some intellectual symbol which my intellect appreciates? Do you not know your activity? But fudge—I cannot say what I want to say, what aches to say itself in me, and so I'll hold up till I see you, and try once more to get some better furtherance by my own effort. Here I am these thirty-one years in life, ignorant in all outward science, but having patient habits of meditation which never know disgust or weariness,

---

his opening sentence), on the theme of "LITERAL CHRISTIANITY, or . . . the doctrine of Jesus, as the suitable outgrowth and completion of the Jewish economy," began only in January 1843 (Habegger, *The Father*, 196), a year later than HJ indicates. Not long after WJ's birth in January 1842, the family moved into 21 Washington Place (their first purchased house), in which HJ was born in 1843. Some of HJ Sr.'s ideas on Emerson are reprinted in Matthiessen, *The James Family*, 434–38; HJ's 1887 essay on Emerson was reprinted in *Partial Portraits* (1888) (*LC* 1, 250–71). See also William T. Stafford, "Emerson and the James Family," *American Literature* 24 (January 1953): 433–61.

285. *Nihil in vita quod non prius in intellectu:* There is nothing in life which is not already in the mind (Lat.).

and feeling a force of impulsive love toward all humanity which will not let me rest wholly mute, a force which grows against all resistance that I can muster against it.[286] What shall I do? Shall I get me a little nook in the country and communicate with my *living* kind—not my talking kind—by life only; a word perhaps of *that* communication, a fit word once a year? Or shall I follow some commoner method—learn science and bring myself first into man's respect, that I may thus the better speak to him? I confess this last theory seems rank with earthliness—to belong to days forever past.[287]

His appeal to Emerson at this hour was, as he elsewhere then puts it, to the "invisible" man in the matter, who affected him as somewhere behind the more or less immediately visible, the beautifully but mystifyingly audible, the Emerson of honeyed lectures and addresses, suggestive and inspiring as that one might be, and who might, as we say to-day, have something, something more at least, for him.[288] "I will tell him that I do not value his substantive discoveries, whatever they may be, perhaps half so largely as he values them, but that I chiefly cherish that erect attitude of mind in him which in God's universe undauntedly seeks the worthiest tidings of God, and calmly defies every mumbling phantom which would challenge its freedom. Should his zeal for realities and contempt of vulgar shows abide the ordeal I have thus contrived for them I shall gladly await his visit to me. So much at least is what I have been saying to myself. Now that I have told it to you also you have become a sort of confidant between me and myself, and so bound to promote harmony there."[289] The corre-

286. Habegger points out that HJ, in quoting this letter, "supposed it was written in 1842 and thus failed to realize that his father's desperate unsettledness was contemporaneous with his own birth" (*The Father*, 200n).

287. This final possibility, quickly dismissed, of becoming a "man of science," foreshadows ironically the future of his eldest son, WJ. He is possibly recalling his Albany tutor and friend Joseph Henry, who belonged to those "days forever past" (see n. 462).

288. HJ here seems to endorse HJ Sr.'s moral and spiritual system of interpreting the phenomenal world in allegorical terms. He is also glossing the opening of the letter from which he earlier quoted: "The Emerson that thinks and feels and lives, this letter is addressed [*sic*]; and not to the Emerson that talks and bewitches one out of his serious thought when one talks to him, by the beautiful serenity of his behaviour. This latter Emerson I shall begin to hate soon for keeping my stupid eyes so continually away from the profounder Emerson who alone can do me any good. But I will now have the true man's ear alone" (letter [1842], bMS Am 1092.9 [4097], Houghton).

289. HJ Sr. seems to value Emerson not for the ideas he propounds but rather for the living example of humanity he sets. The full text of the letter is given in Matthiessen, *The*

spondence expands, however, beyond my space for reporting of it; I but pick out a few passages.[290]

I am cheered by the coming of Carlyle's new book, which Greeley announces, and shall hasten off for it as soon as I have leisure.* The title is provokingly enigmatical, but thought enough there will be in it no doubt, whatever the name;[291] thought heaped up to topheaviness and inevitable lopsidedness, but more interesting to me than comes from any other quarter of Europe—interesting for the man's sake whom it shows. According to my notion he is the very best interpreter of a spiritual philosophy that could be devised for *this age,* the age of transition and conflict; and what renders him so is his natural birth-and-education-place. Just to think of a Scotchman with a heart widened to German spiritualities! To have overcome his educational bigotries far enough to listen to the new ideas, this by itself was wonderful; and then to give all his native shrewdness and humour to the service of making them *tell* to

* *Past and Present,* 1843.

*James Family,* 39–40. Habegger suggests that by HJ's excerpting of "this letter for his memoirs, he picked up the letter's one suggestion of critical detachment—'I will tell you [i.e., you, Emerson] that I do not value his substantive discoveries, whatever they may be, perhaps half so largely as he values them . . . '—and omitted everything that testified to his father's warmly enthusiastic response" (*The Father,* 194n). The letter was HJ Sr.'s first to Emerson, written straight after the latter's opening lecture on 3 March 1842, and it is indeed effusive in its tone.

290. A larger extract from the long letter that follows is given in Matthiessen, *The James Family,* 42–43. It was written on 11 May 1843 and begins with some painful self-analysis: "All that I can at present say is that being better satisfied with you than any man I ever met, I am worst satisfied: which being interpreted means, that while your *life* is of that sort which, so far as I can detect it, lays hold of my profoundest Love, ever and anon some provokingly perverse way of speech breaks forth which does not seem to me to come from the life." The letter concludes with some critical thoughts on the transcendentalist Amos Bronson Alcott (1799–1888) (MS letter, bMS Am 1092.9 [4098], Houghton).

291. Horace Greeley (1811–72), the influential political figure and editor of the *New York Tribune,* was a friend of HJ Sr.'s and published many of his essays. They fell out in 1859 over a debate in the *Tribune* on marriage and free love. Thomas Carlyle (1795–1881), born in Scotland, later to become the "Sage of Chelsea," often a controversial essayist, historian, and philosopher, with a flamboyant style, had a Calvinist background and had been influenced by German philosophical methods. His lifelong friend Emerson arranged for the American publication of *Past and Present.* The "present" of his book's title represents the political and social problems of the Hungry Forties in Britain; the "past" depicts a twelfth-century society, free from utilitarian doctrine and obedient to a power beyond itself.

the minds of his people—what more fortunate thing for the time could there be? You don't look upon Calvinism as a fact at all;[292] wherein you are to my mind philosophically infirm—impaired in your universality. I can see in Carlyle the advantage his familiarity with it gives him over you with a general audience. What is highest in him is built upon that lowest. At least so I read; I believe Jonathan Edwards redivivus in true blue would, after an honest study of the philosophy that has grown up since his day, make the best possible reconciler and critic of this philosophy— far better than Schelling redivivus.[293]

In the autumn of 1843 the "nook in the country" above alluded to had become a question renounced, so far at least as the American country was concerned, and never again afterwards flushed into life.[294] "I think it probable I shall winter in some mild English climate, Devonshire perhaps,

292. Calvinism, a form of Protestantism derived from the teaching of the Swiss divine John Calvin (1509–64), adapted and modified through the centuries, was most prevalent in Scotland, Puritan England, and New England. It insisted on the unregenerate nature of humankind and thus the need for a strict moral code in the quest for individual salvation. The severity shown toward Emerson perhaps arises from HJ Sr.'s own past and his memories of the difficult years of his youth when he resisted the strictures of his father and his high Presbyterianism.

293. Jonathan Edwards (1703–58) was a contentious American theologian who, for instance, declaimed against the freedom of the will. Uncompromising and rigorous, he alienated his congregation and was finally dismissed from his position at Northampton in 1748. Friedrich Wilhelm Joseph von Schelling (1775–1854) was a German philosopher who had close links with the German Romantic movement. In his emphasis on human will he can be regarded as reconciling the philosophical schools associated with idealism and realism. HJ Sr.'s endorsement of the abrasively controversial figure of Edwards reflects his own willingness to engage in debate in such public arenas as the *New York Tribune*. WJ provided a succinct contrast between the two men in his introduction to his father's "Emerson," published in the *Atlantic Monthly* in December 1904 (rpt. in Matthiessen, *The James Family*, 429). See also James Duban, *The Nature of True Virtue: Theology, Psychology, and Politics in the Writings of Henry James, Sr., Henry James, Jr., and William James* (Cranbury, NJ: Fairleigh Dickinson University Press; London: Associated University Presses, 2001). *Redivivus:* restored (Lat.).

294. In the initial passionate stages of his friendship with Emerson, HJ Sr., unsettled, anxious, and having bought an expensive New York house, repeated in his letters the desirability and healthiness of country life. Habegger (*The Father*, 205–9) infers that he hoped for an invitation to come to live near Emerson in rural Concord, a version, as HJ elsewhere smilingly suggests, of Weimar, "our happy equivalent, 'in American money,' for Goethe and Schiller" (*AS*, 264). But he was to be disappointed, and the friendship was not revived until 1847, three years after the family had returned from Europe. The quotations that follow come from a letter of 3 October 1843 (bMS Am 1092.9 [4099], Houghton).

and go on with my studies as at home. I shall miss the stimulus of your candid and generous society, and I confess we don't like the aspect of the journey; but one's destiny puts on many garments as it goes shaping itself in secret—so let us not cling to any particular fashion." Very marked, and above all very characteristic of my father, in this interesting relation, which I may but so imperfectly illustrate, his constant appeal to his so inspired, yet so uninflamed, so irreducible and, as it were, inapplicable, friend for intellectual and, as he would have said, spiritual help of the immediate and adjustable, the more concretely vital, kind, the kind translatable into terms of the real, the particular human terms of action and passion. "Oh you man without a *handle!* Shall one never be able to help himself out of you, according to his needs, and be dependent only upon your fitful tippings-up?"—a remarkably felicitous expression, as it strikes me, of that difficulty often felt by the passionately-living of the earlier time, as they may be called, to draw down their noble philosopher's great overhanging heaven of universal and ethereal answers to the plane of their comparatively terrestrial and personal questions;[295] the note of the answers and their great anticipatory spirit being somehow that they seemed to anticipate everything but the unaccommodating individual case. My father, on his side, bristled with "handles"—there could scarce be a better general account of him—and tipped himself up for you almost before you could take hold of one; of which truth, for that matter, this same letter happens

295. HJ Sr.'s metaphysical conceit illustrates HJ's earlier point regarding his father's "literary" style. HJ Sr.'s impatience with Emerson arose from the philosophical difference between them which rested upon the latter's failure to recognize the power of evil (whose reality HJ Sr. considered to be well represented in *Past and Present*). Emerson embodied, by contrast, as Matthiessen suggests, "an arrested state of innocence, quite wanting in the Blakean energies of experience" (*The James Family*, 428). Yet HJ Sr. also confesses to a personal frustration at Emerson's innate and inaccessible superiority expressed in physical terms: "how soothed and comforted I was by the innocent lovely look of my new acquaintance. . . . and how I used to lock myself up with him in his bed-room, swearing that before the door was opened I would arrive at the secret of his immense superiority to the common herd of literary men!" He found that it was "altogether personal or practical . . . that it came to him by birth or genius like a woman's beauty or charm of manners; that no other account was to be given of it in truth than that Emerson himself was an unsexed woman, a veritable fruit of almighty power in the sphere of our *nature*" ("Mr. Emerson" [1881], rpt. in Matthiessen, *The James Family*, 435). HJ omits the final powerful valediction of this letter: "Farewell then my dear friend—many things spring up to my lips to say besides, but they are only variations of the tune *I love you.*"

to give, even if just trivially, the hint. "Can I do anything for you in the way of taking parcels, no matter how large or expensive?—or for any of your friends? If you see Margaret Fuller ask her to give me some service to render her abroad, the dear noble woman:[296] it seems a real hardship to be leaving the country now that I have just come to talk with her." Emerson, I should add, did offer personally so solid a handle that my father appears to have taken from him two introductions to be made use of in London, one to Carlyle and the other to John Sterling,[297] the result of which shortly afterwards was as vivid and as deeply appropriated an impression of each eminent character as it was probably to be given either of them ever to have made. The impression of Carlyle was recorded but long subsequently, I note, and is included in William's gathering-in of our father's Literary Remains (1885);[298] and of the acquaintance with Sterling no reflection remains but a passage in a letter, under date of Ventnor and of

296. HJ Sr. was introduced to Margaret Fuller (1810–50) by Emerson in 1843; a New England transcendentalist, brilliant scholar, and proponent of women's rights, she edited *The Dial*. HJ elsewhere refers to her as "the imaginative, talkative, intelligent, and finally Italianised and ship-wrecked Margaret Fuller" (*LC* 1, 260). HJ Sr. also records that she was "a most uncomfortable neighbor, from the circumstances of her inordinate self-esteem" (letter to Edmund Tweedy, 24 February 1852, given in Lewis, *The Jameses*, 63n). See also *SBO*, nn. 97–98, 100.

297. John Sterling (1806–1844) was a writer on society and literature, much influenced by Coleridge, who became part owner of the *Athenaeum* magazine. Carlyle met him in 1835 and published his *Life* in 1851. HJ Sr. requests these introductions in this same letter of 3 October 1843.

298. HJ refers to HJ Sr.'s *Recollections of Carlyle*. HJ wrote to WJ from London about how he and Alice, on receiving a copy of the *Literary Remains*, "talked of poor father's fading away into silence and darkness, the waves of the world closing over this System which he tried to offer it, and of how we were touched by this act of yours which will (I am sure) do so much to rescue him from oblivion" (*HJL*, 3:62). Carlyle came to admire HJ Sr., commenting on 17 November 1843 that "James is a very good fellow, better and better as we see him more—something shy and skittish in the man; but a brave heart intrinsically, with sound earnest sense, with plenty of insight and even humour. He confirms an observation of mine, which indeed I find is hundreds of years old, that a stammering man is never a worthless one" (*The Correspondence of Emerson and Carlyle*, ed. Joseph Slater [New York: Columbia University Press, 1964], 352). The novelist's opinion of Carlyle starkly differentiates between man and artist, as appears in a letter of 1884: "Carlyle was a brute, a man of a jealous, grudging, sinister, contemptuous, ungenerous, most invidious soul. . . . But what a genius, painter, humourist, what a literary figure, what a faculty of expression" (*HJL*, 3:55).

the winter of 1843, from the latter to his biographer to be;[299] Carlyle having already mentioned in the Life that "Two American gentlemen, acquaintances also of mine, had been recommended to him, by Emerson most likely"; and that "one morning Sterling appeared here with a strenuous proposal that we should come to Knightsbridge and dine with him and them. . . . And accordingly we went," it goes on. "I remember it as one of the saddest dinners; though Sterling talked copiously, and our friends, Theodore Parker one of them, were pleasant and distinguished men." My father, with Theodore Parker his friend and the date fitting, would quite seem to have been one of the pair were it not that "our conversation was waste and logical, I forget quite on what, not joyful and harmoniously effusive." It is *that* that doesn't fit with any real participation of his— nothing could well do less so; unless the occasion had but too closely conformed to the biographer's darkly and richly prophetic view of it as tragic and ominous, "sad as if one had been dining in a ruin, in the crypt of a mausoleum"—all this "painfully apparent through the bright mask (Sterling) had bound himself to wear."[300] The end of his life was then, to Carlyle's view, in sight; but his own note, in the Isle of Wight, on "Mr. James, your New-England friend," was genial enough—"I saw him several times and liked him. They went on the 24th of last month back to London—or so purposed," he adds, "because there is no pavement here for him to walk on. I want to know where he is, and thought I should be

299. Ventnor, a small town on the Isle of Wight on England's south coast, was regarded as having a suitably mild climate for those affected by lung disease. Sterling was suffering from tuberculosis and would die in September of the following year. Carlyle represented HJ Sr. to Sterling as "an estimable man, full of sense and honest manfulness" (Habegger, *The Father,* 216). HJ Sr. and his family stayed only a few days, leaving Ventnor on 24 November 1843 (ibid.). He had visited the place previously in 1837, before his marriage.

300. Habegger has shown (*The Father,* 216n) that it was not HJ Sr. but Le Baron Russell who was present on this disappointing occasion. Theodore Parker (1810–60), grandson of a Minuteman and influential Unitarian minister who had, like HJ Sr., rejected Calvinism, was also a strong abolitionist. HJ Sr. wrote confidentially to Mrs. Annie Fields, "I am reading Theodore Parker's life with edification. I can't help feeling continually what a capital thing it had been for Theodore if he could only once or twice have honestly suspected what a poor puddle after all his life was, even when it most reflected his busy activity" (quoted in Perry, *Thought and Character of William James,* 1:132). The dinner episode is given in Carlyle's *Life of John Sterling,* part 3, chap. 6. The Sterling family home was in South Place, Knightsbridge, an affluent area of London south of Hyde Park. The house at this time was "empty except of servants," and Sterling had recently lost (within two hours of each other) both his mother and his wife. The letter referred to was written on 7 December 1843.

able to learn from you. I gave him a note for Mill, who may perhaps have seen him."[301]

My main interest in which is, I confess, for the far-off germ of the odd legend, destined much to grow later on, that—already the nucleus of a household—we were New England products; which I think my parents could then have even so much as seemed only to eyes naturally unaware of our American "sectional" differences. My father, when considerably past his thirtieth year, if I am not mistaken, had travelled "East," within our borders, but once in his life—on the occasion of his spending two or three months in Boston as a very young man;[302] there connecting itself with this for me a reminiscence so bedimmed at once and so suggestive as now almost to torment me. It must have been in '67 or '68 that, giving him my arm, of a slippery Boston day, up or down one of the steep streets that used to mount, from behind, and as slightly sullen with the effort, to Beacon Hill, and between which my now relaxed memory rather fails to discriminate, I was arrested by his pointing out to me opposite us a house in which he had for a while had rooms, long before and quite in his early time.[303] I but recall that we were more or less skirting the base of an

301. HJ Sr. would have needed paved surfaces on which to walk owing to his artificial cork leg. His right leg had been amputated above the knee after a childhood accident in which he had suffered severe burns (see *SBO*, nn. 127 and 392). He confided to Julia Ward Howe (in a conversation relating to the death of her three-year-old son and his conviction of an afterlife), "I lost a leg . . . in early youth. I have had a consciousness of the limb itself all my life. Although buried and out of sight, it has always remained a part of me" (Julia Ward Howe, *Reminiscences, 1819–1899* [Boston: Houghton, Mifflin, 1900], 325). As HJ goes on to point out, HJ Sr., despite his association with Emerson and other transcendentalists, was not a New Englander, having been born in Albany. HJ Sr. met John Stuart Mill (1806–73), the English philosopher and economist, though he did not, it seems, fully appreciate Mill's libertarian ideals. On the other hand, his son WJ dedicated *Pragmatism* in 1907 to Mill's memory, recalling his "pragmatic openness of mind" (*William James, Writings 1902–1910*, ed. Bruce Kuklick [New York: Library of America, 1987], 480).

302. HJ refers to HJ Sr.'s dropping out of Union College, escaping from family, and finding employment for a few months in Boston before returning to graduate in 1830 (see also n. 163 above).

303. The James family had moved into Boston from Newport in 1864 to live at 13 Ashburton Place, a small street on Beacon Hill; the later demolition of this house HJ recalls with horror in *AS* (229). Having abandoned Union College, HJ Sr. had found a temporary job with Francis Jenks, who ran the Unitarian journal the *Christian Examiner,* which he edited from his home, 12 Hancock Street, an "elegant four-story house" on Beacon Hill (Habegger, *The Father,* 96). HJ Sr.'s role was "to check every quotation in the scholarly or theological volumes that came across Jenks's desk and to supply notices of new books. 'My

ancient town-reservoir, the seat of the water-supply as then constituted, a monument rugged and dark, massively granitic, perched all perversely, as it seemed to look, on the precipitous slope, and which—at least as I see it through the years—struck quite handsomely the Babylonian note.[304] I at any rate mix up with this frowning object—it had somehow a sinister presence and suggestion—my companion's mention there in front of it that he had anciently taken refuge under its shadow from certain effects of a misunderstanding, if indeed not of a sharp rupture, for the time, with a highly generous but also on occasion strongly protesting parent at Albany, a parent displeased with some course he had taken or had declined to take (there was a tradition among us that he had been for a period quite definitely "wild,") and relief from further discussion with whom he had sought, and had more or less found, on that spot.[305] It was an age in which a flight from Albany to Boston—there being then no Boston and Albany Railroad—counted as a far flight;[306] though it wasn't to occur to me either then or afterwards that the ground of this manœuvre had been any plotted wildness in the Puritan air. What was clear at the moment, and what he remarked upon, was that the street-scene about us showed for all the lapse of time no scrap of change, and I remember well for myself how my first impression of Boston gave it to me under certain aspects as more expressive than I had supposed an American city could be of a seated and rooted social order, an order not complex but sensibly fixed—gathered in or folded back to intensity upon itself; and this, again and again, when the compass of the posture, its narrow field, might almost have made the fold excruciating. It had given however no sign of excruciation—that itself had been part of the Puritan stoicism; which perhaps was exactly why the local look, recognised to the point I speak of by the visitor, was so contained and yet comparatively so full: full, very nearly, I originally fancied, after the appraisable fashion of some composed town-face in one of Balzac's *villes de province*.[307] All of which, I grant, is much to say for the occasion of that

---

ambition is awakened,' he wrote a friend at Union, in late January 1830" (Lewis, *The Jameses*, 22).

304. Boston's Beacon Hill Reservoir, situated on top of the hill, was completed in 1849 and demolished in 1883.

305. HJ Sr.'s self-indulgent student days and his spiritual rebellion against his father are well documented (see above, n. 163), though there is equally clear evidence of the domineering temperament of his father, creator of the extensive family fortune.

306. The Boston-Albany railroad began its original operation in 1833.

307. Provincial towns. When HJ returned to Boston in the early years of the twentieth

dropped confidence, on the sloshy hillside, to which I allude—and part of the action of which was that it had never been dropped before; this circumstance somehow a peculiar source of interest, an interest I the more regret to have lost my grasp of as it must have been sharp, or in other words founded, to account for the long reverberation here noted. I had still—as I was indeed to keep having through life—the good fortune that elements of interest easily sprang, to my incurable sense, from any ghost of a drama at all *presented;* though I of course can't in the least pretend to generalise on what may or may not have constituted living presentation. This felicity occurred, I make out, quite incalculably, just as it could or would; the effect depended on some particular touch of the spring, which was set in motion the instant the touch happened to be right. My father's was always right, to my receptive mind; as receptive, that is, of any scrap of enacted story or evoked picture as it was closed to the dry or the abstract proposition; so that I blush the deeper at not being able, in honour of his reference, to make the latter more vividly flower—I still so feel that I quite thrilled with it and with the standing background at the moment lighted by it. There were things in it, and other persons, old actualities, old meanings and furnishings of the other old Boston, as I by that time couldn't but appraise it; and the really archaic, the overhung and sombre and secret-keeping street, "socially" disconnected, socially mysterious— as I like at any rate to remember it—was there to testify (testify to the ancient time of tension, expansion, sore meditation or whatever) by its positively conscious gloom.[308]

The moral of this, I fear, amounts to little more than that, putting aside the substance of his anecdote, my father had not set foot in New England till toward his thirty-fifth year, and my mother was not to do so till later still; circumstances not in the least preventing the birth of what I have called the falsifying legend. The allusion to the walking at Ventnor touches

---

century he found the place much changed. On a Sunday afternoon on the Common he heard hardly a word of English spoken, and, near the State House "where a great raw clearance has been made, memory met that pang of loss, knew itself sufficiently bereft to see the vanished objects, a scant but adequate cluster of 'nooks,' of such odds and ends as parochial schemes of improvement sweep away, positively overgrown, within one's own spirit, by a wealth of legend" (*AS,* 228).

308. Insofar as HJ refers to the episode of his father's temporarily abandoning college and escaping to Boston, those months have not become any clearer to more recent biographers. How HJ Sr., with his disabled leg, traveled to Boston via New York, when exactly he returned to Schenectady, and what his motives were, remain unanswered questions.

his inability to deal with rural roads and paths, then rougher things than now; by reason of an accident received in early youth and which had so lamed him for life that he could circulate to any convenience but on even surfaces and was indeed mainly reduced to driving—it had made him for all his earlier time an excellent whip. His constitution had been happily of the strongest, but as I look back I see his grave disability, which it took a strong constitution to carry, mainly in the light of a consistency of patience that we were never to have heard broken. The two acceptances melt together for me—that of the limits of his material action, his doing and enjoying, set so narrowly, and that of his scant allowance of "public recognition," or of the support and encouragement that spring, and spring so naturally and rightly, when the relation of effect to cause is close and straight, from any at all attested and glad understanding of a formula, as we say nowadays a message, richly and sincerely urged. Too many such reflections, however, beset me here by the way. My letters jump meanwhile to the summer of 1849, when I find in another of them, addressed to Emerson, a passage as characteristic as possible of one of the writer's liveliest and, as I confess it was ever to seem to me, most genially perverse idiosyncrasies, his distinctly low opinion of "mere" literary men. This note his letters in general again and again strike—not a little to the diver-sion of those who were to have observed and remembered his constant charmed subjection, in the matter of practice, to the masters, even quite the lighter, in the depreciated group. His sensibility to their spell was in fact so marked that it became from an early time a household game with us to detect him in evasive tears over their pages, when these were either real or romantic enough, and to publish without mercy that he had so been caught. There was a period in particular during which this pastime en-joyed, indeed quite revelled in, the form of our dragging to the light, with every circumstance of derision, the fact of his clandestine and deeply moved perusal of G. P. R. James, our nominal congener, at that time ceasing to be prescribed.[309] It was his plea, in the "'fifties," that this romancer had been his idol in the 'forties and the 'thirties, and that under renewed, even if but experimental, surrender the associations of youth flocked back to life—so that *we*, profane about the unduly displaced master, were deplorably the poorer. He loved the novel in fine, he followed

309. George Payne Rainsford James (1799–1860) was a British author who spent some years in the United States (partly as British consul at Norfolk, Virginia) and produced about forty novels.

its constant course in the Revue with a beautiful inconsequence, and the more it was literature loved it the better, which was just how he loved, as well, criticism and journalism; the particular instance, with him, once he was in relation with it, quite sufficiently taking care of the invidiously-viewed type—as this was indeed viewed but *a priori* and at its most general—and making him ever so cheerfully forget to be consistent. Work was verily cut out for the particular instance, as against the type, in an air and at a time favouring so, again and again, and up and down the "literary world," a dire mediocrity. It was the distillers of *that* thinness, the "mere" ones, that must have been present to him when he wrote to Emerson in 1849:[310] "There is nothing I dread so much as literary men, especially *our* literary men; catch them out of the range of mere personal gossip about authors and books and ask them for honest sympathy in your sentiment, or for an honest repugnancy of it, and you will find the company of stage-drivers sweeter and more comforting to your soul.[311] In truth the questions which are beginning to fill the best books, and will fill the best for a long time to come, are not related to what we have called literature, and are as well judged—I think better—by those whom books have at all events not belittled. When a man *lives,* that is lives enough, he can scarcely write. He cannot read, I apprehend, at all. All his writing will be algebraicised, put into the form of sonnets and proverbs, and the community will feel itself insulted to be offered a big bunch of pages, as though it were stupid and wanted tedious drilling like a child." When I begin to quote my father, however, I hang over him perhaps even too historically; for his expression leads me on and on so by its force and felicity that I scarce know where to stop. "The fact is that I am afraid I am in a very bad way, for I cannot heartily engage in any topic in which I shall appear to advantage"[312]—the

310. The extracts that follow in this paragraph come from a long letter of 31 August 1849, a reply to Emerson's invitation to HJ Sr. to lecture at Boston's Town and Country Club; he confessed to feeling "horrified at the prospect of speaking before so urbane an assemblage." He is devotedly keen to distinguish Emerson from these mere "literary men": "Your books are not literature but life, and criticism always strikes me therefore as infinitely laughable when applied to you" (MS letter, bMS Am 1092.9 [4100], Houghton; extracts from the letter are given in Matthiessen, *The James Family,* 44–45). He had considered taking sin as his theme, but the title of his 1 November 1849 lecture was "Socialism and Civilization in Relation to the Development of the Individual Life."

311. HJ Sr. may be referring to what is called in an earlier chapter the "Artless Age" (see n. 110).

312. This may be so, but there is much evidence that HJ Sr. could be disputatious and uncompromising in discussion and debate. His fears here suggest a degree of insecurity.

question having been, *de part et d'autre,*[313] of possible courses of lectures for which the appetite of New York and Boston already announced itself as of the largest. And it still more beguiles me that "my wife and I are obliged—so numerous has waxed our family—to enlarge our house in town and get a country house for the summer." Here came in that earnest dream of the solutional "Europe" with which I have elsewhere noted that my very youngest sensibility was fed.[314] "These things look expensive and temporary to us, besides being an additional care; and so, considering with much pity our four stout boys, who have no play-room within doors and import shocking bad manners from the street, we gravely ponder whether it wouldn't be better to go abroad for a few years with them, allowing them to absorb French and German and get such a sensuous education as they can't get here."[315]

In 1850, however, we had still not departed for Europe—as we were not to do for several years yet;[316] one advantage of which was that my father remained for the time in intercourse by letter with his English friend Dr. J. J. Garth Wilkinson,[317] first known during my parents' con-

313. On both sides.

314. HJ's own childhood experiences of Europe occupy the second half of *SBO;* his father invoked the prospect of Europe frequently for his family.

315. Whatever the benefits of Europe in terms of the experiences it could offer, none of the children received any sustained or continuous education in the years spent out of America. Many of the moves described in *SBO* and in this volume seem to have been dictated by HJ Sr.'s restlessness rather than by the children's needs. Commenting on the minor revisions to HJ Sr.'s letter made by HJ, Habegger contends that America is made to look "more vacuous than vicious" (*The Father,* 287n), thus influencing later biographical emphases. The original reads: "we gravely ponder whether it would not be better to go abroad for a few years with them, allowing them to absorb French & German, and get a better sensuous education than they are likely to get here?" It could be argued, however, that the revision simply neatens HJ Sr.'s punctuation and grammar. In later years Alice James fairly bitterly counseled her brother William to provide a settled environment for his children: "What enrichment of mind and memory can children have without continuity and if they are torn up by the roots every little while as we were! Of all things don't make the mistake wh. brought about our rootless and accidental childhood" (quoted in Lewis, *The Jameses,* 82).

316. The family (along with Aunt Kate) sailed for Liverpool aboard the steamer *Atlantic* on 27 June 1855, and returned to New York on 22 June 1858. They left Newport for Europe once again on 8 October 1859 for a further year.

317. James John Garth Wilkinson (1812–99), a physician as well as a homeopath, published in 1841 some articles on Swedenborg in the British *Monthly Magazine.* They were noticed by HJ Sr. and "within three years Wilkinson had become James's closest

siderable stay in London of several years before, 1843–44; and whose admirable style of expression, in its way as personal and as vivid as Henry James's own, with an added and doubtless more perceptibly full-blooded massiveness, is so attested by his earlier writings,*[318] to say nothing of the rich collection of his letters (1845–55) lately before

* "But, Sir, we have yet one more scene to visit together, connected with all we have previously witnessed: a home scene, Sir Benjamin; and we must now ascend a mountain of pity high enough to command the dewy extense of three kingdoms. From thence we have to look down from every point of our warm hearts with a sight as multifold as the cherubic eyes. We are to see with equal penetration through the diverse thickness of castles, mansions, and cottages, through London and through hamlet, at young wives and at aged mothers, little children, brothers and sisters—all groups and ties that are; and at affianced maidens, ties that were to be. There are rents and tears to-day in the general life: the bulletin of the dead has come, and the groups of sorrow are constituted. Splendid Paris bends as a Niobe or as a Rachel while the corse of her much-enduring Hero is borne to the marble Invalides; other corses go earthward with a shorter procession, helped away by the spades of ruder but more instant sculptors; the rucked sod of the Alma is their urn and monument in one; yet every warrior among them is also buried to-day with swelling greatness of obsequies, if we could see them, in the everlasting ruby vaults of some human heart. You are touched, Sir Benjamin, and are justly religious on this summit. Struck down for a moment from worldliness, we both discourse without an afterthought on the immortal state; we hope that the brave are already welcomed in the land of peace; that our laurels they could not stop to take, and our earned promotion they seem to have missed are clad upon them now by the God of battles in front of the shining armies of the just. We hope also that if their voices could now speak to the mourners, the oil of their sure gladness would heal our faithless sorrow. It is a true strain no doubt, and yet but of momentary power." War, Cholera, and the Ministry of Health. An Appeal to Sir Benjamin Hall and the British People. London, 1854.

———

friend and Swedenborg his newest gospel" (Habegger, *The Father*, 190). Wilky James was named for him, while the Wilkinsons' daughter was named for Mary Walsh James. The families were quite close neighbors during the Jameses' stay at St. John's Wood in winter 1855–56 (see *SBO*, chap. 22). Relations between the two men grew increasingly strained— Wilkinson called HJ Sr. in 1849 "the most genial and unctuous of bullies"—though his *The Human Body and its Connexion with Man* is dedicated to HJ Sr., and twenty of James's letters to Wilkinson were published as *Christianity the Logic of Creation* (1857) (Habegger, *The Father*, 375, 377). HJ is more scathing in a letter of 24 August 1912 to Howard Sturgis: "My dear Father thought J.J.G.W. highly remarkable as a young man (when they both were, and my Father was in England—and indeed J.J. then *was* remarkable); and afterwards, always afterwards, found him very tiresome" (*HJL*, 4:624).

318. In the sample that HJ provides in his footnote, Wilkinson addresses Sir Benjamin Hall (1802–67), a civil engineer and politician who became the first chief commissioner of works when the Metropolitan Board of Works was established in 1851 to deal with environmental and sanitary issues. He goes on to refer to one of the earliest battles of the Crimean

me[319]—notably by The Human Body and its Connection with Man, dedicated in 1851 to my father—that I wonder at the absence of such a master, in more than one happy specimen, from the common educational exhibitions of English prose. Dr. Wilkinson was a friend of Emerson's as well, which leads the latter's New York correspondent to cite to him in February 1850 a highly characteristic passage from one of the London communications.[320]

> Carlyle came up here (presumably to Hampstead) on Monday to see Neuberg, and spoke much of you with very kind recollections.[321] He remembered your metaphysics also and asked with terrible solicitude whether they yet persevered. I couldn't absolutely say that

---

War fought by the allied forces of France and Britain against Russia, the battle of the Alma (20 September 1854). The cause of death for considerable numbers was cholera, among them the French commander, Field Marshall Jacques Leroy Saint-Arnaud (1801–54); he was buried in Les Invalides, which contains the mausoleum for France's military heroes. Wilkinson invokes Niobe in Greek legend as emblematic of maternal grief, and Rachel in the book of Genesis as an example of enduring fidelity in love, a mother who died in childbirth. HJ clearly thought highly of this piece of writing, since he commends it in a letter to Howard Sturgis (24 August 1912, *HJL,* 4:624–25). The essay from which HJ quotes was written as an open letter to promote "homœpathy as the medicine of the future. . . . The reasoning power, the good temper, the wit and *aplomb* which Wilkinson showed in its pages brought him many readers" (Clement John Wilkinson, *James John Garth Wilkinson; a Memoir of His Life, with a Selection from His Letters* [London: Kegan Paul, Trench, Trübner, 1911], 93).

319. In bMS Am 1092.9 (4049–4086), Houghton, there are thirty-eight letters covering the period 1845–82.

320. These lines of Wilkinson's make up part of HJ Sr.'s letter of 26 February 1850 to Emerson, written from New York City. It is perhaps significant that HJ modifies only one word and adjusts some of the punctuation; he is rarely so restrained when dealing with his own family or intimate friends. HJ Sr. had recommended Wilkinson to Emerson when the latter visited Britain in 1847.

321. Wilkinson and his family had lived at 13 Store Street, Bedford Square, Bloomsbury; then at 25 Church Row, Hampstead; in 1851 they moved to 24 Finchley Road, St. John's Wood, where they remained for many years. Joseph Neuberg (1806–67), of German origin, was a naturalized British subject and manufacturer in Nottingham. He helped in the preparation of *Latter-Day Pamphlets,* acted as Carlyle's secretary, and, on occasion, translated his works. "The author's violent attack on the idealisms as well as the respectabilities of the day was not calculated to please either Wilkinson or James" (Perry, *Thought and Character of Willam James,* 1:65 n. 5). Occasionally in the letters he includes in this volume, HJ inserts a comment in parentheses, as here, to serve as explanation or clarification of a point.

they did not, though I did my best to stammer out something about the great social movement. He was suffering dreadfully from *malaise* and indigestion and gave with his usual force his usual putrid theory of the universe. All great men were most miserable; the day on which any man could say he was not miserable, that day he was a scoundrel; God was a Divine Sorrow; to no moment could he, Carlyle, ever say Linger, but only Goodbye and never let me see your face again. And all this interpolated with convulsive laughter, showing that joy would come into him were it even by the path of hysteria and disease. To me he is an unprofitable man, and though he gave me the most kind invitation I have too much respect for my stomach to go much into his company. Where hope is feeble genius and the human voice are on the way to die. By the next boat I will endeavour to send you over my thoughts on his recent pamphlet, the first of a series of Latter-Day-Tracts.[322] He is very rapidly falling out with all his present admirers, for which I like them all the better; and indeed is driving fast toward social views—only his is to be a compulsory, not an attractive, socialism.[323]

After quoting which my father comments: "Never was anything more false than this worship of sorrow by Carlyle; he has picked it up out of past history and spouts it for mere display, as a virtuoso delights in the style of his grandfather. It is the merest babble in him, as everyone who has ever talked an hour with him will acquit him of the least grain of humility. A man who has once uttered a cry of despair should ever after clothe himself in sackcloth and ashes."

The writer was to have meanwhile, before our migration of 1855, a considerable lecturing activity.[324] A confused, yet perfectly recoverable

322. Carlyle's *Latter-Day Pamphlets* was published in 1850 (London: Chapman and Hall).

323. HJ Sr. too would grow disillusioned with Carlyle, as he reveals in an 1856 letter included below.

324. In 1851 HJ Sr. lectured successfully in New York at the Mechanics' Institute on Broadway and also gave six lectures at the Stuyvesant Institute that were later published as *Lectures and Miscellanies* (New York: Redfield, 1852), referred to proudly by young Robertson in chap. 4 above. His topics were "Democracy and its Issues," "Property as a Symbol," "The Principle of Universality in Art," "The Old and New Theology," and "The Scientific Record of Natural and Revealed Religion." In November 1851 he was booked to give six lectures at Boston's Masonic Temple, but withdrew mysteriously at the last minute (Habegger, *The Father*, 324–29), though he had already lectured in the city at the end of

recollection, on my own part, of these years, connects itself with our knowledge that our father engaged in that practice and that he went forth for the purpose, with my mother always in earnest and confident even though slightly fluttered attendance, at about the hour of our upward procession to bed; which fact lent to the proceeding—that is to *his*—a strange air of unnatural riot, quite as of torch-lighted and wind-blown dissipation. We went to plays and to ballets, and they had comparatively speaking no mystery; but at no lecture had we ever been present, and these put on for my fancy at least a richer light and shade, very much as if we ourselves had been on the performing side of the curtain, or the wonder of admiring (in our mother's person) and of being admired (in our father's) had been rolled for us into a single glory. This glory moreover was not menaced, but only made more of a thrill by the prime admirer's anxiety, always displayed at the last, as to whether they were not starting without the feature of features, the *corpus delicti*[325] or manuscript itself; which it was legendary with us that the admired had been known to drive back for in an abashed flurry at the moment we were launched in dreams of him as in full, though mysterious, operation. I can see him now, from the parlour window, at the door of the carriage and under the gusty street-lamp, produce it from a coat-tail pocket and shake it, for her ideal comfort, in the face of his companion. The following, to Emerson, I surmise, is of some early date in the autumn of '52.[326]

I give three lectures in Boston at the Masonic Temple; the first and second on Nov. 5th and 8th respectively. I should be greatly appalled in some respects, but still charmed, to have you for an auditor, seeing thus a hundred empty seats obliterated;[327] but, I beg of you, don't let any engagement suffer by such kindness to me. Looking over the lectures again they horrify me with their loud-mouthed imbecility!—

---

1849 (Le Clair, *Young Henry James,* 55). The series is mentioned in a letter quoted later in the chapter.

325. The body of the crime: an archaic term from jurisprudence relating to the fact that it must be shown that a crime has been committed before someone can be convicted. It is used here ironically, of course.

326. This letter is in fact dated 30 October [1851].

327. HJ Sr. seems here unusually self-deprecating and anxious about the forbidding nature of his audience. According to Habegger, "There would be two or three lectures a week, and tickets for all six nights, costing $1, could be purchased at Boston's two premier bookstores" (*The Father,* 328). Emerson bought two tickets for the ill-fated series, which HJ Sr. suddenly abandoned on grounds of illness.

but I hope they may fall upon less hardened ears in some cases. I am sure that the thought which is in them, or rather seems to me to struggle to be in them, is worthy of all men's rapturous homage, and I will trust that a glimpse of it may somehow befall my patient auditory. The fact is that a vital truth can never be transferred from one mind to another, because life alone appreciates it. The most one can do for another is to plant some rude formula of such truths in his memory, leaving his own spiritual chemistry to set free the germ whenever the demands of his life exact it. The reason why the gods seem so powerless to the sensuous understanding, and suffer themselves to be so long defamed by our crazy theologies, is that they are life, and can consequently be revealed only to life. But life is simply the passage of idea into action; and our crazy theologies forbid ideas to come into action any further than our existing institutions warrant. Hence man leads a mere limping life, and the poor gods who are dependent upon his manliness for their true revelation and for their real knowledge, are doomed to remain forever unknown, and even denied by such solemn pedants as Mr. Atkinson and Miss Martineau.[328] However, I shall try to convert *myself* at least into an army of Goths and Huns, to overcome and destroy our existing sanctities, that the supernal splendours may at length become credible and even visible. Good-bye till we meet in Boston, and cultivate your goodnature according to my extensive needs.

I bridge the interval before our migration of 1855 exactly for the sake of certain further passages addressed to the same correspondent, from London, in the following year. The letter is a long one and highly significant of the writer's familiar frankness, but I must keep down my examples—the first of which glances at his general sense of the men he mainly met.[329]

328. "In 1851 a book appeared in London under the joint authorship of Henry George Atkinson and Harriet Martineau, entitled *Letters on the Laws of Man's Nature and Development*. It was a defense of the positivistic-atheistic position, with special reference to the dependence of mind on body" (Perry, *Thought and Character of William James*, 1:71–72 n. 11). Like Martineau, Henry George Atkinson (1812–90) was a British free thinker, interested also in mesmerism and phrenology; indeed, it was thought that his mesmerism cured the ailing Martineau (whom he met in 1845). Harriet Martineau (1802–76) came from a Unitarian background and was interested in political economy. After a visit to the United States during which she espoused the cause of abolitionism, she produced *Society in America* (1837), which met with some hostility. She was, however, instrumental in promoting abolitionism among the British public.

329. HJ Sr. has found the British men he has met lacking in openness and humanity. In

They are all of them depressed or embittered by the public embarrassments that beset them; deflected, distorted, somehow despoiled of their rich individual manliness by the necessity of providing for these imbecile old inheritances of church and state. Carlyle is the same old sausage, fizzing and sputtering in his own grease, only infinitely *more* unreconciled to the blest Providence which guides human affairs. He names God frequently and alludes to the highest things as if they were realities, but all only as for a picturesque effect, so completely does he seem to regard them as habitually circumvented and set at naught by the politicians.[330] I took our friend M. to see him, and he came away greatly distressed and désillusionné,[331] Carlyle having taken the utmost pains to deny and decry and deride the idea of his having done the least good to anybody, and to profess indeed the utmost contempt for everybody who thought he had, and poor M. being intent on giving him a plenary assurance of this fact in his own case. . . . Arthur Helps seems an amiable kindly little man with friendly offers, but I told him I had no intention to bore him, and would at most apply to him when I might want a good hatter or bootmaker.[332] He fancied a little—at least

---

an elaborate trope he contrasts them with the much admired Emerson: "sure I am meanwhile that you are a matchless summer house, green with clambering vines, and girt with cool piazzas fit to entertain the democratic host as it marches from the old worn out past to the beckoning and blossoming future" (letter marked in pencil "London, 1856," bMS Am 1092.9 [4111], Houghton).

330. For HJ Sr.'s increasing disillusionment with Carlyle and for the views of both HJ and WJ, see Matthiessen, *The James Family,* 459-60.

331. See Perry, *Thought and Character of William James,* 1:83-84 n. 2: "There is an account of this interview in James's published recollections of Carlyle, L.R.H.J. [*The Literary Remains of Henry James*], 466 ff. The friend is Col. James Morrison McKay (later changed to MacKaye, 1805-88), artist, abolitionist, and man of affairs, who moved from Buffalo to Newport about 1850. When James came to reside in Newport the two men became close friends, and James later rented McKay's house for two years (1860-61). William and Henry were schoolmates and playfellows of McKay's son, James Steele McKaye [*sic*], the famous dramatist, actor, and theatrical manager, father of Percy Mac-Kaye, the poet, and James MacKaye, the economist." *Désillusionné:* disillusioned.

332. Edmund Arthur Helps (1813-75), a member of the select Cambridge University Apostles' Club, became a writer and historian and eventually Clerk to the Privy Council. He was a friend of Carlyle's, who—along with others—referred to him as "poor Arthur Helps" (Matthiessen, *The James Family,* 462). Helps's *Social Pressure* was reviewed by HJ in the *Nation* in 1875 (*LC* 1, 1063-64). HJ Sr. had carried a letter of recommendation to him from Emerson.

I thought this was the case—that I was going to make a book, and might be indiscreet enough to put him in!. . . . —— disappoints me, he is so eaten up with the "spirits" and all that.[333] His imagination is so vast as to dwarf all the higher faculties, and his sympathy as narrow as Dr. Cheever's or Brownson's.[334] No reasonable man, it is true, likes the clergy or the philosophers, but ——'s dislike of them seems as envenomed as that between rival tradesmen or rival beauties. One can't endure the nonsense they talk, to be sure, but when one considers the dear human meaning and effort struggling at the bottom of it all one can feel still less any personal separation from the men themselves. ——'s sarcasm is of the fiercest, and on the whole he is only now at last sowing his intellectual wild oats—he will grow more genial in good time. This is it: I think he is but now finding his youth! That which we on our side of the water find so early and exhaust so prodigally he has found thus much later—I mean an emancipation from the shackles of custom; and the kicking up of his heels consequently is proportionate to his greater maturity of muscle. Mrs. —— is a dear little goose of a thing, who fancies the divine providence in closer league with herself than with others, giving her intimations of events about to happen and endowing her with peculiar perspicacity in the intuition of remedies for disease; and ——, the great brawny fellow, sits by and says never a word in abatement of this enormous domestic inflation, though the visitor feels himself crowded by it into the most inconsiderable of corners. A sweet, loving, innocent woman

333. HJ Sr. refers to Garth Wilkinson; given his critical comments and the later remarks about Wilkinson's wife, Emma, it is understandable that HJ would protect their anonymity. Perry points out, "This impression of Wilkinson seems not to have affected his fundamental regard and affection for his old friend. Their correspondence continued on the old terms, and Wilkinson was received as a member of the family when he visited the United States in 1869. This was nothing more than a detachment which was the natural effect of distance and advancing years" (*Thought and Character of William James*, 1:84 n. 3). Habegger suggests, however, that the personal and intellectual differences evident between them at this time were never really reconciled (*The Father*, 376–77).

334. Dr. George Barrell Cheever (1807–90) was a pastor at the Church of the Puritans, New York, 1846–70, a journalist, and temperance reformer, renowned for preaching on controversial social questions. Orestes Augustus Brownson (1803–76), a writer on religious issues, having rejected Calvinism, eventually converted to Catholicism. He became editor of the *Quarterly Review* in 1844. "He was associated with Emerson in the 'Transcendental Club' (1837) and 'The Friends of Universal Progress' (1840), but was never of his intimate circle" (Perry, *Thought and Character of William James*, 1:84 n. 4).

like Mrs. —— oughtn't to grow egotistical in the company of a truly wise man, and this accordingly is another quarrel I have with ——. In short I am getting to the time of life when one values one's friends for what they are more than for what they do. I am just as much impressed as ever by his enormous power, but the goodness out of which it is born and the wisdom by which it is nurtured and bred are things I don't so much see.[335]

The correspondence grew more interspaced, and with the year 1861 and the following, when we were at home again, became a matter of the occasional note. I have before me a series of beautiful examples of Emerson's share in it—during the earlier time copious enough; but these belong essentially to another case. I am all but limited, for any further show of the interesting relation than I have already given, to reproducing a few lines from Emerson's Diary, passages unpublished at the moment I write, and the first of them of April 1850. "I have made no note of these long weary absences at New York and Philadelphia. I am a bad traveller, and the hotels are mortifications to all sense of well-being in me. The people who fill them oppress me with their excessive virility, and would soon become intolerable if it were not for a few friends who, like women, tempered the acrid mass. Henry James was true comfort—wise, gentle, polished, with heroic manners and a serenity like the sun."[336] The hotels of those days may well have been an ordeal—distinct to me still, from no few childish glimpses of their bareness of ease and rudeness of *acceuil*;[337] yet that our justly fastidious friend was not wholly left to their mercy seems signified by my not less vivid remembrance of his staying with us on occasion in New York; some occasion, or occasions, I infer, of his coming on to lecture there. Do I roll several occasions into one, or amplify one beyond reason?—this last being ever, I allow, the waiting pitfall of a chronicler too memory-ridden. I "visualize" at any rate the winter firelight of our back-parlour at dusk and the great Emerson—I knew he was great, greater than any of our friends—sitting in it between my parents, before

335. The letter concludes with a pessimistic vision of British society and the possibility of a working-class revolution: "who knows what lies before us! All that seems certain is that these depraved old nationalities are bound to be destroyed to make way for the humane fellowship of men. The time may be now."

336. *The Journals and Miscellaneous Notebooks of Ralph Waldo Emerson*, vol. 11: *1848–1851*, ed. A. W. Plumstead et al. (Cambridge, Mass.: Belknap Press of Harvard University Press, 1975), 248.

337. Reception, or welcome.

the lamps had been lighted, as a visitor consentingly housed only could have done, and affecting me the more as an apparition sinuously and, I held, elegantly slim, benevolently aquiline, and commanding a tone alien, beautifully alien, to any we heard roundabout, that he bent this benignity upon me by an invitation to draw nearer to him, off the hearth-rug, and know myself as never yet, as I was not indeed to know myself again for years, in touch with the wonder of Boston.[338] The wonder of Boston was above all just then and there for me in the sweetness of the voice and the finish of the speech—this latter through a sort of attenuated emphasis which at the same time made sounds more important, more interesting in themselves, than by any revelation yet vouchsafed us. Was not this my first glimmer of a sense that the human tone *could,* in that independent and original way, be interesting? and didn't it for a long time keep me going, however unwittingly, in that faith, carrying me in fact more or less on to my day of recognising that it took much more than simply not being of New York to produce the music I had listened to.[339] The point was that, however that might be, I had had given me there in the firelight an absolutely abiding measure. If I didn't know from that hour forth quite all it was to *not* utter sounds worth mentioning, I make out that I had at least the opposite knowledge. And all by the operation of those signal moments—the truth of which I find somehow reflected in the fact of my afterwards knowing one of our household rooms for the time—it must have been our only guest-chamber—as "Mr. Emerson's room." The evening firelight played so long for me upon the door—that is to the length probably of three days, the length of a child's impression. But I must not let this carry me beyond the second note of the Diary, this time of May 1852. " 'I do not wish this or that thing my fortune will procure, I wish the great fortune,' said Henry James, and said it in the noblest sense."[340] The report has a beauty to me without my quite understanding it; the union of

338. In *SBO* HJ gives a detailed recollection of these childhood days from 1848 to 1855 when the family lived at 58 West Fourteenth Street. Though born in Boston, Emerson was much associated with Concord, where he had lived for many years.

339. HJ's recollected susceptibility to the subtlest dynamics of a scene, a responsiveness to the tone and timbre of a voice, might illustrate the point he makes earlier in the chapter when he imagines the dramatic potential of the conversation of his parents with Mrs. Chichester.

340. See *Journals of Ralph Waldo Emerson, 1820–1872,* ed. Edward Waldo Emerson and Waldo Emerson Forbes (London: Constable; Boston: Houghton Mifflin, 1913), 8:280, where the final phrase is "in the noble sense."

the two voices in it signifies quite enough. The last very relevant echo of my father's by itself, in the connection, I hasten now to find in a communication that must have been of the summer of 1869, when Dr. Wilkinson paid his only visit to America—this apparently of the briefest.[341] The letter to Emerson from Cambridge notes that his appearance there had been delayed.

He may come to-morrow possibly: if in the morning I will telegraph you; if in the evening I shall try to keep him over Monday that you may meet him here at dinner on that day. But I fear this bothersome Sabbath and its motionless cars may play us a trick. I shall hope for a generous Monday all the same, and if that hope is baulked shall owe Sunday a black-eye—and will pay my debt on the first suitable occasion, I warrant you. What an awkward story (the letter continues) The Nation to-day tells of Charles Sumner! Charles's burly voice has always had for me a dreadfully hollow sound, as if it came from a great copper vat, and I have loved him but with fear and trembling accordingly.[342] Is he *really,* like all American politicians, tricky, or is

341. Emerson to HJ Sr. (7 September 1869): "I hear with great pleasure of Mr Wilkinson's arrival,—why did you not tell me of his coming? I have never heard whisper of it, and shall come, if wheels or feet will bring me, so soon as you send word that he is in your house" (*Letters of Ralph Waldo Emerson,* vol. 9: *1860–1869,* ed. Eleanor M. Tilton [New York: Columbia University Press, 1994], 352). Wilkinson spent the first two weeks of September 1869 in the United States and Canada, sailing up the Hudson to see Albany, then visiting Niagara Falls, Quebec, Lake Champlain, Cambridge, and New York City. He passed a Sunday with the Jameses, where he "renewed the unbroken friendship of old times." The mood seems to have changed when he went to visit Longfellow, who happened to be entertaining Charles Sumner; Sumner was "Chairman of the Committee for Foreign Affairs in the Senate, and notorious at this time for his fierceness over the Alabama Claims. Though he was conciliatory and 'claimed' to be a reader of Wilkinson's works, on the recommendation of Emerson, the conversation ended in an outspoken argument" (C. J. Wilkinson, *Wilkinson Memoir,* 110; see also Wilkinson's letters to HJ Sr., bMS Am 1092.9 [4049–51], and Mary James's letters, bMS Am 1093.1 [34–36], Houghton). The letter that appears in Perry, *Thought and Character of William James,* 1:99–100, is HJ Sr.'s reply to Emerson. It is dated 10 September 1869 (bMS Am 1092.9 [4125], Houghton), and HJ has made only a few cuts and changes to the original.

342. Sumner, an abolitionist, was notoriously beaten on the floor of the Senate during the lead-up to the Civil War by Preston S. Brooks, a congressman from South Carolina. HJ refers to the incident in *William Wetmore Story and his Friends* (2 vols. bound as one, London: Thames and Hudson, n.d.), 2:29–30. (For further detail, see *SBO,* n. 78.) Sumner was most effective during the Civil War, and in later years his political career suffered some decline. "The *Nation* stated that on Jan. 17 and 19, 1869, after the Alabama

The Nation—so careful about facts ordinarily—only slanderous?. . . .
Carlyle nowadays is a palpable nuisance. If he holds to his present
mouthing ways to the end he will find no showman là-bas to match
him, for I hold Barnum a much more innocent personage.[343] I
shouldn't wonder if Barnum grew regenerate in some far off day by ·
mere force of his democracy. But Carlyle's intellectual pride is so
stupid that one can hardly imagine anything able to cope with it.[344]

The following, in so different a key, is of some seven years earlier date—
apparently '62;[345] but I have let it stand over, for reasons, that it may figure
here as the last of the communications addressed to Emerson that I shall
cite. Written at an hotel, the Tremont House, in Boston,[346] it marks his
having come up from Newport for attendance at some meeting of a dining-
club, highly distinguished in composition, as it still happily remains, of
which he was a member—though but so occasionally present that this
circumstance perhaps explains a little the even more than usual vivacity of
his impression.[347] Not indeed, I may add, that mustered reasons or apolo-

---

treaty had arrived in Washington, Sumner wrote to John Bright of the British Cabinet
heartily commending it. On April 13, however, in a vigorous two hours' speech directed
against it, Sumner so influenced the Senate that it rejected the treaty with but one dissent-
ing vote" (Perry, *Thought and Character of William James*, 1:99 n. 24). The influential
pro-abolition *Nation*, which appeared weekly, was for a long time edited by a friend of the
James family, the Irish-born E. L. Godkin (1831–1902); it published much of HJ's earlier
writing from the year it was founded by Godkin, in 1865. HJ Sr. is referring here to
paragraphs in the 9 September 1869 issue of the *Nation* taking to task the Springfield
*Republican* for questioning comments the *Nation* had published about Sumner.

343. *Là-bas:* over there. The phrase is HJ's; HJ Sr. originally gave the English version.
Phineas T. Barnum (1810–91) was the celebrated American showman and publicist.

344. Aside from finding Carlyle's social behavior aggressive and intimidating (see
his "Personal Recollections" of 1881 in *Literary Remains*), HJ Sr.—like many others—
considered Carlyle's increasingly antidemocratic arguments unacceptable.

345. The MS in the Houghton Library has a penciled date of 1861 (bMS Am 1092.9
[4116]), and Habegger agrees with this (*The Father*, 457n). It was written on a Sunday
night from the Tremont House hotel. Matthiessen, who includes this letter in *The James
Family*, dates it in the fall of 1860, soon after the family's return from Europe (479–80).

346. The elegant Tremont House on the corner of Tremont and Beacon streets was well
known for its innovative amenities, including indoor plumbing, running water, and lock-
able rooms.

347. In 1861 HJ Sr. was an invited guest at the Saturday Club, which met regularly on
the last Saturday of the month at the Parker House in Boston; he was elected as a member
toward the end of 1863. The club (which developed out of the Town and Country Club)
included, among other literary men, Sumner, Emerson, Fields, Hawthorne, Lowell, and

gies were ever much called for in any case of the play of that really prime note of his spontaneity.

I go to Concord in the morning, but shall have barely time to see you there, even if I do as much as that; so that I can't forbear to say to you now the word I wanted as to my impression of yesterday about Hawthorne and Ellery Channing.[348] Hawthorne isn't to me a prepossessing figure, nor apparently at all an *enjoying*[349] person in any way: he has all the while the look—or would have to the unknowing— of a rogue who suddenly finds himself in a company of detectives. But in spite of his rusticity I felt a sympathy for him fairly amounting to anguish, and couldn't take my eyes off him all dinner, nor my rapt attention: as that indecisive little Dr. Hedge* [350] found, I am afraid, to his cost, for I hardly heard a word of what he kept on saying to me, and resented his maliciously putting his artificial person between me and the profitable object of study. (It isn't however that I *now* feel any ill-will to him—I could recommend anyone but myself to go and hear him preach. The thing was that Hawthorne seemed to me to possess human substance and not to have dissipated it all away like that culturally debauched ——,[351] or even like good inoffensive comforting Longfellow.) John Forbes[352] and you kept up the human balance at the

* An eminent Unitarian pastor.

Longfellow; HJ Sr. attended irregularly (Habegger, *The Father,* 457-58). See also E. W. Emerson, *Early Years of the Saturday Club,* which gives portraits of its eminent members.

348. William Ellery Channing (1818-1901), the transcendental poet, was the nephew of Dr. Channing, celebrated minister of the Unitarian Church.

349. The MS gives, more appropriately, "*engaging.*"

350. Rev. Dr. Frederic Henry Hedge (1805-90) was also a member of Boston's Examiner Club, where it seems he engaged in close debate with HJ Sr. (for an entertaining account, see Habegger, *The Father,* 459-62).

351. The excised name is that of Charles Eliot Norton (1827-1908) (Matthiessen, *The James Family,* 479). A professor of fine art at Harvard, one of the founders of the *Nation,* he was an important editor and scholar who was an inspirational figure for the young HJ. He had recently begun to coedit the *North American Review,* establishing it as an important voice on moral and political issues. Given the novelist's respect for the man and the fact that one of his sisters, Grace, was still living and a lifelong friend of HJ's, it is not surprising that he suppressed his identity. Later in the letter it is Norton's questing "long antennae" that are referred to.

352. John Murray Forbes (1813-98) was a railroad magnate, abolitionist, and philanthropist; his son married Emerson's daughter Edith.

other end of the table, but my region was a desert with H. for its only oasis. It was so pathetic to see him, contented sprawling Concord owl that he was and always has been, brought blindfold into that brilliant daylight and expected to wink and be lively, like some dapper Tommy Titmouse.[353] I felt him bury his eyes in his plate and eat with such voracity that no one should dare to speak to him. My heart broke for him as his attenuated left-hand neighbour kept putting forth *his* long antennae to stroke his face and try whether his eyes were open. It was heavenly to see him persist in ignoring the spectral smiles—in eating his dinner and doing nothing *but* that, and then go home to his Concord den to fall upon his knees and ask his heavenly Father why it was that an owl couldn't remain an owl and not be forced into the diversions of a canary. I have no doubt that all the tenderest angels saw to his case that night and poured oil into his wounds more soothing than gentlemen ever know. W. Ellery Channing too seemed so human and good—sweet as summer and fragrant as pinewoods. He is more sophisticated than Hawthorne of course, but still he was kin; and I felt the world richer by two *men,* who had not yet lost themselves in mere members of society. This is what I suspect—that we are fast getting so fearful one to another, we "members of society" that we shall ere long begin to kill one another in self-defence and give place in that way at last to a more veracious state of things. The old world is breaking up on all hands: the glimpse of the everlasting granite I caught in H. and W. E. shows me that there is stock enough left for fifty better. Let the old impostors go, bag and baggage, for a very real and substantial one is aching to come in, in which the churl shall not be exalted to a place of dignity, in which innocence shall never be tarnished nor trafficked in, in which every man's freedom shall be respected down to its feeblest filament as the radiant altar of God. To the angels, says Swedenborg, death means resurrection to life; by that necessary rule of inversion which keeps them separate from us and us from them, and so prevents our being mutual nuisances. Let us then accept political and all other distraction that chooses to come; because what is disorder and wrath and contention on the surface is sure to be the greatest peace at the centre, working its way thus to a surface that shall never be disorderly.

353. Tommy Titmouse, a character in a children's story, is a small boy who becomes a great man by working hard and being obedient and good-natured.

But it is in the postscript that the mixture and the transition strike me as most inevitable.

> Weren't you shocked at ——'s engagement? To think of that prim old snuffers imposing himself on that pure young flame![354] What a world, what a world! But once we get rid of Slavery the new heavens and new earth will swim into reality.

No better example could there be, I think, of my father's remarkable and constant belief, proof against all confusion, in the imminence of a transformation-scene in human affairs—"spiritually" speaking of course always—which was to be enacted somehow without gross or vulgar visibility, or at least violence, as I have said, but was none the less straining to the front, and all by reason of the world's being, deep within and at heart, as he conceived, so achingly anxious for it. He had the happiness—though not so untroubled, all the while, doubtless, as some of his declarations would appear to represent—of being able to see his own period and environment as the field of the sensible change, and thereby as a great historic hour; that is, I at once subjoin, I more or less *suppose* he had. His measure of the imminent and immediate, of the socially and historically visible and sensible was not a thing easy to answer for, and when treated to any one of the loud vaticinations or particular revolutionary messages and promises our age was to have so much abounded in, all his sense of proportion and of the whole, of the real and the ridiculous, asserted itself with the last emphasis. In that mixture in him of faith and humour, criticism and conviction, that mark of a love of his kind which fed on discriminations and was never so moved to a certain extravagance as by an exhibited, above all by a cultivated or in the least sententious vagueness in respect to these, dwelt largely the original charm, the peculiarly social and living challenge (in that it was so straight and bright a reflection of life) of his talk and temper. Almost all of my father shines for me at any rate in the above passages, and in another that follows, with their so easy glide from discrimination, as I have called it, that is from analytic play, in the outward sphere, to serenity of synthesis and confidence and high joy in the inward.

354. This refers once more to Charles Eliot Norton; he had recently become engaged to Susan Ridley Sedgwick (1838–72). The original of this letter lacks the postscript that was "tacked onto the version in *Notes of a Son and Brother*," and the allusion to "snuffers" is reminiscent of "the same strikingly repellent image appropriated by Gilbert Osmond in *The Portrait of a Lady*" (Habegger, *The Father*, 457n). A typescript copy of the same letter at Houghton, however, which HJ may conceivably have used, includes the postscript.

It was as if he might have liked so to see his fellow-humans, fellow-diners, fellow-celebrities or whatever, in that acuity of individual salience, in order to proceed thence to some enormous final doubt or dry renouncement— instead of concluding, on the contrary, and on the same free and familiar note, to the eminently "worth while" character of life, or its susceptibility to vast and happy conversions. With which too, more than I can say, have I the sense here of his so finely contentious or genially perverse impulse to carry his wares of observation to the market in which they would on the whole bring least rather than most—where his offering them at all would produce rather a flurry (there might have been markets in which it had been known to produce almost a scandal), and where he would in fact give them away for nothing if thereby he might show that such produce grew. Never was there more of a case of the direct friendliness to startling growths—if so they might be held—of the very soil that lies under our windows. I don't think he liked to scandalize—certainly he didn't in the least for scandal's sake; but nothing inspired him more to the act and the pleasure of appreciation for appropriation, as it might be termed, than the deprecating attitude of others on such ground—that degree of shyness of appropriation on their part which practically left appreciation vague. It was true that the appreciation for a human use, as it might be called—that is for the high optimistic transition—could here carry the writer far.

VII  I find markedly relevant at this point a letter from New-port in the autumn of '61 to another correspondent, one of a series several other examples of which no less successfully appeal to me, even though it involve my going back a little to place three or four of these latter, written at Geneva in 1860. Mrs. William Tappan, primarily Caroline Sturgis of Boston, was for long years and to the end of her life our very great friend and one of my father's most constant and most considered interlocutors, both on the ground of his gravity and on that of his pleasantry.[355] She had spent in Europe with her

355. Caroline Sturgis Tappan came from a privileged background: her father's com-pany, Bryant and Sturgis, prospered, and he had become a "wealthy maritime merchant prince" (Francis B. Dedmond, "The Letters of Caroline Sturgis to Margaret Fuller," *Studies in the American Renaissance, 1988,* ed. Joel Myerson [Charlottesville: University Press of Virginia, 1988], 201). The girl's childhood was blighted, however, by her mother's mental ill health; she suffered from depression after her son drowned and at one point abandoned the family. Caroline's letters have been described as "by turns dreamy, witty,

husband and her two small daughters very much the same years, from early in the summer of '55 till late in the autumn of '60, that we had been spending; and like ourselves, though with less continuity for the time, she had come to live at Newport, where, with no shadow of contention, but with an admirable intelligence, of the incurably ironic or mocking order, she was such a light, free, somewhat intellectually perverse but socially impulsive presence (always for instance insatiably hospitable) as our mustered circle could ill have spared. If play of mind, which she carried to any point of quietly-smiling audacity that might be, had not already become a noted, in fact I think the very most noted, value among us, it would have seated itself there in her person with a nervous animation, a refinement of what might have been called soundable sincerity, that left mere plump assurance in such directions far in the lurch. And she was interesting, she became fairly historic, with the drawing-out of the years, as almost the only survivor of that young band of the ardent and uplifted who had rallied in the other time to the "transcendental" standard, the movement for organised candour of conversation on almost all conceivable or inconceivable things which appeared, with whatever looseness, to find its prime inspirer in Emerson and become more familiarly, if a shade less authentically, vocal in Margaret Fuller.[356] Hungry, ever so cheerfully and confidently hungry, had been much of the New England, and peculiarly the Boston, of those days; but with no such outreaching of the well-scoured empty platter, it probably would have struck one, as by the occasional and quite individual agitation of it from some ruefully-observed doorstep of the best society. It was from such a doorstep that Caroline Sturgis had originally taken her restless flight, just as it was on such another that, after a course of infinite freedom of inquiry and irony, she in the later time, with a fortune inherited, an hospitality extended and a genial gravity of expression confirmed, alighted again, to the no small re-enrichment of a company of friends who had had meanwhile scarce any such intellectual adventures as she was to retain, in a delicate and casual irreverence, the just slightly sharp fragrance or fine asperity of, but who might cultivate

---

whimsical, irreverent, acute, and melancholic . . . one can easily see why the 'gipsy-like' Sturgis, despite her unprepossessing appearance . . . would be attractive to literary people" (Charles Capper, *Margaret Fuller: An American Romantic Life*, vol. 1: *The Private Years* [New York: Oxford University Press, 1992], 273). See also n. 216 above.

356. Tappan, who wrote poetry and moved in transcendentalist circles, became in her youth a protégée and intimate friend of Margaret Fuller as well as enjoying an almost fifty-year friendship with Emerson.

with complacency and in support of the general claim to comprehensive culture and awareness unafraid the legend of her vicarious exposure.

Mr. Frank Sanborn's school, which I have already mentioned and to which the following alludes, was during the years immediately preceding the War, as during those of the War itself, the last word of what was then accounted the undauntedly modern, flourishing as it did under the patronage of the most "advanced" thought.[357] The "coeducational" idea had up to that time, if I mistake not, taken on no such confident and consistent, certainly no such graceful or plausible form; small boys and big boys, boys from near and boys from far, consorted there and cohabited, so far as community of board and lodging and of study and sport went, with little girls and great girls, mainly under the earnest tutoring and elder-sistering of young women accomplished as scholarly accomplishment in such cases was then understood, but with Mr. Sanborn himself of course predominantly active and instructional, and above all with the further felicity of the participation of the generous Emerson family by sympathy and interest and the protective spread of the rich mantle of their presence. The case had been from the first a frank and high-toned experiment,[358] a step down from the tonic air, as was so considerably felt, of radical conviction to the firm ground of radical application, that is of happy demonstration—an admittedly new and trustful thing, but all the brighter and wiser, all the more nobly and beautifully workable for that. With but the scantest direct observation of the attempted demonstration—

357. The school, sponsored by Emerson, was run by Franklin Benjamin Sanborn, a graduate of Harvard, a Boston newspaper man, and a biographer of Emerson, Thoreau, and Hawthorne. He had been "for some years . . . an admirer of 'Henry James's metaphysics,' as expressed in *Putnam's Magazine*" (Lewis, *The Jameses*, 105). The visit allowed HJ Sr. to approach Emerson once more. Le Clair provides further detail: "The building was a small gray structure, about forty feet long and twenty feet wide, with a big stove in the center, three of the walls panelled with blackboards and the entrance wall fronted by the master's desk on a low dais. A central aisle divided the pupils, girls on one side, boys on the other. . . . Surrounding the school house, was the idyllic Concord community, offering picnics at Esterbrook Farm, bathing and skating at Walden Pond, regattas on the river below the old Red Bridge, overnight encampments on Monadnock Mountain" (*Young Henry James*, 339). The school numbered on its roll "the children of some of New England's most renowned intellectuals and idealists" (Maher, *Biography of Broken Fortunes*, 17), but as Strouse points out (*Alice James*, 64), there was never any question of Alice James becoming a pupil. On the school, see also n. 189.

358. "The school had been conducted in an earlier period by the Thoreau brothers" (Lewis, *The Jameses*, 104). Emerson's two daughters, Edith and Ellen, had attended classes for a time.

demonstration, that is, of the excellent fruit such a grafting might produce—I yet imagine the enacted and considerably prolonged scene (it lasted a whole decade) to have heaped perfectly full the measure of what it proposed. The interesting, the curious, the characteristic thing was just, however, I seem to make out—I seemed to have made out even at the time—in the almost complete absence of difficulty. It might almost then be said of the affair that it hadn't been difficult enough for interest even should one insist on treating it as sufficiently complicated or composed for picture. The great War was to leave so many things changed, the country over, so many elements added, to say nothing of others subtracted, in the American consciousness at large, that even though the coeducational idea, taking to itself strength, has during these later years pushed its conquests to the very verge of demonstration of its inevitable limits, my memory speaks to me of the Concord school rather as of a supreme artless word on the part of the old social order than as a charged intimation or announce- ment on the part of the new. The later arrangements, more or less in its likeness and when on a considerable scale, have appeared, to attentive observation, I think, mere endlessly multiplied notes of the range of high spirits in the light heart of communities more aware on the whole of the size and number of their opportunity, of the boundless spaces, the possi- ble undertakings, the uncritical minds and the absent standards about them, than of matters to be closely and preparedly reckoned with. They have been, comparatively speaking, experiments in the void—the great void that may spread so smilingly between wide natural borders before complications have begun to grow. The name of the complication before the fact is very apt to be the discovery—which latter term was so promptly to figure for the faith that living and working more intimately together than had up to then been conceived possible would infinitely improve both the condition and the performance of the brother and sister sexes.[359] It takes

359. In the Notebooks kept in preparation for *AS,* HJ had been considering (in 1905) the roles of men and women and the relations between them, the "values" associated with the country club: "Wasn't the 'sport' image of the young people, the straight brown young men, with strong good figures and homely faces, one of them? I mean as associated with that of the strong, charmless (*work* that 'charmless' right), stalwart, slangy girls, in whom one feels the intimation, the consequence, of the absence of danger, from the men—as one feels throughout, in the N.E., in each sex, the absence of a sense, the absence of the consciousness, of, or of the existence of, danger from the other" (*CN,* 241). In 1907 HJ also published in *Harper's Bazar* "The Manners of American Women" (rpt. in *Henry James on*

long in new communities for discoveries to become complications—though complications become discoveries doubtless often in advance of this; the large vague area, with its vast marginal ease, over which confidence could run riot and new kinds of human relation, elatedly proposed, flourish in the sun, was to shift to different ground the question the Concord school had played with, during its term of life, on its smaller stage, under the great New England elms and maples and in the preoccupied New England air.

The preoccupation had been in a large measure, it is true, exactly with such possibilities, such bright fresh answers to old stale riddles, as Mr. Sanborn and his friends clubbed together to supply; but I can only, for my argument, recover the sense of my single visit to the scene, which must have been in the winter of '62-'63, I think, and which put before me, as I seem now to make out, some suggested fit of perversity—not desperate, quite harmless rather, and almost frivolously futile, on the part of a particular little world that had been thrown back upon itself for very boredom and, after a spell of much admired talking and other beating of the air, wanted for a change to "do" something. The question it "played" with I just advisedly said—for what could my impression have been, personally if indirectly gathered, and with my admirably communicative younger brother to testify,[360] but that if as a school, in strict parlance, the thing was scarce more than naught, as a prolonged pastime it was scarce less than charming and quite filled up in that direction its ample and original measure? I have to reckon, I here allow, with the trick of what I used irrepressibly to read into things in front of which I found myself, for gaping purposes, planted by some unquestioned outer force: it seemed so prescribed to me, so imposed on me, to read more, as through some ever-felt claim for roundness of aspect and intensity of effect in presented matters, whatever they might be, than the conscience of the particular

_Culture: Collected Essays on Politics and the American Social Scene,_ ed. Pierre A. Walker [Lincoln: University of Nebraska Press, 1999], 82–112).

360. Wilky was the last to leave Sanborn's school, at the end of the spring term 1862, and he enlisted on 12 September 1862, so HJ must be at least a year out in his memories. He wrote in a letter of reply to Emerson's son Edward on 4 August 1914, "you remember things (of my own subject,) that I hadn't—like that fantastic little hat, acquired in Paris, that I must have worn to Concord & which lives again for me on your page" (_Henry James: A Life in Letters,_ ed. Philip Horne [London: Allen Lane, Penguin Press, 1999], 541).

affair itself was perhaps developed enough to ask of it. The experience of many of the Concord pupils during the freshness of the experiment must have represented for them a free and yet ever so conveniently conditioned taste of the idyllic—such possibilities of perfect good comradeship between unsuspected and unalarmed youths and maidens (on a comprehensive ground that really exposed the business to a light and put it to a test) as they were never again to see so favoured in every way by circumstance and, one may quite emphatically say, by atmosphere. It is the atmosphere that comes back to me as most of all the making of the story, even when inhaled but by an occasional whiff and from afar—the manner of my own inhaling. In that air of charmed and cultivated good faith nothing for which the beautiful might be so presumingly claimed—if only claimed with a sufficiently brave clean emphasis—wouldn't have *worked,* which was the great thing; every one must have felt that what was aspired to did work, and as I catch the many-voiced report of it again (many-voiced but pretty well suffused with one clear tone, this of inflections irreproducible now) I seem to listen in convinced admiration, though not by any means in stirred envy, to the cheerful clatter of its working. My failure of envy has, however, no mite of historic importance, proving as it does nothing at all but that if we had, in the family sense, so distinctly turned our back on Europe, the distinctness was at no point so marked as in our facing so straight to such a picture, by which I mean to such an exhibition, as my father's letter throws off. Without knowledge of the letter at the time I yet measured the situation much as he did and enjoyed it as he did, because it would have been stupid not to; but from that to any wishful vision of being in it or of it would have been a long jump, of which I was unabashedly incapable. To have broken so personally, so all but catastrophically, with Europe as we had done affected me as the jump sufficient; we had landed somewhere in quite another world or at least on the sharp edge of one; and in the single particular sense could I, as time then went on, feel myself at all moved, with the helpless, the baffled visionary way of it, to push further in. What straight solicitation *that* phase of the American scene could exert—more coercive to the imagination than any we were ever again, as Americans, to know—I shall presently try to explain; but this was an intensely different matter.

I buried two of my children yesterday—at Concord, Mass., and feel so heartbroken this morning that I shall need to adopt two more instantly to supply their place; and lo and behold you and William present yourselves, or if you decline the honour Ellen and Baby.[361] Mary and I trotted forth last Wednesday, bearing Wilky and Bob in our arms to surrender them to the famous Mr. Sanborn. The yellowest sunshine and an atmosphere of balm were all over the goodly land, while the maple, the oak and the dogwood showered such splendours upon the eye as made the Champs Elysées and the Bois appear parvenus and comical.[362] Mrs. Clark is a graceless enough woman outwardly, but so tenderly feathered inwardly, so unaffectedly kind and motherly toward the urchins under her roof, that one was glad to leave them in that provident nest. She has three or four other school-boarders, one of them a daughter of John Brown—tall, erect, long-haired and freckled, as John Brown's daughter has a right to be.[363] I kissed her (inwardly) between the eyes, and inwardly heard the martyred Johannes chuckle over the fat inheritance of love and tenderness he had after all bequeathed to his children in all good men's minds. An arch little Miss Plumley also lives there, with eyes full of laughter and a mouth like a bed of lilies bordered with roses. How it is going to be possible for my two boys to pursue their studies in the midst of that bewilderment I don't clearly see. I am only sure of one thing, which is that if I had had such educational advantages as that in my youth I should probably have been now far more nearly ripe for this world's business. We asked to see Miss Waterman, one of the teachers quartered in the house, in order to say to her how much we should thank her if she would occasionally put out any too lively spark she might see fall on the expectant tinder of my poor boys' bosoms; but

361. This letter (for which *NSB* seems to be the source, see Habegger, *The Father*, 551n) was written to Caroline Sturgis Tappan and dates from the fall of 1860. Burr (*Alice James: Her Brothers*, 3) describes the stagecoach journey from Boston and the exotic appearance of the family members: "A gentleman, brisk of movement and full of energy notwithstanding his artificial leg, was accompanied by two handsome boys of thirteen and fourteen, wearing pea-jackets of a foreign cut and hats and peg-top trousers unlike those seen on other boys in New England." The youngest James son, Robertson, attended the school for one year; the next youngest, Wilky, stayed on for a second year. The family was still living in Newport, and it is recorded that Concord was "a little further off than their mother likes." Both boys were perhaps too old for the school and became "bored and restless" (Habegger, *The Father*, 424, 425). The Tappans' daughters were Ellen and Mary.

362. The Champs Élysées and Bois de Boulogne would be familiar to the traveled Tappans, who had lived in Paris.

363. This could be Sarah Brown, who would have been fourteen (see *CWJ*, 4:91 n. 3).

Miss W. herself proved of so siliceous a quality on inspection[364]—with round tender eyes, young, fair and womanly—that I saw in her only new danger and no promise of safety. My present conviction is that a general conflagration is inevitable, ending in the total combustion of all that I hold dear on that spot. Yet I can't but felicitate our native land that such magnificent experiments in education go on among us.

Then we drove to Emerson's and waded up to our knees through a harvest of apples and pears, which, tired of their mere outward or carnal growth, had descended to the loving bosom of the lawn, there or elsewhere to grow inwardly meet for their heavenly rest in the veins of Ellen the saintly and others; until at last we found the cordial Pan himself in the midst of his household, breezy with hospitality and blowing exhilarating trumpets of welcome.[365] Age has just the least in the world dimmed the lustre we once knew, but an unmistakable breath of the morning still encircles him, and the odour of primaeval woods. Pitchpine is not more pagan than he continues to be, and acorns as little confess the gardener's skill. Still I insist that he is a voluntary Pan, that it is a condition of mere wilfulness and insurrection on his part, contingent upon a mercilessly sound digestion and an uncommon imaginative influx, and I have no doubt that even he, as the years ripen, will at last admit Nature to be tributary and not supreme. However this be, we consumed juicy pears to the diligent music of Pan's pipe, while Ellen and Edith softly gathered themselves upon two low stools in the chimney-corner, saying never a word nor looking a look, but apparently hemming their handkerchiefs; and good Mrs. Stearns, who sat by the window and seemed to be the village dressmaker, ever and anon glanced at us over her spectacles as if to say that never before has she seen this wondrous Pan so glistening with dewdrops. Then and upon the waves of that friendly music we were duly wafted to our educational Zion[366] and carefully made over our good and promising and

364. Given that silica is a mineral substance, this seems an odd choice of adjective; it has been suggested (Habegger, *The Father*, 551n) that HJ may have misread his father's script.

365. Emerson first lived in the Old Manse, the clapboard house his grandfather had built near the North Bridge, before moving to the house on the intersection of the Cambridge Turnpike and Lexington Road, where he remained for almost fifty years. Pan was the Greek god of pastures, flocks, and herds. "I love the mighty PAN," Emerson asserted (Rusk, *Life of Emerson*, 228).

366. Figuratively, Zion is the church of God or the kingdom of heaven.

affectionate boys to the school-master's keeping. Out into the field beside his house Sanborn incontinently took us to show how his girls and boys perform together their worship of Hygeia.[367] It was a glimpse into that new world wherein dwelleth righteousness and which is full surely fast coming upon our children and our children's children; and I could hardly keep myself, as I saw my children's eyes drink in the mingled work and play of the inspiring scene, from shouting out a joyful Nunc Dimittis.[368] The short of the story is that we left them and rode home robbed of our plumage, feeling sore and ugly and only hoping that they wouldn't die, any of these cold winter days, before the parental breast could get there to warm them back to life or cheer them on to a better.

Mrs. William Hunt has just come in to tell the good news of your near advent and that she has found the exact house for you;[369] instigated to that activity by one of your angels, of the Hooper band, with whom she has been in correspondence.[370] I don't thank angel Hooper for putting angel Hunt upon that errand, since I should like to have had the merit of it myself. I suspect the rent is what it ought to be: if it's not I will lay by something every week for you toward it, and have no doubt we shall stagger through the cold weather.

I gather from the above the very flower of my father's irrepressible utterance of his constitutional optimism, that optimism fed so little by any sense of things as they were or are, but rich in its vision of the facility with which they might become almost at any moment or from one day to the other totally and splendidly different. A less vague or vain idealist couldn't, I think, have been encountered; it was given him to catch in the fact at almost any turn right or left some flagrant assurance or promise of the state of man transfigured. The Concord school could be to him for the hour—there were hours and hours!—such a promise; could even figure in

367. Hygeia is the Greek goddess of health.

368. HJ Sr. continues the blend of classical and Judaeo-Christian allusions. The Nunc Dimittis ("Lord, now lettest thou thy servant depart in peace") forms the second liturgical canticle of the Anglican service of evensong.

369. Louisa Perkins Hunt, wife of the painter; the Hunts left Newport for Boston in 1862. The Tappans were in the process of moving from Europe to Newport.

370. Edward William Hooper (1839–1901) and his sisters, Marian, known as Clover (1843–85), and Ellen (1838–87), both of whom suffered mental health problems, were the children of Robert William Hooper (1810–85), a physician. Clover married the historian Henry Adams, and she later killed herself.

that light, to his amplifying sympathy, in a degree disproportionate to its genial, but after all limited, after all not so intensely "inflated," as he would have said, sense of itself. In which light it is that I recognise, and even to elation, how little, practically, of the idea of the Revolution in the vulgar or violent sense was involved in his seeing so many things, in the whole social order about him, and in the interest of their being more or less immediately altered, as lamentably, and yet at the same time and under such a coloured light, as amusingly and illustratively, wrong—wrong, that is, with a blundering helpless human salience that kept criticism humorous, kept it, so to speak, sociable and almost "sympathetic" even when readiest.[371] The case was really of his rather feeling so vast a rightness close at hand or lurking immediately behind actual arrangements that a single turn of the inward wheel, one real response to pressure of the spiritual spring, would bridge the chasms, straighten the distortions, rectify the relations and, in a word, redeem and vivify the whole mass—after a far sounder, yet, one seemed to see, also far subtler, fashion than any that our spasmodic annals had yet shown us. It was of course the old story that we had only to *be* with more intelligence and faith—an immense deal more, certainly—in order to work off, in the happiest manner, the many-sided ugliness of life; which was a process that might go on, blessedly, in the quietest of all quiet ways. *That* wouldn't be blood and fire and tears, or would be none of these things stupidly precipitated; it would simply have taken place by *enjoyed* communication and contact, enjoyed concussion or convulsion even— since pangs and agitations, the very agitations of perception itself, are of the highest privilege of the soul and there is always, thank goodness, a saving sharpness of play or complexity of consequence in the intelligence completely alive. The meaning of which remarks for myself, I must be content to add, is that the optimists of the world, the constructive idealists, as one has mainly known them, have too often struck one as overlooking more of the aspects of the real than they recognise; whereas our indefeasible impression, William's and mine, of our parent was that he by his very constitution and intimate heritage recognised many more of those than he overlooked. What was the finest part of our intercourse with him—that is the most nutritive—but a positive record of that? Such a matter as that the

371. HJ perhaps refers to the range of his father's writing and interests in the sociopolitical field, which sometimes involved him in public debate and controversy. Though he was committed to democratic ideals, his optimistic beliefs in humanity and society led him to adopt a conservative stance. HJ characteristically goes on to recall the "drama," observed in a domestic setting, of his father's creative process.

factitious had absolutely no hold on him was the truest thing about him, and it was all the while present to us, I think, as backing up his moral authority and play of vision that never, for instance, had there been a more numerous and candid exhibition of all the human susceptibilities than in the nest of his original nurture. I have spoken of the fashion in which I still see him, after the years, attentively bent over those much re-written "papers," that we had, even at our stupidest, this warrant for going in vague admiration of that they caught the eye, even the most filially detached, with a final face of wrought clarity, and thereby of beauty, that there *could* be no thinking unimportant—and see him also fall back from the patient posture, again and again, in long fits of remoter consideration, wondering, pondering sessions into which I think I was more often than not moved to read, for the fine interest and colour of it, some story of acute inward difficulty amounting for the time to discouragement. If one wanted drama *there* was drama, and of the most concrete and most immediately offered to one's view and one's suspense; to the point verily, as might often occur, of making one go roundabout it on troubled tiptoe even as one would have held one's breath at the play.

These opposed glimpses, I say, hang before me as I look back, but really fuse together in the vivid picture of the fond scribe separated but by a pane of glass—his particular preference was always directly to face the window—from the general human condition he was so devoutly concerned with. He *saw* it, through the near glass, saw it in such detail and with a feeling for it that broke down nowhere—that was the great thing; which truth it confirmed that his very fallings back and long waits and stays and almost stricken musings witnessed exactly to his intensity, the intensity that would "come out," after all, and make his passionate philosophy and the fullest array of the appearances that couldn't be blinked fit together and harmonise. Detached as I could during all those years perhaps queerly enough believe myself, it would still have done my young mind the very greatest violence to have to suppose that any plane of conclusion for him, however rich and harmonious he might tend to make conclusion, could be in the nature of a fool's paradise. Small vague outsider as I was, I couldn't have borne *that* possibility; and I see, as I return to the case, how little I really could ever have feared it. This would have amounted to fearing it on account of his geniality—a shocking supposition; as if his geniality had been thin and *bête*,[372] patched up and poor, and

372. Foolish.

not by the straightest connections, nominal and other, of the very stuff of his genius. No, I feel myself complacently look back to *my* never having, even at my small poorest, been so *bête,* either, as to conceive he might be "wrong," wrong as a thinker-out, in his own way, of the great mysteries, because of the interest and amusement and vividness his attesting spirit could fling over the immediate ground. What he saw *there* at least could be so enlightening, so evocatory, could fall in so—which was to the most inspiring effect within the range of perception of a scant son who was doubtless, as to the essential, already more than anything else a novelist *en herbe.*[373] If it didn't sound in a manner patronising I should say that I saw that my father saw; and that I couldn't but have given my own case away by not believing, however obscurely, in the virtue of his consequent and ultimate synthesis. Of course I never dreamed of any such name for it—I only thought of it as something very great and fine founded on those forces in him that came home to us and that touched us all the while. As these were extraordinary forces of sympathy and generosity, and that yet knew how to be such without falsifying any minutest measure, the structure raised upon them might well, it would seem, and even to the uppermost sublime reaches, be as valid as it was beautiful. If he so endeared himself wasn't it, one asked as time went on, through his never having sentimentalised or merely meditated away, so to call it, the least embarrassment of the actual about him, and having with a passion peculiarly his own kept together his stream of thought, however transcendent and the stream of life, however humanised? There was a kind of experiential authority in his basis, as he felt his basis—there being no human predicament he couldn't by a sympathy more *like* direct experience than any I have known enter into; and this authority, which concluded so to a widening and brightening of the philosophic—for him the spiritual—sky, made his character, as intercourse disclosed it, in a high degree fascinating. These things, I think, however, are so happily illustrated in his letters that they look out from almost any continuous passage in such a series for instance as those addressed in the earlier time to Mrs. Tappan.[374] His *tone,* that is,

373. Green or unripe.

374. It seems clear that HJ Sr.'s letters, especially those addressed to women in his circle, have an erotic subtext, or at least reflect a desire for emotional intimacy which is facilitated or given legitimacy by the nature of the issues under discussion. Aside from Caroline Tappan, he wrote warm and challengingly frank letters to Elizabeth Cranch, Anna Ward, and Fanny Macdaniel. Habegger comments, "A new pattern was emerging: his closest friendships were not with men interested in socialism but with women interested in

always so effectually looks out, and the living parts of him so singularly hung together, that one may fairly say his philosophy *was* his tone. To cite a few passages here is at the same time to go back to a previous year or two—which my examples, I hold, make worth while. He had been on a visit to Paris toward the winter's end of '60, and had returned to Geneva, whence he writes early in April.[375]

> So sleepy have I been ever since my return from Paris that I am utterly unfit to write letters. I was thoroughly poisoned by tobacco in those horrid railway carriages, and this with want of sleep knocked me down. I am only half awake still, and will not engage consequently in any of those profound inquiries which your remembrance always suggests.
>
> I am very sorry for you that you live in an excommunicated country, or next door to it; and I don't wonder at your wanting to get away.[376] But it is provoking to think that but for your other plan Switzerland might possess you all for the summer. It is doubtless in part this disappointment that will unsettle us in our present moorings and take us probably soon to Germany. What after that I have no idea, and am always so little wilful about our movements that I am ready the young ones should settle them. So we may be in Europe a good while yet, always providing that war keep smooth his wrinkled front and allow us quiet newspapers. They must fight in Italy for some time to come, but between England and France is the main point. If *they* can hold aloof from tearing each other we shall manage; otherwise we go home at once, to escape the universal spatter that must then ensue.[377]

---

his theology," adding that "James was faithful to Mary, but he loved courting his sisters of the spirit, his angel-wives" (*The Father*, 385, 386).

375. As described in chaps. 1 and 2 above, the Jameses spent 1859–60 in Switzerland; three of the boys traveled to Germany for the summer, though their parents and aunt passed much of that time in Paris.

376. Caroline Tappan was living in France at the time; HJ Sr. appears to be referring to the difficulties recently encountered by Napoleon III, his support in principal for the Italian national movement, and the hostility of Catholics across Europe, who feared the consequent downfall of the papacy.

377. England and France had been recent allies in supporting Turkey in the Crimean War. In the changing dynamics of Europe involving the unification of Italy, Napoleon III was closely involved in the process of freeing (for other gains) Lombardy and Venetia from Austrian rule. The British prime minister, Palmerston, while supportive of Cavour's plans for the new Italy, refused to intervene, being keen to avoid any threat to the Austrian empire

What is the meaning of all these wars and rumours of wars? No respectable person ever seems to occupy himself with the question, but I can't help feeling it more interesting than anything in Homer or Plato or the gallery of the Vatican.[378] I long daily with unappeasable longing for a righteous life, such a life as I am sure is implied in every human possibility, and myriads are bearing me company. What does this show but that the issue is near out of all our existing chaos? All our evil is fossil and comes from the mere persistence of diseased institutions in pretending to rule us when we ought to be left free to be living spirits of God. There is no *fresh* evil in the world. No one now steals or commits murder or any other offence with the least relish for it, but only to revenge his poor starved opportunities. The superiority of America in respect to freedom of thought over Europe comes from this fact that she has so nearly achieved her deliverance from such tyrannies. All she now needs to make her right is simply an intelligent recognition of her spiritual whereabouts. If she had this she would put her hand to the work splendidly. You and I when we get home will try to quicken her intelligence in that respect, will do at any rate *our* best to put away this pestilent munching of the tree of knowledge of good and evil, and persuade to the belief of man's unmixed innocence.[379]

Which, it will easily be seen, was optimism with a vengeance, and marked especially in the immediacy, the state of being at hand for him, of a social redemption. What made this the more signal was its being so unattended with visions the least Apocalyptic or convulsional; the better

and suspicious of France and the historical associations even of Napoleon's name. His relationship with Napoleon III cooled from 1858–59 onward.

378. The Vatican galleries or museums date back to 1503.

379. HJ Sr.'s sentiments here presage his imminent return to the United States and perhaps reflect a sense of Europe's indifference toward his ideas and a seemingly binding and unattractive religious orthodoxy. His conviction of mission directs him to the less rigid values of American society: he would never return to Europe. According to Matthiessen's summary, "A second-generation American whose wealth enabled him to recross the sea at will and to be an international cosmopolitan, he grew ever stauncher in his preference for America as the land of the future" (*The James Family*, 11). In his ensuing comments HJ appears keen to underscore the philosophical rigor of his father's progressive ideas, though he is aware too of the irony of HJ Sr.'s optimistic return to America, corresponding almost exactly with the outbreak of its own civil war. According to the book of Genesis, the tree of the knowledge of good and evil was instrumental in causing the fall of humankind from a state of innocence. HJ's "The Tree of Knowledge," a tale of artistic self-deception, was published in 1900.

order slipping in amid the worse, and superseding it, so insidiously, so quietly and, by a fair measure, so easily. It was a faith and an accompanying philosophy that couldn't be said not to be together simplifying; and yet nothing was more unmistakable when we saw them at close range, I repeat, than that they weren't unnourished, weren't what he himself would, as I hear him, have called the "flatulent" fruit of sentimentality.

His correspondent had in a high degree, by her vivacity of expression, the art of challenging his—as is markedly apparent from a letter the date of which fails beyond its being of the same stay at Geneva and of the winter's end.

If I had really imagined that I had bored you and your husband so very little while I was in Paris in December I should long since have repeated the experiment; the more surely that I want so much to see again my darling nieces and delight myself in the abundance of their large-eyed belief. . . . Our Alice is still under discipline—preparing to fulfil some high destiny or other in the future by reducing decimal fractions to their lowest possible rate of subsistence, where they often grow so attenuated under her rapid little fingers that my poor old eyes can no longer see them at all.[380] I shall go before long to England, and then perhaps—! But I shan't promise anything on *her* behalf.

You ask me "why I do not brandish my tomahawk and, like Walt Whitman, raise my barbaric yawp over the roofs of all the houses." It is because I am not yet a "cosmos" as that gentleman avowedly is, but only a very dim nebula, doing its modest best, no doubt, to solidify into cosmical dimensions, but still requiring an "awful sight" of time and pains and patience on the part of its friends.[381] You evidently

380. By "nieces," HJ Sr. refers to Mrs. Tappan's two daughters. Alice was eleven at this time.

381. The correspondents recall lines from Whitman's *Song of Myself*, for instance, his self-characterization as "Walt Whitman, a kosmos, of Manhattan the son, / Turbulent, fleshy, sensual, eating, drinking and breeding, / No sentimentalist, no stander above men and women or apart from them, / No more modest than immodest" (No. 24), and his assertion that, like "the spotted hawk," "I too am not a bit tamed, I too am untranslatable, / I sound my barbaric yawp over the roofs of the world" (No. 52) (*Walt Whitman: Complete Poetry and Collected Prose*, ed. Justin Kaplan [New York: Library of America, 1982], 210, 247). Though HJ was notably dismissive of Whitman in these years (as in his 1865 *Nation* review of "Drum-Taps," *LC* 1, 629–34), his father was clearly much more appreciative. Matthiessen points out that "HJ had thoroughly assimilated his father's disapproval of the selfishness of American competition," but, unlike HJ Sr., he could not celebrate "like

fancy that cosmoses are born to all the faculty they shall ever have, like ducks: no such thing. There is no respectable cosmos but what is born to such a vapoury and even gaseous inheritance as requires long centuries of conflict on its part to overcome the same and become pronounced or educated in its proper mineral, vegetable or animal order. Ducks are born perfect; that is to say they utter the same unmodified unimproved quack on their dying pillow that they uttered on their natal day; whereas cosmoses are destined to a life of such surprising change that you may say their career is an incessant disavowal of their birth, or that their highest maturation consists in their utter renunciation of their natural father and mother. You transcendentalists make the fatal mistake of denying education, of sundering present from past and future from present. These things are indissolubly one, the present deriving its consciousness only from the past, and the future drawing all its distinctive wisdom from our present experience.[382] The law is the same with the individual as it is with the race: none of us can dodge the necessity of regeneration, of disavowing our natural ancestry in order to come forth in our own divinely-given proportions. The secret of this necessity ought to reconcile us to it, however onerous the obligation it imposes; for that secret is nothing more nor less than this, that we cosmoses have a plenary divine origin and are bound eventually to see that divinity reproduced in our most familiar and trivial experience, even down to the length of our shoe-ties.[383] If the Deity were an immense Duck

---

Blake—or Whitman—his own immediate participation in the energy that is 'eternal delight.' HJ's 'only form of riot or revel' was, as he said, 'that of the visiting mind' " (*The James Family*, 244).

382. In Channing's characterization, transcendentalism was "a pilgrimage from the idolatrous world of creeds and rituals to the temple of the Living God in the soul. It was a putting to silence of tradition and formulas, the Sacred Oracle might be heard through intuitions of the single-eyed and pure-hearted" (quoted Habegger, *The Father*, 192). In addition, "Mrs. Tappan's Transcendental credentials were as solid as Emerson's, and like Henry Sr., she went in for 'play of mind,' especially of the 'incurably ironic or mocking order' " (ibid., 424).

383. It is commonly agreed that HJ Sr. rarely separated religion from politics in his social thinking. In its iconoclastic tropes (the deity, for example, likened to an immense duck) and often energetically jarring terms, HJ Sr.'s style can appear comparable with Whitman's, though WJ might not have agreed, since he recalled its " 'great dignity of cadence and full and homely vocabulary' which 'united a sort of inward palpitating human quality, gracious and tender, precise, fierce, scornful, humorous by turns, recalling the rich

capable only of emitting an eternal quack we of course should all have
been born webfooted, each as infallible in his way as the Pope, nor
ever have been at the expense and bother of swimming-schools. But
He is a perfect man, incapable of the slightest quackery, capable only
of every honest and modest and helpful purpose, and these are
perfections to which manifestly no one is born, but only *re*-born. We
come to such states not by learning, only by *unlearning*. No natural
edification issues in spiritual architecture of this splendour, but only a
natural demolition or undoing. I dimly recognise this great truth, and
hence hold more to a present imbecility than to a too eager efficiency. I
feel myself more fit to be knocked about for some time yet and
vastated of my natural vigour than to commence cosmos and raise the
barbaric yawp. Time enough for that when I am fairly finished. Say
what we will, you and I are all the while at school just now. The genial
pedagogue may give you so little of the ferule as to leave you to doubt
whether you really *are* there; but this only proves what a wonderful
pedagogue it is, and how capable of adapting himself to everyone.

His friend in Paris found herself at that time, like many other persons,
much interested in the exercise of automatic writing, of which we have
since so abundantly heard and as to which she had communicated some
striking observations.[384]

> . . . Your letter is full of details that interest but don't fascinate. I
> haven't a doubt of a single experience you allege, and do not agree
> with your friend Count S. (your writing of this name is obscure)[385]
> that the world of spirits is not an element in your writing. I am

vascular temperament of the old English masters, rather than that of an American today' "
(quoted in Perry, *Thought and Character of William James*, 1:125).

384. In terms of psychical research, automatic writing is executed without the volition
of the agent, who may be in a state of trance or indeed apparent consciousness. The 1850s
saw a proliferation of interest in the activity in American spiritualist circles. WJ, incidentally, became interested in spiritualism and psychical research by his later twenties. In the
middle 1880s he was conducting experiments in automatic writing in the belief that "a
person's subconscious can be directly related to the mental activities and forces of others."
While a student at Radcliffe College in the 1890s, Gertrude Stein, who was involved in
these experiments, characteristically complained that "this vehement individual is requested to make herself a perfect blank while someone practices on her as an automaton"
(Gerald E. Myers, *William James: His Life and Thought* [New Haven: Yale University
Press, 1986], 6, 10, 373).

385. Count S. has not been identified.

persuaded now for a long time of the truth of these phenomena and feel no inclination to dispute or disparage them; but at the same time I feel to such a degree my own remoteness from them that I am sure I could never get any personal contact with them. The state of mind exposing one to influences of this nature, and which makes them beneficial to it, is a sceptical state; and this I have never known for a moment. Spiritual existence has always been more real to me (I was going to say) than natural; and when accordingly I am asked to believe in the spiritual world because my senses are getting to reveal it I feel as if the ground of my conviction were going to be weakened rather than strengthened. Of course I should have very little respect for spiritual things which didn't ultimately report themselves to sense, which didn't indeed subside into things of sense as logically as a house into its foundations. But what I deny is that spiritual existence can be directly known on earth—known otherwise than by correspondence or inversely. The letter of every revelation must be directly hostile to its spirit, and only inversely accordant, because the very pretension of revelation is that it's a descent, an absolute coming down, of truth, a humiliation of it from its own elevated and habitual plane to a lower one.

Admit therefore that the facts of "spiritualism" are all true; admit that persons really deceased have been communicating with you about the state of Europe, the approaching crisis and the persons known to us whom you name; in that case I should insist that, to possess the slightest spiritual interest, their revelation should be re-translated into the spiritual tongue by correspondences; because as to any spirit knowing or caring to know those persons, or being bothered about any crisis of ours, that is to me simply incredible. Such matters have in each case doubtless some spiritual or substantial counterpart answering in every particular to its superficial features; and Wilkinson and Emerson, for instance, with the others, are of course shadows of some greater or less spiritual quantities. But I'll be hanged if there's the slightest *sensible* accord between the substance and the semblance on either hand. Your spirits, no doubt, give you the very communications you report to me; only Wilkinson spiritually interpreted and Emerson spiritually interpreted mean things so very different from our two friends of those denominations that if our spiritual eye were for a moment open to discern the difference I think it highly probable—I'm sure it is infinitely possible—we should renounce their acquaintance.

But I have harped on this string long enough; let me change the tune. Your spirits tell you to repose in what they are doing for you and, with a pathos to which I am not insensible, say "Rest now, poor child; your struggles have been great; clasp peace to your bosom at last." And as a general thing our ears are saluted by assurances that these communications are all urged by philanthropy and that everyone so addressing us wants in some way to help and elevate us. But just this is to my mind the unpleasant side of the business. I have been so long accustomed to see the most arrant deviltry transact itself in the name of benevolence that the moment I hear a profession of good-will from almost any quarter I instinctively look about for a constable or place my hand within reach of the bell-rope. My ideal of human intercourse would be a state of things in which no man will ever stand in need of any other man's help, but will derive all his satisfaction from the great social tides which own no individual names. I am sure no man can be put in a position of dependence upon another without that other's very soon becoming—if he accepts the duties of the relation—utterly degraded out of his just human proportions. No man can play the Deity to his fellow man with impunity—I mean spiritual impunity of course. For see: if I am at all satisfied with that relation, if it contents me to be in a position of generosity toward others, I must be remarkably indifferent at bottom to the gross social inequality which permits that position, and instead of resenting the enforced humiliation of my fellow man to myself, in the interests of humanity, I acquiesce in it for the sake of the profit it yields to my own self-complacency. I do hope the reign of benevolence is over; until that event occurs I am sure the reign of God will be impossible.[386] But I have a shocking bad cold that racks my head to bursting almost; I can't think to any purpose. Let me hear soon from you that I have not been misunderstood. I wouldn't for the world seem wilfully to depreciate what you set a high value on. No, I really can't help my judgments. And I always soften them to within an inch of their life as it is.

386. HJ Sr.'s skepticism is evident from at least the beginning of the 1850s when he published some letters in the *New York Tribune*, inviting spirits (in whose existence he believed) to "give us a solution to some of the great questions of the day—the questions of finance, of an increased agricultural production, of the abolition of poverty and crime. Give us an improved medication, say a cure for smallpox, scarlet fever, gout, or even tooth-ache" (quoted in Habegger, *The Father*, 322).

The following, no longer from the Hotel de L'Ecu, but from 5 Quai du Mont Blanc,[387] would indicate that his "Dear Queen Caroline," as he addresses her, was at no loss to defend her own view of the matters in discussion between them: in which warm light indeed it is that I was myself in the after years ever most amusedly to see her.

> Don't scold a fellow so! Exert your royal gifts in exalting only the lowly and humbling only the proud. Precisely what I like, to get extricated from metaphysics, is encouragement from a few persons like yourself, such encouragement as would lie in your intelligent apprehension and acknowledgment of the great *result* of metaphysics, which is a godly and spotless life on earth. If I could find anyone apt to that doctrine I should not work so hard metaphysically to convince the world of its truth. And as for being a metaphysical Jack Horner,[388] the thing is contradictory, as no metaphysician whose studies are sincere ever felt tempted to self-complacency or disposed to reckon himself a good boy. Such exaltations are not for him, but only for the artists and poets, who dazzle the eyes of mankind and *don't* recoil from the darkness they themselves produce—as Dryden says, or Collins.[389]

Mrs. Tappan, spending the month of June in London, continued to impute for the time, I infer (I seem to remember a later complete detachment), a livelier importance to the supernatural authors of her "writing" than her correspondent was disposed to admit; but almost anything was a quickener of the correspondent's own rich, that is always so animated,

387. The family, having spent the winter in Geneva in a suite at the Hôtel de l'Écu, moved in spring 1860 across the Rhône to 5 quai du Mont Blanc (Habegger, *The Father*, 413).

388. HJ Sr. has been compared to the nursery-rhyme figure, who "put in his thumb and pulled out a plum, and said, 'What a good boy am I.'" Perhaps Mrs. Tappan had accused HJ Sr. of selecting only the most choice items from available philosophical systems.

389. HJ Sr. refers to the British poets John Dryden (1631–1700) and William Collins (1721–59). The juxtaposing of sublime insights with a correspondingly fearsome darkness is reminiscent of the rhetorical questions and assertions of Dryden's *The Hind and the Panther*, an allegory addressing contemporary religious controversy: "What weight of antient witness can prevail / If private reason hold the publick scale? / But, gratious God, how well dost thou provide / For erring judgments an unerring Guide? / Thy throne is darkness in th'abyss of light, / A blaze of glory that forbids the sight; / O teach me to believe Thee thus conceal'd, / And search no farther than thy self reveal'd" (*The Poems and Fables of John Dryden*, ed. James Kinsley [London: Oxford University Press, 1962], 356).

earnestness. He had to feel an interlocutor's general sympathy, or recognise a moral relation, even if a disturbed one, for the deep tide of his conviction to rise outwardly higher; but when that happened the tide overflowed indeed.

MY DEAR CAROLINA—Neither North nor South, but an eminently free State, with no exulting shout of master and no groan of captive to be heard in all its borders,[390] but only the cheerful hum of happy husband and children—how do you find London? Here in Geneva we are so saturate with sunshine that we would fain dive to the depths of the lake to learn coolness of the little fishes. Still, we don't envy your two weeks of unbroken rain in dear dismal London. What a preparation for doing justice to Lenox![391] You see I know—through Mary Tweedy, who has a hearty appreciation of her London privileges.[392] How are A. D. and all the rest of them?[393] *Familiar*

390. HJ Sr. recalls for his fellow Yankee the slaveholding states of North and South Carolina. HJ Sr. was not himself an abolitionist: though his view was incompatible with the arguments of many Southerners, he considered that it was the master rather than slave who was degraded by the institution (Habegger, *The Father*, 426). The original of this letter (bMS Am 1092.9 [4275], Houghton) is dated 22 June [1860], and was sent from Geneva; HJ makes a few cuts. I have seen only one other letter from HJ Sr. to Caroline Tappan at Houghton and it is not included in *NSB*. It is possible that HJ's nephew Harry (who had clear ideas about propriety) sorted and selected HJ Sr.'s letters in 1921. Alfred Habegger has informed me that Mary Aspinwall Tappan (Caroline's daughter) wrote to Harry James on 11 January 1921 that she could find only three of WJ's letters to her mother; if she were returning materials to the James family archive at this time, Habegger plausibly suggests, HJ Sr.'s letters may also have been included in this package and passed through Harry's hands.

391. The Tappans had a country estate in Lenox, western Massachusetts (see n. 216 above).

392. Edmund and Mary Tweedy were spending these years in Europe (see n. 113 above).

393. In the MS version HJ Sr. asks, "How is Anna Drew? and Elizabeth, & Samson, and all the rest of them?" As the letter later suggests, Anna had religious interests; she may have been resident in London. Alternatively, Habegger has interestingly suggested that Anna might be Anna Hazard Barker Ward, who became an admired friend of HJ Sr.'s in the 1830s. She was renowned as a great beauty and, in 1857 (to HJ Sr.'s annoyance), converted to Roman Catholicism. Her husband, Samuel Gray Ward, a prosperous banker, took strong care of HJ Sr.'s financial interests, and so "Samson" might be a comic variant on "Sam." The couple had married in 1840 and had four children, one of whom was called Elizabeth. In addition, Anna Barker Ward and Mary Tweedy had long been close friends. Some doubts remain, however: HJ Sr. refers to a "short acquaintance" between Caroline

spirits, are they not, on a short acquaintance?—and how pleasant an aspect it gives to the middle kingdom to think you shall be sure to find there such lovers and friends![394] Only let us keep them at a proper distance. It doesn't do for us ever to accept another only at that other's own estimate of himself. If we do we may as well plunge into Tartarus at once.[395] No human being can afford to commit his happiness to another's keeping, or, what is the same thing, forego his own individuality with all that it imports. The first requisite of our true relationship to each other (spiritually speaking) is that we be wholly independent of each other: then we may give ourselves away as much as we please, we shall do neither them nor ourselves any harm. But until that blessed day comes, by the advance of a scientific society among men, we shall be utterly unworthy to love each other or be loved in return. We shall do nothing but prey upon each other and turn each other's life to perfect weariness.

The more of it then just now the better! The more we bite and devour each other, the more horribly the newspapers abound in all the evidences of our disgusting disorganisation, the disorganisation of the old world, the readier will our dull ears be to listen to the tidings of the new world which is aching to appear, the world wherein dwelleth

---

Tappan and this group, and the reference is to Anna *Drew*. On the other hand, Pierre A. Walker reminds me that the James family were inveterate inventors of nicknames and playful variations on friends' names, and so "Drew" (not necessarily a surname) might fall into this category.

394. HJ Sr.'s terms here are derived from the writings of Swedenborg, who once related that he had been speaking to the still-living Queen of Sweden in the spiritual world. When asked how this could be, he replied: " 'It was not the Queen herself, but her familiar spirit' (*spiritus familiaris*). . . . He then informed me that every man has his good or bad spirit, who is not only constantly near him, but sometimes also withdraws from him, and appears in the spiritual world. . . . Such a familiar spirit has everything perfectly in common with his human companion; he has in the spiritual world visibly the same figure, the same countenance, the same tone of voice; wears also the same garments as the man on earth" (*Documents concerning the Life and Character of Emanuel Swedenborg*, collected, translated, and annotated by R. L. Tafel, 2 vols. (London: Swedenborg Society, British and Foreign, 1877), 2.1.484–85). Swedenborg also claimed that "the middle-space is where those are who are truly Christian; and in its midst . . . is the New Jerusalem" (*The Spiritual Diary of Emanuel Swedenborg*, trans. George Bush and James F. Buss, 5 vols. [London: James Speirs, 1889], 4:418). I am very grateful to Carroll Odhner for his help in directing me to these sources.

395. Tartarus was in Greek mythology the area of the underworld in which the wicked were punished.

righteousness. Don't abuse the newspapers therefore publicly, but tell everybody of the use they are destined to promote, and set others upon the look-out.[396] A. D. is a very good woman, I haven't a doubt, but will fast grow a better one if she would let herself alone, and me also, and all other mere persons, while she diligently inquires about the Lord; that is about that lustrous universal life which God's providence is now forcing upon men's attention and which will obliterate for ever all this exaggeration of our personalities. It is very well for lovers to abase themselves in this way to each other; because love is a *passion* of one's nature—that is to say the lover is not self-possessed, but is lifted for a passing moment to the level of the Lord's life in the race, and so attuned to higher issues ever after in his own proper sphere.[397] But these experiences are purely disciplinary and not final. All passion is a mere inducement to action, and when at last activity really dawns in us we drop this faculty of hallucination that we have been under about persons and see and adore the abounding divinity which is in all persons alike. Who will then ever be caught in that foolish snare again? I did nothing but tumble into it from my boyhood up to my marriage; since which great disillusioning—yes!—I feel that the only lovable person is one who will never permit himself to be loved. But I have written on without any intention and have now no time to say what alone I intended, how charming and kind and long to be remembered you were all those Paris days. Give my love to honest William and tell my small nieces that I pine to pluck again the polished cherries of their cheeks. My wife admires and loves you.

From which I jump considerably forward, for its (privately) historic value, to a communication from Newport of the middle of August '63. My

396. This advice fails to accord with HJ Sr.'s own recent and very public argument in the pages of the *New York Tribune* in spring 1859 when he wrote a series of scathing letters on *Nature and the Supernatural*, by the theologian Horace Bushnell. In this debate HJ Sr. had emphasized the one great aim of philosophy: to reconcile human freedom with human dependence.

397. These views are reminiscent of ideas evident in HJ Sr.'s review of Dr. Marx Edgeworth Lazarus's *Love vs. Marriage* (1852), a book central to the free-love debate of the time. Habegger summarizes HJ Sr.'s argument: "What is a man really doing when he falls in love? He is catching a glimpse, James declared, of his own divine selfhood. The woman he desires is no more than a symbol of his own divinity. Of course, since the man does not understand this symbolism—and also since no wife fulfills 'the promise which the unappropriated woman held out'—he is inevitably disappointed" (*The Father*, 333).

father's two younger sons had, one the previous and one at the beginning of the current, year obtained commissions in the Volunteer Army; as a sequel to which my next younger brother, as Adjutant of the Fifty-fourth Massachusetts, Colonel Robert Shaw's regiment, the first body of coloured soldiers raised in the North, had received two grave wounds in that unsuccessful attack on Fort Wagner from which the gallant young leader of the movement was not to return.[398]

Wilky had a bad day yesterday and kept me busy or I shouldn't have delayed answering your inquiries till to-day. He is very severely wounded both in the ankle and in the side—where he doesn't heal so fast as the doctor wishes in consequence of the shell having made a pouch which collects matter and retards nature. They cut it open yesterday, and to-day he is better, or will be. The wound in the ankle was made by a cannister ball an inch and a half in diameter, which lodged eight days in the foot and was finally dislodged by cutting down through (the foot) and taking it out at the sole. He is excessively

398. Wilky James enlisted with Company F of the 44th Massachusetts Infantry Regiment, then forming in Boston. Bob James had joined the 55th Massachusetts Regiment, the second of two African-American regiments, by mid-June 1863. Wilky went on to serve in the 54th Massachusetts, the first of the black regiments, under the command of Robert Gould Shaw. It was a principled move: the idea of black men as trained soldiers was regarded with contempt by many Northerners, and white officers commanding such troops could expect execution if captured by Confederate forces. Shaw was the son of a strongly abolitionist patrician Boston family, friends of the Jameses. He was killed during the celebrated but ill-fated assault on Fort Wagner in Charleston Bay (18 July 1863) and buried with his men. On the day of the regiment's leaving Boston (subject to both cheers and insults), Shaw's sister Ellen watched from the second-floor balcony at 44 Beacon Street: "When Rob, riding at its head, looked up and kissed his sword, his face was as the face of an angel and I felt perfectly sure he would never come back" (quoted in Peter Burchard, *One Gallant Rush: Robert Gould Shaw and His Brave Black Regiment* [New York: St. Martin's Press, 1965], 93–94). For the episode's significance in marking a shift in the perception of the African-American soldier, see Alice Fahs, *The Imagined Civil War: Popular Literature of the North and South, 1861–1865* (Chapel Hill: University of North Carolina Press, 2001), 169–75. Wilky later wrote "The Assault on Fort Wagner," part of *War Papers,* a collection of war recollections of the Commandery of Wisconsin, Loyal Legion, Milwaukee, 1891, an address earlier published as "Story of the War," 2 December [1888?], in the *Milwaukee Sentinel* (bMS Am 1095, Houghton). Bob wrote "Three Years' Service with the Fifty-Fifth Massachusetts Volunteer Infantry, an address delivered by Robertson James in Concord, Massachusetts, March 10, 1886." For detailed accounts of the two brothers and their Civil War experiences, see Lewis, *The Jameses,* chap. 5; and Maher, *Biography of Broken Fortunes,* chaps. 2 and 3.

weak, unable to do anything but lie passive, even to turn himself on his pillow. He will probably have a slow and tedious recovery—the doctors say of a year at least; but he knows nothing of this himself and speaks, so far as he does talk, but of going back in the Fall.[399] If you write please say nothing of this; he is so distressed at the thought of a long sickness. He is vastly attached to the negro-soldier cause; believes (I think) that the world has existed for it; and is sure that enormous results to civilisation are coming out of it. We heard from Bob this morning at Morris Island; with his regiment, building earthworks and mounting guns.[400] Hot, he says, but breezy; also that the shells make for them every few minutes—while he and his men betake themselves to the trenches and holes in the earth "like so many land-crabs in distress." He writes in the highest spirits. Cabot Russell, Wilky's dearest friend, is, we fear, a prisoner and wounded.[401] We hear nothing decisive, but the indications point that way. Poor Wilky cries aloud for his friends gone and missing, and I could hardly have supposed he might be educated so suddenly up to serious manhood altogether as he appears to have been. I hear from Frank Shaw this morning, and they are all well—and admirable.[402]

399. Wilky was brought home on 31 July 1863. He returned to service too rapidly and was compelled to resign from the regiment on 30 January 1864 because of his wounds. He went back once more, however, on 14 December 1864, and his letters recording the final phase of the war are included in chap. 11 below. Maher points out (*Biography of Broken Fortunes*, 51) that this second phase of recuperation is never recorded by HJ or in letters of the time. Wilky later moved to the Midwest and married, but his health was permanently damaged, and he died of Bright's disease and a weakened heart in 1883, aged thirty-eight. The dying scenes of a wounded young war hero of one of HJ's earliest tales, "The Story of a Year" (1865), are modeled on Wilky's experiences. The soldier's unreliable lover picks up his old army blanket: "A strange earthy smell lingered in that faded old rug, and with it a faint perfume of tobacco. Instantly the young girl's senses were transported as they had never been before to those far-off Southern battlefields. She saw men lying in swamps, puffing their kindly pipes, drawing their blankets closer, canopied with the same luminous dusk that shone down upon her comfortable weakness" (*CT*, 1:91).

400. Morris Island is a long sandy spit of land on the southern side of the entrance to Charleston harbor; the massive earthworks of Fort Wagner were located at its northern end. Southern summer temperatures would have made laboring arduous for these Northern soldiers.

401. He was in fact dead, as HJ relates below.

402. Frank Shaw is Francis G. Shaw (1809–82), who was a supporter of the Fourierist Brook Farm enterprise and also wrote for its associated and brief-lived journal, the *Harbinger* (Perry, *Thought and Character of William James*, 1:31). He was also Robert Gould

This goes beyond the moment I had lately, and doubtless too lingeringly, reached, as I say; just as I shall here find convenience in borrowing a few passages from my small handful of letters of the time to follow—to the extent of its not following by a very long stretch. Such a course keeps these fragments of record together, as scattering them would perhaps conduce to some leakage in their characteristic tone, for which I desire all the fulness it can keep. Impossible moreover not in some degree to yield on the spot to *any* brush of the huge procession of those particular months and years, even though I shall presently take occasion to speak as I may of my own so inevitably contracted consciousness of what the brush, with its tremendous possibilities of violence, could consist of in the given case.[403] I had, under stress, to content myself with knowing it in a more indirect and muffled fashion than might easily have been—even should one speak of it but as a matter of mere vision of the eyes or quickened wonder of the mind or heaviness of the heart, as a matter in fine of the closer and more inquiring, to say nothing of the more agitated, approach. All of which, none the less, was not to prevent the whole quite indescribably intensified time—intensified through all lapses of occasion and frustrations of contact —from remaining with me as a more constituted and sustained act of living, in proportion to my powers and opportunities, than any other homogeneous stretch of experience that my memory now recovers. The case had to be in a peculiar degree, alas, that of living inwardly—like so many of my other cases; in a peculiar degree compared, that is, to the immense and prolonged outwardness, outwardness naturally at the very highest pitch, that was the general sign of the situation. To which I may add that my "alas" just uttered is in the key altogether of my then current consciousness, and not in the least in that of my present appreciation of the same—so that I leave it, even while I thus put my mark against it, as I should restore tenderly to the shelf any odd rococo object that might have slipped from a reliquary. My appreciation of what I presume at the risk of any apparent fatuity to call my "relation to" the War is at present a thing exquisite to me, a thing of the last refinement of romance, whereas it had to be at the time a sore and troubled, a mixed and oppressive thing—though I promptly see, on reflection, how it must frequently have flushed with emotions, with

Shaw's father. HJ, as a "small boy," had gazed on the family in wonder when they were all holidaying on Staten Island, recorded in *SBO*, chap. 3.

403. HJ's oblique reference to the Civil War is characteristic, as if his language is mirroring his detached, observing status, still an influential component of his memories of nearly fifty years earlier.

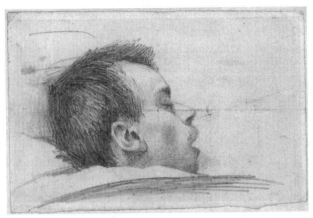

*Sketch of G. W. James brought home wounded from the assault on Fort Wagner.*
*(Houghton Library Harvard University)*

small scraps of direct perception even, with particular sharpnesses in the
generalised pang of participation, that were all but touched in themselves
as with the full experience.[404] Clear as some object presented in high relief
against the evening sky of the west, at all events, is the presence for me
beside the stretcher on which my young brother was to lie for so many
days before he could be moved, and on which he had lain during his boat-
journey from the South to New York and thence again to Newport, of lost

404. Neither HJ nor WJ enlisted, though the two younger James brothers, encouraged
by their father with some of his characteristic inconsistency, did volunteer for service. HJ
and WJ were not alone, of course, in remaining civilians: at Harvard, for instance, "the
pattern of college life changed little. A few students formed drill corps and some did
volunteer general duty. Most of the Southern students returned home to serve in the
Confederate Army, and at the end of each term a few more Northern students dropped out
to enlist in the Union Army, but campus life was affected less than might be expected. Even
the son of President Lincoln calmly continued his studies until his graduation in 1864"
(Gay Wilson Allen, *William James: A Biography* [London: Rupert Hart-Davis, 1967], 77).
Some cousins and a number of other young men of the Jameses' privileged New England
circle, however, did join the Union army, including Oliver Wendell Holmes Jr. (1841–1935)
and John Chipman Gray (1839–1915), both of whom went on to pursue successful careers
in law. James never became one of those described in Holmes's published war letters and
diaries as "touched with fire," and his writing suggests a sense of exclusion, experience
missed, even an aspect of manhood denied. Both WJ and HJ applied to the Boston
Educational Commission in spring 1863, to join a group traveling to Port Royal, South
Carolina, to help and to teach released slaves, but they were rejected as lacking experience
and qualifications. Having been drafted in July of the same year, HJ was exempted from
service because of what the *Newport Mercury* referred to as "various complaints" (presum-

Cabot Russell's stricken father, who, failing, up and down the searched field, in respect of his own irrecoverable boy—then dying, or dead, as afterwards appeared, well within the enemy's works—had with an admirable charity brought Wilky back to a waiting home instead, and merged the parental ache in the next nearest devotion he could find.[405] Vivid to me still is one's almost ashamed sense of this at the hurried disordered time, and of how it was impossible not to impute to his grave steady gentleness and judgment a full awareness of the difference it would have made for him, all the same, to be doing such things with a still more intimate pity. Unobliterated for me, in spite of vaguenesses, this quasi-twilight vision of the good bereft man, bereft, if I rightly recall, of his only son, as he sat

---

ably owing to the back injury described in chap. 9) and may thus have been freed from "any personal anxieties . . . concerning his own individual relationship to the war" (Hoffmann and Hoffmann, "Henry James and the Civil War," 543, 552). See also Paul Jerome Croce, "Calming the Screaming Eagle: William James and His Circle Fight Their Civil War Battles," *New England Quarterly* 76 (March 2003): 5–37. For a consideration of HJ's feelings in relation to his more active younger brothers, see Daniel Aaron, *The Unwritten War: American Writers and the Civil War* (Madison: University of Wisconsin Press, 1987), 110–12. HJ's short story "Owen Wingrave" (1892) (later transformed into an opera by Benjamin Britten, a composer of strongly pacifist convictions) treats the subject of a young man's refusal to enlist and thus engage in a family tradition in which fighting for country helps determine masculinity.

405. The difficulties of locating the injured and dead after battle and the logistical problems for the military authorities in accounting for losses are well documented. HJ misspells the family name. Cabot Jackson Russel (1844–63) was the son of Sarah Cabot Russel and William C. Russel, a Boston lawyer. When he was a child the picture of John Brown hung over the boy's bed. Though he entered Harvard, he was soon suspended, an outcome he regretted. At eighteen he enlisted with the 44th Massachusetts, later to join the 54th, in company with Wilky James. At Fort Wagner, "a ball struck him in the shoulder and he fell. Captain Simkins offered to carry him off. But the boy had become a veteran in a moment, and the answer was, 'No, but you may straighten me out.' As his friend, true to the end, was rendering this last service, a bullet pierced his breast, and his dead body fell over the dying" (*Harvard Memorial Biographies,* 2:457–66). He was buried in a mass pit, along with his commander and many of his black comrades. In his contribution to this memorial essay, Wilky recalled that his "friendship with Cabot began with our joint entrance into military life; and from the first moment to the last of that friendship, it presented him full of honor" (ibid., 465). Wilky had been found by chance by Cabot's father as he lay in the field hospital at Port Royal Harbor. On a difficult journey William Russel brought Wilky back as far as New York by boat; the canister ball in his foot had to be removed during the voyage (Maher, *Biography of Broken Fortunes,* 47–48). In *The Bostonians* (chap. 25), a former Confederate soldier, Basil Ransom, and his companion, Verena Tarrant, pay conciliatory homage to Harvard's dead in the Memorial Hall.

erect and dry-eyed at the guarded feast of *our* relief; and so much doubt-less partly because of the image that hovers to me across the years of Cabot Russell himself, my brother's so close comrade—dark-eyed, youthfully brown, heartily bright, actively handsome, and with the arrested expres-sion, the indefinable shining stigma, worn, to the regard that travels back to them, by those of the young figures of the fallen that memory and fancy, wanting, never ceasing to want, to "do" something for them, set as upright and clear-faced as may be, each in his sacred niche. They have each to such a degree, so ranged, the strange property or privilege—one scarce knows what to call it—of exquisitely, for all *our* time, facing us out, quite blandly ignoring us, looking through us or straight over us at something they partake of together but that we mayn't pretend to know.[406] We walk thus, I think, rather ruefully before them—those of us at least who didn't at the time share more happily their risk. William, during those first critical days, while the stretcher itself, set down with its load just within the entrance to our house, mightn't be moved further, preserved our poor lacerated brother's aspect in a drawing of great and tender truth which I permit myself to reproduce. It tells for me the double story—I mean both of Wilky's then condition and of the draughtsman's admirable hand.

But I find waiting my father's last letter of the small group to Mrs. Tappan. We were by that time, the autumn of 1865, settled in Boston for a couple of years.

MY DEAR CARRY—Are you a carry*atid*[407] that you consider yourself bound to uphold that Lenox edifice through the cold winter as well as the hot summer? Why don't you come to town? I can't *write*

---

406. The configurations of HJ's language, which seem simultaneously both to make living and yet turn to stone the heroic dead—the memory of his brother like an object in high relief, the dead occupying some sacred niche, their seeing past and beyond the living—indicate that HJ's possession of that episode has been affected by the important bronze sculpture by Augustus Saint-Gaudens (1848–1907) on Beacon Street, opposite the Massachusetts State House, known as the Shaw Memorial. WJ was honored to be one of the orators at the monument's unveiling in 1897, and he wrote his brother a detailed account of the occasion (*CWJ*, 3:8–10).

407. This kind of affectionate wordplay, which denotes the flirtatious quality of HJ Sr.'s relationships with certain women of his circle, is often offset by the introduction of a deliberately legitimizing reminder of other roles and protagonists, thus normalizing this level of conversational intimacy. See, e.g., the ending of the earlier letter addressed to "Carolina, Neither North nor South" in which her husband, "honest William," their two daughters, "my small nieces," and HJ Sr.'s own admiring and loving wife are all invoked

what I want to say. My brain is tired, and I gladly forego all writing that costs thought or attention. But I have no day forgotten your question, and am eager always to make a conquest of you; you are so full both of the upper and the nether might as always greatly to excite my interest and make me feel how little is accomplished while you are left not so. I make no prayer to you; I would have no assistance from your own vows; or the pleasure of my intercourse with you would be slain. I would rather outrage than conciliate your sympathies, that I might have all the joy of winning you over at last. Hate me on my ideal side, the side that menaces you, as much as you please meanwhile, but keep a warm corner in your regard for me personally, as I always do for you, until we meet again. It's a delight to know a person of your sense and depth; even the *gaudia certaminis*[408] are more cheering with you than ordinary agreements with other people.

On which note I may leave the exchange in question, feeling how equal an honour it does to the parties.

# VIII

I judge best to place together here several passages from my father's letters belonging to this general period, even though they again carry me to points beyond my story proper. It is not for the story's sake that I am moved to gather them, but for their happy illustration, once more, of something quite else, the human beauty of the writer's spirit and the fine breadth of his expression.[409] This latter virtue is most striking, doubtless, when he addresses his women correspondents, of whom there were many, yet it so pervades for instance various notes, longer and shorter, to Mrs. James T. Fields, wife of the eminent Boston publisher and editor, much commended to us as founder and, for a time, chief conductor of the Atlantic Monthly, our most adopted and enjoyed native *recueil* of that series of

---

after he has tenderly recollected those "charming Paris days" in which she had clearly been a strong attraction. This extract seems deliberately to represent the intellectual debate between HJ Sr. and Mrs. Tappan in terms of something close to romantic struggle.

408. The joys of combat (Lat.).

409. Though it was WJ rather than his brother who had the most intellectual and spiritual sympathy with their father, HJ Sr.'s prose, with its unexpected allusions, daring juxtapositions, gallant tone, and at times mannered pursuit of precise nuance, has something in common with the novelist's late style.

years.[410] The Atlantic seemed somehow, while the good season lasted, to live with us, whereas our relation to the two or three other like organs, homegrown or foreign, of which there could be any question, and most of all, naturally, to the great French Revue,[411] was that we lived with *them.* The light of literature, as we then invoked or at any rate received it, seemed to beat into the delightful Fields salon from a nearer heaven than upon any other scene, and played there over a museum of relics and treasures and apparitions (these last whether reflected and by that time legendary, or directly protrusive and presented, wearers of the bay) with an intensity, I feel again as I look back, every resting ray of which was a challenge to dreaming ambition.[412] I am bound to note, none the less, oddly enough, that my father's communications with the charming mistress of the scene are more often than not a bright profession of sad reasons for inability to mingle in it. He mingled with reluctance in scenes designed and preappointed, and was, I think, mostly content to feel almost anything near at hand become a scene for him from the moment he had happened to cast into the arena (which he preferred without flags or festoons) the golden apple of the unexpected—in humorous talk, that is, in reaction without preparation, in sincerity which was itself sociability.[413] It was not nevertheless that he didn't now and then "accept"— with attenuations.[414]

410. Annie Adams Fields, an author, was the young wife of James T. Fields; after her husband's death she became a companion of the novelist Sarah Orne Jewett (1849–1909), entering one of those relationships known as a "Boston marriage." The two women visited HJ's Lamb House in Rye in 1898. For further detail see above, n. 84. *Recueil:* collection or compilation.

411. The frequently referred to *Revue des deux mondes.*

412. Mr. and Mrs. Fields lived at 148 Charles Street and hosted one of Boston's foremost literary meeting places. It is recalled affectionately in *AS:* "Here, behind the effaced anonymous door, was the little ark of the modern deluge, here still the long drawing-room that looks over the water and toward the sunset, with a seat for every visiting shade" (244–45). In his evaluation of early Boston and Cambridge days and "the confusion of old and doubtless in some cases rather faded importances" (*CN,* 536), the couple and their circle finally emerged in one of his last essays, "Mr. and Mrs. James T. Fields" (1915), written after Mrs. Fields's death (*LC* 1, 160–76).

413. Though HJ Sr. belonged to some of the exclusive Boston clubs of the day, including the Saturday, Radical, and Examiner clubs, his relations with the other members were often uneasy, even quarrelsome, and his attendance was irregular (see Habegger, *The Father,* 457–62).

414. The letter that follows is dated 3 February [1870?] (bMS Am 1092.9 [4133], Houghton).

... If therefore you will let Alice and me come to you on Wednesday evening I shall still rejoice in the benignant fate that befalls my house— even though my wife, indisposed, "feels reluctantly constrained to count herself out of the sphere of your hospitality;" and I will bind myself moreover by solemn vows not to perplex the happy atmosphere which almost reigns in yours by risking a syllable of the incongruous polemic your husband wots of. I will listen devotedly to you and him all the evening if thereby I may early go home repaired in my own esteem, and not dilapidated, as has been hitherto too often the case.

He could resist persuasion even in the insidious form of an expressed desire that he should read something, "something he was writing," to a chosen company.[415]

Your charming note is irresistible at first sight, and I had almost uttered a profligate Yes!—that is a promise irrespective of a power to perform; when my good angel arrested me by the stern inquiry: What have you got to give them? And I could only say in reply to this intermeddling but blest spirit: Nothing, my dear friend, absolutely nothing! Whereupon the veracious one said again: Sit you down immediately therefore and, confessing your literary indigence to this lovely lady, pray her to postpone the fulfilment of her desire to some future flood-tide in the little stream of your inspiration, when you will be ready to serve her.[416]

The following refers to the question of his attending with my mother at some session of a Social Club, at which a prepared performance of some sort was always offered, but of which they had lately found it convenient to cease to be members.[417]

I snatch the pen from my wife's hand to enjoy, myself, the satisfaction of saying to you how good and kind and charming you always are, and how we never grow tired of recounting the fact among ourselves here, and yet how we still shall be unable to accept your hospitality. Why? Simply because we have a due sense of what

415. The MS of this letter is dated 17 April (no year indicated) (bMS Am 1092.9 [4135], Houghton).

416. The letter continues by apologizing that he has nothing suitable currently to "read"—only "a great mass of formless manuscript," along with a lecture prepared on marriage and another on Swedenborg.

417. MS letter dated 8 February (no year indicated) (bMS Am 1092.9 [4134], Houghton).

becomes us after our late secession, and would not willingly be seen at two successive meetings, lest the carnal observer should argue that we had left the Club by the front door of obligation only to be readmitted at the back door of indulgence: I put it as Fields would phrase it. To speak of him always reminds me of various things, so richly endowed is the creature in all good gifts; but the dominant consideration evoked in my mind by his name is just his beautiful home and that atmosphere of faultless womanly worth and dignity which fills it with light and warmth, and makes it a blessing to one's heart whenever one enters its precincts. Please felicitate the wretch for me—!

However earnest these deprecations he could embroider them with a rare grace.[418]

My wife—who has just received your kind note in rapid route for the Dedham Profane Asylum, or something of that sort[419]—begs leave to say, through me as a willing and sensitive medium, that you are one of those *arva beata,*[420] renowned in poetry, which, visit them never so often, one is always glad to *re*visit, which are attractive in all seasons by their own absolute light and without any Emersonian pansies and buttercups to make them so. This enthusiastic Dedhamite says further in effect that while she is duly grateful for your courteous offer of a seat upon your sofa to hear the conquered sage,[421] she yet prefers the material banquet you summon us to in your dining-room, since there we should be out of the mist and able to discern between nature and cookery, between what eats and what is eaten, at all events, and feel a thankful mind that we were in solid comfortable Charles Street, instead of in the vague and wide weltering galaxy, and should be sure to deem A. and J. (*I* am sure of A., and I think my wife feels equally sure of J.),[422] finer fireflies than ever sparkled in the old empyrean. But

418. This is a letter of 11 May [1866?] (bMS Am 1092.9 [4131], Houghton) with a Swampscott address; the Jameses were renting a house for the summer on the coast, fifteen miles north of Boston.

419. Possibly some charitable enterprise whose name HJ Sr. humorously invents; Dedham, in Norfolk County, is on the southwest border of Boston.

420. Blessed lands or regions (Lat.).

421. MS has "the Concord sage," referring to Emerson. HJ may well have dictated (while also revising) this letter to his amanuensis and failed later to correct the mistake.

422. The initials indicate the Fields' given names. In the MS of the letter he refers to Annie and Jamie.

alas who shall control his destiny? Not my wife, whom multitudinous cares enthrall; nor yet myself, whom a couple of months' enforced idleness now constrains to a preternatural activity, lest the world fail of salvation. Please accept then our united apologies and regrets. . . .

*P.S.* Who contrived the comical title for E.'s lectures?— "Philosophy of the People!" May it not have been a joke of J. T. F.'s?[423] It would be no less absurd for Emerson himself to think of philosophising than for the rose to think of botanising. He is the divinely pompous rose of the philosophic garden, gorgeous with colour and fragrance; so what a sad look-out for tulip and violet and lily, and the humbler grasses, if the rose should turn out philosophic gardener as well.

There connects itself with a passage in another letter to the same correspondent a memory of my own that I have always superlatively cherished and that remains in consequence vivid enough for some light reflection here. But I first give the passage, which is of date of November '67. "What a charming impression of Dickens the other night at the Nortons' dinner! How innocent and honest and sweet he is maugre[424] his fame! Fields was merely superb on the occasion, but Dickens was saintly."[425] As a young person of twenty-four I took part, restrictedly yet

423. This was no joke. In the original letter HJ Sr. goes further in protesting his disbelief: "Philosophy of the people too! But that was Fields, or else it was only R.W.E. after dining with F. at the Union Club, and becoming demonalized." Emerson delivered six lectures under the title "Philosophy of the People" in Chickering's Hall, Boston, in 1866 (for a summary of the contents, see J. Elliot Cabot, *A Memoir of Ralph Waldo Emerson* [London: Macmillan, 1887], 2:409–14).

424. In spite of.

425. Dickens first visited America in 1842. He had begun public readings of his works in 1858, and on this second tour of the United States, from November 1867 to May 1868, confined principally to the eastern seaboard, he drew enormous crowds and earned about $140,000 (£20,000). He was already ill, and the dramatic performances further endangered his health. Charles Eliot Norton (see above, n. 351) had married Susan Ridley Sedgwick in 1862, and they lived at their Shady Hill estate in Cambridge in "an enormous house surrounded by fifty acres, just off Kirkland Street to the east of Harvard Yard" (Strouse, *Alice James,* 137). The grounds were "later subdivided into lots. On one of these, WJ built his 95 Irving Street house" (*CWJ,* 4:67 n. 3). The MS letter is dated 30 November 1867 (bMS Am 1092.9 [4132], Houghton). When *NSB* was published, HJ was, incidentally, disappointed at the response of Norton's surviving sister, Grace: "I have the oddest snubbiest & (though not unkindly) letter from poor Grace N., whose lack of intelligence or perception does so always avail itself of any opportunity to come out. She *understands* so

exaltedly, in that occasion—and an immense privilege I held it to slip in at all—from after dinner on; at which stage of the evening I presented myself, in the company of my excellent friend Arthur Sedgwick, brother to our hostess and who still lives to testify, for the honour of introduction to the tremendous guest.[426] How tremendously it had been laid upon young persons of our generation to feel Dickens, down to the soles of our shoes, no more modern instance that I might try to muster would give, I think, the least measure of; I can imagine no actual young person of my then age, and however like myself, so ineffably agitated, so mystically moved, in the presence of any exhibited idol of the mind who should be in that character at all conceivably "like" the author of Pickwick and of Copperfield.[427] There has been since his extinction no corresponding case—as to the relation between benefactor and beneficiary, or debtor and creditor; no other debt in our time has been piled so high, for those carrying it, as the long, the purely "Victorian" pressure of that obligation. It was the pressure, the feeling, that made it—as it made the feeling, and no operation of feeling on any such ground has within my observation so much as attempted to emulate it. So that on the evening I speak of at Shady Hill it was as a slim and shaken vessel of the feeling that one stood there—of the feeling in the first place diffused, public and universal, and in the second place all unfathomably, undemonstrably, unassistedly and, as it were, unrewardedly, proper to one's self as an already groping and fumbling, already dreaming and yearning dabbler in the mystery, the creative, that of comedy, tragedy, evocation, representation, erect and concrete before us there as in a sublimity of mastership.[428] I saw the master—nothing could be more evident—in the light of an intense emotion, and I trembled, I remember, in every limb, while at the same time, by a blest fortune,

---

little, & I seem to myself to have done such honour to old Shady Hill—having to *lend* it things in order to speak of it at all" (HJ to Alice Howe Gibbens James, 18 March 1914, bMS Am 1094 (1745), Houghton).

426. Arthur Sedgwick (1844–1915), lawyer and editor, was a friend both of HJ and WJ. He worked on the *Nation* magazine and later the *New York Evening Post*.

427. HJ recounts his childhood pleasure in attending dramatizations of Dickens's works in New York City, as well as his evading bedtime so that he could listen to the family reading of a recent installment of *David Copperfield*, in *SBO* (chap. 9). Having completed a volume on Hawthorne for Macmillan's Men of Letters series, HJ was later invited to write on Dickens, an offer he eventually declined.

428. At this time HJ had published a range of reviews and some short stories, principally in the *Nation, North American Review,* and *Atlantic Monthly*.

emotion produced no luminous blur, but left him shining indeed, only shining with august particulars. It was to be remarked that those of his dress, which managed to be splendid even while remaining the general spare uniform of the diner-out, had the effect of higher refinements, of accents stronger and better placed, than we had ever in such a connection seen so much as hinted. But the offered inscrutable mask was the great thing, the extremely handsome face, the face of symmetry yet of formidable character, as I at once recognised, and which met my dumb homage with a straight inscrutability, a merciless *military* eye, I might have pronounced it, an automatic hardness, in fine, which at once indicated to me, and in the most interesting way in the world, a kind of economy of apprehension. Wonderful was it thus to see, and thrilling inwardly to note, that since the question was of personal values so great no faintest fraction of the whole could succeed in *not* counting for interest. The confrontation was but of a moment; our introduction, my companion's and mine, once effected, by an arrest in a doorway, nothing followed, as it were, or happened (what *might* have happened it remained in fact impossible to conceive); but intense though the positive perception there was an immensity more left to understand—for the long aftersense, I mean; and one, or the chief, of these later things was that if our hero neither shook hands nor spoke, only meeting us by the barest act, so to say, of the trained eye, the penetration of which, to my sense, revealed again a world, there was a grim beauty, to one's subsequently panting imagination, in that very truth of his then so knowing himself (committed to his monstrous "readings" and with the force required for them ominously ebbing) on the outer edge of his once magnificent margin. So at any rate I was to like for long to consider of it; I was to like to let the essential radiance which had nevertheless reached me measure itself by this accompaniment of the pitying vision. He couldn't loosely spend for grace what he had to keep for life— which was the awful nightly, or all but nightly, exhibition: such the economy, as I have called it, in which I was afterwards to feel sure he had been locked up—in spite of the appearance, in the passage from my father's letter, of the opened gates of the hour or two before. These were but a reason the more, really, for the so exquisitely complicated image which was to remain with me to this day and which couldn't on any other terms have made itself nearly so important. For that was the whole sense of the matter. It hadn't been in the least important that we should have shaken hands or exchanged platitudes—it had only been supremely so that one should have had the essence of the hour, the knowledge enriched by proof that whatever the multifold or absolute reason, no accession to sensibility from any other at all "similar" source could have compared, for penetration, to the intimacy of this particular and prodigious glimpse. It was as if I had carried off my strange treasure just exactly from under the merciless military eye—placed there on guard of the secret. All of which I recount for illustration of the force of action, unless I call it passion, that may reside in a single pulse of time.

I allow myself not to hang back in gathering several passages from another series for fear of their crossing in a manner the line of privacy and giving a distinctness to old intimate things. The distinctness is in the first place all to the honour of the persons and the interests thus glimmering through; and I hold, in the second, that the light touch under which they revive positively adds, by the magic of memory, a composite fineness. The only thing is that to speak of my father's correspondent here is to be more or less involved at once in the vision of her frame and situation, and that to get at all into relation with "the Nortons," as they were known to us at that period, to say nothing of all the years to follow, is to find on my hands a much heavier weight of reference than my scale at this point can carry. The relation had ripened for us with the settlement of my parents at Cambridge in the autumn of '66, and might I attempt even a sketch of the happy fashion in which the University circle consciously accepted, for its better satisfaction, or in other words just from a sense of what was, within its range, in the highest degree interesting, the social predominance of Shady Hill and the master there, and the ladies of the master's family, I should find myself rich in material. That institution and its administrators, however, became at once, under whatever recall of them, a picture of great inclusions and implications; so true is it of any community, and so true above all of one of the American communities best to be studied fifty years ago in their homogeneous form and native essence and identity, that a strong character reinforced by a great culture, a culture great in the given conditions, obeys an inevitable law in simply standing out.[429] Charles

429. Norton, "a friend of Ruskin, an art scholar, a lover of Italy," was a formative figure in HJ's life. A half hour spent with him in December 1864 in the library at Shady Hill came to be regarded as "a positive consecration to letters" (quoted in Edel, *Untried Years*, 208, 210). It is clear that father and son had very divergent feelings about Harvard's professor of fine art. On his 1869–70 visit to Europe, HJ was introduced by Norton to (among others) Darwin, Ruskin, and Rossetti. Norton also guided HJ through the art and culture of Italy when the younger man made his first, revelatory expedition there in the fall of 1869. After Norton's death in 1908, HJ contributed "An American Art-Scholar: Charles Eliot

Eliot Norton stood out, in the air of the place and time—which for that matter, I think, changed much as he changed, and couldn't change much beyond his own range of experiment—with a greater salience, granting his background, I should say, than I have ever known a human figure stand out with from any: an effect involved of course in the nature of the background as well as in that of the figure. He profited at any rate, to a degree that was a lesson in all the civilities, by the fact that he represented an ampler and easier, above all a more curious, play of the civil relation than was to be detected anywhere about, and a play by which that relation had the charming art of becoming extraordinarily multifold and various without appearing to lose the note of rarity. It is not of course through any exhibition of mere multiplicity that the instinct for relations becomes a great example and bears its best fruit; the weight of the example and the nature of the benefit depending so much as they do on the achieved and preserved terms of intercourse. Here it was that the curiosity, as I have called it, of Shady Hill was justified—so did its action prove largely humanising. This was all the witchcraft it had used—that of manners understood with all the extensions at once and all the particularisations to which it is the privilege of the highest conception of manners to lend itself. What it all came back to, naturally, was the fact that, on so happy a ground, the application of such an ideal and such a genius *could* find agents expressive and proportionate, and the least that could be said of the ladies of the house was that they had in perfection the imagination of their opportunity. History still at comparatively close range lays to its lips, I admit, a warning finger—yet how can I help looking it bravely in the face as I name in common courtesy Jane Norton?[430] She distilled civility and sympathy and charm, she exhaled humanity and invitation to friendship, which latter she went through the world leaving at mortal doors as in effect the revelation of a new amenity altogether—something to wait, most other matters being meanwhile suspended, for her to come back on a turn of the genial tide and take up again, according to the stirred desire, with each beneficiary. All this to the extent, moreover, I confess, that it takes the whole of one's measure of her rendered service and her admirable life, cut so much too short—it takes the full list of her fond acclaimers, the shyest

---

Norton" to the *Burlington Magazine*, January 1909 (*Notes on Novelists* [London: Dent, 1914], 327–35).

430. Jane Norton (1824–77), Charles's elder sister, lived with the family and helped raise the children.

with the clearest, those who most waited or most followed, not to think almost more of the way her blest influence went to waste as by its mere uneconomised and selfless spread than of what would have been called (what was by the simply-seeing freely enough called) her achieved success. It was given her at once to shine for the simply-seeing and to abide forever with the subtly; which latter, so far as they survive, are left again to recognise how there plays inveterately within the beautiful, if it but go far enough, the fine strain of the tragic. The household at Shady Hill was leaving that residence early in the summer of '68 for a long stay in Europe, and the following is of that moment.[431]

When I heard the other day that you had been at our house to say farewell I was glad and also sorry, glad because I couldn't say before all the world so easily what I wanted to say to you in parting, and sorry because I longed for another sight of your beautiful countenance. And then I consoled myself with thinking that I should write you the next morning and be able to do my feelings better justice. But when the morning came I saw how you would, with all your wealth of friends, scarcely value a puny chirrup from one of my like, and by no means probably expect it, and so I desisted. And now comes your heavenly letter this moment to renew my happiness in showing me once more your undimmed friendly face. How delightful that face has ever been to me since first I beheld it; how your frank and gracious and healing manners have shed on my soul a celestial dew whenever I have encountered you: I despair to tell you in fitting words. You are the largest and most generous nature I know, and one that remains always, at the same time, so womanly; and while you leave behind you such a memory you needn't fear that our affectionate wishes will ever fail you for a moment. I for my part shall rest in my affection for you till we meet where to love is to live.

Shady Hill was meanwhile occupied by other friends, out of the group of which, especially as reflected in another of my father's letters to Miss Norton,[432] there rise for me beckoning ghosts; against whose deep appeal to me to let them lead me on I have absolutely to steel myself—so far, for the interest of it, I feel that they might take me.

431. This letter is dated 30 June [1868] (bMS Am 1092.9 [4259], Houghton). The Nortons did not return until May 1873.

432. The letter that follows is an undated fragment, most of which HJ quotes (bMS Am 1092.9 [4262], Houghton).

We dined the other night at Shady Hill, where the Gurneys[433] were charming and the company excellent; but there was a perpetual suggestion of the Elysian Fields[434] about the banquet to me, and we seemed met together to celebrate a memory rather than applaud a hope. Godkin and his wife were there,[435] and they heartily lent themselves to discourse of you all. Ever and anon his friendship gave itself such an emphatic *jerk* to your address that you might have heard it on your window-panes if you had not been asleep. As for her—what a great clot she is of womanly health, beauty and benignity! That is a most unwonted word to use in such a connection, but it came of itself, and I won't refuse it, as it means to express a wealth that seems chaotic—seems so because apparently not enough exercised or put to specific use. The Ashburners and Sedgwicks continue your tradition and even ornament or variegate it with their own original force.[436] I go there of a Sunday afternoon, whenever possible, to read anew the gospel of their beautiful life and manners and bring away a text for the good of my own household. No one disputes the authenticity of that gospel, and I have no difficulty in spreading its knowledge.

On which follows, as if inevitably, the tragic note re-echoed; news having come from Dresden, in March '72, of the death of Mrs. Charles Norton, still young, delightful, inestimable.[437]

433. Ephraim Gurney (1829–86), who taught at Harvard and edited the *North American Review,* married Ellen Sturgis Hooper (1837–87), Clover Adams's sister. They took over the Shady Hill estate when the Nortons were in Europe.

434. In Greek poetry, paradise or the Happy Land. The evening was pleasantly untroubled, but holding something of the afterlife presumably.

435. Edwin Lawrence Godkin, during his coeditorship of the *Nation* with Norton, published much of HJ's early writing. He married Frances Elizabeth Foote in 1859. In "The Founding of the 'Nation'" (*Nation,* 8 July 1915; *LC* 1, 177–81), HJ recalls first hearing of Godkin from Charles Eliot Norton.

436. Anne Ashburner (1807–94) and Grace Ashburner (1814–93) were sisters who had moved from Stockbridge, Massachusetts, to Cambridge in 1860. Their sister, Sarah Ashburner Sedgwick, died, and the two aunts raised her four orphaned children, including Arthur, a friend of both WJ and HJ. Arthur had three sisters, Susan (1838–73), who married Charles Eliot Norton; Theodora (1851–1916); and Sara (b. 1839), who married a son of Charles Darwin. When the Jameses moved to Quincy Street on the east side of Harvard Yard in 1866, they were close neighbors of the Ashburners in Kirkland Street.

437. Susan Sedgwick Norton died after the birth of her sixth child. This letter was written on 11 March 1872 (bMS Am 1092.9 [4261], Houghton).

What a blow we have all had in the deeper blow that has prostrated you! I despair to tell you how keen and how real a grief is felt here by all who have heard the desolating news. With my own family the brooding presence of the calamity is almost as obvious as it is in the Kirkland Street home, and I have to make a perpetual effort to reason it down. Reflectively, I confess, I am somewhat surprised that I could have been so *much* surprised by an event of this order. I know very well that death is the secret of life spiritually, and that this outward image of death which has just obtruded itself upon our gaze is *only* an image—is wholly unreal from a spiritual point of view. I know in short that your lovely sister lives at present more livingly than she has ever lived before. And yet my life is so low, habitually, that when I am called upon to put my knowledge into practice I am as superstitious as anybody else and grovel instead of soaring. Keep me in your own sweet and fragrant memory, for nowhere else could I feel myself more embalmed to my own self-respect. Indeed if anything could relieve a personal sorrow to me it would be the sense that it was shared by a being so infinitely tender and true as yourself.

Of the mass of letters by the same hand that I further turn over too many are of a domestic strain inconsistent with other application; but a page here and there emerges clear, with elements of interest and notes of the characteristic that rather invite than deprecate an emphasis. From these I briefly glean, not minding that later dates are involved—no particular hour at that time being far out of touch with any other, and the value of everything gaining here, as I feel, by my keeping my examples together. The following, addressed to me in England early in '69, beautifully illustrates, to my sense, our father's close participation in any once quite positive case that either one or the other of his still somewhat undetermined, but none the less interesting sons—interesting to themselves, to each other and to *him*— might appear for the time to insist on constituting. William had in '68 been appointed to an instructorship in Psychology at Harvard.[438]

---

438. HJ's dating of this letter is inaccurate. In the late 1860s WJ suffered from debilitating backache as well as mental health problems. He returned to New York after an extended tour of Europe only on 18 November 1868. It was a few years before he took up the first of a succession of teaching posts at Harvard. "In 1872 he began as an instructor in anatomy and physiology, his first position after receiving his M.D. from Harvard in 1869 and deciding not to enter medical practice. The following year he was appointed assistant professor of physiology. Three years later he taught his first philosophy courses, and was

He gets on greatly with his teaching; his students—fifty-seven of them—are elated with their luck in having him, and I feel sure he will have next year a still larger number attracted by his fame. He came in the other afternoon while I was sitting alone, and, after walking the floor in an animated way for a moment, broke out: "Bless my soul, what a difference between me as I am now and as I was last spring at this time! Then so hypochondriachal"—he used that word, though perhaps less in substance than form—"and now with my mind so cleared up and restored to sanity. It's the difference between death and life." He had a great effusion. I was afraid of interfering with it, or possibly checking it, but I ventured to ask what especially in his opinion had produced[439] the change. He said several things: the reading of Renouvier (particularly his vindication of the freedom of the will) and of Wordsworth, whom he has been feeding on now for a good while;[440] but more than anything else his having given up the notion that all mental disorder requires to have a physical basis. This had become perfectly untrue to him. He saw that the mind does act irrespectively of material coercion, and could be dealt with therefore at first hand, and this was health to his bones. It was a splendid declaration, and though I had known from unerring signs of the *fact* of the change I never had been more delighted than by hearing of it so unreservedly from his own lips. He has been shaking off his respect for men of mere science as such, and is even more universal and impartial in his mental judgments than I have known him before.

---

appointed assistant professor of philosophy in 1885. In 1889 he was named a professor of psychology, and in 1897 he returned to teaching philosophy until his retirement in 1907" (Myers, *William James,* 3). The letter is dated 18 March [1873] (bMS Am 1092.9 [4199], Houghton). Its first part refers to some appreciative comments on HJ's recent review of *Middlemarch* made by Gail Hamilton (see n. 458)—which HJ modestly omits. The recent marriage of Robertson and Mary Holton ("a little trump") is also mentioned favorably. Among some domestic detail, HJ Sr. is saddened at reports of Emerson's failing memory.

439. HJ Sr. actually wrote "promoted," though HJ makes few changes to this extract.

440. WJ first read the French philosopher Charles Renouvier (1815–1903) in 1868, and he became a major influence on his thinking. "Renouvier's phenomenalism, his pluralism, his fideism, his moralism, and his theism were all congenial to James's mind," and *Some Problems of Philosophy,* published posthumously in 1911, is dedicated to Renouvier by the "endlessly thankful" WJ (Perry, *Thought and Character of William James,* 1:655). WJ records reading "the immortal Wordsworth's *Excursion*" in a letter of 1873 to HJ, and again in 1874 to brother Bob (ibid., 1:337, 355). The poetry of Wordsworth had also had a therapeutic effect on the young John Stuart Mill.

Nothing in such a report could affect me more, at a distance, as indeed nothing shines for me more sacredly now, than the writer's perfect perception of what it would richly say to me, even if a little to my comparative confusion and bewilderment; engaged as I must rightly have appeared in working out, not to say in tentatively playing with, much thinner things. I like to remember, as I do, ineffaceably, that my attention attached itself, intensely and on the spot, to the very picture, with whatever else, conveyed, which for that matter hangs before me still: the vision of my brother, agitated by the growth of his genius, moving in his burst of confidence, his bright earnestness, about the room I knew, which must have been our admirable parent's study—with that admirable parent himself almost holding his breath for the charm and the accepted peace of it, after earlier discussions and reserves; to say nothing too, if charm was in question, of the fact of rarity and beauty I must have felt, or in any case at present feel, in the resource for such an intellectually living and fermenting son of such a spiritually perceiving and responding sire. What was the whole passage but a vision of the fine private luxury of each?—with the fine private luxury of my own almost blurred image of it superadded. Of that same spring of '69 is another page addressed to myself in Europe. My memory must at the very time have connected itself with what had remained to me of our common or certainly of my own inveterate, childish appeal to him, in early New York days, for repetition, in the winter afternoon firelight, of his most personal, most remembering and picture-recovering "story"; that of a visit paid by him about in his nineteenth year, as I make it out, to his Irish relatives, his father's nephews, nieces and cousins, with a younger brother or two perhaps, as I set the scene forth—which it conduced to our liveliest interest to see "Billy Taylor," the negro servant accompanying him from Albany, altogether rule from the point of view of effect.[441] The dignity of this apparition indeed, I must paren-

441. HJ Sr. was in fact twenty-six when he visited Ireland, leaving New York on 20 April 1837 aboard the *Westminster*. He had just completed a second year of study at Princeton Theological Seminary. Landing at Plymouth, he traveled through the West Country en route for London. He stayed there till early August and had a new cork leg fitted. He then moved on to Bailieborough in County Cavan to visit the Irish Jameses. HJ Sr.'s Uncle Robert had died in 1825, leaving a widow and eleven children, some of whom had emigrated to the United States, though three or four remained in the town. HJ Sr. had hoped he might visit Paris, or even Rome and Venice, but left Portsmouth aboard the *Ontario* on 20 September, arriving in New York on 23 October. HJ later goes on to describe the comic, clownlike performance of the servant Billy Taylor, revealing (even with

thesise, would have yielded in general to the source of a glamour still more marked—the very air in which the young emissary would have moved as the son of his father and the representative of an American connection prodigious surely in its power to dazzle. William James of Albany was at that time approaching the term of his remarkably fruitful career, and as I see the fruits of it stated on the morrow of his death—in the New York Evening Post of December 20th 1832, for instance, I find myself envying the friendly youth who could bring his modest Irish kin such a fairytale from over the sea. I attach as I hang upon the passage a melancholy gaze to the cloud of images of what might have been for us all that it distractingly throws off. Our grandfather's energy, exercised in Albany from the great year 1789, appears promptly to have begun with his arrival there. "Every-where we see his footsteps, turn where we may, and these are the results of his informing mind and his vast wealth. His plans of improvement embraced the entire city, and there is scarcely a street or a square which does not exhibit some mark of his hand or some proof of his opulence. With the exception of Mr. Astor," this delightful report goes on to declare, "no other business man has acquired so great a fortune in this State. To his enormous estate of three millions of dollars there are nine surviving heirs. His enterprises have for the last ten years furnished constant employment for hundreds of our mechanics and labourers."[442] The enterprises appear,

---

the quotation marks for the man's name) continuing racial anxieties. An alternative view of Billy Taylor emerges from a friend of HJ Sr.'s, the physicist Joseph Henry, who thought him "a very good fellow in the serving line. He attracts much attention and is quite [a] Lion among the lower classes[,] eats with the family with whom we lodge and would find no difficulty were he not married in getting a white wife" (Habegger, *The Father*, 151–52).

442. HJ's grandfather William James arrived in America in 1789, at the age of eighteen, carrying (according to biographers) a small amount of money and a Latin grammar. His first two wives died; HJ Sr. was the son of his third wife, Catharine Barber. He built up a strong commercial business dealing in commodities such as flour, flax, grain, and vegetables before moving into real estate, eventually buying what was then the village of Syracuse and investing heavily and successfully in the production of salt. He became a respected local figure, delivering an oration at the momentous opening of the eastern section of the Erie Canal linking the Hudson River with Lake Erie in 1823. He died of a stroke on 19 December 1832. The amount of his wealth (based on the obituary quoted by HJ here) has been accepted by all biographers until Habegger, who calculated that "William owned $800,000 in real and $500,00 in personal property. Subtracting his debts of $120,000 leaves a net worth of about $1,200,000" (*The Father*, 112). The report, from which HJ supposedly quotes, appeared in the *Evening Post* (20 December 1832), published in New York. The piece had appeared first in the *Albany Evening Journal* (19 December). HJ makes significant changes to the text, perhaps using other contemporary

alas, to have definitely ceased, or to have fallen into less able hands, with his death—and to the mass of property so handsomely computed the heirs were, more exactly, not nine but a good dozen. Which fact, however, reduces but by a little the rich ambiguity of the question that was to flit before my father's children, as they grew up, with an air of impenetrability that I remember no attempt on his own part to mitigate. I doubt, for that matter, whether he could in the least have appeased our all but haunting wonder as to what had become even in the hands of twelve heirs, he himself naturally being one, of the admirable three millions. The various happy and rapid courses of most of the participants accounted for much, but did they account for the full beautiful value, and would even the furthest stretch of the charming legend of his own early taste for the amusements of the town really tell us what had been the disposition, by such a measure, of *his* share?[443] Our dear parent, we were later quite to

---

obituary material for his first two eulogistic sentences. The *Evening Post* reads: "Mr. William James expired about three o'clock this morning. He had languished, since Saturday, without the slightest hope of recovery; retaining, however, his reason and speech. // Mr. James is a man of great wealth. With the exception of Mr. Astor, no other business man acquired so great a fortune in the State. We learn that his estate is estimated, by intelligent judges, at three millions of dollars. Consisting, however, almost exclusively of real estate, it is more likely to be over than under estimated. To this enormous estate, there are nine surviving heirs. // Mr. James [*sic*] death is a severe loss to the city of Albany. He has done more *to build up* the city than any other individual. His enterprise has, for the last ten years, furnished constant employment for hundreds of our mechanics and laborers.—*Albany Journal.*" The local *Albany Evening Journal* has more detail, with an extra paragraph, which follows the second paragraph above: "Mr. JAMES came to this city in 1789, dependant upon his industry for his means of subsistence. He was a Clerk, for several years, to the late Mr. JOHN ROBINSON, in the old blue store which gave way for Thorp's splendid Marble Buildings. He first commenced for himself, in partnership with Mr. JOHN HORNER, in the Tobacco and Segar business. Their establishment was, we believe, on the corner of Dean st. and Mark Lane, opposite Justus Wright's. He subsequently opened a Dry-Goods and Grocery store in North Market st.; and finally closed his long and prosperous commercial labours about ten years since by retiring from his store in State street." Perhaps most noticeable in these newspaper accounts is the absence of personal detail: the listing of achievements leaves no room for regret, nor for any account of his role as husband, father, or friend.

443. William James's will was contested and, because of the autocratic nature of the conditions he imposed, took fourteen years to go through the New York law courts. It was contested by his wife and by HJ Sr., whose opinions and youthful excesses had been disapproved of. It has been concluded that HJ Sr. received $10,000 per year, not least because this is the amount of the legacy at the center of the plot of *Washington Square* (Lewis, *The Jameses,* 30–31). By any calculation and most standards, HJ Sr. was very well

feel, could have told us very little, in all probability, under whatever pressure, what had become of anything. There had been, by our inference, a general history—not on the whole exhilarating, and pressure for information could never, I think, have been applied; wherefore the question arrests me only through the brightly associated presumption that the Irish visit was made, to its extreme enlivening, in the character of a gilded youth, a youth gilded an inch thick and shining to effulgence on the scene not otherwise brilliant. Which image appeals to my filial fidelity—even though I hasten not to sacrifice the circle evoked, that for which I a trifle unassuredly figure a small town in county Cavan as forming an horizon, and which consisted, we used to delight to hear with every contributive circumstance, of the local lawyer, the doctor and the (let us hope—for we *did* hope) principal "merchant," whose conjoined hospitality appeared, as it was again agreeable to know, to have more than graced the occasion: the main definite pictorial touches that have lingered with me being that all the doors always stood open, with the vistas mostly raking the provision of whiskey on every table, and that these opportunities were much less tempting (to our narrator) than that of the quest of gooseberries in the garden with a certain beautiful Barbara, otherwise anonymous, who was not of the kin but on a visit from a distance at one of the genial houses. We liked to hear about Barbara, liked the sound of her still richer rarer surname; which in spite of the fine Irish harmony it even then struck me as making I have frivolously forgotten. She had been matchlessly fair and she ate gooseberries with a charm that was in itself of the nature of a brogue— so that, as I say, we couldn't have too much of her; yet even her measure dwindled, for our appetite, beside the almost epic shape of black Billy Taylor carrying off at every juncture alike the laurel and the bay. He singularly appealed, it was clear, to the Irish imagination, performing in a manner never to disappoint it; his young master—in those days, even in the North, young mastership hadn't too long since lapsed to have lost every grace of its tradition—had been all cordially acclaimed, but not least, it appeared, *because* so histrionically attended: he had been the ringmaster, as it were, of the American circus, the small circus of two, but the

---

provided for, or, as he commented at the time, "leisured for life" (Lewis, *The Jameses*, 30). Feinstein suggests that HJ Sr. "hid the shameful details of the will from his children," and also, with reference to the inaccuracies of HJ's recollection of his father's trip to Ireland, that "the image not of a disinherited son but of a gilded youth sent as an emissary by his wealthy sire" may have been a "legend" developed by HJ Sr. (*Becoming William James*, 65, 64).

other had been the inimitable clown. My point is that we repaired retro-spectively to the circus as insatiably as our Irish cousins had of old attended it in person—even for the interest of which fact, however, my father's words have led me too far. What here follows, I must neverthe-less add, would carry me on again, for development of reference, should I weakly allow it. The allusion to my brother Wilky's vividly indepen-dent verbal collocations and commentative flights re-echoes afresh, for instance, as one of the fond by-words that spoke most of our whole humorous harmony. Just so might the glance at the next visitor prompt a further raising of the curtain, save that this is a portrait to which, for lack of acquaintance with the original, I have nothing to contribute—beyond repeating again that it was ever the sign of my father's portraits to supply almost more than anything else material for a vision of himself.

Your enjoyment of England reminds me of my feelings on my first visit there forty years ago nearly, when I landed in Devonshire in the month of May or June and was so intoxicated with the roads and lanes and hedges and fields and cottages and castles and inns that I thought I should fairly expire with delight.[444] You can't expatiate too much for our entertainment on your impressions, though you make us want consumedly to go over and follow in your footsteps. Wilky has been at home now for 2 or 3 days and is very philosophic and enthusiastic over your letters.[445] I hoped to remember some of his turns of speech for you, but one chases another out of my memory and it is now all a blank. I will consult Alice's livelier one before I close.

My friend —— is a tropical phenomenon, a favourite of nature whatever his fellow man may say of him.[446] His face and person are handsome rather than otherwise, and it's obvious that he is a very unsoiled and pure piece of humanity in all *personal* regards. And with

444. HJ was in Britain from March to the summer of 1869, and then February to April 1870; this letter was written during this period, though, as Habegger points out (*The Father*, 145n), the original has not been found. "The son was under the impression that his father's first trip had taken place in 1830 and probably substituted 'forty years ago nearly' for whatever Henry Sr. had originally written—possibly 'thirty years ago.'"

445. Wilky was in the final stages of his postwar Florida venture, working a cotton plantation and using paid black labor, an enterprise that originally included Bob. As happened to many other veterans, the experiment failed, and Wilky returned for a time to Cambridge in 1870, having borrowed from his father and incurred debts that may well have permanently depleted the family's capital.

446. Not identified.

such a gift of oratory—such a boundless wealth of diction set off by copious and not ungraceful gesticulation! Here is where he belongs to the tropics, where nature claims him for her own and flings him like a cascade in the face of conventional good-breeding. I can't begin to describe him, he is what I have never before met. I see that he can't help turning out excessively tiresome, but he is not at all vulgar. He has a genius for elocution, that is all; but a real genius and no mistake. In comparison with Mr. F. L. or Mr. Longfellow or the restrained Boston style of address generally, he is what the sunflower is to the snowdrop;[447] but on the whole, if I could kick his shins whenever I should like to and so reduce him to silence, I prefer him to the others.

What mainly commends to me certain other passages of other dates (these still reaching on a little) is doubtless the fact that I myself show in them as the object of attention and even in a manner as a claimant for esthetic aid. This latter active sympathy overflows in a letter of the spring of '70, which would be open to more elucidation than I have, alas, space for. Let the sentence with which it begins merely remind me that Forrest, the American actor, of high renown in his time, and of several of whose appearances toward the close of his career I keep a memory uneffaced— the impression as of a deep-toned thunderous organ, a prodigious instrument pounded by a rank barbarian—had been literally, from what we gathered, an early comrade of our parent: literally, I say, because the association could seem to me, at my hours of ease, so bravely incongruous.[448] By my hours of ease I mean those doubtless too devoted to that habit of wanton dispersed embroidery for which any scrap of the human canvas would serve. From one particular peg, I at the same time allow, the strongest sense of the incongruity depended—my remembrance, long entertained, of my father's relating how, on an occasion, which must have been betimes in the morning, of his calling on the great tragedian, a man of

447. Mr. F.L. has not been identified, though WJ and HJ knew a Francis Lowe of Boston at this time (see *CWJ*, 1:202 n. 4). HJ Sr. had little time for Longfellow, especially, it seems, for his circle's enthusiasm for translating Dante (Habegger, *The Father,* 453).

448. Philadelphia-born Edwin Forrest (1806–72), aside from his acting successes, is remembered for his feud with the British actor Macready which caused the notorious Astor Place riot in New York City in 1849. HJ refers to their hostilities in his "William Charles Macready," which first appeared in the *Nation,* 29 April 1875 (*LC* 1, 1146–51). It seems that HJ Sr. knew Forrest in his earlier Albany days, and later (in company with Edmund Tweedy) became acquainted with his wife Catherine during the infamous divorce case she brought against the actor in 1852 (Habegger, *The Father,* 330).

enormous build and strength, the latter, fresh and dripping from the bath, had entered the room absolutely upside down, or by the rare gymnastic feat of throwing his heels into the air and walking, as with strides, on his hands; an extraordinary performance if kept up for more than a second or two, and the result at any rate of mere exuberance of muscle and pride and robustious joie de vivre.[449] It had affected me, the picture, as one of those notes of high colour that the experience of a young Albany viveur,[450] the like of which I felt I was never to come in for, alone could strike off; but what was of the finer profit in it was less the direct illustration of the mighty mountebank than of its being delightful on the part of a domestic character we so respected to have had, with everything else, a Bohemian past too—since I couldn't have borne at such moments to hear it argued as not Bohemian. What did his having dropped in after such a fashion and at a late breakfast-hour on the glory of the footlights and the idol of the town, what did it fall in with but the kind of thing one had caught glimpses and echoes of from the diaries and memoirs, so far as these had been subject to the passing peep, of the giftedly idle and the fashionably great, the Byrons, the Bulwers, the Pelhams, the Coningsbys, or even, for a nearer vividness perhaps, the N. P. Willises?[451]—of all of whom it was somehow more characteristic than anything else, to the imagination, that they always began their day in some such fashion. Even if I cite this as a fair example of one's instinct for making much of a little—once this little, a chance hand-ful of sand, could show the twinkle of the objective, or even the reflective,

449. Compare this version: "One of the most distinguished philosophical writers of our country, who was a native of Albany and at that time a particular friend of Forrest, has recently been heard to describe with great animation the pleasure he used to take in visiting the actor at this early hour of the morning to see him go through his gymnastic perfor-mances. The metaphysician said he admired the enormous strength displayed by the player, and applauded his fidelity to the conditions for preserving and increasing it, though for his own part he never could bring himself to do anything of the kind" (William Rounseville Alger, *Life of Edwin Forrest, the American Tragedian* [Philadelphia: Lippin-cott, 1877], 1:141).

450. One who lives life to the full.

451. These are proponents of the so-called bohemian life. George, Lord Byron was a British Romantic and satirical poet. Bulwer Lytton (1803–73) was a prolific and once highly popular British novelist; his novel *Pelham* (1828) was inspired by Paris, romance, and dandyism. *Coningsby, or the Younger Generation* (1844) is by Benja-min Disraeli (1804–81), who became British prime minister. Nathaniel Parker Willis (1806–67) was an American poet, writer, and journalist who worked in Boston and New York City.

grain of gold—I still claim value for that instanced felicity, as I felt it, of being able to yearn, thanks to whatever chance support, over Bohemia, and yet to have proof in the paternal presence close at hand of how well even the real frequentation of it, when achieved in romantic youth, might enable a person at last to turn out. The lesson may now indeed seem to have been one of those that rather more strictly adorn a tale than point a moral; but with me, at that period, I think, the moral ever came first and the tale more brilliantly followed. As for the recital, in such detail, of the theme of a possible literary effort which the rest of my letter represents, how could I feel this, when it had reached me, as anything but a sign of the admirable anxiety with which thought could be taken, even though "amateurishly," in my professional interest?—since professional I by that time appeared able to pass for being. And how above all can it not serve as an exhibition again of the manner in which all my benevolent backer's inveterate original *malaise* in face of betrayed symptoms of the impulse to "narrow down" on the part of his young found its solution always, or its almost droll simplification, as soon as the case might reach for him a *personal* enough, or "social" enough, as he would have said, relation to its fruits?[452] Then the malaise might promptly be felt as changed, by a wave of that wand, to the extremity of active and expatiative confidence.

Horatio Alger is writing a Life of Edwin Forrest, and I am afraid will give him a Bowery appreciation.[453] He reports his hero as a very "fine"

452. HJ Sr.'s unwillingness to let his children "narrow down," or establish a field of interest, could be regarded as in keeping with his reluctance to let them attend college and his own inability to describe himself as having any particular occupation. He wrote, "I desire my child . . . to become an upright man, a man in whom goodness shall be induced not by mercenary motives as brute goodness is induced, but by love for it or a sympathetic delight in it. And inasmuch as I know that this character or disposition cannot be forcibly imposed upon him, but must be freely assumed, I surround him as far as possible with an atmosphere of freedom" (*The Nature of Evil*, quoted in Matthiessen, *The James Family*, 70). Though HJ Sr. speaks here in the abstract, it is interesting that there is no space for a mother's view or a daughter's educational needs.

453. This letter, according to HJ, was written in the spring of 1870; its date is 4 March, but the year is 1873 (bMS Am 1092.9 [4198], Houghton; see also Edel et al., *A Bibliography of Henry James*, 25). The letter appears in http://www.dearhenryjames.org/, "Early Letters by Various Correspondents to Henry James," ed. Pierre A. Walker and Greg W. Zacharias. Internal references confirm the year: for instance, the mention of Rosamund Vincy, a character in George Eliot's *Middlemarch*, which began publication in parts only in 1871–72). Horatio Alger (1834–99) was a prolific and popular writer of stories both for and about boys; though he graduated from Harvard in 1860, by 1866 he had moved to New

talker—in which light I myself don't so much recall him, though he had a native breadth—as when telling Alger for example of old Gilbert Stuart's having when in a state of dilapidation asked him to let him paint his portrait.[454] "I consented," said Forrest, "and went to his studio. He was an old white lion, so blind that he had to ask me the colour of my eyes and my hair; but he threw his brush at the canvas, and every stroke was life." Alger talks freely about his own late insanity—which he in fact appears to enjoy as a subject of conversation and in which I believe he has somewhat interested William, who has talked with him a good deal of his experience at the Somerville Asylum.[455] Charles Grinnell—

---

York City, and in 1873 was visiting Europe. But in the original letter, HJ Sr. mentions the "Rev Mr Alger" and is referring to William Rounseville Alger (1822–1905), Horatio's cousin and author of *The Life of Edwin Forrest, the American Tragedian*. HJ is not entirely wrong, however. William Alger's biographer believes that "the work was in fact written by the cousins in collaboration" (Gary Scharnhorst, *A Literary Biography of William Rounseville Alger (1822–1905), a Neglected Member of the Concord Circle* [Lewiston, N.Y.: Edwin Mellen Press, 1990], 2). Scharnhorst and Jack Bales, in *The Lost Life of Horatio Alger, Jr.* (Bloomington: Indiana University Press, 1985), suggest that William Alger "wrote interchapters of theatre history and apparently assigned the job of researching and writing the biographical chapters to his enterprising and ambitious cousin Horatio" (107). The Bowery was a densely populated, racially diverse, rough-and-tumble area of Manhattan's Lower East Side, much favored by Walt Whitman. The "Bowery Boys" had been instrumental in causing the riot at the Astor where Macready was performing Macbeth. HJ devotes a colorful chapter of *AS* to "The Bowery and Thereabouts." See also Gary Scharnhorst, "Henry James and the Reverend William Rounseville Alger," *Henry James Review* 8 (Fall 1986): 71–75.

454. Gilbert Stuart (1755–1828) was perhaps the most celebrated American portrait painter. But Forrest would have had to be very young at the time of this incident, and doubt has been cast on the authenticity of the painting referred to: "There are three portraits of Edwin Forrest in the group at the Museum. One is said, like far too many early American portraits, to have been painted by Gilbert Stuart, as 'the last picture he painted.' As Stuart died in 1828, when Forrest was but twenty-two years old, and as the latter is here represented as a man in middle life, this is impossible" (Arthur Edwin Bye, "Portraits of Actors from the Collection of Edwin Forrest," *Bulletin of the Pennsylvania Museum* 22 [April 1927]: 354–55); there seem to be no portraits extant of Forrest as a young man by Stuart.

455. Details of Horatio Alger's life are difficult to determine—a 1928 biography by Herbert R. Mayes was based on fictitious material—but it is recorded that William Alger suffered a mental breakdown in 1871 when in Europe and that he later spent a period in the McLean Asylum in Somerville (northeast of Cambridge), which would coincide with the date of the letter. The institution, "on a delightful eminence," consisted of "an elegant house for the superintendent, with a wing at each end, handsomely constructed of brick, for the accommodation of the inmates" (R. L. Midgley, *Sights in Boston and Suburbs or Guide to the Stranger* [Boston: Jewett, 1856], 123). There is some evidence that WJ was a

though not à propos of the crazy—has become a great reader and apparently a considerable understander of my productions; Alger aforesaid aussi.[456] Everyone hopes that J. G. hasn't caught a Rosamund Vincy in Miss M. I don't know whether this hope means affection to J. or disaffection to the young lady.[457]

I have written to Gail Hamilton to send me your story;[458] but she

patient (or at least underwent treatment or tests) at McLean (Myers, *William James*, 501 n. 105; Simon, *Genuine Reality*, 121–22n); however, Feinstein comments, "During my research in the Boston area, I was repeatedly told that William James had been hospitalized at McLean in later life. My efforts to gain access to such records or to verify that such records exist were unsuccessful" (*Becoming William James*, 306n). Robertson may also have attended the hospital to counter his alcoholism (Strouse, *Alice James*, 205), so it seems more likely that any conversation took place with William rather than Horatio Alger. Scharnhost and Bales suggest that it was Horatio who had the confessional conversation with WJ (*The Lost Life of Horatio Alger, Jr.*, 70); indeed a charge of pedophilia had been made against him in 1866, which he never contested. It is conceivable that this could be referred to as his "insanity," but the coauthors accept HJ's dating of the letter, which is clearly erroneous. William Alger's psychological ill health began in 1871, and thus he is the much likelier patient. It is interesting that HJ Sr., earlier in this chapter, records WJ's contention, in relation to his own mind and its sanity, that "all mental disorder required to have a physical basis." Scharnhorst suggests that the Rev. Mr. Babcock in *The American* and the Unitarian minister Brand in *The Europeans* may have been modeled on William Alger (*A Literary Biography of William Rounseville Alger*, 105–7).

456. Charles Edward Grinnell (1841–1916), son of Charles Andrews and Anna Almy Cobb Grinnell, was known to the Jameses in Cambridge (*CWJ*, 4:152 n. 4). *Aussi:* also.

457. The pretty but shallow Rosamond Vincy becomes the wife of Dr. Lydgate in George Eliot's *Middlemarch*. "J.G." is John Chipman Gray, one of the younger Jameses' circle and friend of their cousin Minny Temple. He became a lawyer and taught at Harvard. "Miss M." is Anna Lyman Mason (1839–1915); they married in 1873. On 14 January 1873 HJ Sr. wrote to HJ, "John Gray is engaged to Nina Mason—an engagement that excites much wonder, as she is very worldly, it is supposed, and John unworldly" (bMS Am 1092.9 [4197], Houghton).

458. "Gail Hamilton" is the pseudonym of Mary Abigail Dodge (1833–96), a popular American writer, editor of *Wood's Household Magazine* (1872–73), and reformer on behalf of women. HJ records in Paris on 31 November–1 December 1872 that he has completed "The Sweetheart of M. Briseux": "I shall probably send it to the Magazine (*Wood's Household*—degrading connection!) for which Gail Hamilton lately appealed to me" (*CWJ*, 1:180). However, by 1 February 1873, when he is in Rome, he writes to his father, "I yesterday hear from her that she has had bilious fever, *Wood's Magazine* is exploded, and what shall we do with the precious packet? I have written her to send it to you; and would like you to forward it (marked visibly outside with my initials—or even name) to F. P. Church, Editor *Galaxy*" (*HJL*, 1:334). In his letter of 18 March 1873 to his son (see n. 438 above), HJ Sr. quotes Gail Hamilton's words: "Here is a manuscript belonging to that

does it not as yet. I will renew my invitation to her in a day or two if necessary. I went to see Osgood lately about his publishing a selection from your tales.[459] He repeated what he had told you—that he would give you 15 per cent and do all the advertising, etc., you paying for the plates; or he would pay everything and give you 10 per cent on every copy sold after the first thousand. I shall be glad (in case you would like to publish, and I think it time for you to do so) to meet the expense of your stereotyping, and if you will pick out what you would like to be included we shall set to work at once and have the book ready by next autumn. I have meanwhile the materials of a story for you which I was telling William of the other day as a regular Tourgéneff subject,[460] and he urged me to send it off to you at once—he was so struck with it.

Matthew Henry W. was a very cultivated and accomplished young man in Albany at the time I was growing up. He belonged to a highly respectable family of booksellers and publishers and was himself bred to the law;[461] but had such a love of literature, and more especially of the natural sciences, that he never devoted himself strictly to his profession. He was the intimate friend of my dear old tutor, Joseph Henry of the

lovely boy of Yours which he bids me send you—I part from it with regret and only wish I had a magazine to launch, because I am sure such freight would make its fortune." This letter from HJ Sr. to his son in *NSB* is most likely therefore to be a reply to HJ's letter of 1 February 1873. "The Sweetheart of M. Briseux" finally appeared in the *Galaxy* 15 (June 1873): 760–79.

459. This project was not completed until 1875, reflecting HJ's wishes: "I value none of my early tales enough to bring them forth again," he wrote from Rome on 24 March 1873; he preferred to make up a volume of "tales on the theme of American adventurers in Europe, leading off with the *Passionate Pilgrim*" (*HJL*, 1:357). The volume of six tales was published by James Osgood in Boston in 1875; from the evidence of this collection he was already committed to his lifelong practice of extensive revision.

460. HJ became a friend and great admirer of the Russian novelist Ivan Turgenev (1818–83) when he went to Paris at the end of 1875. His essay on Turgenev was first published in 1896 (*LC* 2, 1027–34).

461. This is Matthew Henry Webster, who had a legal office in Albany. The story (HJ Sr.'s narration reveals particularly unappealing sexual attitudes) came out as "Crawford's Consistency" in *Scribner's Monthly*, August 1876, 569–84, described by Habegger as "one of Henry Jr.'s most gentlemanly and dullest stories" (*The Father*, 464). Originally, HJ Sr. had suggested that the outline would make "a good basis for a novel," but it will be noticed that HJ omits the final three words at the end of his extract: perhaps he felt that he could manage only a short story. His habitual problem was that his fictional material expanded beyond expectation.

Smithsonian,[462] and of other distinguished men of science; he corresponded with foreign scientific bodies, and his contributions to science generally were of so original a cast as to suggest great hopes of his future eminence. He was a thorough gentleman, of perfect address and perfect courage—utterly unegotistic, and one's wonder was how he had ever grown up in Albany or resigned himself to living there. One day he invested his money, of which he had a certain quantity, in a scheme much favoured by the president of the bank in which he deposited, and this adventure proved a fortune. There lived near us as well a family of the name of K——, your cousin Mary Minturn Post's stepmother being of its members;[463] and this family reckoned upon a great social sensation in bringing out their youngest daughter, Lydia Sibyl, who had never been seen by mortal eye outside her own immediate circle, save that of a physician who reported that she was fabulously beautiful. She *was* the most beautiful girl I think I ever saw, at a little distance. Well, she made her sensation and brought Matthew Henry promptly to her feet. Her family wanted wealth above all things for her; but here was wealth and something more, very much more, and they smiled upon his suit. Everything went merrily for a while—M. H. was deeply intoxicated with his prize. Never was man so enamoured, and never was beauty better fitted to receive adoration. She was of an exquisite Grecian outline as to face, with a countenance like the tender dawn and form and manners ravishingly graceful. But W. was not content with his adventure—he embarked again and lost almost all he owned. The girl's father—or her mother rather, being the ruler of the family and as hard as the nether world at heart—gave the cue to her daughter and my friend was dismissed. He couldn't believe his senses,

462. The renowned Albany-born scientist Joseph Henry (1797–1878) was professor of mathematics and natural philosophy at the Albany Academy from 1826 to 1832, an institution attended by HJ Sr. and his brothers. He went on to perform pioneering experiments in electricity and magnetism that would lead to the invention of the telegraph, electric motor, and telephone. From 1846 to 1878 he was First Secretary, or director, of the Smithsonian Institution, in Washington, D.C. Joseph Henry may have been the tutor in charge when the young HJ Sr. had the accident that resulted in the amputation of his leg (Habegger, *The Father*, 70).

463. The missing name in the original letter of 4 March 1873 is Kane. HJ's cousin was Mary Ann King (1819–92), daughter of James King (1788–1841) and Ellen James (HJ Sr.'s half-sister), who were married in 1818. Mary Ann later became Mrs. Minturn Post. After his first wife's premature death, King married in 1826 Harriet Clark Kane (c. 1805–54).

he raved and cursed his fate, but it was inexorable. What was to be done? With a bitterness of heart inconceivable he plucked his revenge by marrying at once a stout and blooming jade who was to Lydia Sibyl as a peony to a violet, absolutely nothing but flesh and blood. Her he bore upon his arm at fashionable hours through the streets; her he took to church, preserving his admirable ease and courtesy to everyone, as if absolutely nothing had occurred; and her he pretended to take to his bosom in private, with what a shudder one can imagine. Everybody stood aghast. He went daily about his affairs, as serene and unconscious apparently as the moon in the heavens. Soon his poverty showed itself in certain economies of his attire, which had always been most recherché.[464] Soon again he broke his leg and went about on crutches, but neither poverty nor accident had the least power to ruffle his air of equanimity. He was always superior to his circumstances, met you exactly as he had always done, impressed you always as the best-bred man you knew, and left you wondering what a heart and what a brain lay behind such a fortune. One morning we all read in the newspaper at breakfast that Mr. M. H. W. had appealed the day before to the protection of the police against his wife, who had taken to beating him and whom as a woman he couldn't deal with by striking back; and the police responded properly to his appeal. He went about his affairs as usual that day and every day, never saying a word to any one of his trouble nor even indirectly asking sympathy, but making you feel that here if anywhere was a rare kind of manhood, a self-respect so eminent as to look down with scorn on the refuges open to ordinary human weakness. This lasted five or six years. He never drank or took to other vices, and lived a life of such decorum, so far as his own action was concerned, a life of such interest and science and literature, as to be the most delightful and unconscious of companions even when his coat was at the last shabbiness and you didn't dare to look at him for fear of betraying your own vulgar misintelligence. Finally Lydia Sibyl died smitten with smallpox and all her beauty gone to hideousness. He lingered awhile, his charming manners undismayed still, his eye as undaunted as at the beginning, and then he suddenly died. I never knew his equal for a manly force competent to itself in every emergency and seeking none of the ordinary subterfuges that men so often seek to hide their imbecility. I think it a good basis. . . .

464. Choice or elaborate.

Returning from Europe in June '70, after a stay there of some fifteen months, I had crossed the sea eastward again two years later, with my sister and our admirable aunt as companions—leaving them, I may mention, to return home at the end of six months while I betook myself to Italy, where I chiefly remained till the autumn of '74.[465] The following expresses our father's liberality of recognition and constant tenderness of tone in a manner that no comment need emphasise, but at one or two of his references I allow myself to glance. I happen to remember perfectly for instance the appearance of the novel of Madame Sand's that he so invidiously alludes to in one of the first numbers of the cherished Revue that reached us after the siege of Paris had been raised—such a pathetically scant starved pale number, I quite recall, as expressed the share even of the proud periodical in the late general and so tragic dearth;[466] with which it comes back to me that I had myself a bit critically mused on the characteristic queerness, the oddity of the light thrown on the stricken French consciousness by the prompt sprouting of *such* a flower of the native imagination in the chill air of discipline accepted and after the administration to that consciousness of a supposedly clarifying dose. But I hadn't gone the length of my father, who must have taken up the tale in its republished form, a so slim salmon-coloured volume this time: oh the repeated arrival, during those years, of the salmon-coloured volumes in their habit as they lived, a habit reserved, to my extreme appreciation, for this particular series, and that, enclosing the extraordinarily fresh fruit of their author's benign maturity, left Tamaris and Valvèdre and Mademoiselle La Quintinie in no degree ever "discounted" for us as devotees of the Revue, I make out, by their being but renewals of acquaintance.[467] The sense of the salmon-

465. HJ actually arrived in Cambridge on 10 May 1870, having sailed from the United Kingdom aboard the *Scotia* on 30 April. He left once more on 11 May 1872 with Alice and Aunt Kate and, when in Italy, met up with WJ. He departed Liverpool on the *Atlas* on 25 August 1874; fellow passengers included his friend Oliver Wendell Holmes Jr., traveling with his wife.

466. HJ had an abiding interest in the novelist George Sand (born Amandine-Aurore-Lucile Dupin, 1804–76) and wrote nine essays devoted to her works and her life. HJ is referring here to Sand's *Francia: Un bienfait n'est jamais perdu*, which came out in 1872. It appeared originally in the *Revue des deux mondes* 93 (15 May, 1 June 1871): part 1, 5–29, 193–222; part 2, 369–400. Paris had been besieged from January 1871 during the Franco-Prussian War (1870–71).

467. Sand's *Tamaris* came out in 1862, *Valvèdre* in 1861, *Mademoiselle La Quintinie* in 1863.

coloured[468] distinctive of Madame Sand was even to come back to me long years after on my hearing Edmond de Goncourt speak reminiscentially and, I permit myself to note, not at all reverently, of the *robe de satin fleur-de-pêcher* that the illustrious and infatuated lady, whose more peculiar or native tint, as Blanche Amory used to say, didn't contribute to a harmony, *s'était fait faire* in order to fix as much as possible the attention of Gustave Flaubert at the Dîner Magny;[469] of Gustave Flaubert, who, according to this most invidious of reporters, disembroiled from each other with too scant ease his tangle of possibly incurred ridicule from the declared sentiment of so old a woman, even in a peach-blossom dress, and the glory reflected on him by his admirer's immense distinction. Which vision of a complicated past, recovered even as I write—and of a past indeed contemporary with the early complacencies I attribute to ourselves—doesn't at all blur its also coming back to me that I was to have found my parent "hard on" poor Francia in spite of my own comparative reserves; these being questions and shades that I rejoice to think of our having had so discussionally, and well at home for the most part, the social education of. I see that general period as quite flushed and toned by the salmon-coloured covers; so that a kind of domestic loyalty would ever operate, as we must have all felt, to make us take the thick with the thin and not *y regarder*[470] for

468. This would better read "salmon-colour," as it appears in the British first edition of the volume.

469. The novelist brothers Goncourt, Edmond (1822–96) and Jules (1830–70), recounted Parisian literary life from the 1860s to the 1890s in their often scandalously frank *Journals*. After they were published, HJ wrote a long essay for the *Fortnightly Review* in 1888 (*LC* 2, 404–28). HJ met Edmond de Goncourt at the end of 1875, in company with Turgenev and Flaubert. The Goncourts' *Journal* comments on George Sand are both affectionate and contemptuous: her *robe de satin fleur-de-pêcher* (peach-blossom satin dress) that she *s'était fait faire* (had had made). Blanche Amory, pretty though superficial, attracts the attention of the young eponymous hero of Thackeray's novel *Pendennis* (1849–50). "Tint" is a term associated with Miss Amory: she tells the virtuous Laura, "Your robe was not well made, nor your bonnet very fresh. But you have such beautiful grey eyes, and such a lovely tint." Later the "chief of the kitchen," Monsieur Mirobolant, playfully stressing the French origins of her given name, determines that his dinner will be, like her, "as spotless as the snow": "I sent her up a little *potage à la Reine—à la Reine Blanche* I called it,—as white as her own tint—and confectioned with the most fragrant cream and almonds" ([Harmondsworth: Penguin, 1972], 247, 258). George Sand enjoyed an intimate friendship with the novelist Gustave Flaubert (1821–80), on whom HJ wrote three essays (*LC* 2, 289–346). The restaurant Magny was the premiere meeting place for the bohemian literary life of Paris.

470. To look there.

a Francia the more or the less. When I say all indeed I doubtless have in mind especially my parents and myself, with my sister and our admirable aunt (in her times of presence) thrown in—to the extent of our subjection to the charm of such matters in particular as La Famille de Germandre, La Ville Noire, Nanon and L'Homme de Neige, round which last above all we sat ranged in united ecstasy;[471] so that I was to wonder through the after years, and I think perhaps to this day, how it could come that a case of the "story" strain at its finest and purest, a gush of imaginative force so free and yet so artfully directed, shouldn't have somehow "stood out" more in literary history. Perhaps indeed L'Homme de Neige[472] does essentially stand out in the unwritten parts of that record—which are content to be mere tacit tender tradition; for all the world as if, since there are more or less dreadful perpetuated books, by the hundred, dreadful from whatever baseness or whatever scantness, that for shame, as it were, we never mention, so one may figure others as closeted in dimness (than which there is nothing safer) by the very scruple of respect at its richest. I hover for instance about the closet of L'Homme de Neige, I stand outside a moment as if listening for a breath from within; but I don't open the door, you see—which must mean, in all probability, that I wouldn't for the world inconsiderately finger again one of the three volumes; *that* meaning, in its turn, doubtless, that I have heard the breath I had listened for and that it can only have been what my argument wants, the breath of life unquenched.[473] Isn't it relevant to this that when she was not reading Trollope our dear mother was reading "over" La Famille de Germandre, which, with several of its companions of the same bland period, confirmed her in the sense that there was no one like their author for a "love-story"?—a conviction, however, that when made articulate exposed her to the imputation of a larger tolerance than she doubtless intended to project; till the matter was cleared up by our generally embracing her for so sweetly not knowing about Valentine and Jacques and suchlike, and having

471. The first two of these Sand stories appeared in 1861, and the last two in 1872 and 1859.

472. "The Snowman."

473. Though reassured by the peaceful sound within, HJ avoids, by not opening a figurative door onto the past and the happy family reading experience derived from *L'homme de neige,* any more developed retrospective disappointment. However, as illustrated in the remembered dream of the Galerie d'Apollon in *SBO* (chap. 25), along with other horrific moments in the late short stories, doors and the actions of pushing against or tightly holding them are associated with some mysterious Jamesian psychic panic.

only begun at La Mare au Diable and even thereafter been occasionally obliged to skip.[474]

So far do I let myself go while, to recur to my letter, Chauncey Wright[475] sits for me in his customary corner of the deep library sofa and his strange conflictingly conscious light blue eyes, appealing across the years from under the splendid arch of his fair head, one of the handsomest for representation of amplitude of thought that it was possible to see, seems to say to me with a softness more aimed at the heart than any alarm or any challenge: "But what then are you going to do for me?"[476] I find myself simply ache, I fear, as almost the only answer to this—beyond his figuring for me as the most wasted and doomed, the biggest at once and the gentlest, of the great intending and unproducing (in anything like the just degree) bachelors of philosophy, bachelors of attitude and of life. And as he so sits, loved and befriended and welcomed, valued and invoked and vainly guarded and infinitely pitied, till the end couldn't but come, he renews that appeal to the old kindness left over, as I may say, and which

474. It seems that Mrs. James confined herself (with the somewhat patronizing approval of other family members) to the less controversial regions of Sand's oeuvre, thus avoiding excess of passion or moral complexity. *La famille de Germandre* is one of Sand's most innocent stories. *Valentine* (1832) ends unhappily, the lovers eventually separated by "two different aristocracies," "the aristocracy of birth" and "the aristocracy of the spirit" (Curtis Cate, *George Sand: A Biography* [London: Hamish Hamilton, 1975], 209). In *Jacques* (1834) a husband sacrifices himself for his wife's lover by disappearing while crossing an Alpine glacier (perhaps an influence on the denouement of *Roderick Hudson*). HJ thought both works to be among those showing a "passionate contempt for the institution of marriage" (*LC* 2, 722). *La Mare au Diable* (The devil's pond) is a more tranquil evocation of rural life. In an essay of 1897 for the magazine *The Yellow Book*, he asks of George Sand (thus showing some scorn for the tastes of his late mother), "Do people still handle the works of this master—people other than young ladies studying French with 'La Mare au Diable' and a dictionary?" (*LC* 2, 737). A number of critics have considered the enduring influence of George Sand on HJ's writing, e.g., Patricia Thomson, *George Sand and the Victorians: Her Influence and Reputation in Nineteenth-Century England* (London: Macmillan, 1977), and, in terms of constructs of male identity, Leland S. Person, *Henry James and the Suspense of Masculinity* (Philadelphia: University of Pennsylvania Press, 2003), 18–25.

475. Chauncey Wright (1830–75), a Darwinian philosopher of science and mathematician who graduated from Harvard in 1852, frequently visited the family at Quincy Street and was appreciated for his conversation; he shared many interests with WJ. He met with little worldly success, however.

476. In *AS* HJ frequently imagines the figures of Boston and Cambridge from his earlier life as fleeting, sometimes poignant ghosts, demanding or avoiding attention as he walks familiar streets.

must be more or less known to all of us, for the good society that was helplessly to miss a right chronicler, and the names of which, so full at the time of their fine sense, were yet to be writ in water.[477] Chauncey Wright, of the great imperfectly-attested mind; Jane Norton, of the train, so markedly, of the distinguished, the sacrificial, devoted; exquisite Mrs. Gurney, of the infallible taste, the beautiful hands and the tragic fate; Gurney himself, for so long Dean of the Faculty at Harvard and trusted judge of all judgments (this latter pair the subject of my father's glance at the tenantship of Shady Hill in the Nortons' absence:)[478] they would delightfully adorn a page and appease a piety that is still athirst if I hadn't to let them pass. Harshly condemned to let them pass, and looking wistfully after them as they go, how can I yet not have inconsequently asked them to turn a moment more before disappearing?

My heart turns to you this morning, so radiant in the paternal panoply you wear toward Alice and your aunt, and I would give a great deal to see you.[479] The enclosed scrap of a letter from William is sent to show you how vastly improved are his eyes, especially when you shall have learned that he has written us within the last four or five days twenty pages of like density to these.[480] He would fain persuade us to go to Mount Desert;[481] perhaps later we may go to Quebec, but we are so comfortable together reading Trollope and talking philosophy that we cheerfully drop the future from our regard. Mamma is free and active

477. This is a passing allusion to John Keats's epitaph: "Here lies one whose name was writ in water."

478. Having been professor of history at Harvard, Gurney served as dean of faculty from 1870 to 1875 (see also n. 433 above). His wife, Ellen, had been "reduced to near-madness by the suicide of her sister Clover Adams in December 1885 and the lingering illness and death of her husband . . . the following autumn. Mrs. Gurney slipped out of her sickroom, wandered along the railroad tracks in west Cambridge, and was struck by a freight train" (Lewis, *The Jameses*, 403–4).

479. The letter is dated July 1872 (bMS Am 1092.9 [4193], Houghton). The original begins "My heart yearns to you"; the change may reflect HJ's wish to reduce the effusiveness of HJ Sr.'s style, or may simply result from a mishearing if he were dictating the passage.

480. WJ was on vacation, and this included a stay in Scarboro, near Portland, Maine, in July–August 1872, the time of writing of this letter. Among WJ's physical and mental ailments in these years (including insomnia, backache, and severe depressions) was a propensity to eyestrain, which prevented him from reading for any extended period.

481. Mount Desert is the largest of the many islands off the Maine coast, connected to the mainland even at this time by a bridge.

and bracing. She is a domestic nor'wester, carrying balm and bloom into every nook and corner of her empire. . . . She hangs over The Eustace Diamonds while I try vainly to read George Sand's Francia.[482] I have come across nothing of that lady's that reflects a baser light on her personal history. What must a woman have been through to want to grovel at this time of day in such uncleanness? Don't buy it—I wish I hadn't![483] The new North American is out, with a not too interesting article of Chauncey Wright's on Mivart, a scandalous (in point of taste) essay of Mr. Stirling on Buckle, full of Scotch conceit, insolence and "wut;" a very very laboured article by James Lowell on Dante, in which he determines to exhaust all knowledge; and these are all I have read.[484] Mr. Stirling of course makes Buckle ridiculous, but he stamps himself a shabby creature.

I find the following, addressed to his daughter in August '72, so beautifully characteristic of our parents' always explicit admonition to us, in our dependent years, against too abject an impulse to be frugal in their interests, that I may fairly let it stand as a monument to this particular aspect of their affection.

Your and H.'s last letters bring tears of joy to our eyes.[485] It's a delight above all delights to feel one's children turn out all that the heart covets in children. Your conviction is not up to the truth. Our

482. *The Eustace Diamonds,* the third of Trollope's Palliser novels, was published as a book in 1873. It appeared first in serial form in the *Fortnightly Review,* July 1871 to February 1873, so Mrs. James was reading it by installment.

483. HJ makes a very brief footnote reference to *Francia* in his long essay on Sand published in 1877 (*LC* 2, 728 n. 1), so he presumably ignored his father's advice. In the original HJ Sr.'s language is even stronger: "How bestial a woman ever to have been born, or become, to grovel spontaneously in such filth."

484. All in the *North American Review* 115 (July 1871): Chauncey Wright, "Evolution by Natural Selection: 1 The Origin of Species, etc by Charles Darwin. 2 Evolution and its Consequences, by St. George Mivart. 3 Specific Genesis, by St. George Mivart," 1–30; J. H. Stirling, "Henry Thomas Buckle, his problem and his metaphysics," 65–103; James Lowell, "The Shadow of Dante," a review of Maria Francesca Rossetti's *The Shadow of Dante: Being an Essay towards studying himself, his world, and his pilgrimage* (Boston: Roberts, 1872), 139–209. See also J. Chesley Mathews, "James Russell Lowell's Interest in Dante," *Italica* 36 (June 1959): 77–100.

485. This is a letter, dated 9 August [1872], written not to Alice James but to HJ, with some deletions and judicious editing (bMS Am 1092.9 [4194], Houghton). The reasons for the change of recipient are unclear, unless perhaps HJ felt that the warmth of mutual

"tender thoughts" of you are so constant that I have hardly been able to settle to anything since you have been gone. I can do little else than recount to myself "the tender mercies of the Lord" to me and my household.[486] Still I am not wholly useless; I try to write every day, and though I haven't my daughter at hand to look after my style and occasionally after my ideas, I manage to do a little. Your conscientious economy is excessively touching, but it's a little overstrained. You needn't be afraid of putting us to any embarrassment so long as your expenses don't exceed their present rate; and you can buy all you want in Paris without stretching your tether a particle. This is Mamma's message as well as mine.[487] Charles Atkinson wishes me to say that Monte Genneroso above Lugano Lake—the P.O. Mendrisio—offers a wondrous climate;[488] and Mamma thinks—so fearful is she that you will descend into Italy before the warm weather is over and so compromise your strength—that you had either better go there awhile first or else be ready to retreat on it in case you find the summer heat in Venice impossible.

Nor does this scrap from a letter to myself[489] at the same season breathe a spirit less liberal—so far as the sympathy with whatever might pass for my fondest preoccupations was concerned. These were now quite frankly recognised as the arduous attempt to learn somehow or other to write.[490]

---

affection expressed and evidence of financial dependency were better suited to a twenty-four-year-old daughter than a twenty-nine-year-old son. Pasted into the original MS is a printed clipping that confirms WJ's appointment as instructor in physiology at Harvard for the following year.

486. This may be a paraphrase of Isaiah, 63:7: "I will mention the loving-kindnesses of the Lord and the praises of the Lord, according to all the Lord hath bestowed on us, and the great goodness toward the house of Israel."

487. This relaxed attitude to money is much less evident in Mrs. James's correspondence with HJ where he has sometimes to justify his spending.

488. "Charley," or Charles Follen Atkinson (Harvard class of 1865, d. 1915), was a friend of WJ's and later became a Boston businessman. The area is in the south of Switzerland; Monte Generoso is in the Lepontine Alps, between Lakes Lugano and Como. The reference (according to the Houghton original) is to the post office in Mendrisio just south of Lake Lugano, on the border with Italy.

489. This fragment survives in typescript and is dated "some time in summer of 1872" (bMS Am 1092.9 [4196], Houghton). The review of Droz's *Babolain* referred to appeared in the *Nation*, 15 August 1872.

490. This is HJ's first admission of his professional role as a writer, as opposed to a

I send you The Nation, though there seems nothing in it of your own, and I think I never fail to recognise you. A notice of Gustave Droz's Babolain (by T. S. P., I suppose) there is;[491] which book I read the other day. This fumbling in the cadaver of the old world, however, only disgusts me when so unrelieved as in this case by any contrast or any souffle[492] of inspiration such as you get in Tourguéneff. It's curious to observe how uncertain the author's step is in this story— how he seems always on the look-out for some chance to break away. But it has mastered him, he can't lay the ghost he has conjured.

To which I should limit myself for the commemoration of that group of years by the gentle aid of the always vivid excerpt, were it not that I have before me a considerable cluster of letters addressed by the writer of the foregoing to Mr. J. Eliot Cabot, most accomplished of Bostonians, most "cultivated" even among the cultivated, as we used to say, and of a philosophic acuteness to which my father highly testified, with which indeed he earnestly contended.[493] The correspondence in question covered, during the years I include, philosophic ground and none other; but though no further exhibition of it than this reference may convey is to my purpose I lay it under contribution to the extent of a passage or two just for the pleasure of inviting recognition, as I invite it wherever we meet an instance, of the fashion after which the intensely animated soul can scarce fail of a harmony and a consistency of expression that are nothing less than interesting, that in fact become at once beautiful, in themselves. By which remark I nevertheless do not mean to limit the significance of the writer's side of his long argument with Mr. Eliot Cabot,[494] into

---

gatherer of impressions. Many of his father's letters of these years repeat the admiration expressed, both privately and publicly, for his son's talents. It is clear too from the biographical detail that HJ quickly (and in contrast to his father) recognized what was needed in order to survive as a professional writer.

491. The Frenchman Gustave Droz (1832–95) was both a novelist and painter, popular in Europe and the United States. *Babolain,* a story of a man dragged down by his wife and her mother, was published in 1872. The anonymous *Nation* reviewer was HJ's friend, Thomas Sergeant Perry.

492. Breath.

493. James Elliot Cabot (1821–1903), friend of HJ Sr. and sympathetic toward the ideals of the transcendentalists, edited the works of Emerson and published a two-volume *Memoir* in 1887, reviewed by HJ for *Macmillan's Magazine* in December 1887 (*LC* 1, 250–71).

494. This long letter (HJ quotes about a third), one of five written to Elliot Cabot that have survived, is dated 4 May [1874?] (bMS Am 1092.9 [4092], Houghton).

which I may not pretend to enter, nor the part that in any such case a rare gift for style must inveterately play.

I grant then that I am often tempted to conceive, as I read your letters, that we differ only in your terms being more abstract, mine more concrete; and yet I really don't think this difference is exhaustive. If I thought Philosophy capable ever of being reduced to logical compass or realising itself as science, I should give in at once. But this is just what I cannot think. Philosophy is the doctrine exclusively of the infinite in the finite, and deals with the latter therefore only as a mask, only as *harbouring* the former. But if you formulate it scientifically your terms are necessarily all finite, as furnished by experience, and the infinite is excluded or at most creeps in as the indefinite—Hegel's *becoming* for example.[495] Thus Hegel's dialectic modulates only in the sphere of his distance.[496] His *being* is universal existence, and, as universals have only a logical truth, being in se[497] is equivalent to Nothing. But Nothing hasn't even a logical basis. Lithe as human thought is it can't compass the conception. It is a mere brutum fulmen[498] devised to disguise the absence of thought or its inanition; and Hegel, if he had been wise, would have said no-thought instead of no-thing. For no-thing doesn't express the complete absence of existence. Existence is of two sorts, real and personal, sensible and conscious, quantitative and qualitative. The most you are entitled to say therefore when existence disappears in quantitative, real or sensible, form is that it has been taken up into purely qualitative, personal or conscious form; no-thing being the logical equivalent of all-person. Thus I, who in Hegel's formula presumably extract existence from being, survive the operation as person, and though I am most clearly no-thing I am yet not *being*. Indeed I am not even existence any longer, since by knocking thing out of being I have forfeited my own reality, and consent henceforth to

495. The German philosopher Georg Wilhelm Friedrich Hegel (1770–1831) would have appealed to HJ Sr., partly because of his early interest in the life of Christ as primarily a human, nonmiraculous figure of hope for mankind, though he later came to embrace philosophy rather than religion as a means of approaching the infinite. His *Phenomenology of the Spirit* considers the relation of consciousness to the experience of reality in six categories.

496. The original has, more sensibly, "existence" rather than "distance"—possibly another slip made during HJ's dictation.

497. *In se:* in itself (Lat.).

498. *Brutum fulmen:* unfeeling thunder, i.e. empty threat (Lat.).

be pure personality, *i.e.* phenomenality. And personal or phenomenal existence is constituted by referring itself to a foreign source, or, what is the same thing, confessing itself created: so that the fundamental word of Philosophy, by Hegel's own formula, is creation; which, however, as I understand him, he denies in any objective sense of the word. This then is what I complain of in him—with deference of course to your better knowledge, which, however, you do not urge as yet in what seems to me a silencing way—that he makes existence *essential* to being, so that take existence away and being becomes nothing. It would not be a whit less preposterous in me to say that thought is essential to thing, subject to object, marble to statue, canvas to picture, woman to wife, mother to child. It is literally putting the cart before the horse and converting Philosophy to a practical quagmire. Being implies existence of course just as picture implies canvas, or as personality implies reality, or as chick implies egg; but it implies it only to a lower intelligence than itself, an unspiritual intelligence to wit, which has no direct or inward intuition of being, and requires to be agitated[499] to discerning it. When I recognise the spiritual life of Art I never think of marble or canvas as entering even conditionally into its manifestations.

But I hold my case for a rare command of manner thus proved, and need go no further; the more that I have dropped too many of those threads of my rather niggled tapestry that belong but to the experience of my own weaving hand and the interplay of which represents thereby a certain gained authority. I disentangle these again, if the term be not portentous, though reflecting too, and again with complacency, that though I thus prize them as involved most in my own consciousness, this is just because of their attachment somewhere else to other matters and other lives.

IX   I went up from Newport to Cambridge early in the autumn of '62, and on one of the oddest errands, I think, that, given the several circumstances, I could possibly have undertaken.[500] I was nineteen years old, and it had seemed to me for some time past that some such step as my entering for instance the Harvard Law

499. This should read "educated," not "agitated."

500. The family continued to live in Newport till their move to Boston in 1864. WJ was already "on the scene," as HJ says, a student at the Lawrence Scientific School. Older by

School more or less urgently concerned what I could but try to help myself out by still putting forward as my indispensable education—I am not sure indeed that the claim didn't explicitly figure, or at least successfully dangle, as that of my possibly graceful mere "culture." I had somehow—by which I mean for reasons quite sufficient—to fall back on the merciful "mere" for any statement of my pretensions even to myself: so little they seemed to fit into any scheme of the conventional maximum as compared with those I saw so variously and strongly asserted about me, especially since the outbreak of the War. I am not sure whether I yet made bold to say it, but I should surely be good for nothing, all my days, if not for projecting into the concrete, by hook or by crook—that is my imagination shamelessly aiding—some show of (again) mere life. This impression was not in the least the flag I publicly brandished; in fact I must have come as near as possible to brandishing none whatever, a sound instinct always hinting to me, I gather, that the time for such a performance was much more after than before—before the perfect place had been found for the real planting of the standard and the giving of its folds to the air. No such happy spot had been marked, decidedly, at that period, to my inquiring eye; in consequence of which the emblazoned morsel (hoisted sooner or later by all of us, I think, somehow and somewhere), might have passed for the hour as a light extravagant bandanna rolled into the tight ball that fits it for hiding in the pocket. There it considerably stayed, so far as I was concerned; and all the more easily as I can but have felt how little any particular thing I might meanwhile "do" would matter—save for some specious appearance in it. This last, I recognise, had for me a virtue—principally that of somehow gaining time; though I hasten to add that my approach to the Law School can scarcely, as a means to this end, in the air of it that comes back to me, have been in the least deceptive.[501] By which I

<hr />

one year, William was invariably one step ahead of Henry, a continuous theme in this autobiography and elaborated upon in Edel's highly influential biography. Cambridge was still at that time a tranquil, rural spot. The records of Harvard Law School, established in 1817, show that HJ was enrolled for two terms from 2 September 1862 to 10 July 1863 (Le Clair, *Young Henry James*, 408 n. 3). Law may seem an odd choice, though his options were limited: "Nothing approaching 'liberal arts' existed then, except the rhetoric and oratory taught by Francis J. Child or the French and Spanish taught by James Russell Lowell" (Edel, *Untried Years*, 196).

501. Uncommitted to law from the outset, HJ spent just one year at Dane Hall, Harvard, an experience that confirmed his literary ambitions; at the time he worked on stories, "mainly of a romantic kind," as Sarge Perry recalled (quoted in Habegger, *The Father*,

mean that my appearance of intentions, qualifications, possibilities, or whatever else, in the connection, hadn't surely so much as the grace of the specious. I spoke above of the assumed "indispensability" of some show of my being further subject to the "education" theory, but this was for the moment only under failure to ask to whom, or for what, such a tribute *was* indispensable. The interest to myself would seem to have been, as I recover the sense of the time, that of all the impossibilities of action my proceeding to Cambridge on the very vaguest grounds that probably ever determined a residence there might pass for the least flagrant; as I breathe over again at any rate the comparative confidence in which I so moved I feel it as a confidence in the positive saving virtue of vagueness. Could I but work that force as an ideal I felt it must see me through, for the beauty of it in that form was that it should absolutely superabound. I wouldn't have allowed, either, that it was vaguer to do nothing; for in the first place just staying at home when everyone was on the move couldn't in any degree show the right mark: to be properly and perfectly vague one had to be vague *about* something; mere inaction quite lacked the note—it was nothing but definite and dull. I thought of the Law School experiment, I remember, in all sorts of conceivable connections, but in the connection of dulness surely never for an hour. I thought of it under the head of "life"— by which term at the same time, I blush to confess, I didn't in the least mean free evening access to Boston in a jangling horse-car, with whatever extension this might give to the joy of the liberated senses.[502] I simply meant—well, what was monstrously to happen; which I shall be better inspired here to deal with as a demonstration made in its course than as a premonition relatively crude and at the time still to be verified. Marked in the whole matter, however these things might be, was that irony of fate under the ugly grin of which I found my father reply in the most offhand and liberal manner to my remark that the step in question—my joining, in a sense, my brother at Cambridge—wouldn't be wholly unpracticable. It might have been, from his large assent to it, a masterstroke of high policy. A certain inconsequence in this left me wondering why then if the matter was now so natural it hadn't been to his mind a year before equally simple that I should go to college, and to *that* College, after a more showy, even

---

437). It is possible he enrolled at Harvard as a form of purposeful alternative action to enlisting for the Union army as his two younger brothers had done.

502. Though, having visited and corresponded with WJ, HJ must have been aware of the social pleasures available involving friends and family.

though I see it would have been at the same time a less presumptuous, fashion. To have deprecated the "college course" with such emphasis only so soon afterwards to forswear all emphasis and practically smile, in mild oblivion, on *any* Harvard connection I might find it in me to take up, was to bring it home, I well recall, that the case might originally have been much better managed.

All of which would seem to kick up more dust than need quite have hung about so simple a matter as my setting forth to the Cambridge scene with no design that I could honourably exhibit. A superficial account of the matter would have been that my father had a year or two earlier appeared to think so ill of it as to reduce me, given the "delicacy," the inward, not then the outward, which I have glanced at, to mild renunciation—mild I say because I remember in fact, rather to my mystification now, no great pang of disappointment, no soreness of submission. I didn't want anything so much as I wanted a certain good (or wanted thus supremely *to* want it, if I may say so), with which a conventional going to college wouldn't have so tremendously much to do as for the giving it up to break my heart—or an unconventional not-going so tremendously much either. What I "wanted to want" to be was, all intimately, just *literary;* a decent respect for the standard hadn't yet made my approach so straight that there weren't still difficulties that might seem to meet it, questions it would have to depend on. Passing the Harvard portal positively failed in fact to strike me as the shorter cut to literature; the sounds that rose from the scene as I caught them appeared on the contrary the most detached from any such interest that had ever reached my ear. Merely to open the door of the big square closet, the ample American closet, to the like of which Europe had never treated us, on the shelves and round the walls of which the pink Revues sat with the air, row upon row, of a choir of breathing angels, was to take up that particular, that sacred connection in a way that put the coarser process to shame.[503] The drop of the Harvard question had of a truth really meant, as I recover it, a renewed consecration of the rites of that chapel where the taper always twinkled—which circumstance I mention as not only qualifying my sense of loss, but as symbolising, after a queer fashion, the independence, blest vision (to the extent,

503. HJ hints at his later appreciation of the scale and generosity of American domestic arrangements, as exemplified in *The Ivory Tower.* It seems that the closet full of *Revues des deux mondes,* containing some of the best critical and creative writing of the century, comes close to constituting a college of the liberal arts for the young HJ. His figurative style reiterates the vocational—indeed sanctified—nature of his dedication to the literary.

that is, of its being a closer compact with the life of the imagination), that I should thus both luckily come in for and designingly cultivate: cultivate in other words under the rich cover of obscurity. I have already noted how the independence was, ever so few months later, by so quaint a turn, another mere shake of the tree, to drop into my lap in the form of a great golden apple—a value not a simple windfall only through the fact that my father's hand had after all just lightly loosened it. This accession pointed the moral that there was no difficulty about anything, no intrinsic difficulty; so that, to re-emphasise the sweet bewilderment, I was to "go" where I liked in the Harvard direction and do what I liked in the Harvard relation.[504] Such was the situation as offered me; though as I had to take it and use it I found in it no little difference. Two things and more had come up—the biggest of which, and very wondrous as bearing on any circumstance of mine, as having a grain of weight to spare for it, was the breaking out of the War. The other, the infinitely small affair in comparison, was a passage of personal history the most entirely personal, but between which, as a private catastrophe or difficulty, bristling with embarrassments, and the great public convulsion that announced itself in bigger terms each day, I felt from the very first an association of the closest, yet withal, I fear, almost of the least clearly expressible.[505] Scarce at all to be stated, to begin with, the queer fusion or confusion established in my consciousness during the soft spring of '61 by the firing on Fort Sumter, Mr. Lincoln's instant first call for volunteers and a physical mishap, already referred to as having overtaken me at the same dark hour, and the effects of which were to draw themselves out incalculably and intolerably.[506] Beyond all present notation the interlaced, undivided way in which what had happened to me, by a

504. In the context of HJ Sr.'s diffidence concerning his children's education, HJ earlier recalls—with some gratitude—thus having been "thrown so upon the inward life" (SBO, 50). WJ's changing needs had, it seems, been fully met—if not indulged. Having wished to go to Harvard in the fall of 1861, HJ, aged nineteen, felt much older than the other freshmen (most of them about fifteen years old), as he later acknowledges.

505. It is typical of HJ's late style that he should attempt such a bold juxtaposing, or rather interleaving, of personal and national histories. Later in the chapter he explores the emblematic ramifications of this established fusion of the injury he sustained as a young man and the outbreak of Civil War.

506. The bombardment of Fort Sumter in the middle of Charleston harbor by Confederate troops began on 12 April 1861. With the Northern withdrawal from Fort Sumter, Lincoln called for 75,000 militiamen as volunteers on 15 April 1862. HJ consulted various medical authorities of the time, but received little positive advice or treatment, and his back injury was to become "a part of his private existence" (Novick, *Young Master*, 79).

turn of fortune's hand, in twenty odious minutes, kept company of the most unnatural—I can call it nothing less—with my view of what was happening, with the question of what might still happen, to everyone about me, to the country at large: it so made of these marked disparities a single vast visitation.[507] One had the sense, I mean, of a huge comprehensive ache, and there were hours at which one could scarce have told whether it came most from one's own poor organism, still so young and so meant for better things, but which had suffered particular wrong, or from the enclosing social body, a body rent with a thousand wounds and that thus treated one to the honour of a sort of tragic fellowship. The twenty minutes had sufficed, at all events, to establish a relation—a relation to everything occurring round me not only for the next four years but for long afterward—that was at once extraordinarily intimate and quite awkwardly irrelevant. I must have felt in some befooled way in presence of a crisis— the smoke of Charleston Bay still so acrid in the air—at which the likely young should be up and doing or, as familiarly put, lend a hand much wanted; the willing youths, all round, were mostly starting to their feet, and to have trumped up a lameness at such a juncture could be made to pass in no light for graceful. Jammed into the acute angle between two high fences, where the rhythmic play of my arms, in tune with that of several other pairs, but at a dire disadvantage of position, induced a rural, a rusty, a quasi-extemporised old engine to work and a saving stream to flow, I had done myself, in face of a shabby conflagration, a horrid even if an obscure hurt; and what was interesting from the first was my not doubting in the least its duration—though what seemed equally clear was that I needn't as a matter of course adopt and appropriate it, so to speak, or place it for increase of interest on exhibition.[508] The interest of it, I very presently

507. The phrase seems to echo and thus the event to parallel HJ Sr.'s "vastation," or spiritual crisis (see above, n. 265). The connection was made by Edel (*Untried Years,* 184; see next note).

508. This long, typically tension-building passage recording an event "entirely personal" in its consequences alludes to a Newport fire in which HJ was injured while working as a volunteer fireman. Fires remained a common and dangerous occurrence in these years, and of course HJ Sr. had had a leg amputated as the result of a fire. HJ may also have known "about the nocturnal occasion when his grandfather feverishly worked the pumps on the Albany wharf in a dangerous and unsuccessful attempt to save his shops from being gutted by fire" (Lewis, *The Jameses,* 117). There is some dispute about the date of the fire in Newport. The Hoffmanns, having consulted the *Annual Reports of the City of Newport, 1860–61,* record a conflagration in the early hours of 18 April 1861 that required up to two hundred men to quench it ("Henry James and the Civil War," 532). Edel, seemingly

knew, would certainly be of the greatest, would even in conditions kept as simple as I might make them become little less than absorbing. The shortest account of what was to follow for a long time after is therefore to plead that the interest never did fail. It was naturally what is called a painful one, but it consistently declined, as an influence at play, to drop for a single instant. Circumstances, by a wonderful chance, overwhelmingly favoured it—*as* an interest, an inexhaustible, I mean; since I also felt in the whole enveloping tonic atmosphere a force promoting its growth. Interest, the interest of life and of death, of our national existence, of the fate of those, the vastly numerous, whom it closely concerned, the interest of the extending War, in fine, the hurrying troops, the transfigured scene, formed a cover for every sort of intensity, made tension itself in fact contagious—so that almost any tension would do, would serve for one's share.

I have here, I allow, not a little to foreshorten—have to skip sundry particulars, certain of the steps by which I came to think of my relation to

---

unaware of this information, provides documentation for a date in October 1861 when another fire broke out, but if the latter were the fire at which HJ assisted, he could hardly claim that he sustained an injury at the outbreak of war, in April, unless, as Edel writes, "the blurring of the date" may have "served to minimize his failure during the first six months to spring to the colours with other young men" (*Untried Years*, 180). Given the April date, however, there would be no need to "blur" detail. Such is the grandeur yet indirection of the narrative that the precise nature of his injury has never been established. It seems that HJ became wedged in a fence corner while trying to operate a water pump and thus damaged his spine. It would have been punishing work: "The pumping action, sucking in water to the vacuum chamber on the upstroke and forcing it out through the hose on the downstroke, required bending down to knee level on the downstroke and reaching above the head on the upstroke" (Hoffmann and Hoffmann, "Henry James and the Civil War," 534). Edel enlists a number of critics who have raised (given the nuances of HJ's language) the possibility even of castration or of his being rendered sexually impotent by the accident (*Untried Years*, 179–80). Aaron summarizes Edel by suggesting that HJ was overwhelmed by "a malign invasion of the spirit, something akin to what his father had undergone sixteen years earlier. The Swedenborgians, whose doctrines the elder James professed, described this phenomenon as a 'vastation,' a portmanteau word for Henry James's 'vast visitation.' In other words, he had neither castrated himself nor developed a hernia, but he had suffered a psychic wound" (*The Unwritten War*, 107). For a critique of Edel as overly "psychoanalytical," see Novick, *Young Master*, 465 n. 16. For a summary of ideas on the "obscure hurt" and also "castration anxiety," see Carol Holly, "The Autobiographies: A History of Readings," in *A Companion to Henry James Studies*, ed. Daniel Mark Fogel (Westport, Conn.: Greenwood Press, 1993), 430. Recalling Walt Whitman, Paul John Eakin discusses James as "the *wounded* 'wound-dresser,' " in "Henry James's 'Obscure Hurt': Can Autobiography Serve Biography?" *New Literary History* 19 (Spring 1988): 675–92, on 678.

my injury as a *modus vivendi* workable for the time. These steps had after the first flush of reaction inevitably *had* to be communications of my state, recognitions and admissions;[509] which had the effect, I hasten to add, of producing sympathies, supports and reassurances. I gladly took these things, I perfectly remember, at that value; distinct to me as it still is nevertheless that the indulgence they conveyed lost part of its balm by involving a degree of publication. Direfully distinct have remained to me the conditions of a pilgrimage to Boston made that summer under my father's care for consultation of a great surgeon, the head of his profession there; whose opinion and advice—the more that he was a guaranteed friend of my father's—had seemed the best light to invoke on the less and less bearable affliction with which I had been for three or four months seeking to strike some sort of bargain: mainly, up to that time, under protection of a theory of temporary supine "rest" against which everything inward and outward tended equally to conspire.[510] Agitated scraps of rest, snatched, to my consciousness, by the liveliest violence, were to show for futile almost to the degree in which the effort of our interview with the high expert was afterwards so to show; the truth being that this interview settled my sad business, settled it just in that saddest sense, for ever so long to come. This was so much the case that, as the mere scene of our main appeal, the house from which we had after its making dejectedly emerged put forth to me as I passed it in many a subsequent season an ironic smug symbolism of its action on my fate. That action had come from the complete failure of our approached oracle either to warn, to comfort or to command—to do anything but make quite unassistingly light of the bewilderment exposed to him. In default of other attention or suggestion he might by a mere warning as to gravities only too possible, and already well advanced, have made such a difference; but I have little forgotten how I felt myself, the warning absent, treated but to a comparative pooh-pooh—an impression I long looked back to as a sharp parting of the ways, with an adoption of the wrong one distinctly determined. It was not simply small comfort, it was only a mystification the more, that the

509. In this process of retrospection HJ casts his injury as a part of the national crisis, his own trauma embodying the "tension" about him. His first accommodation of the disability begins by seeking out medical advice. The untypical repetitions of verbs in these two sentences—"I have here . . . have to" and "These steps had . . . inevitably *had* to be"— perhaps point to some unresolved unease in HJ's narrative of private and public crisis.

510. Gordon suggests that this may be Thomas Bigelow, HJ Sr.'s own physician (*A Private Life of Henry James*, 51).

inconvenience of my state had to reckon with the strange fact of there being nothing to speak of the matter with me. The graceful course, on the whole ground again (and where moreover was delicacy, the proposed, the intended, without grace?) was to behave accordingly, in good set terms, as if the assurance were true; since the time left no margin at all for one's gainsaying with the right confidence so high an authority. There were a hundred ways to behave—in the general sense so freely suggested, I mean; and I think of the second half of that summer of '62 as my attempt at selection of the best. The best still remained, under closer comparisons, very much what it had at first seemed, and there was in fact this charm in it that to prepare for an ordeal essentially intellectual, as I surmised, might justly involve, in the public eye, a season of some retirement. The beauty was—I can fairly see it now, through the haze of time, even as beauty!— that studious retirement and preparatory hours did after all supply the supine attitude, did invest the ruefulness, did deck out the cynicism of lying down book in hand with a certain fine plausibility. This was at least a negative of combat, an organised, not a loose and empty one, something definitely and firmly parallel to action in the tented field; and I well recall, for that matter, how, when early in the autumn I had in fact become the queerest of forensic recruits, the bristling horde of my Law School comrades fairly produced the illusion of a mustered army. The Cambridge campus was tented field enough for a conscript starting so compromised; and I can scarce say moreover how easily it let me down that when it came to the point one had still fine fierce young men, in great numbers, for company, there being at the worst so many such who hadn't flown to arms.[511] I was to find my fancy of the merely relative right in any way to figure, or even on such terms just to exist, I was to find it in due course quite drop from me as the Cambridge year played itself out, leaving me all aware that, full though the air might be of stiffer realities, one had yet a rare handful of one's own to face and deal with.

At Cambridge of course, when I got there, I was further to find my brother on the scene and already at a stage of possession of its contents that I was resigned in advance never to reach; so thoroughly I seemed to feel a sort of quickening savoury meal in any cold scrap of his own experience that he might pass on to my palate. This figure has definite truth, that

511. HJ's figurative transformation of Harvard Yard into a military scene filled with similar noncombatant "conscripts" may lack conviction, yet it must be remembered that, though a number of HJ's circle volunteered, many remained civilians (see above, n. 404).

is, but for association at the board literally yielding us nourishment—the happiest as to social composition and freedom of supply of all the *tables d'hôte*[512] of those days, a veritable haunt of conversation ruled by that gently fatuous Miss Upham something of whose angular grace and antique attitude has lived again for us in William's letters. I place him, if not at the moment of my to that extent joining him then at least from a short time afterwards, in quarters that he occupied for the next two or three years— quiet cloistered rooms, as they almost appeared to me, in the comparatively sequestered Divinity Hall of that still virtually rustic age;[513] which, though mainly affected to the use of post-graduates and others, of a Unitarian colour, enrolled under Harvard's theological Faculty, offered chance accommodation, much appreciated for a certain supposedly separate charm, not to say a finer dignity, by the more maturely studious in other branches as well.[514] The superstition or aftertaste of Europe had then neither left me nor hinted that it ever might; yet I recall as a distinct source of interest, to be desperately dealt with, and dealt with somehow to my inward advantage, the special force of the circumstance that I was now for the first time in presence of matters normally, entirely, consistently American, and that more particularly I found myself sniff up straight from the sources, such as they unmistakably were, the sense of that New En-

512. HJ would sit at the table d'hôte, or common dining table, shared with William as well as other guests in Miss Catharine Upham's house in Cambridge at the junction of Kirkland and Oxford streets, just north of Harvard Yard. WJ was enthusiastic about the catering: "Dark aristocratic dining room, with royal cheer 'Fish, roast beef, veal cutlets or pigeons?' says the splendid tall noble looking white armed black eyed Juno of a handmaid, as you sit down. And for dessert, a choice of three, *three* of the most succulent, unctuous (no, not unctuous, unless you imagine a celestial unction without the oil) pie-ey confections, always two plates full—my eye!" (*CWJ*, 4:42).

513. This account cuts some corners: WJ withdrew from the Lawrence Scientific School in spring 1863, to return in the fall term to replace chemistry with anatomy; a letter of 13 September 1863 has him settled in the lodgings of Mrs. Sophie H. Appleton, 616 Main Street; in January–early February 1864 he is staying in the Parker House Hotel, and on 21 February 1864 he is in Divinity Hall; his parents probably left Newport for Boston in May 1864, and then WJ lived at home (*CWJ*, 4:83–90). HJ started out in Divinity Hall but either after "a few days" (Edel, *Untried Years*, 196) or "in the spring term" (Novick, *Young Master*, 86) moved to a house on Winthrop Square.

514. The Harvard Divinity School was characterized by strongly Unitarian convictions, reflecting neighboring Boston's prevailing religious tendencies (see above, n. 256). "The wide street on which Divinity Hall opened was overhung with sycamores. . . . the town of Cambridge was a rural village. . . . It was Hawthorne's New England" (Novick, *Young Master*, 84).

gland which had been to me till then but a name.[515] This from the first instant was what I most took in, and quite apart from the question of what one was going to make of it, of whether one was going, in the simple formula, to like it, and of what would come, could the impression so triumph, of such monstrous assimilations. Clear to me in the light thus kindled that my American consciousness had hitherto been after all and at the best singularly starved, and that Newport for instance, during the couple of years, had fed it but with sips of an adulterated strain. Newport, with its opera-glass turned for ever across the sea—for Newport, or at least *our* Newport, even during the War, lived mainly, and quite visibly, by the opera-glass—was comparatively, and in its degree incurably, cosmopolite; and though on our first alighting there I had more or less successfully, as I fancied, invited the local historic sense to vibrate, it was at present left me to feel myself a poor uninitiated creature.[516] However, an initiation, at least by the intelligence, into some given thing—almost anything really given would do—was essentially what I was, as we nowadays say, after; the fault with my previous data in the American kind had been that they weren't sufficiently given; so that here would be Boston and Cambridge giving as with absolute authority. The War had by itself of course, on the ground I speak of, communicated something of the quality, or rather of the quantity, otherwise deficient; only this was for my case, of which alone I speak, an apprehension without a language or a channel—a revelation as sublime as

515. HJ's hometown was, of course, New York City, a place in which he spent much of his formative American childhood, as he relates in *SBO*. Edel points out pertinently (*Untried Years*, 194) that the terms "*rustic, rural, provincial* figure always in Henry James's picture of New England," though in this newly discovered independence in the environs of Harvard Yard and the company of "fine fierce young men," HJ seems to find a direct, more physical expression of national identity impervious to condescension. He goes on to acknowledge (with appropriate humility) the uniquely defining presence of civil war as part of this subjective process of establishing self in relation to nation.

516. HJ devotes a chapter in *AS* to Newport, the place from his youth he considers to have been best fitted for contemporary American society, the "most favoured resort of its comparative innocence" (*AS*, 219). A similar nostalgia is evident in his biography *William Wetmore Story and His Friends* (1903). The opera glasses (ill suited certainly to frontier life) are trained eastward upon Europe in the hands of its cosmopolitan, traveled residents (such as the Jameses), who are recalled as stretching "fond arms across the sea" (*AS*, 223). After the Civil War "the social life of Newport, which had been rather simple and re- strained for more than half a century, suddenly expanded and became much more sophisti- cated. The city gradually lost much of its southern clientèle and became the summer playground for wealthy northern families" (*Rhode Island*, American Guide Series, 212, quoted in Le Clair, *Young Henry James*, 412 n. 25; see also above, nn. 105-6).

one would like to feel it, but spreading abroad as a whole and not, alas, by any practice of mine, reducible to parts. What I promptly made out at Cambridge was that "America" would be given, as I have called it, to a tune altogether fresh, so that to hear this tune wholly played out might well become on the spot an inspiring privilege. If I indeed, I should add, said to myself "wholly," this was of course not a little straining a point; since, putting my initiation, my grasp of the exhibition, at its conceivable liveliest, far more of the supposed total was I inevitably to miss than to gather to my use. But I might gather what I could, and therein was exactly the adventure. To rinse my mouth of the European aftertaste *in order* to do justice to whatever of the native bitter-sweet might offer itself in congruous vessels—such a brave dash for discovery, and such only, would give a sense to my posture. With which it was unmistakable that I shouldn't in the least have painfully to strive; of such a force of impact was each impression clearly capable that I had much rather to steady myself, at any moment, where I stood, and quite to a sense of the luxury of the occasion, than to cultivate inquiry at the aggressive pitch. There was no need for curiosity—it was met by every object, I seemed to see, so much more than half way; unless indeed I put it better by saying that as *all* my vision partook of that principle the impulse and the object perpetually melted together. It wasn't for instance by the faintest process of inquiry that the *maison* Upham, where I three times daily sat at meat, had scarce to wait an hour to become as vivid a translation into American terms of Balzac's Maison Vauquer, in Le Père Goriot, as I could have desired to deal with.[517]

It would have been at once uplifting to see in the American terms a vast improvement on the prime version, had I not been here a bit baffled by the sense that the correspondence was not quite, after all, of like with like, and that the main scene of Balzac's action was confessedly and curiously sordid

517. The Maison Vauquer is the *pension* in a run-down part of Paris in *Le père Goriot.* HJ goes on to mention three of the novel's male protagonists: the socially aspiring law student Eugène de Rastignac; Goriot, the Lear-like father of two daughters; and Vautrin, a mysteriously fascinating former criminal. HJ greatly admired Balzac and especially this novel, with "the shabby Maison Vauquer" as "the stage of vast dramas" ("Honoré de Balzac" [1875], *LC* 2, 60). The Harvard lodging, however, HJ considers to have other superior features, "*de mieux,*" though, apart from meeting regularly for meals, its occupants lacked the desperation of Balzac's protagonists, all part of the urban mass and poised between respectability and destitution. In *SBO,* HJ frequently revisits his past as reenactments of scenes from other novelists, such as Dickens and Thackeray, as well as Balzac (see also *SBO,* n. 640).

and even sinister, whereas its equivalent under the Harvard elms would rank decidedly as what we had *de mieux,* or in other words of most refined, in the "boarding" line, to show. I must have been further conscious that what we had de mieux in the social line appeared quite liable, on occasion, to board wherever it might—the situation in Balzac's world being on this head as different as possible. No one not deeply distressed or dismally involved or all but fatally compromised could have taken the chances of such an establishment at all; so that to any comparison to our own particular advantage had to be, on reflection, nipped in the bud. There was a generic sameness, none the less, I might still reason; enough of that at least to show the two pictures as each in its way interesting—which was all that was required. The Maison Vauquer, its musty air thick with heavier social elements, might have been more so, for the Harvard elms overhung no strange Vautrin, no old Goriot, no young Rastignac; yet the interest of the Kirkland Street company couldn't, so to speak, help itself either, any more than I could help taking advantage of it. In one respect certainly, in the matter of talk as talk, we shone incomparably brighter; and if it took what we had de mieux to make our so regular resort a scene essentially of conversation, the point was none the less that our materials were there. I found the effect of this, very easily, as American as I liked—liked, that is, to think of it and to make all I might of it for being; about which in truth all difficulty vanished from the moment the local colour of the War broke in. So of course this element did at that season come back to us through every outward opening, and mean enough by contrast had been the questions amid which the Vauquer boarders grubbed. Anything even indirectly touched by our public story, stretching now into volume after volume of the very biggest print, took on that reflected light of dignity, of importance, or of mere gross salience, which passion charged with criticism, and criticism charged with the thousand menaced affections and connections, the whole of the reaction—charged in short with immediate intimate life—have a power, in such conditions, to fling as from a waving torch. The torch flared sufficiently about Miss Upham's board—save that she herself, ancient spinster, pushed it in dismay from her top of the table, blew upon it with vain scared sighs, and would have nothing to do with a matter so disturbing to the right temperature of her *plats.* We others passed it from hand to hand, so that it couldn't quite go out—since I must in fairness add that the element of the casual and the more *generally* ironic, the play of the studious or the irrepressibly social intelligence at large, couldn't fail to insist pretty constantly on its rights. There were quarters as well, I should note, in

which the sense of local colour proceeding at all straight from the source I
have named—reflected, that is, from camp and field—could but very soon
run short; sharply enough do I recall for instance the felt, even if all so
privately felt, limits of *my* poor stream of contributive remark (despite my
habit, so fondly practised in the connection, of expatiating *in petto*).[518] My
poor stream would have trickled, truly, had it been able to trickle at all, from
the most effective of my few occasions of "realising," up to that time, as to
field and camp; literally as to camp in fact, since the occasion had consisted
of a visit paid, or a pilgrimage, rather, ever so piously, so tenderly made, one
August afternoon of the summer just ended, to a vast gathering of invalid
and convalescent troops, under canvas and in roughly improvised shanties,
at some point of the Rhode Island shore that figures to my memory, though
with a certain vagueness, as Portsmouth Grove. (American local names
lend themselves strangely little to retention, I find, if one has happened to
deal for long years with almost any group of European designations—these
latter springing, as it has almost always come to seem, straight from the soil
where natural causes were anciently to root them, each with its rare identity.
The bite into interest of the borrowed, the imposed, the "faked" label,
growing but as by a dab of glue on an article of trade, is inevitably much less
sharp.) Vagueness at best attends, however, the queer experience I glance
at; what lives of it, in the ineffaceable way, being again, by my incurable
perversity, my ambiguous economy, much less a matter of the "facts of the
case," as they should, even though so dead and buried now, revive to help
me through an anecdote, than the prodigiously subjective side of the
experience, thanks to which it still presumes to flush with the grand air of
an adventure.[519] If I had not already so often brazened out my confession of

518. The pervasive topic of conversation at the dining table was what HJ curiously calls
part of the "local colour," the ongoing war. Miss Upham is more concerned with the
temperature of the dishes, or *"plats,"* she serves, while HJ characterizes his own ideas as
internally rehearsed (*in petto,* literally, "within the breast" [It.]).

519. The occasion, as HJ's language suggests, had for him an almost sacramental value,
sustaining a sense of patriotic honor embodied in the sacrificial lives of the young soldiers he
admired. Pilgrimage had been a favored metaphor for travel and its revelatory potential since
his earliest days. He here records the visit as occurring "one August afternoon of the
summer just ended," that is, in 1862, before his enrollment at Harvard. Edel, quoting Sarge
Perry, who accompanied HJ, suggests that the visit to the hospital camp was made a year
earlier (*Untried Years,* 173); however, Charles and Tess Hoffmann indicate ("Henry James
and the Civil War," 540) that HJ made two trips—in summer 1861 for a picnic and a year later
to visit the newly constructed camp that would become Lovell General Hospital. Portsmouth Grove was a small summer resort a few miles north of Newport harbor. HJ complains

the far from "showy" in the terms on which impressions could become indelibly momentous to me I might blush indeed for the thin tatter dragged in thus as an affair of record. It consisted at the time simply of an emotion—though the emotion, I should add, appeared to consist of everything in the whole world that my consciousness could hold. By *that* intensity did it hang as bravely as possible together, and by the title so made good has it handed itself endlessly down.

Owing to which it is that I don't at all know what troops were in question, a "mere" couple of Rhode Island regiments (nothing in those days could be too big to escape the application of the "mere,") or a congeries of the temporarily incapacitated, the more or less broken, picked from the veterans—so far as there already were such—of the East at large and directed upon the Grove as upon a place of stowage and sanitation. Discriminations of the prosaic order had little to do with my first and all but sole vision of the American soldier in his multitude, and above all—for that was markedly the colour of the whole thing—in his depression, his wasted melancholy almost; an effect that somehow corresponds for memory, I bethink myself, with the tender elegiac tone in which Walt Whitman was later on so admirably to commemorate him.[520] The restrictions I

---

of the apparent arbitrariness of American placenames and their synthetic quality; elsewhere, for instance, he prefers, like Walt Whitman, the "pretty native name" of Aquidneck to Rhode Island (*AS*, 210). HJ's semiapologetic introduction for the episode at Portsmouth Grove with its almost incredulous charting of his own deviancy—a "queer experience" reflecting his "incurable perversity" leading to the climax of an experience flushed "with the grand air of an adventure"—typifies his late style and its studied challenging of proprieties. He appropriates and develops the idea of "adventure" in *AS* in its "florid sense," "the sense in which it remains an euphemism" (103), allowing the reader latitude to ponder the nature of the transgressions hinted at. He will go on to recall, in a more coyly concrete way signifying desire, that "the brush of interest against the soldier single and salient was an affair of every day." The feminized role he seems to court finds some confirmation when it is learned that on this August 1862 visit not only was he "following Minny's example" (Gordon, *A Private Life of Henry James,* 52) but his fourteen-year-old sister Alice, Edith and Ellen Emerson, and two other girls also "circled round the groups of convalescing soldiers (with their 'good and interesting faces') for a protracted period, in the unfulfilled hope of starting up a conversation with some of them" (Lewis, *The Jameses,* 119).

520. Such a commemoration is *Drum-Taps,* the sequence of poems based on Whitman's experiences nursing the wounded and dying soldiers of the Civil War which prompted recollections of brotherly and erotic love: "One look I but gave which your dear eyes return'd with a look I shall never forget, / One touch of your hand to mine O boy, reach'd up as you lay on the ground" ("Vigil strange I kept on the field one night," in *Walt Whitman: Complete Poetry and Collected Prose,* 438). HJ's attitude toward Whitman and his poetry

confess to are abject, but both my sense and my aftersense of the exhibition I here allude to had, thanks to my situation, to do all the work they could in the way of representation to me of what was most publicly, most heroically, most wastefully, tragically, terribly going on. It had so to serve for my particular nearest approach to a "contact" with the active drama—I mean of course the collectively and scenically active, since the brush of interest against the soldier single and salient was an affair of every day— that were it not for just one other strange spasm of awareness, scarce relaxed to this hour, I should have been left all but pitifully void of any scrap of a substitute for the concrete experience. The long hot July 1st of '63, on which the huge battle of Gettysburg had begun, could really be— or rather couldn't possibly not be—a scrap of concrete experience for any group of united persons, New York cousins and all, who, in a Newport garden, restlessly strolling, sitting, neither daring quite to move nor quite to rest, quite to go in nor quite to stay out, actually *listened* together, in their almost ignobly safe stillness, as to the boom of far-away guns.[521] This

---

changed with the passing years. Although he dismissed *Drum-Taps* as "an offense against art" in 1865 (*LC* 1, 632), in older age he would read aloud from *Leaves of Grass,* his voice filling "the hushed room like an organ adagio . . . crooning it in a mood of subdued ecstasy," as Edith Wharton recalled from one of HJ's visits to her Massachusetts country house during his American visit of 1904–5: "it was a joy to me to discover that James thought him, as I did, the greatest of American poets" (*A Backward Glance* [New York: Appleton-Century, 1934], 186).

521. The Battle of Gettysburg, 1–3 July 1863, in which the Union Army of the Potomac defeated Robert E. Lee's Confederate forces, was, in terms of numbers, among the greatest conflicts of the war. Fought in southern Pennsylvania, Gettysburg was one of the Civil War's northernmost battles, hence HJ's imagined hearing of the sounds of battle in Newport (a distance of about 340 miles). His cousin William Temple had been killed at Chancellorsville in May, and another valued cousin, Gus Barker, fought at Gettysburg (see Hoffmann and Hoffmann, "Henry James and the Civil War," 546). In *SBO,* HJ refers to the Mason sisters, Lydia, Helen, Gertrude, and Serena, daughters of Lydia Lush and Henry Mason, as his "New York cousinship" (chap. 28). However, the "New York cousins" may include some of the Emmet family, or even the children of Augustus and Elizabeth Bay James, who lived at Rhinebeck, New York State. Newport was still the James family home in 1863. In a letter of 17 September 1913, written from Rye, HJ asked T. S. Perry to check whether the battle had begun on a Sunday, but, as Edel points out, "The first of July 1863 fell on a Wednesday, not a Sunday, and HJ had to sacrifice his artistic need for the Sabbath" (*HJL,* 4:686 n. 3). He also enquired about other specific detail, such as Gus Barker's cavalry regiment, Frank Sanborn's initials, the date when the 54th Massachusetts marched out of Boston, Bob James's first regiment, the date of the attack on Fort Wagner: "It's among ghosts, isn't it, that I ask you to walk, Thomas?" (*HJL,* 4:684–85).

*was*, as it were, the War—the War palpably in Pennsylvania; not less than my hour of a felt rage of repining at my doomed absence from the sight of that march of the 54th Massachusetts out of Boston, "Bob" Shaw at its head and our exalted Wilky among its officers, of which a great sculptor was, on the spot of their vividest passing, to set the image aloft forever.[522] Poor other visitations, comparatively, had had to suffice for me; I could take in fact for amusing, most of all (since that, thank goodness, was high gaiety), a couple of impressions of the brief preliminary camp life at Readville during which we admired the charming composition of the 44th of the same State, under Colonel Frank Lee, and which fairly made romantic for me Wilky's quick spring out of mere juvenility and into such brightly-bristling ranks.[523] He had begun by volunteering in a company that gave him half the ingenuous youth of the circle within our social ken for brothers-in-arms, and it was to that pair of Readville afternoons I must have owed my all so emphasised vision of handsome young Cabot Russell, who, again to be his closest brother-in-arms in the 54th, irrecoverably lost himself, as we have seen, at Fort Wagner.[524] A dry desert, one must suppose, the life in which, for memory and appreciation made one, certain single hours or compressed groups of hours have found their reason for

522. HJ was ill (perhaps with his strained back) on the momentous day (28 May 1863) when the 54th, with its African-American troops commanded by white officers, left Boston, assailed, as Wilky recalls, by "prejudice of the rankest sort" ("Story of the War"). For more on the Shaw Memorial, sculpted by Augustus Saint-Gaudens, see above, n. 406. The names of the black soldiers were added, amid some controversy, in 1981 (Stephen J. Whitfield, " 'Sacred in History and in Art': *The Shaw Memorial*," *New England Quarterly* 60 [March 1987]: 11). See also Richard Powers, "1897, Memorial Day," in *A New Literary History of America*, ed. Greil Marcus and Werner Sollors (Cambridge, Mass.: Belknap Press of Harvard University Press, 2009), 434–40.

523. Camp Meigs at Readville, just south of Boston, was an army training camp (Lewis, *The Jameses*, 134–35). Wilky had originally joined the 44th Massachusetts, before becoming an officer with the 54th (Maher, *Biography of Broken Fortunes*, 35). WJ used to come in from Cambridge to watch his brother drill on Boston Common. Colonel Frank Lee, commander of the 44th, had nominated Wilky, Cabot Russel, and another friend, William Simpkins, to serve as officers with the 54th. Readville became an attraction for visitors: "Many ladies graced the camp with their presence. People came from distant places to witness the novel sight of colored soldiers in quarters and on the drill ground" (Luis F. Emilio, *A Brave Black Regiment: History of the Fifty-Fourth Regiment of Massachusetts Volunteer Infantry, 1863–1865* [Boston: Boston Book Company, 1891], 22–23). HJ's visit to the 44th was in the fall of 1862 (Novick, *Young Master*, 84–85).

524. For HJ's narration of Cabot Russel's death at Fort Wagner and his father's escorting the badly injured Wilky back to New England, see chap. 7 above.

standing out through everything, for insistently living on, in the cabinet of intimate reference, the museum, as it were, of the soul's curiosities—where doubtless at the same time an exhibition of them to mere other eyes or ears or questioning logical minds may effect itself in no plain terms. We recognise such occasions more and more as we go on, and are surely, as a general thing, glad when, for the interest of memory—which it's such a business to *keep* interesting—they constitute something of a cluster. In my queer cluster, at any rate, that flower of the connection which answers to the name of Portsmouth Grove still overtops other members of its class, so that to finger it again for a moment is to make it perceptibly exhale its very principle of life.[525] This was, for me, at the time, neither more nor less than that the American soldier in his multitude was the most attaching and affecting and withal the most amusing figure of romance conceivable; the great sense of my vision being thus that, as the afternoon light of the place and time lingered upon him, both to the seeming enhancement of his quality and of its own, romance of a more confused kind than I shall now attempt words for attended his every movement. It was the charmingest, touchingest, dreadfullest thing in the world that my impression of him should have to be somehow of his abandonment to a rueful humour, to a stoic reserve which could yet melt, a relation with him once established, into a rich communicative confidence; and, in particular, all over the place, of his own scanted and more or less baffled, though constantly and, as I couldn't not have it, pathetically, "knowing" devices.

The great point remained for me at all events that I could afterwards appear to myself to have done nothing but establish with him a relation, that I established it, to my imagination, in several cases—and all in the three or four hours—even to the pitch of the last tenderness of friendship.[526] I recover that, strolling about with honest and so superior fellow-

525. After the extended trope in which the exercise of memory permits entry to the "museum" of his past inner life, HJ's recollection of his visits to military camps employs a more playful and tactile language. His fingering of the "flower of the connection," the visit to the wounded at Portsmouth Grove, having outgrown other experiences, has reached consummation, suggesting the erotic, caressing pleasure of the interchange.

526. This illuminated, composite memory of the American soldier is one of several rhapsodic passages recording HJ's attachment; aside from these more generalized scenes, he includes individual portraits of heroic cousins who died in battle, Gus Barker, Will Temple, and Vernon King. The transgressive possibilities of the homoerotic are contained within the recounting of the elaborate machinery of memory and the immediacy of the narrative voice, that of an aged man engaging with the tragic events of American history. He may assert—however self-indulgently—that he reached "the last tenderness of friendship"

citizens, or sitting with them by the improvised couches of their languid rest, I drew from each his troubled tale, listened to his plaint on his special hard case—taking form, this, in what seemed to me the very poetry of the esoteric vernacular—and sealed the beautiful tie, the responsive sympathy, by an earnest offer, in no instance waved away, of such pecuniary solace as I might at brief notice draw on my poor pocket for.[527] Yet again, as I indulge this memory, do I feel that I might if pushed a little rejoice in having to such an extent coincided with, not to say perhaps positively anticipated, dear old Walt—even if I hadn't come armed like him with oranges and peppermints. I ministered much more summarily, though possibly in proportion to the time and thanks to my better luck more pecuniarily; but I like to treat myself to making out that I can scarce have brought to the occasion (in proportion to the time again and to other elements of the case) less of the consecrating sentiment than he. I like further to put it in a light that, ever so curiously, if the good Walt was most inwardly stirred to his later commemorative accents by his participating in the common Americanism of his hospital friends, the familiar note and shared sound of which formed its ground of appeal, I found myself victim to a like moving force through quite another logic. It was literally, I fear, because our common Americanism carried with it, to my imagination, such a disclosed freshness and strangeness, working, as I might say, over such gulfs of dissociation, that I reached across to *their,* these hospital friends', side of the matter, even at the risk of an imperilled consistency. It had for me, the state in question, colour and form, accent and quality, with scarce less "authority" than if instead of the rough tracks or worn paths of my casual labyrinth I had trod the glazed halls of some school of natural history. What holds me now indeed is that such an institution might have exemplified then almost nothing but the aspects strictly native to our social and seasonal air; so simply and easily conceivable to the kindly

----

with these soldiers characterized by their initial lack of words, part of their mysterious otherness and masculinity, but the rapprochement was evidently brief. The idiosyncratic grammar that coins superlatives like "charmingest, touchingest, dreadfullest" betrays a degree of affectation, perhaps underscoring the querying of gender conventions illustrated by the passage.

527. Not long after writing this paragraph, HJ would find himself fulfilling a similar role in the context of the Great War: "I have been going to a great hospital (St. Bart's), at the request of a medical friend there, to help to give the solace of free talk to a lot of Belgian wounded and sick . . . and have thereby almost discovered my vocation in life to be the beguiling and drawing-out of the suffering soldier" (letter of 21 November 1914, *HJL,* 4:729).

mind were at that time these reciprocities, so great the freedom and pleasure of them compared with the restrictions imposed on directness of sympathy by the awful admixtures of to-day, those which offer to the would-be participant among us, on returns from sojourns wherever homogeneity and its entailed fraternity, its easy contacts, still may be seen to work, the strange shock of such amenities declined on any terms. Really not possible then, I think, the perception now accompanying, on American ground, this shock—the recognition, by any sensibility at all reflective, of the point where our national theory of absorption, assimilation and conversion appallingly breaks down; appallingly, that is, for those to whom the *consecrated* association, of the sort still at play where community has not been blighted, strongly speaks. Which remarks may reinforce the note of my unconsciousness of any difficulty for knowing in the old, the comparatively brothering, conditions what an American at least *was.* Absurd thus, no doubt, that the scant experience over which I perversely linger insists on figuring to me as quite a revel of the right confidence.[528]

The revel, though I didn't for the moment yet know it, was to be renewed for me at Cambridge with less of a romantic intensity perhaps,

528. HJ's comparing of his own visits and offers of small amounts of cash to the years of service devoted to sick and wounded soldiers offered by Walt Whitman, the "Wound Dresser," in both New York and Washington hospitals, recorded in *Specimen Days,* seems inappropriate (for an account of Whitman's contribution, see Jerome Loving, *Walt Whitman: The Song of Himself* [Berkeley: University of California Press, 1999, 2000], 262–71). HJ's untypically familiar epithets for Whitman betray a degree of embarrassment. HJ seems to move beyond the remembered fraternalism both of his own Civil War experience as bystander and witness and of the "dear friends" recorded in Whitman's poetry to recall a nationhood of community sanctified and benignly constituted, whose values have now become eroded, though the term "Americanism" remains elusive. Such a reaching across barriers even then required a dismissal of social convention: he was examining the exhibits, strange and formerly unknown, invoked in the allusion to "some school of natural history." *AS,* with such page headings as "The Ubiquity of the Alien" and "The Scale of the Infusion," illustrates HJ's racial and ethnic anxieties, though it must be remembered that the years of his absence from America, 1882 to 1904, witnessed relentless social change and population growth arising from a policy of open immigration (see also Sara Blair, *Henry James and the Writing of Race and Nation* [Cambridge: Cambridge University Press, 1996]; and Ross Posnock, "Affirming the Alien: The Pragmatist Pluralism of *The American Scene,*" in *The Cambridge Companion to Henry James,* ed. Jonathan Freedman [Cambridge: Cambridge University Press, 1998], 224–46). It is interesting (though perhaps natural in the context) that this nostalgia for a time when American identity appeared more unified and coherent specifies exclusively male experience.

but more usefully, so to put it, and more informingly; surrounded as I presently found myself at the Law School with young types, or rather with young members of a single type, not one of whom but would have enriched my imagined hall of congruous specimens. *That,* with the many months of it, was to be the real disclosure, the larger revelation; that was to be the fresh picture for a young person reaching the age of twenty in wellnigh grotesque unawareness of the properties of the atmosphere in which he but wanted to claim that he had been nourished.[529] Of what I mean by this I shall in a moment have more to say—after pointing a trifle more, for our patience, the sense of my dilatation upon Portsmouth Grove. Perfectly distinct has remained the sail back to Newport by that evening's steamboat; the mere memory of which indeed—and I recall that I felt it inordinately long—must have been for me, just above, the spring of the whole reference. The sail was long, measured by my acute consciousness of paying physically for my excursion—which hadn't answered the least little bit for my impaired state. This last disobliging fact became one, at the same time, with an intensity, indeed a strange rapture, of reflection, which I may not in the least pretend to offer as a clear or coherent or logical thing, and of which I can only say, leaving myself there through the summer twilight, in too scant rest on a deck stool and against the bulwark, that it somehow crowned my little adventure of sympathy and wonder with a shining round of resignation—a realisation, as we nowadays put it, that, measuring wounds against wounds, or the compromised, the particular taxed condition, at the least, against all the rest of the debt then so generally and enormously due, one was no less exaltedly than wastefully engaged in the common fact of endurance. There are memories in truth too fine or too peculiar for notation, too intensely individual and supersubtle—call them what one will; yet which one may thus no more give up confusedly than one may insist on them vainly. Their kind is nothing ever to a present purpose unless they are in a manner statable, but is at the same time ruefully aware of threatened ridicule if they are overstated. Not that I in the least mind such a menace, however, in just adding that, soothed as I have called the admirable ache of my afternoon with that inward interpretation of it, I felt the latter—or rather doubtless simply the

529. Having already imagined the Harvard campus (recalling *Othello*, 1. 3. 86) as the "tented field," HJ characterizes the male student community there as comparable to the military camps he has visited, a group in which he suddenly finds himself wishing to claim his own inherited place.

entire affair—absolutely overarched by the majestic manner in which the distress of our return drew out into the lucid charm of the night.[530] To which I must further add that the hour seemed, by some wondrous secret, to know itself marked and charged and unforgettable—hinting so in its very own terms of cool beauty at something portentous in it, an exquisite claim then and there for lasting value and high authority.

X All of which foregoing makes, I grant, a long parenthesis in my recovery of the more immediate Cambridge impressions. I have left them awaiting me, yet I am happy to say not sensibly the worse for it, in their cluster roundabout Miss Upham and her board of beneficiary images; which latter start up afresh and with the softest submission to any convenient neglect—that ineffably touching and confessed dependence of such apparitions on one's "pleasure," save the mark! for the flicker of restorative light. The image most vividly restored is doubtless that of Professor F. J. Child, head of the "English Department" at Harvard and master of that great modern science of folk-lore to his accomplishment in which his vast and slowly-published collection of the Ballad literature of our language is a recognised monument;[531] delightful man, rounded character, passionate patriot, admirable talker, above all thorough humanist and humorist. He was the genial autocrat of that breakfast-table not only,[532] but of our symposia otherwise timed, and as he comes back to me with the fresh and quite circular countenance of the time before the personal cares and complications of life had gravely thickened for him, his aspect *all* finely circular, with its close rings of the fairest hair,

530. Portsmouth Grove was six to seven miles north of Newport. Sailing down the Sakonnet River, HJ equates his own suffering, his "resignation" to the ensuing pain, with the stoicism of the admired soldiers he has met, thus linking himself to their observed masculinity, an experience inexplicably pleasurable, an "admirable ache," recalled in the radiant twilight.

531. Francis James Child was promoted to be Harvard's first professor of English only in 1876. At this time (1862), when Harvard had about a thousand students and thirty teachers, he taught rhetoric and oratory. His edition of *English and Scottish Ballads* (8 vols.) was published in Boston in 1857–58, and *English and Scottish Popular Ballads* (in 10 parts) in 1882–98. He taught at Harvard for fifty years. See also n. 197.

532. HJ alludes to *The Autocrat of the Breakfast Table*, a collection of essays by Dr. Oliver Wendell Holmes (1809–94), whose son of the same name became a friend of HJ's. Published from 1857 in the *Atlantic Monthly*, they proved highly popular with readers.

its golden rims of the largest glasses, its finished rotundity of figure and attitude,[533] I see that *there* was the American spirit—since I was "after" it—of a quality deeply inbred, beautifully adjusted to all extensions of knowledge and taste and, as seemed to me, quite sublimely quickened by everything that was at the time so tremendously in question. That vision of him was never afterwards to yield to other lights—though these, even had occasion for them been more frequent with me, couldn't much have interfered with it; so that what I still most retain of him is the very flush and mobility, the living expansion and contraction, the bright comedy and almost lunar eclipse, of his cherubic face according as things appeared to be going for the country. I was always just across from him, as my brother, beside whom I took my place, had been, and I remember well how vivid a clock-face it became to me; I found still, as in my younger time, matter enough everywhere for gaping, but greatest of all, I think, while that tense season lasted, was my wonder for the signs and portents, the quips and cranks, the wreathèd smiles, or otherwise the candid obscurations, of our prime talker's presented visage. I set, as it were, the small tick of my own poor watch by it—which private register would thump or intermit in agreement with these indications. I recover it that, thanks to the perpetual play of his sympathy and irony, confidence and scorn, as well as to that of my own less certainly directed sensibility, he struck me on the bad days, which were then so many, as fairly august, cherubism and all, for sincerity of association with every light and shade, every ebb and flow, of our Cause. Where he most shone out, indeed, so that depression then wasn't a gloom in him but a darting flame, was in the icy air of the attitude of the nations to us, that of the couple, the most potent, across the sea, with which we were especially concerned and which, as during the whole earlier half of the War and still longer it more and more defined itself, drew from him at once all the drolleries and all the asperities of his sarcasm.[534]

533. "Bronze bas-relief portraits of Professor Francis James Child and Alexander Agassiz" could be seen in the faculty room in University Hall (John Hays Gardiner, *Harvard* [New York: Oxford University Press, 1914], 93).

534. It is likely that HJ is referring to the United Kingdom and France, both of which nations, driven by economic and industrial considerations, needed to maintain relations (at the least) with the Southern states for the sake of their cotton exports. The large cotton-spinning industries of both countries provide an early example of the growth of global economies in a time when "the nations of the earth would no longer be entirely self-sustaining" (Bruce Catton, *The Coming Fury* [London: Phoenix Press, 1961, 2001], 82). Britain maintained its neutrality, a position resented by the North; relations, made worse by a number of

Nothing more particularly touched me in him, I make out—for it lingers in a light of its own—than the fashion after which he struck me as a fond grave guardian, not so much of the memory and the ashes yet awhile, as of the promise, in all its flower, of the sacrificial young men whom the University connection had passed through his hands and whom he looked out for with a tenderness of interest, a nursing pride, that was as contagious as I could possibly have wished it. I didn't myself know the young men, save three or four, and could only, at our distance, hold my tongue and do them homage; never afterwards (as I even then foreknew would be the case) missing, when I could help it, or failing to pick up, a single brush, a scattered leaf, of their growing or their riper legend. Certain of them whom I had neither seen nor, as they fell in battle, was destined ever to see, have lived for me since just as communicated images, figures created by his tone about them—which, I admit, mightn't or needn't have mattered to me for all the years, yet which couldn't help so doing from the moment the right touch had handed them over to my restless claim.

It was not meanwhile for want of other figures that these were gathered in, for I have again to grant that in those days figures became such for me on easy terms, and that in particular William had only to let the light of *his* attention, his interest, his curiosity, his aversion even (could he indeed have passingly lived in the helplessness of mere aversion) visibly rest on them for me entirely to feel that they must count for as much as might be— so far at least as my perception was concerned, contact being truly another affair. That was the truth at that season, if it wasn't always to remain the truth; I felt his interpretations, his personal allowances, so largely and inveterately liberal, always impose themselves: it was not till ever so much later, and then only little by little, that I came to accept the strange circumstance of my not invariably "liking," in homely parlance, his people, and his not invariably liking mine. The process represented by that word was for each of us, I think, a process so involved with other operations of the spirit, so beautifully complicated and deformed by them, that our results in this sort doubtless eventually lost themselves in the labyrinth of our reasons; which latter, eventually—the labyrinth, I mean—could be a frequent and not other than animated meeting-place in spite of the play of divergence. The true case, I all the while plentifully felt, and still more feel now,

---

incidents, remained poor both during the war and afterward (Ian F. W. Beckett, *The War Correspondents: The American Civil War* [Stroud, U.K.; Dover, N.H.: Alan Sutton, 1993], 1–3). France, of course, also had close historical relations with some Southern states.

was that *I* diverged and my brother almost never; in the sense, that is, that no man can well have cared less for the question, or made less of the consciousness, of dislike—have valued less their developments and comforts. Even the opposite of that complacency scarce seemed a recognised, or at least in any degree a cultivated, state with him; his passion, and that a passion of the intelligence, was justice unafraid—and this, as it were, almost unformulatedly, altogether unpedantically: it simply made him utterly not "mind" numberless things that with most people serve as dim lights, warnings or attractions, in the grope of appreciation or the adventure of instinct. His luminous indifference kept his course thus, as I was later to recognise, extraordinarily straight—to the increase, as I have noted, of my own poor sense of weakly straggling, unaccompanied as this at the same time was by the least envy of such a deficiency in what is roughly called prejudice, and what I, to save my face, in my ups and downs of sociability or curiosity, could perhaps have found no better term for than the play of taste as taste. Wonderful, and to me in the last resort admirable, was William's fine heritage and awareness of that principle without its yet affecting him on the human, the more largely social, just the conversable and workable ground—in presence of some other principle that might do so, whether this validly or but speciously interfered. The triumph over *dis*taste, in one's relations, one's exposures, one's judgments, *that* I could understand as high virtue, strained heroism, the ideal groaningly applied; but what left me always impressed, to put it mildly, was the fact that in my brother's case the incorruptibility of his candour would have had to be explained to him, and with scant presumption too of his taking it in or having patience while one spoke.[535] Such an enterprise, I was well aware, would at any rate have left *me* a sorry enough figure afterwards. What one would have had to be, what one could in the least decently be, *except* candid without alternative—this, with other like matters, I should have had to be prepared to set forth; and, more and more addressed as I eventually found myself to a cultivation of the absolute in taste as taste, to repeat my expression, I was far from the wish to contend for it as against any appearance whatever of a better way. Such was part of the experience, or call it even the discipline, of association with a genius so marked for the process known as giving the benefit of the doubt—and giving it (for that

535. This portrait of his dead brother's virtues may remind us of HJ's initial intentions —to produce a volume of WJ's letters. The letters of the older to the younger brother and WJ's honesty in voicing his dismay at HJ's increasingly difficult prose style provide further evidence of the "incorruptibility of his candour."

was the irritating charm), not in smug charity or for a pointed moral, but through the very nature of a mind incapable of the shut door in any direction and of a habit of hospitality so free that it might again and again have been observed, in contact and intercourse, to supply weaker and less graced vessels with the very means of bringing in response, often absolutely in retort. This last of course was not so much the benefit of the doubt as the displayed unconsciousness of any doubt, a perpetual aid rendered the doubtful, especially when incarnate in persons, to be more right or more true, more clever or more charming or whatever, than mere grudging love of "form," standing by, could at all see it entitled to become. Anything like William's unawareness of exertion after having helped the lame dog of converse over stile after stile I have in no other case met. Together with which, however, I may not forbear to add, the very occasional and comparatively small flare in him of some blest perversity of prejudice that one might enjoy on one's own side the vulgar luxury of naming as such was a thing which, conformably to that elation, one reached out for as one might for the white glint of the rare edelweiss on some high Alpine ledge.

If these remarks illustrate in their number the inevitable bent of the remark to multiply within me as an effect of fraternal evocation I thereby but stick the more to my subject, or in other words to the much-peopled scene, as I found it; which I should scarce have found without him. Peopled as it was with *his* people, which they at first struck me as markedly being, it led me then to take the company, apart from F. J. Child, for whatever he all vividly and possessively pronounced it; I having for a long time but the scantest company of my own, even at the Law School, where my fellow-disciples could bear the name for me only as a troop of actors might have done on that further side of footlights to which I never went round. This last at least with few exceptions, while there were none to the exquisite rule, as I positively to-day feel it, of my apprehension of William's cluster as a concern of his—interesting exactly because of that reference. Any concern of his was thus a thing already charged with life, *his* life over and above its own, if it happened by grace to have any comparable; which, as I pick out the elements again from the savoury Upham shades, could indeed be claimed for several of these. I pick out the ardent and delicate and firm John May, son, as he comes back to me, of a distinguished Abolitionist of New York State[536]—rare bird; and seen by

536. John (or Joe) May was a friend of WJ's, the son of a New York abolitionist, according to Edel (*Untried Years*, 198).

that fact in a sort of glamour of picturesque justification, an air deriving colour from the pre-established gallantry, yet the quiet and gentlemanly triumph, of his attitude. So at least do I read back into blurred visions the richest meanings they could have. I pick out for a not less baffled tribute a particular friend of my brother's and a comrade of May's, whom I identify on the superficial side but by his name of Salter and the fact of his studentship in theology;[537] which pursuit, it comes over me as I write, he must have shared, of homely, almost of sickly, New England type as he was, with May of the fine features, the handsome smile, by my resolute recollection, the developed moustache and short dark pointed beard, the property of vaguely recalling in fine some old portrait supposedly Spanish (supposedly, and perhaps to a fantastic tune, by *me*—or I dare say it was by no one else). Salter had no such references—it even appalled me to have a bit intelligently to imagine to what origins starved of amenity or colour his aspect and air, the slope of his shoulders, the mode of growth of his hair, the relation of his clothes to his person and the relation of his person to the inevitable needs of intercourse, might refer him; but there played about him a bright force in the highest and extraordinarily quick flares of which one felt nothing, while the exhibition lasted, but his intellectual elegance. He had the distinction of wit—so rare, we ever feel it to be, when we see it beautifully act; and I remember well how, as that was indeed for me almost the whole of intellectual elegance, I fell back on the idea that such an odd assortment of marks in him was at least picturesque, or much in the Maison Vauquer line: pinched as I must have been by the question of whether a person of that type and cut had the "right" to be witty. On what else but the power the right rested I couldn't doubtless have said; I but recall my sense that wit was somehow the finest of all social matters and that it seemed impossible to be less connected with such than this product of New England at its sparest and dryest; which fact was a sort of bad mark for the higher civilisation. I was prepared to recognise that you might be witty and ugly, ugly with the highest finish of ugliness—hadn't the celebrated Voltaire been one of the scrappiest of men as well as of the most immortally quoted?[538]—but it cost a wrench to have to take it that you could shine to admiration out of such a platitude of the mere "plain." It was William in especial who guaranteed to me Salter's

537. See above, n. 261.

538. Voltaire (1694–1778), a poet, philosopher, and essayist of the French Enlightenment, was most famous perhaps for *Candide* (1759). His skin was scarred by smallpox, and he is said to have had a long nose and to have been very thin.

superior gift, of which in the free commerce of Divinity Hall he had frequent illustration—so that what I really most apprehended, I think, was the circumstance of *his* apprehending: this too with a much finer intellectual need and competence than mine, after all, and in the course of debates and discussions, ardent young symposia of the spirit, which struck me as falling in with all I had ever curiously conceived of those hours that foster the generous youth of minds preappointed to greatness. *There* was the note of the effective quaint on which I could put my finger:[539] catch a poor student only dreary enough and then light in him the flame of irony at its intensest, the range of question and the command of figure at their bravest, and one might, with one's appetite for character, feed on the bold antithesis. I had only to like for my brother, and verily almost with pride, his assured experience of any queer concretion—his experience of abstractions I was to rise to much more feebly and belatedly, scarce more indeed ever than most imperfectly—to find the very scene of action, or at least of passion, enjoyed by these my elders and betters, enriched and toned and consecrated after the fashion of places referred to in literature and legend.

I thus live back of a sudden—for I insist on just yielding to it—into the odd hours when the poor little old Divinity Hall of the overgrown present faced me as through the haze of all the past Indian summers it had opened its brooding study-windows to; when the "avenue" of approach to it from the outer world was a thing of dignity, a positive vista in a composition; when the Norton woods, near by, massed themselves in scarlet and orange, and when to penetrate and mount a stair and knock at a door and, enjoying response, then sink into a window-bench and inhale at once the vague golden November and the thick suggestion of the room where nascent "thought" had again and again piped or wailed, was to taste as I had never done before the poetry of the prime initiation and of associated growth.[540] With cards of such pale pasteboard could the trick, to my vision,

539. "Quaint" in substantive form does not exist in modern English. HJ may imply an abstraction or have omitted some noun (such as "thing").

540. "Initiation" is a favored term for HJ's most heightened experiences from this period. Here it relates to his awareness of creativity (the fiction he was reading and penning) as well as his awakened sense of New England, more physically and sensuously present than it had been in Newport, a place seemingly wedded to Europe. In one of the 1904–5 American notebooks, he refers to a further, unforgettable revelation, "*l'initiation première* (the divine, the unique)" (*CN*, 238), to which Novick (*Young Master*, 109–10) attributes a sexual connotation, in HJ's relationship with Oliver Wendell Holmes Jr. The notes he made of his 1904–5 return to Boston and Cambridge and those "far-off unspeak-

play itself—by which I mean that I admire under this memory the constant "dodges" of an imagination reduced to such straits for picking up a living. It was as if one's sense of "Europe," sufficiently sure of itself to risk the strategic retreat, had backed away on tiptoe just to see how the sense of what was there facing one would manage without it—manage for luxury, that is, with the mere indispensable doubtless otherwise provided for. That the sense in question did manage beautifully, when at last so hard pressed, and that the plasticity and variety of my vision draw from me now this murmur of elation, are truths constituting together for me the perhaps even overloaded moral of my tale. With which I scarce need note that so elastic a fancy, so perverse a little passion for finding good in everything—good for what I thought of as history, which was the consideration of life, while the given thing, whatever it was, had only to be before me—was inevitably to work a storage of other material for memory close-packed enough to make such disengagement as I thus attempt at the end of time almost an act of violence. I couldn't do without the *scene,* as I have elsewhere had occasion to hint, whether actually or but possibly peopled (the people always calling for the background and the background insisting on the people); and thanks to this harmless extravagance, or thanks in other words to the visionary liberties I constantly took (so that the plate of sense was at the time I speak of more overscored and figured for me than sense was in the least practically required to have it), my path is even now beset to inconvenience with the personal image unextinct. It presents itself, I feel, beyond reason, and yet if I turn from it the ease is less, and I am divided when I further press the spring between compunction at not pausing before some shade that seems individually and even hopefully to wait, and the fear of its feeling after all scanted of service should I name it only to leave it. I name for instance, just to hover a little, silent Vanderpool, the mutest presence at the Upham board, and quite with no sense of the invidious in so doing.[541] He was save for myself, by my remembrance, the only member of the Law School there present; I see him moreover altogether remarkably, just incorruptibly and exquisitely dumb, though with a "gentlemanly" presence, a quasi-conservative New Jersey finish (so delicate those dim discrimina-

---

able past years" in preparation for a chapter in *AS* are filled with an anguished regret for that "pathetic, heroic little *personal* prime of my own" (*CN,* 238).

541. Beach Vanderpool Jr. came from Newark, New Jersey (see also Edel, *Untried Years,* 199). The contemporary Boston and Cambridge of *AS* is similarly filled with ghosts and shades, diffident yet pleading, contained within old secrets and stories he refrains from detailing.

tions!) that would have seemed naturally to go with a certain forensic assurance. He looked so as if he came from "good people"—which was no very common appearance on the Harvard scene of those days, as indeed it is to a positive degree no so very common appearance on any scene at any time: it was a note of aspect which one in any case found one's self, to whatever vague tune, apt quite to treasure or save up. So it was impossible not to recognise in our soundless *commensal*[542] the very finest flower of shyness, the very richest shade of the deprecating blush, that one had perhaps ever encountered; one ended in fact by fairly hanging on the question of whether the perfection of his modesty—for it was all a true welter of modesty, not a grain of it anything stiffer—would beautifully hold out or would give way to comparatively brute pressure from some point of our circle. I longed to bet on him, to see him through without a lapse; and this in fact was so thoroughly reserved to me that my eventual relief and homage doubtless account for the blest roundness of my impression. He had so much "for" him, was tall and fine, equipped and appointed, born, quite to an effect of ultimately basking, in the light of the Law, acquainted, one couldn't fail of seeing, with a tradition of manners, not to mention that of the forensic as aforesaid, and not to name either the use of "means," equally imputable: how rare accordingly would be the *quality*, letting even the quantity alone, of his inhibitions, and how interesting in the event the fact that he was absolutely never to have deviated! He disappeared without having spoken, and yet why should I now be noting it if he hadn't nevertheless admirably expressed himself? What this consisted of was that there was scarce anything he wouldn't have done for us had it been possible, and I think, in view of the distinctness with which he still faces me, the tenderness with which he inspires my muse and the assurance with which I have "gone into" him, that I can never in all my life since have seen so precious a message delivered under such difficulties. Admirable, ineffaceable, because so essentially all *decipherable,* Vanderpool![543]

542. Sharing a table or eating together. Compare HJ's 9 February 1911 letter to Edith Wharton: "share me generously with your I am sure not infrequent *commensaux* Walter B. and Morton F." (*HJL,* 4:573).

543. The innocent, silent, yet "readable" figure of Vanderpool, who so charmed the young HJ that he recalls him over fifty years later, would have made a sharp contrast to the boisterous James brothers at home. Edward Emerson recalled the cut and thrust of the male members of the family at dinner and the reassurances of Mrs. James: "Don't be disturbed, Edward; they won't stab each other" (E. W. Emerson, *Early Years of the Saturday Club,* 328).

It wasn't either that John Bancroft tossed the ball of talk—which but for the presence of the supremely retentive agent just commemorated would have appeared on occasion to remain in his keeping by a preference, on its own part, not to be outwitted; this more or less at all times too, but especially during the first weeks of his dawning on us straight out of Germany and France, flushed with the alarm, as one might have read it, of having to justify rare opportunities and account for the time he had inordinately, obscurely, or at least not a little mysteriously, spent—the implication of every inch of him being that he had spent it seriously.[544] Odd enough it certainly was that we should have been appointed to unveil, so far as we might, a *pair* of such marked monuments to modesty, marble statues, as they might have been, on either side of the portal of talk; what I at any rate preserve of my immediate vision of Bancroft—whose very promptest identity indeed had been his sonship to the eminent historian of our country and earlier and later diplomatist—was an opposition, trying to me rather than engaging as its like had been in the composition of Vanderpool, between what we somehow wanted from him (or what I at least did) and what we too scantly gathered. This excellent friend, as he was later on to become, with his handsome high head, large colourable brow and eyes widely divided—brave contribution ever to a fine countenance—sat there in a sort of glory of experience which, had he been capable of anything so akin to a demonstration, he would have appeared all unsociably to repudiate. It was bruited of him that, like John La Farge, whose friend he was admiringly to become—for he too had a Newport connection—he "painted," that is persisted (which was the wondrous thing!) in painting; and that this practice had grown upon him in France, where, *en province*,[545] his brother had entirely taken root and where the whole art-life, as well as the rural life, of the country had been opened to him; besides its a little later coming to light that he had romantically practised at Dusseldorf, where too he had personally known and tremendously liked George du Maurier, whose first so distinguished appearances as an illustrator had already engaged our fondest attention—were they

544. John Chandler Bancroft (1835–1901), son of the historian and diplomat George Bancroft (1800–1891), graduated from Harvard in 1859. A talented painter, he traveled in Europe, studying art in Düsseldorf and Paris, and became fluent in French and German. Later, having invested in mines in Michigan, he succeeded in business. His *New York Times* obituary (17 August 1901) was written by John La Farge.

545. In the countryside.

most dawningly in the early Cornhill, or in Punch, or in Once a Week?[546] They glimmer upon me, darkly and richly, as from the pages of the last named. Not to be rendered, I may again parenthesise, our little thrilled awareness, William's and mine, though mine indeed but panting after his, of such peeping phenomena of the European day as the outbreak of a "new man" upon our yearning view of the field of letters and of the arts. I am moved to wonder at how we came by it, shifting all for ourselves, and with the parental *flair*, so far as the sensibility of home was concerned, turned but to directions of its own and much less restless on the whole than ours. More touching to me now than I can say, at all events, this recapture of the hour at which Du Maurier, consecrated to much later, to then still far-off intimate affection, became the new man so significantly as to make a great importance of John Bancroft's news of him, which already bore, among many marvels, upon the supreme wonder of his working, as he was all his life bravely to work, under impaired and gravely menaced eyesight. When I speak, as just above, of what, through so many veils, "came to light," I should further add, I use a figure representing a considerable lapse of time and shading off, for full evocation, into more associations than I can here make place for. Nothing in this connection came *soon* to light at least but that endless amazement might lie in the strange facts of difference between our companion and his distinguished sire—the latter so supremely, so quaintly yet so brilliantly, social a figure, I apprehended, when gaped at, a still more angular, but more polished and pacific Don Quixote, on the sleekest of Rosinantes, with white-tipped chin protrusive, with high sharp elbows raised and long straight legs beautifully pointed, all after the gallantest fashion, against the clear sunset sky of old Newport cavalcades.[547] Mr. Bancroft the elder, the "great," was a comfort, that is a

546. The Düsseldorf school of art was an influential center in the 1830s and 1840s. Advocating a Romantic style, it attracted many American painters who later became members of the Hudson River school (see also *SBO,* n. 433). For George du Maurier, see above, n. 40. As HJ goes on to say, Du Maurier suffered from severe eye problems that threatened his career as an artist. He provided illustrations for all three of these popular magazines: from fall 1860 for *Once a Week,* and for the *Cornhill* from 1863 to 1886. Having published cartoons and drawings in *Punch* for several years, he became a staff member in 1865.

547. HJ originally met John Bancroft at Newport, where his father owned Rosecliff Mansion. Bancroft himself had a five-story house built there in 1895. Don Quixote is the chivalrous but unbalanced hero of Cervantes's picaresque fiction of that name, and Rosinante is his horse; HJ has already likened another Newport inhabitant of the time, the painter William Morris Hunt, to the same fictional figure (see above, n. 126). The physical

fine high identity, a cluster of strong accents, the sort of thing one's vision followed, in the light of history, if not of mere misguided fancy, for illustration of conceived type—type, say in this case, of superior person of the ancient and the more or less alien public order, the world of affairs transacted at courts and *chancelleries*,[548] in which renown, one had gathered from the perusal of memoirs, allowed for much development of detail and much incision of outline, when not even directly resting on them. As it had been a positive bliss to me that words and names might prove in extremity sources of support, so it comes back to me that I had drawn mystic strength from just obscurely sighing "Metternich!" or "Talleyrand!" as Mr. Bancroft bounced by me—so far as a pair of widely-opened compasses might bounce—in the August gloaming.[549] The value of which, for reflection, moreover, was not in the least in its being that if his son remained so long pleadingly inscrutable any derived Metternich suggestion had contributed to keep him so—for quite *there* was the curiosity of the case, that among the imputations John appeared most to repudiate was that of having at any moment breathed the air either of records or of protocols. If he persisted in painting for years after his return to America without, as the legend grew, the smallest disclosure of his work or confession of his progress to human eye or ear, he drew the rigour of this course wholly from his singleness of nature, in the aftertime to be so much approved to us. However, I pause before the aftertime, into the lap of which more than one sort of stored soundness and sweetness was to fall from him drop by drop.

I scarce know whether my impulse to lead forth these most shrinking of my apparitions be more perverse or more natural—mainly feeling, I confess, however it appear, that the rest of my impression of the animated Cambridge scene, so far as I could take it in, was anything but a vision of unasserted forces. It was only I, as now appears to me, who, ready as yet to assert nothing, hung back, and for reasons even more appreciable to me

---

detail of HJ's comparison may also reveal the influence of Gustave Doré's illustrations for the Cervantes novel.

548. Offices attached to an embassy or consulate.

549. The reference to a pair of compasses must relate to George Bancroft's thin, angular form and the comparable shape of his horse. The Austrian prince Klemens Wenzel von Metternich (1773-1859) was an eminent politician and diplomat involved in replanning Europe after the Napoleonic wars; he and Charles Maurice de Talleyrand-Périgord (1754-1838), who survived the French Revolution and prospered in the succeeding monarchy, were presumably known to George Bancroft.

to-day than then; wondering, almost regretting as I do, that I didn't with a still sharper promptness throw up the sponge for stoppage of the absurd little boxing-match within me between the ostensible and the real—this I mean because I might afterwards thereby have winced a couple of times the less in haunting remembrance of exhibited inaptitude. My condition of having nothing to exhibit was blessedly one that there was nobody to quarrel with—and I couldn't have sufficiently let it alone. I didn't in truth, under a misleading light, reconsider it much; yet I have kept to this hour a black little memory of my having attempted to argue one afternoon, by way of exercise and under what seemed to me a perfect glare of publicity, the fierce light of a "moot-court," some case proposed to me by a fellow-student—who can only have been one of the most benign of men unless he was darkly the designingest, and to whom I was at any rate to owe it that I figured my shame for years much in the image of my having stood forth before an audience with a fiddle and bow and trusted myself to rub them together desperately enough (after the fashion of Rousseau in a passage of the Confessions,) to make some appearance of music.[550] My music, I recall, before the look on the faces around me, quavered away into mere collapse and cessation, a void now engulfing memory itself, so that I liken it all to a merciful fall of the curtain on some actor stricken and stammering. The sense of the brief glare, as I have called the luckless exposure, revives even on this hither side of the wide gulf of time; but I must have outlived every witness—I was so obviously there the very youngest of all aspirants—and, in truth, save for one or two minor and merely comparative miscarriages of the sacrificial act before my false gods, my connection with the temple was to remain as consistently superficial as could be possible to a relation still restlessly perceptive through all its profaneness.[551] Perceiving, even with its accompaniments of noting, wondering,

550. *The Confessions* of Jean-Jacques Rousseau (1712–78), the French Enlightenment philosopher and writer, were published posthumously in 1782 and represent one of the earliest forms of autobiography. Rousseau was a self-taught musician and composer and in book 4 of the *Confessions* recalls setting himself up in Lausanne as a music master—quite unqualified—and writing a symphony within two weeks for performance. His public humiliation was complete: "never since the days of French opera, never in all the world, has such a cacophony been heard" (trans. Angela Scholar [Oxford: Oxford University Press, 2000], 145).

551. The moot court was staged by the Marshall Club. To be fair to HJ, "James's nephew many years later, seeking to discover more about this incident, learned that a classmate, George Gray, was the 'judge' who found against the defendant, and that the case apparently was such that a real lawyer in a real court could have stood no chance of

fantasticating, kicked up no glare, but went on much rather under richest shades or in many-coloured lights—a *tone* of opportunity that I look back on as somehow at once deliciously soothing to myself and favourable to the clearness of each item of the picture even as the cool grey sky of a landscape is equalising. That was of course especially when I had let everything slide—everything but the mere act of rather difficultly living (by reason of my scant physical ease,) and fallen back again on the hard sofa of certain ancient rooms in the Winthrop Square, contracted nook, of a local order now quite abolished, and held to my nose for long and sustaining sniffs the scented flower of independence.[552] I took my independence for romantic, or at least for a happy form of yawning vessel into which romance, even should it perforce consist but of mere loose observational play, might drop in the shape of ripe fruit from a shaken tree. Winthrop Square, as I had occasion to note a couple of years since, is a forgotten name, and the disappearance of my lodging spares me doubtless a reminder, possibly ironic, of the debility of those few constructional and pictorial elements that, mustering a wondrous good-will, I had invited myself to rejoice in as "colonial." The house was indeed very old, as antiquity in Cambridge went, with everything in it slanting and gaping and creaking, but with humble antique "points" and a dignity in its decay; above all with the deep recess or alcove, a sweet "irregularity" (so could irregularities of architectural conception then and there count,) thrust forth from its sitting-room toward what I supposed to be the Brighton hills[553] and forming, by the aid of a large window and that commanding view, not to mention the grace of an ancient expansive bureau or secretary-desk (this such a piece, I now venture to figure, as would to-day be pounced on at any cunning dealer's,) a veritable bower toward which even so shy a dreamer as I still then had to take myself for might perhaps hope to woo the muse. The muse was of course the muse of prose fiction— never for the briefest hour in my case the presumable, not to say the presuming, the much-taking-for-granted muse of rhyme, with whom I had

winning" (Edel, *Untried Years*, 200). Thus the fellow student who proposed the case may have been more "designing" than HJ allows.

552. Winthrop Square (now built over) was south of Harvard Square. HJ was still suffering, evidently, from the back problem that had been "pooh-poohed" by a Boston physician.

553. Brighton was the first stop on the Boston and Worcester Railroad, "five miles from Boston . . . a pleasant town on the south side of the Charles River" (Midgley, *Sights in Boston and Suburbs,* 87).

never had, even in thought, the faintest flirtation; and she did, in the event, I note, yield to the seduction of so appointed a nook—as to which romantic passage, however, I may not here anticipate. I but lose myself in the recovered sense of what it richly "meant" to me just to *have* a place where I could so handsomely receive her, where I could remark with complacency that the distant horizon, an horizon long since rudely obliterated, was not, after all, too humble to be blue, purple, tawny, changeable in short, everything an horizon should be, and that over the intervening marshes of the Charles (if I don't go astray in so much geography)[554] there was all the fine complicated cloud-scenery I could wish—so extravagantly did I then conceive more or less associational cloud-scenery, after the fashion, I mean, of that feature of remembered English and Boulognese water-colours,[555] to promote the atmosphere of literary composition as the act had begun to glimmer for me.

Everything, however, meant, as I say, more quite other things than I can pretend now to treat of. The mere fact of a sudden rupture, as by the happiest thought, with the "form" of bringing home from the Law-library sheepskin volumes that might give my table, if not, for sufficiency of emphasis, my afflicted self, a temporary countenance, heaped up the measure of my general intention—from the moment I embraced instead of it the practice of resorting to Gore Hall exclusively for my reading-matter;[556] a practice in the light of which my general intention took on the

554. The changing of the landscape on the banks of the Charles River began in the second half of the nineteenth century; the landfill work that transformed Boston's Back Bay (and the views from the rear of the Fields' house on Charles Street, which would serve as Olive Chancellor's home in *The Bostonians*) was initiated in 1857 and continued for many years.

555. HJ may be thinking of the watercolors of such English painters as John Sell Cotman (1782–1842) and Richard Parkes Bonington (1802–28). In an 1878 essay, "The Norwich School," he refers with admiration to a Cotman watercolor with a "great watery, wind-stirred sky." Bonington was, in his pre-1824 phase, much inspired by the landscapes of Normandy. In "The Wallace Collection in Bethnal Green," HJ commends his work, feeling that his art "draws true melody; his taste, his eye, as the French say, are unsurpassable" (*Painter's Eye*, 154, 73).

556. Gore Hall, named in honor of the Federalist politician and diplomat Christopher Gore (1758–1827), was the college library from 1838. Its outer walls were "of rough Quincy granite laid in regular courses, with hammered stone buttresses, towers, pinnacles, drip stones, &c" (Midgley, *Sights in Boston and Suburbs,* 133). It was later demolished to make way for the Widener Memorial Library, which opened in 1915. When Basil Ransom visits in company with Verena Tarrant, he admires the "wealth and wisdom of the place." It is slyly described as "a diminished copy of the chapel of King's College, at the greater

air of absolutely basking. To get somehow, and in spite of everything, in spite especially of being so much disabled, at life, *that* was my brooding purpose, straight out of which the College library, with its sparse bristle of aspiring granite, stood open to far more enchanted distances than any represented by the leathery walls, with never a breach amid their labelled and numbered blocks, that I might pretend to beat against in the other quarter. Yet, happily enough, on this basis of general rather than of special culture, I still loosely rejoiced in being where I was, and by way of proof that it was all right the swim into my ken of Sainte-Beuve, for whose presence on my table, in still other literary company, Gore Hall aiding, I succeeded in not at all blushing, became in the highest degree congruous with regular attendance at lectures.[557] The forenoon lectures at Dane Hall I never in all my time missed,[558] that I can recollect, and I look back on it now as quite prodigious that I should have been so systematically faithful to them without my understanding the first word of what they were about. They contrived—or at least my attendance at them did, inimitably—to be "life;" and as my wondering dips into the vast deep well of the French critic to whom all my roused response went out brought up that mystery to me in cupfuls of extraordinary savour, where was the incongruity of the two rites? That the Causeries du Lundi,[559] wholly fresh then to my grateful lips, should so have overflowed for me was certainly no marvel—that prime acquaintance absolutely *having,* by my measure, to form a really sacred date in the development of any historic or aesthetic consciousness worth mentioning; but that I could be to the very end more or less thrilled by simply sitting, all stupid and sentient, in the thick company of my merely nominal associates and under the strange ministrations of Dr. Theophilus Parsons, "Governor" Washburn and Professor Joel Parker,

Cambridge," yet still "a rich and impressive institution" (*The Bostonians* [Harmondsworth: Penguin, 1966], 208).

557. Charles Augustin Sainte-Beuve (1804–69) revolutionized the critical methods of the nineteenth century. In an essay of 1875 HJ referred to him as "the acutest critic the world has seen" (*"Premiers lundis"*; *LC*, 2, 669; see also *SBO*, n. 542).

558. Dane Hall, later demolished, was erected for the law school in 1829. It was a building "designed in the Greek Revival style, its portico ornamented by four wooden pillars, on a corner of the College Yard just off the street" (Novick, *Young Master*, 83).

559. Sainte-Beuve's articles, the *Causeries du lundi,* were published weekly in the newspapers *Le Constitutionnel,* and later *Le Moniteur* and *Le Temps.* They appeared in fifteen volumes in 1851–62. *Nouveaux lundis* came out in thirteen volumes in 1861–69, and later in book form.

would have appeared to defy explanation only for those by whom the phenomena of certain kinds of living and working sensibility are unsuspected.[560] For myself at any rate there was no anomaly—the anomaly would have been much rather in any prompter consciousness of a sated perception; I knew why I liked to "go," I knew even why I could unabashedly keep going in face of the fact that if I had learned my reason I had learned, and was still to learn, absolutely nothing else; and that sufficiently supported me through a stretch of bodily overstrain that I only afterwards allowed myself dejectedly to measure. The mere sitting at attention for two or three hours—such attention as I achieved—was paid for by sorry pain; yet it was but later on that I wondered how I could have found what I "got" an equivalent for the condition produced. The condition was one of many, and the others for the most part declared themselves with much of an equal, though a different, sharpness. It was acute, that is, that one was so incommoded, but it had broken upon me with force from the first of my taking my seat—which had the advantage, I acknowledge, of the rim of the circle, symbolising thereby all the detachment I had been foredoomed to—that the whole scene was going to be, and again and again, as "American," and above all as suffused with New England colour, however one might finally estimate that, as I could possibly have wished. Such was the effect of one's offering such a plate for impressions to play on at their will; as well as of one's so failing to ask in advance what they would matter, so taking for granted that they would all matter somehow. It would matter somehow for instance that just a queer dusky half smothered light, as from windows placed too low, or too many interposing heads, should hang upon our old auditorium—long since voided of its then use and, with all its accessory chambers, seated elsewhere afresh and in much greater state; which glimpse of a scheme of values might well have given the measure of the sort of profit I was, or rather wasn't, to derive. It doubtless quite ought to have confounded me that I had come up to *faire mon droit*[561] by appreciations predominantly of the local chiaroscuro and other like quantities; but I remember no alarm—I only remember with

560. These three men "made up the entire law faculty, successful and unimaginative lawyers all" (Novick, *Young Master*, 83). Theophilus Parsons (1797–1882) was Dane Professor of Law from 1848 to 1870, Governor Emory Washburn (1800–77, the last Whig governor of Massachusetts) was on the faculty from 1855 to 1876, and Judge Joel Parker (1795–1875), considered by many to be dry and uninteresting, was Royall Professor of Law from 1847 to 1868.

561. To read, or study, law.

what complacency my range of perception on those general lines was able to spread.

It mattered, by the same law, no end that Dr. Theophilus Parsons, whose rich, if slightly quavering, old accents were the first to fall upon my ear from the chair of instruction beneath a huge hot portrait of Daniel Webster[562] should at once approve himself a vivid and curiously-composed person, an *illustrative* figure, as who should say—exactly with all the marks one might have wished him, marks of a social order, a general air, a whole history of things, or in other words of people; since there was nothing one mightn't, by my sentiment, do with such a subject from the moment it gave out character. Character thus was all over the place, as it could scarce fail to be when the general subject, the one gone in for, had become identical with the persons of all its votaries. Such was the interest of the source of edification just named, not one ray of whose merely professed value so much as entered my mind. Governor Washburn was of a different, but of a no less complete consistency—queer, ingenuous, more candidly confiding, especially as to his own pleasant fallibility, than I had ever before known a chaired dispenser of knowledge, and all after a fashion that endeared him to his young hearers, whose resounding relish of the frequent tangle of his apologetic returns upon himself, quite, almost always, to inextricability, was really affectionate in its freedom. I could understand and admire that—it seemed to have for me legendary precedents; whereas of the third of our instructors I mainly recall that he represented dryness and hardness, prose unrelieved, at their deadliest— partly perhaps because he was most master of his subject. He was none the less placeable for these things withal, and what mainly comes back to me of him is the full sufficiency with which he made me ask myself how I *could* for a moment have seen myself really browse in any field where the marks of the shepherd were such an oblong dome of a bare cranium, such a fringe of dropping little ringlets toward its base, and a mouth so meanly retentive, so ignorant of style, as I made out, above a chin so indifferent to the duty, or at least to the opportunity, of chins. If I had put it to myself that there was no excuse for the presence of a young person so affected by the idea of how people looked on a scene where the issue was altogether what they usefully taught, as well as intelligently learned and wanted to learn, I feel I should, after my first flush of confusion, have replied assuredly enough that just the

562. Daniel Webster (1782–1852), the celebrated New England lawyer, orator, and statesman, trained for the law in Boston under Christopher Gore.

beauty of the former of these questions was in its being of equal application everywhere; which was far from the case with the latter. The question of how people looked, and of how their look counted for a thousand relations, had risen before me too early and kept me company too long for me not to have made a fight over it, from the very shame of appearing at all likely to give it up, had some fleeting delusion led me to cast a slur upon it. It would do, I was already sure, half the work of carrying me through life, and where was better proof of all it would have to give than just in the fact of what it was then and there doing? It worked for appreciation—not one of the uses of which as an act of intelligence had, all round, finer connections; and on the day, in short, when one should cease to live in large measure by one's eyes (with the imagination of course all the while waiting on this) one would have taken the longest step towards not living at all.[563] My companions—however scantly indeed they were to become such— were subject to my so practising in a degree which represented well-nigh the whole of my relation with them, small reciprocity for them as there may have been in it; since vision, and nothing but vision, was from beginning to end the fruit of my situation among them. There was not one of them as to whom it didn't matter that he "looked," by my fancy of him, thus or so; the key to this disposition of the accents being for me to such an extent that, as I have said, I was with all intensity taking in New England and that I knew no better *immediate* way than to take it in by my senses. What that name really comprehended had been a mystery, daily growing less, to which everything that fell upon those senses referred itself, making the innumerable appearances hang together ever so densely. Theophilus Parsons, with his tone, his unction, his homage still to some ancient superstition, some standard of manners, reached back as to a state of provincialism rounded and compact, quite self-supporting, which gave it serenity and quality, something comparatively rich and urban; the good ex-Governor, on the other hand, of whom I think with singular tenderness, opened through every note of aspect and expression straight into those depths of rusticity which more and more unmistakably underlay the social order at large and out of which one felt it to have emerged in any degree but at scattered

563. Earlier in the chapter HJ likened himself to a plate, presumably a photographic plate, and located himself in a seat on "the rim of the circle." His recollections of his tutors record physical features and eccentricities of manner, the results of his observational vantage point, rather than their ideas or the content of their teaching. A similar process occurs in relation to his fellow students.

points. Where it did emerge, I seemed to see, it held itself as high as possible, conscious, panting a little, elate with the fact of having cleared its skirts, saved its life, consolidated its Boston, yet as with wastes unredeemed, roundabout it, propping up and pushing in—all so insistently that the light in which one for the most part considered the scene was strongly coloured by their action. This was one's clue to the labyrinth, if labyrinth it was to be called—a generalisation into which everything fitted, first to surprise and then indubitably to relief, from the moment one had begun to make it. Under its law the Puritan capital, however visibly disposed to spread and take on new disguises, affected me as a rural centre even to a point at which I had never known anything as rural; there being involved with this too much further food for curiosity and wonder. Boston was in a manner of its own stoutly and vividly urban, not only a town, but a town of history—so that how did it manage to be such different things at the same time? That was doubtless its secret—more and more interesting to study in proportion as, on closer acquaintance, yet an acquaintance before which the sense of one's preferred view from outside never gave way, one felt the equilibrium attained as on the whole an odd fusion and intermixture, of the chemical sort as it were, and not a matter of elements or aspects sharply alternating. There was in the exhibition at its best distinctly a savour—an excellent thing for a community to have, and part of the savour was, as who should say, the breath of the fields and woods and waters, though at their domesticated and familiarised stage, or the echo of a tone which had somehow become that of the most educated of our societies without ceasing to be that of the village.

Of so much from the first I felt sure, and this all the more that by my recollection of New York, even indeed by my recollection of Albany, we had been aware in those places of no such strain. New York at least had been whatever disagreeable, not to say whatever agreeable, other thing one might have declared it—it might even have been vulgar, though that cheap substitute for an account of anything didn't, I think, in the connection, then exist for me; but the last reference to its nature likely to crop up in its social soil was beyond question the flower of the homely. New England had, by one's impression, cropped up there, but had done so just *as* New England, New England unabsorbed and unreconciled; which was exactly a note in the striated, the piebald or, more gracefully, cosmopolite local character. I am not sure that the comparatively—I say comparatively— market-town suggestion of the city by the Charles came out for me as a positive richness, but it did essentially contribute to what had become so highly desirable, the reinforcement of my vision of American life by the idea of variety. I apparently required of anything I should take to my heart that it should be, approached at different angles, "like" as many other things as possible—in accordance with which it made for a various "America" that Boston should seem really strong, really quaint and amusing and beguiling or whatever, in not having, for better or worse, the same irrepressible likenesses as New York.[564] I invoked, I called down the revelation of, new likenesses by the simple act of threading the Boston streets, whether by garish day (the afterglow of the great snowfalls of winter was to turn in particular to a blinding glare, an unequalled hardness of light,) or under that mantle of night which draped as with the garb of adventure our long-drawn townward little rumbles in the interest of the theatre or of Parker's[565]—oh the sordid, yet never in the least deterrent conditions of transit in that age of the unabbreviated, the dividing desert and the primitive horse-car! (The desert is indeed, despite other local developments and the general theory of the rate at which civilisation spreads and ugliness wanes, still very much what it was in the last mid-century, but the act of passage through it has been made to some extent easier.)[566] Parker's played in the intercourse of Cambridge with Boston a part of a preponderance that I look back upon, I confess, as the very condition of the purest felicity we knew—I knew at any rate myself none, whether of a finer or a grosser strain, that competed with this precious relation. Competition has thickened since and proportions have altered—to no small darkening of the air,

564. This record of HJ's assimilation of Boston, in which he recognizes a tangible colonial past less evident in New York or Albany, its cultural and intellectual assets, its fusion of the urban with the homely, its proliferation of social movements, introduces a more developed sense of what New England came to mean for him. As he was leaving for Europe the social constitution of the city was changing; with the arrival of many Irish immigrants, increasing social divisions developed from the 1860s onward. HJ's impressions of the place in the early twentieth century narrated in *AS* are shaded with racial and social anxieties.

565. The Parker House was a hotel at 60 School Street, Boston.

566. The Boston-Cambridge horsecar service was introduced in 1856. A more mechanized form of transportation was developed in the last decade of the century. The emphatically European Eugenia in *The Europeans* (1878) observes from her window "a huge, low omnibus, painted in brilliant colours, and decorated apparently with jingling bells. . . . When it reached a certain point the people in front of the grave-yard . . . projected themselves upon it . . . a movement suggesting the scramble for places in a life-boat at sea— and were engulfed in its large interior" ([Harmondsworth: Penguin, 1964], 6).

but the time was surely happier; a single such *point de repère*[567] not only sufficed but richly heaped up the measure. Parker's, on the whole side of the joy of life, *was* Boston—speaking as under the thrill of early occasions recaptured; Boston could be therefore, in the acutest connections, those of young comradeship and young esthetic experience, heaven save the mark, fondly prepared or properly crowned, but the enjoyed and shared repast, literally the American feast, as I then appraised such values; a basis of native abundance on which everything else rested. The theatre, resorted to whenever possible, rested indeed doubtless most, though with its heaviest weight thrown perhaps at a somewhat later time; the theatre my uncanny appetite for which strikes me as almost abnormal in the light of what I braved to reach it from the studious suburb, or more particularly braved to return from it. I touch alas no spring that doesn't make a hum of memories, and pick them over as I will three or four of that scenic strain linger on my sense. The extraordinary fact about these—which plays into my gener-alisation a little way back—was that, for all the connection of such occa-sions with the great interest of the theatre at large, there was scarce an impression of the stage wrung from current opportunity that didn't some-how underscore itself with the special Boston emphasis; and this in spite of the fact that plays and performers in those days were but a shade less raggedly itinerant over the land than they are now. The implication of the provincial in the theatric air, and of the rustic in the provincial, may have been a matter of the "house" itself, with its twenty kinds of redolence of barbarism—with the kind determined by the very audience perhaps in-deed plainest;[568] vivid to me at all events is it how I felt even at the time, in repairing to the Howard Atheneum to admire Miss Maggie Mitchell and Miss Kate Bateman, that one would have had only to scratch a little below the surface of the affair to come upon the but half-buried Puritan curse not so very long before devoted to such perversities.[569] Wasn't the curse still in

567. Reference point, benchmark.

568. HJ is, of course, judging Boston's theater in the light of his earlier experiences in London and, more importantly, Paris, home of the Théâtre Français. Compare Hyacinth Robinson's reaction to an "inanimate revival" of a play in London: "he had been at the Théâtre Français and the tradition of that house was still sufficiently present to him to make any other style of interpretation of comedy appear at the best but a confident form of horseplay" (*The Princess Casamassima*, 355).

569. Theaters still felt the need to stress their respectability, hence names such as lyceum and athenaeum. The Howard Athenaeum opened in 1845 and closed in 1953. Though in its earlier years it staged Shakespeare and classic plays ("one of the most

the air, and could anything less than a curse, weighing from far back on the general conscience, have accounted for one could scarce say what want of self-respect in the total exhibition?—for that intimation more than anything else perhaps of the underhand snicker with which one sat so oddly associated. By the blest law of youth and fancy withal one did admire the actress—the young need to admire as flatly as one could broke through all crowding apprehensions. I like to put it down that nothing in the world qualified my wonder at the rendering by the first of the performers I have named of the figure of "Fanchon the Cricket" in a piece so entitled, an artless translation from a German original, if I rightly remember, which original had been an arrangement for the stage of La Petite Fadette, George Sand's charming rustic idyll.[570] I like to put it down that Miss Maggie Mitchell's having for years, as I gathered, twanged that one string and none other, every night of her theatric life, over the huge country, before she was revealed to us—just as Mr. Joe Jefferson, with no word of audible reprehension ever once addressed to him, was to have twanged his[571]—did nothing to bedim the brightness of our vision or the apparent freshness of her art, and that above all it seemed a privilege critically to disengage the delicacy of this art and the rare effect of the natural in it from the baseness in which it was framed: so golden a glimmer is shed, as one looks back, from any shaky little torch lighted, by whatever fond stretch, at the high esthetic flame. Upon these faint sparks in the night of time would I gently breathe, just to see them again distinguishably glow, rather than leave their momentary function uncommemorated. Strange doubtless were some of the things that represented these momentary functions—strange I mean in proportion to the fires they lighted. The small bower of the muse in Winthrop Square was first to know the fluttered descent of the goddess to

---

comfortable places of amusement in the city, and . . . deservedly popular" [Midgley, *Sights in Boston and Suburbs,* 111]), it later became better known for burlesque. Margaret Julia Mitchell (1832–1918) was most famous for her role in *Fanchon the Cricket,* with which she toured America. For more on Kate Bateman (1842–1917), whom HJ had seen perform as a child, see *SBO,* chap. 7.

570. *Fanchon the Cricket* was a performing version (one of several) of a German translation of George Sand's tale *La petite Fadette* (1848), whose plot is itself a juvenile variation on *The Taming of the Shrew.* Kate Bateman used an adaptation by Charlotte Birch Pfeiffer.

571. The American actor-playwright Joseph Jefferson (1829–1905) (who also visited England and Australia) was famous as a comic character performer; he became particularly associated with the role of Rip Van Winkle in Dion Boucicault's adaptation of Washington Irving's story.

my appeal for her aid in the composition of a letter from which the admired Miss Maggie should gather the full force of my impression. Particularly do I incline even now to mention that she testified to her having gratefully gathered it by the despatch to me in return of a little printed copy of the play, a scant pamphlet of "acting edition" humility, addressed in a hand which assumed a romantic cast as soon as I had bethought myself of finding for it a happy precedent in that of Pendennis's Miss Fotheringay.[572]

It had been perhaps to the person of this heroine that Pendennis especially rendered homage, while I, without illusions, or at least without confusions, was fain to discriminate in favour of the magic of method, that is of genius, itself; which exactly, more than anything else could have done (success, as I considered, crowning my demonstration,) contributed to consecrate to an exquisite use, *the* exquisite, my auspicious *réduit* afore-said.[573] For an esthetic vibration to whatever touch had but to be intense enough to tremble on into other reactions under other blest contacts and commotions. It was by the operation again of the impulse shaking me up to an expression of what the elder star of the Howard Atheneum had artis-tically "meant" to me that I first sat down beside my view of the Brighton hills to enrol myself in the bright band of the fondly hoping and fearfully doubting who count the days after the despatch of manuscripts. I formally addressed myself under the protection, not to say the inspiration, of Winthrop Square to the profession of literature, though nothing would induce me now to name the periodical on whose protracted silence I had thus begun to hang with my own treasures of reserve to match it.[574] The bearing of which shy ecstasies—shy of exhibition then, that is, save as achievements recognized—is on their having thus begun, at any rate, to supply all the undertone one needed to whatever positive perfunctory

572. In Thackeray's novel *Pendennis*, the nineteen-year-old Arthur Pendennis has fallen in love with the thirty-year-old actor, Miss Fotheringay. With typical irony, however, it is revealed that she has very limited understanding of the plays in which she appears and that even her replies to Pendennis's ardent letters were written for her by a third party.

573. HJ had long been fascinated by the art of acting, as he revealed in a conversation with a friend, the novelist Mary (Mrs. Humphry) Ward, whose novella *Miss Bretherton*, modeled on the performances of Mary Anderson, appeared in 1884 (*CN*, 28). His own later work *The Tragic Muse* offers a more searching examination of the actor "type." *Réduit:* retreat or nook.

574. Novick has shown that the anonymous first-night review, "Miss Maggie Mitchell in 'Fanchon the Cricket,'" that appeared in Boston's *Daily Traveller* on 6 January 1863 was by HJ. His commentary on "Henry James's first published work" and the review itself forms the appendix to *Henry James: The Young Master*, 431–33.

show; the show proceeding as it could, all the while, thanks to much help from the undertone, which felt called upon at times to be copious. It is not, I allow, that memory may pretend for me to keep the two elements of the under and the over always quite distinct—it would have been a pity all round, in truth, should they have altogether escaped mixing and fraternising. The positive perfunctory show, at all events, to repeat my term, hitched itself along from point to point, and could have no lack of outside support to complain of, I reflect, from the moment I could make my own every image and incitement—those, as I have noted, of the supply breaking upon me with my first glimpse of the Cambridge scene. If I seem to make too much of these it is because I at the time made still more, more even than my pious record has presumed to set down. The air of truth doubtless hangs uneasy, as the matter stands, over so queer a case as my having, by my intimation above, found appreciability in life at the Law School even under the failure for me of everything generally drawn upon for it, whether the glee of study, the ardour of battle or the joy of associated adventure. Not to have felt earlier sated with the mere mechanic amusement or vain form of regularity at lectures would strike me to-day as a fact too "rum" for belief if certain gathered flowers by the way, flowers of perverse appreciation though they might but be, didn't give out again as I turn them over their unspeakable freshness.[575] They were perforce gathered (what makes

575. In this opaque passage the tensions and pleasures HJ touches upon emerge as tellingly in his figurative terms as in his more direct summary of a situation. He has already established at the beginning of the chapter his adopted peripheral role, on the rim of a circle, as a photographic plate, open to myriad impressions in this newly realized version of America. By this stage, in the all-male enclave in which he has no genuine place (the study of law and the pile of impressive textbooks are merely a front), his terms cohere to suggest covertness and privacy full of their own riches as he inhabits a secret garden or nook. The theme emerges only gradually and coyly as his fellow male students (or as he calls them—in the manner of Dickens—"the young appearances") become, rather than the study of law, the absorbing subject; they are individuals distinguishing themselves as brothers or other near relatives, of the same "precious clay" as their military peers witnessing the Civil War. Other pleasingly distinctive and different versions emerge—"special cases of elegant deviation"—whose provenance may be more exotic than New England, but all appealing to "fancy," and all introducing varieties of "Americanism" in a Whitmanesque vision of desirable masculinity. The discourse parades the deviance of its insights, self-consciously characteristic of the late James, as it refers to "so queer a case," gathering "flowers of perverse appreciation," collecting "pearls of differentiation," detecting the dissolution of "stiff" laws of identity as prone to failure and appreciating the "thick stem" beneath, which allows for varieties of maleness. HJ blames his "fond imagination" for these flights, implying both foolishness and affection. For a reading of this passage that regards HJ as posing

it still more wondrous) all too languidly; yet they massed themselves for my sense, through the lapsing months, to the final semblance of an intimate secret garden. Such was the odd, the almost overwhelming consequence— or one of these, for they are many—of an imagination to which literally everything obligingly signified. One of the actual penalties of this is that so few of such ancient importances remain definable or presentable. It may in the fulness of time simply sound *bête*[576] that, with the crash of greater questions about one, I should have been positively occupied with such an affair as the degree and the exact shade to which the blest figures in the School array, each quite for himself, might settle and fix the weight, the interest, the function, as it were, of his Americanism. I could scarce have cleared up even for myself, I dare say, the profit, or more pertinently the charm, of that extravagance—and the fact was of course that I didn't feel it as extravagance, but quite as homely thrift, moral, social, esthetic, or indeed, as I might have been quite ready to say, practical and professional. It was practical at least in the sense that it probably more helped to pass the time than all other pursuits together. The real proof of which would be of course my being able now to string together for exhibition some of these pearls of differentiation—since it was to differentiation exactly that I was then, in my innocence, most prompted; not dreaming of the stiff law by which, on the whole American ground, division of *type,* in the light of opposition and contrast, was more and more to break down for me and fail: so that verily the recital of my mere concomitant efforts to pick it up again and piece its parts together and make them somehow show and serve would be a record of clinging courage. I may note at once, however, as a light on the anomaly, that there hung about *all* young appearances at that period something ever so finely derivative and which at this day rather defies re-expression—the common character or shared function of the precious clay so largely making up the holocausts of battle; an advantage working for them circuitously or perhaps ambiguously enough, I grant, but still placing them more or less under the play of its wing even when the arts of peace happened for the hour to engage them. They potentially, they conceivably, they indirectly paid, and nothing was for the most part more ascertainable of them individually than that, with brothers or other near

---

"questions of gender and sexuality" and the possibilities of "improvisation, or perfor-mance," indeed as illustrating "the phallic power of his imagination to convert robust young men into flowers," see Person, *Henry James and the Suspense of Masculinity,* 7–8.

576. Stupid, silly.

relatives in the ranks or in commands, they came, to their credit, of paying families. All of which again may represent the high pitch of one's associated sensibility—there having been occasions of crisis, were they worth recovering, when under its action places, persons, objects animate or not, glimmered alike but through the grand idealising, the generalising, blur. At moments of less fine a strain, it may be added, the sources of interest presented themselves in looser formation. The young appearances, as I like to continue to call them, could be pleasingly, or at least robustly homogeneous, and yet, for livelier appeal to fancy, flower here and there into special cases of elegant deviation—"sports," of exotic complexion, one enjoyed denominating these (or would have enjoyed had the happy figure then flourished) thrown off from the thick stem that was rooted under our feet. Even these rare exceptions, the few apparitions referring themselves to other producing conditions than the New England, wrought by contrast no havoc in the various quantities for which that section was responsible; it was certainly refreshing—always to the fond imagination—that there were, for a change, imprints in the stuff of youth that didn't square with the imprint, virtually *one* throughout, imposed by Springfield or Worcester, by Providence or Portland, or whatever rural wastes might lie between;[577] yet the variations, I none the less gather as I strive to recall them, beguiled the spirit (talking always of my own) rather than coerced it, and this even though fitting into life as one had already more or less known it, fitting in, that is, with more points of contact and more reciprocation of understanding than the New England relation seemed able to produce. It could in fact fairly blind me to the implication of an inferior immediate *portée*[578] that such and such a shape of the New York heterogeneity, however simplified by silliness, or at least by special stupidity (though who was I to note *that*?) pressed a certain spring of association, waiting as I always was for such echoes, rather than left it either just soundless or bunglingly touched.

It was for example a link with the larger life, as I am afraid I must have privately called it, that a certain young New Yorker, an outsider of still more unmistakable hue than I could suppose even myself, came and went before us with an effect of cultivated detachment that I admired at the time for its perfect consistency, and that caused him, it was positively thrilling

577. Springfield and Worcester are towns in central Massachusetts; the college town of Providence is in Rhode Island; the large city of Portland is further north, on the coast of Maine.

578. Bearing, effect.

to note, not in the least to forfeit sympathy, but to shine in the high light of public favour. The richest reflections sprang for me from this, some of them inspiring even beyond the promptly grasped truth, a comparative commonplace, that the variation or opposition sufficiently embodied, the line of divergence sharply enough drawn, always achieves some triumph by the fact of its emphasis, by its putting itself through at any cost, any cost in particular of ridicule. So much one had often observed; but what really enriched the dear induction and made our friend's instance thus remain with me was the part played by the utter blandness itself of his protest, such an exhibition of the sweet in the imperturbable. This it was that enshrined him, by my vision, in a popularity than which nothing could have seemed in advance less indicated, and that makes me wonder to-day whether he was simply the luckiest of gamblers or just a conscious and consummate artist. He reappears to me as a finished fop, finished to possibilities we hadn't then dreamt of, and as taking his stand, or rather taking all his walks, on *that*, the magician's wand of his ideally tight umbrella under his arm and the magician's familiar of his bristling toy-terrier at his heels.[579] He became thus an apparition entrancing to the mind. His clothes were of a perfection never known nor divined in that sphere, a revelation, straight and blindingly authentic, of Savile Row in its prime;[580] his single eyeglass alone, and his inspired, his infinite use of it as at once a defensive crystal wall and a lucid window of hospitality, one couldn't say most which, might well have foredoomed him, by all likelihood, to execration and destruction. He became none the less, as I recover him, our general pride and joy; his entrances and exits were acclaimed beyond all others, and it was his rare privilege to cause the note of derision and the note of affection to melt together, beyond separation, in vague but virtual homage to the refreshment of felt type. To see it dawn upon rude breasts (for rude, comparatively, *were* the breasts of the type-less, or at the best of the typed but in one character, throughout the same,) that defiant and confident difference carried far enough might avert the impulse to slay, was to muse ever so agreeably on the queer means by which great morals, picking up a life as they may, can still get themselves

---

579. The dandy, or fop, was of course a significant figure most notably in nineteenth-century French artistic life. Perry identified this New York fop as Sam D. Craig (see Edel, *Untried Years*, 199).

580. Savile Row, near Regent Street in London's West End, is still regarded as representing the best in men's bespoke tailoring.

pointed.[581] The "connotation" of the trivial, it was thus attaching to remark, could perfectly serve when that of the important, roughly speaking, failed for a grateful *connection*—from the moment some such was massed invitingly in view. The difficulty with the type about me was that, in its monotony, beginning and ending with itself, it *had* no connections and suggested none; whereas the grace of the salient apparition I have perhaps too earnestly presented lay in its bridging over our separation from worlds, from great far-off reservoirs, of a different mixture altogether, another civility and complexity. Young as I was, I myself clearly recognised that ground of reference, saw it even to some extent in the light of experience—so could I stretch any scrap of contact; kept hold of it by fifty clues, recalls and reminders that dangled for me mainly out of books and magazines and heard talk, things of picture and story, things of prose and verse and anecdotal vividness in fine, and, as I have elsewhere allowed, for the most part hoardedly English and French. Our "character man" of the priceless monocle and the trotting terrier was "like" some type in a collection of types—that was the word for it; and, there being no collection, nor the ghost of one, roundabout us, was a lone courageous creature in the desert of our bald reiterations.[582] The charm of which conclusion was exactly, as I have said, that the common voice did, by every show, bless him for rendered service, his dropped hint of an ideal containing the germ of other ideals—and confessed by that fact to more appetites and inward yearnings than it the least bit consciously counted up.

Not quite the same service was rendered by G. A. J., who had no ridicule to brave, and I can speak with confidence but of the connections, rather confused if they were, opened up to me by his splendid aspect

581. This affectionate portrait and quasi-sociological evaluation of the exoticism of the "fop" in relation to the surrounding "typeless" young men might be regarded as a variant on the discreet deviance HJ has explored in himself. In his further consideration of the young man as a "type" he attributes his recognition of its features to his exposure to European infuences; indeed, he implies the French use of the term, which can include the sense of "chap" or "bloke." Interestingly, a *drôle de type* signifies a "queer chap" or "rum stick"—dated epithets HJ has himself recently employed.

582. If these young New England provincials had no manual to consult in deciphering the type, a typically French equivalent might have answered their needs, a volume that HJ mentions in *SBO*, chap. 25. It is a collection of brief essays with accompanying illustrations, designed to survey the range of national types, titled *Les français peints par eux-mêmes: Encyclopédie morale du dix-neuvième siècle* [The French painted by themselves: a moral encyclopedia of the nineteenth century] (1839–42), published in Paris by Léon Curmer and released in 422 weekly installments.

and which had absolutely nothing in common with the others that hung near.[583] It was brilliant to a degree that none other had by so much as a single shade the secret of, and it carried the mooning fancy to a further reach even, on the whole, than the figure of surprise I have just commemorated; this last comparatively scant in itself and rich only by what it made us read into it, and G. A. J. on the other hand intrinsically and actively ample and making us read wonders, as it were, into whatever it might be that was, as we used to say, "back of" him. He had such a flush of life and presence as to make that reference mysteriously and inscrutably loom— and the fascinating thing about this, as we again would have said, was that it could strike me as so beguilingly American. That too was part of the glamour, that its being so could kick up a mystery which one might have pushed on to explore, whereas our New York friend only kicked up a certainty (for those properly prepared) and left not exploration, but mere assured satisfaction, the mark of the case. G. A. J. reached westward,

583. G.A.J. is, as HJ revealed to his American publisher (*HJL*, 4:737), George Abbott James, born in Ohio in 1838 and the "sole member of the Harvard law class whose friendship the novelist cherished in later life" (Edel, *Untried Years*, 199). The two had corresponded since the 1870s. Though they did not meet on HJ's 1904–5 U.S. visit, he had recently seen the widower in the excessively hot summer of 1911 during his stay in America after WJ's death. HJ was in a state of depression, referring in a letter of 10 May 1911 to his "accursèd necessity of falling back into deep dark holes" which seemed to him "endless & unutterable." He wrote gratefully on his return, "I don't know, dearest George, what I should have done without you—you were the best of all good Samaritans at the worst of all melancholy seasons. I have only to lean back a little, as I say, to live over again each day & each hour of the romantic time; for romantic it already has become to me, across the separating sea—& the sweet savour of the whole fond episode will cling always to my spiritual palate" (12–13 August 1911; bMS Am 1094.1 [147, 149], Houghton). G. A. James lived at Lowland House, Nahant, on the bay north of Boston. HJ later wrote that there, " 'at the tip end of the Nahant promontory, quite out at sea, where, amid gardens & groves & on a vast breezy verandah, my life was most mercifully saved. . . .' He was to look back on this as 'Paradise': 'the blest time.' He took in 'the great restorative breath' of the sea; heard 'the soft boom of the surge' upon the rocks. There on his couch, he exchanged 'the hot poison-cup for a long draught of the coolest and sweetest elixir!' // Thrust in the furnace, melting down to mere 'mass,' with a 'blest' glimpse of 'Paradise,' he came to the edge of existence. He walked naked at Nahant like an Ancient Mariner under the eye of the sun" (Gordon, *A Private Life of Henry James*, 345–46). The Nahant peninsula, "one of the most pleasant and delightful watering places in the world" (Midgley, *Sights in Boston and Suburbs*, 180), is granted a complete chapter to itself in many guidebooks. Clearly HJ wished to acknowledge his still-living friend without compromising his privacy (see also his letters and references to G. A. James in *The Letters of Henry James*, ed. Percy Lubbock, 2 vols. [London: Macmillan, 1920], 2:114–15, 116–17, 198).

westward even of New York, and southward at least as far as Virginia; teeming facts that I discovered, so to speak, by my own unaided intelligence—so little were they responsibly communicated. Little was communicated that I recover—it would have had to drop from too great a personal height; so that the fun, as I may call it, was the greater for my opening all by myself to perceptions. I was getting furiously American, in the big sense I invoked, through this felt growth of an ability to reach out westward, southward, anywhere, everywhere, on that apprehension of finding myself but patriotically charmed. Thus there dawned upon me the grand possibility that, charm for charm, the American, the assumed, the postulated, would, in the particular case of its really acting, count double; whereas the European paid for being less precarious by being also less miraculous. It counted single, as one might say, and only made up for that by counting almost always. It mightn't be anything like almost always, even at the best, no doubt, that an American-grown value of aspect would so entirely emerge as G. A. J.'s seemed to do; but what did this exactly point to unless that the rarity so implied would be in the nature of the splendid?[584] That at least was the way the cultivation of patriotism as a resource was the cultivation of workable aids to the same, however ingenious these. (Just to glow belligerently with one's country was no resource, but a primitive instinct breaking through; and besides this resources were cooling, not heating.) It might have seemed that I might after all perfectly dispense with friends when simple acquaintances, and rather feared ones at that, though feared but for excess of lustre, could kindle in the mind such bonfires of thought, feeding the flame with gestures and sounds and light accidents of passage so beyond their own supposing. In spite of all which, however, G. A. J. was marked for a friend and taken for a kinsman from the day when his blaze of colour should have sufficiently cleared itself up for me to distinguish the component shades.

584. This recognition of the richness and potential of the American character, a more mysterious element than its European equivalent presumably because of HJ's formative years spent traveling, is predicated upon the young American male, specifically here George James. HJ's becoming "furiously American" occurred within the camaraderie (however tentatively explored) of the Harvard Law School—ironically, since the nation itself was engaged in civil self-destruction. Bearing in mind the novelist's consequent long-term removal to Europe, these feelings may more fully represent the older HJ; in the final decade of his life (and evident in *The Ivory Tower*) it seems that (along with severe misgivings) he discovered something of the "romance," the incalculable promise of his native country.

**XI**      I am fully aware while I go, I should mention, of all that flows from the principle governing, by my measure, these recoveries and reflections—even to the effect, hoped for at least, of stringing their apparently dispersed and disordered parts upon a fine silver thread; none other than the principle of response to a long-sought occasion, now gratefully recognised, for making trial of the recording and figuring act on behalf of some case of the imaginative faculty under cultivation. The personal history, as it were, of an imagination, a lively one of course, in a given and favourable case, had always struck me as a task that a teller of tales might rejoice in, his advance through it conceivably causing at every step some rich precipitation—unless it be rather that the play of strong imaginative passion, passion strong enough to *be,* for its subject or victim, the very interest of life, constitutes in itself an endless crisis. Fed by every contact and every apprehension, and feeding in turn every motion and every act, wouldn't the light in which it might so cause the whole scene of life to unroll inevitably become as fine a thing as possible to represent? The idea of some pretext for such an attempt had again and again, naturally, haunted me; the man of imagination, and of an "awfully good" one, showed, as the creature of that force or the sport of that fate or the wielder of that arm, for the hero of a hundred possible fields—if one could but first "catch" him, after the fashion of the hare in the famous receipt.[585] Who and what might he prove, when caught, in respect to *other* signs and conditions? He might take, it would seem, some finding and launching, let alone much handling—which itself, however, would be exactly part of the pleasure. Meanwhile, it no less appeared, there were other subjects to go on with, and even if one had to wait for him he would still perhaps come. It happened for me that he *was* belatedly to come, but that he was to turn up then in a shape almost too familiar at first for recognition, the shape of one of those residual substitutes that engage doubting eyes the day after the fair. He had been with me all the while, and only too obscurely and intimately—I had not found him in the market as an exhibited or *offered* value. I had in a word to draw him forth from within rather than meet him in the world before me, the more convenient sphere of the objective, and to make him objective, in short, had to turn

---

585. HJ refers to the famous opening line of the recipe for jugged hare in which you must first catch your hare. Though often associated with Isabella Beeton (1836–65) and her *Book of Household Management,* the advice is probably proverbial.

nothing less than myself inside out.[586] What was *I* thus, within and essentially, what had I ever been and could I ever be but a man of imagination at the active pitch?—so that if it was a question of treating *some* happy case, any that would give me what, artistically speaking, I wanted, here on the very spot was one at hand in default of a better. It wasn't what I should have preferred, yet it was after all the example I knew best and should feel most at home with—granting always that objectivity, the prize to be won, shouldn't just be frightened away by the odd terms of the affair. It is of course for my reader to say whether or no what I have done *has* meant defeat; yet even if this should be his judgment I fall back on the interest, at the worst, of certain sorts of failure. I shall have brought up from the deep many things probably not to have been arrived at for the benefit of these pages without my particular attempt. Sundry of such I seem still to recognise, and not least just now those involved in that visionary "assistance"[587] at the drama of the War, from however far off, which had become a habit for us without ceasing to be a strain. I am sure I thought more things under that head, with the fine visionary ache, than I thought in all other connections together; for the simple reason that one had to *ask* leave—of one's own spirit—for these last intermissions, whereas one but took it, with both hands free, for one's sense of the bigger cause. There was not in that the least complication of consciousness. I have sufficiently noted how my apprehension of the bigger cause was at the same time, and this all through, at once quickened and kept low; to the point that positively my whole acquaintance of the personal sort even with such a matter as my brother Wilky's enrolment in the 44th Massachusetts was to reduce itself to but a single visit to him in camp.

I recall an afternoon at Readville, near Boston, and the fashion in which his state of juniority gave way, for me, on the spot, to immensities of superior difference, immensities that were at the same time intensities, varieties, supremacies, of the enviable in the all-difficult and the delightful in the impossible:[588] such a fairy-tale seemed it, and withal such a flat revolution, that this soft companion of my childhood should have such romantic chances and should have mastered, by the mere aid of his native

586. The likeliest fictional figure, so intimately related to HJ himself, would seem to be Lambert Strether in *The Ambassadors* (1903). As the passage develops, however, it is possible that, with much self-deprecation, HJ refers to his own presence in this quasi-autobiographical genre, which records impressions gathered by an aspiring artist.

587. In the French sense of being present at, or witnessing, an event.

588. This episode has already been recorded in chap. 9 above.

gaiety and sociability, such mysteries, such engines, such arts. To become first a happy soldier and then an easy officer was in particular for G. W. J.[589] an exercise of sociability—and that above all was my extract of the Readville scene, which most came home to me as a picture, an interplay of bright breezy air and high shanty-covered levels with blue horizons, and laughing, welcoming, sunburnt young men, who seemed mainly to bristle, through their welcome, with Boston genealogies,[590] and who had all alike turned handsome, only less handsome than their tawny-bearded Colonel,[591] under I couldn't have said what common grace of clear blue toggery imperfectly and hitchingly donned in the midst of the camp labours that I gaped at (by the blessing of heaven I could in default of other adventures still gape) as at shining revels. I couldn't "do things," I couldn't indefinitely hang about, though on occasion I did so, as it comes back to me, verily to desperation; which had to be my dim explanation—dim as to my ever insisting on it—of so rare a snatch at opportunity for gapings the liveliest, or in better terms admirations the crudest, that I could have presumed to encumber the scene with. Scarce credible to me now, even under recall of my frustrations, that I was able in all this stretch of time to respond but to a single other summons to admire at any cost, which I think must have come again from Readville, and the occasion of which, that of my brother's assumed adjutancy of the so dramatically, so much more radically recruited 54th involved a view superficially less harmonious.[592] The whole situation was more wound up and girded then,

589. Garth Wilkinson James.

590. Jane Maher, in *Biography of Broken Fortunes* (31) describes the officers of the 54th and 55th, rather than the 44th, regiments (which HJ actually refers to at the end of the previous paragraph) as containing "some of New England's most illustrious families: Shaw, Russell, Higginson, two Appletons, two Hallowells, two Jameses. Two sons of Frederick Douglass served in the Fifty-fourth."

591. Major Francis L. Lee had been commissioned a colonel.

592. Wilky had originally enlisted with the 44th Massachusetts Infantry Regiment, sailing for North Carolina on 22 October 1862; he was promoted to corporal and later sergeant. On 23 March 1863 he and his friend Cabot Russel transferred to the 54th Massachusetts Regiment, then being set up under the authority of Massachusetts governor John Andrew and commanded by Robert Gould Shaw. Zenas T. Haines, a corporal in the 44th and a former journalist, reported for the *Boston Herald* that "the Boston regiment of colored men has excited much interest here. Some of our best men have accepted commissions in it. Among these are Lieut. [Albert S.] Hartwell, Sergts. [Garth W.] James and [Cabot J.] Russell [*sic*], of Co. F. We shall part with these men with great regret, and at the same time give them a hearty Godspeed in their brave and self-sacrificing undertaking" (*"In the Country of the Enemy": The Civil War Reports of a Massachusetts Corporal*, ed.

the formation of negro regiments affected us as a tremendous War measure, and I have glanced in another place at the consequence of it that was at the end of a few months most pointedly to touch ourselves.[593] That second aspect of the weeks of preparation before the departure of the regiment can not at all have suggested a frolic, though at the time I don't remember it as grim, and can only gather that, as the other impression had been of something quite luminous and beautiful, so this was vaguely sinister and sad—perhaps simply through the fact that, though our sympathies, our own as a family's, were, in the current phrase, all enlisted on behalf of the race that had sat in bondage, it was impossible for the mustered presence of more specimens of it, and of stranger, than I had ever seen together, not to make the young men who were about to lead them appear sacrificed to the general tragic need in a degree beyond that of their more orthodox appearances.[594] The air of sacrifice was, however, so to brighten as to confound itself with that of splendid privilege on the day (May 28th, '63) of the march of the 54th out of Boston, its fairest of young commanders at its head, to great reverberations of music, of fluttering banners, launched benedictions and every public sound; only from that scene, when it took place, I had to be helplessly absent[595]—just as I

---

William C. Harris [Gainesville: University Press of Florida, 1999], 136). This must have been HJ's final visit to Readville, according to Maher (*Biography of Broken Fortunes,* 36). HJ was later to admit that, "I am always very much struck by the sight of a uniform. . . . I watched the soldiers whenever an opportunity offered. . . . When, of a summer afternoon, they scatter themselves abroad in undress uniform—with their tight red jackets and tight blue trousers following the swelling lines of their manly shapes, and their little visorless caps perched neatly askew on the summit of their six feet two of stature—it is impossible not to be impressed, and almost abashed, by the sight of such a consciousness of neatly-displayed physical advantages and by such an air of superior valor" ("The British Soldier," *Lippincott's Magazine* 22 [1878]; rpt. in *Henry James on Culture,* 5–8). See also Peter Rawlings, "Grotesque Encounters in the Travel Writing of Henry James," *Yearbook of English Studies* 34 (2004): 182.

593. HJ may be referring to Wilky's being severely injured in the assault on Fort Wagner (see chap. 7 above).

594. Owing to the racial views of the time, it had been difficult to recruit officers to lead African-American troops, and those who were selected were carefully chosen. In addition, of course, black soldiers were still untried in battle, and the public, even in the North, was frequently hostile to the idea. Though many of the abolitionists and pragmatists of the North had supported the idea of enlisting black soldiers for the military, in the days before Lincoln's Emancipation Proclamation the subject was politically delicate.

595. See n. 522. The scene is described in Peter Burchard's *One Gallant Rush,* 93–95. The regiment was posted to Port Royal Island off the South Carolina coast.

see myself in a like dismal manner deprived of any nearness of view of my still younger brother's military metamorphosis and contemporary initiation. I vainly question memory for some such picture of *him,* at this stage of his adventure, as would have been certain to hang itself, for reasons of wonder and envy again, in my innermost cabinet. Our differently compacted and more variously endowed Bob, who had strained much at every tether, was so eager and ardent that it made for him a positive authority; but what most recurs to me of his start in the 45th, or of my baffled vision of it, is the marvel of our not having all just wept, more than anything else, either for his being so absurdly young or his being so absurdly strenuous —we might have had our choice of pretexts and protests. It seemed so short a time since he had been l'ingénieux petit Robertson of the domestic schoolroom, pairing with our small sister as I paired with Wilky.[596] We didn't in the least weep, however—we smiled as over the interest of childhood at its highest bloom, and that my parents, with their consistent tenderness, should have found their surrender of their latest born so workable is doubtless a proof that we were all lifted together as on a wave that might bear us where it would. Our ingenious Robertson was but seventeen years old, but I suspect his ingenuity of having, in so good a cause, anticipated his next birthday by a few months. The 45th was a nine-months regiment, but he got himself passed out of it, in advance of its discharge, to a lieutenancy in the 55th U.S.C.T.,[597] Colonel A. P. Hallowell (transferred from lieutenant-colonelcy of the 54th) commanding; though not before he had been involved in the siege of Charleston, whence the visionary, the quite Edgar Poeish look, for my entertainment, of the camp-

596. The French governess, Mademoiselle Danse, had described Bob as "clever little Robertson" during the family's stay in Paris in 1856 (see *SBO*, 258). HJ seems momentarily to have moved away from the usual dynamics within his family whereby he aligns himself with, or rather subordinates himself to, the older WJ.

597. To help with enlistment in the Union army, Congress passed in July 1862 a militia act that increased the length of time that state militias could be called into federal service from the ninety days specified by the 1795 militia act to nine months. By August 1862 the War Department required states to furnish a specified number of nine-month militia regiments: Massachusetts raised about ten regiments at this time, including the 44th. The 54th was a three-year regiment. I am grateful to James M. McPherson and Joseph E. Glatthaar for this information; more generally, see *The Oxford Companion to American Military History,* editor in chief John Whiteclay Chambers II (Oxford: Oxford University Press, 1999), 135. U.S.C.T. were the United States Colored Troops; after the second stage of Lincoln's Emancipation Proclamation in January 1863, the recruitment of African-American soldiers began.

covered "Folly Island" of his letters.[598] While his regiment was engaged in Seymour's raid on Florida he suffered a serious sunstroke,[599] with such consequences that he was recommended for discharge; of which he declined to avail himself, obtaining instead a position on General Ames's staff and enjoying thus for six months the relief of being mounted. But he returned to his regiment in front of Charleston (after service with the Tenth Army Corps, part of the Army of the James, before Petersburg and Richmond);[600] and though I have too scant an echo of his letters from that scene one of the passages that I do recover is of the happiest. "It was when the line wavered and I saw Gen'l Hartwell's horse on my right rear up with a shell exploding under him that I rammed my spurs into my own beast, who, maddened with pain, carried me on through the line, throwing men down, and over the Rebel works some distance ahead of our troops."[601]

598. Colonel Norwood Penrose Hallowell (not A. P. Hallowell) (1839–1914), brother of Edward Needles Hallowell (1836–1871) and a close friend of Oliver Wendell Holmes Jr., became lieutenant colonel of the 54th Massachusetts on 17 April 1863, and on 30 May 1863 colonel of the newly organized 55th. After the war he became a banker. The siege of Charleston (a city known as "the Cradle of Secession" and heavily fortified on its coastal side) carried on through the latter part of 1863. Folly Island (to the southwest of Morris Island) lies off the much larger James Island, all on the southwestern approach to Charleston harbor. Poe's "The Gold-Bug" (mentioned in *SBO*, chap. 5) begins near Charleston.

599. The raid was led by Brigadier General Truman Seymour (1824–1891). The battle of Olustee, also known as Ocean Pond, near Jacksonville, took place in February 1864 and was a failure for the Union forces, as indeed was the planned conquest of Florida (David J. Eicher, *The Longest Night: A Military History of the Civil War* [New York: Simon and Schuster, 2001], 639–40). Bob later recalled the disaster: "Exhausted as was our black regiment, it was still necessary to cover the retreat of our men as best we might. During the night I occupied with the men under my command a strong stockade which protected the only road upon which the stricken forces could defile in their retreat. . . . Of that well organized body of five thousand men which had gone into the fight at Olustee, in the morning 2,200 did not return" ("Three Years' Service with the Fifty-Fifth Massachusetts Volunteer Infantry," quoted in Maher, *Biography of Broken Fortunes*, 68).

600. For information about many of the military commanders referred to in this chapter I am indebted to John H. Eicher and David J. Eicher's *Civil War High Commands* (Stanford: Stanford University Press, 2001). Brigadier General Adelbert Ames (1835–1933) had fought at the Battle of Gettysburg. In the spring of 1864 he was commanding a division of the 10th Corps of Major General Ben Butler's Army of the James, in the region of Richmond and Petersburg, Virginia. The 39,000 Union forces accomplished little: "the campaign was a fiasco from the outset" (Eicher, *The Longest Night*, 680).

601. Major General Alfred Stedman Hartwell (1836–1912) had transferred from the 54th to the 55th Massachusetts. Maher points out that, according to Bob's own account in "Three Years' Service with the Fifty-Fifth Massachusetts Volunteer Infantry," this heroism belonged to a colleague called Dewhurst and Bob was not involved, though he did become

For this action he was breveted captain; and the 55th, later on, was the first body of troops to enter Charleston and march through its streets—which term of his experience, as it unfolded, presents him to my memory as again on staff duty; with Brigadier-Generals Potter, Rufus Hatch and his old superior and, at my present writing, gallant and vivid survivor, Alfred Hartwell,[602] who had been his captain and his lieut.-colonel in the 45th and the 55th respectively.*[603]

*My youngest brother's ingenuity was to know as little rest during much of his life as his strong faculty of agitation—to the employment of which it was indeed not least remarkably applied. Many illustrations of it would be to give, had I more margin; and not one of them anything less than striking, thanks to the vivacity of his intelligence, the variety of his gifts and the native ability in which he was himself so much less interested than was the case with everyone he met, however casually, that he became, many years before his death in 1910, our one gentleman of leisure: so far as this condition might consort with the easiest aptitude for admirable talk, charged with natural life, perception, humour and colour, that I have perhaps ever known. There were times when Bob's spoken overflow struck me as the equivalent, for fine animation, of William's epistolary. The note of the ingenious in him spent itself as he went, but I find an echo of one of its many incidents in the passage of verse that I am here moved to rescue from undue obscurity. It is too "amateurish" and has too many irregular lines, but images admirably the play of spirit in him which after ranging through much misadventure could at last drop to an almost effective grasp of the happiest relation.

> Although I lie so low and still
> Here came I by the Master's will;
> He smote at last to make me free,
> As He was smitten on the tree
> And nailèd there. He knew of old
> The human heart, and mine is cold;
> And I know now that all we gain
> Until we come to Him is vain.
> Thy hands have never wrought a deed,
> Thy heart has never known a need,
> That went astray in His great plan
> Since far-off days when youth began.
> For in that vast and perfect plan
> Where time is but an empty span
> Our Master waits. He knows our want,

---

a captain at this time. "Henry's crediting Bob with the deed may simply have been an error; however, Henry frequently used his *Autobiography* to portray his family in the way *he* wanted them to be seen" (*Biography of Broken Fortunes*, 69).

602. Brigadier general Edward Elmer Potter (1823–1889) and John Porter (not Rufus) Hatch (1822–1901). Potter served principally as General Foster's chief-of-staff during the war (Leonne M. Hudson, "The Role of the 54th. Massachusetts Regiment in Potter's Raid," *Historical Journal of Massachusetts* 30 [Summer 2002]: 181–97).

I can at all events speak perfectly of my own sense of the uplifting wave just alluded to during the couple of years that the "boys' " letters from the field came in to us—with the one abatement of glamour for them the fact that so much of their substance was in the whole air of life and their young reports of sharp experience but a minor pipe in the huge mixed concert

------

We know not his—till pale and gaunt
With weariness of life we come
And say to Him, What shall I be?
Oh Master, smite, but make me free
Perchance in these far worlds to know
The better thing we sought to be.

And then upon thy couch lie down
And fold the hands which have not sown;
And as thou liest there alone
Perhaps some breath from seraph blown
As soft as dew upon the rose
Will fall upon thee at life's close.
So thou wilt say, At last, at last!
All pain is love when pain is past!
And to the Master once again:
Oh keep my heart too weak to pray;
I ask no longer questions vain
Of life and love, of loss and gain—
These for the living are and strong;
I go to Thee, to Thee belong.
Once was I wakened by Thy light,
But years have passed, and now the night
Takes me to Thee. I am content;
So be it in Thy perfect plan
A mansion is where I am sent
To dwell among the innocent.

603. Bob led a difficult life after the war. Initially, he had wished to train as an architect, but this aspiration was not entertained by his parents. After an abortive attempt to run a cotton-growing enterprise with Wilky in Florida, he moved to Milwaukee and worked (like Wilky) as a clerk on the St. Paul Railway. He married Mary Holton in November 1872, and they had two children. Over time he was plagued by alcoholism, spending five years in the Dansville Asylum in New York State; his philandering led to the couple's spending much time apart, and he eventually lived for many years in Concord (where he is buried). Contact with HJ also became limited. Suffering from heart trouble, Bob died on 3 July 1910. With no permanent employment, he did a little writing, which is perhaps why HJ refers to his being a "gentleman of leisure." In the later 1870s Bob sent HJ some of his poems; the novelist wrote to their mother: "They have great and real beauty, in spite of their queerness and irregularity of form, and I shall be curious to see whether this form will grow more

always in our ears. Faded and touching pages, these letters are in some abundance before me now, breathing confidence and extraordinary cheer —though surviving principally but in Wilky's admirable hand, of all those I knew at that time the most humiliating to a feebler yet elder fist;[604] and with their liveliest present action to recompose for me not by any means so much the scenes and circumstances, the passages of history concerned, as to make me know again and reinhabit the places, the hours, the stilled or stirred conditions through which I took them in. These conditions seem indeed mostly to have settled for me into the single sense of what I missed, compared to what the authors of our bulletins gained, in wondrous opportunity of vision, that is *appreciation of the thing seen*[605]—there being clearly such a lot of this, and all of it, by my conviction, portentous and prodigious. The key to which assurance was that I longed to live by my eyes, in the midst of such far-spreading chances, in greater measure than I then had help to, and that the measure in which *they* had it gloriously overflowed. This capacity in them to deal with such an affluence of life stood out from every line, and images sprung up about them at every turn of the story. The story, the general one, of the great surge of action on which they were so early carried, was to take still other turns during the years I now speak of, some of these not of the happiest; but with the same relation to it on my own part too depressingly prolonged—that of seeing,

---

perfect. They are soft as moonbeams in a room at night—strangely pure in feeling" (31 January 1877, quoted in Maher, *Biography of Broken Fortunes*, 175). The poem included by HJ in his footnote has a religious emphasis typical of Bob: he was "strongly atracted to the Catholic church while at Dansville and wrote lengthy letters about its teachings, but it is not clear whether or not he actually converted. He later followed the teachings of the Christian Scientists, and finally he returned to Swedenborg" (ibid., 187).

604. Having apparently requested Wilky's letters of the 1860s, HJ wrote to thank his widow, Caroline (Carrie) Cary James, while also confessing the pain of revisiting the "faraway and yet so intimate ghostly past where everything and everyone lives again but to become lost over again, and what seems most to come forth are the old pains and suffering and mistakes. And yet Wilky's war letters are an extraordinary picture of young courage and cheery and happy reaction of every kind—making me recall so vividly the times we received them and all that convulsed public and private history, that they seem a story of another's life and world altogether" (*Alice James: Her Brothers*, 64). Indeed, as Lewis justly suggests, these letters constitute "Wilky's contribution to the family's literary achievement" (*The Jameses*, 127). The Houghton Library holds a number of Wilky's letters, written between December 1864 and May 1865 (bMS Am 1095 [5–11]); others are held by Mr. David James.

605. HJ may be alluding to Victor Hugo's *Choses vues*, the title for the large collection of Hugo's unpublished works which appeared posthumously in 1887.

sharing, envying, applauding, pitying, all from too far-off, and with the queer sense that, whether or no they would prove to have had the time of their lives, it seemed that the only time I should have had would stand or fall by theirs. This was to be yet more deplorably the case later on—I like to give a twitch to the curtain of a future reduced to the humility of a past: when, the War being over and we confronted with all the personal questions it had showily muffled up only to make them step forth with their sharper angles well upon us, our father, easily beguiled, acquired by purchase and for the benefit of his younger sons divers cottonlands in Florida;[606] which scene of blighted hopes it perhaps was that cast upon me, at its defiant distance, the most provoking spell. There was provocation, at those subsequent seasons, in the very place-name of Serenola, beautiful to ear and eye;[607] unforgettable were to remain the times, while the vain experiment dragged on for our anxiety and curiosity, and finally to our great discomfiture, when my still ingenuous young brothers, occupied in raising and selling crops that refused alike, it seemed, to come and to go, wafted northward their fluctuating faith, their constant hospitality and above all, for one of the number at home, their large unconscious evocations. The mere borrowed, and so brokenly borrowed, impression of southern fields basking in a light we didn't know, of scented sub-tropic nights, of a situation suffused with economic and social drama of the strangest and sharpest, worked in me, I dare say most deceptively, as a sign of material wasted, my material not being in the least the crops unproduced or unsold, but the precious store of images ungathered.[608] However,

606. Early in February 1866, Wilky and Bob James "joined five other onetime Union officers in purchasing 3,100 acres of land in Alachua County, in north central Florida, some miles above Gainesville. At $4.50 an acre, the transaction cost about $15,000, payable over three years; of this, the elder James was prepared to contribute some $4,300 for his two sons' share" (Lewis, *The Jameses,* 163). Though there is little definite information, Maher suggests (*Biography of Broken Fortunes,* 82) that there may have been other sponsors as well. Paul Fisher indicates that "Aunt Kate, too, contributed some of her carefully hoarded money" (*House of Wits: An Intimate Portrait of the James Family* [London: Little, Brown, 2008], 218). For a general account, see also Feinstein, *Becoming William James,* 285–93.

607. When crops proved disappointing in Waldo, Wilky then bought more land (with capital provided by his father) at Serenola, twenty miles to the north. Bob had withdrawn by this time and was unhappily working in Iowa. It is thought that this outlay of funds seriously and permanently depleted the fortune HJ Sr. had originally inherited.

608. One of HJ's earliest stories reflects this sentiment; see above, n. 399. The time spent in the reconstructing South was difficult for both the younger boys, however. Apart from difficult conditions, arduous labor, and illness, they had to contend with awkward

the vicarious sensation had, as I say, been intense enough, from point to point, before that; a series of Wilky's letters of the autumn of '62 and the following winter during operations in North Carolina intended apparently to clear an approach to Charleston overflow with the vivacity of his interest in whatever befell, and still more in whatever promised, and reflect, in this freshness of young assurances and young delusions, the general public fatuity.[609] The thread of interest for me here would certainly be much more in an exhibition of some such artless notes of the period, with their faded marks upon them, than in that of the spirit of my own poor perusal of them—were it not that those things shrink after years to the common measure when not testifying to some rarity of experience and expression. All experience in the field struck me indeed as then rare, and I wondered at both my brothers' military mastery of statement, through which played, on the part of the elder, a whimsicality of "turn," an oddity of verbal colloca-tion, that we had ever cherished, in the family circle, as the sign of his address. "The next fight we have, I expect," he writes from Newberne, N.C., on New Year's Day '63, "will be a pretty big one, but I am confident

---

colleagues and local hostility. The final failure of the enterprise replicated many North-erners' attempts to be part of a new agricultural economy.

609. At this time Wilky was in New Bern, east central North Carolina. He quickly became involved in skirmishes with Southern troops, and also witnessed his colleagues succumbing to fever and malaria. New Bern, at the mouth of the Neuse River, "was a point of much military importance. It was near the head of an extensive and navigable arm of the sea, and was connected by railway with Beaufort harbor at Morehead City, and Raleigh, the capital of the state." When Wilky arrived, "the coasts of North Carolina were in the possession of the National troops. Its ports were closed, either by actual occupation or by blockading vessels, and its commerce ceased entirely, excepting such as was carried on by British blockade-runners," as Benson J. Lossing records in his partisan but impressively detailed *Pictorial Field Book of the Civil War: Journeys through the Battlefields in the Wake of Conflict* (1870), 3 vols. (Baltimore: Johns Hopkins University Press, 1997), 2:305 n. 2, 315. Charleston was an important strategic goal, since the capture of "the very city in which the secession movement began would surely be psychologically damaging to the Con-federacy" (Eicher, *The Longest Night*, 564). It was, however, powerfully defended by coastal forts and batteries—as Wilky would discover in April 1863 when the 54th Mas-sachusetts mounted an attack on Fort Wagner. HJ made his first visit to Charleston in February 1905. As he stood on the Battery, "The Forts, faintly blue on the twinkling sea, looked like vague marine flowers; innocence, pleasantness ruled the prospect: it was as if the compromised slate, sponged clean of all the wicked words and hung up on the wall for better use, dangled there so vacantly as almost to look foolish. Ah, there again was the word: the air still just tasted of the antique folly" (*AS*, 413–14).

that under Foster[610] and our gunboats we will rid the State of these miserable wretches whom the Divine Providence has created in its wisdom to make men wish——! Send on then, open yourselves a recruiting establishment if necessary—all we want is numbers! *They* are the greatest help to the individual soldier on the battle-field. If he feels he has 30,000 men behind him pushing on steadily to back him he is in much more fighting trim than when away in the rear with 10,000 ahead of him fighting like madmen. It seems that Halleck[611] told Foster when F. was in Washington that he scarcely slept for a week after learning that we were near Goldsboro', having heard previously that a reinforcement of 40,000 Rebels were coming down there to whip us. Long live Foster!"[612]

"It was so cold this morning," he writes at another and earlier date, "that Divine service was held in our barracks instead of out-of-doors, as it generally is, and it was the most impressive that I have ever heard. The sermon was on profanity, and the chaplain, after making all the observations and doing by mouth and action as much as he could to rid the regiment of the curse, sat down, credulous being, thinking he had settled the question for ever. Colonel Lee then rose and said that the chaplain the other day accused him—most properly—of profanity and of its setting a very bad example to the regiment; also that when he took the command he

610. The veteran major general John G. Foster, "of Fort Sumter fame," was "in command of the troops in North Carolina" in 1862, and "in command of the coast islands of South Carolina when Sherman was engaged in the Georgia campaign" (Lossing, *Pictorial Field Book*, 2:167, 3:181, 412 n. 1).

611. Major General Henry W. Halleck was appointed on 23 July 1862 by President Lincoln to be general in chief of all U.S. armies. "Halleck would act as a sort of filter through which commanders in the field would communicate to the secretary of war and the president" (Eicher, *The Longest Night*, 304).

612. General Foster had set out for Goldsboro on 11 December 1862 to attack "the railway that connected Richmond with the Carolinas." After several skirmishes and quite heavy losses, the bridge over the Neuse River carrying the Weldon and Wilmington railway was destroyed, as well as "several other bridges, about six miles of the railway, and a half-finished iron-clad gun-boat" (Lossing, *Pictorial Field Book*, 3:181–83). The Confederate opposition was strong, though their numbers never reached 40,000. On 14 December Wilky and his regiment were involved "in an engagement of some intensity near Kinston, about forty miles inland from New Bern. . . . the very next day they marched seventeen miles to a spot near Whitehall, a small village on the Neuse, where the bloodiest episode in the small campaign took place." The following day they were engaged in action "at a point just below the village of Goldsboro, eighteen miles beyond Whitehall. The troops, under heavy fire, managed to destroy the railroad bridge across the Neuse" (Lewis, *The Jameses*, 128–29).

had felt how very bad the thing would be in its influence on all around him. He felt that it would be the great conflict of his life. At this point his head drooped and he lifted his handkerchief to his face; but he went on in conclusion: 'Now boys, let us try one and all to vindicate the sublime principles our chaplain has just so eloquently expressed, and I will do *my* best. I hope to God I have wounded no man's feelings by an oath; if I have I humbly beg his pardon.' Here he finished." How this passage impressed me at the time signifies little; but I find myself now feel in its illustration of what could then happen among soldiers of the old Puritan Common-wealth a rich recall of some story from Cromwellian ranks.[613] Striking the continuity, and not unworthy of it my brother's further comment. "I leave you to imagine which of these appeals did most good, the conventional address of the pastor or the honest manly heart-touching acknowledgment of our Colonel. That is the man through and through, and I heard myself say afterwards: 'Let him swear to all eternity if he *is* that sort of man, and if profanity makes such, for goodness' sake let us all swear.' This may be a bad doctrine, but is one that might after all undergo discussion."[614] From which letter I cull further: "I really begin to think you've been hard in your judgments of McClellan.[615] You don't know what an enemy we have to conquer. Every secesh[616] I've seen, and all the rebel prisoners here, talk of the War with such callous earnestness." A letter from Newberne of December 2nd contains a "pathetic" record of momentary faith, the sort so abundant at the time in what was not at all to be able to happen. Moreover a name rings out of it which it is a kind of privilege to give again

613. HJ links the moral values of the Puritan period in seventeenth-century England, when Oliver Cromwell (1599–1658) became head of the Commonwealth, with those of the soldiers of civil war in the new world. For the idea of a national providentialism in the American Civil War period, see Nicholas Guyatt, *Providence and the Invention of the United States, 1607–1876* (Cambridge: Cambridge University Press, 2007), 259–98.

614. This reads very much as if appealing to the taste of HJ Sr. and the kind of discussion that might occur at home.

615. Major General George Brinton McClellan (1826–85), from May 1861 to March 1862 general in chief of the Union armies, was then assigned to lead the Department and Army of the Potomac from September to November 1862. Generally thought to have been disastrously tentative and indecisive as a commander (though greatly admired by the men who served under him), he was removed by Lincoln and never returned to military service. The female protagonist of HJ's "The Story of a Year" has a photograph of the general in her bedroom. Always politically involved, he was later rehabilitated in the guise of Democratic presidential candidate in 1864.

616. "Secesh," or secessionist.

to the air—when one can do so with some approach to an association signified; so much did Charles Lowell's virtue and value and death represent at the season soon to come for those who stood within sight of them, and with such still unextinct emotion may the few of these who now survive turn to his admirably inspired kinsman's Harvard Commemoration Ode and find it infinitely and tenderly suffused with pride. Two gallantest nephews, particularly radiant to memory, had James Russell Lowell to commemorate.[617]

> I sweep for them a pæan, but they wane
> > Again and yet again
> Into a dirge and die away in pain.
> In these brave ranks I only see the gaps,
> Thinking of dear ones whom the dumb turf wraps,
> Dark to the triumph which they died to gain.

Cabot has had news that Mr. Amos Lawrence of Boston is getting up a cavalry regiment (Wilky writes),[618] and he has sent home to try for a commission as 2nd lieutenant. Now if we could only *both* get such a commission in that regiment you can judge yourself how desirable it would be. Perkins will probably have one in the Massachusetts 2nd and our orderly stands a pretty good chance

617. Brigadier General Charles Russell Lowell (1835–64) was a nephew of James Russell Lowell, the husband of Josephine (Effie) Shaw Lowell, sister of Robert Gould Shaw; he belonged to the Harvard class of 1854. "Lowell, also known as Beau Sabreur, was one of the most romantically dashing of Union officers; he had thirteen horses shot from under him before he was mortally wounded at Cedar Creek, Virginia, in October 1864" (Lewis, *The Jameses*, 129n). The Cedar Creek engagement in the Shenandoah Valley in October 1864 brought heavy casualties to both sides; having been hit in the arm and lungs, Lowell died the next day (Eicher, *The Longest Night*, 752). Charles's brother James Jackson Lowell (aged twenty-three when the war broke out) left the Dane Law School at Harvard in 1861 (a year before HJ arrived) to enlist. On McClellan's retreat to the Potomac he was killed at Glendale (see Edward Everett Hale, *James Russell Lowell and His Friends* [London: Constable, 1899], 183–84; and for a highly informed account of the entire family, Bundy's *The Nature of Sacrifice*). According to the memorial tablets in Harvard's Memorial Hall, Lowell was of the class of 1858 and died on 4 July 1862. James Russell Lowell's "Ode recited at the Harvard Commemoration, 21 July 1865" was a poem that HJ greatly admired, fascinated by the way in which "the air of the study mingles with the hot breath of passion" ("James Russell Lowell," *Atlantic Monthly*, January 1892; *LC*, 1:529).

618. Amos Lawrence (1814–86) was the son of a Boston philanthropist of the same name and a prominent abolitionist.

of one in the 44th.[619] This cavalry colonelcy will probably be for Cabot's cousin, Charles Lowell.[620]

There is a report that we start this week for Kinston, and if so we shall doubtless have a good little fight.[621] We have just received 2 new Mass. Regiments, the 8th and the 51st. We have absolutely no time to ourselves; and what time we do have we want much more to give to lying down than to anything else. But try your best for me now, and I promise you to do *my* best wherever I am.

A homelier truth is in a few lines three weeks later.

The men as a general thing think war a mean piece of business as it's carried on in this State; we march 20 or 30 miles and find the enemy entrenched in riflepits or hidden away in some out-of-the-way place; we send our artillery forward, and after a brisk skirmish ahead the foe is driven back into the woods, and we march on for 20 miles more to find the same luck. We were all on the last march praying for a fight, so that we might halt and throw off our knapsacks. I don't pretend I am eager to make friends with bullets, but at Whitehall,[622] after marching some 20 miles, I was on this account really glad when I heard cannonading ahead and the column was halted and the fight began.

The details of this engagement are missing from the letter, but we found matter of interest in two or three other passages—one in particular recording a December day's march with 15,000 men, "not including artillerymen," 70 pieces of artillery and 1100 cavalry; which, "on account of obstructions on the roads," had achieved by night but seventeen miles and resulted in a bivouac "in 3 immense cotton-fields, one about as large as Easton's Pond at Newport."[623]

We began to see the camp fires of the advance brigade about 4 miles ahead of us, and I assure you those miles were soon got over. I think

619. This refers to William E. Perkins, who became a lieutenant with the 2nd Massachusetts Infantry.

620. Cabot Russel's maternal aunt was Anna Cabot Jackson, wife of Charles Russell Lowell Sr. and mother of Charles Russell Lowell Jr.

621. A later letter recounts this episode below.

622. A small village on the Neuse River. This is part of the same North Carolina engagement detailed in n. 609 above.

623. Easton's North Pond and South Pond are to the northeast of Newport, not far from where the Jameses had lived.

Willy's artistic eye would have enjoyed the sight—it seemed so as if the world were on fire. When we arrived on the field the stacks were made, the ranks broken and the men sent after rail fences, which fortunately abound in this region and are the only comfort we have at night. A long fire is made, the length of the stacks, and one rank is placed on one side of it and the other opposite. I try to make a picture you see, but scratch it out in despair. The fires made, we sit down and make our coffee in our tin dippers, and often is one of these pushed over by some careless wretch who hasn't noticed it on the coals or has been too tired to look. The coffee and the hard tack consumed we spread our rubber blankets and sleep as sound as any house in Christendom. At about 5 the fearful reveille calls us to our feet, we make more coffee, drink it in a hurry, sling our knapsacks and spank down the road in one of Foster's regular old quicksteps.

Thrilling at our fireside of course were the particulars of the Kinston engagement,[624] and still more, doubtless, the happy freshness of the writer.

At 8 A.M. we were on the road, and had hardly marched 3 miles when we knew by sounds ahead that the ball had opened. We were ordered up and deployed in an open field on the right of the road, where we remained some half an hour. Then we were moved some hundred yards further, but resumed our former position in another field. Here Foster came up to the Major, who was directly in the rear of our company and told him to advance our left wing to support Morrison's[625] battery, which was about half a mile ahead. He also said he was pressing the Rebs hard and that they were retiring at every shell from our side. On we went, the left flank company taking the lead, and many a bullet and shell whizzed over our heads in that longest half-mile of my life. We seemed to be nearing the fun, for

624. "[General] Foster then pressed on toward Kinston, skirmishing heavily on the way, and when within a mile of that village, he encountered a larger force (about six thousand) . . . well posted between the Neuse River and an impassable swamp. After a sharp fight the Confederates were driven across the river. They fired the bridge behind them, but the flames were put out, and about four hundred of the fugitives were made prisoners, with eleven guns and a large amount of commissary stores" (Lossing, *Pictorial Field Book,* 3:183). The same area, incidentally, would see further action during Sherman's sweep northward from Georgia near the end of the war, in March 1865.

625. I have found no other information on this Union officer.

wounded men were being carried to the rear and dead ones lay on each side of us in the woods. We were taken into another field on the left of the road, and before us were deployed the 23rd Mass., who were firing in great style. First we were ordered to lie down, and then in 5 or 10 minutes ordered up again, when we charged down that field in a manner creditable to any Waterloo legion. I felt as if this moment was the greatest of my life and as if all the devils of the Inferno were my benighted system. We halted after having charged some 60 yards, when what should we see on our left, just out of the woods and stuck up on a rail, but a flag of truce, placing under its protecting wing some 50 or 60 poor cowering wretches who, in their zeal for recognition, not only pulled out all their pocket handkerchiefs, but in the case of one man spread out his white shirt-flaps and offered them pacifically to the winds. The most demonic shouts and yells were raised by the 23rd ahead of us at this sight, in which the 44th joined; while the regiments on our right, and that of the road, greeted in the same frightful manner 200 prisoners they had cut off from retreat by the bridge. So far I was alive and the thing had lasted perhaps 3 hours; all the enemy but the 200 just named had got away over the bridge to Kinston and our cavalry were in hot pursuit. I don't think Sergeant G. W. has ever known greater glee in all his born days. At about 3 P.M. we crossed the bridge and got into the town. All along the road from bridge to town Rebel equipments, guns and cartridge-boxes lay thick, and within the place dead men and horses thickened too. We were taken ahead through the town to support the New York 3rd Artillery beyond, where it was shelling the woods around and ridding the place for the night of any troublesome wanderers. The Union pickets posted out ahead that night said the shrieks of women and children further on in the wood could be heard perfectly all night long, these unfortunates having taken refuge there from the threatened town. That night we lived like fighting-cocks—molasses, pork, butter, cheese and all sorts of different delicacies being foraged for and houses entered regardless of the commonest dues of life, and others set on fire to show Kinston was our own.[626] She belonged to our army, and almost every man

626. On a much worse scale, Wilky and his 54th Massachusetts were notoriously commanded to loot and burn the town of Darien, on the Altamaha River in Georgia, to the disgust of their commander, Colonel Shaw. He was obeying the orders of the "eccentric Kansas jayhawker Col. James Montgomery," who told him, "'I shall burn this town,' explaining that the Southerners 'must be made to feel that this was a real war, and that they

claimed a house. If I had only had your orders beforehand for trophies I could have satisfied you with anything named, from a gold watch to an old brickbat. This is the ugly part of war. A too victorious army soon goes down; but we luckily didn't have time for big demoralisation, as the next day in the afternoon we found ourselves some 17 miles away and bivouacking in a single prodigious cornfield.

To which I don't resist subjoining another characteristic passage from the same general scene as a wind-up to that small chapter of history.

The report has gained ground to-day that we leave to-morrow, and if so I suppose the next three months will be important ones in the history of the War. Four ironclads and a great many gunboats are in Beaufort Harbour;[627] we have at present a force of 50,000 infantry, an immense artillery and upwards of 800 cavalry. Transports innumerable are filling up every spare inch of our harbour, and every man's pity and charity are exercised upon Charleston, Mobile or Wilmington.[628] We are the only nine-months regiment going, a fact which to the sensitive is highly gratifying, showing Foster's evident high opinion of us. The expedition, I imagine, will be pretty interesting, for we shall have excitement enough without the fearful marches. To-day is Sunday, and I've been reading Hugo's account of Waterloo in Les Misérables and preparing my mind for something of the same sort at Wilmington.[629] God grant the battle may do as much harm to the Rebels as Waterloo did to the French. If it does the fight will be worth the dreadful carnage it may involve, and the experience for the survivors an immense treasure. Men will fight forever if they are well treated. Give them little marching and keep the wounded away from

were to be swept away by the hand of God like the Jews of old'" (Eicher, *The Longest Night*, 499). According to Wilky, Montgomery felt such methods "a fitting compensation for all these early sufferings of the abolitionists" ("Story of the War").

627. Beaufort, sixty miles south of Charleston, was "a delightful city on Port Royal Island, where the most aristocratic portion of South Carolina society had summer residences" (Lossing, *Pictorial Field Book*, 2:124). The Confederates were driven out on 7 November 1861, and the place was taken over by Union forces who used it as a supply and repair center.

628. Major Southern ports in South Carolina, Alabama, and North Carolina blockaded during the war (though Wilmington was the last Confederate port to fall—as late as January 1865).

629. In Victor Hugo's *Les misérables* (1862), "Cosette," the second of five sections, treats the Battle of Waterloo at considerable length.

them, and they'll do anything. I am very well and in capital spirits, though now and then rather blue about home. But only 5 months more and then heaven! General Foster has just issued an order permitting us to inscribe Goldsboro, Kinston and Whitehall on our banner.

On the discharge of the 44th after the term of nine months for which it had engaged and my brother's return home, he at once sought service again in the Massachusetts 54th, his connection with which I have already recorded, as well as his injuries in the assault on Fort Wagner fruitlessly made by that regiment in the summer of '63. He recovered with difficulty, but at last sufficiently, from his wounds (with one effect of which he had for the rest of his short life grievously to reckon),[630] and made haste to rejoin his regiment in the field—to the promotion of my gathering a few more notes. From "off Graham's Point, Tillapenny River, Headquarters 2nd Brigade," he writes in December '64.[631]

We started last night from the riflepits in the front of Deveaux Neck to cross the Tillapenny and make a reconnaissance on this side and try and get round the enemy's works. It is now half-past 10 A.M., and I have been trying to wash some of my mud off.[632] We are all a sorry

630. As HJ indicates later in the chapter, Wilky would afterward walk with a limp.

631. Wilky, having undergone a second convalescence, had returned to the 54th on Morris Island only at the beginning of December 1864. Moving inland south toward Pocotaligo, twenty-five miles from Beauport and close to the Charleston-Savannah railroad, part of the regiment met up with General Sherman's forces, and the city of Savannah would be surrendered on the night of 20 December. When Wilky wrote to one of his Albany relatives, Jeannette Gourlay, on 28 December, his morale was understandably affected by the difficult physical conditions: "For the last 3 weeks the Coast Division of 4 Brigades have been making an unsuccessful movement in cooperation with Sherman. They started fresh & in good spirits with 6000 effective men; they have fought 4 battles, been whipped once & lost 2000 men. Such in brief is the eventful but fruitless history of the grand diversion in favor of Gen'l Sherman, recorded by one its most fearless & prominent participators. If I was not quite so muddy & dirty & sleepy & hungry, I might be able to tell you more, but mud & dirt are fearful impediments to sleep & hunger terribly demoralizing faculties. Suffice it to say that when the time comes for us to draw in our pickets & pull up our stakes here, & once more turn faceward to Morris Island & there get clean, get food & sleep your humble servt will try & tell you something more of this memorable campaign up the Tillapenny.—" (MS letter, bMS Am 1095 [8], Houghton).

632. Deveaux or, more usually, Deveaux's Neck lies between the Tulifinny (rather than Tillapenny) River and the Coosawhatchie River in Jasper County, South Carolina, just north of Savannah. Compare Emilio (who also mentions the incessant rain): "Potter's and

crowd of beggars—I don't look as I did the night we left home. I am much of the time mud from head to foot, and my spirit is getting muddled also. But I am in excellent condition as regards my wounds and astonish myself by my powers. I rode some 26 miles yesterday and walked some 3 in thick mud, but don't feel a bit the worse for it. We're only waiting here an hour or two to get a relief of horses, when we shall start again. We shan't have a fight of any kind to-day, but to-morrow expect to give them a little trouble at Pocotaligo. Colonel Hallowell commands this reconnaissance. We have only 4 regiments and a section of artillery from the 2nd Brigade with us. We heard some fine music from the Rebel lines yesterday. They have got a stunning band over there. Prisoners tell us it's a militia band from Georgia.[633] Most all the troops in our front are militia composed of old men and boys, the flower of the chivalry being just now engaged with Sherman at Savannah. We hear very heavy firing in that direction this morning, and I guess the chivalry is getting the worst of it. The taking of Fort McAllister the other day was a splendid thing—we got 280 prisoners and made them go out and pick up the torpedoes round the fort.[634] Sherman was up at Oguchee and Ossahaw yesterday on another consultation with Foster.[635] We had called our whole army out the

------

the Naval Brigade landed on the 6th at Deveaux's Neck, and with the howitzers pushed toward the railroad, which, crossing the Neck by means of a bridge over the Coosa-whatchie, ran over the peninsula and left it by another bridge spanning the Tullifinny River. Potter, leading his skirmishers, forced back the enemy's light troops, making a few cap-tures" (*A Brave Black Regiment*, 256). HJ was probably dependent on Wilky's spelling of the Tullifinny River, though in fact he spells it in a number of ways. See also n. 663 below.

633. "At the beginning of the war, brass bands accompanied many units into service, and they were constant sources of entertainment throughout the conflict" (Gallagher et al., *This Mighty Scourge of War*, 149–50).

634. The attack on Fort McAllister in Bryan County, Georgia, south of Savannah, took place on 12 December 1864 and was accomplished in thirteen minutes. The 54th heard the news on the evening of 14 December. When it was taken, Sherman could establish contact with the Union fleet as well as threaten Savannah with destruction, "a brilliant ending of the Great March from the Chattahoochee to the sea," as Lossing believed (*Pictorial Field Book*, 3:412–13). In the event, Major General William Joseph Hardee (1815–73), the Con-federate commander, slipped away from Savannah with 15,000 men, heading for Charles-ton and abandoning the city to the Northern forces. On 22 December Sherman famously wrote to Lincoln: "I beg to present you as a Christmas gift the City of Savannah with 150 heavy guns & plenty of ammunition & also about 25,000 bales of cotton" (Eicher, *The Longest Night*, 768). The torpedoes mentioned by Wilky were crude landmines.

635. The 230-mile Ogeechee (rather than Oguchee) River reaches the ocean sixteen

night before in front of our works to give him three cheers. This had a marvellous effect upon the Rebs. About 20 men came in the night into our lines, thinking we had got reinforcements and were going to advance. *Later.* A scout has just come in and tells us the enemy are intrenched about 4 miles off, so that we *shall* have to-day a shindy of some kind. Our headquarters are now in a large house once owned by Judge Graham.[636] The coloured troops are in high spirits and have done splendidly this campaign.

The high spirits of the coloured troops appear naturally to have been shared by their officers—"in the field, Tillapenny River," late at night on December 23rd, '64.

We have just received such bully news to comfort us that I can't help rising from my slumbers to drop you a line. A despatch just received tells us that Sherman has captured 150 guns, 250,000 dols. worth of cotton at Savannah, that Forrest is killed and routed by Rousseau, and that Thomas has walked into Hood and given him the worst kind of fits.[637] I imagine the poor Rebel outposts in our front feel pretty blue to-night, for what with that and the thermometer at about zero I guess the night won't pass without robbing their army of some of its best and bravest. We suffer a good deal from the cold, but are now sitting round our camp fire in as good spirits as men could possibly be. A despatch received early this evening tells us to look out sharp for Hardee, but this latest news knocks that to a cocked hat, and we are only just remembering that that gentleman is round.[638] My foot is bully.

---

miles south of Savannah; Fort McAllister was built on the south bank near its mouth, regarded by Sherman "as a proper avenue of future supply for his troops, from the sea" (Lossing, *Pictorial Field Book,* 3:411). Ossabaw (rather than Ossahaw) Sound, where river and ocean meet, is the largest sound on the coast of Georgia.

636. "Graham's Neck . . . is the point of land between the Tullifinny and Pocotaligo rivers" (Emilio, *A Brave Black Regiment,* 263), just south of Deveaux's Neck. Presumably Judge Graham owned the estate originally.

637. Wilky refers to decisive events in Tennessee. The Confederate commander brigadier general Nathan Bedford Forrest (1821–77) and his troops were routed by the Union general Lovell Harrison Rousseau (1818–69) at Pulaski and later at Columbia; after a series of engagements, Union forces under Major General George Henry Thomas (1816–70) defeated Confederate troops led by Major General John Bell Hood (1831–79) in battle at Nashville on 15 December 1864.

638. Hardee, having moved northward, would evacuate a ruined Charleston in February 1865.

As regards that impaired member, on which he was ever afterwards considerably to limp, he opines three days later, on Christmas evening,[639] that "even in the palmy days of old it never *felt* better than now." And he goes on:

Though Savannah is taken I fear we shan't get much credit for having helped to take it. Yet night and day we have been at it hammer and tongs, and as we are away from the main army and somewhat isolated and cut off our work has been pretty hard. We have had only 1,200 effective men in our brigade, and out of that number have had regularly 400 on picket night and day, and the fatigue and extra guard duty have nearly used them up. Twice we have been attacked and both times held our own. Twice we attacked and once have been driven. The only prisoners we have captured on the whole expedition have been taken by this part of the column, and on the whole though we didn't march into Savannah I know you will give us a little credit for having hastened its downfall. Three prisoners that we took the other night slept at our Hdqrs, and we had a good long talk with them. We could get out of them nothing at all that helps from a military point of view, but their stories about the Confederacy were most hopeless. They were 3 officers and gentlemen of a crack S.C. cavalry company which has been used during the War simply to guard this coast, and their language and state of mind were those of the true Southern chevalier.[640] They confessed to a great scare on finding themselves hemmed in by coloured troops, and all agree that the niggers are the worst enemies they have had to face. On Thursday we turned them over to the Provost-Marshal at Deveaux Neck, who took them to Gen'l Hatch.[641] The General had got our despatch announcing we could get

639. Presumably HJ means one, or possibly two days later.
640. Wilky makes further reference to this incident in his 13 January 1865 letter to Ellen Shaw: "From several prisoners taken at this fight we learnt some curious facts in regard to the organization of this corps. It seems that they were all 'landed gentry' from the District of Beaufort & St Johns whose only duty had been since the beginning of the war to guard the coast & their own firesides. They supplied their own horses & arms & equipments, and every two men were allowed to have a cart & horse to carry round their tents & household goods. // I should judge from what I saw & heard of them, that they were the fiercest kind of rebels. Men who as yet had suffered very little from the war, either in battle or in worldly possessions & who had become more & more envenomed with sectional hatred as the lines tightened round their domain" (bMS Am 1095 [31], Houghton).
641. Brigadier General John Porter Hatch.

nothing at all out of them, and he came down on them most ruthlessly and told them to draw lots, as one would have to swing before night. He told them he had got the affidavit of an escaped Union prisoner, a man captured at Honey Hill[642] and who had come into our lines the day previous, to the effect that he had witnessed the hanging of a negro soldier belonging to the 26th U.S.C.T., and that he had determined one of them should answer for it. Two seemed very much moved, but the third, Lee by name (cousin of Gen'l Stephen Lee of the cavalry),[643] said he knew nothing about it, but if it was so, so it might be. The other two were taken from each other and Gen'l Hatch managed to draw a good deal of information from them about our position, that is the force and nature of the enemy and works in our front. Lee refused to the last to answer any question whatever, and they all 3 now await at Hilton Head the issue of the law.[644] The hanging of the negro seems a perfectly ascertained fact—he was hung by the 48th Georgia Infty, and the story has naturally much stirred up our coloured troops. If Hardee should decide to come down on us I believe he would get the worst of it, and only hope now that our men won't take a prisoner alive. They certainly make a great mistake at Washington in not attending to these little matters, and I am sure the moral effect of an order from the President announcing that such things have happened, and that the coloured troops have taken them thoroughly to heart, would be greater on the Rebels than any physical blow we can deal them.

When I read again, "in the field before Pocotaligo," toward the middle of January '65, that "Sherman leaves to-night from Beaufort with Logan's Corps[645] to cross Beaufort Ferry and come up on our right flank and push on to Pocotaligo bridge," the stir as from great things rises again for me,

642. "Three miles south of Grahamville Station, South Carolina, at Honey Hill, Hatch attacked and fought a bloody action against Gustavus Smith's 1,400 Georgia militia troops on November 30 [1864]" (Eicher, *The Longest Night*, 766-77). This was a major engagement for the 54th (Emilio, *A Brave Black Regiment*, 236-53).

643. Lieutenant General Stephen Dill Lee (1833-1908) of the Confederacy.

644. The Union headquarters, the Department of the South, was located at Hilton Head on the South Carolina coast, north of Savannah. It was the base for the Union's blockading of Southern ports; many former slaves also found refuge there.

645. General John Alexander Logan (1826-86), who had been given charge of the Army of the Tennessee the previous year after Major General James B. McPherson (1828-64) had been killed at Atlanta.

wraps about Sherman's name as with the huge hum that then surrounded it, and in short makes me give the passage such honour as I may.[646] "We are waiting anxiously for the sound of his musketry announcing him." I was never in my life to wait for any such sound, but *how* at that juncture I hung about with privileged Wilky! "We all propose at Hdqrs to take our stores out and ride up to the bank of the river and watch the fight on the other side. We are praying to be relieved here—our men are dying for want of clothing; and when we see Morris Island again we shall utterly rejoice." He writes three days later from headquarters established in a plantation the name of which, as well as that of the stream, of whatever magnitude, that they had crossed to reach it, happens to be marked by an illegibility quite unprecedented in his splendid script—to the effect of a still intenser evocation (as was then to be felt at any rate) of all the bignesses involved. "Sherman's whole army is in our front, and they expect to move on Charleston at any moment."[647] Sherman's whole army!—it affected me from afar off as a vast epic vision. The old vibration lives again,

646. HJ's feelings about Sherman are, many years later, more divided. Writing about Saint-Gaudens's public memorial to Sherman at the southeast end of New York's Central Park, he believed the sculptor had tried to reconcile the general's too disparate roles as destroyer and benefactor: "I would have had a Sherman of the terrible march (the 'immortal' march, in all abundance, if that be the needed note), not irradiating benevolence, but signifying, by every ingenious device, the misery, the ruin and the vengeance of his track" (*AS*, 173–74). Wilky wrote to Ellen (Nelly) Shaw on 13 January 1865, "Since this reconnaissance we have sent out 5 or 6 others & the last one made by the 54th. has I think been the most satisfactory one. They got nearer to Pocotaligo than the Union Army have ever been. Col. Harper with 180 men started on Saturday with orders to devellope the enemies lines & if possible skirmish them out of their outposts. He advanced some 3 miles, avoided the causeway where 3 years before Gen'l Mitchell lost 900 men, & came up within musket shot of their advanced works. The rebels gave us here some 10 or 12 rounds of musketry, & retired to support their artillery on the knoll behind their outer works. We got valuable information here in regard to the disposition of their defenses & to the number of their troops, and retired in poor condition, but just in time to save ourselves. From information drawn from this reconnaissance & previous ones in the same direction, I think that the long delayed destruction of the bridge is more reasonably accounted for than it has ever been before" (bMS Am 1095 [31], Houghton).

647. Sherman had ensured that his goals in South Carolina, the state regarded as the breeding ground of rebellion, would remain unclear. "On February 14, Sherman's men crossed the Congaree River and moved on Columbia, not 'wasting time' with Charleston, as Sherman termed it" (Eicher, *The Longest Night*, 799). Columbia was decimated by fire; Charleston was evacuated at the same time, ruined by Hardee and his retreating troops so that as little as possible would be left for Union forces.

but with it also that of the smaller and nearer, the more intimate notes—
such for instance as: "I shall go up to the 20th Corps to-morrow and try
for a sight of Billy Perkins and Sam Storrow in the 2nd Mass."[648] Into
which I somehow read, under the touch of a ghostly hand no more
"weirdly" laid than *that,* more volumes than I can the least account for or
than I have doubtless any business to.

My visionary yearning must however, I think, have drawn most to feed
on from the first of a series of missives dated from Headquarters, Department of the South, Hilton Head S.C., this particular one of the middle of
February. "I write in a great hurry to tell you I have been placed on
General Gillmore's staff as A.D.C. It is just the very thing for my foot
under present circumstances, and I consider myself most fortunate.[649] I
greatly like the General, who is most kind and genial and very considerate.
My duties will be principally the carrying of orders to Savannah, Morris
Island, Fortress Monroe, Combalee (?) Florida,[650] and the General's correspondence. Charleston is ours," he goes on two days later: "it surrendered to a negro regiment yesterday at 9 A.M.[651] We have just come
up from Sumter, where we have hoisted the American flag. We were lying
off Bull's Bay[652] yesterday noon waiting for this when the General saw
through his glass the stars and stripes suddenly flown from the town hall.
We immediately steamed up to Sumter and ran up the colours there. Old

648. For Billy Perkins, see above, n. 619. Samuel Storrow, born in 1843, was killed at
Averyborough (Black Creek) in North Carolina on 16 March 1865. See *Memoirs of the War
of '61: Colonel Charles Russell Lowell, Friends and Cousins* [compiled by Elizabeth Cabot
Putnam] (Boston: Ellis, 1920), 57.

649. General Quincy Adams Gillmore (1825–88). "On a reconnaissance in later January, Wilky was thrown from his horse and partially redamaged his foot. He was immediately transferred to the headquarters of the Department of the South at Hilton Head, and
made aide-de-camp to his old chief, General Gillmore. His new duties, which he found not
without interest, had him shuttling up and down the departmental area from South Carolina to Florida" (Lewis, *The Jameses,* 153). In February 1865 he was promoted to captain.

650. Fort (or Fortress) Monroe on the southeastern border of Virginia, "situated at the
tip of the finger of land between the York and James rivers known as the Peninsula"
(Gallagher et al., *This Mighty Scourge of War,* 46), occupied an important strategic position. The "most extensive military work in the country," it acted, according to Lossing, as
"the massive key to the waters of Maryland, Virginia, and Upper North Carolina" (Lossing, *Pictorial Field Book,* 1:499). Though HJ transcribes "Combalee," Wilky may have
been referring to the Combahee River in South Carolina.

651. The 55th Massachusetts, in which Bob had become a captain.

652. Bull's Bay is a wide bay on the coast north of Charleston.

Gillmore was in fine feather and I am in consummate joy."[653] The joy nevertheless, I may add, doesn't prevent the remark after a couple of days more that "Charleston isn't on the whole such a very great material victory; in fact the capture of the place is of value only in that its moral effect tends to strengthen the Union cause." After which he proceeds:

Governor Aiken of S.C.[654] came up to Hdqrs to-day to call on the Gen'l, and they had a long talk. He is a "gradual Emancipationist" and says the worst of the President's acts was his sweeping Proclamation.[655]

653. Maher (*Biography of Broken Fortunes,* 53) quotes from two newspaper accounts from correspondents of the *Boston Journal* and the *Tribune* which record Wilky's proud but sad memories of the assault on Fort Wagner. The writer for the *Boston Journal* observed, for instance, "a young officer, looking musingly and long toward Morris Island—sitting there, the old flag floating over his head, apparently unconscious of everything around him. He walked away at last—rather haltingly, for he was lame and wounded—still gazing toward Wagner. It was Lieut. James." Wilky reported events to his sister, Alice, on 22 February 1865, on returning to the Department of the South after visiting Charleston: "We stopped at Sumpter [*sic*] on the way back & the band with the old flag played Yankee Doodle and the Star Spangled banner. Charleston looks pretty well used up, our shot & shell during the last year having hastened somewhat the destruction which the city was eventually to fall heir to. It was without exception the proudest moment of my life when we stepped into Fort Sumpter & Genl Gillmore took of [*sic*] his hat & with the whole staff around him called for nine rousing cheers for the good old flag which waved above us. We took 200 pieces of artillery & plenty of ordnance supplies. The cotton was nearly all burned. The rebs just before leaving set fire to one of the arsenals & killed 250 men women & children. Such is the barbarity of these cursed wretches. // The town is full of poor whites & negroes & the latters enthusiasm cannot be quenched. I never saw anything like them, they fall about you & cling to you fairly with delight" (MS letter, bMS Am 1095 [11], Houghton).

654. William Aiken Jr. (1806–87) was a rice planter and, with 700 slaves, one of the largest slave owners of the South. He became governor of South Carolina in 1844 for a two-year term, and was elected to the U.S. Congress from 1851 to 1857. He took no part in secession and treated his slaves so humanely that many chose to remain with him during Reconstruction. Various biographical resources itemize his enduring wealth. Wilky's comments about the governor's shortage of clothes and indeed that he was disappointed at "the ingratitude of the Negro" may refer to a temporary condition.

655. Lincoln's Emancipation Proclamation came into effect on New Year's Day 1863, declaring that all slaves held within the named states which had rebelled against the United States (and over which, of course, Lincoln had dubious authority) should be "then, thenceforward, and forever free; and the executive government of the United States, including the military and naval authority thereof, will recognize and maintain the freedom of such persons and will do no act or acts to repress such persons, or any of them, in any efforts they may make for their actual freedom" (*The American Civil War: Literary Sources*

Before that every one in this State was ready to come back on the gradual system, and would have done so if Lincoln's act hadn't driven them to madness. This is all fine talk, but there is nothing in it. They had at least 5 months' warning and could have in that time perfectly returned within the fold; in fact the strong Abolitionists of the North were afraid the President had made the thing but too easy for them and that they would get ahead of us and themselves emancipate. This poor gentleman is simple crazy and weakminded. Between Davis[656] and us he is puzzled beyond measure, and doesn't know what line to take. One thing though troubled him most, namely the ingratitude of the negro. He can't conceive how the creatures he has treated with such extraordinary kindness and taken such care of should all be willing to leave him. He says he was the first man in the South to introduce religion among the blacks and that his plantation of 600 of them was a model of civilisation and peace. Just think of this immense slaveholder telling me as I drove him home that the coat be had on had been turned three times and his pantaloons the only ones he possessed. He stated this so simply and touchingly that I couldn't help offering him a pair of mine—which he refused, however. There are some 10,000 people in the town, mostly women and negroes, and it's tremendously ravaged by our shell, about which they have naturally lied from beginning to end.

"Bob has just come down from Charleston," he writes in March—"he has been commissioned captain in the 103rd U.S.C.T. I am sorry he has left his regiment, still he seemed bent on doing so and offers all kinds of reasons for it. He may judge rightly, but I fear he's hasty;" and indeed this might appear from a glimpse of our younger brother at his ease given by him in a letter of some days before, written at two o'clock in the morning and recording a day spent in a somewhat arduously performed visit to Charleston. "I drove out to the entrenchments to-day to see B., and found him with Hartwell (R. J.'s[657] colonel) smoking their long pipes on the verandah of a neat country cottage with a beautiful garden in front of them and the birds chirping and rambling around. Bob looks remarkably well and seemed very nice indeed. He speaks very highly of Hartwell, and the latter the same of him. They seemed settled in remarkable comfort at

---

and Documents, ed. Jon Roper [Mountfield, East Sussex: Helm Information, 2000], 2:301–2).

656. Jefferson Davis (1808–89) was the Confederate president.

657. Robertson (Bob) James.

Charleston and to be taking life easy after their 180 miles march through South Carolina."[658] He mentions further that his visit to the captured city,[659] begun the previous day, had been made in interesting conditions; there is in fact matter for quotation throughout the letter, the last of the small group from which I shall borrow. He had, with his general, accompanied a "large Senatorial delegation from Washington and shown them round the place." He records the delegation's "delight" in what they saw; how "a large crowd of young ladies" were of the party, so that the Senatorial presences were "somewhat relieved and lightened to the members of the staff;" and also that they all went over to Forts Sumter and Moultrie and the adjacent works.[660] The pleasure of the whole company in the scene of desolation thus presented is one of those ingenuous historic strokes that the time-spirit, after a sufficient interval, permits itself to smile at—and is not the only such, it may be noted, in the sincere young statement.

> To-morrow they go to Savannah, returning here in the evening, when there is to be a grand reception for them at Hdqrs. We expect Gen'l Robert Anderson (the loyalist commandant at Sumter when originally fired upon) by the next steamer, with Gideon Welles (secretary of the Navy) and a number of other notables from Washington. Anderson is going to raise the old flag on Sumter, and of course there will be a great shindy here—I only wish you were with us to join in it.[661] I never go to

658. Bob had traveled to Columbia, South Carolina, with General Hartwell and his troops. It was a city ruined by fire; there is a degree of doubt about the extent to which Sherman's advancing forces caused the devastation (see, e.g., Bruce Catton, *Never Call Retreat,* vol. 3 of *The Centennial History of the American Civil War* [London: Phoenix Press, 1963, 2001], 434–35; and Gallagher et al., *This Mighty Scourge of War,* 286).

659. Wilky wrote to Alice that Charleston "looks pretty well used up, our shot & shell during the last year having hastened somewhat the destruction which the city was eventually to fall heir to" (MS letter, 22 February 1865, bMS Am 1095 [11], Houghton).

660. Two of the numerous forts and batteries surrounding Charleston. Fort Sumter, standing in the middle of the harbor entrance, the largest of the forts, and the starting point for the war, was little more than a ruin. Fort Moultrie was on Sullivan's Island, three or four miles from the city.

661. Gideon Welles (1802–78) Compare Lossing: "A few weeks after the fall of Charleston, and on the anniversary of the evacuation of Fort Sumter, four years before, the identical flag which was then taken down, folded up and borne away by Major Anderson, the brave defender of the post, was, by the same hand, again flung to the breeze over that fortress, which had been reduced to an almost shapeless mass of rubbish. Major Anderson had borne away the tattered flag, with a resolution to raise it again over the fortress, or be

Sumter without the deepest exhilaration—so many scenes come to my mind. It's the centre of the nest, and for one to *be* there is to feel that the whole game is up. These people have always insisted that there the last gun should be fired. But the suffering and desolation of this land is the worst feature of the whole thing. If you could see what they are reduced to you couldn't help being touched. The best people are in utter penury; they look like the poorest of the poor and they talk like them also. They are deeply demoralised, in fact degraded. Charleston is more forsaken and stricken than I can describe; it reminds me when I go through the streets of some old doomed city on which the wrath of God has rested from far back, and if it ever revives will do so simply through the infinite mercy and charity of the North. But for this generation at least the inhabitants are done for. Can't H. come down and pay us a visit of 2 or 3 weeks? I can get him a War Dept. pass approved by General Gillmore.

H. knew and well remembers the pang of his inability to accept this invitation, to the value of which for emphasis of tragic life on the scene of the great drama the next passage adds a touch. Mrs. William Young, the lady alluded to, was a friend we had known almost only on the European stage and amid the bright associations of Paris in particular.[662] Whom did we suppose he had met on the arrival of a steamer from the North but this more or less distracted acquaintance of other days?—who had come down

---

wrapped in it as his winding sheet, at the last. He was permitted to raise it there again, before the war had ended, and then to bear it away a second time, for the next office to which he had dedicated it." "When the multitude were assembled around the flag-staff, William B. Bradbury led them in singing his song of *Victory at Last,* followed by *Rally Round the Flag"* (*Pictorial Field Book,* 3:465 and n. 5).

662. HJ here anticipates the episode narrated by Wilky below. Mrs. Young may have traveled with the group of young ladies mentioned earlier. Lossing records that "a large number of citizens went from the harbor of New York in the steamer *Oceanus,* to assist in the ceremonies" (*Pictorial Field Book,* 3:465 n. 5), though this was only one of a number of such expeditions at the time: "The symbolic reappropriation of the nation was best expressed by the frequent trips wealthy New Yorkers took to the South" (Sven Beckert, *The Monied Metropolis: New York City and the Consolidation of the American Bourgeoisie, 1850–1896* [Cambridge: Cambridge University Press, 2001], 143). Mrs. William Young does not figure in the published biographical material relating to the James family, but Pierre A. Walker has suggested that she may be the person mentioned by HJ in a letter written to his mother from Paris on 8 or 9 June 1876, "your old friend Mrs. Young" who "sent much love to father & you." HJ reported that she and her husband "have lived here many years. Mrs. Y. is redfaced, stout & plain" (MS letter, bMS Am 1094 [1837], Houghton).

"to try and get her stepmother into our lines and take her home. She is accompanied by a friend from New York, and expects to succeed in her undertaking. I hardly think she will, however, as her mother is 90 miles out of our lines and a very old woman. We have sent a negro out to give her Mrs. Young's news, but how can this poor old thing travel such a distance on foot and sleep in the swamp besides? It's an absurd idea, but I shall do everything in my power to facilitate it." Of what further befell I gather no account; but I remember how a later time was to cause me to remark on the manner in which even dire tragedy may lapse, in the individual life, and leave no trace on the ground it has ravaged—none at least apparent unless pushingly searched for. The last thing to infer from appearances, on much subsequent renewal of contact with Mrs. Young in Paris again, was that this tension of a reach forth across great war-wasted and swamp-smothered spaces for recovery of an aged and half-starved pedestrian female relative counted for her as a chapter of experience: the experience of Paris dressmakers and other like matters had so revived and super-vened. But let me add that I speak here of mere appearances, and have ever inclined to the more ironic and more complicating vision of them. It would doubtless have been too simple for wonder that our elegant friend should have lived, as it were, under the cloud of reminiscence—and wonder had always somewhere to come in.[663]

XII  It had been, however, neither at Newport nor at Cambridge—the Cambridge at least of that single year—that the plot began most to thicken for me: I figure it as a sudden stride into conditions of a sort to minister and inspire much more, all round, that we early in 1864 migrated, as a family, to Boston, and that I

663. From a letter HJ wrote on 16 February 1915 to Scribner's, his American publishers, it is clear that they had been contacted by a reader, Professor Burt G. Wilder, who had pointed out a number of inaccuracies in the names of places and people mentioned in this Civil War chapter. HJ is loftily apologetic: "My Tillapenny shall certainly be Tullafinny on the next opportunity. . . . So again there shall on the same occasion be found a *b*, instead of my *h*, in Ossabaw, as there shall be two middle *e*'s instead of my *u*, in Ogeechee. What a pity these changes, however, should make the words rather more than less resemble throat-clearing and sneezing! // I thank your correspondent particularly for setting right my mistake in using U.S.C.T. when I should have named the 55th Massachusetts, an error for which I blush, feeling it now, as Prof. Wilder says, a bad one. . . . Colonel Hallowell's first initial *shall* be N, and I am at a loss to trace the fantastic Rufus attributed to General John P. Hatch save by some sharp interference with association" (*HJL*, 4:736–37).

now seem to see the scene of our existence there for a couple of years packed with drama of a finer consistency than any I had yet tasted.[664] We settled for the interesting time in Ashburton Place—the "sympathetic" old house we occupied, one of a pair of tallish brick fronts based, as to its ground floor, upon the dignity of time-darkened granite, was lately swept away in the interest of I know not what grander cause;[665] and when I wish to think of such intercourse as I have enjoyed with the good city at its closest and, as who should say its kindest, though this comes doubtless but to saying at its freshest, I live over again the story of that sojourn, a period bristling, while I recover my sense of it, with an unprecedented number of simultaneous particulars. To stick, as I can only do, to the point from which my own young outlook worked, the things going on for me so tremendously all at once were in the first place the last impressions of the War, a whole social relation to it crowding upon us there as for many reasons, all of the best, it couldn't have done elsewhere; and then, more personally speaking, the prodigious little assurance I found myself gathering as from one day to another that fortune had in store some response to my deeply reserved but quite unabashed design of becoming as "literary" as might be.[666] It was as if, our whole new medium of existence aiding, I had begun to see much further into the question of how that end was gained. The vision, quickened by a wealth, a great mixture, of new appearances, became such a throbbing affair that my memory of the time from the spring of '64 to the autumn of '66 moves as through an apartment hung with garlands and lights—where I have but to breathe for an instant on the flowers again to see them flush with colour, and but tenderly to snuff the candles to see them twinkle afresh. Things happened, and happened repeatedly, the mere brush or side-wind of which was the stir of life; and the fact that I see, when I consider, how it was mostly the mere side-wind I got, doesn't draw from the picture a shade of its virtue. I

664. The Jameses moved from Newport to 13 Ashburton Place, on Beacon Hill near the statehouse, in May 1864 and rented it for two years. "Curiously, the Jameses' new home, on the North Slope of the hill, stood nearer to the African Meeting House on Joy Street than to the Brahmin mansions several blocks away in Louisburg Square" (Fisher, *House of Wits*, 201).

665. During his 1904–5 visit the house was demolished within a few weeks. HJ's horror is described in *AS;* it seems he felt his own identity to be under threat: "It was as if the bottom had fallen out of one's own biography, and one plunged backward into space without meeting anything" (229).

666. HJ refers to his understated ambition as "just *literary*" in chap. 9 (238).

literally, and under whatever felt restriction of my power to knock about, formed independent relations—several; and two or three of them, as I then thought, of the very most momentous. I may not attempt just here to go far into these, save for the exception of the easiest to treat, which I also, by good fortune, win back as by no means the least absorbing—the beautiful, the entrancing presumption that I should have but to write with sufficient difficulty and sufficient felicity to get once for all (that was the point) into the incredibility of print. I see before me, in the rich, the many-hued light of my room that overhung dear Ashburton Place from our third floor, the very greenbacks, to the total value of twelve dollars, into which I had changed the cheque representing my first earned wage. I had earned it, I couldn't but feel, with fabulous felicity: a circumstance so strangely mixed with the fact that literary composition of a high order had, at that very table where the greenbacks were spread out, quite viciously declined, and with the air of its being also once for all, to "come" on any save its own essential terms, which it seemed to distinguish in the most invidious manner conceivable from mine. It was to insist through all my course on this distinction, and sordid gain thereby never again to seem so easy as in that prime handling of my fee.[667] Other guerdons, of the same queer, the same often rather greasy, complexion followed; for what had I done, to the accompaniment of a thrill the most ineffable, an agitation that, as I recapture it, affects me as never exceeded in all my life for fineness, but go one beautiful morning out to Shady Hill at Cambridge and there drink to the lees the offered cup of editorial sweetness?—none ever again to be more delicately mixed. I had addressed in trembling hope my first fond attempt at literary criticism to Charles Eliot Norton, who had lately, and with the highest, brightest competence, come to the rescue of the North American Review, submerged in a stale tradition and gasping for life, and he had not only published it in his very next number—the interval for me of breathless brevity—but had expressed the liveliest further hospitality, the gage of which was thus at once his welcome to me at home.[668] I was to grow fond of regarding as a positive consecration to letters that half-hour in the long

667. HJ published two pieces in 1864, the short story "A Tragedy of Error" in *Continental Monthly* 5 (February): 204–16, and a review of Nassau W. Senior's *Essays on Fiction* in the *North American Review* 99 (October): 580–87, both unsigned. The following year he published another piece of fiction, "The Story of a Year," and fifteen reviews, principally in the *North American Review* and the newly created *Nation*.

668. For the influential Charles Eliot Norton, owner of Shady Hill, see above, nn. 351 and 425.

library at Shady Hill, where the winter sunshine touched serene book-shelves and arrayed pictures, the whole embrowned composition of objects in my view, with I knew not what golden light of promise, what assurance of things to come: there was to be nothing exactly like it later on—the conditions of perfect rightness for a certain fresh felicity, certain decisive pressures of the spring, *can* occur, it would seem, but once. This was on the other hand the beginning of so many intentions that it mattered little if the particular occasion was not repeated; for what did I do again and again, through all the years, but handle in plenty what I might have called the small change of it?[669]

I despair, however, as I look back, of rendering the *fusions* in that much-mixed little time, every feature of which had something of the quality and interest of every other, and the more salient, the more "epoch-making"—I apply with complacency the portentous term—to drape themselves romantically in the purple folds of the whole. I think it must have been the sense of the various climaxes, the enjoyed, because so long postponed, revenges of the War, that lifted the moment in the largest embrace: the general consciousness was of such big things at last in sight, the huge national emergence, the widening assurance, however overdarkened, it is true, by the vast black cost of what General Grant (no light-handed artist he!) was doing for us.[670] He was at all events working to an end, and something strange and immense, even like the light of a new day rising above a definite rim, shot its rays through the chinks of the immediate, the high-piled screen of sacrifice behind which he wrought. I fail to seize again, to my wonder, the particular scene of our acclamation of Lee's surrender, but I feel in the air the exhalation of our relief, which mingled, near and far, with the breath of the springtime itself and positively seemed to become over the land, over the world at large in fact, an element of

669. HJ's old friend Grace Norton, one of the residents of Shady Hill, must have thought he exaggerated the atmosphere of the house and perhaps misremembered some events, since in a letter of 7 April 1914 he refers to her "gentle rectification" and justifies his approach: "What my remarks come to is that Shady Hill was from the date of the beginning of the war (though at the very first perhaps but in germ) the most agreeable and graceful and civilized house in a scantly civilized place, and though you wave off the soft impeachment with a magnificence of humility and chronology I defy you to break it down" (*HJL*, 4:710).

670. HJ refers to the enduringly heroic Union commander Ulysses S. Grant (1822–85). In *AS* he offers a powerful elegiac portrait of the man after visiting his tomb on Riverside Heights, overlooking the Hudson River, in New York City (144–46).

reviving Nature.[671] Sensible again are certain other sharpest vibrations then communicated from the public consciousness: Ashburton Place resounds for me with a wild cry, rocks as from a convulsed breast, on that early morning of our news of Lincoln's death by murder;[672] and, in a different order, but also darkening the early day, there associates itself with my cherished chamber of application the fact that of a sudden, and while we were always and as much as ever awaiting him, Hawthorne was dead. What I have called the fusion strikes me as indeed beyond any rendering when I think of the peculiar assault on my private consciousness of *that* news: I sit once more, half-dressed, late of a summer morning and in a bedimmed light which is somehow at once that of dear old green American shutters drawn to against openest windows and that of a moral shadow projected as with violence—I sit on my belated bed, I say, and yield to the pang that made me positively and loyally cry.[673] I didn't rise early in those days of scant ease—I now even ask myself how sometimes I rose at all; which ungrudged license withal, I thus make out, was not less blessedly effective in the harmony I glance at than several showier facts. To tell at all adequately why the pang was fine would nevertheless too closely involve my going back, as we have learned to say, on the whole rich interpenetration. I fondly felt it in those days invaluable that I had during

671. The Confederate commander Robert E. Lee (1807–70) formally surrendered at Appomattox Court House, Virginia, on 9 April 1865.

672. Lincoln was assassinated at Ford's Theatre, Washington D.C., by John Wilkes Booth on 14 April 1865. Wilky James, writing to his parents from Hilton Head, offers a soldier's perspective on the event, though he also sees the president's removal as providential, believing him insufficiently severe to deal with what he deemed necessary postwar retribution: "The effect of poor Lincoln's death has given a life-long lesson to those who watch it, & the effect that his death has made upon the army is truly very touching. Every man feels that his own well being has been trampled on, that his own honor has been violated. . . . I see Gods wise Providence & justice ridding the sinner of a too pure-minded & clement judge, & putting over him a less worthy & more competent & timely one. He knew that Lincoln never would give the hell to these men that they had been preparing themselves for, & consequently arranged this aright" (27 April 1865, bMS Am 1095 [5], Houghton).

673. Nathaniel Hawthorne died on 19 May 1864. HJ's grief at this identifiably American moment (with the old green shutters and Whitman-like openness of emotion) might be regarded as another seminal moment in his life—a recognition of his own coming role in American letters. Richard Brodhead considers that the passage hints darkly that "James does not so much follow Hawthorne as replace him, implying as it does a link between James's metaphorical birth as an artist and Hawthorne's literal death" (*The School of Hawthorne* [New York: Oxford University Press, 1986], 122).

certain last and otherwise rather blank months at Newport taken in for the first time and at one straight draught the full sweet sense of our one fine romancer's work—for sweet it then above all seemed to me; and I remember well how, while the process day after day drew itself admirably out, I found the actual exquisite taste of it, the strain of the revelation, justify up to the notch whatever had been weak in my delay. This prolonged hanging off from true knowledge had been the more odd, so that I couldn't have explained it, I felt, through the fact that The Wonder-Book and Twice-Told Tales had helped to enchant our childhood;[674] the consequence at any rate seemed happy, since without it, very measurably, the sudden sense of recognition would have been less uplifting a wave. The joy of the recognition was to know at the time no lapse—was in fact through the years never to know one, and this by some rare action of a principle or a sentiment, I scarce know whether to call it a clinging consistency or a singular silliness, that placed the Seven Gables, the Blithedale Romance and the story of Donatello and Miriam (the accepted title of which I dislike to use, not the "marble" but very particularly the human Faun being throughout in question) somewhere on a shelf unvisited by harsh inquiry.[675] The feeling had perhaps at the time been marked by presumption, by a touch of the fatuity of patronage; yet wasn't well-nigh the best charm of a relation with the works just named in the impulse, known from the first, somehow to stand in *between* them and harsh inquiry? If I had asked myself what I meant by that term, at which freedom of appreciation, in fact of intelligence, might have looked askance, I hope I should have

674. Hawthorne's *A Wonder-Book for Boys and Girls,* stories of ancient Greek mythology, was published in 1852; *Twice-Told Tales,* eighteen stories and sketches, was published in 1837.

675. Hawthorne's *The House of the Seven Gables* came out in 1851, *The Blithedale Romance* in 1852, and *The Marble Faun,* or *Transformation* as it was called in England, in 1860. All are sympathetically discussed in HJ's 1879 monograph on Hawthorne, though even then he granted *The Marble Faun,* which is set in Italy, "a slighter value than its companions": "I am far from regarding it as the masterpiece of the author, a position to which we sometimes hear it assigned." He also raised the same misgivings about the work's title: he regarded the American alternative as "rather singular, for it completely fails to characterise the story, the subject of which is the living faun . . . the unfortunate Donatello. His marble counterpart is mentioned only in the opening chapter. On the other hand Hawthorne complained that *Transformation,* 'gives one the idea of Harlequin in a pantomime' " (*Hawthorne; LC* 1, 444). It seems that his American publishers, Ticknor and Fields, came up with *The Marble Faun* as a title.

found a sufficient answer in the mere plea of a sort of *bêtise*[676] of tenderness. I recall how once, in the air of Rome at a time ever so long subsequent, a friend and countryman now no more, who had spent most of his life in Italy and who remains for me, with his accomplishment, his distinction, his extraordinary play of mind and his too early and too tragic death, the clearest case of "cosmopolitan culture" I was to have known, exclaimed with surprise on my happening to speak as from an ancient fondness for Hawthorne's treatment of the Roman scene: "Why, can you read *that* thing, and *here?*—to me it means nothing at all!"[677] I remember well that under the breath of this disallowance of any possibility of association, and quite most of such a one as I had from far back positively cultivated, the gentle perforated book tumbled before me from its shelf very much as old Polonius, at the thrust of Hamlet's sword, must have collapsed behind the pictured arras.[678] Of course I might have picked it up and brushed it off, but I seem to feel again that I didn't so much as want to, lost as I could only have been in the sense that the note of harsh inquiry, or in other words of the very stroke I had anciently wished to avert, *there* fell straight upon my ear. It represented everything I had so early known we must have none of; though there was interest galore at the same time (as there almost always is in lively oppositions of sensibility, with the sharpness of each, its special exclusions, well exhibited), in an

676. Stupidity, silliness.

677. As HJ goes on to explain, this is Henry Bennet Brewster (1850–1908), an American born and educated in Paris who spent much of his life in Italy. It was thought at one stage that he was a model for Gilbert Osmond in *The Portrait of a Lady* (1881), but this was dismissed when it was proved that the two men met only in 1889. For further detail, see Henry Brewster (his grandson), "Henry James and the Gallo-American" and "Henry James: Fourteen Letters," *Botteghe oscure* 19 (Spring 1957): 170–81, 182–94; these letters cover the period from February 1891 to February 1898. Henry Bennet Brewster provides a somewhat poignant insight into the older James: "H.J. dined with me last night. I had an impression of great goodness and kindness, almost tenderness; of an immense bienveillance and yet of fastidious discrimination; something delicate and strong morally. But the fumbling for words is worse than ever; you know how patient I am; well sometimes I could have screamed. Surely this must be nervousness; it is not possible that he should talk thus with the people that he sees daily" (letter to Dame Ethel Smyth, 1 June 1907, quoted in Martin Halpern, "Henry B. Brewster (1850–1908): An Introduction," *American Quarterly* 14 [Autumn 1962]: 480).

678. This somewhat far-fetched allusion is to *Hamlet*, 3.4, when Hamlet, believing his stepfather Claudius to be concealed behind the arras in his mother's room, stabs the unfortunate Polonius by mistake. HJ felt torn between loyalty to Hawthorne's American genius and (what was at threat in his novel) the beautiful reality of Rome.

"American" measure that could so reject our beautiful genius and in a Roman, as it were, that could so little see he had done anything for Rome. H. B. Brewster in truth, literary master of three tongues at least, was scarce American at all; homely superstitions had no hold on him; he was French, Italian, above all perhaps German; and there would have been small use, even had there been any importance, in my trying to tell him for instance why it had particularly been, in the gentle time, that I had settled once for all to take our author's case as simply exquisite and not budge from that taking. Which indeed scarce bears telling now, with matters of relative (if *but* of relative!) urgence on hand—consisting as it mainly did in the fact that his work was all charged with a *tone*, a full and rare tone of prose, and that this made for it an extraordinary value in an air in which absolutely nobody's else was or has shown since any aptitude for being. And the tone had been, in its beauty—for me at least—ever so appreciably American; which proved to what a use American matter could be put by an American hand: a consummation involving, it appeared, the happiest moral. For the moral was that an American could be an artist, one of the finest, without "going outside" about it, as I liked to say; quite in fact as if Hawthorne had become one just by being American *enough,* by the felicity of how the artist in him missed nothing, suspected nothing, that the ambient air didn't affect him as containing.[679] Thus he was at once so clear and so entire—clear without thinness, for he might have seemed underfed, it was his danger; and entire without heterogeneity, which might, with less luck and to the discredit of our sufficing manners, have had to be his help. These remarks, as I say, were those I couldn't, or at any rate didn't, make to my Roman critic; if only because I was so held by the other case he offered me—that of a culture for which, in the dense medium around us, Miriam and Donatello and their friends hadn't the virtue that shines or pushes through.[680] I tried to feel that this *constatation*[681] left me musing—

679. HJ makes similar claims for Hawthorne in his early monograph, believing that, of the novels, "the pure, natural quality of the imaginative strain is their great merit." *The House of the Seven Gables* vindicates its American inspiration, rendering, "to an initiated reader, the impression of a summer afternoon in an elm-shadowed New England town" (*Hawthorne, LC* 1, 412). In *AS* the "elm-shaded" character of the New England village reveals its "most exemplary state:" "you have said so much . . . that little else remains" (38).

680. Miriam is the aspiring American artist who comes to Rome and becomes involved in the secret, murderous event that also taints the loving Donatello's life. Hilda and Kenyon are the other friends.

681. Verification or establishment (of fact).

and perhaps in truth it did; though doubtless if my attachment to the arranger of those images had involved, to repeat, my not budging, my meditation, whatever it was, respected that condition.

It has renewed itself, however, but too much on this spot, and the scene viewed from Ashburton Place claims at the best more filling in than I can give it. Any illustration of anything worth illustrating has beauty, to my vision, largely by its developments; and developments, alas, are the whole flowering of the plant, while what really meets such attention as one may hope to beguile is at the best but a plucked and tossed sprig or two. That my elder brother was during these months away with Professor Agassiz, a member of the party recruited by that great naturalist for a prolonged exploration of Brazil, is one of the few blooms, I see, that I must content myself with detaching—the main sense of it being for myself, no doubt, that his absence (and he had never been at anything like such a distance from us,) left me the more exposed, and thereby the more responsive, to contact with impressions that had to learn to suffice for me in their uncorrected, when not still more in their inspiringly emphasised, state.[682] The main sense for William himself is recorded in a series of letters from him addressed to us at home and for which, against my hope, these pages succeed in affording no space—they are to have ampler presentation;[683] but the arrival of which at irregular intervals for the greater part of a year comes back to me as perhaps a fuller enrichment of my consciousness than it owed for the time to any other single source. We all still hung so together that this replete organ could yet go on helping itself, with whatever awkwardness, from the conception or projection of others of a like

682. WJ (funded with $600 from Aunt Kate) set out from New York with a number of other Harvard students on 31 March 1865 aboard the Pacific Company liner *Colorado*, bound for Rio de Janeiro. The aim of the expedition, led by the eminent Professor Louis Agassiz (see above, n. 195) and his wife, was to gather specimens from the Amazon River. En route off the Virginia coast they could see the smoke of a burning Richmond. WJ was ill soon after arriving in Brazil, but stayed on, returning to Cambridge in February 1866.

683. It had been HJ's original intention to include a selection of WJ's Brazil letters. At some stage, however, they were cut, though (while unwell) he did revise them in preparation, experiencing, as he told his nephew Harry, "a *morbid* anxiety," "a desperation of nervousness in the whole connection" (quoted by Tamara Follini, "Pandora's Box: The Family Correspondence in *Notes of a Son and Brother*," *Cambridge Quarterly* 25, no. 1 [1996]: 33). The two-volume *Letters of William James,* edited by his son, include somes of WJ's letters written during his trip to Brazil (1:56–70); see also Carlton Sprague Smith, "William James in Brazil," *Four Papers Presented in the Institute for Brazilian Studies,* ed. Charles Wagley et al. (Nashville: Vanderbilt University Press, 1951), 97–138.

*general* strain, such as those of one's brothers might appear; thanks to which constant hum of borrowed experience, in addition to the quicker play of whatever could pass as more honestly earned, my stage of life knew no drop of the curtain. I literally came and went, I had never practised such coming and going; I went in particular, during summer weeks, and even if carrying my general difficulty with me, to the White Mountains of New Hampshire, with some repetition, and again and again back to Newport, on visits to John La Farge and to the Edmund Tweedys (*their* house almost a second summer home to us;)[684] to say nothing of winter attempts, a little weak, but still more or less achieved, upon New York—which city was rapidly taking on the capital quality, the large worldly sense that dear old London and dear old Paris, with other matters in hand for them as time went on, the time they were "biding" for me, indulgently didn't grudge it. The matters they had in hand wandered indeed as stray vague airs across to us—this I think I have noted; but Boston itself could easily rule, in default even of New York, when to "go," in particular, was an act of such easy virtue. To go from Ashburton Place was to go verily round the corner not less than further afield; to go to the Athenæum, to the Museum, to a certain door of importances, in fact of immensities, defiant of vulgar notation, in Charles Street, at the opposite end from Beacon.[685] The fruit

684. Oliver Wendell Holmes and HJ visited the White Mountains in August 1865, traveling by rail from Boston and then carriage, following the Saco River to North Conway. The Temple sisters, including, most significantly, Minny, spent the summer there, possibly with their Albany great-aunt Ellen Gourlay (though the editors of *CWJ* [4:609] suggest that this may have been Jeannette Barber Gourlay). It was perhaps the first of several visits (involving "some repetition") by HJ; see below, n. 778. Edmund and Mary Tweedy lived at Bellevue Court, Newport, while the artist John La Farge "was now living on a farm near Newport, overlooking the sea" (Novick, *Young Master*, 120).

685. The Boston Athenaeum, on Beacon Street near the State House, "exquisite institution, to fond memory, joy of the aspiring prime" (*AS*, 232), is built "of Patterson freestone, and in the Palladian style of architecture." A sculpture gallery occupies the first floor, a library the second, and a picture gallery the third story. Not far away, on Tremont Street, the Boston Museum was run by Moses Kemball. It was regarded as "a spacious and superb building, its front adorned by elegant balconies and rows of grand glass globes, like enormous pearls, which at night are luminous with gas. Three tiers of elegantly arched windows admit light into the building." Also located here was the Boston Museum Theater (Midgley, *Sights in Boston and Suburbs,* 41–44, 36–39). In 1856 admission to the Athenaeum and to the museum was twenty-five cents; by 1867 it had risen to thirty cents. The theater is fondly recalled in *AS* (242–43). Novick points out that "the door at the opposite end of Charles Street from Beacon was the Holmeses'" (*Young Master*, 468 n. 14). Thus HJ discreetly alludes to his friendship with Oliver Wendell Holmes. It is

of these mixed proceedings I found abundant at the time, and I think quite inveterately sweet, but to gather it in again now—by which I mean set it forth as a banquet for imaginations already provided—would be to presume too far; not least indeed even on my own cultivated art of exhibition. The fruit of golden youth is all and always golden—it touches to gold what it gathers;[686] this was so the essence of the case that in the first place everything was in some degree an adventure, and in the second any differences of degree guiding my selection would be imperceptible at this end of time to the cold eye of criticism. Not least moreover in the third place the very terms would fail, under whatever ingenuity, for my really justifying so bland an account of the period at large. Do I speak of it as a thumping sum but to show it in the small change, the handful of separate copper and silver coin, the scattered occasions reduced to their individual cash value, that, spread upon the table as a treasure of reminiscence, might only excite derision? *Why* was "staying at Newport" so absurdly, insistently romantic, romantic out of all proportion, as we say—why unless I can truly tell in proportion to what it became so? It consisted often in my "sitting" to John La Farge, within his own precincts and in the open air of attenuated summer days,[687] and lounging thereby just passive to the surge of culture that broke upon me in waves the most desultory and disjointed, it was true, but to an absolute effect of unceasingly scented spray. Particular hours and old (that is young!) ineffable reactions come back to me; it's like putting one's ear, doctor-fashion, to the breast of time—or say as the subtle savage puts his to the ground—and catching at its start some vibratory hum that has been going on more or less for the fifty years since. Newport, the barren isle of our return from Europe, had thus become— and at no such great expense if the shock of public affairs, everywhere making interests start to their feet, be counted out of the process—a source of fifty suggestions to me; which it would have been much less,

interesting that the term "importances" in relation to James and Annie Fields and their circle in Charles Street comes up in HJ's Notebooks (see above, n. 412).

686. Compare HJ's impressions of the "young men of business" whom he noticed on the New Jersey ferry on his 1904–5 visit: "It was perhaps this simple sense of treasure to be gathered in, it was doubtless this very confidence in the objective reality of impressions, so that they could deliciously be left to ripen, like golden apples, on the tree—it was all this that gave a charm to one's sitting in the orchard, gave a strange and inordinate charm both to the prospect of the Jersey shore and to every inch of the entertainment, so divinely inexpensive, by the way" (*AS*, 6).

687. Only one portrait, in oils, by John La Farge has survived. See above, n. 103.

however, I hasten to add, if the call of La Farge hadn't worked in with our other most standing attraction, and this in turn hadn't practically been part of the positive affluence of certain elements of spectacle. Why again I should have been able to see the pictorial so freely suggested, that pictorial which was ever for me the dramatic, the social, the effectively human aspect, would be doubtless a baffling inquiry in presence of the queer and dear old phenomena themselves; those that, taken together, may be described at the best, I suppose, rather as a much-mixed grope or halting struggle, call it even a competitive scramble, toward the larger, the ideal elegance, the traditional forms of good society in possession, than as a presentation of great noble assurances.

Spectacle in any case broke out, spectacle accumulated, by our then measure, many thicknesses deep, flushing in the sovereign light, as one felt it, of the waning Rhode Island afternoons of August and September with the most "evolved" material civilisation our American world could then show; the vividest note of this in those years, unconscious, even to an artless innocence, of the wider wings still to spread, being the long daily *corso*[688] or processional drive (with cavaliers and amazons not otherwise than conveniently intermixed,) which, with a different direction for different days, offered doubtless as good an example of that gregarious exercise at any cost distinguishing "fashionable life" as was anywhere on the globe to be observed. The price paid for the sticking together was what emphasised, I mean, the wondrous resolve to stick, however scant and narrow and unadjusted for processional effect the various fields of evolution. The variety moreover was short, just as the incongruities of composition in the yearning array were marked; but the tender grace of old sunset hours, the happier breadth of old shining sands under favour of friendly tides, the glitter *quand même*[689] of "caparisoned" animals, appointed vehicles and approved charioteers, to say nothing of the other and more freely exchanged and interrelated brightnesses then at play (in the softer ease of women, the more moustachio'd swagger of men, the braver bonhomie of the social aspect at large), melted together for fond fancy into a tone, a rhythm, a representational virtue charged, as to the amenities, with authority. The amenities thus sought their occasion to multiply even to the sound of far cannonades, and I well remember at once reflecting, in such maturity as I could muster, that the luckier half of a nation able to

688. Run or trip (It.).
689. Notwithstanding.

carry a huge war-burden without sacrifice of amusement might well overcome the fraction that had to feed but on shrinkage and privation; at the
same time that the so sad and handsome face of the most frequent of our
hostesses, Mary Temple the elder as she had been,[690] now the apt image of
a stern priestess of the public altar, was to leave with me for the years to
come the grand expression and tragic irony of its revulsion from those
who, offering us some high entertainment during days of particular tension, could fiddle, as she scathingly said, while Rome was burning. Blest
again the state of youth which could appreciate that admirable look and
preserve it for illustration of one of the forms of ancient piety lost to us,
and yet at the same time stow away as part of the poetry of the general
drama just the luxury and pride, overhanging summer seas and projecting
into summer nights great shafts of light and sound, that prompted the
noble scorn. The "round of pleasure" all this with a grand good conscience of course—for it always in the like case has that, had it at least
when arranging performances, dramatic and musical, at ever so much a
ticket, under the advantage of rare amateur talent, in aid of the great
Sanitary Commission that walked in the footsteps and renewed in various
forms the example of Florence Nightingale;[691] these exhibitions taking
place indeed more particularly in the tributary cities, New York, Philadelphia, Boston (we were then shut up to those,) but with the shining stars
marked for triumphant appearance announced in advance on the Newport
scene and glittering there as beauties, as élégantes,[692] as vocalists, as

690. "Mary Temple the elder" was Mary Tweedy, wife of HJ Sr.'s friend Edmund
Tweedy. She was an older sister of Colonel Robert Temple, who had married HJ's paternal
aunt Catherine, whose deaths HJ recalls in *SBO*, chap. 13 (see also *SBO*, n. 21). Mary
Temple the younger was HJ's cousin Minny.

691. During her time in the Crimea (1854–56), Florence Nightingale (1820–1910)
had revolutionized nursing practices and sanitary standards. The Sanitary Commission,
founded in the United States in 1861 and run mainly by women volunteers, promoted clean
and healthy conditions in the Union army camps of the Civil War. In addition, such
organizations (including the Women's Aid Societies and the nursing corps) "provided a
sense of social usefulness for people who were excluded from active participation in the
war by virtue of age, sex, leisured status, or all three" (Strouse, *Alice James*, 79n). HJ wrote
to T. S. Perry on 25 March 1864, "I walk a little every day, and by sitting and standing and
staring and lingering and sniffing the air, contrive to get a certain amount of exercise. The
great event since you went off has been a grand sanitary concert. . . . Here your humble
servant performed the duties of one: attired like an English footman, he showed folks to
their seats" (*HJL*, 1:50).

692. Women of fashion.

heroines of European legend. Hadn't there broken upon us, under public stress, a refluent wave from Paris, the mid-Empire Paris of the highest pitch, which was to raise our social water-mark to a point unprecedented and there strikingly leave it? We were learning new lessons in every branch —that was the sense of the so immensely quickened general pace; and though my examples may seem rather spectral I like to believe this bigger breathing of the freshness of the future to have been what the collective rumble and shimmer of the whole business most meant. It exhaled an artless confidence which yet momently increased; it had no great sense of a direction, but gratefully took any of which the least hint was given, gathering up by the way and after the fact whatever account of itself a vague voice might strike off. There were times when the account of itself as flooding Lawton's Valley for afternoon tea was doubtless what it would most comfortably have welcomed—Lawton's Valley, at a good drive's length from the seaward quarter, being the scene of villeggiatura of the Boston muse,[693] as it were, and the Boston muse having in those after all battle-haunted seasons an authority and a finish of accent beyond any other Tyrtaean[694] strain. The New York and perhaps still more the Philadelphia of the time fumbled more helplessly, even if aspiringly, with the Boston evidences in general, I think, than they were to be reduced to doing later on; and by the happy pretext, certainly, that these superior signs had then a bravery they were not perhaps on their own side indefinitely to keep up.

They rustled, with the other leafage of the umbrageous grove, in the summer airs that hung over the long tea-tables; afternoon tea was itself but a new and romantic possibility, with the lesson of it gratefully learnt at

693. The muse of Boston was Julia Ward Howe (1819–1910), writer and reformer immortalized by her Civil War lyrics "The Battle Hymn of the Republic." In his late essay on James and Annie Fields, HJ recalls how "that immemorial and inextinguishable lady" had performed for him "that 'Battle-hymn of the Republic,' which she had caused to be chanted half a century before and still could accompany with a real breadth of gesture, her great clap of hands and indication of the complementary step, on the triumphant line, 'Be swift my hands to welcome him, be jubilant my feet!'" (*LC* 1, 176). As Novick points out, "Lawton's Valley was a summer place the Howes had purchased very cheaply just before the war . . . it held a small, tumbledown farmhouse with just enough room for them and their three children" (*Young Master,* 118). It is located in Portsmouth, ten miles north of Newport; they cultivated the land and gorge round about and, because space was limited, entertained guests outside. "To Lawton's Valley she brought the new English fashion for afternoon tea, perfectly suited to outdoor entertaining on summer afternoons." *Villeggiatura:* holiday home (It.).

694. Tyrtaeus was a Greek martial poet of the 7th century BCE.

hands that dispensed, with the tea and sugar and in the charmingest voice perhaps then to be heard among us, a tone of talk that New York took for exotic and inimitable, yet all the more felt "good," much better than it might if left *all* to itself, for thus flocking in every sort of conveyance to listen to. The Valley was deep, winding and pastoral—or at least looks so now to my attached vision; the infancy of a finer self-consciousness seemed cradled there; the inconsequent vehicles fraternised, the dim, the more dejected, with the burnished and upstanding; so that I may really perhaps take most for the note of the hour the first tremor of the sense on the part of fashion that, if it could, as it already more or less suspected, get its thinking and reading and writing, almost everything in fact but its arithmetic, a bit dingily, but just by that sign cleverly, done for it, so occasion seemed easy, after all, for a nearer view, without responsibility, of the odd performers of the service. When these last were not literally all Bostonians they were New Yorkers who might have been mistaken for such—never indeed by Bostonians themselves, but only by other New Yorkers, the rich and guileless;[695] so the effect as of a vague tribute to culture the most authentic (if I speak not too portentously) was left over for the aftertaste of simple and subtle alike. Those were comparatively thin seasons, I recognise, in the so ample career of Mrs. Howe, mistress of the Valley and wife of the eminent, the militant Phil-Hellene, Dr. S. G. of the honoured name, who reached back to the Byronic time and had dedicated his own later to still more distinguished liberating work on behalf of deaf mutes;[696] for if she was thus the most attuned of interlocutors, most urbane of disputants, most insidious of wits, even before her gathered fame as Julia Ward and the established fortune of her elegant Battle-Hymn, she was perhaps to have served the State scarce better through final organised activities and shining optimisms and great lucky lyric hits than by having in her vale of heterogeneous hospitality undermined the blank assurance of her thicker contingent—after all too but to an *amusing* vague unrest—and thereby scattered the first rare seed of new assimila-

695. HJ's ironic comment perhaps reflects the contemporary rivalry between the two cities as New York continued to grow and become increasingly influential.

696. The philanthropist and "Phil-Hellene" (lover of Greece) Samuel Gridley Howe (1801–76) took part in the Greek fight for independence (as well as the Polish revolution); a physician, he opened and ran a school for the blind and those referred to at the time as feeble-minded. He went on to achieve "world-wide renown by teaching sign-language to a blind, deaf and dumb child. Charles Dickens had written an account of this achievement, and Dr. Howe had become a transatlantic celebrity" (Novick, *Young Master,* 117).

tions. I am moved to add that, by the old terminology, the Avenue might have been figured, in the connection, as descending into the glen to meet the Point—which, save for a very small number of the rarest representatives of the latter, it could meet nowhere else. The difficulty was that of an encounter of birds and fishes; the two tribes were native to elements as opposed as air and water, the Avenue essentially nothing if not exalted on wheels or otherwise expertly mounted, and the Point hopelessly pedestrian and unequipped with stables, so that the very levels at which they materially moved were but upper and lower, dreadfully lower, parallels.[697] And indeed the way to see the Point—which, without playing on the word, naturally became our highest law—was *at* the Point, where it appeared to much higher advantage than in its trudge through the purple haze or golden dust of supercilious parades. Of the advantage to which it did so appear, off in its own more languorous climate and on its own ground, we fairly cultivated a conviction, rejoicing by that aid very much as in certain old French towns it was possible to distinguish invidiously the Ville from the Cité.[698] The Point was our *cité*, the primal aboriginal Newport—which, striking us on a first acquaintance as not other than dilapidated, might well have been "restored" quite as M. Viollet-le-Duc was even then restoring Carcassonne;[699] and this all the more because our elder Newport, the only seat of history, had a dismantled grassy fort or archaic citadel that dozed over the waterside and that might (though I do take the vision, at close quarters, for horrible) be smartly waked up.[700]

697. The Avenue is Newport's Belle Vue Avenue, which overlooks the town, home to the wealthy and usually recently arrived families, whose luxurious mansions dismay HJ in *AS* (224–25). The small wooden houses of the Point, at the heart of the colonial Old Town, "felicitous cottages . . . their pleasure-boats at their little wharves" harbored those "less fashionable . . . but also the more cultivated and the more artistic" (*AS*, 216). Without stables, they would have no carriages. HJ's wordplay on "the point" is repeated from *AS:* "we had admired the Old Town too for the emphasis of its peculiar point, *the* Point; a quarter distinguished . . . by a really refined interest" (215).

698. The *cité* is usually the older part of a town.

699. The French architect and writer on architecture Eugène Emmanuel Viollet-le-Duc (1814–79), renowned as a restorer of Gothic buildings, began work on restoring the fortifications of Carcassonne in southwest France in 1849.

700. The opening ceremony for Fort Adams at the mouth of Newport harbor took place on 4 July 1799. "This structure stands on a point of land opposite the wharves of Newport. A sail of ten minutes duration from Bannister's pier conveys the visitor to the opposite shore. There he may walk round the ramparts, see the beautiful view which it commands of town and bay and bold sea shore, without any intervening obstacles" (*A*

The waterside, which was that of the inner bay, the ample reach toward Providence,[701] so much more susceptible of quality than the extravagant open sea, the "old houses," the old elms, the old Quaker faces at the small-paned old windows, the appointedness of the scene for the literary and artistic people, who, by our fond constructive theory, lodged and boarded with the Quakers, always thrifty these, for the sake of all the sweetness and quaintness, for the sake above all somehow of *our* hungry felicity of view, by which I mean mine and that of a trusty friend or two, T. S. Perry in especial—those attributes, meeting a want, as the phrase is, of the decent imagination, made us perhaps overdramatise the sphere of the clever people, but made them at least also, when they unmistakably hovered, affect us as truly the finest touches in the picture. For they were in their way ironic about the rest, and that was a tremendous lift in face of an Avenue that not only, as one could see at a glance, had no irony, but hadn't yet risen, the magazines and the Point aiding, to so much as a suspicion of the effect, familiar to later generations, with which the word can conversationally come in. Oh the old clever people, with their difference of shade from that of the clever old ones—some few of these to have been discerned, no doubt, as of Avenue position: I read back into their various presences I know not what queer little functional value the exercise and privilege of which, uncontested, uncontrasted (save with the absence of everything but stables) represents a felicity for the individual that is lost to our age. It could count as functional then, it could count as felicitous, to have been reabsorbed into Boston, or to propose to absorb even, for the first time, New York, under cover of the mantle, the old artistic draped cloak, that had almost in each case trailed round in Florence, in Rome, in Venice,[702] in conversations with Landor, in pencilled commemoration, a little niggling possibly but withal so sincere, of the "haunts" of Dante, in a general claim of having known the Brownings (ah "the Brownings" of those days!) in a disposition to arrange readings of these and the most oddly associated other poets about the great bleak parlours of the hotels.[703] I despair, however, of any really right register of the art with which

*Handbook of Newport, and Rhode Island* [Newport: C. E. Hammett Jr., 1852], 140). See also George Champlin Mason, *Reminiscences of Newport* (Newport: Charles E. Hammett Jr., 1884), 294–98.

701. Across Narragansett Bay, about thirty miles north of Newport.

702. HJ has already recorded the European proclivities of Newport's inhabitants in chap. 4 (see n. 106).

703. The English poet and author of *Imaginary Conversations* (5 vols., 1824–29),

the cité ingratiated itself with me in this character of a vivid missionary Bohemia; I met it of course more than half way, as I met everything in the faintest degree ingratiating, even suggesting to it with an art of my own that it should become so—though in this matter I rather missed, I fear, a happy conversion, as if the authenticity were there but my sort of personal dash too absent.

I appear to myself none the less to have had dash for approaches to a confidence more largely seated; since I recall how, having commenced critic under Charles Norton's weighty protection, I was to find myself, on all but the very morrow, invited to the high glory, as I felt it, of aiding to launch, though on the obscurer side of the enterprise, a weekly journal which, putting forth its first leaves in the summer of '65 and under the highest auspices, was soon to enjoy a fortune and achieve an authority and a dignity of which neither newspaper nor critical review among us had hitherto so much as hinted the possibility. The New York Nation had from the first, to the enlivening of several persons consciously and ruefully astray in our desert, made no secret of a literary leaning; and indeed its few foremost months shine most for me in the light of their bestowal of one of the longest and happiest friendships of my life, a relation with Edwin Lawrence Godkin, the Nation incarnate as he was to become, which bore fruit of affection for years after it had ceased to involve the comparatively poorer exercise.[704] Godkin's paper, Godkin's occasional presence and

Walter Savage Landor (1775-1864) led a tempestuous life, often much involved in political controversy, and spent many years in Italy. Having returned to Tuscany in poor health toward the end of his life, he was supported by expatriates like the sculptor William Wetmore Story and Robert and Elizabeth Barrett Browning. Some of their letters and reminiscences of 1859-60, included in the second volume of HJ's *William Wetmore Story and His Friends* (6-29), make frequent reference to "poor Landor." Study of the Italian poet Dante Alighieri (1265-1321) formed, of course, part of a liberal education of the day, and indeed Charles Eliot Norton (not to mention another member of the Cambridge Dante circle, Longfellow) produced translations of the poet. Mainly because of Elizabeth Barrett Browning's fragile health, the Brownings lived principally in Florence after their marriage in 1846. The young HJ met the aging Robert Browning in London, finding that "there are two Brownings—an esoteric and an exoteric" (Edel, *Conquest of London*, 330)—and thus a *donnée* for a short story, "The Private Life" (1892) (see also *TMY*, n. 92). HJ stayed in an apartment attached to the Casa Alvisi in Venice which belonged to Katherine De Kay Bronson; Browning had also accepted her hospitality. In his gentle mocking of a social group with which he had so much in common—even though he half-admits his integration—HJ is perhaps being disingenuous.

704. The *Nation*, to which HJ was to contribute numerous reviews from 1865 onward, was edited by Godkin. "Vol. I, No. I contained unsigned reviews by both father and son—

interesting history and vivid ability and, above all, admirably aggressive and ironic editorial humour, of a quality and authority new in the air of a journalism that had meant for the most part the heavy hand alone, these things, with the sudden sweet discovery that I might for my own part acceptedly stammer a style, are so many shades and shifting tints in the positive historic iridescence that flings itself for my memory, as I have noted, over the "period" of Ashburton Place. Wherever I dip, again, I pull out a plum from under the tooth of time—this at least so to my own rapt sense that had I more space I might pull both freely and at a venture. The strongest savour of the feast—with the fumes of a feast it comes back— was, I need scarce once more insist, the very taste of the War as ending and ended; through which blessing, more and more, the quantity of military life or at least the images of military experience seemed all about us, quite paradoxically, to grow greater. This I take to have been a result, first of the impending, and then of the effective, break-up of the vast veteran Army, swamping much of the scene as with the flow of a monster tide and bringing literally home to us, in bronzed, matured faces and even more in bronzed, matured characters, above all in the absolutely acquired and stored resource of overwhelming reference, reference usually of most substance the less it was immediately explicit, the more in fact it was faded and jaded to indifference, what was meant by having patiently served. The very smell of having so served was somehow, at least to my supersensitive nostril, in the larger and cooler air, where it might have been an emana- tion, the most masculine, the most communicative as to associated far-off things (according to the nature, ever, of elements vaguely exhaled), from the operation of the general huge gesture of relief—from worn toggery put off, from old army-cloth and other fittings at a discount, from swordbelts and buckles, from a myriad saturated articles now not even lying about but brushed away with an effect upon the passing breeze and all relegated to the dim state of some mere theoretic commemorative panoply that was

---

Henry Junior's review of a novel by Henry Kingsley and Henry Senior's review of Carlyle's *Frederick the Great*. From then on the junior Henry was a consistent writer for the *Nation*, first of reviews, later of travel sketches. For a brief period he was all but a staff member in New York; still later he was the *Nation*'s informal correspondent-at-large in England. . . . In later years his contributions to the journal tapered off, especially after Godkin relin- quished the editorship; yet his connection with it can be said to cover almost half a century" (Edel, *Untried Years*, 224). At the end of his life HJ published an essay "The Founding of the 'Nation' " (the play on words is continued in the text) in which he recalled the "blest element" of his relationship with Godkin (*Nation*, 8 July 1915; *LC* 1, 180).

never in the event to be objectively disposed.[705] The generalisation grew richly or, as it were, quite adorably familiar, that life was ever so handsomely reinforced, and manners, not to say manner at large, refreshed, and personal aspects and types accented, and categories multiplied (no category, for the dreaming painter of things, could our scene afford not to grab at on the chance), just by the fact of the discharge upon society of such an amount of out-of-the-way experience, as it might roughly be termed—such a quantity and variety of possession and assimilation of unprecedented history. It had been unprecedented at least among ourselves, we had had it in our own highly original conditions—or "they," to be more exact, had had it admirably in theirs; and I think I was never to know a case in which his having been directly touched by it, or, in a word, having consistently "soldiered," learnt all about it and exhausted it, wasn't to count all the while on behalf of the happy man for one's own individual impression or attention; call it again, as everything came back to that, one's own need to interpret. The discharge upon "society" is moreover what I especially mean; it being the sense of how society in *our* image of the word was taking it all in that I was most concerned with; plenty of other images figured of course for other entertainers of such. The world immediately roundabout us at any rate bristled with more of the young, or the younger, cases I speak of, cases of "things seen" and felt, and a delectable difference in the man thereby made imputable, than I could begin here to name even had I kept the record. I think I fairly cultivated the perceiving of it all, so that nothing of it, under some face or other, shouldn't brush my sense and add to my impression; yet my point is more particularly that the body social itself was for the time so permeated, in the light I glance at, that it became to its own consciousness more interesting. As so many existent parts of it, however unstoried yet, to their minor credit, various thrilled persons could inhale the interest to their fullest capacity and feel that they too had been pushed forward—and were even to find themselves by so much the more pushable yet.

I resort thus to the lift and the push as the most expressive figures for that immensely *remonté* state which coincided for us all with the great disconcerting irony of the hour, the unforgettable death of Lincoln. I think

705. HJ's olfactory-inspired memories of postwar life, "the very smell of having served" —an episode exploited in "The Story of a Year" (see above, n. 399)—and his observations of the "worn toggery" all around must, given the harsh conditions endured by many surviving veterans, seem strangely beside the point, even though it is conceded that the society he had known had been changed irrevocably, or at least made "more interesting."

of the springtime of '65 as it breathed through Boston streets—my remembrance of all those days is a matter, strangely enough, of the out-of-door vision, of one's constantly dropping down from Beacon Hill, to the brave edge of which we clung, for appreciation of those premonitory gusts of April that one felt most perhaps where Park Street Church stood dominant,[706] where the mouth of the Common itself uttered promises, more signs and portents than one could count, more prodigies than one could keep apart, and where further strange matters seemed to charge up out of the lower districts and of the "business world," generative as never before of news. The streets were restless, the meeting of the seasons couldn't but be inordinately so, and one's own poor pulses matched—at the supreme pitch of that fusion, for instance, which condensed itself to blackness roundabout the dawn of April 15th: I was fairly to go in shame of its being my birthday.[707] These would have been the hours of the streets if none others had been—when the huge general gasp filled them like a great earth-shudder and people's eyes met people's eyes without the vulgarity of speech. Even this was, all so strangely, part of the lift and the swell, as tragedy has but to be of a pure enough strain and a high enough connection to sow with its dark hand the seed of greater life. The collective sense of what had occurred was of a sadness too noble not somehow to inspire, and it was truly in the air that, whatever we had as a nation produced or failed to produce, we could at least gather round this perfection of a classic woe. True enough, as we were to see, the immediate harvest of our loss was almost too ugly to be borne—for nothing more sharply comes back to me than the tune to which the "esthetic sense," if one glanced but from *that* high window (which was after all one of many too), recoiled in dismay from the sight of Mr. Andrew Johnson perched on the stricken scene.[708] We had given ourselves a figure-head, and the figure-head sat there in its habit as it lived, and we were to have it in our eyes for three or

706. Park Street Church, just opposite the northeastern corner of Boston Common on Park and Tremont streets, has been, since 1809, the venue for a number of historic events. For HJ it was "a happy landmark . . . with its mild recall, by its spire, of Wren's bold London examples, the comparatively thin echo of a far-away song—playing its part, however, for harmonious effect, as perfectly as possible" (*AS*, 239).

707. The day on which news arrived of Lincoln's assassination on 14 April.

708. Andrew Johnson (1808–75) became the seventeenth president of the United States on the death of Lincoln. During the period of Reconstruction he narrowly but justly escaped impeachment in a contentious power struggle in which (contravening the Tenure of Office act) he had dismissed his secretary of war, Edwin M. Stanton.

four years and to ask ourselves in horror what monstrous thing we had done. I speak but of aspects, those aspects which, under a certain turn of them, may be all but everything; gathered together they become a symbol of what is behind, and it was open to us to waver at shop-windows exposing the new photograph, exposing, that is, *the* photograph, and ask ourselves what we had been guilty of as a people, when all was said, to deserve the infliction of that form. It was vain to say that we had deliberately invoked the "common" in authority and must drink the wine we had drawn. No countenance, no salience of aspect nor composed symbol, could superficially have referred itself less than Lincoln's mould-smashing mask to any mere matter-of-course type of propriety; but his admirable unrelated head had itself revealed a type—as if by the very fact that what made in it for roughness of kind looked out only less than what made in it for splendid final stamp, in other words for commanding Style.[709] The result thus determined had been precious for representation, and above all for fine suggestional function, in a degree that left behind every medal we had ever played at striking; whereas before the image now substituted representation veiled her head in silence and the element of the suggested was exactly the direst. What, however, on the further view, was to be more refreshing than to find that there were excesses of native habit which truly we couldn't bear? so that it was for the next two or three years fairly sustaining to consider that, let the reasons publicly given for the impeachment of the official in question be any that would serve, the grand inward logic or mystic law had been that we really couldn't go on offering each other before the nations the consciousness of such a presence. That was at any rate the style of reflection to which the humiliating case reduced me; just this withal now especially working, I feel, into that image of our generally quickened activity of spirit, our having by the turn of events more ideas to apply and even to play with, that I have tried to throw off. Everything I recover, I again risk repeating, fits into the vast miscellany— the detail of which I may well seem, however, too poorly to have handled.

Let it serve then for a scrap of detail that the appearance of William's further fortune enjoyed thereabouts a grasp of my attention scarce menaced even by the call on that faculty of such appearances of my own as I had naturally in some degree also to take for graces of the banquet. I

709. HJ seems to be suggesting that the characteristically rough-hewn but heroic features of Lincoln which had promised integrity and truth, thus asserting the value of "Style," had been replaced by a much shabbier example of leadership which threatened humiliation for the nation.

associate the sense of his being, in a great cause, far away on the billow with that clearance of the air through the tremendous draught, from sea to sea, of the Northern triumph, which seemed to make a good-natured infinitude of room for all the individual interests and personal lives that might help the pot to bubble—if the expression be not too mean for the size of our confidence; that the cause on which the Agassiz expedition to South America embarked *was* of the greatest being happily a presumption altogether within my scope.[710] It reawoke the mild divinatory rage with which I had followed, with so little to show for it, the military fortune of my younger brothers—feeding the gentle passion indeed, it must be added, thanks to the letter-writing grace of which the case had now the benefit, with report and picture of a vividness greater than any ever to be shed from a like source upon our waiting circle. Everything of the kind, for me, was company; but I dwelt, for that matter and as I put it all together, in company so constant and so enchanting that this amounted to moving, in whatever direction, with the mass—more and more aware as I was of the "fun" (to express it grossly) of living by my imagination and thereby finding that company, in countless different forms, could only swarm about me.[711] Seeing further into the figurable world *made* company of persons and places, objects and subjects alike: it gave them all without exception chances to be somehow or other interesting, and the imaginative ply of finding interest once taken (I think I had by that time got much beyond looking for it), the whole conspiracy of aspects danced round me in a ring. It formed, by my present vision of it, a shining escort to one's possibly often hampered or mystified, but never long stayed and absolutely never wasted, steps; it hung about, after the fashion of winter evening adumbrations just outside the reach of the lamplight, while one sat writing, reading, listening, watching—perhaps even again, incurably, but dawdling and gaping; and most of all doubtless, if it supplied with colour

710. The expedition set out "with the purpose of netting and classifying the many hitherto unknown species of fish which Agassiz believed could be found there—he was first of all an ichthyologist, and his earliest scientific works were extremely well-informed studies of Brazilian and then of Central European fish" (Lewis, *The Jameses,* 171). Agassiz (who never accepted Darwin's theory of evolution) and his wife, Elizabeth Cabot Cary Agassiz, published in 1868 their account of the expedition, *A Journey in Brazil.*

711. This might be regarded as further endorsement of the power of imagination in exploiting vicarious experience. The term "fun" recalls the seminal moment in the Galerie d'Apollon at the Louvre when HJ the boy glimpsed the creative possibilities, indeed the "sporting" life, ahead of him (see *SBO,* chap. 25).

people and things often by themselves, I dare say, neutral enough, how it painted thick, how it fairly smothered, any surface that did it the turn of showing positive and intrinsic life! Ah the things and the people, the hours and scenes and circumstances, the *inénarrables*[712] occasions and relations, that I might still present in its light if I would, and with the enormous advantage now (for this I should unblushingly claim), of being able to mark for present irony or pity or wonder, or just for a better intelligence, or again for the high humour or extreme strangeness of the thing, the rare indebtedness, calculated by the long run, in which it could leave particular cases! This necessity I was under that everything should be interesting—for fear of the collapse otherwise of one's sustaining intention—would have confessed doubtless to a closest connection, of all the connections, with the small inkpot in which I seemed at last definitely destined to dip to the exclusion of any stream more Pactolean:[713] a modest manner of saying that difficulty and slowness of composition were clearly by this time not in the least appointed to blight me, however inveterate they were likely to prove; that production, such as it was, floundered on in spite of them; and that, to put it frankly, if I enjoyed as much company as I have said no small part of it was of my very own earning. The freshness of first creations—since we are exalted, in art, to these arrogant expressions—never fails, I take it, to beguile the creator, in default of any other victim, even to the last extravagance; so that what happened was that one found all the swarm of one's intentions, one's projected images, quite "good enough" to mix with the rest of one's society, setting up with it terms of interpenetration, an admirable commerce of borrowing and lending, taking and giving, not to say stealing and keeping.[714] Did it verily *all*, this freshness of felt contact, of curiosity and wonder, come back perhaps to certain small

712. Beyond words, untellable. One of HJ's favorite epithets, "unspeakable," usually denotes for him inexpressible excitement rather than moral condemnation; taken in its literal application, the term might be regarded as an extreme expression of linguistic inadequacy or failure, related to the novelist's stammer, inherited from his father. However, the idea of HJ's speech hesitation has been regarded by some biographers as "apocryphal" (Edel, *Untried Years*, 285).

713. Presumably "golden": the Pactolus River in Lydia was famous in classical times for its golden sands.

714. HJ refers perhaps to his early short stories rather than the urbane and confident reviews he was providing for the periodicals. The extent of his "stealing" is arguable, though Habegger's *Henry James and the "Woman Business"* offers interesting parallels with the contemporary "agonists"—the popular American women novelists who wrote of unhappy women and loveless marriages.

and relatively ridiculous achievements of "production" as aforesaid?—
ridiculous causes, I mean, of such prodigious effects. I am divided between the shame on the one hand of claiming for them, these concocted
"short stories," that they played so great a part, and a downright admiring
tenderness on the other for their holding up their stiff little heads in such a
bustle of life and traffic of affairs. I of course really and truly cared for
them, as we say, more than for aught else whatever—cared for them with
that kind of care, infatuated though it may seem, that makes it bliss for the
fond votary never to so much as speak of the loved object, makes it a
refinement of piety to perform his rites under cover of a perfect freedom of
mind as to everything *but* them.[715] These secrets of the imaginative life
were in fact more various than I may dream of trying to tell; they referred
to actual concretions of existence as well as to the supposititious; the joy of
life indeed, drawbacks and all, was just in the constant quick flit of association, to and fro, and through a hundred open doors, between the two
great chambers (if it be not absurd, or even base, to separate them) of
direct and indirect experience. If it is of the great comprehensive *fusion*
that I speak as the richest note of all those hours, what could truly have
been more in the sense of it than exactly such a perfect muddle of pleasure
for instance as my having (and, as I seem to remember, at his positive
invitation) addressed the most presuming as yet of my fictional bids to my
distinguished friend of a virtual lifetime, as he was to become, William
Dean Howells, whom I rejoice to name here and who had shortly before
returned from a considerable term of exile in Venice and was in the act of
taking all but complete charge of the Boston "Atlantic"?[716] The confusion

715. Speaking of HJ's 112 tales, Maqbool Aziz comments that "most were given book
status by James himself, some receiving the honour more than once, in the collections
which he issued from time to time. Only fifty-five stories, however, found their way into the
'definitive' New York Edition" (*The Tales of Henry James*, vol. 1: *1864–1869*, ed. Aziz
[Oxford: Clarendon Press, 1973], xvii). The earliest tales found only limited favor with
their author: of the 14 tales in Aziz's volume covering the years 1864–69, only 6 were
reprinted in HJ's lifetime.

716. William Dean Howells (1837–1920), who had been American consul at Venice,
came from the Midwest. He began working on the *Atlantic Monthly* (edited by James
Fields) in 1865. His novels introduced a realist vein in fiction; his "canvas is not of a
dazzling brightness," HJ commented, invoking Zola, in his 1886 essay on Howells (*LC* 1,
503). The two men became close friends in the mid-1860s, taking regular Sunday walks
together, though HJ rarely felt able to appreciate Howells's predominantly American
subject matter. It was Howells who wrote to HJ accepting his story "Poor Richard" for
publication and inviting more submissions. The British novelist George Moore is reported

was, to be plain, of more things than can hope to go into my picture with any effect of keeping distinct there—the felt felicity, literally, in my performance, the felt ecstasy, the still greater, in my receipt of Howells's message; and then, naturally, most of all, the at once to be recorded blest violence in the break upon my consciousness of his glittering response after perusal.

There was still more in it all than that, however—which is the point of my mild demonstration; I associate the passage, to press closer, with a long summer, from May to November, spent at the then rural retreat of Swampscott, forty minutes by train northward from Boston,[717] and that scene of fermentation, in its turn, I invest with unspeakable memories. It was the summer of '66 and of the campaign of Sadowa across the sea[718]— we had by that time got sufficiently away from our own campaigns to take some notice of those of other combatants, on which we bestowed in fact, I think, the highest competence of attention then anywhere at play; a sympathetic sense that bore us even over to the Franco-German war four years later and helped us to know what we meant when we "felt strongly" about it.[719] No strength of feeling indeed of which the vibration had remained to us from the other time could have been greater than our woe-stricken vision of the plight of France under the portent of Sedan;[720] I had been

---

to have commented scathingly that while HJ went abroad and read Turgenev, Howells stayed at home and read HJ (Edel, *Untried Years*, 280).

717. For Swampscott, see above, n. 260. In one of the surviving American journals, written in March 1905 on the Californian coast, HJ records that distant summer of 1866, "the memory of lying on my bed at Swampscott . . . and reading, in ever so thrilled a state, George Eliot's *Felix Holt*, just out, and of which I was to write, and *did* write, a review in the *Nation*. (I had just come back from a bad little 'sick' visit to the Temples somewhere—I have forgotten the name of the place—in the White Mountains; and the Gourlays were staying with us at S[wampscott], and I was miserably stricken by my poor broken, all but unbearable, and unsurvivable *back* of those [and still, under fatigue, even of these] years.) To read over the opening pages of *Felix Holt* makes even now the whole time softly and shyly live again. Oh, strange little intensities of history, of ineffaceability; oh, delicate little odd links in the long chain, kept unbroken for the fingers of one's tenderest touch! Sanctities, pieties, treasures, abysses!" (*CN*, 239).

718. At the battle of Sadowa, or Königgrätz, 3 July 1866, Austria was defeated by Prussia after the Seven Weeks' War, part of growing Prussian dominance in Europe and also a blow to French national credibility.

719. France declared war (which had been partly orchestrated by Bismarck) on Germany on 19 July 1870. Peace was restored in spring 1871.

720. The surrender of Sedan in the Ardennes region of northern France on 2 September 1870 marked the collapse of Napoleon III's government. It was portentous because it marked Prussian military superiority and the eventual siege and bombardment of Paris in

back to that country and some of its neighbourhoods for some fifteen months during the previous interval,[721] and I recover again no share in a great collective pang more vividly than our particular appalled state, that of a whole company of us, while we gaped out at the cry of reiterated bulletins from the shade of an August verandah, and then again from amid boskages of more immediate consolation, during the Saratoga and the Newport seasons of 1870.[722] I had happened to repair to Saratoga, of all inconsequent places, on my return from the Paris and the London of the weeks immediately preceding the war, and though it was not there that the worst sound of the first crash reached us, I feel around me still all the air of our dismay—which was, in the queerest way in the world, that of something so alien mixed, to the increase of horror, with something so cherished: the great hot glare of vulgarity of the aligned hotels of the place and period drenching with its crude light the apparent collapse of everything we had supposed most massive. Which forward stretch on the part of this chronicle represents, I recognise, the practice of the discursive well-nigh overmastering its principle—or would do so, rather, weren't it that the fitful and the flickering, the extravagant advance and the corrective retreat from it, the law and the lovely art of foreshortening, have had here throughout most to serve me. It is under countenance of that law that I still grasp my capricious clue, making a jump for the moment over two or three years and brushing aside by the way quite numberless appeals, claims upon tenderness of memory not less than pleas for charm of interest, against which I must steel myself, even though I account this rank dis-

---

1871. Kaplan points out that "it seemed clear to Henry that the French rather than the Germans were at fault in the initiation of the war. // He did, though, prefer French republicanism to Prussian autocracy" (*The Imagination of Genius*, 125). *The History of David Grieve* (1892), a long novel by HJ's friend Mrs. Humphry Ward, recounts these Parisian scenes from the perspective of Henri Regnault, the real-life painter who appears in the novel and who was heroically killed at Buzenval, before the walls of Paris. HJ reviewed his letters, published posthumously, in the *Nation* (2 January 1873; *LC* 2, 619–27).

721. HJ had traveled alone to Europe in February 1869, returning to Cambridge in May 1870. He visited England, France, Switzerland, and Italy.

722. Having visited health spas in England for his digestive problems, HJ also made a trip in July 1870 to try the mineral springs at the resort of Saratoga Springs, in the Hudson Valley twenty-five miles north of Albany. Its famed hotels were numerous and large, and he stayed at the Grand Union, writing a travel sketch called "Saratoga," one of a series for the *Nation* magazine (August 1870) (*Henry James: Travel Writings: Britain and America*, 750–58). In August he went on to Newport, by this time a fashionable place in which to escape the heat of the summer months.

loyalty to each. There is no quarter to which I have inclined in my brief recovery of the high tide of impression flooding the "period" of Ashburton Place that might not have drawn me on and on; so that I confess I feel myself here drag my mantle, right and left, from the clutch of suppliant hands—voluminous as it may doubtless yet appear in spite of my sense of its raggedness. Wrapped in tatters it is therefore that, with three or four of William's letters of '67 and '68 kept before me, I make my stride, not only for the sake of what I still regard as their admirable interest, but for the way they bring back again to me everything they figured at the time, every flame of faith they rekindled, every gage they held out for the future. Present for me are still others than these in particular, which I keep over for another introducing, but even the pages I here preserve overflow with connections—so many that, extravagant as it may sound, I have to make an effort to breast them. These are with a hundred matters of our then actual life—little as that virtue may perhaps show on their face; but above all just with the huge small fact that the writer was by the blest description "in Europe," and that this had verily still its way of meaning for me more than aught else beside.[723] For what sprang in especial from his situation was the proof, with its positive air, that a like, when all was said, might become again one's own; that such luck wasn't going to be for evermore perversely out of the question with us, and that in fine I too was already in a manner transported by the intimacy with which I partook of his having been. I shouldn't have overstated it, I think, in saying that I really preferred such a form of experience (of this particular one) to the simpler—given most of our current conditions; there was somehow a greater richness, a larger accession of knowledge, vision, life, whatever one might have called it, in "having him there," as we said, and in my individually getting the good of this with the peculiar degree of ease that reinforced the general quest of a

723. WJ sailed for Europe in April 1867, returning in November 1868. Having stayed in Paris in May, he moved on to Dresden in the summer. August was spent in Teplitz (then in Bohemia), and from September to January 1868 he remained in Berlin. In early 1868 he was back in Teplitz, and then from March to June in Dresden. In the summer he briefly visited Heidelberg before returning to Berlin. From August to October he stayed at Divonne-les-Bains in the French Savoie before visiting Geneva and Paris. His motives for the trip (aside from improving his German) were at least twofold. This was a period of chronic ill health for WJ; he suffered from digestive disorders, insomnia, significant eye problems, back pain, and, as a consequence, serious depression. At Teplitz he took the baths for his back problem, a cure he also tried at Divonne. However, he also wished to develop his interest in experimental physiology, an area of study for which German universities were renowned.

*"The cold water cure at Divonne—excellent for melancholia."—*
*From a letter of William James (page 350). (Houghton Library, Harvard University)*

special sufficiency of that boon to which I was during those years rigidly, and yet on the whole by no means abjectly, reduced.

Our parents had in the autumn of '66 settled, virtually for the rest of their days, at Cambridge,[724] and William had concomitantly with this, that is from soon after his return from Brazil, entered upon a season of study at the Harvard Medical School, then keeping its terms in Boston and under the wide wing of—as one supposed it, or as I at any rate did—the Massachusetts General Hospital.[725] I have to disengage my mantle here with a

724. In October the Jameses moved to 20 Quincy Street, on the east side of Harvard Yard, opposite the home of the university's president, Thomas Hill. It was a "square frame house on a little rise of ground, overhung by trees . . . after the noise and bustle of Boston it seemed like a country retreat, a cloister" (Novick, *Young Master,* 142). The owner was Louis Thies, who had been curator of prints at Harvard (see also above, n. 190). HJ Sr. bought the house in 1870, and he and Mary James did not move again. In November 1867 HJ wrote to WJ (who was then in Berlin), "Life here in Cambridge—or in this house, at least, is about as lively as the inner sepulchre" (*CWJ,* 1:25). The house has since been replaced by the Harvard Faculty Club.

725. The Massachusetts General Hospital (designed originally by Charles Bulfinch) had been extended in 1846. "Near the hospital in Allen Street . . . stands the MASSACHUSETTS MEDICAL COLLEGE. This building will accommodate more than three hundred students. . . . This institution is properly a branch of Harvard College; . . . it

force in which I invite my reader to believe—for I push through a thicket of memories in which the thousand-fingered branches arrestingly catch; otherwise I should surrender, and with a passionate sense of the logic in it, to that long and crowded Swampscott summer at which its graceless name has already failed to keep me from having glanced. The place, smothered in a dense prose of prosperity now, may have been even in those days, by any high measure, a weak enough apology for an offered breast of Nature: nevertheless it ministered to me as the only "American country" save the silky Newport fringes with which my growing imagination, not to mention my specious energy, had met at all continuous occasion to play—so that I should have but to let myself go a little, as I say, to sit up to my neck again in the warm depth of its deposit. Out of this I should lift great handfuls of variety of vision; it was to have been in its way too a season of coming and going,[726] and with its main mark, I make out, that it somehow absurdly flowered, first and last, into some intenser example of every sort of intimation up to then vouchsafed me, whether by the inward or the outward life. I think of it thus as a big bouquet of blooms the most mixed—yet from which it is to the point just here to detach the sole reminiscence, coloured to a shade I may not reproduce, of a day's excursion to see my brother up at the Hospital. Had I not now been warned off too many of the prime images brought, for their confusion, to the final proof, I should almost risk ever so briefly "evoking" the impression this mere snatch was to leave with me, the picture as of sublime activities and prodigious possibilities, of genial communities of consideration and acquisition, all in a great bright porticoed and gardened setting, that was to hang itself in my crazy cabinet

---

may be doubted whether any seminary in the country offers the means of a more complete professional education than may be obtained in the medical school of Boston" (Midgley, *Sights in Boston and Suburbs*, 124).

726. In addition to HJ's own summer spent in such places as Newport, Swampscott (where the whole family had moved temporarily), and the White Mountains, and the independent movements of his brothers, Oliver Wendell Holmes Jr., to whom he was much attached, had gone to Europe. HJ passionately recalls in his American journal ("here, here, only here") the "particular little thrills and throbs and daydreams" of that late summer. He had gone to Charles Street "for news of O.W.H., then on his 1st flushed and charming visit to England, and saw his mother in the cool dim matted drawingroom of that house (passed, *never,* since, without the *sense*), and got the news, of all his London, his general English, success and felicity, and *vibrated* so with the wonder and romance and curiosity and dim weak tender (oh, tender!) envy of it, that my walk up the hill, afterwards, up Mount Vernon St. and probably to Athenaeum was all coloured and gilded, and humming with it" (*CN,* 239).

for as long as the light of the hour might allow.[727] I put my hand on the piece still—in its now so deeply obscured corner; though the true point of my reference would seem to be in the fact that if William studied medicine long enough to qualify and to take his degree (so as to have become as roundedly "scientific" as possible)[728] he was yet immediately afterwards, by one of those quick shifts of the scene with which we were familiar, beginning philosophic study in Germany and again writing home letters of an interest that could be but re-emphasised by our having him planted out as a reflector of impressions where impressions were both strong and as different as possible from those that more directly beat upon us. I myself could do well enough with these last, I may parenthesise, so long as none others were in question; but that complacency shrank just in proportion as we were reached by the report of difference and of the foreign note, the report particularly favourable—which was indeed what any and every report perforce appeared to me. William's, from anywhere, had ever an authority for me that attended none others; even if this be not the place for more than a word of light on the apparent disconnection of his actual course. It comes back to me that the purpose of practising medicine had at no season been flagrant in him, and he was in fact, his hospital connection once over, never to practise for a day. He was on the other hand to remain grateful for his intimate experience of the laboratory and the clinic, and I was as constantly to feel that the varieties of his application had been as little wasted for him as those of my vagueness had really been for me. His months at Dresden and his winter in Berlin were of a new variety—this last even with that tinge of the old in it which came from his sharing quarters with T. S. Perry, who, his four years at Harvard ended and his ensuing grand tour of Europe,[729] as

727. "The premises [of the hospital] have been improved by the planting of ornamental trees and shrubs, and the extension of the gravel walks for those patients whose health will admit of exercise in the open air, while a high fence gives retirement to a spot that should be always still" (Midgley, *Sights in Boston and Suburbs,* 122).

728. WJ, having (with interruptions) served the three years necessary, presented himself for final examination in June 1869. He was tested in anatomy by Dr. Oliver Wendell Holmes (Sr.): "The doctor asked the candidate a single question, and when William answered correctly, Holmes, according to a local tradition, said: 'That's enough! If you know *that,* you must know everything. Now tell me—how is your dear old father?'" (Lewis, *The Jameses,* 200).

729. Though the idea of a gentleman's education being completed by a grand tour of Europe (with Italy as the prime destination) is very much an aristocratic convention from an earlier era, it is clear that many of the well-connected young men of New England enjoyed a similar privilege while also engaging in formal learning.

then comprehensively carried out, performed, was giving the Universities of Berlin and Paris a highly competent attention.[730] To whatever else of method may have underlain the apparently lawless strain of our sequences I should add the action of a sharp lapse of health on my brother's part which the tension of a year at the dissecting table seemed to have done much to determine; as well as the fond fact that Europe was again from that crisis forth to take its place for us as a standing remedy, a regular mitigation of all suffered, or at least of all wrong, stress. Of which remarks but a couple of letters addressed to myself, I have to recognise, form here the occasion; these only, in that order, have survived the accidents of time, as I the more regret that I have in my mind's eye still much of the matter of certain others; notably of one from Paris (on his way further) recounting a pair of evenings at the theatre, first for the younger Dumas and Les Idées de Madame Aubray, with Pasca and Delaporte, this latter of an exquisite truth to him, and then for something of the Palais Royal with *four* comedians, as he emphatically noted, who were each, wonderful to say, "de la force of Warren of the Boston Museum."[731] He spent the summer of '67 partly in

730. Though he enjoyed Perry's company—"you've no idea how it lightens the burden of life to have some one to talk to an hour or two a day"—WJ considered the younger man had not "made as much intellectual progress as he might have done since he left home and has not outgrown his old laziness. This damned Parisian feuilleton & chronique literature I think has harmed him" (letter to HJ, 17 October 1867, *CWJ*, 1:22–23). The two were sharing quarters in Berlin in the winter of 1867, and WJ confessed on 26 December, "My great lack now is companionship. T.S.P. is too young and Grimm is too old, and I often long with a perfect vengeance for an evening at Cambridge." Hermann Grimm was "a son of one of the great Germanists ('the brothers G.')" (Perry, *Thought and Character of William James*, 254, 253).

731. The letter to which HJ refers was written on 3 May 1867 and obviously did survive. The original version in French is included in *CWJ*, 1:11–13. The letter's first half, translated into English, is given in Perry, *Thought and Character of William James*, 235–36. The four-act comedy by Alexandre Dumas *fils* (1824–95) *Les idées de Madame Aubray* was first performed on 16 March 1867 at the Gymnase-Dramatique theater in Paris. WJ's letter makes no mention of either Madame Pasca or Madame Delaporte, who had leading roles in the play. The Théâtre du Palais-Royal was associated with popular comedy. WJ mentions not four, but five "low-comedians"—though HJ's memory after more than forty years is still impressive. William Warren (1812–88) "played for thirty-seven years at the Boston Museum, and was not only a Boston institution, but one of the best actors of broad comedy in his time" (Perry, *Thought and Character of William James*, 235 n. 11). The Boston Museum Theater was founded in 1846 (see also *SBO*, n. 282). The beautiful building also housed a range of curiosities and exhibits (Donald C. King, *The Theatres of Boston: A Stage and Screen History* [Jefferson, N.C.: McFarland, 2005], 26, 32–36; and

Dresden and partly at Bad-Teplitz in Bohemia, where he had been recommended the waters; he was to return for these again after a few months and was also to seek treatment by hydropathy at the establishment of Divonne, in the French back-country of Lake Leman, where a drawing sent home in a letter, and which I do my best to reproduce, very comically represents him as surrounded by the listening fair.[732] I remember supposing even his Dresden of the empty weeks to bristle with precious images and every form of local character—this a little perhaps because of his treating us first of all to a pair of whimsical crayoned views of certain animated housetops seen from his window. It is the old names in the old letters, however, that now always most rewrite themselves to my eyes in colour—shades alas that defy plain notation, and if the two with which the following begins, and especially the first of them, only ask me to tell their story I but turn my back on the whole company of which they are part.

. . . I got last week an excellent letter from Frank Washburn who writes in such a manly way.[733] But the greatest delight I've had was the loan of 5 Weekly Transcripts from Dick Derby.[734] It's strange how quickly one grows away from one's old surroundings. I never should have believed that in so few months the tone of a Boston paper would seem so outlandish to me. As it was, I was in one squeal of amusement, surprise and satisfaction until deep in the night, when I went to bed tired out with patriotism. The boisterous animal good-humour, familiarity, reckless energy and self-confidence, unprincipled

---

William C. Young, *Documents of American Theater History: Famous American Play-houses, 1716–1899* [Chicago: American Library Association, 1973], 1:104). *De la force:* of the calibre.

732. Lake Leman is more commonly known as Lake Geneva. Susan E. Gunter suggests that "the image can be read as William's desire to mesmerize women with accounts of his ailments and cures, or perhaps it is a self-ironizing record of a real event. When Henry found the drawing again decades later, he called it 'the comic (so very charming) thing of the listening young ladies at the Divonne water cure'" (*Alice in Jamesland: The Story of Alice Howe Gibbens James* [Lincoln: University of Nebraska Press, 2009], 37).

733. WJ writes to his "dearest Family." The letter is dated 24 July 1867; he was staying with Frau Kayser in Dresden (*CWJ* 4:182). Francis Tucker Washburn (1843–73) graduated from Harvard in 1864 and later became a Unitarian clergyman.

734. WJ refers to the *Boston Weekly Transcript*. Richard Henry Derby (1844–1907) was a physician who "graduated from Harvard in 1864" and "studied in Europe from 1867 to the summer of 1870" (*CWJ*, 4:606). Elsewhere, however, WJ, referring to "that poor creature" Derby, confesses that he "cannot stomach him" (*CWJ*, 4:234, 177).

optimism, esthetic saplessness and intellectual imbecility, made a mixture hard to characterise, but totally different from the tone of things here and, as the Germans would say, whose "Existenz so völlig dasteht,"[735] that there was nothing to do but to let yourself feel it. The Americans themselves here too amuse me much; they have such a hungry, restless look and seem so unhooked somehow from the general framework. The other afternoon as I was sitting on the Terrace, a gentleman and two young ladies came and sat down quite near me. I knew them for Americans at a glance, and the man interested me by his exceedingly American expression: a reddish moustache and tuft on chin, a powerful nose, a small light eye, half insolent and *all* sagacious, and a sort of rowdy air of superiority that made me proud to claim him as a brother. In a few minutes I recognised him as General M'Clellan,[736] rather different from his photographs of the War-time, but still not to be mistaken (and I afterwards learned he is here). Whatever his faults may be that of not being "one of us" is not among them.

This next is the note of a slightly earlier impression.[737]

The Germans are certainly a most gemüthlich people. The way all the old women told me how "freundlich" their rooms were—so "freundlich mobilirt" and so forth—melted my heart.[738] Whenever you tell an inferior here to do anything (*e.g.* a cabman) he or she replies "Schön!" or rather "Schehn!" with an accent not quick like a Frenchman's "Bien!"[739] but so protracted, soothing and reassuring to you that you feel as if he were adopting you into his family. You say I've said nothing of the people of this house, but there is nothing to tell about them.[740] The Doctor is an open-hearted excellent man as

---

735. Whose existence is so totally present (Ger.).

736. Spelling as in first edition. McClellan stood as a Democratic presidential candidate in 1864, but lost to Lincoln. After the war he spent much of his time abroad.

737. What follows is an extract from a letter written to HJ, 27 June 1867, and sent from Dresden (see *CWJ*, 1:16–18).

738. *Gemüthlich* (or *gemütlich*): good-natured; *so freundlich mobilirt* (or *möbliert*): furnished in such a friendly, congenial way.

739. *Schön:* fine ("schehn" is an attempt to render the local Dresden accent); *bien:* fine.

740. WJ was staying with the Semler family in Dresden. Dr. Semler is "Christian Semler (b. 1828) who published several works on Shakespeare and Homer. He was WJ's first landlord in Dresden. Dresden directories show a J. Jacob Christian Semler residing at Christianstrasse" (*CWJ*, 1:18 n. 3).

ever was, and wrapped up in his children; Frau Semler is a sickly, miserly, petty-spirited nonentity. The children are quite uninteresting, though the younger, Anna or Aennchen, aged five, is very handsome and fat. The following short colloquy, which I overheard one day after breakfast a few days since, may serve you as a piece of local colour. Aennchen drops a book she is carrying across the room and exclaims "Herr Jesus!"

Mother: "Ach, das sagen *Kinder* nicht, Anna!"

Aennchen (reflectively to herself, sotto voce): "Nicht fur Kinder!" . . . [741]

What here follows from Divonne—of fourteen months later—is too full and too various to need contribution or comment.[742]

You must have envied within the last few weeks my revisiting of the sacred scenes of our youth, the shores of Leman, the Écu de Genève, the sloping Corraterie, etc.[743] My only pang in it all has been caused by your absence, or rather by the fact of my presence instead of yours; for I think your abstemious and poetic soul would have got much more good of the things I've seen than my hardening and definite-growing nature. I wrote a few words about Nürnberg to Alice from Montreux.[744] I found that about as pleasant an impression as any I have had since being abroad—and this because I didn't expect it. The Americans at Dresden had told me it was quite uninteresting. I enclose you a few stereographs I got there—I don't know why, for they are totally irrelevant to the real effect of the place. This it would take Théophile Gautier to describe, so I renounce.[745] It was strange to find how little I remembered at Geneva—I couldn't find the way I used to

741. *Ach, das sagen Kinder nicht:* Oh, *children* don't say that; *nicht fur [für] Kinder:* not for children (the little girl hinting at adult double standards).

742. WJ to HJ, Divonne, 26 August [1868] (*CWJ*, 1:54).

743. WJ refers to the family's stay in Geneva, most recently in 1859-60, recalled by HJ in chap. 1 above. They had stayed in the Hôtel de l'Écu; the "sloping Corraterie" is a street.

744. Nürnberg (or Nuremberg) is a historic town of Bavaria in southern Germany; Montreux, a Swiss town, lies at the eastern end of Lake Geneva. Though two letters from WJ to Alice, written from Dresden in June and July 1868, have survived, no letter from this period written from Montreux is given or referred to in *CWJ*, 4.

745. A stereograph was a picture representing an object so that is appears to be solid. Pierre Jules Théophile Gautier (1811-72) was a poet, novelist, and journalist, also famed for his travel writings, particularly on Spain and Russia.

take up to the Academy, and the shops and houses of the Rue du Rhône visible from our old windows[746] left me uncertain whether they were the same or new ones. Kohler has set up a new hotel on the Quai du Mont-Blanc—you remember he's the brother of our old Madame Buscarlet there; but I went for association's sake to the Écu. The dining-room was differently hung, and the only thing in my whole 24 hours in the place that stung me, so to speak, with memory, was that kind of chinese-patterned dessert-service we used to have. So runs the world away. I didn't try to look up Ritter, Chantre or any of ces messieurs, but started off here the next morning, where I have now been a week.[747]

My impression on gradually coming from a German into a French atmosphere of things was rather unexpected and not in all respects happy. I have been in Germany half amused and half impatient with the slowness of proceeding and the uncouthness of taste and expression that prevail there so largely in all things, but on exchanging it for the brightness and shipshapeness of these quasi-French arrangements of life and for the tart fire-cracker-like speech of those who make them I found myself inclined to retreat again on what I had left, and had for a few days quite a homesickness for the easy, ugly, substantial German ways. The "'tarnal" smartness in which the railway refreshment counters, for example, are dressed up, the tight waists and "tasteful" white caps of the female servants, the everlasting monsieur and madame, and especially the quickness and snappishness of enunciation, suggesting such an inward impatience, quite absurdly gave on my nerves. But I am getting used to it all, and the French people who sit near me here at table and who repelled me at first by the apparently cold-blooded artificiality of their address to each other, now seem less heartless and inhuman. I am struck more than ever I was with the hopelessness of us English, and *a fortiori* the Germans, ever competing with the French in matters of form or finite taste of any sort. They are sensitive to things that simply don't exist for us. I notice it here in manners and speech: how can a people who speak with no tonic accents in their words *help* being cleaner and neater in expressing themselves? On the other hand the limitations of *reach* in the French mind strike me more and more; their delight in

746. The Hôtel de l'Écu where they had stayed was in the place du Rhône.

747. Charles Ritter (1838–1908) was a Swiss scholar, Ernest Chantre (1843–1924) a French anthropologist; both had become friends of WJ during his schooldays in Switzerland.

rallying round an official standard in all matters, in counting and dating everything from certain great names, their use and love of catchwords and current phrases, their sacrifice of independence of mind for the mere sake of meeting their hearer or reader on common ground, their metaphysical incapacity not only to deal with questions but to know what the questions are, stand out plainer and plainer the more headway I make in German. One wonders where the "Versöhnung"[748] or conciliation of all these rival national qualities is going to take place. I imagine we English stand rather between the French and the Germans both in taste and in spiritual intuition. In Germany, while unable to avoid respecting that solidity of the national mind which causes such a mass of permanent work to be produced there annually, I couldn't help consoling myself by the thought that whatever, after all, they might *do,* the Germans were a plebeian crowd and could never *be* such gentlemen as we were. I now find myself getting over the French superiority by an exactly inverse process of thought. The Frenchman must sneer at us even more than we sneer at the Germans—and which sneer is final, his at us two, or ours at him, or the Germans' at us? It seems an insoluble question, which I fortunately haven't got to settle.

I've read several novels lately, some of the irrepressible George's: La Daniella and the Beaux Messieurs de Bois-Doré.[749] (Was it thee, by the bye, that wrotest the Nation notices on her, on W. Morris's new poem and on The Spanish Gypsy? They came to me unmarked, but the thoughts seemed such as you would entertain, and the style in some places like yours—in others not.)[750] George Sand babbles her improvisations on so that I never begin to believe a word of what she says. I've also read The Woman in White,[751] a couple of Balzac's, etc., and a volume of tales by Mérimée which I will send you if I can by Frank Washburn. He is a big man; but the things which have given me most pleasure have been some sketches of travel by Th. Gautier. What

748. Reconciliation (Ger.).

749. George Sand's *La Daniella* was published in 1865, *Les beaux messieurs de Bois-Doré* in 1857.

750. HJ reviewed for the *Nation* in July 1868 George Sand's *Mademoiselle Merquem* (*LC* 2, 696–701), William Morris's *The Earthly Paradise* (*LC* 1, 1182–86), and George Eliot's poem *The Spanish Gypsy* (*LC* 1, 933–41); he also published a lengthy review of *The Spanish Gypsy* in the *North American Review* in October 1868 (*LC* 1, 941–58).

751. *The Woman in White,* by the British novelist Wilkie Collins (1824–89), was published in 1860.

an absolute thing genius is! That this creature, with no more soul than a healthy poodle-dog, no philosophy, no morality, no information (for I doubt exceedingly if his knowledge of architectural terms and suchlike is accurate) should give one a finer enjoyment than his betters in all these respects by mere force of good-nature, clear eyesight and felicity of phrase! His style seems to me perfect, and I should think it would pay you to study it with love—principally in the most trivial of these collections of notes of travel. T. S. P.[752] has a couple of them for you, and another, which I've read here and is called Caprices et Zigzags, is worth buying. It contains wonderful French (in the classic sense, I mean, with all those associations) descriptions of London. I'm not sure if you know Gautier at all save by the delicious Capitaine Fracasse.[753] But these republished feuilletons[754] are all of as charming a quality and I should think would last as long as the language.

There are 70 or 80 people in this etablissement,[755] no one of whom I have as yet particularly cottoned up to. It's incredible how even so slight a barrier as the difference of language with most of them, and still more as the absence of local and personal associations, range of gibes and other common ground to stand on, counts against one's scraping acquaintance. It's disgusting and humiliating. There is a lovely maiden of *etwa*[756] 19 sits in sight of me at the table with whom I am falling deeply in love. She has never looked at me yet, and I really believe I should be quite incapable of conversing with her even were I "introduced," from a sense of the above difficulties and because one doesn't know what subjects or allusions may be possible with a jeune fille.[757] I suppose my life for the past year would have furnished you, as the great American nouvelliste, a good many "motives" and subjects of observation—especially so in this place. I wish I could pass them over to you—such as they are you'd profit by them more than I and gather in a great many more. I should like full well an hour's, or even longer, interview with you, and with the Parents and the Sister and the Aunt and all; just so as to start afresh on a clean basis. Give my

752. Thomas Sergeant Perry.

753. *Caprices et zigzags* (1845) deals in part with English life; *Capitaine Fracasse* (1863) is a picaresque mystery novel.

754. Serial stories.

755. Establishment.

756. About (Ger.).

757. Young girl.

love to Wendell Holmes. I've seen —— —— several times;[758] but what a cold-blooded cuss he is! Write me your impression of T. S. P., who will probably reach you before this letter. If Frank Washburn ever gets home be friendly to him. He is much aged by travel and experience, and is a most charming character and generous mind.

# XIII

If I add to the foregoing a few lines more from my brother's hand, these are of a day separated by long years from that time of our youth of which I have treated. Addressed after the immense interval to an admirable friend whom I shall not name here,[759] they yet so vividly refer—and with something I can only feel as the first authority—to one of the most prized interests of our youth that, under the need of still failing to rescue so many of these values from the dark gulf, I find myself insist the more on a place here, before I close, for that presence in our early lives as to which my brother's few words say so much. To have so promptly and earnestly spoken of Mary Temple the younger in this volume is indeed I think to have offered a gage for my not simply leaving her there. The opportunity not so to leave her comes at any rate very preciously into my hands, and I can not better round off this record than by making the most of it.[760] The

758. In the original, WJ refers to John Chipman Gray, who was still alive at the time of *NSB*'s publication; he died in 1915.

759. John Chipman Gray (1839–1915) was a lawyer and professor at Harvard Law School. Again without revealing Gray's identity, HJ recalls seeing him in the distance—but not speaking to him—when he revisited Harvard on his 1904–5 trip to the United States: "I went into the new Law Library, immense and supreme—in the shadow of which I caught myself sniffing the very dust, pre-historic but still pungent, of the old. I saw in the distance a distinguished friend, all alone, belatedly working there, but to go to him I should have had to cross the bridge that spans the gulf of time, and, with a suspicion of weak places, I was nervous about its bearing me" (*AS*, 59).

760. HJ received a cache of twenty-three letters (of which he used nineteen) written by Minny Temple to John Chipman Gray when he was three-quarters of the way through *NSB*. "Wrapped . . . in the beauty and dignity of art," as HJ comments at the end of the chapter, his cousin became an inspiration for Isabel Archer in *The Portrait of a Lady*, who (unlike Minny) goes to Europe and "affronts" her destiny, and also for Milly Theale, the dying heroine of *The Wings of the Dove*. Anticipating the latter novel, he recorded in his Notebook over twenty-four years after her death "the little idea of the situation of some young creature . . . who, at 20 . . . is suddenly condemned to death. . . . She learns that she has but a short time to live, and she rebels, she is terrified, she cries out in her anguish, her tragic young despair. She is in love with life . . . and she clings to it with passion, with

letter to which William alludes is one that my reader will presently recognise. It had come back to him thus clearly at the far end of time.[761]

I am deeply thankful to you for sending me this letter, which revives all sorts of poignant memories and makes her live again in all her lightness and freedom. Few spirits have been more free than hers. I find myself wishing so that she could know me as I am now. As for knowing her as *she* is now—??!! I find that she means as much in the way of human character for me now as she ever did, being unique and with no analogue in all my subsequent experience of people. Thank you once more for what you have done.

The testimony so acknowledged was a letter in a copious succession, the product of little more than one year, January '69 to February '70, sacredly preserved by the recipient; who was not long after the day of my brother's acknowledgment to do me the honour of communicating to me the whole series.[762] He could have done nothing to accord more with the spirit in which I have tried to gather up something of the sense of our far-off past, his own as well as that of the rest of us; and no loose clue that I have been able to recover unaided touches into life anything like such a tract of the time-smothered consciousness. More charming and interesting things emerge for me than I can point to in their order—but they will make, I think, their own appeal. It need only further be premised that our delightful young cousin had had from some months back to begin to reckon with the progressive pulmonary weakness of which the letters tell

supplication. 'I don't want to die—I won't, I won't, oh, let me live; oh, save me!' . . . If she only could live just a little; just a little more—just a little longer" (*CN,* 102–3).

761. The letter from WJ to Gray that follows is dated 17 March, but without indicating a year. Clearly, it was written in his later years, and WJ died in August 1910. The surviving MS is in the hand of Alice Howe Gibbens James (bMS Am 1092.1 [39], Houghton). The Minny Temple letter that Gray sent to him is probably the one dated 27 January 1869 where she speaks warmly and admiringly of her cousin (see also *Letters of William James,* 1:36–37). It is evident that Gray had been thinking of Minny and these letters for a number of years before going to see Alice James in 1913, though HJ goes on to say that the time between the writing of WJ's letter and the handing over of the letters was "not long." The letter appears in appendix 2 of *CWJ,* 12:673.

762. It would be impracticable to indicate and comment on all the changes made by HJ to the following letters, but the copies, originally made by Alice Howe Gibbens James and her daughter, have been included in the collection of Mary Temple's letters appended to this volume. It was, of course, HJ's sister-in-law who enabled him to read the letters.

the sad story.[763] Also, I can scarce help saying, the whole world of the old New York, that of the earlier dancing years, shimmers out for me from the least of her allusions.

I will write you as nice a letter as I can, but would much rather have a good talk with you.[764] As I can't have the best thing I am putting up with the second-best, contrary to my pet theory. I feel as if I were in heaven to-day—all because the day is splendid and I have been driving about all the morning in a small sleigh in the fresh air and sunshine, until I found that I had in spite of myself, for the time being, stopped asking the usual inward question of why I was born. I am not going to Canada—I know no better reason for this than because I said I *was* going.[765] My brother-in-law makes such a clamour when I propose departure that I am easily overcome by his kindness and my own want of energy.[766] Besides, it is great fun to live here; the weather just now

763. Like both her parents, Mary Temple died of tuberculosis. The New England region "was generally recognized as 'miasmic' " and the disease "was responsible for one-fifth of all deaths" (Bundy, *The Nature of Sacrifice*, 104).

764. This letter is written from Pelham, near New Rochelle, a suburb of New York City, the home of her sister Kitty, married to Richard Stockton Emmet. It is dated 7 January 1869.

765. Visiting Canada, Minny had "stayed with Sir John Rose (1820–88), a statesman and financier, known as 'Rose of Montreal' " (Gordon, *A Private Life of Henry James*, 42). It was a second marriage both for him and for Minny's aunt Charlotte, who was the sister of her father, Robert, and of Mary Tweedy, who became her guardian (see also *A Life in Letters*, 151 n. 4).

766. Kitty had married her rather older husband Richard on 29 September 1868, and they were living in a large country house. Another sister, Ellen (Elly), went on to marry Richard's similarly wealthy brother, Christopher Temple Emmet (1822–84), a railroad baron, twenty-eight years older than his bride. Mary Walsh James had written to HJ on 21 September 1869, "You know they have been living (I mean Elly & Mr. E.) in the house together for several months and he had been in the habit of lavishing presents upon her and jestingly saying what he was going to give her when she became his 'little wife'—No one thought of the possibility of such a thing. In this way they both became accustomed to the thought. He told Kitty that when he found Elly's fascinations exerting such power over him he made up his mind that it could not be and that he must tear himself away—but he could not do it—And it seems there was no need, the fascination was mutual—I only trust that it. has not been his good things (for it seems he has prospects of great wealth) that have seduced Elly" (bMS Am 1093.1 [37], Houghton). These age differences were a cause of general surprise within the family and a possible reason (aside from a few critical comments among the generally favorable) for the surviving sisters' unhappiness about the publication of Minny's letters of the time. Some biographers have speculated that Kitty married partly to provide a home for her younger sisters.

is grand, and I knock about all day in a sleigh, and do nothing but enjoy it and meditate. Then we are so near town that we often go in for the day to shop and lunch with some of our numerous friends, returning with a double relish for the country. We all went in on a spree the other night and stayed at the Everett House; from which, as a starting-point, we poured ourselves in strong force upon Mrs. Gracie King's ball—a very grand affair, given for a very pretty Miss King, at Delmonico's.[767] Our raid consisted of thirteen Emmets and a moderate supply of Temples, and the ball was a great success. It was two years since I had been to one and I enjoyed it so much that I mean very soon to repeat the experiment—at the next Assembly if possible. The men in society, in New York, this winter, are principally a lot of feeble-minded boys; but I was fortunate enough to escape them, as my partner for the German[768] was a man of thirty-five, the solitary *man*, I believe, in the room. Curiously enough, I had danced my last German, two years before, in that very place and with the same person. He is a Mr. Lee, who has spent nearly all his life abroad; two of his sisters have married German princes, and from knocking about so much he has become a thorough cosmopolite. As he is intelligent, with nothing to do but amuse himself, he is a very agreeable partner, and I mean to dance with him again as soon as possible.[769] I don't know why I have tried your patience by writing so about a person you have never seen; unless it's to show you that I haven't irrevocably given up the world, the flesh and the devil, but am conscious of a

767. Everett House was a New York City hotel on the northwest corner of Union Square. Delmonico's is a famous Manhattan restaurant, which had moved to Fourteenth Street and Fifth Avenue in 1862 and later transferred to Twenty-sixth Street. "Archibald Gracie King was the first man in New York Society to give a ball elsewhere than under his own roof. In the early '70's, he decided to celebrate the début of one of his daughters not at his home but at Delmonico's, then at Fourteenth Street and Fifth Avenue. Accordingly, he interviewed Charley Delmonico and told that shocked purveyor to the appetites of the élite that he wished his largest rooms for a dance and supper. Delmonico expostulated and then surrendered" (Mrs. John King Van Rensselaer in collaboration with Frederic Van de Water, *The Social Ladder* [New York: Henry Holt, 1924; rpt. New York: Arno Press, 1975], 37–38). See also Beckert, *The Monied Metropolis*, 156.

768. The German *cotillon*, a kind of dance.

769. David Bradley Lee would have been an appropriate age; he died, according to a *New York Times* obituary of 26 August 1903, at the age of seventy. His wealth was based on the wholesale grocery market in New York City, and he continued to make frequent visits to Europe. His sisters were the Countess von Waldersee and the Baroness de Wechter.

faint charm about them still when taken in small doses. I agree with you perfectly about Uncle Henry—I should think he would be very irritating to the legal mind; he is not at all satisfactory even to mine.[770] Have you seen much of Willy James lately? That is a rare creature, and one in whom my intellect, if you will pardon the misapplication of the word, takes more solid satisfaction than in almost anybody.[771] I haven't read Browning's new book—I mean to wait till you are by to explain it to me—which reminds me, along with what you say about wishing for the spring, that we shall go to North Conway next summer,[772] and that in that case you may as well make up your mind to come and see us there. I can't wait longer than that for the Browning readings. (Which would have been of The Ring and the Book.)[773] Arthur

770. Minny Temple's relationship with both James parents (and, to an extent, their daughter Alice) seems to have been an uneasy one. In having ideas and being willing to express them, she clearly challenged Mary James's views on women and their appropriate behavior. Lilla Cabot, another intelligent and creative young woman (she married Sarge Perry and became a successful painter), knew the family and criticized "the poky banality of the James house, ruled by Mrs James." She regarded Alice as "clever but coldly self-absorbed" and dismissed Mrs. James and Aunt Kate as "large florid stupid-seeming ladies" (quoted by Edel in the introduction to Alice James, *Diary*, 5–6). Minny had visited the Cambridge household near the end of 1869 and found little consolation in her uncle's spiritual ideas; she was, it seems, lectured by him, as she records in one of the letters toward the end of this chapter. Though HJ made numerous emendations to her letters, and was in general protective of his father's memory, he allowed these critical comments to stand. For an interpretation of this familial relationship, of the tension between HJ's vision of woman and orphanhood, and of the translation of Minny Temple into a fantasized fictional figure, see Habegger, *Henry James and the "Woman Business"*, chap. 6: "Minnie Temple's Death and the Birth of Henry James's Imagination."

771. The relationship between the cousins had been difficult, as a letter of WJ's to HJ, written on 5 December 1869, indicates: "M. Temple was here for a week a fortnight since. She was delightful in all respects, and although very thin, very cheerful. I am conscious of having done her a good deal of injustice for some years past, in nourishing a sort of unsympathetic hostility to her. She is after all a most honest little phenomenon, and there is a true respectability in the courage with which she keeps 'true to her own instincts'—I mean it has a certain religious side with her. Moreover she is more devoid of 'meanness,' of anything petty in her character than any one I know, perhaps either male or female. *Je tiens à* telling you this, as I recollect last winter abusing her to you rather virulently" (*CWJ*, 1:129). According to Philip Horne, Minny arrived on 19 November 1869 (*A Life in Letters*, 36 n. 1).

772. North Conway is in the Mount Washington valley of the White Mountains, New Hampshire.

773. As previously mentioned, these occasional parenthetical notes (including the odd

Sedgwick[774] has sent me Matthew Arnold's photograph, which Harry had pronounced so disappointing. I don't myself, on the whole, find it so; on the contrary, after having looked at it much, I like it—it quite harmonises with my notion of him, and I have always had an affection for him.[775] You must tell me something that you are *sure* is true—I don't care much what it may be, I will take your word for it. Things get into a muddle with me—how can I give you "a start on the way of righteousness"? You know that way better than I do, and the only advice I can give you is not to stop saying your prayers. I hope God may bless you, and beyond those things I hardly know what is right, and therefore what to wish you. Good-bye.

"North Conway" in the foregoing has almost the force for me of a wizard's wand; the figures spring up again and move in a harmony that is not of the fierce present; the sense in particular of the August of '65 shuts me in to its blest unawarenesses not less than to all that was then exquisite in its current certainties and felicities; the fraternising, endlessly conversing group of us gather under the rustling pines—and I admire, precisely, the arrival, the bright revelation as I recover it, of the so handsome young man, marked with military distinction but already, with our light American promptitude, addressed to that high art of peace in which a greater eminence awaited him, of whom this most attaching member of the circle was to make four years later so wise and steady a confidant.[776] Our

---

one in square brackets) are HJ's. *The Ring and the Book* was published between November 1868 and February 1869 (see also HJ's essay, delivered as part of the Browning centenary celebrations, "The Novel in 'The Ring and the Book,'" *Transactions of the Royal Society of Literature,* 2nd ser., 31, no. 4 [1912]; *LC* 1, 791–811). Browning is, of course, notorious for his sometimes difficult and obscure style.

774. See above, n. 426.

775. The middle and late sixties saw the publication of some of Arnold's great prose works, notably the *Essays in Criticism* (1st ser., 1865) and *Culture and Anarchy* (1869). HJ reviewed the former for the *North American Review* (*LC,* 1:711–19), earning Arnold's respect; he was "unaware that it was the work of a twenty-two-year-old novice" (*HJL,* 1:58 n. 2). HJ would first meet Arnold in 1873 at William Wetmore Story's apartment in the Palazzo Barberini, Rome.

776. The "so handsome young man" is John Chipman Gray. Oliver Wendell Holmes was also in the group, and it seems that he and HJ had to share a room, if not a bed, in the lodgings Minny had found for them (*HJL,* 1:60–61). The four Temple sisters were there: Kitty Temple aged twenty-two, Minny twenty, Elly fifteen, and Henrietta twelve. The idyllic setting and group of young people, the romantic possibilities, the memory of a recently finished war may all have inspired HJ to write "Poor Richard" (1867), as Edel

circle I fondly call it, and doubtless then called it, because in the light of that description I could most rejoice in it, and I think of it now as having formed a little world of easy and happy interchange, of unrestricted and yet all so instinctively sane and secure association and conversation, with all its liberties and delicacies, all its mirth and its earnestness protected

---

suggests in *Untried Years* (231–39). More recently, however, Novick (*Young Master*, 474–75 n. 26) has offered a revised account, claiming to straighten the record of this "canonical scene" accepted by "a generation of commentators." He argues that Edel's account is overly derived from the short story rather than historical events, specifically in focusing on the tensions between two ex–Civil War heroes and the humiliation felt by "poor Richard," the noncombatant, as the three men vie for the favor of the central female character. "Gray was not present on this visit. HJ says that Gray came 'a little later,' at Holmes's invitation . . . and this is confirmed by what I have been able to learn of Gray's movements. Gray probably first visited North Conway the next year, in the summer of 1866. When Gray eventually did make the acquaintance of the Temple girls, he seems to have taken an interest in Kitty, rather than Minny. In short, rather than three young men competing for Minny Temple on one traumatic summer afternoon, we have HJ bringing Holmes to meet her, her two sisters, and a maiden aunt. . . . There is no evidence that the scene of the three men competing for Minny Temple's attention ever happened; and there is very good reason to think that it was Holmes, rather than Minny, with whom HJ was in 'love.' " There are, of course, dangers in speculating, as both biographers do, on the emotional dynamics of the episode. Novick's version, however, does seem to ignore elements in HJ's own autobiographical account. Here HJ invites Holmes, who, in turn, introduced "a little later the great friend of *his* then expanding situation"; Holmes and Gray thus made an "interesting pair . . . possessed . . . of a quantity of common fine experience" (i.e., the war). The "most attaching member of the circle," Minny Temple, would "four years later" make Gray her confidant. The male visitors ("three quite exceptional young men," as he jokingly says) engaged in "the final sublime coach-drive of other days." HJ refers to the last five miles from Conway to North Conway, the rest of the journey being taken from Boston by railroad. This is what Edel implies, but he is unnecessarily corrected by Novick, who points out that "there was no 'old carriage road' from Boston to North Conway." The events (as HJ narrates them—with whatever inaccuracies of memory) thus coincide much more closely with Edel's than with Novick's account, some of it based on eccentric readings of phrases like "a little later" to imply a year's difference. HJ's letter of 1914, written to Henrietta Temple, seems entirely to verify Edel's account: "Do *you* remember that far-away old 1st summer at North Conway & the Blue Blinds, with J.G. & O.W.H. & Aunt Charlotte & H.I., in short all of us, or were you too juvenile a little shrimp?" (S. P. Rosenbaum, "Letters to the Pell-Clarkes from Their 'Old Cousin and Friend' Henry James," *American Literature* 31 [March 1959]: 46–58, on 54). The Blue Blinds was one of the many lodging houses in North Conway. In the early twentieth century, HJ would return—with a touch of nostalgia—to the White Mountains, this time in Edith Wharton's automobile: "The old informal earthy coach-road was a firm highway, wide and white—

and directed so much more from within than from without, that I ask myself, perhaps too fatuously, whether any such right conditions for the play of young intelligence and young friendship, the reading of Matthew Arnold and Browning, the discussion of a hundred human and personal things, the sense of the splendid American summer drawn out to its last generosity, survives to this more complicated age. I doubt if there be circles to-day, and seem rather to distinguish confusedly gangs and crowds and camps, more propitious, I dare say, to material affluence and physical riot than anything we knew, but not nearly so appointed for ingenious and ingenuous talk. I think of our interplay of relation as attuned to that fruitful freedom of what we took for speculation, what we didn't recoil from as boundless curiosity—as the consideration of life, that is, the personal, the moral inquiry and adventure at large, so far as matter for them had up to then met our view—I think of this fine quality in our scene with no small confidence in its having been rare, or to be more exact perhaps, in its having been possible to the general American felicity and immunity as it couldn't otherwise or elsewhere have begun to be. Merely to say, as an assurance, that such relations shone with the light of "innocence" is of itself to breathe on them wrongly or rudely, is uncouthly to "defend" them—as if the very air that consciously conceived and produced them didn't all tenderly and amusedly take care of them. I at any rate figure again, to my customary positive piety, all the aspects now; that in especial of my young orphaned cousins as mainly composing the maiden train and seeming as if they still had but yesterday brushed the morning dew of the dear old Albany naturalness;[777] that of the venerable, genial, erect great-aunt, their more immediately active guardian, a model of antique spinsterhood appointed to cares such as even renewals of wedlock could scarce more have multiplied for her, and thus, among her many ancient and curious national references—one was tempted to call them—most impressive by her striking resemblance to the portraits, the most benignant, of General Washington. She might have represented the mother, no less adequately than he represented the father, of their country.[778] I can only feel, however, that what particularly drew the desired

---

and ground to dust, for all its firmness, by the whirling motor; without which I might have followed it, back and back, into the near, into the far, country of youth" (*AS*, 27).

777. Both their parents had died in 1854; HJ had witnessed as a child these scenes of adult tragedy (see *SBO*, chap. 13).

778. There are differing views concerning the identity of the elderly female relative of the Temple girls who accompanied them to North Conway in summer 1865. The "great-

circle sharpest for me was the contribution to it that I had been able to effect by introducing the companion of my own pilgrimage, who was in turn to introduce a little later the great friend of *his* then expanding situation, restored with the close of the War to civil pursuits and already deep in them; the interesting pair possessed after this fashion of a quantity of common fine experience that glittered as so much acquired and enjoyed luxury—all of a sort that I had no acquisition whatever to match. I remember being happy in that I might repeatedly point our moral, under permission (for we were always pointing morals), with this brilliant advantage of theirs even if I might with none of my own; and I of course knew—what was half the beauty—that if we were just the most delightful loose band conceivable, and immersed in a regular revel of all the harmonies, it was largely by grace of the three quite exceptional young men who, thanks in part to the final sublime coach-drive of other days, had travelled up from Boston with their preparation to admire inevitably quickened. I was quite willing to offer myself as exceptional through being able to promote such exceptions and see them justified to waiting apprehension. There was a dangling fringe, there were graceful accessories and hovering shades, but, essentially, we of the true connection made up the drama, or in other words, for the benefit of my imagination, reduced the fond figment of the Circle to terms of daily experience. If drama we could indeed feel this as being, I hasten to add, we owed it most of all to our just having such a heroine that everything else inevitably came. Mary Temple was beautifully and indescribably *that*—in the technical or logical as distinguished from the pompous or romantic sense of the word; wholly without effort or

---

aunt" is not named by HJ, though Novick (*Young Master*, 474) asserts that she is Ellen Gourlay, "one of the Albany great-aunts" (120). The Gourlays did live in Albany, and the four spinster sisters were the daughters of HJ's great-aunt (sister of his grandmother: see *CWJ*, 4:609). The Temple girls had spent much time there in their youth and so would have known the Gourlays. Lyndall Gordon, however, offers an alternative when she names the great-aunt as Miss Charlotte Perkins, and adds that they were all staying at the Blue Blinds (*A Private Life of Henry James*, 71), information available in Rosenbaum's "Letters to the Pell-Clarkes." His note offers a different relative: " 'Aunt Charlotte' possibly refers to Charlotte Temple Sweeney [i.e. Sweeny], a sister of Henrietta's father; she and another aunt, Mary Temple Tweedy, served as guardians for the Temples after the deaths of their parents in 1854" (54n). This is the aunt who lived in Canada and married Sir John Rose of Montreal (see n. 766 above), but the reference is to a great-aunt, not an aunt. Aunt Charlotte is mentioned a number of times in Minny's letters to John Gray as being in failing health (see below, pp. 487, 492, and 494).

desire on her part—for never was a girl less consciously or consentingly or vulgarly dominant—everything that took place around her took place as if primarily in relation to her and in her interest: that is in the interest of drawing her out and displaying her the more. This too without her in the least caring, as I say—in the deep, the morally nostalgic indifferences that were the most finally characteristic thing about her—whether such an effect took place or not; she liked nothing in the world so much as to see others fairly exhibited; not as they might best please her by being, but as they might most fully reveal themselves, their stuff and their truth: which was the only thing that, after any first flutter for the superficial air or grace in an acquaintance, could in the least fix her attention. She had beyond any equally young creature I have known a sense for verity of character and play of life in others, for their acting out of their force or their weakness, whatever either might be, at no matter what cost to herself; and it was this instinct that made her care so for life in general, just as it was her being thereby so engaged in that tangle that made her, as I have expressed it, ever the heroine of the scene. Life claimed her and used her and beset her—made her range in her groping, her naturally immature and un-lighted way from end to end of the scale. No one felt more the charm of the actual—only the actual comprised for her kinds of reality (those to which her letters perhaps most of all testify), that she saw treated round her for the most part either as irrelevant or as unpleasant. She was absolutely afraid of nothing she might come to by living with enough sincerity and enough wonder; and I think it is because one was to see her launched on that adventure in such bedimmed, such almost tragically compromised conditions that one is caught by her title to the heroic and pathetic mark. It is always difficult for us after the fact not to see young things who were soon to be lost to us as already distinguished by their fate; this particular victim of it at all events might well have made the near witness ask within himself how her restlessness of spirit, the finest reckless impatience, was to be assuaged or "met" by the common lot. One somehow saw it no-where about us as up to her terrible young standard of the interesting—even if to say this suggests an air of tension, a sharpness of importunity, than which nothing could have been less like her. The charming, irresist-ible fact was that one had never seen a creature with such lightness of forms, a lightness all her own, so inconsequently grave at the core, or an asker of endless questions with such apparent lapses of care. It is true that as an effect of the state of health which during the year '69 grew steadily worse the anxious note and serious mind sound in her less intermittently than by her former wont.[779]

    This might be headed with that line of a hymn, "Hark, from the tombs etc.!"—but perhaps it won't prove as bad as that.[780] It looks pretty doubtful still, but I have a sort of feeling that I shall come round this one time more; by which I don't mean to brag! The "it" of which I speak is of course my old enemy hemorrhage, of which I have had within the last week seven pretty big ones and several smaller, hardly worth mentioning. I don't know what has come over me—I can't stop them; but, as I said, I mean to try and beat them yet. Of course I am in bed, where I shall be indefinitely—not allowed to speak one word, literally, even in a whisper. The reason I write this is because I don't think it will hurt me at all—if I take it easy and stop when I feel tired. It is a pleasant break in the monotony of gruel and of thinking of the grave—and then too a few words from somebody who is strong and active in the good old world (as it seems to me now) would be very refreshing. But don't tell anyone I have written, because it will be sure to reach the ears of my dear relatives and will cause them to sniff the air and flounce! You see I am a good deal of a baby—in the sense of not wanting the reproaches of my relatives on this or any other subject. . . . All the Emmets are so good and kind that I found, when it came to the point, that there was a good deal to make life attractive, and that if the choice were given me I would much rather stay up here on the solid earth, in the air and sunshine, with an occasional sympathetic glimpse of another person's soul, than to be put down underground and say good-bye for ever to humanity, with all its laughter and its sadness. Yet you mustn't think me now in any *special* danger of dying, or even in low spirits, for it isn't so—the doctor tells me I am *not* in danger, even if the hemorrhages should keep on.

779. Two of HJ's letters, one to his mother, the other to WJ, written from England on hearing of Minny's death, are given in *HJL*, 1:218–29. At one stage he considered including them (without attribution) in this volume. He already foresaw her significance, writing to his brother, "She lives as a steady unfaltering luminary in the mind rather than as a flickering wasting earth-stifled lamp. Among all my thoughts and conceptions I am sure I shall never have one of greater sereneness and purity: her image will preside in my intellect, in fact, as a sort of measure and standard of brightness and repose" (227).

780. This letter is dated 27 January 1869 and the address is Pelham. Minny refers to a funeral hymn by Isaac Watts (1674–1748): "Hark! from the tombs a doleful sound; / Mine ears, attend the cry; / 'Ye living men, come view the ground / Where you must surely lie.'"

However, "you can't fool a regular boarder," as Mr. Holmes would say, and I can't see why there is any reason to think they will heal a week hence, when I shall be still weaker, if they can't heal now. Still, they *may* be going to stop—I haven't had one since yesterday at 4, and now it's 3; nearly twenty-four hours. I am of a hopeful temperament and not easily scared, which is in my favour. If this *should* prove to be the last letter you get from me, why take it for a good-bye; I'll keep on the lookout for you in the spirit world, and shall be glad to see you when you come there, provided it's a better place than this. Elly is in New York, enjoying herself immensely, and I haven't let her know how ill I have been, as there were to be several parties this last week and I was afraid it might spoil her fun. I didn't mean you to infer from my particularising Willy James's intellect that the rest of him isn't to my liking—he is one of the very few people in this world that I love. He has the largest heart as well as the largest head, and is thoroughly interesting to me. He is generous and affectionate and full of sympathy and humanity—though you mustn't tell him I say so, lest he should think I have been telling you a lie to serve my own purposes. Good-bye.

I should have little heart, I confess, for what is essentially the record of a rapid illness if it were not at the same time the image of an admirable soul. Surrounded as she was with affection she had yet greatly to help herself, and nothing is thus more penetrating than the sense, as one reads, that a method of care would have been followed for her to-day, and perhaps followed with signal success, that was not in the healing or nursing range of forty years ago.

It is a week ago to-day, I think, since I last wrote to you, and I have only had one more hemorrhage—the day after.[781] I feel pretty sure they have stopped for the present, and I am sitting up in my room, as bright as possible. Yesterday when I walked across it I thought I should never be strong again, but now it's quite different, and so nice to be out of bed that my spirits go up absurdly. As soon as I am able I am to be taken to town for another examination, and then when I know my fate I will do the best I can. This climate is trying, to be sure, but such as it is I've got to take my chance in it, as there is no one I care enough for, or who cares enough for me, to take charge of me to

781. Letter written from Pelham, 3 February 1869.

Italy, or to the south anywhere. I don't believe any climate, however good, would be of the least use to me with people I don't care for.[782] You may let your moustache grow down to your toes if you like, and I shall but smile scornfully at your futile precautions.

Of the following, in spite of its length, I can bring myself to abate nothing.[783]

. . . . Well, "to make a long story short," as Hannah (her old nurse) says, I caught a cold, and it went to the weak spot, and I had another slight attack of hemorrhage; but I took the necessary steps at once, stayed in bed and didn't speak for six days, and then it stopped and I felt better than I had at all since I was first taken ill. But I began to tire so of such constant confinement to my room that they promised to take me to town as soon as I was well enough, and perhaps to the Opera. This of course would have been a wild excitement for me, and I had charming little plans of music by day and by night, for a week, which I meant to spend with Mrs. Griswold.[784] Accordingly a cavalcade set out from here on Monday, consisting of myself escorted by sisters and friends, who were to see me safely installed in my new quarters and leave me. I arrived, bundled up, at Mrs. Griswold's, and had begun to consider myself already quite emancipated from bondage—so that I was discussing with my brother-in-law the propriety of my going that evening to hear Faust,[785] this but the

782. Referring to these final three sentences, Habegger writes that "this passage corresponds to nothing in Minny's letters to Gray (or to James) and was almost certainly composed by James himself" ("Henry James's Rewriting of Minny Temple's Letters," *American Literature* 58 [May 1986]: 176).

783. Letter written from Pelham, 4 March 1869. HJ in fact omits a significant amount of the letter.

784. Probably a family friend and relative of Minny's. In a letter of 6 August 1867, Alice James mentions that Wilky "has just returned from Newport where he has been spending a few days at the Griswolds with Kitty Temple" (*CWJ*, 4:189–90). The wife of the eminent merchant and financier John Noble Alsop Griswold was Jane Emmet Griswold (b. 1832), a descendant of Thomas Addis Emmet (Minny's great-grandfather: see also *SBO*, n. 65). As well as living in New York City, they had a house built on Bellevue Avenue in Newport in 1864. John Griswold is listed among New York City's wealthiest as a "merchant . . . long . . . interested in a London line of packets" (*The Wealth and Biography of the Wealthy Citizens of the City of New York*, 11th ed. [New York, published at the Sun Office, 1846], 13).

785. *Faust* (1859), a frequently performed lyric comic opera by Charles François Gounod (1818–93), was being performed at the New York Academy of Music as part of

beginning of a mad career on which I proposed to rush headlong—when Dr. Bassett arrived, who is the medical man that I had meant to consult during my stay *incidentally* and between the pauses in the music.[786] The first thing he said was: "What are you doing here? Go directly back to the place you came from and don't come up again till the warm weather. As for music, you mustn't hear of it or even think of it for two months." This was pleasant, but there was nothing to be done but obey; which I did a few hours later, with my trunk still unpacked and my immediate plan of life somewhat limited.

I say my immediate plan because my permanent found itself by no means curtailed, but on the contrary expanded and varied in a manner I had not even dared to hope. This came from what Dr. B. said subsequently, when he had examined my lungs; that is to say after he had laid his head affectionately first under one of my shoulders and then the other, and there kept it solemnly for about ten minutes, in a way that was irresistibly ludicrous, especially with Kitty as spectator. His verdict was that my lungs were *sound,* that he couldn't detect the least evidence of disease, and that hemorrhage couldn't have come from the lung itself, but from their membraneous lining, and that of the throat, whatever this may be. So he gave me to understand that I have as sound a pair of lungs at present as the next person; in fact from what he said one would have thought them a pair that a prize-fighter might covet. At the same time he sent me flying back to the country, with orders not to get excited, nor to listen to music, nor to speak with anybody I care for, nor to do anything in short that the unregenerate nature longs for. This struck my untutored mind as somewhat inconsistent, and I ventured a gentle remonstrance, which however was not even listened to, and I was ignominiously thrust into a car and borne back to Pelham. The problem still bothers me: either sound lungs are a very dangerous thing to have, or there is a foul conspiracy on foot to oppress me. Still, I cling to the consoling thought of my matchless lungs, and this obliterates my present sufferings.

Max Maretzek's Italian opera season in February 1869 (T. Allston Brown, *A History of the New York Stage, 1732 to 1901* [New York: Dodd, Mead, 1903], 2:61). This, incidentally, is the work being performed at the same venue at the beginning of Edith Wharton's *The Age of Innocence.*

786. A John S. Bassett, "physician," is listed at 11 West 31st Street in *Trow's New York City Directory . . . for the year ending May 1, 1871* (New York: John F. Trow, 1870).

Harry came to see me before he sailed for Europe; I'm very glad he has gone, though I don't expect to see him again for a good many years.[787] I don't think he will come back for a long time, and I hope it will do him good and that he will enjoy himself—which he hasn't done for several years. I haven't read all of Faust, but I think I know the scenes you call divine—at least I know some that are exquisite.[788] But why do you speak so disparagingly of King David, whom I always had a weakness for? Think how charming and lovable a person he must have been, poet, musician and so much else combined—with however their attendant imperfections.[789] I don't think I should have cared to be *Queen* David exactly. I am possessed with an overpowering admiration and affection for George Eliot. I don't know why this has so suddenly come over me, but everything I look at of hers nowadays makes me take a deeper interest in her. I should love to see her, and I hope Harry will; I asked him to give my love to her.[790] But I don't remember ever to have heard *you* speak of her. Good-bye. I wish conventionality would invent some other way of ending a letter than "yours truly"; I am so tired of it, and as one says it to one's shoemaker it would be rather more complimentary to one's friends to dispense with it altogether and just sign one's name without anything, after the

787. HJ accompanied Aunt Kate to New York, where she stayed on with her cousin Helen Perkins on Fourteenth Street; they would later travel to Italy (Novick, *Young Master*, 169). He spent two days in the city before boarding the *China* for Liverpool on 17 February 1869 (Edel, *Untried Years*, 287). In the event, he returned from Europe in 1870, leaving on 30 April aboard the *Scotia*. Minny died on 8 March 1870.

788. The drama *Faust* (part 1, 1808; part 2, 1832) by Johann Wolfgang von Goethe (1749–1832).

789. David, king of Israel in the Old Testament, was a warrior and musician, but also known for his adultery with Bathsheba and the murder of her husband, Uriah. In a later letter of Minny's there is a reference to a Browning poem, "Bishop Blougram's Apology," first published in volume 1 of *Men and Women* (1855); if she had also been reading volume 2 she might have read "Saul," in which David figures as harpist and prophet, acting as a curative moral force for King Saul. The original letter has Minny refer to "Mrs D." rather than "Queen David."

790. Though George Eliot had published a great deal by this time, the late 1860s were a period principally devoted to poetry; the mature masterpieces such as *Middlemarch* and *Daniel Deronda* (which profoundly influenced HJ) did not appear till the next decade. Thanks to his links with the Norton family, HJ met George Eliot in London in May 1869, a meeting he refers to in *TMY*, chap. 5, below. "George Eliot was an important influence and model during Henry's youthful scribbling. . . . but he did not return to her in his old age" (Edel, *Untried Years*, 266–67).

manner of Miss Emerson[791] and other free Boston citizens. But I am a slave to conventionality, and after all *am* yours truly. . . .

Singularly present has remained to "Harry," as may be imagined, the rapid visit he paid her at Pelham that February; he was spending a couple of days in New York, on a quick decision, before taking ship for England. I was then to make in Europe no such stay as she had forecast—I was away but for fifteen months; though I can well believe my appetite must have struck her as open to the boundless, and can easily be touched again by her generous thought of this as the right compensatory thing for me. That indeed is what I mainly recall of the hour I spent with her—so unforgettable none the less in its general value; our so beautifully agreeing that quite the same course would be the right thing for *her* and that it was wholly detestable I should be voyaging off without her. But the precious question and the bright aspect of her own still waiting chance made our talk for the time all gaiety; it was, strangely enough, a laughing hour altogether, coloured with the vision of the next winter in Rome, where we should romantically meet: the appearance then being of particular protective friends with Roman designs, under whose wing she might happily travel.[792] She had at that moment been for many weeks as ill as will here have been shown; but such is the priceless good faith of youth that we perfectly kept at bay together the significance of this. I recall no mortal note—nothing but the bright extravagance of her envy; and see her again, in the old-time Pelham parlours, ever so erectly slight and so more than needfully, so transparently, fair (I fatuously took this for "becoming"), glide as swiftly, toss her head as characteristically, laugh to as free a disclosure of the handsome largeish teeth that made her mouth almost the

791. Or Ellen Emerson, the eldest of Emerson's daughters, as the original letter has it. She may have inherited some qualities from her great-aunt, Miss Mary Moody Emerson of Concord, of small stature (four feet, three inches tall) and indomitable: "There is a famous story of the call made upon her by Thoreau's mother, who, in honor of the occasion, had adorned her best cap with bright pink ribbons. Miss Emerson came forward to greet her guest and then sat down, shut her eyes, and kept them shut. After a short call, the visitor rose to take leave. 'You noticed I closed my eyes?' Miss Emerson said. 'Yes, Madam, I noticed it.' 'It is because I did not wish to look upon those ribbons—so unsuitable at your time of life and to a person of your serious character!'" (*Alice James: Her Brothers*, 14).

792. Later in the year, on 15 August, Minny wrote to HJ to tell him that "she was about to take a 'strange step'. . . . A Mr and Mrs Jones had agreed to take her to Rome next winter, and she meant to stay for a year at least: 'Think, my dear of the pleasure we would have together in Rome—I am crazy at the mere thought'" (Gordon, *A Private Life of Henry James*, 101).

main fact of her face, as if no corner of the veil of the future had been lifted. The house was quiet and spacious for the day, after the manner of all American houses of that age at those hours, and yet spoke of such a possible muster at need of generous, gregarious, neighbouring, sympathising Emmets; in spite of which, withal, the impression was to come back to me as of a child struggling with her ignorance in a sort of pathless desert of the genial and the casual. Three months before I returned to America the struggle had ended. I *was*, as happened, soon to see in London her admiration, and my own, the great George Eliot—a brief glimpse then, but a very impressive, and wellnigh my main satisfaction in which was that I should have my cousin to tell of it. I found the Charles Nortons settled for the time in London, with social contacts and penetrations, a give and take of hospitality, that I felt as wondrous and of some elements of which they offered me, in their great kindness, the benefit;[793] so that I was long to value having owed them in the springtime of '69 five separate impressions of distinguished persons, then in the full flush of activity and authority, that affected my young provincialism as a positive fairytale of privilege. I had a Sunday afternoon hour with Mrs. Lewes at North Bank, no second visitor but my gentle introducer, the younger Miss Norton, sharing the revelation,[794] which had some odd and for myself peculiarly thrilling accompaniments; and then the opportunity of dining with Mr. Ruskin at Denmark Hill,[795] an impression of uneffaced intensity and followed by a like—and yet so unlike—evening of hospitality from William Morris in the medieval mise-en-scène of Queen Square.[796] This had been preceded by a luncheon

793. The Norton family sailed for Europe in July 1868 and did not return to the United States until May 1873.

794. George Eliot lived happily with the already married writer and journalist George Henry Lewes (1817–78) (whose wife had deserted him) for twenty-four years. In referring to her as "Mrs. Lewes," HJ follows George Eliot's own practice. Between 1863 and 1876 they lived at The Priory, 21 North Bank, Regent's Park, not far from the house rented by the Jameses during their London stay of 1855–56 (see *SBO*, chap. 22, especially n. 493). The younger Miss Norton was Grace (1834–1926), HJ's lifelong correspondent (not Susan, Charles Eliot Norton's wife, as Novick [*Young Master*, 187] has it).

795. John Ruskin (1819–1900), the influential art and social critic, supporter of the Pre-Raphaelite movement, lived at 163 Denmark Hill in south London between 1847 and 1872. On meeting him in March 1869, HJ characterized Ruskin as "scared back by the grim face of reality into the world of unreason and illusion," wandering there "without a compass and a guide—or any light save the fitful flashes of his beautiful genius." On his visit HJ most enjoyed—"cold-blooded villain that I am"—a Titian portrait (*HJL*, 1:103).

796. William Morris (1834–96), poet, artist, and designer, lived (and worked) at 26

with Charles Darwin, beautifully benignant, sublimely simple, at Down;[797] a memory to which I find attached our incidental wondrous walk—Mrs. Charles Norton, the too near term of her earthly span then smoothly out of sight,[798] being my guide for the happy excursion—across a private park of great oaks, which I conceive to have been the admirable Holwood[799] and where I knew my first sense of a matter afterwards, through fortunate years, to be more fully disclosed: the springtime in such places, the adored footpath, the first primroses, the stir and scent of renascence in the watered sunshine and under spreading boughs that were somehow before aught else the still reach of remembered lines of Tennyson, ached over in nostalgic years.[800] The rarest hour of all perhaps, or at least the strangest, strange verily to the pitch of the sinister, was a vision, provided by the same care, of D. G. Rossetti in the vernal dusk of Queen's House Chelsea[801]— among his pictures, amid his poetry itself, his whole haunting "esthetic," and yet above all bristling with his personality, with his perversity, with anything, as it rather awfully seemed to me, but his sympathy, though it at

---

Queen Square, Bloomsbury. His designs were strongly influenced by medieval subjects and conventions. HJ gives a detailed account of this visit in a letter to his sister, Alice (10 March 1869, *HJL*, 1:89–98).

797. Charles Robert Darwin (1809–82), the naturalist, developed in his *Origin of Species* (1859) the theory of evolution; its application ranged far beyond its scientific origins, especially in its impact on Victorian religious orthodoxies. Down House is in Bromley on the borders of southeast London and Kent. This was HJ's only meeting with Darwin.

798. Charles's wife, Susan, died in Dresden. The family had not been able to accompany her body home, but HJ attended the funeral at Shady Hill and the interment at Mount Auburn Cemetery: "An unusually bright spring had relapsed into winter, Harry James wrote Charles; and, as the mourners stood at the grave, heavy snowflakes began to drop from a silent, leaden sky" (James Turner, *The Liberal Education of Charles Eliot Norton* [Baltimore: Johns Hopkins University Press, 1999], 246).

799. Holwood Park, on the edge of Farnborough, is a short distance from Down.

800. Alfred, 1st Baron Tennyson (1809–92), frequently evokes simple and idyllic English pastoral scenes in his poetry, but HJ seems to have had no specific poem in mind. Elsewhere he admired "Tennyson's solid verbal felicities, his unerring sense of the romantic, his acute perception of everything in nature that may contribute to his fund of exquisite imagery, his refinement, his literary tone, his aroma of English lawns and English libraries" ("Mr. Tennyson's Drama" [1875], *Henry James: Essays on Art and Drama,* ed. Peter Rawlings [Aldershot: Scolar Press; Brookfield, Vt.: Ashgate, 1996], 100).

801. Dante Gabriel Rossetti (1828–82), poet and painter, was another (founding) member of the Pre-Raphaelite brotherhood; he lived at the Queen's House, 16 Cheyne Walk. In his later years HJ had an apartment at 21 Carlyle Mansions, Cheyne Walk.

the same time left one oddly desirous of more of him. These impressions heaped up the measure, goodness knew, of what would serve for Minnie's curiosity—she was familiarly Minnie to us; the point remaining all along, however, that, impatient at having overmuch to wait, I rejoiced in possession of the exact vivid terms in which I should image George Eliot to her.[802] I was much later on to renew acquaintance with that great lady, but I think I scarce exceed in saying that with my so interested cousin's death half the savour of my appreciation had lost itself. Just in those days, that month of April, the latter had made a weak ineffectual move to Philadelphia in quest of physical relief—which expressed at the same time even more one of those reachings out for appeasement of the soul which were never too publicly indulged in, but by which her power to interest the true subjects of her attraction was infinitely quickened. It represented wonderments, I might well indeed have said to myself, even beyond any inspired by the high muse of North Bank.

I suppose I ought to have something special to say after having been suddenly transplanted to a new place and among new people, yet there isn't much to tell.[803] I came because they all thought at home that the climate might do me good; I don't feel, however, any difference in my sensations between this and New York—if I do it's in favour of New York. I wish it might turn out that an inland climate isn't after all necessary for me, as I like the other sort much better and really think I feel stronger in it too. My doctor told me that Boston would kill me in six months—though he is possibly mistaken. I am going to try it a little longer here, and then go back to Pelham, where I'm pretty sure I shall find myself better again. It may be that the mental atmosphere is more to me than any other, for I feel homesick here all the while, or at least what I call so, being away from what is most *like* home to me, and what if I were there I should call tired. The chief object I had in coming was to listen to Phillips Brooks;[804] I have heard him several times and am not, I think, disappointed. To be sure

802. HJ famously did "image" George Eliot in a letter to his father of 10 May 1869: "she is magnificently ugly—deliciously hideous. She has a low forehead, a dull grey eye, a vast pendulous nose, a huge mouth, full of uneven teeth and a chin and jaw-bone *qui n'en finissent pas*" (*HJL*, 1:116).

803. Letter written from Philadelphia, 2 April 1869.

804. Phillips Brooks (1835–93) was an influential member of the Episcopal Church. Though he became rector of Philadelphia's Church of the Holy Trinity in the 1860s, he returned to Boston and to Trinity Church in 1869, as Minny touches on in a later letter.

he didn't say anything new or startling, but I certainly oughtn't to have expected that, though I believe I did have a secret hope that he was going to expound to me the old beliefs with a clearness that would convince me for ever and banish doubt. I had placed all my hopes in him as the one man I had heard of who, progressive in all other ways, had yet been able to keep his faith firm in the things that most earnest men have left far behind them. Yet in preaching to his congregation he doesn't, or didn't, touch the real difficulties at all. He was leading them forward instead of trying to make it clear to *me* that I have any good reason for my feelings. Still, it was something to feel that he has them too, and isn't afraid to trust them and live for them. I wonder what he really does believe or think about it all, and whether he knows the reaction that comes to me about Thursday, after the enthusiasm and confidence made by his eloquence and earnestness on Sunday. To-morrow will be Saturday, and I shall be glad when Sunday comes to wind me up again. I feel sadly run down to-night and as if I should like to see some honest old pagan and shake him by the hand. It will seem all right and easy again soon, I know, but is it always thus? Is there no more of that undoubting faith in the world that there used to be? But I won't talk any more about it now, or I shan't sleep; it is getting late and all themes but the least interesting must be put away.

"Quaint," as we now say, it at this end of time seems to me that Phillips Brooks, the great Episcopal light of the period, first in Philadelphia and then in Boston, and superior character, excellent, even ardent, thoughtful, genial, practical man, should have appeared to play before her a light possibly of the clear strain, the rich abundance, the straight incidence, that she so desired to think attainable. A large, in fact an enormous, softly massive and sociably active presence, of capacious attention and comforting suggestion, he was a brave worker among those who didn't too passionately press their questions and claims—half the office of such a minister being, no doubt, to abate the high pitch, and the high pitch being by the same token too much Minnie's tendency. She was left with it in the smug Philadelphia visibly on her hands; she had found there after all but a closed door, to which she was blandly directed, rather than an open, and the sigh of her falling back with her disappointment seems still to reach one's ears. She found them too much all round, the stiff blank barriers that, for whatever thumping, didn't "give;" and in fine I like not too faintly to colour this image of her as failing, in her avid young sincerity, to draw from the honest pastor of more satisfied souls any assurance that she could herself honestly apply. I confess that her particular recorded case, slender enough in its lonely unrest, suggests to me a force, or at least a play, of effective criticism more vivid to-day than either of the several rich monuments, honourably as these survive, to Phillips Brooks's positive "success." She had no occasion or no chance to find the delightful harmonising friend in him—which was part of the success for so many others. But her letter goes on after a couple of days—she had apparently not sent the previous part, and it brings her back, we can rejoicingly note, to George Eliot, whose poem, alluded to, must have been The Spanish Gypsy. This work may indeed much less have counted for her than the all-engulfing Mill on the Floss,[805] incomparably privileged production, which shone for young persons of that contemporaneity with a nobleness that nothing under our actual star begins in like case to match. These are great recognitions, but how can I slight for them a mention that has again and again all but broken through in my pages?—that of Francis Boott and his daughter (she to become later on Mrs. Frank Duveneck and to yield to the same dismal decree of death before her time that rested on so many of the friends of our youth).[806] When I turn in thought to the happiness that our kinswoman

805. *The Spanish Gypsy,* an extended poem, met with great success on its publication in 1868; *The Mill on the Floss* appeared in 1860.

806. Francis Boott (1813–1904) was a musician and amateur composer who graduated from Harvard in 1831; his wealth was derived from New England textile mills. After the deaths of his wife (in 1847) and an infant son, he and his daughter, Lizzie, spent many years in Italy, though they returned to Cambridge for a time, living there between 1865 and 1871. Lizzie Boott (1846–88) was a talented artist. She joined William Morris Hunt's painting class in Boston and later became a pupil of the artist Frank Duveneck (1848–1919), whom she married in 1886. HJ admired his work, commenting in a *Galaxy* piece of 1875 that "we shall take it hard if he fails to do something of the first degree of importance" ("On Some Pictures Lately Exhibited," *Painter's Eye,* 99). This promise (according to HJ in an opinion expressed in his last dictated letter, to his niece Mary Margaret) was not fulfilled: "His only good work was done in his very few first years, nearly fifty of these ago—at least the long interval since has always looked like a deadly desert. I daresay, however, in fact I must often have heard, that he has flourished at Cincinnati during a large part of that time as an excellent teacher so it's doubtless all right" (1 December 1915, *HJL,* 4:783). Lizzie gave birth to a son at the end of 1886, but died suddenly of pneumonia in March 1888. There is a fine portrait of Francis Boott (1881) by Duveneck in the Art Museum at Cincinnati, his hometown; the Boston Museum of Fine Arts has a tomb effigy of Lizzie in marble by Duveneck and Clement J. Barnhorn (modeled 1891, carved 1894; the bronze monument is in the Allori Cemetery in Florence). Having received photographs of the sculpture, HJ wrote to Francis Boott: "what a meaning and eloquence the whole thing

was still to have known in her short life, for all her disaster, Elizabeth Boott, delightful, devoted and infinitely under the charm, at once hovers for me; this all the more, I hasten to add, that we too on our side, and not least Mary Temple herself, were under the charm, and that *that* charm, if less immediately pointed, affected all our young collective sensibility as a wondrous composite thing. There was the charm for us—if I must not again speak in assurance but for myself—that "Europe," the irrepressible even as the *ewig Weibliche*[807] of literary allusion was irrepressible, had more than anything else to do with; and then there was the other that, strange to say (strange as I, once more, found myself feeling it) owed nothing of its authority to anything so markedly out of the picture. The spell to which I in any case most piously sacrificed, most cultivated the sense of, was ever of this second cast—and for the simple reason that the other, serene in its virtue, fairly insolent in its pride, needed no rites and no care. It must be allowed that there was nothing composite in any spell proceeding, whether directly or indirectly, from the great Albany connection:[808] this form of the agreeable, through whatever appeals, could certainly not have been more of a piece, as we say—more of a single superfused complexion, an element or principle that we could in the usual case ever so easily and pleasantly account for. The case of that one in the large number of my cousins whom we have seen to be so incomparably the most interesting was of course anything but the usual; yet the Albany origin, the woodnote wild,[809] sounded out even amid her various voices and kept her true, in her way, to something we could only have called local, or perhaps family, type. Essentially, however, she had been a free incalculable product, a vivid exception to rules and precedents; so far as she had at all the value of the "composite" it was on her own lines altogether—the composition

___

has—and one is touched to tears by this particular example which comes home to one so—of the jolly great truth that it is *art* alone that triumphs over fate. Poor long-silent Lizzie speaks and lives there again" (letter of 14 July 1893, *HJL*, 3:417–18). As HJ later acknowledges, father and daughter provided some inspiration for Gilbert and Pansy Osmond in *The Portrait of a Lady*.

807. Eternally female (Ger.). HJ may have been influenced by Minny Temple's earlier reference to Goethe's *Faust*, because the term derives from the poem's final line invoking woman's transcendent power: "Das Ewig-Weibliche zieht uns hinan" (The eternally female draws us upward).

808. The Temple children had spent much time in Albany, and Minny was eventually buried in Albany Rural Cemetery with her parents.

809. John Milton (1608–74) refers to "sweetest Shakespeare fancy's child," warbling "his native wood-notes wild," in *L'Allegro* (1631?) (133–34).

was of things that had lain nearest to hand. It mattered enormously for such a pair as the Bootts, intimately associated father and daughter, that what had lain nearest *their* hand, or at least that of conspiring nature and fortune in preparing them for our consumption, had been the things of old Italy, of the inconceivable Tuscany, that of the but lately expropriated Grand Dukes in particular,[810] and that when originally alighting among us *en plein*[811] Newport they had seemed fairly to reek with a saturation, esthetic, historic, romantic, that everything roundabout made precious. I was to apprehend in due course, and not without dismay, that what they really most reeked with was the delight of finding us ourselves exactly as we were; they fell so into the wondrous class of inverted romantics, several other odd flowers of which I was later on to have anxiously to deal with: we and our large crude scene of barbaric plenty, as it might have been called, beguiled them to appreciations such as made our tribute to themselves excite at moments their impatience and strike them as almost silly. It was *our* conditions that were picturesque, and I had to make the best of a time when they themselves appeared to consent to remain so but by the beautiful gaiety of their preference. This, I remember well, I found disconcerting, so that my main affectionate business with them became, under amusement by the way, that of keeping them true to type. What above all contributed was that they really couldn't help their case, try as they would to shake off the old infection;[812] they were of "old world" production through steps it was too late to retrace; and they were in the practical way and in the course of the very next years to plead as guilty to this as the highest proper standard for them could have prescribed. They "went

810. HJ liked to play, as here, with the name of the Bootts; elsewhere he referred to them as the "easy-fitting Bootts" (Edel, *Untried Years,* 259). Having been a collection of city states and independent principalities, and subject to a variety of foreign influences, Italy was in the process of becoming one nation. The grand Duchy of Tuscany (with an illustrious family history that included the Medicis) ceased to exist from December 1859.

811. In the middle of.

812. HJ had himself succumbed to the baneful, complicating influence of Europe, having felt his "European gains sinking gradually out of sight and sound and American experience closing *bunchily* together over them, as flesh over a bullet—the simile is *àpropos!*" (letter to Grace Norton, 26 September [1870], *HJL,* 1:245–46). He records a similar wound, in an appropriately New World trope, when feeling in his side "buried and unextracted, the head of one of those well-directed shafts from the European quiver to which, of old, tender American flesh was . . . helplessly and bleedingly exposed"; almost from birth, as he says, "that poison had entered my veins" (Preface to New York Edition of *The Reverberator,* "Madame de Mauves," . . . "Louisa Pallant," *LC* 2, 1205).

back," and again and again, with a charming, smiling, pleading inconsequence—any pretext but the real one, the fact that the prime poison was in their veins, serving them at need; so that, as the case turned, all my own earlier sense, on the spot, of Florence and Rome[813] was to mix itself with their delightfully rueful presence there. I could then perfectly put up with that flame of passion for Boston and Newport in them which still left so perfect their adaptability to Italian installations that would have been impossible save for subtle Italian reasons.

I speak of course but of the whole original view: time brings strange revenges and contradictions, and all the later history was to be a chapter by itself and of the fullest. We had been all alike accessible in the first instance to the call of those references which played through their walk and conversation with an effect that their qualifying ironies and amusing reactions, where such memories were concerned, couldn't in the least abate; for nothing in fact lent them a happier colour than just this ability to afford so carelessly to cheapen the certain treasure of their past. They had enough of that treasure to give it perpetually away—in our subsequently to be more determined, our present, sense; in short we had the fondest use for their leavings even when they themselves hadn't. Mary Temple, with her own fine quality so far from composite, rejoiced in the perception, however unassisted by any sort of experience, of what their background had "meant"; she would have liked to be able to know just that for herself, as I have already hinted, and I actually find her image most touching per- haps by its so speaking of what she with a peculiar naturalness dreamed of and missed. Of clear old English stock on her father's side, her sense for what was English in life—so we used to simplify—was an intimate part of her, little chance as it enjoyed for happy verifications.[814] In the Bootts,

813. In "From a Roman Note-book" HJ records the Christmas season 1872 and the following spring of 1873, a period spent in Rome, when he took pleasant walks with Lizzie Boott (*Italian Hours*, 177, 181, 190).

814. For the Temple family, see *CWJ*, 2:173–74 n. 6. HJ told WJ that Robert Temple the elder (1783–1834), Minny's grandfather, was "a *bastard* son of Sir John Temple, the 'founder' of the family in America, & he hanged himself after burning the public office of which he was in charge, to cover the tracks of his peculations" (*CWJ*, 2:172). The editors of *CWJ* write that he "collected pensions in the names of Revolutionary War veterans but failed to send the money to the pensioners. He shot himself after burning his papers." The Temples understandably preferred to be associated with earlier family members, such as "Sir William Temple (1628–99), British statesman and author, who in about 1680 built Moor Park, near Farnham, Surrey, by digging a canal and designing a Dutch garden around it. The park became famous through Jonathan Swift who, as Temple's secretary,

despite their still ampler and more recently attested share in that racial strain, the foreign tradition had exceedingly damped the English, which didn't however in the least prevent her being caught up by it as it had stamped itself upon the admirable, the infinitely civilised and sympathetic, the markedly *produced* Lizzie. This delightful girl, educated, cultivated, accomplished, toned above all, as from steeping in a rich old medium, to a degree of the rarest among her coevals "on our side," had the further, the supreme grace that she melted into American opportunities of friendship —and small blame to her, given such as she then met—with the glee of a sudden scarce believing discoverer. Tuscany could only swoon away under comparison of its starved sociabilities and complacent puerilities, the stress of which her previous years had so known, with the multiplied welcomes and freedoms, the exquisite and easy fellowships that glorified to her the home scene. Into not the least of these quick affinities had her prompt acquaintance with Mary Temple confidently ripened; and with no one in the aftertime, so long as that too escaped the waiting shears, was I to find it more a blest and sacred rite, guarded by no stiff approaches, to celebrate my cousin's memory. That really is my apology for this evocation—which might under straighter connections have let me in still deeper; since if I have glanced on another page of the present miscellany at the traps too often successfully set for my wandering feet my reader will doubtless here recognise a perfect illustration of our danger and will accuse me of treating an inch of canvas to an acre of embroidery. Let the poor canvas figure time and the embroidery figure consciousness —the proportion will perhaps then not strike us as so wrong. Consciousness accordingly still grips me to the point of a felt pressure of interest in such a matter as the recoverable history—history in the esthetic connection at least—of its insistent dealings with a given case. How in the course of time for instance was it not insistently to deal, for a purpose of application, with the fine prime image deposited all unwittingly by the "picturesque" (as I absolutely required to feel it) Boott situation or Boott *data?* The direct or vital value of these last, in so many ways, was experiential, a stored and assimilated thing; but the seed of suggestion proved after long years to have kept itself apart in order that it should develop under a particular breath. A not other than lonely and bereft American, addicted

lived there for many years." Robert Temple the elder, mentioned by HJ, was born in Boston and unrelated to Sir William: "the relation of the American Temples to their noble namesakes in Britain is not clear" (ibid., 173–74 n. 6).

to the arts and endowed for them, housed to an effect of long expatriation in a massive old Florentine villa with a treasured and tended little daughter by his side,[815] *that* was the germ which for reasons beyond my sounding the case of Frank Boott had been appointed to plant deep down in my vision of things. So lodged it waited, but the special instance, as I say, had lodged it, and it lost no vitality—on the contrary it acquired every patience—by the fact that little by little each of its connections above ground, so to speak, was successively cut. Then at last after years it raised its own head into the air and found its full use for the imagination. An Italianate bereft American with a little moulded daughter in the setting of a massive old Tuscan residence was at the end of years exactly what was required by a situation of my own—conceived in the light of the Novel; and I *had* it there, in the authenticated way, with its essential fund of truth, at once all the more because my admirable old friend had given it to me and none the less because he had no single note of character or temper, not a grain of the non-essential, in common with my Gilbert Osmond. This combination of facts has its shy interest, I think, in the general imaginative or reproductive connection—testifying as it so happens to do on that whole question of the "putting of people into books" as to which any ineptitude of judgment appears always in order. I probably shouldn't have had the Gilbert Osmonds at all without the early "form" of the Frank Bootts, but I still more certainly shouldn't have had them with the *sense* of my old inspirers. The form had to be disembarrassed of that sense and to take in a thoroughly other; thanks to which account of the matter I am left feeling that I scarce know whether most to admire, for support of one's beautiful business of the picture of life, the relation of "people" to art or the relation of art to people. Adorable each time the mystery of which of these factors, as we say, has the more prevailingly conduced to a given effect—and too much adored, at any rate, I allow, when carrying me so very far away. I retrace my steps with this next.

I have made several attempts lately to write you a letter, but I have given it up after two or three pages, because I have always been in a blue state of mind at the time, and have each time charitably decided before

815. Francis and Lizzie lived for long periods in a part of the Villa Castellani on Bellosguardo Hill, overlooking Florence; HJ visited in the fall of 1877 and makes discreet reference to the place in *Italian Hours* (111) (see also Peter Collister, "Levels of Disclosure: Voices and People in Henry James's *Italian Hours*," *Yearbook of English Studies* 35 [2004]: 199–200).

it was too late to spare you.[816] But if I were to wait until things change to rose-colour I might perhaps wait till I die, or longer even, in which case your next communication from me would be a spiritual one. I am going to Newport in the early part of May to meet the Bootts[817]—Henrietta has just come back from there delighted with her visit; why, heaven knows, I suppose, but I don't—except that she is in that blissful state of babyhood peculiar to herself where everything seems delightful. . . . I like George Eliot not through her poem so much, not nearly so much, as through her prose. The creature interests me personally, and I feel a desire to know something of her life; how far her lofty moral sentiments have served her practically—for instance in her dealings with Lewes. I see that she understands the character of a *generous* woman, that is of a woman who believes in generosity and who must be that or nothing, and who feels keenly, notwithstanding, how hard it is practically to follow this out, and how (looking at it from the point of view of comfort as far as this world goes) it "pays" not at all. We are having weather quite like summer and rather depressing; I don't feel very well and am always catching cold—that is I suppose I am, as I have a cough nearly all the time. As for Phillips Brooks, what you say of him is, no doubt, all true—he didn't touch the main point when *I* heard him, at all events, and that satisfaction you so kindly wish me is, I am afraid, not to be got from any man. The mystery of this world grows and grows, and sticks out of every apparently trivial thing, instead of lessening. I hope this feeling may not be the incipient stage of insanity. Paul told the truth when he said that now we see through a glass, *very* darkly.[818] I hope and trust that the rest may be equally true, and that some day we shall see face to face. You say it is easy to drown thought by well-doing, and is it not also the soundest philosophy (so long of course as one doesn't humbug oneself); since by simply thinking out a religion who has ever

816. Letter written from Pelham, 24 April 1869.
817. She was also going to Newport "to see an ailing aunt, Miss Clarke" (Gordon, *A Private Life of Henry James,* 99).
818. A reference to a famous passage of the First Epistle of St. Paul to the Corinthians on the theme of love, or charity: "When I was a child, I spake as a child, I thought as a child: but when I became a man, I put away childish things. For now we see through a glass, darkly; but then face to face: now I know in part; but then shall I know even as also I am known. And now abideth faith, hope, charity, these three; but the greatest of these is charity" (13:11–13).

arrived at anything that did not leave one's heart empty? Do you ever see Willy James? Good-bye.

Needless enough surely to declare that such pages were essentially not love-letters: that they could scarce have been less so seems exactly part of their noble inevitability, as well as a proof singularly interesting and charming that confident friendship may obey its force and insist on its say quite as much as the sentiment we are apt to take, as to many of its occasions, for the supremely vocal. We have so often seen this latter beat distressfully about the bush for something still deficient, something in the line of positive esteem or constructive respect, whether offered or enjoyed, that an esteem and a respect such as we here apprehend, explicit enough on either side to dispense with those superlatives in which graceless reaction has been known insidiously to lurk, peculiarly refresh and instruct us. The fine special quietude of the relation thus promoted in a general consciousness of unrest—and even if it could breed questions too, since a relation that breeds none at all is not a living one—was of the highest value to the author of my letters, who had already sufficiently "lived," in her generous way, to know well enough in how different a quarter to look for the grand inconclusive. The directness, the ease, the extent of the high consideration, the felt need of it as a support, indeed one may almost say as an inspiration, in trouble, and the free gift of it as a delightful act of intelligence and justice, render the whole exhibition, to my sense, admirable in its kind. Questions luckily *could* haunt it, as I say and as we shall presently see, but only to illustrate the more all the equilibrium preserved. I confess I can imagine no tribute to a manly nature from a feminine more final even than the confidence in "mere" consideration here embodied— the comfort of the consideration being in the fact that the character with which the feminine nature was dealing lent it, could it but come, such weight. We seem to see play through the whole appeal of the younger person to the somewhat older an invocation of the weight suspended, weight of judgment, weight of experience and authority, and which may ever so quietly drop. How kindly in another relation it had been in fact capable of dropping comes back to me in the mention of my brother Wilky, as to whom this aspect of his admiring friendship for our young relative's correspondent, the fruit of their common military service roundabout Charleston, again comprehensively testifies.[819] That comradeship was a

819. During the Civil War John Chipman Gray rose to the rank of major and become judge-advocate general of U.S. volunteers in the Department of the South at Hilton Head,

privilege that Wilky strongly cherished, as well as what one particularly liked to think for him of his having known—he was to have known nothing more fortunate. In no less a degree was our elder brother to come to prize *his* like share in the association—this being sufficiently indicated, for that matter, in the note I have quoted from him. That I have prized my own share in it let my use of this benefit derived strongly represent. But again for Minnie herself the sadder admonition is sharp, and I find I know not what lonely pluck in her relapses shaken off as with the jangle of silver bells, her expert little efforts to live them down, Newport and other matters aiding and the general preoccupied good will all vainly at her service. Pitiful in particular her carrying her trouble experimentally back to the Newport of the first gladness of her girlhood and of the old bright spectacle.

> I know quite well I don't owe you a letter, and that the custom for maidens is to mete out strictly letter for letter;[820] but if you don't mind it I don't, and if you *do* mind that kind of thing you had better learn not to at once—if you propose to be a friend of mine; or else have your feelings from time to time severely shocked. After which preamble I will say that there is a special reason in this case, though there might not be in another.

She mentions having seen a common friend, in great bereavement and trouble, who has charged her with a message to her correspondent "if you know of anything to comfort a person when the one they love best dies, for heaven's sake say it to her—*I* hadn't a word to say." And she goes on:

> I wrote to you that I was going to Newport, and I meant to go next Tuesday, but I had another hemorrhage last night, and it is impossible to say when I shall be able to leave here. I think I was feeling ill when I last wrote to you, and ever since have been coughing and feeling wretchedly, until finally the hemorrhage has come. If that goes over well I think I shall be better. I am in bed now, on the old plan of gruel and silence, and I may get off without any worse attack this time. It is a perfect day, like summer—my windows are up and the birds sing. It seems quite out of keeping that I should be in bed. I should be all right if I could only get rid of coughing. The warm weather will set me

South Carolina. This would have been when he met up with Wilky James, though he makes no mention of it in, e.g., *War Letters 1862–1865 of John Chipman Gray and John Codman Ropes* (Boston: Houghton Mifflin, 1927).

820. Letter written from Pelham, 9 May 1869.

up again. I wonder what you are doing to-day. Probably taking a solitary walk and meditating—on what? Good-bye.

But she went to Newport after a few days apparently; whence comes this.

I believe I was in bed when I last wrote to you, but that attack didn't prove nearly so bad a one as the previous;[821] I rather bullied it, and after the fourth hemorrhage it ceased; moreover my cough is better since I came here. But I am, to tell the truth, a little homesick— and am afraid I am becoming too much of a baby. Whether it's from illness or from the natural bent I know not, but there is no comfort in life away from people who care for you—not an heroic statement, I am fully aware. I hear that Wilky is at home, and dare say he will have the kindness to run down and see me while I am here; at least I hope so. But I am not in the mood for writing to-day—I am tired and can only bore you if I kept on. It is just a year since we began to write, and aren't you by this time a little tired of it? If you are, say so like a man— don't be afraid of me. Now I am going to lie down before dressing for dinner. Good-bye.

This passage more than a month later makes me ask myself of which of the correspondents it strikes me as most characteristic. The gay clearness of the one looks out—as it always looked out on the least chance given—at the several apparent screens of the other; each of which is indeed disconnectedly, independently clear, but tells too small a part (at least for her pitch of lucidity) of what they together enclose, and what was *quand même* of so fine an implication. Delightful at the same time any page from her that is not one of the huddled milestones of her rate of decline.

How can I write to you when I have forgotten all about you?[822]—if one *can* forget what one has never known. However, I am not quite sure whether it isn't knowing you too much rather than too little that seems to prevent. Do you comprehend the difficulty? Of course you don't, so I will explain. The trouble is, I think, that to me you have no distinct personality. I don't feel sure to whom I am writing when I say to myself that I will write to you. I see mentally three men, all answering to your name, each liable to read my letters and yet differing so much from each other that if it is proper for one of them it's quite

821. Letter written from Newport, 20 May 1869.
822. Letter written from Pelham, 27 June 1869.

unsuitable to the others. Do you see? If you can once settle for me the question of which gets my letters I shall know better what to say in them. Is it the man I used to see (I can't say know) at Conway, who had a beard, I think, and might have been middle-aged,[823] and who discussed Trollope's novels with Kitty and Elly? This was doubtless one of the best of men, but he didn't *interest* me, I never felt disposed to speak to him, and used to get so sleepy in his society at about eight o'clock that I wondered how the other girls could stay awake till eleven. Is it *that* person who reads my letters? Or is it the young man I recently saw at Newport, with a priestly countenance, calm and critical, with whom I had certainly no fault to find as a chance companion for three or four days, but whom I should never have dreamt of writing to or bothering with my affairs one way or the other, happiness or no happiness, as he would doubtless at once despise me for my nonsense and wonder at me for my gravity? Does *he* get my letters?—or is it finally the being who has from time to time himself written to me, signing by the same name that the other gentlemen appropriate? If my correspondent is this last I know where I stand— and, please heaven, shall stand there some time longer. Him I won't describe, but he's the only one of the three I care anything about. My only doubt is because I always address him at Pemberton Square,[824] and I think him the least likely of the three to go there much. But good-bye, whichever you are!

It was not at any rate to be said of her that she didn't live surrounded, even though she had to go so far afield—very far it may at moments have appeared to her—for the freedom of talk that was her greatest need of all. How happily and hilariously surrounded this next, of the end of the following August, and still more its sequel of the mid-September, abun-

823. Gray was six years older than Minny and thus twenty-nine at the time of the letter's writing, "a partner in a Boston law firm, and about to start his lifelong career at Harvard Law School" (Gordon, *A Private Life of Henry James,* 92). The firm he cofounded still thrives.

824. In the original letter Mary Temple refers to "Mr Gray's office." The address given in her letter of 7 January 1869 is 4 Pemberton Square, Boston, Massachusetts (see p. 484 below). At this time the square was an elegant terrace of substantial row houses, home to a number of eminent Boston families. Gray and his partner, John Codman Ropes, established their legal firm in January 1866 at 20 State Street; they moved to Pemberton Square in 1868, staying there till 1876 (Albert Boyden, *Ropes-Gray, 1865–1940* [Boston: privately printed, 1942]).

dantly bring back to me; so in the habit were the numerous Emmets, it might almost be said, of marrying the numerous young women of our own then kinship: they at all events formed mainly by themselves at that time the figures and the action of her immediate scene. The marriage of her younger sister was as yet but an engagement—to the brother-in-law of the eldest, already united to Richard Emmet and with Temple kinship, into the bargain, playing between the pairs. All of which animation of prospective and past wedding-bells, with whatever consolidation of pleasant ties, couldn't quench her ceaseless instinct for the obscurer connections of things or keep passionate reflections from awaiting her at every turn. This disposition in her, and the way in which, at the least push, the gate of thought opened for her to its widest, which was to the prospect of the soul and the question of interests on *its* part that wouldn't be ignored, by no means fails to put to me that she might well have found the mystifications of life, had she been appointed to enjoy more of them, much in excess of its contentments. It easily comes up for us over the relics of those we have seen beaten, this sense that it was not for nothing they missed the ampler experience, but in no case that I have known has it come up for me so much. In none other have I so felt the naturalness of our asking ourselves what such spirits would have done with their extension and what would have satisfied them; since dire as their defeat may have been we don't see them, in the ambiguous light of some of their possibilities, at peace with victory.[825] This may be perhaps an illusion of our interest in them, a mere part of its ingenuity; and I allow that if our doubt is excessive it does them a great wrong—which is another way in which they were not to have been righted. We soothe a little with it at any rate our sense of the tragic.

... The irretrievableness of the step (her sister E.'s marriage)[826] comes over my mind from time to time in such an overwhelming way that it's most depressing, and I have to be constantly on my guard not

825. Even at the time of her death HJ shockingly argued with himself that Minny had lived fully, that her death was fitting: "The more I think of her the more perfectly satisfied I am to have her translated from this changing realm of fact to the steady realm of thought. There she may bloom into a beauty more radiant than our dull eyes will avail to contemplate." In his last conversation with her at Pelham he had asked how she slept, and he goes on to cast death as the ultimate, paradoxical awakening: " 'Sleep,' she said, 'Oh, I don't sleep. *I've given it up.*' And I well remember the laugh with which she made this sad attempt at humor. And so she went on, sleeping less and less, waking wider and wider, until she waked absolutely!" (letter to WJ, 29 March 1870, *HJL*, 1:226–67).

826. This is HJ's parenthesis.

to let Temple and Elly see it, as it would naturally not please them.[827] After all, since they are not appalled at what they've done, and are quite sure of each other, as they evidently are, why should I worry myself? I am well aware that if all other women felt the seriousness of the matter to the extent I do, hardly any would *ever* marry, and the human race would stop short. So I ought perhaps to be glad so many people can find and take that "little ease" that Clough talks about, without consciously giving up the "highest thing."[828] And may not this majority of people be the truly wise and my own notions of the subject simply fanatical and impracticable? I clearly see in how small a minority I am, and that the other side has, with Bishop Blougram, the best of it from one point of view;[829] but I can't help that, can I? We must be true to *ourselves*, mustn't we? though all the rest of humanity be of a contrary opinion, or else throw discredit upon the wisdom of God, who made us as we are and not like the next person. Do you remember my old hobby of the "remote possibility of the best thing" being better than a clear certainty of the second best? Well, I believe it more than ever, every day I live. Indeed I don't believe anything else— but is not that everything? And isn't it exactly what Christianity means? Wasn't Christ the only man who ever lived and died *entirely* for his faith, without a shadow of selfishness? And isn't that reason enough why we should all turn to Him after having tried everything else and found it wanting?—turn to Him as the only pure and *unmixed* manifestation of God in humanity? And if I believe this, which I think I do, how utterly inconsistent and detestable is the life I lead, which, so far from being a loving and cheerful surrender of itself once for all to God's service, is at best but a base compromise— a few moments or acts or thoughts consciously and with difficulty divested of actual selfishness. Must this always be so? Is it owing to

827. Letter written from Pelham, 29 August 1869. Elly's husband, Christopher Temple Emmet, was always known as Temple within the family.

828. Arthur Hugh Clough (1819–61): "I have seen higher, holier things than these, / And therefore must to these refuse my heart, / Yet am I panting for a little ease; / I'll take and so depart" (no. 10 of the sequence "Blank Misgivings of a Creature moving about in Worlds not realised" (*Poems of Arthur Hugh Clough,* 2nd ed., ed. F. L. Muhlhauser [Oxford: Clarendon Press, 1974], 33).

829. Essentially, Browning's Bishop Blougram (supposedly modeled on Cardinal Wiseman) in the poem "Bishop Blougram's Apology" stands for a compromised kind of Christianity in which expediency—choosing belief over doubt—offers the most acceptable, if hypocritical, outcome.

the indissoluble mixture of the divine and the diabolical in us all, or is it because I myself am hopelessly frivolous and trifling? Or is it finally that I really don't *believe,* that I have still a doubt in my mind whether religion *is* the one exclusive thing to live for, as Christ taught us, or whether it will prove to be only *one* of the influences, though a great one, which educate the human race and help it along in that culture which Matthew Arnold thinks the most desirable thing in the world?[830] In fine is it the meaning and end of our lives, or only a moral principle bearing a certain part in our development—?

Since I wrote this I have been having my tea and sitting on the piazza looking at the stars and thinking it most unfaithful and disloyal of me even to speak as I did just now, admitting the possibility of that faith not being everything which yet at moments is so divinely true as to light up the whole of life suddenly and make everything clear. I know the trouble is with *me* when doubt and despondency come, but on the other hand I can't altogether believe it wrong of me to have written as I have, for then what becomes of my principle of saying what one really thinks and leaving it to God to take care of his own glory? The truth will vindicate itself in spite of my voice to the contrary. If you think I am letting myself go this way without sufficient excuse I won't do it again; but I can't help it this time, I have nobody else to speak to about serious things. If by chance I say anything or ask a question that lies at all near my heart my sisters all tell me I am "queer" and that they "wouldn't be me for anything"—which is, no doubt, sensible on their part, but which puts an end to anything but conversation of the most superficial kind on mine. You know one gets lonely after a while on such a plan of living, so in sheer desperation I break out where I perhaps more safely can.

Such is the magic of old letters on its subtlest occasions that I recon-stitute in every detail, to a vivid probability—even if I may not again proportionately project the bristling image—our scene of next mention; drawing for this upon my uneffaced impression of a like one, my cousin

830. The views attributed to Matthew Arnold by Minny on culture belong to the earlier 1860s. Though to an extent he identified culture (or literature) as encapsulating the emotional or moral aspects of religious experience, the argument of *Culture and Anarchy* (published in January 1869), with its twin strands of Hellenism and Hebraism, anticipates a position in which he observed religion and culture as occupying distinctive and indepen-dent roles.

Katharine Temple's bright nuptials, in the same general setting, very much before, and in addition seeming to see the very muse of history take a fresh scroll in order to prepare to cover it, in her very handsomest hand, well before my eyes. Covered is it now for me with that abounding and interesting life of the generations then to come at the pair of preliminary flourishes ushering in the record of which I thus feel myself still assist.

But a line to-day to tell you that Elly was safely married on Wednesday.[831] She looked simply beautiful in her wedding garment, and behaved herself throughout with a composure that was as delightful as it was surprising. I send you a photograph of myself that I had taken a few weeks ago. It looks perhaps a trifle melancholy, but I can't help that—I did the best I could. But I won't write more—it wouldn't be enlivening. Everything looks grey and blue in the world nowadays. It will all be bright again in time, I have no doubt; there is no special reason for it; I think I am simply tired with knocking about. Yet my week in Newport might have been pleasant enough if the dentist hadn't taken that occasion to break my bones for me in a barbarous manner. You are very kind and friendly to me—you don't know how much happiness your letters give me. You will be surprised, I dare say, but I shall not, at the last day, when the accounts are all settled, to find how much this counts in your favour. Good-bye.

I find my story so attaching that I prize every step of its course, each note of which hangs together with all the others. The writer is expressed to my vision in every word, and the resulting image so worth preserving. Much of one's service to it is thus a gathering-in of the ever so faded ashes of the happiness that did come to her after all in snatches. Everything could well, on occasion, look "grey and blue," as she says; yet there were stretches, even if of the briefest, when other things still were present than the active symptoms of her state. The photograph that she speaks of above is before me as I write and blessedly helpful to memory—so that I am moved to reproduce it only till I feel again how the fondness of memory must strike the light for apprehension. The plan of the journey to California for the advantage of the climate there was, with other plans taken up and helplessly dropped,[832] but beguiling for the day, to accompany her almost to the end.

831. Letter written from Pelham, 17 September 1869.

832. WJ to HJ, 5–6 December 1869: "Letter fm. Minny to Alice yest. saying Temple Emmet had telegraphed her not to come to Cal. as he was coming East in December" (*CWJ*, 1:131).

The Temple-Emmet caravan have advanced as far as Newport and now propose to retreat again to Pelham without stopping at Boston or anywhere else.[833] My brother-in-law has business in New York and can't be away any longer. I haven't been well of late, or I should have run up to Boston for a day or two to take a sad farewell of all I love in that city and thereabouts before I cross the Rocky Mountains. This little trip has been made out for me by my friends; I have determined to go, and shall probably start with Elly and Temple in about ten days, possibly not for a fortnight, to spend the winter in San Francisco. I can't be enthusiastic about it, but suppose I might as well take all the means I can to get better: a winter in a warm climate *may* be good for me. In short I am going, and now what I want *you* to do about it is simply to come and see us before that. Kitty is going to send you a line to add her voice—perhaps that may bring you. You may never see me again, you know, and if I were to die so far away you'd be sorry you hadn't taken leave of me, wouldn't you?

The idea of California held, and with other pleasant matters really occupied the scene; out of which moreover insist on shining to me accessory connections, or connections that then were to be: intensely distinct for example the figure of Miss Crawford, afterwards Madame von Rabe, sister of my eminent friend F. Marion of the name and, in her essence, I think, but by a few shades less entire a figure than he—which is saying much.[834] The most endowed and accomplished of men Frank Crawford, so that I have scarcely known another who had more aboundingly lived and wrought, about whom moreover there was singularly

833. Letter written from Newport, 4 October 1869.

834. Annie Crawford (b. 1846) and her brother Frank Marion Crawford (1854–1909) were children of the sculptor Thomas Crawford (1814–57), who lived much in Italy; Julia Ward Howe was their aunt. Miss Crawford became the Countess von Rabe, while her brother found success as a prolific and popular novelist. HJ considered his highly successful *To Leeward* (1883) "contemptibly bad & ignoble" (*A Life in Letters,* 152). Their mother, Louisa, later married the American painter Luther Terry (his works regarded by HJ as "the queerest old survivals of the American art of thirty years ago" [*HJL,* 1:335]). In 1873 HJ visited the family in Rome, where they lived in the stone-built Odescalchi Palace. "The presiding genius of the Terry household was Annie Crawford, who, Henry wrote home, 'has every gift (including a face so mobile and expressive that it amounts almost to beauty), but she is as hard as flint and I am pretty sure she will never have an adorer. He will have to be a real lion-tamer.' The judgment was shrewder than he knew. Not long after, Annie married Erich von Rabe, a Junker baron with a dominating will, an estate in Prussia and violent anti-English prejudices" (Edel, *Conquest of London,* 95).

more to be said, it struck me, than at all found voice at the time he might have been commemorated. Therefore if the young lady alluded to in my cousin's anecdote was at all of the same personal style and proportion— well, I should draw the moral if it didn't represent here too speciously the mouth of a trap, one of those I have already done penance for; the effect of my yielding to which would be a shaft sunk so straight down into matters interesting and admirable and sad and strange that, with everything that was futurity to the occasion noted in our letter and is an infinitely mixed and a heavily closed past now, I hurry on without so much as a glance.

The present plan is to send me to California in about three weeks by water, under the care of one of the Emmet boys and Temple's valet—for nurse; and by the time I get there, early in December, they will be settled in San Francisco for the winter.[835] The idea of a twenty-one days' sea-voyage is rather appalling—what do you think of it? This day is but too heavenly here. I haven't been to church, but walking by myself, as happy as possible. When one sleeps well and the sun shines, what happiness to live! I wish you were here— wouldn't I show you Pelham at high tide, on a day that is simply intoxicating, with a fresh breeze blown through the red and yellow leaves and sunshine "on field and hill, in heart and brain," as Mr. Lowell says.[836] I suppose you remember the pony I drove, and Punch, the little Scotch terrier that tried so to insinuate himself into your affections, on the piazza, the morning you left. The former has been "cutting up," the latter *cut* up, since then. You wouldn't believe me when I told you the pony was a highly nervous creature—but she behaved as one the other day when I took the Roman Miss Crawford, who has been staying near here, a ride. She shied at a dog that frightened her, and dragged the cart into a ditch, and tried to get over a stone wall, waggon and all. I of course had to hang on to the reins, but I suggested to Miss Crawford that she should get out, as the cart was pretty steady while the horse's forefeet were on top of the wall; which she did, into a mud-puddle, and soiled her pretty striped stockings and shoes in a horrible way. It ended by the dear little

835. Letter written from Pelham, 24 October 1869.

836. From J. R. Lowell's "Palinode: Autumn": "Still thirteen years: 'tis autumn now / On field and hill, in heart and brain; / The naked trees at evening sough; / The leaf to the forsaken bough / Sighs not,—'Auf wiedersehen!' " (*Poetical Works of James Russell Lowell*, ed. Marjorie R. Kaufmann [Boston: Houghton Mifflin, 1978], 308).

beast's consenting to get back upon all fours, but I found it very amusing and have liked her better ever since. . . . How does Mr. Holmes persevere about smoking? I pity him if he can't sleep, and wish *I* had a vicious habit so that I might give it up. But I must finish my tale of the quadruped Punch, who was called upon in the dead of night by five dogs of the neighbourhood and torn to pieces by them. The coachman heard him crying in the night, and in the morning we found him—that is to say we gathered him together, his dear little tail from one place and his head from another etc! So went out a very sweet little spirit—I wonder where it is now. Don't tell me he hadn't more of a soul than that Kaufmann, the fat oysterman.[837]

I find bribes to recognition and recovery quite mercilessly multiply, and with the effort to brush past them more and more difficult; with the sense for me at any rate (whatever that may be worth for wisdom or comfort) of sitting rather queerly safe and alone, though as with a dangle of legs over the edge of a precipice, on the hither side of great gulfs of history. But these things, dated toward the end of that November, speak now in a manner for themselves.

My passage for California is taken for the 4th of December;[838] Elly and Temple have written to me to come at once—they are settled in San Francisco for the winter. My brother-in-law here has been promised that I shall be made so comfortable I shan't want to tear myself from the ship when I arrive. The captain is a friend of Temple's, and also of my uncle Captain Temple,[839] and both of them are going to arrange so for me that I fully expect the ship to be hung with banners and flowers when I step on board. . . . I enjoyed my time in Boston far more than I had expected—in fact immensely, and wouldn't have missed it for anything;[840] I feel now as if it had *necessarily* had to

837. Presumably a local figure. Oysters constituted cheap fare at the time, and oyster saloons were popular.

838. Letter written from Pelham, 21 November 1869.

839. Minny's grandfather, Robert Temple of Rutland, Vermont, had five children with his first wife, Clarina Hawkins; one of the younger was William Grenville Temple (1824–94), who became a rear admiral in the U.S. navy (Temple Prime, *Some Account of the Temple Family*, 3rd ed. [New York: n.p., 1896], 56–57); he may have been a sea captain at this time.

840. Minny went to stay with the Jameses in Cambridge on 19 November 1869, at Mrs. James's invitation (see *CWJ*, 1:121 n. 7): "She had gone to say goodbye before embarking

happen.[841] I don't know how I should have done the winter, and especially started off for an indefinitely long absence in the west without the impetus that it gave me in certain directions—the settling down and shaking up, the dissipating of certain impressions that I had thought fixed and the strengthening of others that I hadn't been so sure of: an epoch in short. I dare say you have had such—in which a good deal of living was done in a short time, to be turned over and made fruitful in days to come. I saw Mr. Holmes once, and was very glad of that glimpse, short as it was. I went home by way of Newport, where I stayed two days—and where I was surprised to hear of Fred Jones's engagement to Miss Rawle of Philadelphia.[842] Do you know her? When I got to New York I went to the Hones' to ask something about Fred and his affairs and found that Miss Rawle was staying next door with Mrs. Willy Duncan;[843] so I went in to see her on the spur of the moment, very much

on a three-week voyage to join Elly and Emmet, who preceded her overland to California" (Gordon, *A Private Life of Henry James*, 110–11).

841. Bearing in mind her longing for Europe, it is clear that Minny was reluctant to go, as she wrote to HJ on 7 November 1869: " 'When shall we meet again, / Dearest & best, / Thou going Easterly / I to the West?' as the song saith" (Robert C. Le Clair, "Henry James and Minny Temple," *American Literature* 21 [March 1949]: 47).

842. In her letter of 7 November 1869, Minny recorded the engagement of "my friend Fred Jones to Miss Minnie Rawle of Philadelphia, a handsome and brilliant young lady" (Le Clair, "Henry James and Minny Temple," 48). Minnie, or Mary Cadwalader Rawle (1850–1935), was the daughter of William Henry Rawle, listed as an attorney-at-law, 710 Walnut Street, Philadelphia (*McElroy's Philadelphia City Directory . . . for the year ending May 1, 1867* [Philadelphia: A. McElroy, 1867]); his legal practice was one of the country's most distinguished. Frederic Rhinelander Jones (1846–1918) was the eldest brother of Edith Jones, who would become HJ's eminent friend Edith Wharton. The whole Jones family had gone to Europe in November 1866, to remain there for six years, leaving Fred in New York. His marriage to Mary lasted for about twelve years. Whether or not HJ encountered Miss Rawle in 1869 remains uncertain, but they certainly met in 1883 and, as Mary Cadwalader Jones, she became an important and enduring friend and correspondent, resident in New York City (see also *Dear Munificent Friends*, 123–88).

843. In Alice Howe Gibbens James's transcription the name is not "Hones" but "Hows" (see p. 507 below). Frederick W. Dupee, editor of *Henry James: Autobiography* (1956; Princeton: Princeton University Press, 1983), gives the name as "Jones" (533), which has a degree of logic in the context, though no reason is given for the change of name from the first American and English editions. In fact, Robert L. Hones is listed as living at 247 Fifth Avenue, while resident at 249 Fifth Avenue is William Butler Duncan, a prosperous banker (*Trow's New York City Directory . . . for the year ending May 1, 1867*), who was married to Jane Percy Sargent, a cousin of the painter John Singer Sargent (Bertram Wyatt-Brown, *The House of Percy: Honor, Melancholy, and Imagination in a Southern*

as I had come from the boat, not particularly presentable for a first call: however, I thought if she had a soul she wouldn't mind it—and such I found the case. . . . Lizzie Boott was as sweet and good to me as ever; I think she is at once the most unselfish and most unegotistical girl I know—they don't always go together.

What follows here has, in its order, I think, that it still so testifies to life—if one doesn't see in it indeed rather perhaps the instinct on the writer's part, though a scarce conscious one, to wind up the affairs of her spirit, as it were, and be able to turn over with a sigh of supreme relief for an end intimately felt as at hand. The moral fermentation breaking through the bustle of outward questions even at a time when she might have thrown herself, as one feels, on the great soft breast of equalising Nature, or taken her chance of not being too wrong, is a great stroke of truth. No one really could be less "morbid"; yet she would take no chance—it wasn't in her—of not being right with the right persons; among whom she so ranked her correspondent.

My address at San Francisco will be simply Care of C. Temple Emmet, Esq.;[844] and I am surely off this time unless heaven interposes in a miraculous way between now and Saturday. I've no great courage about it, but after all it's much the same to me where I am; life is always full of interest and mystery and happiness to me, and as for the voyage, the idea of three weeks of comparative solitude between sea and sky isn't unattractive. . . . I know that by my question [as to why he had written, apparently, that she was, of her nature, "far off" from him][845] I am putting an end to that delightful immunity I have enjoyed so much with you from sickening introspection, analysis of myself and yourself, that exhausting and nauseating subjectivity, with which most of my other friends see fit to deluge me, thereby taking much that is refreshing out of life. Don't be afraid of "hurting my feelings" by anything you can say. Our friendship has always been to my mind a one-sided thing, and if you should tell me you find me in any way

*Family* [New York: Oxford University Press, 1996], 344). In later years Sargent became a friend of HJ's. Mrs. Duncan became one of the most famous and beautiful of society hostesses in New York City. Though her family had southern roots, she came from Philadelphia, and would therefore have known the Rawles.

844. Letter written from Pelham, 30 November 1869.

845. HJ inserts this parenthesis and also reorganizes some of the letter's content (see pp. 509–10 below).

unsympathetic or unsatisfactory it won't disappoint me, and I won't even allow myself to think I'm sorry. I feel so clearly that God knows best, and that we ought neither of us surely to wish to distort his creatures from the uses he made them for, just to serve our own purposes—that is to get a little more sympathy and comfort. We must each of us, after all, live out our own lives apart from everyone else; and yet, this being once understood as a fundamental truth, there is nobody's sympathy and approval that would encourage me so much as yours. I mean that if one's heart and motives could be known by another as God knows them, without disguise or extenuation, and if it should *then* prove that on the *whole* you didn't think well of me, it would, more than anything else could, shake my confidence in my own instincts, which must after all forever be my guide. And yet, as I said before, I am quite prepared for the worst, and shall listen to it, if necessary, quite humbly. I am very much inclined to trust your opinion before my own.

An hour later. *Sold* again, by all that's wonderful—I had almost said by all that's damnable, though it isn't exactly that. My brother Dick[846] has just walked in with a telegram from Temple: "I shall be back in December—don't send M." A tremendous revulsion of feeling and a general sigh of relief have taken place on this announcement, and it's all right, I'm sure, though when I wrote you an hour ago I thought the same of the other prospect.

One catches one's breath a little, frankly, at what was to follow the above within a few days—implying as it does that she had drawn upon herself some fairly direct statement of her correspondent's reserves of view as to her human or "intellectual" composition. To have *had* such reserves at such an hour, and to have responded to the invitation to express them— for invitation there had been—is something that our actual larger light quite helps us to flatter ourselves *we* shouldn't have been capable of. But what was of the essence between these admirable persons was exactly the tone of truth; the larger light was all to wait for, and the real bearings of the hour were as unapparent as the interlocutors themselves were at home in clearness, so far as they might bring that ideal about. And whatever turn their conversation took is to the honour always of the generous girl's passion for truth. As this long letter admirably illustrates that, I withdraw from it almost nothing. The record of the rare commerce would be in-

846. That is, her brother-in-law Richard Emmet.

complete without it; all the more perhaps for the wonder and pain of our seeing the noble and pathetic young creature have, of all things, in her predicament, to plead for extenuations, to excuse and justify herself.

I understood your letter perfectly well—it was better than I feared it might be, but bad enough.[847] Better because I knew already all it told me, and had been afraid there might be some new and horrible development in store for me which I hadn't myself felt; but bad enough because I find it in itself, new or old, such a disgusting fact that I am intellectually so unsympathetic. It is a fault I feel profoundly conscious of, but one that, strange to say, I have only of late been conscious of *as* a fault. I dare say I have always known, in a general way, that I am very unobservant about things and take very little interest in subjects upon which my mind doesn't naturally dwell; but it had never occurred to me before that it is a fault that ought to be corrected. Whether because I have never been given to studying myself much, but have just let myself go the way my mind was most inclined to, more interested in the subject itself than in the fact that it interested me; or whether because one is averse to set oneself down as indolent and egotistic I don't know; at all events I have of late seen the thing in all its unattractiveness, and I wish I could get over it. Do you think that, now I am fully roused to the fact, my case is hopeless? Or that if I should try hard for the next twenty-five years I might succeed in modifying it? I am speaking now of a want of interest in *all* the rest of the world; of not having the desire to investigate subjects, naturally uninteresting to me, just because they are interesting to some other human being whom I don't particularly owe anything to except that he *is* a human being, and so his thoughts and feelings ought to be respected by me and sympathised with. Not to do this is, I know, unphilosophic and selfish, conceited and altogether inhuman. To be unselfish, to live for other people, to mould our lives as much as possible on the model of Christ's all-embracing humanity, seems most clearly to my mind the one thing worth living for; and yet it is still the hardest thing for me to do, and I think I do it less than anybody else who feels the necessity of it strongly at all.

I am glad you still go to an occasional ball—I should rather like to meet you at one myself; it's a phase of life we have seen so little of together. I have been feeling so well lately that I don't know what to

847. Letter written from Pelham, 12 December 1869.

make of it. I don't remember ever in my life being in such good spirits. Not that they are not in general pretty natural to me when there is the slightest excuse for them, but now everything seems bright and happy, my life so full of interest, my time so thoroughly filled and such a delicious calm to have settled down on my usually restless spirit. Such an enjoyment of the *present*, such a grateful contentment, is in each new day as I see it dawn in the east, that I can only be thankful and say to myself: "Make a note of this—you are happy; don't forget it, nor to be thankful for this beautiful gift of life." This is Sunday morning, and I wonder whether you are listening to Phillips Brooks. I understand how you feel about his preaching—that it is all feeling and no reason; I found it so myself last winter in Philadelphia: he was good for those within the pale, but not good to convince outsiders that they should come in. I am glad, however, that he preaches in this way—I think his power lies in it; for it seems to me, after all, that what comfort we get from religion, and what light we have upon it, come to us through feeling, that is through trusting our instinct as the voice of God, the Holy Ghost, though it may at the same time appear to us directly against what our intellect teaches us. I don't mean by this that we should deny the conclusions arrived at by our intellect—which on the contrary I believe we should trust and stand by to the bitter end, whenever this may be. But let us fearlessly trust our *whole* nature, showing our faith in God by being true to ourselves all through, and not dishonouring Him by ignoring what our heart says because it is not carried out by our intellect, or by wilfully blunting our intellectual perception because it happens to run against some cherished wish of our heart.

"But," you will say, "how can a man live torn to pieces this way by these contrary currents?" Well, I know it is hard to keep our faith *sure* of a standpoint where these apparent inconsistencies are all reconciled and the jangle and discord sound the sweetest harmony; but I do believe there *is* one, in God, and that we must only try to have that faith and never mind how great the inconsistency may seem, nor how perplexing the maze it leads us through. Let us never give up one element of the problem for the sake of coming to a comfortable solution of it in this world. I don't blame those eager minds that are always worrying, studying, investigating, to *find* the solution here below; it is a noble work, and let them follow it out (and without a bit of compromise) to whom God has given the work. But whether we find it or not I would have them and all of us feel that it is to *be* found, if God wills—and through no other means surely than by our being *true*. Blessed are they who have not seen and who have yet believed.[848] But I am going out now for a walk! We have had the most delightful weather this whole week, and capital sleighing, and I have spent most of my time driving myself about with that same dear little pony. I went to town yesterday to a matinée of William Tell;[849] it was delightful and I slept all night after it too. I am reading German a little every day, and it's beginning to go pretty well. Good-bye. Don't tire yourself out between work and dissipation.

I find myself quite sit up to her, as we have it to-day, while she sits there without inconvenience, after all that has happened, under the dead weight of William Tell; the relief of seeing her sublimely capable of which, with the reprieve from her formidable flight to the Pacific doubtless not a little contributing, helps to draw down again the vision, or more exactly the sound, of the old New York and Boston Opera as our young generation knew and artlessly admired it; admired it, by my quite broken memories of the early time, in Brignoli the sweet and vague, in Susini the deep and rich, in Miss Kellogg the native and charming, in Adelaide Phillipps the universal,[850] to say nothing of other acclaimed warblers (they appear to me to have warbled then so much more than since) whom I am afraid of not placing in the right perspective. They warbled Faust a dozen times, it comes back to me, for once of anything else; Miss Kellogg and Brignoli heaped up the measure of that success, and I well remember the great

848. These are Jesus' words to the doubting apostle, Thomas: "because thou hast seen me, thou hast believed: blessed are they that have not seen, and yet have believed" (John 20:29).

849. *Guillaume Tell* (1829), the French grand opera based on Schiller's play, by Gioacchino Rossini (1792–1868). Performed at the New York Academy of Music as part of the Italian opera season in November–December 1869 (Brown, *New York Stage*, 2:63), it proved a great success.

850. The operatic stars of the day, Italian tenor Pasquale Brignoli (1824–84), Italian bass Agostino Susini (1825–83), soprano Clara-Louise Kellogg (1842–1916), and contralto Adelaide Phillipps (or Phillips, 1833–82). They performed chiefly at the Academy of Music, which, replacing the Astor Place Opera House, was established in 1854. The first building for the New York Metropolitan Opera did not open till 1883 (Henry Edward Krehbiel, *Chapters of Opera* [New York: Holt, 1909], 64, 92). Though musical and theatrical venues and small performing groups proliferated in these years, I have found no reference to a company such as the New York and Boston Opera, and HJ may well simply be referring to the traditions of opera in those cities. He was evidently never a keen operagoer or music lover.

yearning with which I heard my cousin describe her first enchanted sense of it. The next in date of the letters before me, of the last day but one of December '69, is mainly an interesting expression of the part that music plays in her mental economy—though but tentatively offered to her correspondent, who, she fears, may not be musical enough to understand her, understand how much "spiritual truth has been 'borne in' upon me by means of harmony: the relation of the part to the whole, the absolute value of the individual, the absolute necessity of uncompromising and unfaltering truth, the different ways in which we like our likes and our unlikes," things all that have been so made clearer to her. Of a singular grace in movement and attitude, a grace of free mobility and activity, as original and "unconventional" as it was carelessly natural, she never looked more possessed of her best resources than at the piano in which she delighted, at which she had ardently worked, and where, slim and straight, her shoulders and head constantly, sympathetically swaying, she discoursed with an admirable touch and a long surrender that was like a profession of the safest relation she could know. Comparatively safe though it might have been, however, in the better time, she was allowed now, I gather, but little playing, and she is deep again toward the end of January '70 in a quite other exposure, the old familiar exposure to the "demon," as she calls it, "of the Why, Whence, Whither?" Long as the letter is I feel it a case again for presentation whole; the last thoughts of her life, as they appear, breathe in it with such elevation. They seem to give us her last words and impulses, and, with what follows of the middle of February, constitute the moving climax of her rich short story.

There have been times (and they will come again no doubt) when I could write to you about ordinary things in a way at least not depressing;[851] but for a good while now I have felt so tired out, bodily and mentally, that I couldn't conscientiously ask you to share my mood. The life I live here in the country, and so very much alone, is capable of being the happiest or the unhappiest of existences, as it all depends so on oneself and is so very little interfered with by outside influences. Perhaps I am more than usually subject to extremes of happiness and of depression, yet I suppose everyone must have moments, even in the most varied and distracting life, when the old questioning spirit, the demon of the Why, Whence, Whither? stalks in like the skeleton at the feast and takes a seat beside him. I say everyone, but I must except those

851. Letter written from Pelham, 25 January 1870.

rare and happy souls who really believe in Christianity, who no longer strive after even goodness as it comes from one's own effort, but take refuge in the mysterious sacrifice of Christ, his merit sufficing, and in short throw themselves in the orthodox way on the consoling truth of the Atonement—to me hitherto neither comprehensible nor desirable. These people, having completely surrendered self, having lost their lives, as it were in Christ, must truly have found them, must know the rest that comes from literally casting their care of doubt and strife and thought upon the Lord.

I say hitherto the doctrine of the vicarious suffering of Christ has been to me not only incomprehensible but also unconsoling; I didn't want it and didn't understand even intellectually the feeling of people who do. I don't mean to say that the life and death of Christ and the example they set for us have not been to me always the brightest spot in history—for they have; but they have stood rather as an example that we must try to follow, that we must by constant and ceaseless effort bring our lives nearer to—but always, to some extent at least, through ourselves, that is through ourselves with God's help, got by asking Him for it and by His giving it to us straight and with no mediation. When I have seen as time went by my own shortcomings all the more instead of the less frequent, I have thought: "Well, you don't try hard enough; you are not really in earnest in thinking that you believe in the Christian life as the only true one." The more I tried, nevertheless, the less it seemed like the model life;[852] the best things I did continued to be the more spontaneous ones; the greatest efforts had the least success; until finally I couldn't but see that if this was Christianity it was not the "rest" that Christ had promised his disciples—it was nothing more than a pagan life with a high ideal, only an ideal so high that nothing but failure and unhappiness came from trying to follow it. And one night when I was awake through all the hours it occurred to me: What if this were the need that Christianity came to fill up in our hearts? What if, after all, that old meaningless form of words that had been sounded in my unheeding ears all my days were suddenly to become invested with spirit and truth? What if this were the good tidings that have made so many hearts secure and

852. The original transcript has "moral life"; the change seems more likely to have been the result of HJ's reading aloud rather than a misreading of Minny's handwriting (see p. 517 below).

happy in the most trying situations? For if morality and virtue were the test of a Christian, certainly Christ would never have likened the kingdom of heaven to a little child, in whose heart is no struggle, no conscious battle between right and wrong, but only unthinking love and trust.[853]

However it may turn out, whether it shall seem true or untrue to me finally, I am at least glad to be able to put myself intellectually into the place of the long line of Christians who have felt the need and the comfort of this belief. It throws a light upon Uncle Henry's talk, which has seemed to me hitherto neither reasonable nor consoling. When I was with him it so far disgusted me that I fear I showed him plainly that I found it not only highly unpractical, but ignoble and shirking. I knew all the while that he disliked what he called my pride and conceit, but felt all the same that his views didn't touch my case a bit, didn't give me the least comfort or practical help, and seemed to me wanting in earnestness and strength. *Now* I say to myself: What if the good gentleman had all along really got hold of the higher truth, the purer spirituality? Verily there are two sides to everything in this world, and one becomes more charitable the older one grows. However, if I write at this length it is because I am feeling to-day too seedy for anything else. I had a hemorrhage a week ago, which rather took the life out of me; but as it was the only one I feel I should by this time be coming round again—and probably might if I hadn't got into a sleepless state which completely knocks me up. The old consolatory remark, "Patience, neighbour, and shuffle the cards," ought to impart a little hope to me, I suppose; but it's a long time since I've had any trumps in my hand, and you know that with the best luck the game always tired me. Willy James sometimes tells me to behave like a man and a gentleman if I wish to outwit fate. What a *real* person he is! He is to me in nearly all respects a head and shoulders above other people. How is Wendell Holmes? Elly is having the gayest winter in Washington and wants me to go to them there,[854] which I

853. The Gospel of St. Matthew contains a number of passages invoking the exemplary innocence of children; Minny may be referring to 19:13–14: "Then there were brought unto him little children, that he should put his hands on them, and pray; and the disciples rebuked them. But Jesus said, Suffer little children, and forbid them not, to come unto me: for of such is the kingdom of heaven."

854. Minny's original plan to join Elly and her husband in California was overtaken when they returned to the East Coast in December 1869.

had meant to do before the return of my last winter's illness. But it's not for me now.

Later.—I have kept my letter a day or two, thinking I might feel in tune for writing you a better one and not sending this at all. But alas I shall have to wait some time before I am like my old self again, so I may as well let this go. You see I'm not in a condition, mentally or physically, to take bright and healthy views of life. But if you really care you may as well see this mood as another, for heaven only knows when I shall get out of it. Can you understand the utter weariness of thinking about one thing all the time, so that when you wake up in the morning consciousness comes back with a sigh of "Oh yes, here it is again; another day of doubting and worrying, hoping and fearing has begun." If I don't get any sleep at all, which is too frequently the case, the strain is a "leetle" bit too hard, and I am sometimes tempted to take a drop of "pison" to put me to sleep in earnest. That momentary vision of redemption from thinking and striving, of a happy rest this side of eternity, has vanished away again. I can't help it; peaceful, desirable as it may be, the truth is that practically I don't believe it. It was such a sudden thing, such an entire change from anything that had ever come to me before, that it seemed almost like an inspiration, and I waited, almost expecting it to continue, to be permanent. But it doesn't stay, and so back swings the universe to the old place—paganism, naturalism, or whatever you call the belief whose watchword is "God and our own soul." And who shall say there is not comfort in it? One at least feels that here one breathes one's native air, welcoming back the old *human* feeling, with its beautiful pride and its striving, its despair, its mystery and its faith. Write to me and tell me whether, as one goes on, one must still be tossed about more and more by these conflicting feelings, or whether they finally settle themselves quietly one way or the other and take only their proper share at least of one's life. This day is like summer, but I should enjoy it more if last night hadn't been quite the most unpleasant I ever spent. I got so thoroughly tired about two in the morning that I made up my mind in despair to give the morphine another trial, and as one dose had no effect took two; the consequence of which is that I feel as ill to-day as one could desire. I can tell you, sir, you had better prize the gift of sleep as it deserves while you have it. If I don't never write to you no more you'll know it's because I really wish to treat you kindly. But one of these days you'll get another kind of letter, brim-full perhaps with health and happiness and thoroughly ashamed of my present self. I had a long letter yesterday from Harry James at Florence[855]—enjoying Italy but homesick. Did you see those verses in the North American translated from the Persian?[856] Good-bye.

The last of all is full both of realities and illusions, the latter insistently living through all the distress of the former. And I should like to say, or to believe, that they remained with her to the end, which was near.

Don't be alarmed at my pencil—I am not in bed but only bundled-up on the piazza by order of the doctor.[857] . . . I started for New York feeling a good deal knocked up, but hoping to get better from the change; I was to stay there over Sunday and see Dr. Metcalfe, who has a high reputation and was a friend of my father's. I left a request at his office that he would come to me on Sunday P.M.;[858] but in the meantime my cousin Mrs. Minturn Post, with whom I was staying, urged upon me her physician, Dr. Taylor, who came on Saturday night, just as I was going to bed, and, after sounding my lungs, told me very dreadful things about them.[859] As his verdict was worse than Metcalfe's proved I will tell you what he said first. He began very solemnly: "My dear young lady, your right lung is diseased; all your hemorrhages have come from there. It must have been bad for at least a year before they began. You must go to Europe as soon as possible." This was not cheerful, as I had been idiot enough to believe some time ago such a different explanation. But of course I wanted to learn what he absolutely thought, and told him I wasn't a bit afraid. If there weren't tubercles was I curable and if there *were* was I hopeless? I

855. Having spent October 1869 in Florence, HJ returned to the city briefly in December–January 1870, en route for England again.

856. In the *North American Review* 109, no. 225 (October 1869): 565–84, one of the "Critical Notices" deals with *Les Quatrains de Khèyam, traduits du Persan* and *Rubáiyát of Omar Khayyám, the Astronomer-Poet of Persia*.

857. Letter written from Pelham, 16 February 1870.

858. Dr. John T. Metcalfe's office was at 86 Fifth Avenue (*Complete Letters of HJ, 1855–72*, 2:354n).

859. A cousin to both Minny and Henry, Mary Ann King (1819–92) married Minturn Post, a New York City physician, in 1844 (for the relationship, see n. 463). Dr. Post died in 1869; in *Trow's New York City Directory . . . for the year ending May 1, 1871*, Mary A. Post, widow of Minturn, is listed as living at 30 West Twenty-fifth Street. In the same directory there are nine Taylors listed as physicians, four of whom also appear in the same series "for the year ending May 1, 1867": Charles F. Taylor, George H. Taylor, Isaac E. Taylor, and Samuel W. Taylor.

asked him for the very worst view he had conscientiously to take, but didn't mean definitely to ask how long I should live, and so was rather unprepared for his reply of "Two or three years." I didn't however wish to make him regret his frankness, so I said, "Well, Doctor, even if my right lung were all gone I should make a stand with my left," and then, by way of showing how valiant the stand would be, fainted away. This, I should say, was owing a good deal to my previous used-up condition from want of sleep. It made him at any rate hasten to assure me that there was every possibility of my case being not after all so bad—with which he took his departure; to my great relief as I didn't think him at all nice. His grammar was bad, and he made himself generally objectionable.

The next night dear Dr. Metcalfe came, whom I love for the gentlest and kindest soul I have ever seen. To start with he's a gentleman, as well as an excellent physician, and to end with he and my father were fond of each other at West Point,[860] and he takes a sort of paternal interest in me. He told me that my right lung is decidedly weaker than my left, which is quite sound, and that the hemorrhage has been a good thing for it and kept it from actual disease; and also that if I can keep up my general health I may get all right again. He has known a ten times worse case get entirely well. He urged me not to go to Washington, but decidedly to go to Europe; so this last is what I am to do with my cousin Mrs. Post if I am not dead before June. In a fortnight I'm to go back to New York to be for some time under Metcalfe's care. I feel tired out and hardly able to stir, but my courage is good, and I don't propose to lose it if I can help, for I know it all depends on myself whether I get through or not. That is if I begin to be indifferent to what happens I shall go down the hill fast. I have fortunately, through my mother's father,[861] enough Irish blood in me rather to enjoy a good fight. I feel the greatest longing for summer or spring; I should like it to be always spring for the rest of my life and to have all the people I care for always with me! But who *wouldn't* like it so? Good-bye.

860. The U.S. Military Academy is on the west bank of the Hudson River, forty miles north of New York City. HJ records seeing it in a "strong silver light, all simplifying and ennobling . . . as a cluster of high promontories, of the last classic elegance, overhanging vast receding reaches of river, mountain-guarded and dim" (*AS*, 150).

861. HJ's grandfather as well, William James of Albany.

To the gallantry and beauty of which there is little surely to add. But there came a moment, almost immediately after, when all illusion failed; which it is not good to think of or linger on, and yet not pitiful not to note. One may have wondered rather doubtingly—and I have expressed that— what life would have had for her and how her exquisite faculty of chal- lenge could have "worked in" with what she was likely otherwise to have encountered or been confined to. None the less did she in fact cling to consciousness; death, at the last, was dreadful to her; she would have given anything to live—and the image of this, which was long to remain with me, appeared so of the essence of tragedy that I was in the far-off aftertime to seek to lay the ghost by wrapping it, a particular occasion aiding, in the beauty and dignity of art. The figure that was to hover as the ghost has at any rate been of an extreme pertinence, I feel, to my doubtless too loose and confused general picture, vitiated perhaps by the effort to comprehend more than it contains. Much as this cherished companion's presence among us had represented for William and myself—and it is on *his* behalf I especially speak—her death made a mark that must stand here for a too waiting conclusion. We felt it together as the end of our youth.

THE END

# THE MIDDLE YEARS

*Henry James from a drawing kindly lent by Mr. W. Rothenstein.*

## CHAPTER SUMMARIES

In reminiscing, Henry James can range freely and be highly allusive, so these brief notes may help the reader locate specific subjects and events. Where possible, approximate dates have been provided.

The following pages represent all that Henry James lived to write of a volume of autobiographical reminiscences to which he had given the name of one of his own short stories, *The Middle Years*. It was designed to follow on *Notes of a Son and Brother* and to extend to about the same length. The chapters here printed were dictated during the autumn of 1914.[1] They were laid aside for other work toward the end of the year and were not revised by the author. A few quite evident slips have been corrected and the marking of the paragraphs—which he usually deferred till the final revision—has been completed.

In dictating *The Middle Years* he used no notes, and beyond an allusion or two in the unfinished volume itself there is no indication of the course which the book would have taken or the precise period it was intended to cover.

Percy Lubbock.[2]

I
If the author of this meandering record has noted elsewhere* that an event occurring early in 1870 was to mark the end of his youth, he is moved here at once to qualify in one or two respects that emphasis.[3] Everything depends in such a view on what one means by one's youth—so shifting a consciousness is this, and so related at the same

* "Notes of a Son and Brother," 1914.

1. This third volume of autobiographical writing, like a number of other works, remains incomplete. These last years mark a period of declining health for HJ, witnessed in the diaries, which record ongoing appointments with eminent physicians. In addition, the outbreak of the Great War in Europe in August 1914, in which a number of the young men of his circle (including his manservant, Burgess Noakes) and the sons of old friends served (and all too frequently died), caused him considerable anguish. The novelist became involved in two charities, one devoted to raising money for Belgian refugees, the other, the American Volunteer Motor-Ambulance Corps. For HJ's "Writings on World War I, 1914–1917," see *Henry James on Culture*, 131–85.

2. The job of preparing *The Middle Years* for posthumous publication was entrusted by the James family to Percy Lubbock, who, in this brief note, usefully sketches the circumstances of its composition as well as his own seemingly limited role as editor. Lubbock (1879–1965) was one of the younger generation of writers and critics who gathered round HJ in his later years. His study of the novel as a form, *The Craft of Fiction* (London: Jonathan Cape, 1921) follows Jamesian critical premises. For his role in preparing *TMY* for publication, see "A Note on This Edition," in this volume.

3. The end of youth was denoted in the final chapter of *NSB* by the death of Minny Temple in March 1870. Having there pursued the narrative of Minny Temple's final year,

time to many different matters. We are never old, that is we never cease easily to be young, for *all* life at the same time: youth is an army, the whole battalion of our faculties and our freshnesses, our passions and our illusions, on a considerably reluctant march into the enemy's country, the country of the general lost freshness; and I think it throws out at least as many stragglers behind as skirmishers ahead—stragglers who often catch up but belatedly with the main body, and even in many a case never catch up at all. Or under another figure it is a book in several volumes, and even at this a mere instalment of the large library of life, with a volume here and there closing, as something in the clap of its covers may assure us, while another remains either completely agape or kept open by a fond finger thrust in between the leaves. A volume, and a most substantial, *had* felt its pages very gravely pressed together before the winter's end that I have spoken of, but a restriction may still bear, and blessedly enough, as I gather from memory, on my sense of the whole year then terminated—a year seen by me now in the light of agitations, explorations, initiations (I scarce know how endearingly enough to name them!) which I should call fairly infantine in their indifference to proportions and aims, had they not still more left with me effects and possessions that even yet lend themselves to estimation.

It was at any rate impossible to have been younger, in spite of whatever inevitable submissions to the rather violent push forward at certain particular points and on lines corresponding with them, than I found myself, from the first day of March 1869, in the face of an opportunity that affected me then and there as the happiest, the most interesting, the most alluring and beguiling, that could ever have opened before a somewhat disabled young man[4] who was about to complete his twenty-sixth year. Treasures

---

HJ now returns to March 1869, when, having called on her en route for New York City, he left for England at the beginning of what extended to a fifteen-month tour, a series of what he calls "initiations," when he visited Europe—and, most importantly, Italy. Like WJ, he was in search of remedies for his chronic physical ailments, most notably his back trouble and constipation, but as he quickly establishes in this volume, it was a period of aesthetic enrichment and confirmation of his calling to register most fully and profoundly the impressions by which he continues to be importuned.

4. Even in his letter to WJ on Minny's death, HJ refers to his "invalidism," and Edel comments: "There is abundant evidence that HJ thought himself in his youth more sickly than he was—much of his illness was a state of melancholy induced by the war. He himself describes in *Notes of a Son and Brother* how quickly he revived when the war was ended (chap. 9) and thereafter he led a strenuous life of travel and work for many years until beset

of susceptibility, treasures not only unconscious of the remotest approach to exhaustion, but, given the dazzling possibilities, positively and ideally intact, I now recognise—I in fact long ago recognised—on the part of that intensely "reacting" small organism; which couldn't have been in higher spirits or made more inward fuss about the matter if it had come into a property measured not by mere impressions and visions, occasions for play of perception and imagination, mind and soul, but by dollars and "shares", lands and houses or flocks and herds. It is to the account of that immense fantastication that I set down a state of mind so out of proportion to anything it could point to round about save by the vaguest of foolish-looking gestures; and it would perhaps in truth be hard to say whether in the mixture of spirit and sense so determined the fact of innocence or that of intelligence most prevailed. I like to recover this really prodigious flush—as my reader, clearly, must perceive I do; I like fairly to hang about a particular small hour of that momentous March day—which I have glanced at too, I believe, on some other and less separated page than this—for the sake of the extraordinary gage of experience that it seemed on the spot to offer, and that I had but to take straight up:[5] my life, on so complacently near a view as I now treat myself to, having veritably con-sisted but in the prolongation of that act. I took up the gage, and as I look back the fullest as well as simplest account of the interval till now strikes me as being that I have never, in common honour, let it drop again. And the small hour was just that of my having landed at Liverpool in the gusty,

---

by the infirmities of old age." He regretted too that "she never knew how sick and disordered a creature I was" and looked forward to the time when he might be "more active and masculine" (*HJL*, 1:229 n. 1, 224).

5. It is in his essay "London" that HJ describes his disembarking at Liverpool and subsequent journey to "the murky modern Babylon" of London in 1869—his first inde-pendent, adult stay in the capital (*Century Magazine*, December 1888; *Travel Writings: Great Britain and America*, 13). The London of that essay is the mid-Victorian city of Mayhew and Dickens. On 22 June 1903 HJ committed himself to write a book on "London Town" for the publisher Macmillan. It was never written—HJ offered his autobiographical volumes instead—but the surviving notes of topographical and architectural detail from 1908–9 indicate that its method might have been similar to that of *AS* (see *CN*, 273–80). The description of Lambert Strether's arrival at the port of Liverpool at the opening of *The Ambassadors* (1903) must have been indebted to this early experience. As for the original date of HJ's disembarking, Novick comments that "in TMY, James says very positively that he arrived on March 1, a Monday, but the chronology of his arrival and a letter to his mother dated March 2, from 7 Half Moon Street, make Saturday, February 27, a more likely date" (*Young Master*, 483 n. 6).

cloudy, overwhelmingly English morning and pursued, with immediate intensities of appreciation, as I may call the muffled accompaniment for fear of almost indecently overnaming it, a course which had seated me at a late breakfast in the coffee-room of the old Adelphi Hotel ("Radley's," as I had to deplore its lately having ceased to be dubbed,)[6] and handed me over without a scruple to my fate. This doom of inordinate exposure to appearances, aspects, images, every protrusive item almost, in the great beheld sum of things, I regard in other words as having settled upon me once for all while I observed for instance that in England the plate of buttered muffin and its cover were sacredly set upon the slop-bowl after hot water had been ingenuously poured into the same, and had seen that circumstance in a perfect cloud of accompaniments. I must have had with my tea and my muffin a boiled egg or two and a dab of marmalade, but it was from a far other store of condiments I most liberally helped myself. I was lucidly aware of so gorging—esoterically, as it were, while I drew out the gustatory process; and I must have said in that lost reference to this scene of my dedication which I mentioned above that I was again and again in the aftertime to win back the homeliest notes of the impression, the damp and darksome light washed in from the steep, black, bricky street, the crackle of the strong draught of the British "sea-coal" fire, much more confident of its function, I thought, than the fires I had left, the rustle of the thick, stiff, loudly unfolded and refolded "Times", the incomparable truth to type of the waiter, truth to history, to literature, to poetry, to Dickens, to Thackeray, positively to Smollett and to Hogarth,[7] to every connection that could help me to appropriate him and his setting, an arrangement of things hanging together with a romantic rightness that had the force of a revelation.

To what end appropriation became thus eager and romance thus easy one could have asked one's self only if the idea of connectibility as stretching away and away hadn't of a sudden taken on such a wealth of suggestion; it represented at once a chain stretching off to heaven knew where, but far

6. James Radley opened a hotel in 1826 that was later renamed the Adelphi Hotel; rebuilt in 1912, it was remarkable for its luxury and modernity. In the nineteenth century, Liverpool was the major point of departure and arrival for transatlantic travelers.

7. "Sea-coal" can be variously mineral coal found on the seashore, or coal shipped by sea and therefore of high quality. The waiter features as a national type in the works of all these British writers and artists. Tobias George Smollett (1721–71) was a comic, picaresque novelist, William Hogarth (1697–1764) a painter of scenes of contemporary life with a powerful satirical application.

into one's future at least, one's possibilities of life, and every link and pulse of which it was going accordingly to be indispensable, besides being delightful and wonderful, to recognise. Recognition, I dare say, was what remained, through the adventure of the months to come, the liveliest principle at work; both as bearing on the already known, on things unforgotten and of a sense intensely cultivated and cherished from my younger time, and on the imagined, the unimagined and the unimaginable, a quantity that divided itself somehow into the double muster of its elements, an endless vista or waiting array, down the middle of which I should inconceivably pass—inconceivably save for being sure of some thrilled arrest, some exchange of assurance and response, at every step. Obviously half the charm, as I can but thinly describe it, of the substantially continuous experience the first passages of which I thus note was in the fact that, immensely moved by it as I was, and having so to deal with it—in the anticipatory way or to the whatevers and wherevers and whenevers within me that should find it in order—I yet felt it in no degree as strange or obscure, baffling or unrecognising on its own side; everything was so far from impenetrable that my most general notion was the very ecstasy of understanding and that really wherever I looked, and still more wherever I pressed, I sank in and in up to my nose. This in particular was of the perfect felicity, that while the fact of difference all round me was immense the embarrassment of it was nil—as if the getting into relation with the least waste had been prepared from so far back that a sort of divine economy now fairly ruled. It was doubtless a part of the total fatuity, and perhaps its sublimest mark, that I knew what everything meant, not simply then but for weeks and months after, and was to know less only with increase of knowledge. That must indeed have been of the essence of the general effect and the particular felicity—only not grotesque because, for want of occasion, not immediately exhibited: a consciousness not other than that of a person abruptly introduced into a preoccupied and animated circle and yet so miraculously aware of the matters conversed about as to need no word of explanation before joining in. To say of such a person that he hadn't lost time would, I knew, be feebly to express his advantage; my likeness to him, at any rate, probably fell short of an absurd one through the chapter of accidents, mostly of the happiest in their way too, which, restraining the personal impulse for me, kept appearances and pretensions down. The feast, as it more and more opened out, was all of the objective, as we have learned so comfortably to say; or at least of its convenient opposite only in so far as this undertook to interpret it for myself alone.

To return at all across the years to the gates of the paradise of the first larger initiations is to be ever so tempted to pass them, to push in again and breathe the air of this, that and the other plot of rising ground particularly associated, for memory and gratitude, with the quickening process.[8] The trouble is that with these sacred spots, to later appreciation, the garden of youth is apt inordinately to bristle, and that one's account of them has to shake them together fairly hard, making a coherent thing of them, to profit by the contribution of each. In speaking of my earliest renewal of the vision of Europe, if I may give so grand a name to a scarce more than merely enlarged and uplifted gape, I have, I confess, truly to jerk myself over the ground, to wrench myself with violence from memories and images, stages and phases and branching arms, that catch and hold me as I pass them by. Such a matter as my recovery of contact with London for a few weeks, the contact broken off some nine years before, lays so many plausible traps for me that discretion half warns me to stand off the ground and walk round it altogether. I stop my ears to the advice, however, under the pleading reminder that just those days began a business for me that was to go ever so much further than I then dreamed and planted a seed that was, by my own measure, singularly to sprout and flourish—the harvest of which, I almost permit myself to believe, has even yet not all been gathered. I foresee moreover how little I shall be able to resist, throughout these Notes, the force of persuasion expressed in the individual *vivid* image of the past wherever encountered, these images having always such terms of their own, such subtle secrets and insidious arts for keeping us in relation with them, for bribing us by the beauty, the authority, the wonder of their saved intensity. They have saved it, they seem to say to us, from such a welter of death and darkness and ruin that this alone makes a value and a light and a dignity for them, something indeed of an argument that our story, since we attempt to tell one, has lapses and gaps without them. Not to be denied also, over and above this, is the downright pleasure of the illusion yet again created, the *apparent* transfer from the past to the present of the particular combination of things that did at its hour ever so directly operate and that isn't after all

8. HJ's rhetorical disquiet at his need (yet reluctance) to select from the richly insistent material of the past is characteristic of all his autobiographical writing. Whether his thoughts on the recalled sensation of being "at home" with these new experiences of independence in Britain typify the aging narrator in retrospection or the susceptible young man he once was is, of course, impossible to gauge.

then drained of virtue, wholly wasted and lost, for sensation, for participation in the act of life, in the attesting sights, sounds, smells, the illusion, as I say, of the recording senses.

What began, during the springtime of my actual reference, in a couple of dusky ground-floor rooms at number 7 Half-Moon Street,[9] was simply an establishment all in a few days of a personal relation with London that was not of course measurable at the moment—I saw in my bedazzled state of comparative freedom too many other relations ahead, a fairly intoxicated vision of choice and range—but that none the less set going a more intimately inner consciousness, a wheel within the wheels, and led to my departing, the actual, the general incident closed, in possession of a return-ticket "good", as we say, for a longer interval than I could then dream about, and that the first really earnest fumble of after years brought surprisingly to light. I think it must have been the very proportions themselves of the invitation and the interest that kept down, under the immense impression, everything in the nature of calculation and presumption; dark, huge and prodigious the other party to our relation, London's and mine, as I called it, loomed and spread—much too mighty a Goliath for the present in any conceivable ambition even of a fast-growing David.[10] My earlier apprehension, fed at the season as from a thousand outstretched silver spoons—for these all shone to me with that effect of the handsomest hospitality—piled up the monster to such a height that I could somehow only fear him as much as I admired and that his proportions in fact reached away quite beyond my expectation.[11] He was always the great

9. After the phrase "lands and houses or flocks and herds" on p. 411 above, the version of *TMY* which appeared in *Scribner's Magazine* (see "A Note on This Edition") makes a cut to this point. It is the first of many such changes, presumably designed to make for less demanding reading.

10. This street, then occupied by a number of lodging houses, is still rather gloomy because of the unbroken rooflines of its five- or six-story buildings; it runs north from Piccadilly. Not far from Berkeley Square, it would have been familiar to HJ from his boyhood stay in England in 1855–56. He rented the rooms for a month and complained to his lifelong friend George Abbott James on 20 March 1869 that London seemed "the darkest & dingiest of cities—especially when seen, as I see it now, from the basement of an ancient lodging house in a narrow, albeit highly respectable street, with the brightness of heaven obscured at once by a steady deluge of rain & a vast wire screen" (*Complete Letters of HJ, 1855–72*, 1:252).

11. As HJ mentions in the final chapter of *NSB*, his entrée into London's intellectual and literary circles—to whatever extent he looks back on himself as an underdog—was expe-

figure of London, and I was for no small time, as the years followed, to be kept at my awestruck distance for taking him on that sort of trust: I had crept about his ankles, I had glanced adventurously up at his knees, and wasn't the moral for the most part the mere question of whether I should ever be big enough to so much as guess where he stopped?

Odd enough was it, I make out, that I was to feel no wonder of that kind or degree play in the coming time over such other social aspects, such superficially more colourable scenes as I paid, in repetition as frequent as possible, my respects and my compliments to: they might meet me with wreathed smiles and splendid promises and deep divinations of my own desire, a thousand graces and gages, in fine, that I couldn't pretend to have picked up within the circle, however experimentally widened, of which Half-Moon Street was the centre, and nothing therefore could have exceeded the splendour of these successive and multiplied assurances. What it none the less infinitely beguiles me to recognise to-day is that such exhibitions, for all their greater direct radiance, and still more for all their general implication of a store of meaning and mystery and beauty that they alone, from example to example, from prodigy to prodigy, had to open out, left me comparatively little crushed by the impression of their concerning me further than my own action perhaps could make good. It was as if I had seen that all there was for me of these great things I should sooner or later take; the amount would be immense, yet, as who should say, all on the same plane and the same connection, the aesthetic, the "artistic", the romantic in the looser sense, or in other words in the air of the passions of the intelligence. What other passions of a deeper strain, whether personal or racial, and thereby more superstitiously importunate, I must have felt involved in the question of an effective experience of English life I was doubtless then altogether unprepared to say; it probably came, however, I seem actually to make out, very much to this particular perception, exactly, that any penetration of the London scene would *be* experience after a fashion that an exercise of one's "mere intellectual curiosity" wherever else wouldn't begin to represent, glittering as the rewards to such curiosity amid alien peoples of genius might thoroughly appear. On the other hand it was of course going to be nothing less than a superlative help that one would have but to reach out straight and in the full measure of one's passion for these rewards, to find one's self carried all the way by one's

---

dited by Charles Eliot Norton and his family. He was not to take "possession" of the city until the winter of 1876.

active, one's contemplative concern with them—this delightful affair, fraught with increase of light, of joy and wonder, of possibilities of adventure for the mind, in fine, inevitably exhausting the relation.

II Let me not here withal appear to pretend to say how far I then foresaw myself likely to proceed, as it were, with the inimitable France and the incomparable Italy;[12] my real point is altogether in the simple fact that they hovered before me, even in their scrappy foretastes, to a great effect of ease and inspiration, whereas I shouldn't at all have resented the charge of fairly hiding behind the lowly door of Mr. Lazarus Fox—so unmistakeably did it open into complications tremendous. This excellent man, my Half-Moon Street landlord—I surrender, I can't keep away from him—figures to me now as but one of the thousand forms of pressure in the collective assault, but he couldn't have been more carefully chosen for his office had he consciously undertaken to express to me in a concentrated manner most of the things I was "after".[13] The case was rather indeed perhaps that he himself by his own mere perfection put me up to much of what I should most confidently look for, and that the right lines of observation and enjoyment, of local and social contact, as I may call it, were most of all those that started out from him and came back to him. It was as if nothing I saw could have done without him, as if nothing he was could have done without everything else. The very quarters I occupied under his protection happened, for that matter, to swarm —as I estimated swarming—with intensities of suggestion—aware as I now encourage myself to become that the first note of the numberless reverberations I was to pick up in the aftertime had

12. Though HJ had lived for extended periods in France as a child, he had not yet visited Italy. He would get to know both countries well and publish such volumes as *Portraits of Places* (1883) (travel essays on Italy, France, Britain and America), *A Little Tour in France* (1884), and *Italian Hours* (1909).

13. HJ wrote to his mother at the time, "My landlord is a very finished specimen and I wish you could see him. He is an old servant of some genteel family, who lets out his three floors to gentlemen and waits upon them with the most obsequious punctuality. He does everything for me—won't let me raise a finger for myself—is butler, landlord, valet, guide, philosopher and friend all at once. I am completely comfortable, save that his tremendous respectability and officiousness are somewhat oppressive. Nevertheless, in this matter of lodgings, esteem me most happy and fortunate" (quoted in Edel, *Untried Years,* 290–91). HJ comments a little later in this chapter that Fox had been an employee of the Rutson family, one of whose sons lodged on the second floor.

definitely been struck for me as under the wave of his conducting little wand. He flourished it modestly enough, ancient worthy of an immemorial order that he was—old pensioned servant, of course, of a Cumberland (as I believe) family, a kind, slim, celibate, informing and informed member of which occupied his second floor apartments; a friend indeed whom I had met on the very first occasion of my sallying forth from Morley's Hotel in Trafalgar Square to dine at a house of sustaining, of inspiring hospitality in the Kensington quarter.[14] Succumbing thus to my tangle of memories, from which I discern no escape, I recognise further that if the endlessly befriending Charles Nortons introduced me to Albert Rutson, and Albert Rutson introduced me to his feudal retainer, so it was in no small degree through the confidence borrowed from the latter's interest in the decent appearance I should make, an interest of a consistency not to have been prefigured by any at all like instance in my past, that I so far maintained my dizzy balance as to be able to ascend to the second floor under the thrill of sundry invitations to breakfast. I dare say it is the invitations to breakfast that hold me at this moment by their spell—so do they breathe to me across the age the note of a London world that we have left far behind; in consequence of which I the more yearningly steal back to it, as on sneaking tiptoe, and shut myself up there without interference.[15] It is embalmed in disconnections, in differences, that I cultivate

14. On reaching the capital HJ stayed at Morley's Hotel, on the east side of Trafalgar Square (now the site of South Africa House), a traditional old establishment recommended to him by a garrulous fellow traveler on the slow Sunday train south from Liverpool. It was raining when he arrived at Euston Station, the terminus for the northwest, and he took a cab for the mile and a quarter journey to Trafalgar Square: "The low black houses were as inanimate as so many rows of coal-scuttles, save where at frequent corners, from a gin-shop, there was a flare of light more brutal still than the darkness." By contrast, Morley's was "a ruddy spot; brilliant, in my recollection, is the coffee-room fire, the hospitable mahogany, the sense that in the stupendous city this, at any rate for the hour, was a shelter and a point of view" ("London," *Henry James: Travel Writings: Great Britain and America*, 15). HJ dined with the Nortons on their extended European tour; they were renting an apartment on Queen's Gate Terrace, south of Kensington Gardens in South Kensington. Here he met Albert Rutson, private secretary to Henry Austin Bruce, 1st Baron Aberdare, and home secretary in Gladstone's government of 1868 (*HJL*, 1:91, 97 n. 12).

15. Meeting up for a late-morning or noontime breakfast was not uncommon. For the young men HJ met who held political jobs, the main work of the day was geared to the later afternoon when Parliament sat. As he goes on to suggest, such conventions typify a period when the city's self-confidence was unassailed. HJ writes to WJ on 19 March 1869 of Rutson, "He entertained me this morning with a certain Hon George Broderick (a son of Lord Middleton, you know)—an extremely pleasant & intelligent man. (Rutson has just

a free fancy for pronouncing advantageous to it: sunk already was the shaft by which I should descend into the years, and my inspiration is in touching as many as possible of the points of the other tradition, retracing as many as possible of the features of the old face, eventually to be blurred again even before my own eyes, and with the materials for a portrait thereby accessible but to those who were present up to the time of the change.

I don't pretend to date this change which still allows me to catch my younger observation and submission at play on the far side of it; I make it fall into the right perspective, however, I think, when I place it where I began to shudder before a confidence, not to say an impudence, of diminution in the aspects by which the British capital differed so from those of all the foreign together as to present throughout the straight contradiction to them. That straight contradiction, testifying invaluably at every turn, had been from far back the thing, romantically speaking, to clutch and keep the clue and the logic of; thanks to it the whole picture, every element, objects and figures, background and actors, nature and art, hung consummately together, appealing in their own light and under their own law—interesting ever in every case by instituting comparisons, sticking on the contrary to their true instinct and suggesting only contrast. They were the *opposite*, the assured, the absolute, the unashamed, in respect to whatever might be of a generally similar intention elsewhere: this was their dignity, their beauty and their strength—to look back on which is to wonder if one didn't quite consciously tremble, before the exhibition, for any menaced or mitigated symptom in it. I honestly think one did, even in the first flushes of recognition, more or less so tremble; I remember at least that in spite of such disconcertments, such dismays, as certain of the most thoroughly Victorian *choses vues*[16] originally treated me to, something yet deeper and finer than observation admonished me to like them just as they were, or at least not too fatuously to dislike—since it somehow glimmered upon me that if they had lacked their oddity, their monstrosity, as it even might be, their unabashed insular conformity, other things that belong to them, as they belong to these, might have loomed less large and massed less thick, which effect was wholly to be deprecated. To catch that secret, I make out

stopped in to ask me again for Sunday. He is indeed as my landlord describes him— 'wrapped up in goodness & kindness.[']')" George Charles Brodrick (1831–1903) was a "British journalist, later warden of Merton College, Oxford" (*CWJ*, 1:59, 60 n. 2).

16. Things seen or witnessed. HJ may have taken the term from Victor Hugo (see *NSB*, n. 605).

the more I think of it, was to have perhaps the smokiest, but none the less the steadiest, light to walk by; the "clue", as I have called it, was to be one's appreciation of an England that should turn its back directly enough, and without fear of doing it too much, on examples and ideas not strictly homebred—since she did her own sort of thing with such authority and was even then to be noted as sometimes trying other people's with a *kind* of disaster not recorded, at the worst, among themselves.

I must of course disavow pretending to have read this vivid philosophy into my most immediate impressions, and I may in fact perhaps not claim to have been really aware of its seed till a considerable time had passed, till apprehensions and reflections had taken place in quantity, immeasurable quantity, so to speak, and a great stir-up of the imagination been incurred. Undoubtedly is it in part the new—that is, more strictly, the elder—acuteness that I touch all the prime profit with; I didn't know at the time either how much appearances were all the while in the melting-pot or what wealth of reaction on them I was laying up. I cherish, for love of the unbroken interest, all the same, the theory of certain then positive and effective prefigurements, because it leaves me thus free for remarking that I knew where I was, as I may put it, from the moment I saw the state of the London to come brought down with the weight of her abdication of her genius. It not unnaturally may be said that it hasn't been till to-day that we *see* her genius in its fulness—throwing up in a hundred lights, matters we practically acknowledge, such a plastic side as we had never dreamed she possessed. The genius of accommodation is what we had last expected of her—accommodation to anything but her portentous self, for in *that* connection she was ever remarkable; and certainly the air of the generalised, the emulous smart modern capital has come to be written upon her larger and larger even while we look.

The unaccommodating and unaccommodated city remains none the less closely consecrated to one's fondest notion of her—the city too indifferent, too proud, too unaware, too stupid even if one will, to enter any lists that involved her moving from her base and that thereby, when one approached her from the alien *positive* places (I don't speak of the American, in those days too negative to be related at all) enjoyed the enormous "pull", for making her impression, of ignoring everything but her own perversities and then of driving these home with an emphasis not to be gainsaid. Since she didn't emulate, as I have termed it, so she practised her own arts altogether, and both these ways and these consequences were in the flattest opposition (*that* was the happy point!) to foreign felicities or foreign standards, so that the effect in every case was of the straightest reversal of them—with black for the foreign white and white for the foreign black, wet for the foreign dry and dry for the foreign wet, big for the foreign small and small for the foreign big: I needn't extend the catalogue. *Her* idiosyncrasy was never in the least to have been inferred or presumed; it could only, in general, make the outsider provisionally gape. She sat thus imperturbable in her felicities, and if that is how, remounting the stream of time, I like most to think of her, this is because if her interest is still undeniable—as that of overgrown things goes—it has yet lost its fineness of quality. Phenomena may be interesting, thank goodness, without being phenomena of elegant expression or of any other form of restless smartness, and when once type is strong, when once it plays up from deep sources, every show of its sincerity delivers us a message and we hang, to real suspense, on its continuance of energy, on its again and yet again consistently acquitting itself. So it keeps in tune, and, as the French adage says, *c'est le ton qui fait la chanson*.[17] The mid-Victorian London was sincere—that was a vast virtue and a vast appeal; the contemporary is sceptical, and most so when most plausible; the turn of the tide could verily be fixed to an hour—the hour at which the new plausibility began to exceed the old sincerities by so much as a single sign. They could truly have been arrayed face to face, I think, for an attentive eye—and I risk even saying that my own, bent upon them, as was to come to pass, with a habit of anxiety that I should scarce be able to overstate, had its unrecorded penetrations, its alarms and recoveries, even perhaps its very lapses of faith, though always redeemed afresh by still fonder fanaticisms, to a pitch that shall perhaps present itself, when they expose it all the way, as that of tiresome extravagance. Exposing it all the way is none the less, I see, exactly what I plot against it—or, otherwise expressed, in favour of the fine truth of history, so far as a throb of that awful pulse has been matter of one's own life; in favour too of the mere returns derivable from more inordinate curiosity. These Notes would enjoy small self-respect, I think, if that principle, not to call it that passion, didn't almost furiously ride them.[18]

17. Literally, "It is the tone that makes the song," i.e., "It's not what you say but the way you say it."

18. It is tempting to regard this reflection on London in its distant mid-Victorian heyday and national obliviousness to alternative influences as material that might have been developed in "London Town," though the extant notes are (understandably) more a record of sights and vistas, many detailing the churches of one of its most historic quarters, the City.

**III** I was at any rate in the midst of sincerities enough, sincerities of emphasis and "composition"; perversities, idiosyncrasies, incalculabilities, delightful all as densities at first insoluble, delightful even indeed as so much mere bewilderment and shock. When was the shock, I ask myself as I look back, not so deadened by the general atmospheric richness as not to melt more or less immediately into some succulence for the mind, something that could feed the historic sense almost to sweetness? I don't mean that it was a shock to be invited to breakfast—there were stronger ones than that; but was in fact the *trait de moeurs*[19] that disconnected me with most rapidity and intensity from all I had left on the other side of the sea. To be so disconnected, for the time, and in the most insidious manner, was above all what I had come out for, and every appearance that might help it was to be artfully and gratefully cultivated. I recollect well how many of these combined as I sat at quite punctual fried sole and marmalade in the comparatively disengaged sitting-room of the second floor—the occupancy of the first has remained vague to me; disengaged from the mantle of gloom the folds of which draped most heavily the feet of the house, as it were, and thereby promoted in my own bower the chronic dusk favourable to mural decoration consisting mainly of framed and glazed "coloured" excisions from Christmas numbers of the Illustrated London News that had been at their hour quite modern miracles.[20] Was it for that matter into a sudden splendour of the modern that I ascendingly emerged under the hospitality of my kind fellow-tenant, or was it rather into the fine classicism of a bygone age, as literature and the arts had handed down that memory? Such were the questions whisked at every turn under my nose and reducing me by their obscure charm but to bewildered brooding, I fear, when I should have been myself, to repay these attentions, quite forward and informing and affirmative.

There were eminent gentlemen, as I was sure they could only be, to

19. Cultural feature.

20. The *Illustrated London News,* founded in 1842 by Herbert Ingram and Mark Lemon (editor of *Punch* magazine), became, after initial difficulties, a great success, featuring woodcuts based on the work of some of the most eminent artists and illustrators. It serves as an impressive social record of its time. From 1855 onward, the magazine produced a special Christmas number with illustrations in color. The air of London at the time was polluted by domestic coal fires and industrial discharge; smog and "pea soupers" were frequent and so lower-story rooms would be deprived of light.

"meet" and, alas, awfully to interrogate me—for vivid has remained to me, as the best of my bewilderment, the strangeness of finding that I could be of interest to *them:* not indeed to call it rather the proved humiliation of my impotence. My identity for myself was *all* in my sensibility to their own exhibition, with not a scrap left over for a personal show; which made it as inconvenient as it was queer that I should be treated as a specimen and have in the most unexpected manner to prove that I was a good one. I knew myself the very worst conceivable, but how to give to such other persons a decent or coherent reason for my being so required more presence of mind than I could in the least muster—the consequence of which failure had to be for me, I fear, under all that confused first flush, rather an abject acceptance of the air of imbecility. There were, it appeared, things of interest taking place in America, and I had had, in this absurd manner, to come to England to learn it: I had had over there on the ground itself no conception of any such matter—nothing of the smallest interest, by any perception of mine, as I suppose I should still blush to recall, had taken place in America since the War. How *could* anything, I really wanted to ask—anything comparable, that is, to what was taking place under my eyes in Half-Moon Street and at dear softly presiding Rutson's table of talk. It doubtless essentially belonged to the exactly right type and tone and general figure of my fellow-breakfasters from the Temple, from the Home Office, the Foreign Office, the House of Commons, from goodness knew what other scarce discernible Olympian altitudes, it belonged to the very cut of their hair and their waistcoats and their whiskers—for it was still more or less a whiskered age—that they should desire from me much distinctness about General Grant's first cabinet, upon the formation of which the light of the newspaper happened then to beat;[21] yet at the same time that I asked myself if it was to such cold communities, such flat

21. It is unsurprising that Rutson's guests, from legal and political circles, were concerned with contemporary developments in Anglo-American relations, which remained tense. The most contentious issue related to Britain's having supplied to the Confederacy the warship *Alabama,* which inflicted devastating damage on Union shipping. The United States continued to make claims for reparation for losses: "By 1869, these had still not been settled, and President Ulysses S. Grant told the British Minister to Washington, Edward Thornton, that 'the *Alabama* claims were the only grave question which the United States had at issue with any nation'" (Kathleen Burk, *Old World, New World: The Story of Britain and America* [London: Little, Brown, 2007], 273). The deadlock between the two governments was not broken until November 1870.

frustrations as were so proposed, that I had sought to lift my head again in European air, I found the crisis enriched by sundry other apprehensions.

They melted together in it to that increase of savour I have already noted, yet leaving me vividly admonished that the blankness of my mind as to the Washington candidates relegated me to some class unencountered as yet by any one of my conversers, a class only not perfectly ridiculous because perfectly insignificant. Also that politics walked abroad in England, so that one might supremely bump against them, as much as, by my fond impression, they took their exercise in America but through the back streets and the ways otherwise untrodden and the very darkness of night; that further all lively attestations were *ipso facto* interesting, and that finally and in the supreme degree, the authenticity of whatever one was going to learn in the world would probably always have for its sign that one got it at some personal cost. To this generalisation mightn't one even add that in proportion as the cost was great, or became fairly excruciating, the lesson, the value acquired would probably be a thing to treasure? I remember really going so far as to wonder if any act of acquisition of the life-loving, life-searching sort that most appealed to me wouldn't mostly be fallacious if unaccompanied by that tag of the price paid in personal discomfort, in some self-exposure and some none too impossible consequent discomfiture, for the sake of it. Didn't I even on occasion mount to the very height of seeing it written that these bad moments were the downright consecration of knowledge, that is of perception and, essentially, of exploration, always dangerous and treacherous, and so might afterwards come to figure to memory, each in its order, as the silver nail on the wall of the temple where the trophy is hung up? All of which remark, I freely grant, is a great ado about the long since so bedimmed little Half-Moon Street breakfasts, and is moreover quite wide of the mark if suggesting that the joys of recognition, those of imaginatively, of projectively fitting in and fitting out every piece in the puzzle and every recruit to the force of a further understanding weren't in themselves a most bustling and cheering business.

It was bustling at least, assuredly, if not quite always in the same degree exhilarating, to breakfast out at all, as distinguished from lunching, without its being what the Harvard scene made of it, one of the incidents of "boarding";[22] it was association at a jump with the ghosts of Byron

22. Presumably HJ is recalling his meals taken with WJ at Miss Upham's board in Cambridge (*NSB*, 246–47).

and Sheridan and Scott and Moore and Lockhart and Rogers and *tutti quanti*[23]—as well as the exciting note of a social order in which everyone wasn't hurled straight, with the momentum of rising, upon an office or a store. The mere vision in numbers of persons embodying and in various ways sharply illustrating a clear alternative to that passivity told a tale that would be more and more worth the reading with every turn of the page. So at all events I fantasticated[24] while harassed by my necessity to weave into my general tapestry every thread that would conduce to a pattern, and so the thread for instance of the great little difference of my literally never having but once "at home" been invited to breakfast on types as well as on toast and its accessories could suggest an effect of silk or silver when absolutely dangled before me. That single occasion at home came back in a light that fairly brought tears to my eyes, for it was touching now to the last wanness that the lady of the winter morn of the Massachusetts Sabbath, one of those, as I recover it, of 1868, to reach whose board we had waded through snowdrifts, had been herself fondling a reminiscence, though I can scarce imagine supposing herself to offer for our consumption any other type than her own. It was for that matter but the sweet staleness of her reminiscence that made her a type, and I remember how it had had to do thereby all the work: *she,* of an age to reach so considerably back, had breakfasted out, in London, and with Mr. Rogers himself—that was the point; which I am bound to say did for the hour and on that spot supply richness of reference enough.[25] And I am caught up, I find, in the very act of this claim for my prior scantness of experience by a memory

23. All such people, or the whole lot (It.). HJ lists the celebrated, occasionally notorious, literary men of an earlier era: Byron was a friend of the Irish writer Thomas Moore (1779–1852), who enjoyed great popularity through his songs. In 1830 Moore published the *Letters and Journals of Lord Byron.* Richard Brinsley Sheridan (1751–1816) was a politician as well as playwright. A biography of the Scottish novelist and poet Sir Walter Scott was published in ten volumes in 1839 (2nd ed.) by another Scot, John Gibson Lockhart (1794–1854), who also wrote for *Blackwood's Magazine* (a periodical famous for attacking the work of the Romantic poets). The poet Samuel Rogers (1763–1855) maintained a high social profile and was well known for entertaining fellow writers at breakfast. His *Table Talk,* illustrating his conversational talents and packed with famous historical names, was published in 1856.

24. This is a term HJ seems to have favored at this time; it occurs elsewhere in *TMY,* chaps. 1 and 7.

25. It has not been possible to identify this woman. She was clearly aged, had visited England, and mixed in literary circles—like many of her social class. I have found no likely reference in Samuel Rogers's memoirs.

that makes it not a little less perfect and which is oddly enough again associated with a struggle, on an empty stomach, through the massed New England whiteness of the prime Sunday hour. I still cherish the vision, which couldn't then have faded from me, of my having, during the age of innocence—I mean of my own—breakfasted with W. D. Howells, insidious disturber and fertiliser of that state in me, to "meet" Bayard Taylor and Arthur Sedgwick all in the Venetian manner, the delightful Venetian manner which toward the later 'sixties draped any motion on our host's part as with a habit still appropriate.[26] *He* had risen that morning under the momentum of his but recently concluded consular term in Venice, where margin, if only that of the great loungeable piazza, had a breadth, and though Sedgwick and I had rather, as it were, to take the jump standing, this was yet under the inspiration of feeling the case most special. Only it had *been* Venetian, snow-shoes and all; I had stored it sacredly away as not American at all, and was of course to learn in Half-Moon Street how little it had been English either.

What must have seemed to me of a fine international mixture, during those weeks, was my thrilling opportunity to sit one morning, beside Mrs. Charles Norton's tea-urn, in Queen's Gate Terrace, opposite to Frederic Harrison, eminent to me at the moment as one of the subjects of Matthew Arnold's early fine banter, one of his too confidently roaring "young lions" of the periodical press.[27] Has any gilding ray since that happy

26. For Howells, see *NSB*, n. 716. During the Civil War he served as U.S. consul-general in Venice, and his sketches, *Venetian Life*, were published in 1866. For Arthur Sedgwick, see *NSB*, n. 426. The American writer, poet, and renowned traveler Bayard Taylor (1825-1878), brought out a translation of Goethe's *Faust* in two volumes in 1871. In 1865 HJ wrote a piece on his *John Godfrey's Fortunes; Related by Himself; A Story of American Life* for the *North American Review*, but it was not published until 1957, by the *Harvard Library Bulletin* (*LC* 1, 621-25, 1449n).

27. The tea urn belongs to Charles Norton's mother, who, having let Shady Hill in Cambridge, accompanied the family on their tour of Europe (Novick, *Young Master*, 174). Frederic Harrison (1831-1923), who became editor of the *Fortnightly Review*, was a leading positivist and follower of the ideas of Auguste Comte. In later years HJ would describe him as one "who in spite of his aspect, complexion, hair-brushing etc, as of a provincial second rate dandy, is very good company. The contrast between Harrison's Comtism, communism etc, and his highly ornate and conventional appearance, is most singular" (letter to Alice James, 17 February [1878], *HJL*, 2:158). Harrison had recently dismissed Arnold's characterization of culture as "the silliest cant of the day," and the latter had amusedly responded in his five essays on "anarchy and authority" composed between June 1867 and August 1868, which later became chaps. 2-6 of *Culture and Anarchy* (Park Honan, *Matthew Arnold: A Life* [London: Weidenfeld and Nicolson, 1981], 345, 347).

season rested here and there with the sovereign charm of interest, of drollery, of felicity and infelicity taken on by scattered selected objects in that writer's bright critical dawn?—an element in which we had the sense of sitting gratefully bathed, so that we fairly took out our young minds and dabbled and soaked them in it as we were to do again in no other.[28] The beauty was thus at such a rate that people had references, and that a reference was then, to my mind, whether in a person or an object, the most glittering, the most becoming ornament possible, a style of decoration one seemed likely to perceive figures here and there, whether animate or not, quite groan under the accumulation and the weight of. One had scarcely met it before—that I now understood; at the same time that there was perhaps a wan joy in one's never having missed it, by all appearance, having on the contrary ever instinctively caught it, on the least glimmer of its presence. Even when present, or what in the other time I had taken for present, it had been of the thinnest, whereas all about me hereafter it would be by all appearance almost glutinously thick—to the point even of one's on occasion sticking fast in it; that is finding intelligibility smothered in quantity. I lost breath in fact, no doubt, again and again, with this latter increase, but was to go on and on for a long time before any first glimmer of reaction against so special a source of interest. It attached itself to objects often, I saw, by no merit or virtue—above all, repeatedly, by no "cleverness"—of their own, but just by the luck of history, by the action of multiplicity of circumstance. Condemned the human particle "over here" was to *live*, on whatever terms, in thickness—instead of being free, comparatively, or as I at once ruefully and exquisitely found myself, only to feel and to think in it. Ruefully because there were clearly a thousand contacts

---

Harrison appears consistently as a representative figure in Arnold's argument. *Culture and Anarchy* was published in book form "in 1869 concurrently with James's London visit" (*Henry James: Autobiography*, 609n). Later in his London life (in 1881), HJ recorded that he was pleased to hear that Arnold had "told a friend of mine the other day that 'Henry James is a de-ah!'" (*HJL*, 2:342). According to a letter written to WJ, Professor Edward Spencer Beesly (1831–1915) was also present, another of the "political economists of the *Fortnightly Review*" (*HJL*, 1:99).

28. What follows as a consequence of breakfast and other gatherings (though HJ remains in a predominantly abstract mode, despite occasional concrete tropes) seems based upon "the fine international mixture" which he found in the British capital. HJ regarded the situations and settings as almost as important as the protagonists in this new and refreshing cultural scene. He observes an inherited self-confidence that applies critical or ironic rigor not inward but predominantly to external developments in contemporary culture.

and sensations, of the strong direct order, that one lost by not so living; exquisitely because of the equal number of immunities and independences, blest independences of perception and judgment, blest liberties of range for the intellectual adventure, that accrued by the same stroke. These at least had the advantage, one of the most distinguished conceivable, that when enjoyed with a certain intensity they might produce the illusion of the other intensity, that of being involved in the composition and the picture itself, in the situations, the complications, the circumstances, admirable and dreadful; while no corresponding illusion, none making for the ideal play of reflection, conclusion, comparison, however one should incline to appraise the luxury, seemed likely to attend the immersed or engaged condition.

Whatever fatuity might at any rate have resided in these complacencies of view, I made them my own with the best conscience in the world, and I meet them again quite to extravagance of interest wherever on the whole extent of the scene my retrospect sets me down. It wasn't in the least at the same time that encountered celebrities only thus provoked the shifting play of my small lamp, and this too even though they were easily celebrated, by my measure, and though from the very first I owed an individual here and there among them, as was highly proper, the benefit of impression at the highest pitch. On the great supporting and enclosing scene itself, the big generalised picture, painted in layer upon layer and tone upon tone, one's fancy was all the while feeding; objects and items, illustrations and aspects might perpetually overlap or mutually interfere, but never without leaving consistency the more marked and character the more unmistakeable. The place, the places, bristled so for every glance with expressive particulars, that I really conversed with them, at happy moments, more than with the figures that moved in them, which affected me so often as but submissive articles of furniture, "put in" by an artist duly careful of effect and yet duly respectful of proportion. The great impression was doubtless no other then and there than what it is under every sky and before every scene that remind one afresh, at the given moment, of all the ways in which producing causes and produced creatures correspond and interdepend; but I think I must have believed at that time that these cross references kept up their game in the English air with a frankness and a good faith that kept the process, in all probability, the most traceable of its kind on the globe.

What was the secret of the force of that suggestion?—which was not, I may say, to be invalidated, to my eyes, by the further observation of cases and conditions. Was it that the enormous "pull" enjoyed at every point of the general surface the stoutness of the underlying belief in what was behind all surfaces?—so that the particular visible, audible, palpable fact, however small and subsidiary, was incomparably absolute, or had, so to speak, such a conscience and a confidence, such an absence of reserve and latent doubts about itself, as was not elsewhere to be found. Didn't such elements as that represent, in the heart of things, possibilities of scepticism, of mockery, of irony, of the return of the matter, whatever it might be, on itself, by some play or other of the questioning spirit, the spirit therefore weakening to entire comfort of affirmations? Didn't I see that humour itself, which might seem elsewhere corrosive and subversive, was, as an English faculty, turned outward altogether and never turned inward?—by which convenient circumstance subversion, or in other words alteration and variation were not promoted. Such truths were wondrous things to make out in such connections as my experience was then, and for no small time after, to be confined to; but I positively catch myself listening to them, even with my half-awakened ears, as if they had been all so many sermons of the very stones of London.[29] *There*, to come back to it, was exactly the force with which these stones were to build me capaciously round: I invited them, I besought them, to say all they would, and—to return to my figure of a while back—it was soon so thoroughly as if they had understood that, once having begun, they were to keep year after year fairly chattering to me. Many of these pages, I fondly foresee, must consist but

29. HJ is perhaps echoing the title of one of John Ruskin's most important works, *The Stones of Venice* (1851–53). Just as Ruskin regarded art and architecture as expressing, by means of the artist, the moral ethos of his civilization (invariably invoked in male terms), so HJ considers London's stones with their "sermons" as emblematic in expressing something of contemporary values. Many of HJ's comments on Ruskin are quite slighting (as is evident in *Italian Hours*), but his views on art were undoubtedly indebted to the British critic of art and society. HJ was understandably flattered when told by Charles Eliot Norton in 1873 that Ruskin (an old friend of Norton's) had admired his writing on Italian art, especially on the Venetian painter Tintoretto. Norton observed, "It would have been pleasant for you to see the cordial admiration he felt for your work, and to hear his warm expression of the good it did him to find such sympathies and such appreciations, and to know that you were to be added to the little list of those who intelligently and earnestly care for the same things that you have touched him most deeply and influenced his life most powerfully. You may be pleased from your heart to have given not merely pleasure, but stimulus to a man of genius very solitary and with very few friends who care for what he cares for." As Edel points out in his note, "Ruskin, said Norton, had been 'eager' that HJ might have been appointed Slade Professor of Fine Arts at Cambridge instead of Sidney Colvin, lately named" (*HJL*, 1:361 n. 3).

of the record of their chatter. What was most of all happening, I take it, was that under an absurd special stress I was having, as who should say, to improvise a local medium and to arrange a local consciousness. Against my due appropriation of those originally closest at my hand inevitable accidents had conspired—and, to conclude in respect to all this, if a considerable time was to be wanted, in the event, for ideal certainty of adjustment, half the terms required by this could then put forth the touching plea that they had quite achingly waited.

IV It may perhaps seem strange that the soil should have been watered by such an incident as Mr. Lazarus Fox's reply, in the earliest rich dusk, to my inquiry as to whither, while I occupied his rooms, I had best betake myself most regularly for my dinner: "Well, there is the Bath Hotel, sir, a very short walk away, where I should think you would be very comfortable indeed. Mr. So-and-So dines at his club, sir—but there is also the Albany in Piccadilly, to which I believe many gentlemen go."[30] I think I measured on the spot "all that it took" to make my friend most advisedly—for it was clearly what he did— see me seated in lone state, for my evening meal, at the heavy mahogany of the stodgy little hotel that in those days and for long after occupied the north-west corner of Arlington Street and to which, in common with many compatriots, I repeatedly resorted during the years immediately following. We *suffered*, however, on those occasions, the unmitigated coffee-room of Mr. Fox's prescription—it was part of a strange inevitability, a concomitant of necessary shelter and we hadn't at least gone forth to invoke its austere charm. I tried it, in that singular way, at the hour I speak of—and I well remember forecasting the interest of a social and moral order in which it could be supposed of me that, having tried it once, I should sublimely try it again. My success in doing so would indeed have been sublime, but a finer shade of the quality still attached somehow to my landlord's confidence in it; and this was one of the threads that, as I have

30. The Bath Hotel was a genteel establishment at 25 Arlington Street, off Piccadilly. The fictional Amy March stayed there on her European visit in Louisa M. Alcott's *Little Women,* and HJ himself used it when he returned to London in spring 1870. The Albany eating house, so redolent of a bygone England, appears as the Red-Lion in "A Passionate Pilgrim" (1871), in which the narrator, "having dreamed of lamb and spinach, and a charlotte russe . . . sat down in penitence to a mutton-chop and a rice pudding" (*CT,* 2:228).

called them, I was to tuck away for future picking-up again and unrolling. I fell back on the Albany, which long ago passed away and which I seem to have brushed with a touch of reminiscence in some anticipation of the present indulgence that is itself quite ancient history. It was a small eating-house of the very old English tradition, as I then supposed at least, just opposite the much greater establishment of the same name, which latter it had borrowed,[31] and I remember wondering whether the tenants of the classic chambers, the beadle-guarded cluster of which was impressive even to the deprecated approach, found their conception of the "restaurant"—we still pronounced it in the French manner—met by the small compartments, narrow as horse-stalls, formed by the high straight backs of hard wooden benches and accommodating respectively two pairs of feeders, who were thus so closely face to face as fairly to threaten with knife and fork each others' more forward features.

The scene was sordid, the arrangements primitive, the detail of the procedure, as it struck me, wellnigh of the rudest; yet I remember rejoicing in it all—as one indeed might perfectly rejoice in the juiciness of joints and the abundance of accessory pudding; for I said to myself under every shock and at the hint of every savour that this was what it was for an exhibition to reek with local colour, and one could dispense with a napkin, with a crusty roll, with room for one's elbows or one's feet, with an immunity from intermittance of the "plain boiled", much better than one could dispense with that. There were restaurants galore even at that time in New York and in Boston, but I had never before had to do with an eating-house and had not yet seen the little old English world of Dickens, let alone of the ever-haunting Hogarth, of Smollett and of Boswell, drenched with such a flood of light.[32] As one sat there one *understood;* one drew out the severe séance not to stay the assault of precious conspiring truths, not to break the current of in-rushing telltale suggestion. Every face was a documentary scrap, half a dozen broken words to piece with half a dozen others, and so on and on; every sound was strong, whether rich and

31. The Albany, originally built in 1770, was converted into chambers for bachelors by Henry Holland in 1802. It stood next to the Royal Academy, opposite Fortnum and Mason's.

32. The restaurant (in the modern sense) emerged first in post-Revolutionary France. The eating house offered less refined fare (usually substantial meat dishes) and often catered to local workers. The artists and writers mentioned were always associated for HJ with the city life of Britain; James Boswell (1740–95) was a Scottish lawyer best remembered for his *Life of Samuel Johnson* (1791).

fine or only queer and coarse; everything in this order drew a positive sweetness from never being—whatever else it was—gracelessly flat. The very rudeness was ripe, the very commonness was conscious—that is not related to mere other forms of the same, but to matters as different as possible, into which it shaded off and off or up and up; the image in fine was organic, rounded and complete, as definite as a Dutch picture of low life hung on a museum wall.[33] "Low" I say in respect to the life; but that was the point for me, that whereas the smartness and newness beyond the sea supposedly disavowed the low, they did so but thinly and vainly, falling markedly short of the high; which the little boxed and boiled Albany attained to some effect of, after a fashion of its own, just by having its so thoroughly appreciable note-value in a scheme of manners. It was imbedded, so to speak, in the scheme, and it borrowed lights, it borrowed even glooms, from so much neighbouring distinction. The places across the sea, as they to my then eyes faintly after-glowed, had no impinging borders but those of the desert to borrow *from*.[34] And if it be asked of me whether all the while I insist, for demonstration of the complacency with which I desire to revert, on not regretting the disappearance of such too long surviving sordidries as those I have evoked, I can but answer that blind emotion, in whichever sense directed, has nothing to say to the question and that the sense of what we just *could* confidently live by at a given far-away hour is a simple stout fact of relief.

Relief, again, I say, from the too enormous present accretions and alternatives—which we witlessly thought so innumerable then, which we

33. HJ was an admirer of Dutch painting, deriving in 1873, for instance, "a deep satisfaction from these delectable realists—the satisfaction produced by the sight of a perfect accord between the aim and the result" ("The Wallace Collection in Bethnal Green," *Painter's Eye*, 77). In *Adam Bede* (1859), George Eliot's narrator feels obliged to defend a liking for a genre despised by the "lofty-minded" (though not without a degree of condescension) which offers "faithful pictures of a monotonous homely existence": "I turn . . . from cloud-borne angels, from prophets, sibyls, and heroic warriors, to an old woman bending over her flower-pot, or eating her solitary dinner, while the noonday light, softened perhaps by a screen of leaves, falls on her mob-cap, and just touches the rim of her spinning-wheel, and her stone jug, and all those cheap common things which are the precious necessaries of life to her" ([Harmondsworth: Penguin, 1980], 223) Thomas Hardy also subtitled his early pastoral novel *Under the Greenwood Tree* (1872), a "Rural Painting of the Dutch School."

34. It seems that even vulgar British scenes derived substance from accumulated history in HJ's eyes when compared to the comparatively impoverished traditions of American society.

artlessly found so much of the interest of *in* an immeasurable multiplicity and which I now feel myself thus grope for ghostly touch of in the name, neither more nor less, of poetic justice. I wasn't doubtless at the time so very sure, after all, of the comparative felicity of our state, that of the rare *moment* for the fond fancy—I doubtless even a bit greedily missed certain quantities, not to call them certain qualities, here and there, and the best of my actual purpose is to make amends for that blasphemy. There isn't a thing I can imagine having missed that I don't quite ache to miss again; and it remains at all events an odd stroke that, having of old most felt the thrill of the place in its mighty muchness, I have lived to adore it backward for its sweet simplicity. I find myself in fact at the present writing only too sorry when not able to minimise conscientiously this, that or the other of the old sources of impression. The thing is indeed admirably possible in a *general* way, though much of the exhibition was none the less undeniably, was absolutely large: how can I for instance recall the great cab-rank, mainly formed of delightful hansoms, that stretched along Piccadilly from the top of the Green Park unendingly down, without having to take it for unsurpassably modern and majestic?[35] How can I think—I select my examples at hazard—of the "run" of the more successful of Mr. Robertson's comedies at the "dear little old" Prince of Wales's Theatre in Tottenham Court Road as anything less than one of the wonders of our age?[36] How, by the same token, can I not lose myself still more in the glory of a time that was to watch the drawn-out procession of Henry Irving's Shakespearean splendours at the transcendent Lyceum?[37] or how, in the same general line, not recognise that to live through the extravagant youth

35. Green Park lies to the south of Piccadilly as it stretches west to Hyde Park Corner. By this time many of HJ's urban journeys were made on the underground railway, "ploughing along in a vast circle thro' the bowels of London, and giving you egress to the upper earth in magnificent stations" (*HJL*, 1:91).

36. Thomas William Robertson (1829–71), an Anglo-Irish playwright, achieved West End fame with his comedies written in a realistic medium, beginning with *Society* in 1865. A number of his plays were successful in the following years of the decade, and they were generally performed at the Prince of Wales's Theatre. Tottenham Court Road runs north from Oxford Street at its junction with Charing Cross Road. The small and fashionable Prince of Wales's Theatre was in Tottenham Street, just off Tottenham Court Road.

37. Sir Henry Irving (1838–1905) began his association with the Lyceum Theatre in Wellington Street in 1871, and he was highly successful in playing the major tragic roles of Shakespeare. He assumed the management of the Lyceum in 1878 when *Hamlet* and *The Merchant of Venice* were performed; his productions were famous for their elaborate scenery and rich costumes.

of the aesthetic era, whether as embodied in the then apparently inexhaustible vein of the Gilbert and Sullivan operas or as more monotonously
expressed in those "last words" of the *raffiné* that were chanted and
crooned in the damask-hung temple of the Grosvenor Gallery, was to
seem privileged to such immensities as history would find left to her to
record but with bated breath?[38]

These latter triumphs of taste, however, though lost in the abysm now,
had then a good many years to wait and I alight for illustrative support of
my present mild thesis on the comparative humility, say, of the inward
aspects, in a large measure, of the old National Gallery,[39] where memory
mixes for me together so many elements of the sense of an antique world.
The great element was of course that I well-nigh incredibly stood again in

38. HJ himself became involved in the late decadent days of the aesthetic movement
when, in the 1890s, some of his fiction was published in the *Yellow Book*, a quarterly
referred to by the London *Times* as "a mixture of English rowdyism and French lubricity"
(William Gaunt, *The Aesthetic Adventure* [London: Jonathan Cape, 1945], 140), also famous for cultivating the talent of Aubrey Beardsley (for the aesthetic movement, see also
*NSB*, n. 136). The still popular comic operettas (rather than operas) of Sir William
Schwenk Gilbert (1836–1911) and Sir Arthur Sullivan (1842–1900) mark a twenty-year
collaboration that began in 1871 with *Thespis; or, The Gods Grown Old*. Their *Patience*,
produced in 1881, is a parody of rival aesthetes, and Reginald Bunthorne is modeled partly
on Oscar Wilde when he sings, "Though the Philistines may jostle, you will rank as an
apostle in the high aesthetic band, / If you walk down Piccadilly with a poppy or a lily in
your medieval hand." The Grosvenor Gallery, at 135–37 New Bond Street, whose proprietor was Sir Coutts Lindsay (1839–1913), opened in 1877 and closed in 1890. HJ was
present at its opening, along with the Prince of Wales, Gladstone, Ruskin, and Wilde; the
latter approved of its walls, "hung with scarlet damask above a dado of dull green gold"
(Richard Ellmann, *Oscar Wilde* [London: Penguin, 1988], 75), though HJ in his review
disliked their "savage red" color ("The Picture Season in London," *Painter's Eye*, 147).
The gallery was established to counter the exclusiveness of the Royal Academy, exhibiting
the works, for instance, of a number of significant Pre-Raphaelite painters. Ellmann (*Oscar
Wilde*, 76–78) contrasts HJ's review with Wilde's "The Grosvenor Gallery," written for the
*Dublin University Magazine*. For the Grosvenor Gallery, see also C. E. Hallé, *Notes from a
Painter's Life* (London: Murray, 1909), 108–14. *Raffiné:* someone of subtle taste.

39. London's National Gallery was originally established at 100, Pall Mall in 1824,
transferring to its site overlooking Trafalgar Square (designed by William Wilkins) in 1838.
HJ seems to refer to the much-needed building improvements, completed in 1877, when
half a dozen new rooms were added and the paintings "at last arranged and distributed in a
manner worthy of itself and of the nation" ("The National Gallery," *Painter's Eye*, 122).
Though a comparatively small collection, its quality is unrivaled. After the founding of the
Tate Gallery in 1897, many of the National Gallery's post-1790 paintings were transferred,
leaving increased space for the remaining works.

the immediate presence of Titian and Rembrandt, of Rubens and Paul Veronese, and that the cup of sensation was thereby filled to overflowing;[40] but I look at it to-day as concomitantly warm and closed-in and, as who should say, cosy that the ancient order and contracted state and thick-coloured dimness, all unconscious of rearrangements and reversals, blighting new lights and invidious shattering comparisons, still prevailed and kept contemplation comfortably confused and serenely superstitious, when not indeed at its sharpest moments quite fevered with incoherences. The place looks to me across the half century richly dim, yet at the same time both perversely plain and heavily violent—violent through indifference to the separations and selections that have become a tribute to modern nerves; but I cherish exactly those facts of benightedness, seeming as they do to have positively and blessedly conditioned the particular sweetness of wonder with which I haunted the Family of Darius, the Bacchus and Ariadne, or the so-called portrait of Ariosto.[41] Could one in those days feel anything with force, whether for pleasure or for pain, without feeling it as an immense little act or event of life, and as therefore taking place on a scene and in circumstances scarce at all to be separated from its own sense and impact?—so that to recover it is to recover the whole medium, the material pressure of things, and find it most marked for preservation as an aspect, even, distinguishably, a "composition."[42]

*What* a composition, for instance again I am capable at this hour of exclaiming, the conditions of felicity in which I became aware, one afternoon during a renewed gape before the Bacchus and Ariadne, first that a little gentleman beside me and talking with the greatest vivacity to another gentleman was extremely remarkable, second that he had the largest and

40. Titian (Tiziano Vecellio, d. 1576), painter of the Venetian school; Rembrandt Harmensz van Rijn (1606–69), Dutch painter of portraits and biblical scenes; Peter Paul Rubens (1577–1640), painter in the Flemish baroque style; Paolo Veronese (1528–88), painter of the Veronese and Venetian schools.

41. *The Family of Darius* is by Veronese; in May 1869 HJ thought Titian's *Bacchus and Ariadne* "one of the great facts of the Universe" (*CWJ*, 1:73). There is still doubt as to whether Titian's *Portrait of a Man* in the National Gallery has Ariosto as its subject. HJ wrote to WJ: "I admire Rafael: I enjoy Rubens; but I passionately love Titian" (ibid.), though elsewhere he suggested, "There are fine painters and coarse painters, and Rubens belonged to the latter category; he reigned in it with magnificent supremacy" ("Les Maîtres d'Autrefois," *Painter's Eye*, 119).

42. In the *Scribner's Magazine* version (62 [October 1917]: 469), a question mark replaces the less appropriate period here.

most *chevelu*[43] auburn head I had ever seen perched on a scarce perceptible body, third that I held some scrap of a clue to his identity, which couldn't fail to be eminent, fourth that this tag of association was with nothing less than a small photograph sent me westward across the sea a few months before, and fifth that the sitter for the photograph had been the author of Atalanta in Calydon and Poems and Ballads![44] I thrilled, it perfectly comes back to me, with the prodigy of this circumstance that I should be admiring Titian in the same breath with Mr. Swinburne—that is in the same breath in which *he* admired Titian and in which I also admired *him,* the whole constituting on the spot between us, for appreciation, that is for mine, a fact of intercourse, such a fact as could stamp and colour the whole passage ineffaceably, and this even though the more illustrious party to it had within the minute turned off and left me shaken. I was shaken, but I was satisfied—that was the point; I didn't ask more to interweave another touch in my pattern, and as I once more gather in the impression I am struck with my having deserved truly as many of the like as possible. I was welcome to them, it may well be said, on such easy terms—and yet I ask myself whether, after all, it didn't take on my own part some doing, as we nowadays say, to make them so well worth having. They themselves took, I even at the time felt, little enough trouble for it, and the virtue of the business was repeatedly, no doubt, a good deal more in what I brought than in what I took.

I apply this remark indeed to those extractions of the quintessence that had for their occasion either one's more undirected though never fruitless walks and wanderings or one's earnest, one's positively pious approach to whatever consecrated ground or shrine of pilgrimage that might be at the moment in order. There was not a regular prescribed "sight" that I during those weeks neglected—I remember haunting the museums in especial, though the South Kensington was then scarce more than embryonic,[45]

43. Long-haired.

44. The dramatic poem *Atalanta in Calydon,* by Algernon Charles Swinburne (1837–1909), was an immediate success on its appearance in 1865; his collection *Poems and Ballads* was published the following year. Much of the poet's work was considered morally scandalous: he was described by John Morley (later a friend) as "the libidinous laureate of a pack of satyrs" (Ian Fletcher, *Swinburne* [London: Longman, 1973], 13). HJ may have signaled the poet's reputed sadomasochistic interests in his earlier question as to his own feelings of the time and their potential "for pleasure or for pain."

45. Originally called the Museum of Manufactures on its establishment after the Great

with a sense of duty and of excitement that I was never again to know combined in equal measure, I think, and that it might really have taken some element of personal danger to account for. There *was* the element, in a manner, to season the cup with sharpness—the danger, all the while, that my freedom might be brief and my experience broken, that I was under the menace of uncertainty and subject in fine to interruption. The fact of having been so long gravely unwell sufficed by itself to keep apprehension alive; it was our idea, or at least quite intensely mine, that what I was doing, could I but put it through, would be intimately good for me—only the putting it through was the difficulty, and I sometimes faltered by the way. This makes now for a general air on the part of all the objects of vision that I recover, and almost as much in those of accidental encounter as in the breathlessly invoked, of being looked at for the last time and giving out their message and story as with the still, collected passion of an only chance. This feeling about them, not to say, as I might have imputed it, *in* them, wonderfully helped, as may be believed, the extraction of quintessences—which sprang at me of themselves, for that matter, out of any appearance that confessed to the least value in the compound, the least office in the harmony. If the commonest street-vista was a fairly heart-shaking contributive image, if the incidents of the thick renascent light anywhere, and the perpetual excitement of never knowing, between it and the historic and determined gloom, which was which and which one would most "back" for the general outcome and picture, so the great sought-out compositions, the Hampton Courts and the Windsors, the Richmonds, the Dulwiches,[46] even the very Hampstead Heaths and

---

Exhibition of 1851, the South Kensington Museum reopened in Cromwell Gardens in 1857. It was renamed the Victoria and Albert Museum in 1899, the world's largest collection of decorative arts and design.

46. These are places of historic interest on the periphery of London. Hampton Court, to the southwest, is dominated by its Tudor palace erected by Cardinal Wolsey and acquired by Henry VIII in 1526. HJ found it "of a sufficient and comfortable antiquity" when he visited on a gloomy afternoon, "a proper day to wander thro' an old deserted palace, to tread the terraces of an ancient garden and survey generally the haunts of departed and mortalized royalty" (*HJL*, 1:103–4). It provides the location for an early scene in "A Passionate Pilgrim." Windsor, a town twenty miles west of London, is famous for its ancient castle, still a royal residence. The James family rented a cottage in Windsor Great Park in 1844, the location for HJ Sr.'s "vastation" (see *SBO*, n. 150). Richmond, an attractive town on the banks of the Thames, is twelve miles southwest of London. Dulwich, in south London, is well known for its fine picture gallery, part of Dulwich College: "One long gallery, lit from an

Putney Commons,[47] to say nothing of the Towers, the Temples, the Cathedrals and the strange penetrabilities of the City, ranged themselves like the rows of great figures in a sum, an amount immeasurably huge, that one would draw on if not quite as long as one lived, yet as soon as ever one should seriously get to work. That, to a tune of the most beautiful melancholy—at least as I catch it again now—was the way all values came out: they were charged somehow with a useability the most immediate, the most urgent, and which, I seemed to see, would keep me restless till I should have done something of my very own with them.

This was indeed perhaps what most painted them over with the admonitory appeal: there were truly moments at which they seemed not to answer for it that I should get all the good of them, and the finest—what I was so extravagantly, so fantastically after—unless I could somehow at once indite my sonnet and prove my title. The difficulty was all in there being so much of them—I might myself have been less restless if they could only have been less vivid. This they absolutely declined at any moment and in any connection to be, and it was ever so long till they abated a jot of the refusal. Thereby, in consequence, as may easily be judged, they were to keep me in alarms to which my measures practically taken, my catastrophes anxiously averted, remained not quite proportionate. I recall a most interesting young man who had been my shipmate on the homeward-bound "China", shortly before—I could go at length into my reasons for having been so struck with him, but I forbear[48]—who, on

---

old fashioned ceiling, paved with brick tile and lined with very fair specimens of most of the great masters" (*HJL,* 1:100). It is said to be England's oldest public art gallery.

47. Hampstead Heath is an extensive tract on elevated ground in north London, preserved as an open space since 1871. In the same year Wimbledon and Putney commons, south of the Thames, were protected from encroaching building schemes.

48. The young man was presumably British, and therefore "homeward bound." The SS *China* went into service in 1862 for the Cunard company. HJ's treatment of these years, the emphasis given here to his remembered conviction of the rich potential of experience available, a preference, too, for mysterious references or introspective moments of revelation or private emotion, illustrates how distinct is his autobiographical method from that of other, more conventional and anecdotal memoirs (as exemplified, say, in Edith Wharton's *A Backward Glance*). There is no doubt, however, that, as these chapters progress and HJ recalls George Eliot and Tennyson, he moves into a more anecdotal mode, leaving behind the original premises of the "Family Book." He remains highly selective nevertheless; the letters of these years are, in contrast, full of meetings and events and eminent names. It is surprising, for example, that no mention is made here of Leslie Stephen, his

our talking, to my intense trepidation of curiosity, of where I might advisedly "go" in London, let me know that he always went to Craven Street Strand, where bachelor lodgings were highly convenient, and whence I in fact then saw them flush at me over the cold grey sea with an authenticity almost fierce.[49] I didn't in the event, as has been seen, go to Craven Street for rooms, but I did go, on the very first occasion, for atmosphere, neither more nor less—the young man of the ship, building so much better than he knew, had guaranteed me such a rightness of that; and it belongs to this reminiscence, for the triviality of which I should apologize did I find myself at my present pitch capable of apologizing for anything, that I had on the very spot there one of those hallucinations as to the precious effect dreadful to lose and yet impossible to render which interfused the aesthetic dream in presence of its subject with the mortal drop of despair (as I should insist at least didn't the despair itself seem to have acted here as the preservative.) The precious effect in the case of Craven Street was that it absolutely reeked, to my fond fancy, with associations born of the particular ancient piety embodied in one's private altar to Dickens; and that this upstart little truth alone would revel in explanations that I should for the time have feverishly to forego. The exquisite matter was not the identification with the scene of special shades or names; it was just that the whole Dickens procession marched up and down, the whole Dickens world looked out of its queer, quite sinister windows—for it was the socially sinister Dickens, I am afraid, rather than the socially encouraging or confoundingly comic who still at that moment was most apt to meet me with his reasons.[50] Such a reason was just that look of the inscrutable riverward street, packed to blackness with accumulations of suffered experience, these, indescribably, disavowed and confessed at one and the same time, and with the fact of its blocked old Thames-side termination, a mere fact of more oppressive enclosure now, telling all sorts of vague loose stories about it.

---

first wife, and his sister-in-law (both daughters of the much-admired Thackeray), who showed him considerable kindness.

49. Craven Street, which runs down from the Strand near Charing Cross toward the Thames, was well known for its lodging houses in the nineteenth century. Some years earlier, in 1849, HJ's countryman Herman Melville had stayed at number 25.

50. In this momentary descent into the darker, deprived levels of London society, HJ may have anticipated (as Edel points out in *Untried Years*, 291) the scenes and protagonists of his most Dickensian novel, *The Princess Casamassima.*

V Why, however, should I pick up so small a crumb from that mere brief first course at a banquet of initiation which was in the event to prolong itself through years and years?—unless indeed as a scrap of a specimen, chosen at hazard, of the prompt activity of a process by which my intelligence afterwards came to find itself more fed, I think, than from any other source at all, or, for that matter, from all other sources put together. A hundred more suchlike modest memories breathe upon me, each with its own dim little plea, as I turn to face them, but my idea is to deal somehow more conveniently with the whole gathered mass of my subsequent impressions in this order, a fruitage that I feel to have been only too abundantly stored. Half a dozen of those of a larger and more immediate dignity, incidents more particularly of the rather invidiously so-called social contact, pull my sleeve as I pass; but the long, backward-drawn train of the later life drags them along with it, lost and smothered in its spread—only one of them stands out or remains over, insisting on its place and hour, its felt distinguishability. To this day I feel again *that* roused emotion, my unsurpassably prized admission to the presence of the great George Eliot, whom I was taken to see, by one of the kind door-opening Norton ladies, by whom Mrs. Lewes's guarded portal at North Bank appeared especially penetrable, on a Sunday afternoon of April '69.[51] Later occasions, after a considerable lapse, were not to overlay the absolute face-value, as I may call it, of all the appearances then and there presented me—which were taken home by a young spirit almost abjectly grateful, at any rate all devoutly prepared, for them. I find it idle even to wonder what "place" the author of Silas Marner and Middle-

51. On this visit, which took place on Sunday, 9 May 1869, HJ was accompanied by Grace Norton, and also, according to Gordon S. Haight (*George Eliot: A Biography* [Oxford: Clarendon Press, 1968], 416), by Sara Sedgwick, Charles Eliot Norton's sister-in-law. With the passing years Lewes became increasingly protective of Eliot, hence the reference to the "guarded portal." Norton described the house, called the Priory, as "a little, square, two-story dwelling standing in a half garden, surrounded with one of those high brick walls of which one grows so impatient in England" (*Letters of Charles Eliot Norton, with Biographical Comment by His Daughter Sara Norton and M. A. DeWolfe Howe*, 2 vols. [Boston: Houghton Mifflin, 1913; rpt. New York: AMS Press, 1973], 1:317). HJ had returned from a three-week stay at a health spa in the Malvern Hills in search of relief from his various ailments, followed by visits to places of historic interest on the Anglo-Welsh borders, before taking in Salisbury, Ely, Blenheim, Winchester, and Oxford (HJL, 1:108–14). Over the years he would write many sketches of rural and provincial England, collected finally in *English Hours* (1905).

march[52] may be conceived to have in the pride of our literature—so settled and consecrated in the individual range of view is many such a case free at last to find itself, free after ups and downs, after fluctuations of fame or whatever, which have divested judgment of any relevance that isn't most of all the relevance of a living and recorded *relation*. It has ceased then to know itself in any degree as an estimate, has shaken off the anxieties of circumspection and comparison and just grown happy to act as an attachment pure and simple, an effect of life's own logic, but in the ashes of which the wonted fires of youth need but to be blown upon for betrayal of a glow. Reflective appreciation may have originally been concerned, whether at its most or at its least, but it is well over, to our infinite relief—yes, to our immortal comfort, I think; the interval back cannot again be bridged. We simply sit with our enjoyed gain, our residual rounded possession in our lap; a safe old treasure, which has ceased to shrink, if indeed also perhaps greatly to swell, and all that further touches it is the fine vibration set up if the name we know it all by is called into question—perhaps however little.[53]

It was by George Eliot's name that I was to go on knowing, was never to cease to know, a great treasure of beauty and humanity, of applied and achieved art, a testimony, historic as well as aesthetic, to the deeper interest of the intricate English aspects; and I now allow the vibration, as I have called it, all its play—quite as if I had been wronged even by my own hesitation as to whether to pick up my anecdote. That scruple wholly fades with the sense of how I must at the very time have foreseen that here was one of those associations that would determine in the far future an exquisite inability to revise it. Middlemarch had not then appeared—we of the faith were still to enjoy that saturation, and Felix Holt the radical was upwards of three years old; the impetus proceeding from this work, however, was still fresh enough in my pulses to have quickened the palpitation

---

52. *Silas Marner* was published in 1861; HJ reviewed *Middlemarch* for the *Galaxy* in March 1873, proclaiming it "at once one of the strongest and one of the weakest of English novels" (*LC* 1, 958).

53. HJ's thoughts on George Eliot's posthumous reputation—she remains a "safe old treasure"—may have been influenced by his own disillusionment as a novelist. In these years—as, indeed, earlier in his career—he was aware of a limited readership, of difficulty in placing some of the short stories, and of the neglect accorded to the recent monumental New York Edition of his fiction (1907–9), whose Prefaces constitute both an evolved critical position and a revisiting of his personal history.

of my finding myself in presence. I had rejoiced without reserve in Felix Holt—the illusion of reading which, outstretched on my then too frequently inevitable bed at Swampscott during a couple of very hot days of the summer of 1866, comes back to me, followed by that in sooth of sitting up again, at no great ease, to indite with all promptness a review of the delightful thing, the place of appearance of which nothing could now induce me to name, shameless about the general fact as I may have been at the hour itself:[54] over such a feast of fine rich natural tone did I feel myself earnestly bend. Quite unforgettable to me the art and truth with which the note of this tone was struck in the beautiful prologue and the bygone appearances, a hundred of the outward and visible signs of the author's own young rural and midmost England, made to hold us by their harmony.[55] The book was not, if I rightly remember, altogether genially greeted,[56] but I was to hold fast to the charm I had thankfully suffered it, I had been conscious of absolutely needing it, to work.

Exquisite the remembrance of how it wouldn't have "done" for me at all, in relation to other inward matters, not to strain from the case the last drop of its happiest sense. And I had even with the cooling of the first glow so little gone back upon it, as we have nowadays learned to say, had in fact so gone forward, floated by its wave of superlative intended benignity, that, once in the cool quiet drawing-room at North Bank I knew myself steeped in still deeper depths of the medium. G. H. Lewes was absent for the time

54. For HJ's stay at Swampscott, see *NSB*, p. 341. *Felix Holt* was published in 1866, and HJ's review appeared in the *Nation* on 16 August 1866 (*LC* 1, 907–12). It is not clear why HJ should be reluctant to name the magazine in which it came out, unless it be that his review is in fact far from effusive, his praise diluted by some strong misgivings. He admires the novelist's humanity and "extensive human sympathy," but begins by invoking "her closely wedded talent and foibles. Her plots have always been artificial—clumsily artificial—the conduct of her story slow, and her style diffuse" (*LC* 1, 907).

55. The novel's introduction refers to a period "five-and-thirty years ago" when "the glory had not yet departed from the old coach-roads," though it also goes on to recount unrepealed corn-laws, pauperism and a lack of electoral representation (*Felix Holt, the Radical* [London: Penguin, 1995], 3). HJ uses a familiar phrase, derived from St. Augustine, from the catechism of the Anglican Book of Common Prayer in which a sacrament is described as the outward and visible sign of an inward and invisible grace.

56. The novel did not, in fact, sell very well, and the critics had reservations: "Between the divided structure of *Felix Holt* on the one hand and the incredibly complicated legal plot on the other, they did not find the dramatic unity they were looking for. . . . The curious thing is that however much the critics attack the novel they remain convinced that it is an important and impressive work" (introduction to *George Eliot: The Critical Heritage*, ed. David Carroll [London: Routledge and Kegan Paul, 1971], 25–26).

on an urgent errand; one of his sons, on a visit at the house, had been suddenly taken with a violent attack of pain, the heritage of a bad accident not
long before in the West Indies, a suffered onset from an angry bull, I seem
to recall, who had tossed or otherwise mauled him, and, though beaten
off, left him considerably compromised[57]—these facts being promptly
imparted to us, in no small flutter, by our distinguished lady, who came in
to us from another room, where she had been with the hapless young man
while his father appealed to the nearest good chemist for some known
specific. It infinitely moved me to see so great a celebrity quite humanly
and familiarly agitated—even with something clear and noble in it too, to
which, as well as to the extraordinarily interesting dignity of her whole odd
personal conformation, I remember thinking her black silk dress and the
lace mantilla attached to her head and keeping company on either side
with the low-falling thickness of her dark hair effectively contributed.[58] I
have found myself, my life long, attaching value to every noted thing in
respect to a great person—and George Eliot struck me on the spot as
somehow *illustratively* great; never at any rate has the impression of those
troubled moments faded from me, nor that at once of a certain high grace
in her anxiety and a frank immediate appreciation of our presence, modest
embarrassed folk as we were. It took me no long time to thrill with the

57. Lewes had three sons, two of whom spent time in Africa, rather than the West
Indies. It seems that the incident with an angry bull may be HJ's invention—referring to
this episode, Haight comments on his "tendency to fictionalize" (*George Eliot*, 416n). All
three boys enjoyed a warm relationship with George Eliot. Thornton, or "Thornie," his
second son, had just returned in ill health, suffering from "an injury of the spine received
four years ago, in a fall while wrestling" (George Eliot to John Blackwood, 11 May 1869,
*The George Eliot Letters*, ed. Gordon S. Haight [London: Oxford University Press; New
Haven: Yale University Press, 1956–78], 5:34–35). This, it seems, had developed into
tuberculosis of the spine, and he endured an agonizing few months, nursed by Lewes and
Eliot, before dying on 19 October 1869, recorded by Eliot: "He went quite peacefully. For
three days he was not more than fitfully and imperfectly conscious of the things around
him. He went to Natal on the 17th October 1863, and came back to us ill on the 8th May
1869. Through the six months of his illness, his frank impulsive mind disclosed no trace of
evil feeling. He was a sweet-natured boy—still a boy, though he had lived for twenty-five
years and a half. On the 9th of August he had an attack of paraplegia, and although he
partially recovered from it, it made a marked change in him. After that he lost a great deal of
his vivacity, but he suffered less pain. This death seems to me the beginning of our own"
(*George Eliot's Life as Related in Her Letters and Journals*, arranged and edited by her
husband, J. W. Cross [1885; Edinburgh: Blackwood, n.d.], 454).

58. This remains the most familiar representation of George Eliot in portraits from her
later years.

sense, sublime in its unexpectedness, that we were perhaps, or indeed quite clearly, helping her to pass the time till Mr. Lewes's return—after which he would again post off for Mr. Paget the pre-eminent surgeon;[59] and I see involved with this the perfect amenity of her assisting us, as it were, to assist her, through unrelinquished proper talk, due responsible remark and report, in the last degree suggestive to me, on a short holiday taken with Mr. Lewes in the south of France, whence they had just returned. Yes indeed, the lightest words of great persons are so little as any words of others are that I catch myself again inordinately struck with her dropping it off-hand that the mistral, scourge of their excursion, had blown them into Avignon, where they had gone, I think, to see J. S. Mill,[60] only to blow them straight out again—the figure put it so before us; as well as with the moral interest, the absence of the *banal,* in their having, on the whole scene, found pleasure further poisoned by the frequency in all those parts of "evil faces: oh the evil faces!" *That* recorded source of suffering enormously affected me—I felt it as beautifully characteristic: I had never heard an *impression de voyage*[61] so little tainted with the superficial or the vulgar. I was myself at the time in the thick of impressions, and it was true that they would have seemed to me rather to fail of life, of their own doubtless inferior kind, if submitting beyond a certain point to be touched with that sad or, as who should say, that grey colour: Mrs. Lewes's were, it appeared, predominantly so touched, and I could at once admire it in

59. Sir James Paget (1814–99) was an eminent physiologist and pathologist who began in practice near Cavendish Square in 1851. An old friend of the couple and an admirer of Eliot's writing, he served as surgeon extraordinary to Queen Victoria and surgeon in ordinary to the Prince of Wales (*George Eliot's Life,* 582). He attended to Thornie on that Sunday evening and, indeed, would treat G. H. Lewes in his last illness in 1878.

60. The couple's nine-week trip to southern France and Italy took place in March–May 1869. John Stuart Mill had a villa at St. Véran, near Avignon, where his wife was buried. He was associated with the *Westminster Review,* a radical journal of which George Eliot later became assistant editor (1851–53), the period during which she met Lewes.

61. Travel impression. On an earlier visit to northern Germany, Eliot also recorded how "we were constantly pained by meeting peasants who looked underfed and miserable" (*George Eliot's Life,* 430). HJ's friend Mary Ward remembered as an eighteen-year-old hearing George Eliot talk of her Spanish travels during a visit to Mark Pattison at Lincoln College, Oxford, in 1870 (HJ had lunched there, incidentally, the previous year): she spoke "for about twenty minutes, with perfect ease and finish, without misplacing a word or dropping a sentence, and I realised at last that I was in the presence of a great writer. Not a great *talker*" (Mrs. Humphry Ward, *A Writer's Recollections* [London: Collins, 1918], 108).

them and wonder if they didn't pay for this by some lack of intensity on other sides. Why I didn't more impute to her, or to them, that possible lack is more than I can say, since under the law of moral earnestness the vulgar and the trivial would be then involved in the poor observations of my own making—a conclusion sufficiently depressing.

However, I didn't find myself depressed, and I didn't find the great mind that was so good as to shine upon us at that awkward moment however dimly anything but augmented; what was its sensibility to the evil faces but part of the large old tenderness which the occasion had caused to overflow and on which we were presently floated back into the room she had left?—where we might perhaps beguile a little the impatience of the sufferer waiting for relief. We ventured in our flutter to doubt whether we *should* beguile, we held back with a certain delicacy from this irruption, and if there was a momentary wonderful and beautiful conflict I remember how our yielding struck me as crowned with the finest grace it could possibly have, that of the prodigious privilege of humouring, yes literally humouring so renowned a spirit at a moment when we could really match our judgment with hers. For the injured young man, in the other and the larger room, simply lay stretched on his back on the floor, the posture apparently least painful to him—though painful enough at the best I easily saw on kneeling beside him, after my first dismay, to ask if I could in any way ease him. I see his face again, fair and young and flushed, with its vague little smile and its moist brow; I recover the moment or two during which we sought to make natural conversation in his presence, and my question as to what conversation *was* natural; and then as his father's return still failed my having the inspiration that at once terminated the strain of the scene and yet prolonged the sublime connection. Mightn't *I* then hurry off for Mr. Paget?—on whom, as fast as a cab could carry me, I would wait with the request that he would come at the first possible moment to the rescue. Mrs. Lewes's and our stricken companion's instant appreciation of this offer lent me wings on which I again feel myself borne very much as if suddenly acting as a messenger of the gods—surely I had never come so near to performing in that character. I shook off my fellow visitor for swifter cleaving of the air, and I recall still feeling that I cleft it even in the dull four-wheeler of other days[62] which, on getting out of the house, I recognised as the only object animating, at a distance, the long blank Sunday vista beside the walled-out Regent's Park. I crawled to

62. This would be a brougham, a one-horse, four-wheeled closed carriage.

Hanover Square—or was it Cavendish?[63] I let the question stand—and, after learning at the great man's door that though he was not at home he was soon expected back and would receive my message without delay, cherished for the rest of the day the particular quality of my vibration.

It was doubtless even excessive in proportion to its cause—yet in what else but that consisted the force and the use of vibrations? It was by their excess that one knew them for such, as one for that matter only knew things in general worth knowing. I didn't know what I had expected as an effect of our offered homage, but I had somehow not, at the best, expected a relation—and now a relation had been dramatically determined. It would exist for me if I should never again in all the world ask a feather's weight of it; for myself, that is, it would simply never be able not somehow to act. Its virtue was not in truth at all flagrantly to be put to the proof—any opportunity for that underwent at the best a considerable lapse; but why wasn't it intensely acting, none the less, during the time when, before being in London again for any length of stay, I found it intimately concerned in my perusal of Middlemarch, so soon then to appear, and even in that of Deronda, its intervention on behalf of which defied any chill of time?[64] And to these references I can but subjoin that they obviously most illustrate the operation of a sense for drama. The process of appropriation of the two fictions was experience, in great intensity, and roundabout the field was drawn the distinguishable ring of something that belonged equally to this condition and that embraced and further vivified the imaged mass, playing in upon it lights of surpassing fineness. So it was, at any rate, that my "relation"—for I didn't go so far as to call it "ours"—helped me to squeeze further values from the intrinsic substance of the copious final productions I have named, a weight of variety, dignity and beauty of which I have never allowed my measure to shrink.

Even this example of a rage for connections, I may also remark, doesn't deter me from the mention here, somewhat out of its order of time, of another of those in which my whole privilege of reference to Mrs. Lewes, such as it remained, was to look to be preserved. I stretch over the years a little to overtake it, and it calls up at once another person, the ornament, or

63. Both squares are in Mayfair, south of Oxford Street, almost two miles from St. John's Wood.

64. *Middlemarch* was published in 1871–72; Eliot's last novel, *Daniel Deronda,* was published in 1874–76. Following F. R. Leavis in *The Great Tradition* (London: Chatto and Windus, 1948)—who also includes as an appendix HJ's 1876 dialogue "*Daniel Deronda:* A Conversation"—many critics have discussed the links between Eliot's and HJ's heroines.

at least the diversion, of a society long since extinct to me, but who, in common with every bearer of a name I yield to the temptation of writing, insists on profiting promptly by the fact of inscription—very much as if first tricking me into it and then proving it upon me. The extinct societies that once were so sure of themselves, how can they *not* stir again if the right touch, that of a hand they actually knew, however little they may have happened to heed it, reaches tenderly back to them? The touch *is* the retrieval, so far as it goes, setting up as it does heaven knows what undefeated continuity. I must have been present among the faithful at North Bank during a Sunday afternoon or two of the winter of '77 and '78—I was to see the great lady alone but on a single occasion before her death; but those attestations are all but lost to me now in the livelier pitch of a scene, as I can only call it, of which I feel myself again, all amusedly, rather as sacrificed witness. I had driven over with Mrs. Greville from Milford Cottage, in Surrey, to the villa George Eliot and George Lewes had not long before built themselves, and which they much inhabited, at Witley[65]—this indeed, I well remember, in no great flush of assurance

---

65. Mrs. Richard Greville (1823–82, née Sabine Matilda Thellusson) had a country home, The Cottage, Milford, Godalming, Surrey, as well as a house in London, 23 Wilton Crescent, Knightsbridge. She was a society hostess; "charming Mrs Thellusson and her daughter, Mrs Greville, who lived between Witley and Godalming, were especial friends" of Eliot and Lewes (*George Eliot's Life*, 577). In 1862 she had married Richard Greville, a relative of Charles C. F. Greville, whose *A Journal of the Reigns of King George IV and King William IV* HJ reviewed for the *Nation* in 1875 (*LC* 1, 1023–29). Eliot and Lewes bought The Heights, at Witley, near Godalming, at the end of 1876: "It stands on a gentle hill, overlooking a lovely bit of characteristic English scenery. In the foreground green fields, prettily timbered, undulate up to the high ground of Haslemere in front, with Blackdown (where Tennyson lives) on the left hand, and Hind Head on the right. . . . The walks and drives in the neighbourhood are enchanting" (*George Eliot's Life*, 557–58). Of an earlier visit, in April 1878, HJ wrote WJ, "The Leweses were very urbane & friendly & I think that I shall have the right *dorénavant* to consider myself a Sunday *habitué*. The great G.E. herself is both sweet and superior, & has a delightful expression in her large, long, pale equine face. I had my turn at sitting beside her & being conversed with in a low, but most harmonious tone; & bating a tendency to *aborder* only the highest themes I have no fault to find with her" (*CWJ*, 1:301). Elsewhere HJ refers less chivalrously, if affectionately, to Mrs. Greville as "crazy, stage-struck, scatter-brained, . . . on the whole the greatest fool I have ever known," adding, "Her mother, Mrs. Thélusson, who is one of the nicest women I have seen, is a simply delicious and exquisite goose, and her sister Lady Probyn is touchingly devoid of common sense" (*HJL*, 2:241). She was the "most frequent caller" at the home of Lewes and Eliot and "popped in without warning." This visit with HJ took place on 1 November 1878 (Haight, *George Eliot: A Biography*, 513–14).

that my own measure of our intended felicity would be quite that of my buoyant hostess. But here exactly comes, with my memory of Mrs. Greville, from which numberless by-memories dangle, the interesting question that makes for my recall why things happened, under her much-waved wing, not in any too coherent fashion—and this even though it was never once given her, I surmise, to guess that they anywhere fell short. So gently used, all round indeed, was this large, elegant, extremely near-sighted and extremely demonstrative lady, whose genius was all for friend-ship, admiration, declamation and expenditure, that one doubted whether in the whole course of her career she had ever once been brought up, as it were, against a recognised reality; other at least perhaps than the tiresome cost of the materially agreeable in life and the perverse appearance, at times, that though she "said" things, otherwise recited choice morceaux, whether French or English, with a marked oddity of manner, of "attack", a general incongruity of drawing-room art, the various contributive elements, hour, scene, persuaded patience and hushed attention, were perforce a precarious quantity.

It is in that bygone old grace of the unexploded factitious, the air of a thousand dimmed illusions and more or less early Victorian beatitudes on the part of the blandly idle and the supposedly accomplished, that Mrs. Greville, with her exquisite goodnature and her innocent fatuity, is embalmed for me; so that she becomes in that light a truly shining specimen, almost the image or compendium of a whole side of a social order.[66] Just so she has happy suggestion; just so, whether or no by a twist of my mind toward the enviability of certain complacencies of faith and taste that we would yet neither live back into if we could, nor can catch again if we would, I see my forgotten friend of that moist autumn afternoon of our call, and of another, on the morrow, which I shall not pass over, as having rustled and gushed and protested and performed through her term under a kind of protection by the easy-going gods that is not of this fierce age.

66. This portrait of Mrs. Greville was admired by Virginia Woolf in her 1917 review of *The Middle Years;* she regarded her as "a type of the enthusiastic sisterhood which, with all its extravagances and generosities and what we might unkindly, but not without the authority of Henry James, call absurdity, now seems extinct" ("The Old Order," in *The Death of the Moth and Other Essays* [London: Hogarth Press, 1942], 89–90). Indeed, HJ extends the portrait of the individual to invoke an entire era of privilege and benevolence, a pattern of life, which typifies Victorian England. The impressionistic writing and choice of tangible detail from the domestic scene anticipate something of Woolf's style.

Amiabilities and absurdities, harmless serenities and vanities, pretensions and undertakings unashamed, still profited by the mildness of the critical air and the benignity of the social—on the right side at least of the social line. It had struck me from the first that nowhere so much as in England was it fortunate to *be* fortunate, and that against that condition, once it had somehow been handed down and determined, a number of the sharp truths that one might privately apprehend beat themselves beautifully in vain. I say beautifully for I confess without scruple to have found again and again at that time an attaching charm in the general exhibition of enjoyed immunity, paid for as it was almost always by the personal amenity, the practice of all sorts of pleasantness; if it kept the gods themselves for the time in goodhumour, one was willing enough, or at least I was, to be on the side of the gods. Unmistakeable too, as I seem to recover it, was the positive interest of watching and noting, roundabout one, for the turn, or rather for the blest continuity, of their benevolence: such an appeal proceeded, in this, that and the other particular case, from the fool's paradise really rounded and preserved, before one's eyes, for those who were so good as to animate it. There was always the question of how long they would be left to, and the growth of one's fine suspense, not to say one's frank little gratitude, as the miracle repeated itself.

All of which, I admit, dresses in many reflections the small circumstance that Milford Cottage, with its innumerable red candles and candleshades, had affected me as the most embowered retreat for social innocence that it was possible to conceive, and as absolutely settling the question of whether the practice of pleasantness mightn't quite ideally pay for the fantastic protectedness. The red candles in the red shades have remained with me, inexplicably, as a vivid note of this pitch, shedding their rosy light, with the autumn gale, the averted reality, all shut out, upon such felicities of feminine helplessness as I couldn't have prefigured in advance and as exemplified, for further gathering in, the possibilities of the old tone. Nowhere had the evening curtains seemed so drawn, nowhere the copious service so soft, nowhere the second volume of the new novel, "half-uncut", so close to one's hand, nowhere the exquisite head and incomparable brush of the domesticated collie such an attestation of *that* standard at least, nowhere the harmonies of accident—of intention was more than one could say—so incapable of a wrong deflection. That society would lack the highest finish without some such distributed clusters of the thoroughly gentle, the mildly presumptuous and the inveterately mistaken, was brought home to me there, in fine, to a tune with which I had no quarrel, perverse enough as I had been from an early time to know but the impulse to egg on society to the fullest discharge of any material stirring within its breast and not making for cruelty or brutality, mere baseness or mere stupidity, that would fall into a picture or a scene. The quality of serene anxiety on the part for instance of exquisite Mrs. Thellusson, Mrs. Greville's mother,[67] was by itself a plea for any privilege one should fancy her perched upon; and I scarce know if this be more or be less true because the anxiety—at least as I culled its fragrance—was all about the most secondary and superfluous small matters alone. It struck me, I remember, as a new and unexpected form of the pathetic altogether; and there was no form of the pathetic, any more than of the tragic or the comic, that didn't serve as another pearl for one's lengthening string. And I pass over what was doubtless the happiest stroke in the composition, the fact of its involving, as all-distinguished husband of the other daughter, an illustrious soldier and servant of his sovereign, of his sovereigns that were successively to be, than against whose patient handsome bearded presence the whole complexus of femininities and futilities couldn't have been left in more tolerated and more contrasted relief;[68] pass it over to remind myself of how, in my particular friend of the three, the comic and the tragic were presented in a confusion that made the least intended of them at any moment take effectively the place of the most. The impression, that is, was never that of the sentiment operating—save indeed perhaps when the dear lady applied her faculty for frank imitation of the ridiculous, which she then quite directly and remarkably achieved; but that she could be comic, that she *was* comic, was what least appeased her unrest, and there were reasons enough, in a word, why her failure of the grand manner or the penetrating note should evoke the idea of their opposites perfectly achieved. She sat, alike in adoration and emulation, at the feet of my admirable old friend Fanny Kemble,[69] the goodnature of whose consent to

67. Born Marie Macnaghten (1803–81), she married Thomas Robarts Thellusson (1801–69).

68. Mrs. Greville's sister, Letitia Maria Thellusson (b. 1825, d. before 1901), married Sir Dighton Macnaghten Probyn (1833–1924) in 1872. He was a highly esteemed army officer and courtier, becoming knight general officer of the royal household, secretary to the Prince of Wales, and general and keeper of the Privy Purse.

69. The celebrated actor and writer Frances Anne (Fanny) Kemble (1809–93) was a close friend of Mrs Greville's. Mrs. Kemble met HJ in Rome in 1873, and they remained friends until her death. She provided the *données* for some of his fiction, including *Wash-*

"hear" her was equalled only by the immediately consequent action of the splendidly corrective spring on the part of that unsurpassed subject of the dramatic afflatus fairly, or, as I should perhaps above all say, contradictiously provoked. Then aspirant and auditor, rash adventurer and shy alarmist, were swept away together in the gust of magnificent rightness and beauty, no scrap of the far-scattered prime proposal being left to pick up.

Which detail of reminiscence has again stayed my course to the Witley Villa, when even on the way I quaked a little with my sense of what *generally* most awaited or overtook my companion's prime proposals. What had come most to characterise the Leweses to my apprehension was that there couldn't be a thing in the world about which they weren't, and on the most conceded and assured grounds, almost scientifically particular; which presumption, however, only added to the relevance of one's learning how such a matter as their relation with Mrs. Greville could in accordance with noble consistencies be carried on. I could trust *her* for it perfectly, as she knew no law but that of innocent and exquisite aberration, never wanting and never less than consecrating, and I fear I but took refuge for the rest in declining all responsibility. I remember trying to say to myself that, even such as we were, our visit couldn't but scatter a little the weight of cloud on the Olympus we scaled—given the dreadful drenching afternoon we were after all an imaginable short solace there; and this indeed would have borne me through to the end save for an incident which, with a quite ideal logic, left our adventure an approved ruin. I see again our bland, benign, commiserating hostess beside the fire in a chill desert of a room where the master of the house guarded the opposite hearthstone, and I catch once more the impression of no occurrence of anything at all appreciable but their liking us to have come, with our terribly trivial contribution, mainly from a prevision of how they should more devoutly like it when we departed. It is remarkable, but the occasion yields me no single echo of a remark on the part of any of us— nothing more than the sense that our great author herself peculiarly suffered from the fury of the elements, and that they had about them rather the minimum of the paraphernalia of reading and writing, not to speak of that of tea, a conceivable feature of the hour, but which was not provided

*ington Square* (see *CN*, 11–12; and *SBO*, n. 526). HJ reviewed her *Record of a Girlhood* for the *Nation* in 1878 and after her death wrote a long essay, "Frances Anne Kemble," which appeared in *Temple Bar* (*LC* 1, 1069–71; 1071–97).

for. Again I felt touched with privilege, but not, as in '69, with a form of it redeemed from barrenness by a motion of my own, and the taste of barrenness was in fact in my mouth under the effect of our taking leave. We did so with considerable flourish till we had passed out to the hall again, indeed to the door of the waiting carriage, toward which G. H. Lewes himself all sociably, *then* above all conversingly, wafted us—yet staying me by a sudden remembrance before I had entered the brougham and signing me to wait while he repaired his omission. I returned to the doorstep, whence I still see him reissue from the room we had just left and hurry toward me across the hall shaking high the pair of blue-bound volumes his allusion to the uninvited, the verily importunate loan of which by Mrs. Greville had lingered on the air after his dash in quest of them; "Ah those books—take them away, please, away, away!" I hear him unreservedly plead while he thrusts them again at me, and I scurry back into our conveyance, where, and where only, settled afresh with my companion, I venture to assure myself of the horrid truth that had squinted at me as I relieved our good friend of his superfluity. What indeed was this superfluity but the two volumes of my own precious "last"—we were still in the blest age of volumes[70]—presented by its author to the lady of Milford Cottage, and by her, misguided votary, dropped with the best conscience in the world into the Witley abyss, out of which it had jumped with violence, under the touch of accident, straight up again into my own exposed face?

The bruise inflicted there I remember feeling for the moment only as sharp, such a mixture of delightful small questions at once salved it over and such a charm in particular for me to my recognising that this particular wrong—inflicted all unawares, which exactly made it sublime—was the only rightness of our visit. Our hosts hadn't so much as connected book

70. Though Kaplan in his biography of HJ (*The Imagination of Genius*, 195) says this work is *The American,* HJ's "latest" work was *The Europeans,* first published in two volumes on 18 September 1878, the English edition covered in "bright blue sand-grain cloth" (Edel et al., *Bibliography of Henry James,* 37). *The American* appeared in only one volume. The famous Victorian "three-decker" format for novels ended in the 1890s, and earlier James novels, such as *The Portrait of a Lady, The Bostonians, The Princess Casamassima,* and *The Tragic Muse,* were first published in multiple volumes. However, HJ's twentieth-century novels, such as *The Wings of the Dove* (1902) and *The Golden Bowl* (1904), also appeared initially in three volumes. HJ uses similarly benedictory terms on recalling empty days in Boulogne-sur-Mer when the "blest novel in three volumes exercised through its form . . . an appeal that made it do with me what it would," and he would surrender himself at the lending library to such "rich individual trinities" (*SBO,* 325–26).

with author, or author with visitor, or visitor with anything but the convenience of his ridding them of an unconsidered trifle; grudging as they so justifiedly did the impingement of such matters on their consciousness. The vivid demonstration of one's failure to penetrate there had been in the sweep of Lewes's gesture, which could scarce have been bettered by his actually wielding a broom.[71] I think nothing passed between us in the brougham on revelation of the identity of the offered treat so emphatically declined—I see that I couldn't have laughed at it to the confusion of my gentle neighbour. But I quite recall my grasp of the *interest* of our distinguished friends' inaccessibility to the unattended plea, with the light it seemed to throw on what it was really to *be* attended. Never, never save as attended—by presumptions, that is, far other than any then hanging about one—would one so much as desire *not* to be pushed out of sight. I needn't attempt, however, to supply all the links in the chain of association which led to my finally just qualified beatitude: I had been served right enough in all conscience, but the pity was that Mrs. Greville had been. This I never wanted for her; and I may add, in the connection, that I discover now no grain of false humility in my having enjoyed in my own person adorning such a tale. There was positively a fine high thrill in thinking of persons— or at least of a person, for any fact about Lewes was but derivative— engaged in my own pursuit and yet detached, by what I conceived, detached by a pitch of intellectual life, from all that made it actual to myself. *There* was the lift of contemplation, there the inspiring image and the big supporting truth; the pitch of intellectual life in the very fact of which we seemed, my hostess and I, to have caught our celebrities sitting in that queer bleak way wouldn't have bullied me in the least if it hadn't been the centre of such a circle of gorgeous creation. It was the fashion

71. Autolycus was a "snapper-up of unconsidered triffles" in Shakespeare's *The Winter's Tale* (4.3.26). Though most biographers follow HJ in emphasizing his humiliation here, Haight suggests he may have misread the incident. Mrs. Greville had loaned the couple HJ's novel on 19 October, and they wished to return it before leaving Witley ten days later: "James fills several pages of *The Middle Years* with impressions of the bruise this episode inflicted on his ego, already sore from his brother William's disappointment with the book. His assumption that the Leweses did not connect it with him and had not read it was wrong. They had. But they failed to realize James's projected vision of the occasion, in which George Eliot should recognize that he too was doing 'her sort of work.' . . . Focused on his own feelings, James's mind failed to sense the tragic misery on that sad hearthstone" (*George Eliot: A Biography*, 514). Despite this explanation, it might have been kind of such a respected figure at least to acknowledge the presence of a younger writer. More importantly, however, Lewes was dead within the month, succumbing to enteritis on 30 November 1878.

among the profane in short either to misdoubt, before George Eliot's canvas, the latter's backing of rich thought, or else to hold that this matter of philosophy, and even if but of the philosophic vocabulary, thrust itself through to the confounding of the picture. But with that thin criticism I wasn't, as I have already intimated, to have a moment's patience; I was to become, I was to remain—I take pleasure in repeating—even a very Derondist of Derondists, for my own wanton joy:[72] which amounts to saying that I found the figured, coloured tapestry *always* vivid enough to brave no matter what complication of the stitch.

## VI

I take courage to confess moreover that I am carried further still by the current on which Mrs. Greville, friend of the supereminent, happens to have launched me; for I can neither forbear a glance at one or two of the other adventures promoted by her, nor in the least dissociate her from that long aftertaste of them, such as

72. HJ asserts his extreme admiration for Eliot in associating himself with her final novel, *Daniel Deronda,* which, because of its mixed qualities (the intimate portrayal of a young woman's sensibility, the somewhat idealizing vision of Jewish culture) has provoked some critical disagreement. Indeed HJ himself at the time regarded its hero as "a dead, though amiable failure," while appreciating the work as "a great *exposé* of the female mind" (*HJL,* 2:59, 91). On the other hand, the anecdote (a rare item in HJ's autobiographical mode), told so frankly against himself, and in spite of his limited knowledge of the situation, defines something of the earnest, even self-important and self-absorbed, atmosphere of the Lewes-Eliot household. In a more private context, Alice James offers a characteristically trenchant response to the third volume of J. W. Cross's biography: "what a monument of ponderous dreariness is the book! What a lifeless, diseased, self-conscious being she must have been! Not one burst of joy, not one ray of humour, not one living breath in one of her letters or journals. . . . Whether it is that her dank, moaning features haunt and pursue one thro' the book, or not, but she makes upon me the impression, morally and physically, of mildew, or some morbid growth—a fungus of a pendulous shape, or as of something damp to the touch. . . . Then to think of those books compact of wisdom, humour, and the richest humanity, and of her as the creator of the immortal *Maggie,* in short, what a horrible disillusion! . . . the possession of what genius and what knowledge could reconcile one to the supreme boredom of having to take oneself with that superlative solemnity!" (*Diary,* 41–42). In his review of Cross's *Life,* published in the *Atlantic Monthly* in 1885, though he notes in passing "the absence of free aesthetic life," HJ is understandably more measured, concluding, "What *is* remarkable, extraordinary . . . is that this quiet, anxious, sedentary, serious, invalidical English lady, without animal spirits, without adventures or sensations, should have made us believe that nothing in the world was alien to her; should have produced such rich, deep, masterly pictures of the multiform life of man" ("The Life of George Eliot," *LC* 1, 1002–3, 1010).

they were, which I have positively cultivated. I ask myself first, however, whether or no our drive to Aldworth, on the noble height of Blackdown, had been preceded by the couple of occasions in London on which I was to feel I saw the Laureate most at his ease, yet on reflection concluding that the first of these—and the fewest days must have separated them—formed my prime introduction to the poet I had earliest known and best loved.[73] The revelational evening I speak of is peopled, to my memory, not a little, yet with a confusedness out of which Tennyson's own presence doesn't at all distinctly emerge; he was occupying a house in Eaton Place,[74] as appeared then his wont, for the earlier weeks of the spring, and I seem to recover that I had "gone on" to it, after dining somewhere else, under protection of my supremely kind old friend the late Lord Houghton, to whom I was indebted in those years for a most promiscuous befriending.[75] He must have been of the party, and Mrs. Greville quite independently must, since I catch again the vision of her, so expansively and voluminously seated that she might fairly have been couchant, so to say, for the proposed characteristic act—there was a deliberation about it that

73. Tennyson succeeded Wordsworth as poet laureate in 1850. He oversaw the building of Aldworth in Surrey, a French-style Gothic mansion, in 1867. For decades the poet enjoyed the greatest national recognition. HJ wrote reviews of Tennyson's dramas *Queen Mary* and *Harold* for the *Galaxy* and *Nation* in the mid-seventies (*Henry James: Essays on Art and Drama*, 87–118; 185–93).

74. Eaton Place, between Belgrave and Eaton squares, is in the heart of London's Belgravia. Between 1875 and 1882 the Tennyson family took a London house for the spring (February to Easter) in various locations, including Wimpole Street, Upper Belgrave Street, Eaton Place, and Eaton Square (Hallam Tennyson, *Alfred Lord Tennyson: A Memoir by His Son* [London: Macmillan, 1897], 604).

75. Richard Monckton Milnes, 1st Baron Houghton (1809–85), had (with Tennyson) been elected a member of the elite Apostles Club at Cambridge University; became a biographer of John Keats, champion of the poetry of Swinburne, a bibliophile and collector of erotica; a Conservative then a Liberal member of Parliament; and was at the heart of London's literary life and famous for the breakfasts he gave. In 1877 HJ had been provided with a letter of introduction by his friend Henry Adams, whom HJ had met as editor of the *North American Review*, though Houghton had preempted its use by calling on him first (see also Novick, *Young Master*, 508 n. 29). HJ was bowled over: "Lord Houghton has been my guide, philosopher and friend—he has breakfasted me, dined me, conversatzioned me, absolutely caressed me. He has been really most kind and paternal, and I have seen, under his wing, a great variety of interesting and remarkable people" (*HJL*, 2:110). A couple of years later, in 1879, HJ's enthusiasm is only slightly more tempered: "He is a battered and world-wrinkled old mortal, with a restless and fidgety vanity, but with an immense fund of real kindness and humane feeling" (ibid., 208).

precluded the idea of a spring; that, namely, of addressing something of the Laureate's very own to the Laureate's very face. Beyond the sense that he took these things with a gruff philosophy—and could always repay them, on the spot, in heavily-shovelled coin of the same mint, since it *was* a question of his genius—I gather in again no determined impression, unless it may have been, as could only be probable, the effect of fond prefigurements utterly blighted.

The fond prefigurements of youthful piety are predestined more often than not, I think, experience interfering, to strange and violent shocks; from which no general appeal is conceivable save by the prompt preclusion either of faith or of knowledge, a sad choice at the best. No other such illustration recurs to me of the possible refusal of those two conditions of an acquaintance to recognise each other at a given hour as the silent crash of which I was to be conscious several years later, in Paris, when placed in presence of M. Ernest Renan,[76] from the surpassing distinction of whose literary face, with its exquisite finish of every feature, I had from far back extracted every sort of shining gage, a presumption general and positive. Widely enough to sink all interest—that was the dreadful thing—opened there the chasm between the implied, as I had taken it, and the attested, as I had, at the first blush, to take it; so that one was in fact scarce to know what might have happened if interest hadn't by good fortune already reached such a compass as to stick half way down the descent. What interest *can* survive becomes thus, surely, as much one of the lessons of life as the number of ways in which it remains impossible. What comes up in

76. Joseph-Ernest Renan (1823–92) was a French philologist, historian, and critic who wrote a life of Jesus as well as an important autobiography, *Souvenirs d'enfance et de jeunesse*. He was renowned for the elegance of his style. HJ recorded his dining with the Renans for WJ in 1876: "Renan is hideous and charming—more hideous even than his photos. & more charming even than his writing. His talk at table was really exquisite for urbanity, finesse & wit—all quite without show-off. I talked with him for three quarters of an hour, in the corner, after dinner, told him that I couldn't measure his writings on the side of erudition, but that they had always been for me (& all my family!!) 'la plus haute perfection de l'expression,' & he treated me as if I were a distinguished savant." WJ had been reading the French author in 1882, and commented rather more directly than his brother, "Renan is really deliquescent with putrefaction,—but who can putrefy with such a fine old flavor as he?" (*CWJ*, 1:252, 333). HJ wrote a number of notes and reviews of Renan; as *Souvenirs* was appearing in 1882, he commented that its author was "a queer mixture. He has an enchanting mind, but it needs ventilation, awfully" (letter to Theodore Child, 5 December 1882, *A Life in Letters*, 143); HJ's substantial essay on the autobiography was published in the *Atlantic Monthly* in August 1883 (*LC* 2, 633–45).

face of the shocks, as I have called them, is the question of a shift of every supposition, a change of base under fire, as it were; which must take place successfully if one's advance be not abandoned altogether. I remember that I saw the Tennyson directly presented as just utterly other than the Tennyson indirectly, and if the readjustment, for acquaintance, was less difficult than it was to prove in the case of the realised Renan the obligation to accept the difference—wholly as difference and without reference to strict loss or gain—was like a rap on the knuckles of a sweet superstition. Fine, fine, fine could he only be[77]—fine in the sense of that quality in the texture of his verse, which had appealed all along by its most inward principle to one's taste, and had by the same stroke shown with what a force of lyric energy and sincerity the kind of beauty so engaged for could be associated. Was it that I had preconceived him in that light as pale and penetrating, as emphasising in every aspect the fact that he was fastidious? was it that I had supposed him more fastidious than really *could* have been—at the best for that effect? was it that the grace of the man *couldn't*, by my measure, but march somehow with the grace of the poet, given a perfection of this grace? was it in fine that style of a particular kind, when so highly developed, seemed logically to leave no room for other quite contradictious kinds? These were considerations of which I recall the pressure, at the same time that I fear I have no account of them to give after they have fairly faced the full, the monstrous demonstration that Tennyson was not Tennysonian.[78] The desperate sequel to that was that he thereby

77. HJ is perhaps echoing the opening line of one of Tennyson's most famous lyrics, which begins: "Break, break, break, / On thy cold gray stones, O Sea! / And I would that my tongue could utter / The thoughts that arise in me" (*The Poems of Tennyson*, ed. Christopher Ricks [London: Longman, 1969, 1987], 2:24).

78. HJ seems to have first coined this paradox in a letter to Charles Eliot Norton: "Shall I even mention to you that . . . I went to lunch with Tennyson (I was staying, near him, with an amiable and clever, but fantastic and ridiculous, Mrs. Greville) and that he took me up into his study and read aloud—not very well—"Locksley Hall," from beginning to end? I don't know whether you saw anything of this author who personally is less agreeable than his works—having a manner that is rather bad than good. But whenever I feel disposed to reflect that Tennyson is not personally Tennysonian, I summon up the image of Browning, and this has the effect of making me check my complaints" (17 November [1878], *HJL*, 2:196). Anne Thackeray Ritchie (1837–1919), a novelist and old friend of HJ's (and Thackeray's daughter), was displeased at his portrayal of Tennyson in *TMY*, as she revealed to the wife of the American ambassador Walter Hines Page and reported to Hallam, the poet's son: "I said I loved Henry James but that I was very angry with him for the way he had written of your Father—She said she also cared very much for Henry James, but that never

changed one's own state too, one's beguiled, one's aesthetic; for what *could* this strange apprehension do but reduce the Tennysonian amount altogether? It dried up, to a certain extent, that is, in my own vessel of sympathy—leaving me so to ask whether it was before or after that I should take myself for the bigger fool. There had been folly somewhere; yet let me add that once I recognised this, once I felt the old fond pitch drop of itself, not alone inevitably, but very soon quite conveniently and while I magnanimously granted that the error had been mine and no-body's else at all, an odd prosaic pleasantness set itself straight up, sub-stitutionally, over the whole ground, which it swept clear of every single premeditated effect. It made one's perceptive condition purely profane, reduced it somehow to having rather the excess of awkwardness than the excess of felicity to reckon with; yet still again, as I say, enabled a compro-mise to work.

The compromise in fact worked beautifully under my renewal of impression—for which a second visit at Eaton Place offered occasion; and this even though I had to interweave with the scene as best I might a highly complicating influence. To speak of James Russell Lowell's influence as above all complicating on any scene to the interest of which he contrib-uted may superficially seem a perverse appreciation of it;[79] and yet in the

---

were two persons more apart, that Henry was absolutely incapable of understanding Tennysons spiritual greatness & *might*—that Henry could not even conceive with all his fine intuition and humanity & perception of tangible things, the great inspiration that she felt more & more & that others were realizing more every day." Hallam Tennyson, invari-ably protective of his father's reputation, agreed: "Your description of Mrs Pages talk touched me. My Father was very kind to Henry James, & I am sorry that he has requited the kindness in the way he apparently has done" (John Aplin, *"A True Affection": Anne Thackeray Ritchie and the Tennysons* [Lincoln, U.K.: Tennyson Society, 2006], 66 and n. 121). Both correspondents seem to undervalue a general point HJ was making—the impos-sibly subtle being he had created from the experience of reading the poetry, quite at odds with the strong physical reality of the man's presence—and the salutary if chastening realization that he must adjust his original, undeniably naive assumptions. On the other hand, HJ's references to Tennyson "spouting" his poetry are uncharacteristically collo-quial and typify the equivocal tone of this portrait.

79. Lowell, having served as ambassador to Spain since 1877, became U.S. minister to the Court of St. James's from May 1880 until 1885. In his personal notes, HJ frequently refers to the older man as "dear Lowell"; standing on a bluff near Mount Auburn in Cambridge during his American trip of 1904–5 and looking across the Charles River to Soldiers Field on the Boston side, HJ reaches out a commemorative hand to Lowell, "the very genius of the spot" (*AS*, 69). He regarded him as "New England accomplished and articulate" (*LC* 1, 541). The novelist's affection emerges most poignantly in the last letter

light of that truth only do I recover the full sense of his value, his interest, the moving moral of his London adventure—to find myself already bumping so straight against which gives me, I confess, a sufficiently portentous shake. He comes in, as it were, by a force not to be denied, as soon as I look at him again—as soon as I find him for instance on the doorstep in Eaton Place at the hour of my too approaching it for luncheon as he had just done. There he is, with the whole question of him, at once before me, and literally superimposed by that fact on any minor essence. I quake, positively, with the apprehension of the commemorative dance he may lead me; but for the moment, just here, I steady myself with an effort and go in with him to his having the Laureate's personal acquaintance, by every symptom, and rather to my surprise, all to make. Mrs. Tennyson's luncheon table was an open feast, with places for possible when not assured guests; and no one but the American Minister, scarce more than just installed, and his extremely attached compatriot sat down at first with our gracious hostess.[80] The board considerably stretched, and after it had been indicated to Lowell that he had best sit at the end near the window, where the Bard would presently join him, I remained, near our hostess, separated from him for some little time by an unpeopled waste. Hallam came in all genially and auspiciously, yet only to brush us with his blessing and say he was lunching elsewhere, and my wonder meanwhile hung about the representative of my country, who, though partaking of offered food, appeared doomed to disconnection from us. I may say at once that my wonder was always unable *not* to hang about this admired and cherished friend when other persons, especially of the eminent order, were concerned in the scene. The case was quite other for the unshared relation, or when it was shared by one or other of three or four of our common friends who had the gift of determining happily the pitch of ease; suspense, not to say anxiety, as to the possible turn or drift of the affair quite

---

(20 July 1891) he wrote to the dying man: "I have, somehow a vision of you which makes my heart ache a good deal—and makes me brush from my eye the tear in which old London pictures—other pictures—are reflected. Your non-arrival—this spring—made me for the first time in my life willing to say that I 'realised' a situation. I seemed to see that you were tied down by pain and weakness, that you were suffering often and suffering much. I don't like to ask for fear of a yes, and I don't like not to ask for fear of your noticing my silence" (*HJL*, 3:346). HJ's substantial memorial essay appeared in the *Atlantic Monthly* in January 1892 (*LC* 1, 516–40).

80. Tennyson had married Emily Sarah Sellwood (1813–96) in 1850, after a long engagement.

dropped—I rested then, we alike rested, I ever felt, in a golden confidence. This last was so definitely not the note of my attention to him, so far as I might indulge it, in the wider social world, that I shall not scruple, occasion offering, to inquire into the reasons of the difference. For I can only see the ghosts of my friends, by this token, as "my" J. R. L. and whoever; which means that my imagination, of the wanton life of which these remarks pretend but to form the record, had appropriated them, under the prime contact—from the moment the prime contact had successfully worked—once for all, and contributed the light in which they were constantly exposed.

Yes, delightful I shall undertake finding it, and perhaps even making it, to read J. R. L.'s exposure back into *its* light; which I in fact see begin to shine for me more amply during those very minutes of our wait for our distinguished host and even the several that followed the latter's arrival and his seating himself opposite the unknown guest, whose identity he had failed to grasp. Nothing, exactly, could have made dear Lowell more "my" Lowell, as I have presumed to figure him, than the stretch of uncertainty so supervening and which, in its form of silence at first completely unbroken between the two poets, rapidly took on for me monstrous proportions. I conversed with my gentle neighbour during what seemed an eternity—really but hearing, as the minutes sped, all that Tennyson didn't say to Lowell and all that Lowell wouldn't on any such compulsion as that say to Tennyson. I like, however, to hang again upon the hush—for the sweetness of the relief of its break by the fine Tennysonian growl. I had never dreamed, no, of a growling Tennyson—I had too utterly otherwise fantasticated; but no line of Locksley Hall[81] rolled out as I was to happen soon after to hear it, could have been sweeter than the interrogative sound of "Do you know anything about *Lowell*?" launched on the chance across the table and crowned at once by Mrs. Tennyson's anxious quaver: "Why, my dear, this *is* Mr. Lowell!" The clearance took place successfully enough, and the incident, I am quite aware, seems to shrink with it; in spite of which I still cherish the reduced reminiscence for its connections: so far as my vision of Lowell was concerned they began at that moment so

81. A poem that Tennyson considered to be one of his most important, "Locksley Hall" (1842), offers an optimistic vision of the coming era, a prospect of political and industrial progress, witnessed by a hero who will transcend personal disappointment by means of public service. In a letter of 1870 to WJ, HJ repeats one of the poem's most famous (if technically misinformed) metaphors derived from the age of the railway: "God speed you. I see you booked indelibly for the ringing grooves of change" (*CWJ*, 1:143).

to multiply. A belated guest or two more came in, and I wish I could for my modesty's sake refer to this circumstance alone the fact that nothing more of the occasion survives for me save the intense but restricted glow of certain instants, in another room, to which we had adjourned for smoking and where my alarmed sense of the Bard's restriction to giving what he had as a bard only became under a single turn of his hand a vision of quite general munificence. Incredibly, inconceivably, he had *read*—and not only read but admired, and not only admired but understandingly referred; referred, time and some accident aiding, the appreciated object, a short tale I had lately put forth, to its actually present author, who could scarce believe his ears on hearing the thing superlatively commended; pronounced, that is, by the illustrious speaker, more to his taste than no matter what other like attempt. Nothing would induce me to disclose the title of the piece, which has little to do with the matter; my point is but in its having on the spot been matter of pure romance to me that I was there and positively so addressed.[82] For it was a solution, the happiest in the world, and from which I at once extracted enormities of pleasure: my relation to whatever had bewildered me simply became perfect: the author of In Memoriam[83] had "liked" my own twenty pages, and his doing so was a gage of his grace in which I felt I should rest forever—in which I have in fact rested to this hour. My own basis of liking—such a blessed supersession of all worryings and wonderings!—was accordingly established, and has met every demand made of it.

Greatest was to have been, I dare say, the demand to which I felt it exposed by the drive over to Aldworth with Mrs. Greville which I noted above and which took place, if I am not mistaken, on the morrow of our drive to Witley.[84] A different shade of confidence and comfort, I make out, accompanied this experiment: I believed more, for reasons I shall not now attempt to recover, in the furthermost maintenance of our flying bridge,

82. Dupee (*Henry James: Autobiography*, 609) suggests that the story admired by Tennyson was "Madame de Mauves" (which appeared in the *Galaxy* in spring 1874), a tale of conflicting European-American values in which the hero must renounce any hopes of loving the pure but mistreated young wife of the title.

83. One of the classic documents of Victorian faith and doubt, *In Memoriam A.H.H.*, a sequence of elegiac poems arising from Tennyson's intense grief at the sudden death of his friend Arthur Henry Hallam and charting "the way of the soul," was published in 1850.

84. Compare letter of 14 November 1878 from HJ to WJ: "I went into the country the other day to stay with a friend a couple of days (Mrs. Greville) & went with her to lunch with Tennyson, who, after lunch, read us Locksley Hall. The next day went to Geo. Eliot's" (*CWJ*, 1:309).

the final piers of which, it was indubitable, *had* at Witley given way. What could have been moreover less like G. H. Lewes's valedictory hurl back upon us of the printed appeal in which I was primarily concerned than that so recent and so directly opposed passage of the Eaton Place smoking-room, thanks to which I could nurse a certified security all along the road?[85] I surrendered to security, I perhaps even grossly took my ease in it; and I was to breathe from beginning to end of our visit, which began with our sitting again at luncheon, an air—so unlike that of Witley!—in which it seemed to me frankly that nothing but the blest obvious, or at

85. HJ makes some apology for "confusedness" about dates and memories at the beginning of this chapter, and he might have clarified the sequence of events had he revised the text. A brief chronology based partly on this chapter may help. There is evidence of two closely grouped springtime meetings between HJ and Tennyson in London. HJ made one evening visit in company with Lord Houghton and Mrs. Greville; she recited some of the poet's work to him and he reciprocated. (It seems that she enjoyed reciting Tennyson: George Eliot records in her diary for 1 October 1879 that "Mrs. Greville came and recited the Revenge" [*The George Eliot Letters*, 7:202]). The laureate did not live up to HJ's preconception. This was most likely to have been in 1877, since HJ records what was presumably the other meeting with the poet on 28 March (a seemingly all-male occasion and with no poetry reading) in a letter to WJ of 29 March 1877: "Yesterday I dined with Lord Houghton—with Gladstone, Tennyson, Dr. Schliemann (the excavator of old Mycenae &c) & half a dozen other men of 'high culture.' I sat next but one to the Bard, & heard most of his talk which was all about port-wine & tobacco: he seems to know much about them, & can drink a whole bottle of port at a sitting with no incommodity. He is very swarthy & scraggy & strikes one at first as much less handsome than his photos.: but gradually you see that it's a face of genius. He had I know not what simplicity, speaks with a strange rustic accent & seemed altogether like a creature of some primordial English stock, a 1000 miles away from American manufacture" (*CWJ*, 1:283). Another luncheon meeting at Eaton Square, which included James Russell Lowell, occurred (given the date of Lowell's taking up his appointment in London) sometime in May 1880, or a little later. Once again, Tennyson gave a reading of "Locksley Hall," a repeat of the performance of 30 October 1878 (*HJL*, 2:190; see also *CWJ*, 1:309). Tennyson complimented HJ on one of his short stories in the smoking room at Eaton Square—this must have been (since their adjourning to smoke is mentioned) the luncheon visit with Lowell. HJ implies that it compensated for the return of the two volumes by Lewes and Eliot in November 1878, but his description of that incident as "so recent and so directly opposed" seems misleading in that there was a gap of two years. Those visits to Witley (the Lewes-Eliot house) and to Aldworth (the Tennysons') took place on consecutive days. He recalls that the Aldworth visit occurred, "if I am not mistaken, on the morrow of our drive to Witley" (i.e., the day after), the sequence that Edel follows (*Conquest of London*, 374). However two letters of the time—one to Lizzie Boott (*HJL*, 2:390), the other to WJ (*CWJ*, 1:309)—indicate that he saw the Tennysons first.

least the blest outright, could so much as attempt to live. These elements hung sociably and all auspiciously about us—it was a large and simple and almost empty occasion; yet empty without embarrassment, rather as from a certain high guardedness or defensiveness of situation, literally indeed from the material, the local sublimity, the fact of our all upliftedly hanging together over one of the grandest sweeps of view in England.[86] Remembered passages again people, however, in their proportion, the excess of opportunity; each with that conclusive note of the outright all unadorned. What could have partaken more of this quality for instance than the question I was startled to hear launched before we had left the table by the chance of Mrs. Greville's having happened to mention in some connection one of her French relatives, Mademoiselle Laure de Sade?[87] It had fallen on my own ear—the mention at least had—with a certain effect of unconscious provocation; but this was as nothing to its effect on the ear of our host. "De Sade?" he at once exclaimed with interest—and with the consequence, I may frankly add, of my wondering almost to ecstasy, that is to the ecstasy of curiosity, to what length he would proceed. He proceeded admirably—admirably for the triumph of simplification—to the very greatest length imaginable, as was signally promoted by the fact that clearly no one present, with a single exception, recognised the name or the nature of the scandalous, the long ignored, the at last all but unnameable author;[88] least of all the gentle relative of Mademoiselle Laure, who listened with the blankest grace to her friend's enumeration of his titles to infamy, among which that of his most notorious work was pronounced. It

86. Blackdown is the highest hill in the county of Sussex; situated close to the Surrey border, it offers panoramic views of the surrounding countryside. Anne Thackeray Ritchie describes Aldworth "on the summit of a high, lonely hill in Surrey. . . . It is a white stone house with many broad windows facing a great view and a long terrace, like some one of those at Siena or Perugia, with a low parapet of stone, where ivies and roses are trained, making a foreground to the lovely haze of the distance" (*Records of Tennyson, Ruskin, Browning* [New York: Harper, 1892], 55).

87. Laure de Sade (1860–1936) was a descendant of the Marquis de Sade and a member of the aristocratic, fashionable Parisian set of the end of the nineteenth century. She became the Comtesse de Chevigné and apparently inspired Marcel Proust in *À la recherche du temps perdu.*

88. Louis-Donatien Aldonze, Marquis de Sade (1740–1814), was a French aristocrat who led a notoriously dissolute life. His writings, often pornographic, contain scenes of sexual violence, hence the term *sadism.* His most famous work is perhaps *Les 120 journées de Sodome* (1782–85).

was the homeliest, frankest, most domestic passage, as who should say, and most remarkable for leaving none of us save myself, by my impression, in the least embarrassed or bewildered; largely, I think, because of the failure—a failure the most charmingly flat—of all measure on the part of auditors and speaker alike of what might be intended or understood, of what, in fine, the latter was talking about.

He struck me in truth as neither knowing nor communicating knowledge, and I recall how I felt this note in his own case to belong to that general intimation with which the whole air was charged of the want of proportion between the great spaces and reaches and echoes commanded, the great eminence attained, and the quantity and variety of experience supposable. So to discriminate was in a manner to put one's hand on the key, and thereby to find one's self in presence of a rare and anomalous, but still scarcely the less beautiful fact. The assured and achieved conditions, the serenity, the security, the success, to put it vulgarly, shone in the light of their easiest law—that by which they emerge early from the complication of life, the great adventure of sensibility, and find themselves determined once for all, fortunately fixed, all consecrated and consecrating. If I should speak of this impression as that of glory without history, that of the poetic character more worn than paid for, or at least more saved than spent, I should doubtless much over-emphasise; but such, or something like it, was none the less the explanation that met one's own fond fancy of the scene after one had cast about for it. For I allow myself thus to repeat that I was so moved to cast about, and perhaps at no moment more than during the friendly analysis of the reputation of M. de Sade. Was I not present at some undreamed-of demonstration of the absence of the remoter real, the real other than immediate and exquisite, other than guaranteed and enclosed, in landscape, friendship, fame, above all in consciousness of awaited and admired and self-consistent inspiration?

The question was indeed to be effectively answered for me, and everything meanwhile continued to play into this prevision—even to the pleasant growling note heard behind me, as the Bard followed with Mrs. Greville, who had permitted herself apparently some mild extravagance of homage: "Oh yes, you may do what you like—so long as you don't kiss me before the cabman!" The allusion was explained for us, if I remember—a matter of some more or less recent leave-taking of admirer and admired in London on his putting her down at her door after being taken to the play or wherever; between the rugged humour of which reference and the other just commemorated there wasn't a pin to choose, it struck me, for a certain old-time Lincolnshire ease or comfortable stay-at-home license.[89] But it was later on, when, my introductress having accompanied us, I sat upstairs with him in his study, that he might read to us some poem of his own that we should venture to propose, it was then that mystifications dropped, that everything in the least dislocated fell into its place, and that image and picture stamped themselves strongly and finally, or to the point even, as I recover it, of leaving me almost too little to wonder about. He had not got a third of the way through Locksley Hall, which, my choice given me, I had made bold to suggest he should spout—for I had already heard him spout in Eaton Place—before I had begun to wonder that I didn't wonder, didn't at least wonder more consumedly; as a very little while back I should have made sure of my doing on any such prodigious occasion. I sat at one of the windows that hung over space, noting how the windy, watery autumn day, sometimes sheeting it all with rain, called up the dreary, dreary moorland or the long dun wolds;[90] I pinched myself for the determination of my identity and hung on the reader's deep-voiced chant for the credibility of his: I asked myself in fine why, in complete deviation from everything that would have seemed from far back certain for the case, I failed to swoon away under the heaviest pressure I had doubtless ever known the romantic situation bring to bear. So lucidly all the while I considered, so detachedly I judged, so dissentingly, to tell the whole truth, I listened; pinching myself, as I say, not at all to keep from swooning, but much rather to set up some rush of sensibility. It was all interesting, it was at least all odd; but why in the name of poetic justice had one anciently heaved and flushed with one's own recital of the splendid stuff if one was now only to sigh in secret "Oh dear, oh dear"? The author lowered the whole pitch, that of expression, that of interpretation above all; I heard him, in cool surprise, take even more out of his verse than he had put in, and so bring me back to the point I had immediately and privately made, the point that he wasn't Tennysonian. I felt him as he went on and on lose that character beyond repair, and no effect of the organ-roll, of monotonous majesty, no suggestion of the long echo, availed at all to save it. What the case came to for me, I take it—and by the case I mean

89. Tennyson was a native of Somersby in Lincolnshire, on the east coast of England in the region of the Wash.

90. HJ perhaps recalls the opening scene of "Locksley Hall": " 'Tis the place, and all around it, as of old, the curlews call, / Dreary gleams about the moorland flying over Locksley Hall" (*The Poems of Tennyson*, 2:120). A "wold," a hilly tract of land, is more commonly associated with Yorkshire and Lincolnshire.

the intellectual, the artistic—was that it lacked the intelligence, the play of discrimination, I should have taken for granted in it, and thereby, brooding monster that I was, born to discriminate *à tout propos*,[91] lacked the interest.

Detached I have mentioned that I had become, and it was doubtless at such a rate high time for that; though I hasten to repeat that with the close of the incident I was happily able to feel a new sense in the whole connection established. My critical reaction hadn't in the least invalidated our great man's being a Bard—it had in fact made him and left him more a Bard than ever: it had only settled to my perception as not before what a Bard might and mightn't be. The character was just a rigid idiosyncrasy, to which everything in the man conformed, but which supplied nothing outside of itself, and which above all was not intellectually wasteful or heterogeneous, conscious as it could only be of its intrinsic breadth and weight. On two or three occasions of the aftertime I was to hear Browning read out certain of his finest pages, and this exactly with all the exhibition of point and authority, the expressive particularisation, so to speak, that I had missed on the part of the Laureate; an observation through which the author of Men and Women appeared, in spite of the beauty and force of his demonstration, as little as possible a Bard.[92] He particularised if ever a man did, was heterogeneous and profane, composed of pieces and patches that betrayed some creak of joints, and addicted to the excursions from which these were brought home; so that he had to *prove* himself a

91. At every turn.

92. For *Men and Women*, see *NSB*, n. 141. The contrast he makes is reminiscent of HJ's views in the letter of 17 November 1878 to Charles Eliot Norton quoted above (*TMY*, n. 78), yet he is here perhaps referring to the physical presence of the poets as much as to their performance of their own work. Edel points out that "Henry held Browning in high esteem; and if at moments he was depreciatory, he was to recognize, when he recalled the contrasting figures of the Laureate and Mr Browning, that there was a distinct difference of temperament—that the scales weighted in favour of the latter." This may be so, though when Edel goes on to record HJ's opinion of Browning's reading aloud, it emerges as no less severe: "One of my latest sensations was going one day to Lady Airlie's to hear Browning read his own poems—with the comfort of finding that, at least if you don't understand them, he himself apparently understands them even less. He read them as if he hated them and would like to bite them to pieces" (*Conquest of London*, 376). It is thought that Browning may have inspired HJ's short story "The Private Life" (1892), an examination of the discrepancies between a playwright's pedestrian public persona and his other unseen being, the creator: "One is the genius, the other's the bourgeois, and it's only the bourgeois whom we personally know. He talks, he circulates, he's awfully popular, he flirts with you" (*CT*, 8:210).

poet, almost against all presumptions, and with all the assurance and all the character he could use. Was not this last in especial, the character, so close to the surface, with which Browning fairly bristled, what was most to come out in his personal delivery of the fruit of his genius? It came out almost to harshness; but the result was that what he read showed extraordinary life. During that audition at Aldworth the question seemed on the contrary not of life at all—save, that is, of one's own; which was exactly not the question. With all the resonance of the chant, the whole thing was yet *still,* with all the long swing of its motion it yet remained where it was— heaving doubtless grandly enough up and down and beautiful to watch as through the superposed veils of its long self-consciousness. By all of which I don't mean to say that I was not, on the day at Aldworth, thoroughly reconciled to learning what a Bard consisted of; for that came as soon as I had swallowed my own mistake—the mistake of having supposed Tennyson something subtly other than one. I had supposed, probably, such an impossibility, had, to repeat my term, so absurdly fantasticated, that the long journey round and about the truth no more than served me right; just as after all it at last left me quite content.

VII　It left me moreover, I become aware—or at least it now leaves me—fingering the loose ends of this particular free stretch of my tapestry; so that, with my perhaps even extravagant aversion to loose ends, I can but try for a moment to interweave them. There dangles again for me least confusedly, I think, the vision of a dinner at Mrs. Greville's—and I like even to remember that Cadogan Place,[93] where memories hang thick for me, was the scene of it— which took its light from the presence of Louisa Lady Waterford, who took hers in turn from that combination of rare beauty with rare talent which the previous Victorian age had for many years not ceased to acclaim.[94] It insists on coming back to me with the utmost vividness

93. Cadogan Place is in the Knightsbridge area of west London, but there is no record of Mrs. Greville having lived there at this time. Her house was 23 Wilton Crescent, Knightsbridge, less than a quarter of a mile away (see n. 65 above).

94. Louisa, marchioness of Waterford (1818–91), mixed with HJ's friends Fanny Kemble and Mrs. Greville during these years. Her London address was 30 Charles Street, St. James's. Louisa and her sister, Charlotte, Lady Canning, daughters of Sir Charles Stuart, 1st and last Baron Stuart de Rothesay, British ambassador to France and Russia,

that Lady Waterford was illustrational, historically, preciously so, meeting one's largest demand for the blest recovery, when possible, of some glimmer of the sense of personal beauty, to say nothing of personal "accomplishment", as our fathers were appointed to enjoy it. Scarce to be sated that form of wonder, to my own imagination, I confess—so that I fairly believe there was no moment at which I wouldn't have been ready to turn my back for the time even on the most triumphant actuality of form and feature if a chance apprehension of a like force as it played on the sensibility of the past had competed. And this for a reason I fear I can scarce explain—unless, when I come to consider it, by the perversity of a conviction that the conditions of beauty have improved, though those of character, in the fine old sense, may not, and that with these the measure of it is more just, the appreciation, as who should say, more competent and the effect more completely attained.

What the question seems thus to come to would be a consuming curiosity as to any cited old case of the spell in the very interest of one's catching it comparatively "out"; in the interest positively of the likelihood of one's doing so, and this in the face of so many great testifying portraits. My private perversity, as I here glance at it, has had its difficulties—most of all possibly that of one's addiction, in growing older, to allowing a supreme force to one's earlier, even one's earliest, estimates of physical felicity; or in other words that of the felt impulse to leave the palm for good looks to those who have reached out to it through the medium of our own history. If the conditions *grow* better for them why then should we have almost the habit of thinking better of our handsome folk dead than of our living?—and even to the very point of not resenting on the part of others similarly affected the wail of wonder as to what has strangely "become" of the happy types *d'antan*.[95] I dodge that inquiry just now—we may meet it again; noting simply the fact that "old" pretenders to the particular crown I speak of—and in the sense especially of the pretension made rather for than by them—offered to my eyes a greater interest than the new, whom I was ready enough to take for granted, as one for the most part easily could; belonging as it exactly did on the other hand to the interest of their elders that *this* couldn't be so taken. That was just the attraction of the latter

------

were distinguished figures in Victorian society (Novick, *Young Master,* 359–61; and Augustus J. C. Hare, *The Story of Two Noble Lives,* 3 vols. [London: George Allen, 1893]).

95. Former times, "days of yore" (archaic).

claim—that the grounds of it had to be made out, puzzled out verily on occasion, but that when they were recognised they had a force all their own. One would have liked to be able to clear the distinction between the new and the old of all ambiguity—explain, that is, how little the super-ficially invidious term was sometimes noted as having in common with the elderly: so much was it a clear light held up to the question that truly beautiful persons might be old without being elderly. Their juniors couldn't be new, unfortunately, without being youthful—unfortunately because the fact of youth, so far from dispelling ambiguity, positively introduced it. One made up one's mind thus that the only sure specimens were, and had to be, those acquainted with time, and with whom time, on its side, was acquainted; those in fine who had borne the test and still looked at it face to face. These were of one's own period of course—one looked at *them* face to face; one blessedly hadn't to consider them by hearsay or to refer to any portrait of them for proof: indeed in presence of the resisting, the gained, cases one found one's self practically averse to old facts or old traditions of portraiture, accompanied by no matter what names.[96]

All of which leads by an avenue I trust not unduly majestic up to that hour of contemplation during which I could see quite enough for the major interest what was meant by Lady Waterford's great reputation. Nothing could in fact have been more informing than so to see what was meant, than so copiously to share with admirers who had had their vision and passed on; for if I spoke above of her image as illustrational this is because it affected me on the spot as so diffusing information. My impression was of course but the old story—to which my reader will feel himself treated, I fear, to satiety: when once I had drawn the curtain for the light

96. HJ's musings on an earlier epoch with its nostalgia-inducing potential for inflating impressions of beauty to the detriment of later times and customs nevertheless recognizes the greatness of character that attaches to the great women (*grandes dames* perhaps) of earlier, Victorian days. Lady Louisa seemingly played no very significant part in his life, but it is clear that she represents the values and even appearance of a period to which he felt drawn. In this mood, it is possible that HJ intended to go on to memorialize Mrs. Fanny Kemble, a more important figure in his life, the center of a dynamic social network, with recollections of life on both sides of the Atlantic. In a less constrained but more sinister fictional medium, his incomplete novel *The Sense of the Past* explores the attractions of travel into a past that, despite its romantic attractions, can prove treacherous and poten-tially destructive, equipped to detect and unveil any discrepancies or transgressions in the appearance or behavior (his secret self) of the time-traveling hero from the present.

shed by this or that or the other personal presence upon the society more or less intimately concerned in producing it the last thing I could think of was to darken the scene again. For this right or this wrong reason then Mrs. Greville's admirable guest struck me as flooding it; indebted in the highest degree to every art by which a commended appearance may have formed the habit of still suggesting commendation, she certainly—to my imagination at least—triumphed over time in the sense that if the years, in their generosity, went on helping her to live her grace returned the favour by paying life back to them. I mean that she reanimated for the fond analyst the age in which persons of her type could so greatly flourish—it being ever so pertinently of her type, or at least of that of the age, that she was regarded as having cast the spell of genius as well as of beauty. She painted, and on the largest scale, with all confidence and facility, and nothing could have contributed more, by my sense, to what I glance at again as her illustrational value than the apparently widespread appreciation of this fact—taken together, that is, with one's own impression of the work of her hand. There it was that, like Mrs. Greville herself, yet in a still higher degree, she bore witness to the fine old felicity of the fortunate and the "great" under the "old" order which would have made it so good then to live could one but have been in their shoes. She determined in me, I remember, a renewed perception of the old order, a renewed insistence on one's having come just in time to see it begin to stretch back: a little earlier one wouldn't have had the light for this perhaps, and a little later it would have receded too much.[97]

The precious persons, the surviving figures, who held up, as I may call it, the light were still here and there to be met; my sense being that the last of them, at least for any vision of mine, has now quite gone and that illustration—not to let that term slip—accordingly fails. We all now illustrate together, in higgledy-piggledy fashion, or as a vast monotonous mob, our own wonderful period and order, and nothing else; whereby the

97. Anne Thackeray Ritchie's stepniece Virginia Woolf admired HJ's broad characterization of Mrs. Greville and Lady Waterford: "He recalls the high-handed manner in which these ladies took their way through life, baffling the very stroke of age and disaster with their unquenchable optimism, ladling out with both hands every sort of gift upon their passage, and bringing to port in their tow the most incongruous and battered of derelicts. . . . Personality, whatever one may mean by it, seems to have been accorded a licence for the expression of itself for which we can find no parallel in the present day" ("The Old Order," 90-91).

historic imagination, under its acuter need of facing backward, gropes before it with a vain gesture, missing, or all but missing, the concrete *other,* always other, specimen which has volumes to give where hearsay has only snippets. The old, as we call it, I recognise, doesn't disappear all at once; the *ancien régime* of our commonest reference survived the Revolution of our most horrific in patches and scraps, and I bring myself to say that even at my present writing I am aware of more than one individual on the scene about me touched *comparatively* with the elder grace. (I think of the difference between these persons and so nearly all other persons as a grace for reasons that become perfectly clear in the immediate presence of the former, but of which a generalising account is difficult.) None the less it used to be one of the finest of pleasures to acclaim and cherish, in case of meeting them, one and another of the *complete* examples of the conditions irrecoverable, even if, as I have already noted, they were themselves least intelligently conscious of these; and for the enjoyment of that critical emotion to draw one's own wanton line between the past and the present. The happy effect of such apparitions as Lady Waterford, to whom I thus undisseverably cling, though I might give her after all much like company, was that they made one draw it just where they might most profit from it. They profited in that they recruited my group of the fatuously fortunate, the class, as I seemed to see it, that had had the longest and happiest innings in history—happier and longer, on the whole, even than their congeners of the old French time— and for whom the future wasn't going to be, by most signs, anything like as bland and benedictory as the past. They placed *themselves* in the right perspective for appreciation, and did it quite without knowing, which was half the interest; did it simply by showing themselves with all the right grace and the right assurance. It was as if they had come up to the very edge of the ground that was going to begin to fail them; yet looking over it, looking on and on always, with a confidence still unalarmed. One would have turned away certainly from the sight of any actual catastrophe, wouldn't have watched the ground nearly fail, in a particular case, without a sense of gross indelicacy. I can scarcely say how vivid I felt the drama so preparing might become—that of the lapse of immemorial protection, that of the finally complete exposure of the immemorially protected.[98] It might

98. Given HJ's perspective here on the overlapping phases of history and the comparatively untroubled years of the late-Victorian era, it is hardly surprising that, soon after

take place rather more intensely before the footlights of one's inner vision than on the trodden stage of Cadogan Place or wherever, but it corresponded none the less to realities all the while in course of enactment and which only wanted the attentive enough spectator. Nothing should I evermore see comparable to the large fond consensus of admiration enjoyed by my beatific fellow-guest's imputed command of the very palette of the Venetian and other masters—Titian's, Bonifazio's, Rubens's, where did the delightful agreement on the subject stop? and never again should a noble lady be lifted so still further aloft on the ecstatic breath of connoisseurship.[99]

This last consciousness, confirming my impression of a climax that could only decline, didn't break upon me all at once but spread itself through a couple of subsequent occasions into which my remembrance of the dinner at Mrs. Greville's was richly to play. The first of these was a visit to an exhibition of Lady Waterford's paintings held, in Carlton House Terrace,[100] under the roof of a friend of the artist, and, as it enriched the hour also to be able to feel, a friend, one of the most generously gracious, of my own; during which the reflection that "they" had indeed had their innings, and were still splendidly using for the purpose the very fag-end of the waning time, mixed itself for me with all the "wonderful colour" framed and arrayed, that blazed from the walls of the kindly great room, lent for the advantage of a charity, and lost itself in the general chorus of immense comparison and tender consecration. Later on a few days spent

---

the time of writing, he would feel overwhelmed at the cataclysm of the Great War and its wholesale slaughter of young men. He recorded in his Diary in early August 1914, "Everything blackened over and for the time blighted by the hideous Public situation. This is (Monday) the Aug. Bank Holiday—but with horrible suspense and the worst possibilities in the air" (*CN*, 407–8). As if repeating his Civil War experiences, HJ made hospital visits to wounded soldiers as his own health also deteriorated ("The Long Wards" [1916], *Henry James on Culture*, 169–76).

99. Bonifazio (not Paolo) Veronese (1487–1553) was born in Verona Bonifazio de' Pitati. Lady Louisa Waterford was an accomplished watercolorist and had been taught drawing by Ruskin.

100. Carlton House Terrace, an exclusive address in the St. James's area, housed a number of prime ministers in the Victorian period. Lady Louisa's family bought 4 Carlton House Terrace in 1837, five years before her marriage. She exhibited her work quite regularly at a variety of venues, including the Grosvenor Gallery. HJ is referring here to number 17, the home of Russell Sturgis, the wealthy father of Howard Sturgis, whom HJ frequently visited at Queen's Acre, Windsor.

at a house of the greatest beauty and interest in Northumberland did wonders to round off my view; the place, occupied for the time by genial tenants, belonged to the family of Lady Waterford's husband[101] and fairly bristled, it might be said, with coloured designs from her brush . . .[102]

101. Lady Louisa Waterford's husband was an Irish nobleman, Henry de la Poer Beresford, 3rd Marquess of Waterford. When he died in a riding accident, Ford Castle, in the village of Ford, Northumberland, passed to her, and from 1859 she began an extensive restoration of the building and became involved in local philanthropic work. She spent much of her time there until her death; there is no mention of other tenants of the castle in biographical sources.

102. Virginia Woolf's brilliant review of the incomplete volume offers appropriately elegiac insights, while acutely observing HJ's incurable revisionary need: "Although we are aware that we shall hear his voice no more, there is no hint of exhaustion or of leave-taking; the tone is as rich and deliberate as if time were unending and matter infinite; what we have seems to be but the prelude to what we are to have, but a crumb, as he says, of a banquet now forever withheld. Someone speaking once incautiously in his presence of his 'completed' works drew from him the emphatic assertion that never, never so long as he lived could there be any talk of completion; his work would end only with his life; and it seems in accord with this spirit that we should feel ourselves pausing, at the end of a paragraph, while in imagination the next great wave of the wonderful voice curves into fullness" ("The Old Order," 86). Edel, however, suggests that the volume's incompletion resulted not from the increasing infirmities of age but from a lack of motive: HJ had reached the point in this account where his subject had become the independent professional writer, living alone and established in the Old World. *TMY* "was never completed, although Henry lived long enough and had the vigour to write it. He had achieved solitude in his art; but the subject of his art had always been family relations, and personal relations. In reality there was no personal autobiography that he wanted to write, once removed from the frame of Family" (*The Master*, 451–52). HJ's typescript ends with a simple period: the three periods of the first edition, emphasizing incompletion, are Lubbock's, which, Hannah Sullivan argues in "Passionate Correction: The Theory and Practice of Modernist Revision" (Ph.D. diss., Harvard University, 2008), helped further justify his case for publication of *TMY*.

# "DEAR BRIGHT LITTLE MINNY"

## Mary Temple's Twenty-Three Letters to John Chipman Gray, 1869–1870

Henry James received some of his best reviews for *Notes of a Son and Brother*, many critics agreeing that the final chapter, which presents a selection of Mary Temple's letters, formed an appropriate climax to the work.[1] The twenty-three letters cover the final months of her life and were written between 7 January 1869 and 16 February 1870; she died three weeks later, aged twenty-four. They might never have been included had their recipient, John Chipman Gray, elderly and in ill health, not called round to see James's sister-in-law, Alice Howe Gibbens James, in Irving Street, Cambridge, in May 1913.[2] It was with Alice James that the question of what should happen to the letters resided, and it was she who was instrumental in their finally appearing in *Notes of a Son and Brother*. In their record of Mary Temple's search for spiritual solace, her determined resolution not to be defeated by consumption, and her all-too-short enjoyment of everyday pleasures, the letters make moving reading. But the circumstances of their early twentieth-century publication in one of the last complete works of a highly respected author are also redolent of age and a sense of lives reaching conclusion.

Just a few years earlier Gray had shown William James one of the letters in which he was admiringly mentioned. William replied,

> I am deeply grateful to you for sending me this letter, which revives all sorts of poignant memories, and makes Minny live again in all her lightness and freedom. Few spirits have been *freer* than hers. I find myself wishing so that she could know me as I am now—as for knowing her as *she* is now—??!!!—
>
> I find that she means as much, in the way of human character, for me now as ever she did, being unique, and with no analogue in all my subsequent experience of people. Thank you once more, dear John, for what you have done![3]

By the time of Gray's 1913 visit to Alice, William had died, and Gray, feeling himself close to death, sought his widow's advice: should he destroy this substantial collection? His sharing of the letters with her indicates a conviction that they should, in some way, be preserved.

Writing to her brother-in-law after Gray's visit, Alice James recounts the circumstances of the visit, and why she feels the letters should be entrusted to another surviving member of that circle—Henry James himself, still engaged in the "Family Book," the project he had been encouraged to begin after William's death:

> I was telephoned one morning to know if I should be at home that afternoon early when Mr Gray would call. After he had rested a bit he told me why he had come, that he had some letters from Minnie Temple which he was uncertain how to dispose of. "Perhaps I ought to burn them but I shrink from doing it," and he went on to say that he would give them to me, to keep or to destroy. He does not wish them given to her family. Of course I asked if I might give them to you. He only half assented, repeating "You must read them first, you must be responsible". "*Here they are—*" and he drew the packet from some pocket where I had seen no sign of them.
>
> I did read them—ah, so tenderly—Any one might read them—then I went to see Mr Gray and tell him how beautiful I thought them and again ask him to let me send them to you. He agreed. He said "I have been reading *A Small Boy* and I can trust his taste and judgment."
>
> It is a gallant and haunting record—almost too perfect to be broken up—but you will know how to use it for some memorial of her. The second time I saw him I promised to show him the copies of your letters, the two written on hearing of Minnie's death[4]—it seemed the only generous thing to do after he had given you the right to use his— and I felt as if you would say "Do it." He thought your letters most beautiful and just, and he added slowly, "I too was never in love with her." I liked better to write to her than to see her." She was the only *just* woman I have ever known. Her friendship is one of the things in my life which I best like to remember." If only he could have given the letters to William! How he would have prized them![5]

It is understandable that Alice felt that William would have made an appropriate guardian of the letters, which indeed make fuller reference to him than to Henry.[6] It is also clear that she recognized the importance of her own role in dealing with them appropriately. In a letter of 14 March 1914, congratulating James on his achievement in evoking that distant time, she writes that she regards herself as a part of the same generation, but unlike Minny, she was granted a long and fulfilling life: "I love to think that in ever so humble a way I could help this record to see the light. You may not understand in the least how I feel but it almost seems as if I had had all that she deserved. Were you ever haunted by a 'vicarious atonement' feeling? That some one else was going without that you might be blessed?"[7]

Henry, despite his increasingly fragile physical and mental condition, had acted quickly, incorporating a selection of the letters into his current volume, as he later recalled:

> They came, & when I had read them (with *such* irresistible tears!) I recognized my chance to do what I had always longed in some way to do without seeing quite how—reserve & preserve in some way from oblivion, commemorate & a little *enshrine,* the image of our admirable & exquisite, our noble and unique little Minnie. . . . that last chapter of the book has been extraordinarily acclaimed (with all the rest) in this country—where I can best judge of the impression, & dear Minnie's name is *really* now, in the most touching way, I think, silvered over & set apart.[8]

As with so many of Henry James's dealings with letters (not to mention comparable scenes in his fiction), strong feelings were aroused as he examined these surviving documents; he characterizes elsewhere the potency of such materials: "Boxfuls of ghosts and echoes, a swarm of apparitions and reverberations as dense as any set free by the lifted lid of Pandora."[9] Their content was still capable (Pandora-like) of causing hurt even after so many years, with relatives of the people mentioned still living. And the novelist's seeming obliviousness to the sensitivities of surviving and interested members of the family added to the potential for revived pain. Minny's younger sister Ellen, for instance, was understandably offended that neither she nor her other surviving sister, Henrietta—legally having some rights over the letters)—had been consulted about the material or its publication. The fault may not have been entirely James's on this occasion: Gray had stipulated that on no account must the documents be returned to any surviving relatives of Minny. It was a condition James found easy to comply with. He privately (and scathingly) commented of Ellen that he couldn't, in any case, communicate "over such depths of illiteracy as surround her" (*HJL*, 4:707).

Dismissive of any close family claims, James next took the kind of irrevocable action familiar from some of the more sensational moments of his own fiction. Having selected and edited Mary Temple's correspondence, he bypassed John Chipman Gray, Alice Howe Gibbens James, and any claims of the original Temple family by destroying the originals: they would survive only through the medium of his "life" account. However calculated this action—it may have seemed to him routine in that he invariably destroyed material once published—James's intention was thwarted. Transcripts of the originals can be seen at the Houghton Library, Harvard University, preserved in the distinctive handwriting of Alice James and her daughter, Mary Margaret. Before mailing them to her brother-in-law, Alice had the foresight to copy out Minny's originals—a laborious though not that unusual a task for the time. It has been suggested that, aware of his abiding need to maintain personal privacy (though it is hardly compromised in these letters), she accurately anticipated James's final move and determined to conserve the letters. This may be so, though given their sentimental value and the trust that Gray had placed in her, it is conceivable (recalling the recent fate of the *Titanic*) that she was also ensuring their survival in light of the dangers of a long voyage across the Atlantic. What she thought on learning of the destruction of the originals is not recorded, but she remained devoted to her brother-in-law, traveling to London to care for him during his final illness, as her dying husband had requested. On the brown manila envelope that contains the letters at the Houghton Library, however, a penciled comment has survived: "The originals of these letters were given by J.C.G. to A.H.J.—She sent them to H.J. who used them & afterwards destroyed them without saying a word to her." Alice Howe James's handwriting appears on the envelope, but these accusatory words, in another hand, were probably written by her son Harry, who had had his own tense exchanges with his uncle concerning the latter's use and sometimes questionable treatment of his father's letters in *Notes of a Son and Brother*.

When *Notes of a Son and Brother* appeared—whatever the family hurts or editorial sleights of hand—the Mary Temple letters were highly regarded. This clearly pleased James, all too aware as he was of the impending world war and the contrast with the days when the letters were written. He wrote to his sister-in-law on 18 March 1914, "I hope you will think that the use I have made of M.T.'s letters is as interesting as it *could* have been, & that J.G. will think so, poor dear man—if, ill & detached as he is, he still thinks or cares about anything. The whole working-in of Minnie was difficult & delicate—highly so; but I seem already to gather here that my evocation of her appears by her touchingness & beauty, the 'stroke,' or success, of the book."[10] Her letters perhaps suggest some of the qualities attributed to that more traveled and richer young woman who (unlike Minny) did reach Europe and for whom she served as a model, Milly Theale (another M.T.). In terms of their moral and emotional insight they might be thought to compensate in some way for our sense of loss as readers at the end of *The Wings of the Dover* when we are left to imagine the contents of the letter the dying Milly Theale left for Morton Densher.

### THE TEXT OF THE LETTERS

We can do no more than assume that Alice and Mary Margaret's transcriptions are accurate. The women seem to have shared the task of copying the letters fairly equally, and I have retained the minor orthographic features that characterize each. Alice transcribed the first five letters (7 January to 2 April 1869), Margaret Mary the next twelve (24 April to November 1869); the last six letters were split evenly between mother and daughter, Alice copying those of 21 and 30 November 1869 and 25 January 1870 (with its covering letter of 27 January), Margaret Mary the letters of 12 and 30 December 1869 and 16 February 1870.

An examination of these documents will allow readers to draw comparisons with the extracts that appear in the final chapter of *Notes of a Son and Brother*.[11] The entire sequence has never before been published;[12] it becomes clear in the comparison that in James's text Mary Temple appears more formal, earnest, and grammatically correct. The letters are fascinating and important for what they reveal of the dynamics of a young woman's life of the period and, on a more introspective level, for their representation of issues of belief and faith, and for the evidence of human courage and resilience they offer.

The letters appear without editorial notes; those portions included in the text of *Notes of a Son and Brother* have, of course, already received some editorial attention.[13]

### A NOTE ON TRANSCRIPTION

Alice Howe James tends to place punctuation outside quotation marks while Mary Margaret places punctuation within. Her mother sometimes separates (as James himself did) elided words (e.g., "does n't"), a fairly common practice at the time; I have retained this feature. Alice's lower- and uppercase letters are sometimes indistinguishable. Other punctuation marks are inconsistently used: dashes often replace periods, but commas too can be indicated just by a small horizontal mark. When necessary, or where the mark is ambiguous, I have simply used my judgment. I have not indicated the occasional crossing out or amending of a word, since it is unlikely to reflect a change made by the original author. Mary Margaret rarely indents the openings of paragraphs, but, for the sake of clarity, I have indented them. The occasional nonstandard spelling, punctuation, or usage is noted simply by a *sic* in square brackets. Sometimes a small space is left between two sentences within a line and, from the sense, I have taken this to indicate a paragraph break. Dates of letters have been given as they appear in the transcripts. In the letter dated 12 December 1869, transcribed by Mary Margaret, which discusses the preaching of Phillips Brooks, I have amended one sentence in accordance with the transcriber's intentions. It reads, "I felt so myself last winter about it, in Philadelphia," but the transcriber has written the figures "2" and "1" over two of the phrases indicating a reversal of order, presumably having mis-copied Mary Temple's original sentence, which would have read, "I felt so myself about it, last winter in Philadelphia." Alice James concludes her transcription of Letter 4 by continuing its final line up the left-hand margin of the page.

NOTES

The title comes from Mary James's words on Mary Temple's death, quoted by HJ (*HJL*, 1:219).

1. For a list of British periodicals in which *NSB* (as well as *SBO*) was reviewed, see Carol Holly, "The British Reception of Henry James's Autobiographies," *American Literature* 57 (December 1985): 573.

2. For an account of Alice James's life and her role in the James family, see Susan E. Gunter, *Alice in Jamesland: The Story of Alice Howe Gibbens James* (Lincoln: University of Nebraska Press, 2009).

3. William James to John Chipman Gray, 17 March [no year], bMS Am 1092.1 (39), Houghton. HJ gives the letter, with just a few changes, in *NSB*, chap. 13.

4. One to his mother, 26 March 1870, and one to WJ, 29 March 1870 (*Complete Letters of Henry James, 1855–1872*, ed. Pierre A. Walker and Greg W. Zacharias [Lincoln: University of Nebraska Press, 2006], 2:335–41; 341–49).

5. MS letter from Alice Howe Gibbens James to Henry James, 17 May 1913, bMS Am 1092.11 (53), Houghton; punctuation matches the original.

6. For a discussion of William James's relationship with Mary Temple, see Robert Richardson, *William James: In the Maelstrom of American Modernism* (Boston: Houghton Mifflin, 2007), 96–99, 108–13. On first hearing of Mary's death, "On a page of his

diary all by itself he drew a crude grave marker with the initials M.T. and the date of her death" (ibid., 112).

7. See bMS Am 1092.11 (54), Houghton.

8. S. P. Rosenbaum, "Letters to the Pell-Clarkes from Their 'Old Cousin and Friend' Henry James," *American Literature* 31 (March 1959): 53. The letter, of 5 May 1914, was written to Henrietta Pell-Clarke, Minny's youngest sister.

9. HJ, *William Wetmore Story and His Friends* (2 vols. bound as one, London: Thames and Hudson, n.d.), 1:14.

10. See bMS Am 1094 (1745), Houghton.

11. For HJ's practice of revising letters, see *HJL*, 4:793–804; William Hoffa, "The Final Preface: Henry James's Autobiography," *Sewanee Review* 77 (Spring 1969): 277–93; Alfred Habegger, "Henry James's Rewriting of Minny Temple's Letters," *American Literature* 58 (May 1986): 159–80; and Tamara Follini, "Pandora's Box: The Family Correspondence in *Notes of a Son and Brother*," *Cambridge Quarterly* 25, no. 1 (1996): 26–40.

12. Held at the Houghton Library, bMS Am 1092.12 (in four folders). Habegger reproduced the first four letters after discussing their revisions in "Henry James's Rewriting of Minny Temple's Letters." He considers "what Minnie meant for James" as well as her other extant letters in *Henry James and the "Woman Business"* ([Cambridge: Cambridge University, 1989], 126–49).

13. Four of the letters from Mary Temple to HJ, incidentally, were published in Robert C. Le Clair, "Henry James and Minny Temple," *American Literature* 21 (March 1949): 35–48. They contain a few transcription errors, according to Leon Edel; HJ's letters to Minny have not survived (*Henry James: The Untried Years, 1843–1870* [London: Rupert Hart-Davis, 1953], 318, 351n).

# Twenty-three Letters from Mary Temple to John Chipman Gray

LETTER 1

Pelham January 7*th* 1869

Dear Mr Gray—

I will write you as nice a letter as I know how, but I would much rather have a nice talk with you. As I can't have the best thing, however, I must (contrary to my pet theory) put up with the second best. But for fear you should follow in my footsteps, let me repeat, emphatically that this is a wicked thing to do, on general principles—I got your letter a few days ago, and I hope you remark the forgiving way in which I answer in *two* days' time, charitably ignoring the *years* that yours took in coming. But I am afraid my charity begins at home, in this case—I feel as if I were in Heaven today. And all because the day is fine, and I have been driving about all the morning in a little sleigh, in the fresh air and sunshine, until in spite of myself, I found I had stopped asking for the time being, the usual mental question of why I was born—I am not going to Canada—I know no better reason for this, than because I said I *was* going. I like to be out here in the country, and Kitty likes to have me with her. This being the case, her husband makes such a clamor when I propose to leave, that I am easily persuaded, by his kindness and my own want of energy, to stay where I am. It is great fun living out here. The weather you know is fine & I knock about all day in a sleigh, & do nothing but enjoy the sunshine, & meditate. Then we are so near the town, that we go in very often, for the day, & do a little shopping, lunch with some of our numerous friends, and come out again, with a double relish for the country. We all went in, on a spree, the other night, & stayed at the Everett House, from which, as a starting point, we poured in, in strong force, upon Mrs Gracie King's ball—a very grand affair, given for a very pretty Miss King, at Del Monico's. On this occasion the raiding party consisted of thirteen Emmets, & a moderate supply of Temples. The ball was a great success—I had not been to one before in two years, & I liked it very much. So much that I mean to try it again very soon, at the next Assembly—The men in Society, in New York, this winter, are principally a lot of feeble-minded boys—but I was fortunate enough to escape them, as my partner for the German was a man of about 35—the solitary *man* I believe in the room—and curiously enough, I had danced my last German, two years ago before, in that very place, with the same person. He is a Mr Lee, a man who has spent nearly all his life abroad. Two of his sisters have married German princes—& he from knocking about so much has become a thorough man of the world, and as he is intelligent, with nothing to do but amuse himself, he is a very agreeable partner for the German, & I mean to dance another with him soon—I don't know why I have tried your patience by writing about an individual that you have never seen. This is merely to show you that I have not retired irrevocably from the world, the flesh & the devil. I am conscious of a very faint Charm about it still, when taken in small doses. So you think Lizzie Boott more wide awake than she used to be. It is only that you are getting to know her better. I do not wonder that *two* such undemonstrative creatures as you two are, can't make much of each other. I agree with you perfectly about Uncle Henry. I should think he would be very irritating to the legal mind—He is not at all satisfactory even to mine. Have you seen much of Willy James lately? That is a rare creature, and one in whom my *intellect* (if you will pardon the mis-application of the word) takes more solid satisfaction than in almost anybody—I had begun to think that you did n't mean to write anymore, and that *name* which you called me at parting, must have been expressive of your greatest disapprobation—"Pyramid" I think it was, which, as far as I can make out is a cold, hard, unsympathetic, uninteresting body. I am sure I am much obliged to you, Sir, for your opinion of me—When I go in to town, I generally meet Mrs Clymer in the cars. She is quite a pretty woman, I think, & I always feel very sorry for her. There is something pathetic to me about her. She has had a legal divorce, I hear, so you can marry her now, if you like, but perhaps, being a lawyer, you had something to do with getting her out of it. Oh, by the way, I hope you got something pretty for yourself with the forty-two dollars (was n't it?) that I saw you had received from the public treasury, some time ago—How gratifying and consoling it is, when our friends don't write to us, to have the newspaper furnish us with these interesting items about them. I have n't read Browning's new book—I mean to wait till you are by to explain it to me—which reminds me, along with what you say about wishing for the spring, that I mean to go to Conway next summer. Mr Boott says he will take Lizzie there, if we go, so I think it very likely that Aunt Charlotte will go, with Elly, Henrietta & myself. In that case, you may as well make up your mind to a little visit there yourself, as I can't wait any longer than that to have Browning read to me. Arthur Sedgwick sent me Matthew Arnold's likeness, which Harry had said was very disappointing—but I do not, on the whole, find it so—

on the contrary, after having looked at it a good many times, I like it. It quite harmonizes with my notion of him, & I always had an affection for him. So Christmas has come and gone again, and we are beginning another year—I am glad it is fairly over. Anniversaries are apt to be sad things when one gets as old as I am. As for wishes and hopes for the new year you have my best. I can only say that I hope you may be happier this year than you have ever been before, (as indeed you ought to be, if you take that great step.) You must write to me and tell me something that you are *sure* is true. I don't care much what it is, & I will take your word for it. Things get into a muddle with me—How can I give you "a start on the way of righteousness"? I think you know that way better than I do. The only thing that I can say is—Don't stop saying your prayers—& God bless you. Inside of that, I hardly know what is right or what wish to give you for the new year. You told me not to write you a sheet and a half, in a big hand—Have I not obeyed you with a vengeance? If you don't like such a long letter, I give you leave to retaliate in the same manner—tit-for-tat. And now goodbye—Address to Pelham—I am here, indefinitely—and Believe me always yours

Most sincerely

Mary Temple.

("Kitty" took rooms at the Blue Blinds Conway)

Addressed to
John C. Gray jr Esq.
No 4 Pemberton Square
Boston Massachusetts.


LETTER 2

Pelham, January 27*th* 1869

Dear Mr Gray,

This might be headed with that line of a hymn, "Hark, from the tombs!" &c—but perhaps it won't prove as bad as that. It looks pretty doubtful still, but I have a sort of feeling that I shall get the better of it, this one time more—by which I don't mean to brag, or I may have to pay for my proud boastings. The "it," of which I speak, is, of course, my old enemy, hemorrhage, of which I have had plenty within the last week— seven pretty big ones, & several little ones, hardly worth the name. I don't know what has come over me—I can't stop them—but as I said, I mean to try & beat them yet. Of course I am in bed, where I shall be, indefinitely—

not allowed to speak one word, literally, even in a whisper—The reason I write this, is because I don't think it will hurt me at all, if I take it easy, & stop when I feel tired. It is a pleasant break in the monotony of eating gruel, and thinking of the proximity of the grave—and then too, it was so nice to get your letter this morning, that I want another—I would n't be such a baby, or such an Oliver Twist as to cry for more, if I were not ill and weak, indeed I would n't, but I think a few words from somebody who is strong and active, in the good old world, (it seems to me now,) would be very refreshing—And you'll write to me, won't you, even if it does take a little time away from the law, or from Miss Adams—and one thing I want to say before I go any further—Don't tell anybody I wrote this letter to you—because it will be sure to reach the ears of my dear relatives—& it will cause them to sniff the air, & flounce, &c. I mean, of course, only this letter, while I am ill. You will no doubt hear of my illness from other quarters, Lizzie Boott, perhaps, as I wrote a letter to her about a week ago, in which I told her that I had had a very slight hemorrhage, the day before, but I had not gone to bed, & thought nothing of it. Of course this was all wrong—if I had taken care of myself, it might have stopped there—A day or two ago, I found that my letter had not gone, & I added a line to say that the hemorrhages had gone on getting worse & worse. So she will probably tell you, & so you won't perhaps have to tell a lie about it. You see I *am* a good deal of a baby & don't want hear the reproaches of my relatives, on this, or any other subject. Kitty says I may write to you—& that is enough—She takes good care of me—& all the Emmets are so good & kind, that I found, when it came to the point, that there was a good deal that made life attractive, & that if the choice were given to me, I would a good deal rather stay up here, on the solid earth, in the air and sunshine, with an occasional sympathetic glimpse of another person's soul, than to be put down, under the earth, and say good bye forever to humanity— with all its laughter and its sadness. But you must n't think that I am in any special danger of dying just at present, or that I am in low spirits—for it is not so. The Dr. tells me that I am not in any danger, even if the hemor- rhages should keep on—"but you can't fool a regular boarder" as Mr Holmes would say, & I can't see why there is any reason to think they will heal, a week later, when I shall be weaker than now, if they can't heal now—however, *I* think they are going to stop *now*. I haven't had one since yesterday at *four*, & now it is three o'clock, nearly twenty four hours. I am of a hopeful temperament, & not easily frightened, which is in my favor. If this *should* prove to be the last letter you get from me, why take it for a good-bye—I'll keep on the look-out for you in the spirit-world, and shall be glad to see you when you come there, provided it is a better place than this—So Robert Winthrop has got Miss Mason after all. May they be 'appy—You had better look out how you talk about too strict a rule—You may "catch a tartar" yet. My praiseworthy effort to cultivate society, has been snubbed by Heaven, apparently, and the snub has been so effectual, that I am afraid it will be a long time before I shall make another attempt. Elly is in town enjoying herself immensely. I have n't let her know how ill I have been, because there were several parties in the last week & I was afraid it might spoil her fun. But Kitty wrote her a note today—& I think she will come to me soon. I did not mean you to infer from my particularizing Willy James'es *intellect,* that the rest of him was not to my liking. He is one of the very few people in this world that I love—"& no mistake." He has the largest heart as well as the largest head—and is thoroughly interesting to me—and he is generous & affectionate & full of sympathy & *humanity.* Don't tell him I said so, though—or he would think I had been telling you a lie, to serve my own purposes. I believe I have written enough now—but I have rested several times, between— Good bye—Mind what I said about not telling anybody that I wrote to you while I was ill—& reward me for the exertion by writing soon to me—

Yours—

Mary Temple

LETTER 3

Pelham February 3rd 1869

Dear Mr Gray—

I can never tell you how much good your letter did me. It was just what I needed, just what I wanted—It did comfort me, & make me happy, and it was impossible to make me think the world was hard to me, at the very moment that you were making me feel the very best thing in it. I see now more than ever that with every trouble there comes a compensating happiness—for how should I ever have known how good and kind you are if I had not been ill?—It is no good to talk about it, but I don't believe you know how far down in my heart I feel it. I wrote a note to you yesterday, in pencil, as I was lying down still, but this morning I decided not to send it, because I feel so much better today, and I think it did not give a bright enough view of the case. It is a week ago today, since I wrote my last letter, I think, & I have only had one more hemorrhage, since—and that was the day after I wrote you. Since then, they have stopped entirely, and I feel pretty sure that I shall have no more this time. I am sitting up in my room today, and I feel as bright as possible. Yesterday when I walked across the room, I felt as if I should never be strong again, but today it is quite different, & I feel that, now that I am fairly out of bed, I shall soon get over being weak—It is so nice to be up again, that my spirits go up, absurdly— It does n't take much to make me forget that I have ever been so ill. Of course you know how much pleasure your letters give me, but I can't help feeling selfish in letting you write. I know I've got no business to keep bothering you, and perhaps, after a while I may have strength of mind enough to stop writing to you, thereby, giving you a chance to stop too. But must I be a Spartan just yet? How can I help liking to get your letters when they are so kind—Perhaps if you were to snub me a little in your next, it might "let me down easy"—As soon as I am able, I am to be taken to town to have my lungs examined, and then when I know my fate, I will do the best I can.

*No* sentiment? And pray, sir, how do you think you are ever going to meet your fate, if this is the way you behave? Remember you are to tell me about it, when the fatal day arrives. The Conway plan has fallen through already—Aunt Charlotte is not well enough to think of taking us—My own plans all depend upon whether I get strong again—And now good-bye. I have compunctions about taking your time, *not* from Miss Adams, I confess, but from criticisms on Mrs Bradwell, & the like. I have n't seen the whole of that yet, but I shall soon have the Review. You really need n't write again, if you don't want to. I shan't think it unfriendly, after your last letter. If you were to get tired & never speak to me again, I should n't mind it—because I can't thank you enough for what you have done already & moreover, sir, you may now let your moustache grow down to your toes, if you like—and I will but smile scornfully at your futile precautions. Here is the end of my paper & only room to sign myself—Yours—M. Temple.

LETTER 4
Pelham March 4*th* 1869
Dear Mr Gray,

I was very glad to get your letter yesterday—I supposed that you might meet Lizzie Boott often, & that she would tell you how I was, as she has been a very constant correspondent, since I have been ill, & I have sent her weekly bulletins concerning myself. And then you know that I told you that as soon as I was well again, I would give you a little holiday—So I kept my word—but I might have kept my promise and still given myself the pleasure of writing to you, when I got ill again after about a ten days' triumph—only I thought that as I had no good news to tell, I would n't write at all—I thought that illness even was hardly a good enough excuse for behaving like a baby, when one had reached the advanced age of twenty-three—and at all Events, I could not quite reconcile it to my conscience, that you, an unprotected man, having done nothing to deserve such treatment at my hands, should be the victim—fine sentiment, wasn't it? Please give me the credit for it.

Well, "to make a long story short" as Hannah says, I caught a cold, & it went to the weak spot, & I had another slight attack of hemorrhage, but I took the necessary steps at once, & stayed in bed & did n't speak for five or six days, & then it stopped, & I felt better than I had at all, since I was first taken ill. This last illness did n't amount to much, and I did n't mind it at all—but I began to get very tired of the constant confinement to my bedroom, and they promised me to take me to town as soon as I was well enough, and perhaps to the opera. This of course would have been a wild excitement for me, and I had charming little plans of music by day & by night, for a week, which I meant to spend with Mrs Griswold. Accordingly a cavalcade set out from here on Monday—consisting of myself, escorted by my sisters and friends, who were to see me safely installed in my new quarters & leave me—I arrived, bundled up, at Mrs Griswold's, & had begun to consider myself already as fairly emancipated from invalidism & nursing—& I was discussing, with Mr Emmet the propriety of my going that evening to hear Faust, which was but the beginning of the mad career upon which I proposed to rush headlong—when Dr Bassett arrived, who is the medical man, that I had meant to consult, *incidentally*, between the pauses in the music, during my stay there. The first thing he said was, "What are you doing here?"—Go directly back to the place you came from, & don't come to the city again till warm weather comes. And as for music, you must n't hear it or even think of it for two months." This was pleasant, but there was nothing to be done, but obey—which I did a few hours later with my trunk which had not been unpacked, and with my immediate plan of life somewhat limited. I say my *immediate* plan because my permanent plan of life was by no means curtailed, but on the contrary expanded & varied in a manner I had not even dared to hope—This came from what the Doctor said subsequently, when he had examined my lungs, that is to say, after he had laid his head affectionately first on one of my shoulders & then on the other, and there kept it solemnly for about ten minutes, in a way that was irresistibly ludicrous, especially with Kitty as spectator. This, I am aware, is a highly indecorous, not to say frivolous view to take of it, but I am proud to say that I controlled my desire to laugh, and awaited his verdict with becoming gravity. He said my lungs were *sound*—that he could not detect the slightest evidences of disease, and that the hemorrhage could not have come from the lung itself, but from the membraneous lining of the lungs and throat—whatever that may be—I know not, but I suppose he does. At all events he gave me to understand that I had as sound a pair of lungs, at present, as the next person—in fact from what he said, one would have thought them a pair that a prize-fighter might covet. At the same time he sent me flying back to the Country, with orders not to get excited, nor to listen to music, nor to speak to anybody I care about, nor to do anything in short that the unregenerate nature longs for. This struck my untutored mind as somewhat inconsistent, and I ventured a gentle remonstrance, which however was not even listened to, and I was ignominiously thrust into a car and borne back to Pelham. The problem still bothers me—Either sound lungs are a very dangerous thing to possess, or there is a foul conspiracy on foot to oppress me—But I cling to the consoling thought of my matchless lungs—& this obliterates my present sufferings.

Pray *why* do you overwork yourself? Is it for the love of *drudging* for its own sake, or have you the starving wife & bare-footed children in view?—I suspect it must be the latter which imparts a magical glow to your intellect. I think it is but natural that you should wish to be able to hold out hopes to that young person to whom you talked an hour and a half the other night, that you would not eventually allow her to starve, if you could help it.

Harry came to see me before he sailed—I am very glad that he has gone, although I don't expect to see him again in a good many years. I do not think he will come back for a long time. I hope it will do him good, & that he will enjoy himself, which he has n't done for several years, I think. I have n't read all of Faust—but I think I know the scenes you call divine, at least I know some that are exquisite. But I don't know the play well enough to judge of Faust's character—Why do you speak so disparagingly of King David, whom I always had a weakness for? Think how charming and loveable a person he must have been—poet, musician & so much else combined—with however their attendant imperfections. I don't think I should care to have been Mrs D. exactly. I am possessed with an overpowering admiration and affection for George Eliot. I don't know why it has so suddenly come over me, but everything I see of hers now-a-days makes me feel a deeper interest in her. I should love to see her—& I hope Harry will—I told him to give my love to her. Do you like her too? I don't remember ever hearing you speak of her. Goodbye. I wish that conventionality would invent some other way of ending a letter than "Yours truly." I am so tired of it, & as one says it to one's shoe-maker it is rather more complimentary to one's friend to dispense with it altogether & sign one's name abruptly, after the manner of Ellen Emerson & other free Boston citizens. But I am a slave to conventionality and therefore again sign myself Yours truly Mary Temple—But conceived with somewhat more of warmth than I would say it to my shoemaker!

LETTER 5
Philadelphia April *2nd* 1869
Dear Mr Gray,
Kitty sent on your last letter to me, as it came after I had left home—Elly and I have been here now for more than a fortnight and are going back to Pelham early next week. I suppose I ought to have something special to say, after having been suddenly transplanted to a new place and among new people, but I believe there is nothing to tell. I came here, because they all thought that the climate might do me good—I don't find however that I feel any difference in my sensations, between this & New York—if I do, it is in favor of New York. I wish it might turn out that an inland climate was not after all necessary for me, as I like the other sort much better, & really think that I feel stronger in it, too. The Doctor told me that Boston would kill me in six months, but that might possibly be a mistake too—I am going to try it a little longer, & then try the Pelham climate again.—I think I shall find I am stronger there than here—It may be that the mental atmosphere is more important than any other—& the truth is I feel homesick nearly all the time—or at least what I call homesick, being away from what is most like home to me—& if I were there, what I should call tired— The Whites are the kindest creatures imaginable, & do everything to make me comfortable, and the worst of it is, that they won't let us go home—and I can't tell them that I am tired out & want to go back to Kitty, because that would n't be civil, and as they won't let us go till I give them a good reason, and as there *is* no good reason why I should *ever* go, except that I want to, I am distraught with the consciousness of my own feeble-mindedness & inability to cope with these peculiar circumstances. The chief object I had in coming, was to hear Phillips Brooks. And I have heard him several times—and I think I was not disappointed. To be sure

he did not say anything new or startling, but I certainly ought not to have expected that, though I believe I did have a secret hope that he was going to expound to me the old beliefs with a clearness that would convince me & forever banish doubt. I had placed all my hopes in Phillips Brooks, as the one man I had heard of, who, progressive in all other ways, had yet been able to keep his faith firm in things that most earnest men have left far behind them—but of course, in preaching to his congregation he did not touch upon the real difficulties at all. He was leading them forward, instead of trying to make it clear to me that I had any good reason for the *feeling* that I *have*—But it was something at least to feel that he had the feeling too—and was not afraid to trust it—& live for it. I wonder what he really does think about it all—and whether he ever feels the reaction I feel about Thursday which is sure to follow the enthusiasm & confidence made by his eloquence & earnestness on Sunday—Tomorrow will be Saturday, and I shall be glad when Sunday comes to wind me up again for I feel sadly run down tonight, and as if I should like to see some honest old pagan & shake him by the hand. It will seem all right and easy again soon, I know, but is it always so?—Is there no more of that undoubting Faith in the world that used to be? But I won't talk any more about it now, or I shan't sleep, as it is getting late now, & all themes except utterly dull ones should be put away—so I'll tell you about the people here. Mr White, you remember of old. He looks as much as ever like a contemplative & ancient monkey. William White is still the soul of kindness, and flies wildly about doing little errands of mercy—thrusting little benches under my feet, & cushions behind my back, & making me generally comfortable—I have seen several of the Philadelphia men, who are supposed to be ornaments of society—none of them are at all striking however—the only one I care to see again is a disconsolate widower with three children—He is only 29 & very melancholy & excites my pity. He is only your age, and just think how much he has gone through already. I am going to Newport the latter part of this month. Lizzie Boott and her father are to be there at the same time. There is a great deal more I should like to say to you—but I am awfully tired, and I believe I must stop. How is Mr Holmes now-a-days? Tell him, when you see him, with affectionate regards from me, (you might say *kind* regards) that I drank his health on the 8*th* of March and wished him three times twenty-eight years. I am going to Pelham on Monday if can accomplish it, and if not, as soon as may be. "So write" to me at Pelham and believe me always yours, Mary Temple. This letter is altogether the most *disgusting* letter in its appearance that I have ever seen. Pray excuse it. I have folded it about a dozen times—& it is too unladylike for anything. If I had a bit of strength remaining I would write it over—but I can't do it.

LETTER 6
Pelham April 24*th* 1869
Dear Mr Gray—

I have made several attempts lately to write you a letter, but I have given it up after two or three pages, because I have always been in a blue state of mind at the time, & I have each time charitably decided before it was too late, to spare you. But if I were to wait until things change to rose-color, I might perhaps wait till I die, or longer even, in which case your next communication from me would be a spiritual one. I am going to Newport in the early part of May, to meet the Bootts. Henrietta has just come back from there, delighted with her visit, why Heaven knows I suppose—but I don't—except that she is in that blissful state of babyhood peculiar to herself where everything seems delightful. I was afraid she would find it gloomy, Aunt Charlotte being so ill, & there being no young people in the house. But she didn't mind it, & was enchanted with everything. She is such a good little girlie—"long may she wave!—" I had a letter yesterday from Lizzie Boott, from Cambridge, where she is staying with her cousin, Miss Greenough—which name, by the way of the time I saw you a year ago, when I was teasing you to tell me the name of a certain individual, do you remember? & Miss Greenough was one that I pounced upon in my promiscuous guessing, because she had *light hair,* among other characteristics. My curiosity was great then, and is as great now, not to know her name, but her fate—I mean in your regard—Is she just where she was, or has she gone up or down, upon nearer view? Is she head and shoulders above all other women in the world to you, or has another one arisen, and overtopped her?—Do you think it impertinent for me to ask such a question?—If you do, don't mind telling me to hold my tongue—But you know I take an interest in this affair, & you must remember that a whole year has gone by since I saw you in Newport, and in these affairs one doesn't stand still a year, at your age, & there has been ample time for further developement [*sic*] one way or the other—Don't forget to tell me in your next letter, whether you still love her "best"—Alas! I fear me, that I shall hear that you don't—that like everything else, it was a delusion, pleasing while it lasted—

I like George Eliot, not through her poem so much, or nearly so much as her prose—While I was ill I read The Mill on the Floss, which I liked very much, & Felix Holt, I remember I liked immensely—The creature interests me, personally, & I feel a desire to know something about her life—how far her lofty moral sentiments have served her practically—for instance in her dealings with Lewes—I see that she understands the character of a *generous* woman, that is, of a woman who believes in generosity, & who must be that or nothing, & who feels keenly, notwithstanding, how hard it is practically to follow it out, & how, (looking at it from the point of view of comfort as far as this world goes,) it "pays" not at all—

We are having warm weather here quite like summer, & rather depressing—I don't feel very well, & am always catching cold—that is I suppose I am, as I have a cough nearly all the time, & am not by any means as strong as Sampson.

As for Mr Brooks, what you say of him is no doubt, all true—He did not touch the main point when I heard him, at all events—& that satisfaction that you so kindly wish me, is, I am afraid, not to be got from any man. The mystery of this world grows and grows, & sticks out of every apparently trivial thing, instead of lessening. I hope this feeling may not be the incipient stages of insanity! Paul told the truth when he said that "now we see through a glass, very darkly"—I hope and trust that the rest may be equally true, & that some day we may see "face to face".

You say it is easy to drown thought by well doing. But is it not also the soundest philosophy, (so long of course as one doesn't humbug one'self.) Since by simply thinking out a religion, who has ever arrived at anything that did not leave one's heart empty?

Do you ever see Willy James? Good-bye. Write soon—and believe me, Yours most sincerely Mary Temple.

LETTER 7
Pelham May 9*th* 1869
Dear Mr Gray,

I know quite well that I do not owe you a letter, & that the custom is for maidens to mete out strictly letter for letter—but if you don't mind it, I don't, & if you *do* mind that kind of thing, you had better learn not to at once, if you propose to be a friend of mine, or else have your feelings from time to time severely shocked. After which preamble, I will say that there is a special reason in this case, though there might not be in another. Mrs Clymer's mother died about a fort-night ago, and Mrs Clymer feels her death very deeply. I went to see her a few days ago, as I was feeling very very sorry for her, & I found her very sad & depressed—Her's seems to be a hard lot in life. She asked me if I ever wrote to you, & if I would tell you that her mother was dead, as she would like you to know it, but did not feel quite equal to writing to you herself. I told her I would do so, & so that is the chief occasion of this letter. This is very hard for poor Mrs. Clymer. It seems to me that she has very little happiness left in life. By the way I don't know whether she has been divorced from that man or not. I have heard it contradicted. Poor old Mr Snelling is completely broken down by his wife's death. They have decided to leave New Rochelle, & are going to town, to board somewhere in Madison Ave. Mrs Clymer told me to tell you that Mrs Peter's address is 73 Madison Avenue. If you know of anything to comfort a person when the one they love best dies, for Heaven's sake, say it to her. I hadn't a word to say. I wrote you that I was going to Newport, & I meant to go next Tuesday night, but I had another hemorrhage last night, and it is impossible to say when I shall be able to leave here. I think I was feeling ill when I wrote last to you—I caught a dreadful cold in Philadelphia, & ever since, I have been coughing and feeling wretchedly, until finally the hemorrhage has come, & if that goes over well, I think I shall be better.

Lizzie Boott & her father are going to Newport on the 17th. & I am in hopes that I may be well enough to get there by that time. I am in bed now, on the old plan of gruel and silence, and I may get off without any worse attack this time. I feel as if I ought to get to Newport as soon as possible, because Aunt Charlotte is so ill. I ought to tell you that Mrs Snelling died of typhoid pneumonia. It is a perfect day, like summer—My windows are up, & the birds are singing. It seems quite out of keeping that I should be in bed. I should be all right, if I could only get rid of coughing—the warm weather will set me up again—I wonder what you are doing to-day— probably taking a solitary walk & meditating—on what? Good-bye & believe me

Yours—

Mary Temple

LETTER 8

Newport. May 1869 Friday.

Dear Mr Gray,

I forgot to say to you yesterday that I should like you to send me the things of my brother's that you spoke of, to Newport—just in care of Mr Tweedy—Mr Tweedy is going to Boston to-day, and if you happen to see him, he would bring it down to me—but it will come all right by Express, if you don't—I feel better to-day than I have for a month. Thank you very much for taking the trouble to send me those things of Willy's.

Yours most truly

Mary Temple.


LETTER 9

Newport. May 20*th* 1869.

Dear Mr Gray,

I got your letter this morning, forwarded from Pelham—I came from New York last Monday night with Mr Tweedy—as I did not like to delay it any longer, having made so many attempts to get here. I believe I was in bed when I last wrote to you, but this attack did not prove nearly as bad a one as the first—I rather bullied it, & after the fourth one, it departed— and I think my cough is better since I came here. The Bootts came down last night. I shall go home the latter part of next week. I am a little homesick—to tell the truth. I am afraid I am getting to be too much of a baby—whether it is from illness or from the natural bent I know not, but there is no comfort in life away from people who care for you. It is not heroic, I am aware, but natural, notwithstanding.

I hear that Wilky is home, & I daresay he will have the kindness to run down & see me while I am here—at least I hope so. Old Mrs Snelling was a very nice woman. I always liked her—and Mrs Clymer's position is a particularly sad one because her mother's death breaks up her home, & takes away what was apparently the least unpleasant phase of her life—She always had a very nice way with her mother, & they seemed to be very fond of each other. I don't think I am in the mood for writing to-day. I am tired, and should only bore you if I kept on. But your letters are not stupid, so write me some more of them. It is just a year since we began to write to each other. Aren't you getting a little tired of it? If you are, say so, like a man. Don't be afraid of me. Now I am going to lie down for five minutes before dressing for dinner. Good-bye.

Believe me, Yours sincerely

Mary Temple.


LETTER 10

Pelham June 27*th* 1869

Dear Mr Gray,

How can I write to you, when I have forgotten all about you? But how can one forget what one has never known—but then I am not quite sure whether I know you too little or too much to be able to write to you. Do you comprehend the difficulty? Of course you don't, so I will explain. The trouble is, I think, that to me you have no distinct personality—I don't feel sure to whom I am writing. When I say to myself that I will write to Mr Gray, I mentally see three men, all answering to that name, & each liable to read the letter I write, & yet differing so much from each other that the letter which I might with all propriety write to one of them, would be quite unsuitable to send to the other. Do you see? If you can once settle for me the question "who gets my letters?" I shall know better what to say in them—Is it the middle-aged man I used to see at Conway, (I cannot say know,) with a beard, I think, smoking and gravely discussing Trollope's novels with Elly or Kitty, good, perhaps, but not interesting (to me) to whom I never felt disposed to speak, & in whose society I used to get sleepy at eight o'clock, & wonder how the other girls could stay awake till eleven.

Is it that man that reads my letters? or is it the young man I saw recently at Newport—with a priestly countenance—calm and critical, with whom I have certainly no fault to find, as a chance companion for three or four days, but whom I should never dream of writing to, or bothering with my affairs one way or the other, happinesses or unhappinesses, as he would doubtless despise me for my nonsense & wonder at me for my seriousness. Does that man get my letters? or is it finally the same man who has from time to time written me letters, signed by the name that the other two gentlemen appropriate? If it is the last man, I know where I stand, & please Heaven, I mean to stand there some time longer. This last one I won't describe, but he is the only one of the three that I care anything about, and it is altogether a pleasure & sometimes a comfort to write to him & hear from him. He is very different to the other two. I hope he is the one that gets my letters, but I have my fears because I always address them to Mr Gray's office & I think *my* friend is the least likely of the three to go every day to the office. I hope you appreciate, dear Mr Gray, how perplexing a position I am in. Won't you solve the mystery for me *very* soon? Do write & tell me those other two men don't see my letters, & then I'll write to you as of old & tell you what I am about. In the mean time good-bye whatever you are. If the first or the second man should open this I beg leave to sign myself his very truly—

Mary Temple

(But if it should happen to be the third man, he may read instead of truly, *affectionately*)

LETTER 11

Pelham July 7*th* 1869.

Dear Mr Gray,

I got your letter yesterday, and I think I will feel "aisier" in my mind if I answer it at once. There is so much to say that I hardly know where to begin. I am afraid I have made you feel badly, with my nonsense, but you might have known that unless I cared a good deal for the remaining "third" of you which I said nothing about, I would not have pitched into the other two thirds in the way I did—and after all, this last third of you, which you call the "fraction over" is in reality pretty nearly the whole thing, to my mind, & the other two parts that I spoke of, are the fraction over. I am afraid from the sound of those words in your letter "verily you are a plain-spoken young woman," that you are angry with me. Are you? Please don't be angry. If you were here I should make you "make up" with me in a minute, was I rude, & thoughtless & unkind to say so many uncomplimentary things, & none of the other kind to make up for it? Well, as I said before, you ought to have known that I would not have said what I did, unless there was a great deal more that I might have said on the other side. All that I meant to say was, that I really seem to be farther off from you when you are talking to me than when you are writing to me. That is about what all that nonsense meant that I wrote you—I mean that when I am away from you I forget all about the accidents of your age & sex & temperament etc. etc., which naturally force themselves upon my notice when we are together, & I think of you only as a friend who is always kind & sympathetic & gentle, & also far wiser than I am & so a great help & comfort to me in this weary world, where it is so hard for one soul to know another, under all the necessary & unnecessary disguises that keep them apart. But when I saw you, I realized all the hindrances that exist to a friendship between you & me. It seemed such a one-sided affair. If I were a man, & could be practically a friend to you that could ever help you or serve you in any way, it would be of some use. But as it is, I am afraid it is a very one-sided affair. What good can the friendship of a woman with "narrow sympathies," & not a particularly cultivated intellect do you? I felt this when I was with you, & also, that I must bore you with my nonsense & my seriousness alike—(I mean by *you* in this instance the young man, at Newport, & not the other man that writes to me) For certainly you never have been anything but kind and good to me through all my various moods, with which I have from time to time inflicted you. I don't think I am saying what I want to say to you—but I despair of ever doing that in this world. Wait patiently till we both get to Heaven & then we will have a good talk, & understand each other—and in the meantime if I don't understand you here, don't mind it—it is only because I am not worth it. I mean capable of it—but if I can't understand you, I can at least feel certain points in your character as well as I shall in Heaven, I think—and now there is one other thing—You say that you are accustomed to having people learn to care less for you instead of more as time goes on, and you seem to think that it has been so in my case—But it has been an exceptional one, as I have gone on liking you better, slowly but surely, since I first began to really know you, about two years ago, until now I have got so into the habit of it, that I should find it hard to stop. Therefore, such as it is, you have my friendship, to make use of if it can possibly be of any service to you ever, & to throw away, if you find it in your way—Write to me that you are not angry with me, and that you do not altogether hate me—I am glad you like Lizzie Boott. You will be sure to like her still better when you know more of her. I am pretty well again, now-a-days—but I had a doleful time of it in Newport for nearly a fortnight, after you left. I was ill in bed nearly all the time. I have followed your advice & begun to take drawing lessons, of a Frenchman, named Roudel—whom I think a very good teacher. He talks to me in French, & I reply in monosyllables, which I hope in time to extend into fluent conversation. So you see I am killing two birds with one stone—I like my lessons very much—but find it impossible in the beginning, to draw a tree, which I mean to make my chief study, till I learn to do it. I take three lessons a week—long ones, of two or three hours, so that I have the opportunity, if I only have the energy to really improve. I had a letter from Harry yesterday from Switzerland. He saw George Eliot in London, & as he says was "completely fascinated with her—" She is ugly, however, but has a charming voice & manner, but I haven't time to tell you any more of his letter now. I want to say, as I shan't write again before your birthday, that I shall think of you on that day, & wish you a great many good wishes. Thirty does seem to be a turning point. I hope you may be as happy as you deserve, which is the best thing I can say, & that the next friend you have may treat you better than I did in my last letter. But indeed I was more in fun than in earnest, & you won't mind it, will you? Please write & tell me so, & believe that I am always

    Affectionately yours
    Mary Temple

LETTER 12

Pelham. July 29*th* 1869

Dear Mr Gray,

Your letter gave me much pleasure. You are a sensible man, & I like you. It is all right—and I'll be good, and try never to bother you any more. Don't ever forget that I do feel a sincere friendship for you. A great event has happened with us, since I wrote to you. I am the proud possessor of a little nephew—Kitty has a son born yesterday at two o'clock—I don't suppose you care to hear that he weighs 8½ pounds, or that his hair is dark brown & curly, & his nose straight & beautiful—but these are very interesting details to his doting aunt. Kitty is doing very well now, but she was very very ill, and gave us all a terrible fright. The boy roars most of the time—but he is a most attractive child notwithstanding. He is not a bit an Emmet, but exactly like Kitty. I part his hair in the middle & brush it up each side, in a very becoming manner—& as he has no clients to conciliate, he lets me arrange his hair as I like without a murmur. Now that he is safely in the world, I think I should like a little change from Pelham, that is, after Kitty gets well. Elly means to go to Newport about the middle of August, to stay with Mrs Phinney—I would rather go to the mountains somewhere. Won't you dress yourself up like an old woman, & take me to Lenox with you? There is a test of friendship. Do you know I have had to give up my drawing, after all—My teacher backed out of it, because he could not get anybody to join me, & he found that he couldn't afford to come every day from the village for me alone—I was very sorry, but of course there was no help for it—the fates seem to be against my taking lessons in drawing. But *some* of these days, when everything else happens that one would like, that will no doubt come in too; in the meantime my genius must remain uncultivated—Lizzie Boott has been at Pomfret with the Jameses for a month, & has fallen quite in love (or should I say *into* love) with them—especially Uncle Henry & Willy. She is going to Lenox next week, to stay with the Tappans. I am glad Mr Holmes is going to Newport. A little of that kind of life would be good for him, I think. Aren't you going to devote some of your September vacation to making the acquaintance of my nephew? He will be able to hold his head up by that time, & will be delighted to see you. And now I must go up to see him, before I go to bed, so I will say good-night to you. I feel very much like thanking you for being so good to me, & asking you at the same time not to stop—but you would probably think me very weak-minded, so I won't say anything about it—Good-bye—Write soon. Don't work too hard in this warm weather. And believe me always

Yours affectionately

Mary Temple.

LETTER 13

Pelham. August 29*th* 1889 [corrected in pencil to 1869]

Dear Mr Gray,

I believe it is really not very long since I last wrote to you, but it seems a good while to me, probably because so important an event as Elly's engagement has happened in the meantime. You must have heard it some time ago, in Lenox—& since then from Elly herself. Of course I suppose you were surprized—we all were—but we are becoming accustomed to it, as the weeks go on. She has only a little over two weeks more, before her marriage. Mr Emmet thinks he may have to start for California the day after the wedding, the 16th., & his sudden step is rather a shock to us all, as we had not expected to have Elly whisked off to the other end of the world so soon—but of course there is nothing to be said—since she has decided to cast her fate with his, for better for worse, till death parts them, it must of course matter very little to her where she is so long as she is with him—and we must try and console ourselves with the thought that he will take good care of her. I am sure he will be kind and good to her always—& she is very happy, so there is no more to be said—but, at best, this marrying is a very solemn thing, as it may possible have occurred to you—The irretrievableness of the step comes over my mind from time to time in such an overwhelming way that it is very depressing—and I have to be constantly on my guard not to let Temple & Elly see it, as it would not please them, naturally. And after all, since they are not appalled by it, & & [*sic*] are quite sure of each other, as they are—why should I worry myself about it?—I am aware that if all other women felt the eternal significance of matrimony to the extent that I do, that hardly any of them would get married at all, & the human race would come to a stand-still—so I ought to be glad perhaps that so many people can find and take that "little ease" that Clough talks about, without consciously giving up the "highest thing"—And may not the greater part of the human race of the present day be the truly wise ones, and my own notions of the subject simply fanatical and impracticable? I clearly see that I am in the minority, & that the other side has, with Bishop Blougram, the best of it, from one point of view—but I can't help that, can I. We must be true to ourselves mustn't we, though all the rest of humanity be of a contrary opinion, or else throw discredit upon the wisdom of God who made us as we are & not like the next person. Do you remember my old hobby of the "remote possibility" of the best thing, being better than a clear certainty of the second best? Well, I believe it more than ever, every day I live. Indeed I don't believe anything else—but is not that everything? And isn't it exactly what Christianity means. Wasn't Christ the only man that ever lived and died *entirely* for his faith, without a shadow of selfishness? And isn't that reason enough why we should all turn to him, after having tried everything else & found it unsatisfactory, as the only pure & unmixed manifestation of God, in humanity? And if I believe this, which I think I do, how utterly inconsistent and detestable is the life I lead, which so far from being a loving & cheerful surrendering of itself once for all, to God's service, is at best but a base compromise. A few moments or acts or thoughts out of my whole life, consciously & with difficulty divested of actual selfishness. Must this always be so? Is it owing to the indissoluble mixture of the devine [*sic*] & the diabolical in us all, or is it because *I* am hopelessly frivolous & trifling? Or is it finally that I really don't believe—that I have still a doubt in my mind whether religion *is* the one exclusive thing to live for, as Christ taught us, or whether it will prove to be only *one* of the influences, though a great one, which educate the human Race, and help it along in that culture which Matthew Arnold thinks the most desirable thing in the world. In fine, is it the meaning & end of our lives, or only a moral principle bearing a certain part in our developement? — — — — —

Since I wrote this I have been having my tea, & sitting on the piazza looking at the stars—& thinking that it is very unfaithful & disloyal of me even to speak as I have just now, admitting the possibility of that faith not being everything which at moments is so devinely true a thing to me, as to light up the whole of life suddenly, & make everything clear. I know that the trouble is with *me*, when the doubt & despondency comes, & yet, on the other hand I can't altogether believe it wrong for me to have said to you what I did, for then what becomes of my principle to say what you really think, & leave it to God to take care of his own glory. I think the truth will vindicate itself, in spite of my voice to the contrary. If you think I am writing all this to you without sufficient excuse, I won't do it again— But I can't help it—I have nobody to speak to about serious things. If by chance I say anything or ask a question that lies at all near my heart, Kitty & Elly both tell me that I am "queer" & that "they wouldn't be me for anything", which is no doubt sensible on their part, but which puts an end to anything but conversation of the most superficial kind on my part—& you know one gets lonely after a while on this plan of living & so in sheer desperation I turn to the one that is least likely to mind my troubling him, which is yourself, sir—But enough of this—I want to say a few words about Elly's marriage. Don't suppose that I don't like it for I do, since she is so happy, & they are both so fond of each other, I know, that he will make her a kind & devoted husband & he is a good, intelligent, honorable man, & I am very fond of him. They have, I think, as fair a chance of happiness as any couple I know. That other notion, Plato's, wasn't it? of waiting to marry till you find that other half which *exactly* fits, is no doubt a delusion & a snare, & not to be realized here below—which is wise perhaps, if we are expected to wish to go to a better world—for "Earth being so good, would Heaven seem best?" What kind of a fortnight have you had at Lenox? Did you see anybody that you liked? My heart has been in my throat for the last week about the Boat Race—not altogether with disappointment at the result, altho' I was disappointed; but it seems to have stirred up all the old feeling within me, which has been slumbering since the war. It is the pluck and manliness of the Harvard boys that goes to my heart. I can stand having them beaten, & I acknowledge that those "Blasted Britishers" have won a fair victory, altho' Simmons & Loring were ill, because their very illness was the result of their inferior knowledge in training. This has been a capital lesson for them, & next year I believe we could beat them on their own ground & I should like to try it again this year on neutral ground. But I am as proud of them as if they had won the race. They behaved like men from beginning to end, God bless them & have made my heart glow more than ever with patriotic pride. How do you feel about it? The baby is growing finely, & Kitty is very well. I think that I shall stay here now until after Elly is married unless I should decide to go to Newport to see my dentist, in which case I should run up to Cambridge for a few days, & come back in time for the wedding. Elly wrote to you some time ago. I daresay you have already answered it. I have not been feeling very well of late, & have had a good deal of something like Pleurisy, which is not a comfortable thing, but I am better now. Write to me & tell me what you are doing with yourself. I have written you too long a letter I know—but I won't do it again & I know that you are good enough to forgive me—and believe me Yours sincerely & affly Mary Temple

LETTER 14

Pelham. September 17*th* 1869.

Dear Mr Gray,

I am only going to write you a line to-day, just to tell you that Elly was safely married on Wednesday. She looked simply beautiful in her wedding garment, & behaved herself throughout with a composure that was as delightful as it was surprizing. Her voice did not even tremble when she made the responses, and the whole thing was most successful. They went to Saratoga—& will be home on Monday. I send you a photograph of myself that I had taken a few weeks ago. It looks perhaps a trifle melancholy, but I can't help that. I did the best I could. I won't write any more to-day because it would not be enlivening. Everything looks gray & blue in the world now-a-days. It will all be bright again in time, I have no doubt. There is no special reason for it—only I think I am a little tired with knocking about. I have been on the go for the last ten days—having spent a week in Newport which might have been pleasant enough if the Dentist had not taken that occasion to break my bones for me in a barbarous manner. Perhaps I may see you soon—Kitty & Dick propose to make a little trip, with me & the baby, to Newport & Lenox. We shall probably start on Thursday, & spend one night in Boston. We will let you know when we are there—& you can repair to wherever we may be, & Kitty will take pleasure & pride in displaying her infant to you. Elly got your earrings just before she was married & will no doubt write you a line, when she gets back. I think they were extremely pretty. Your taste & mine seem to have been much alike, as I gave her a pair of earrings, also gold & pearls, but of a different pattern. I got your letter the morning Elly was married. You are very kind & good & friendly to me. You don't know how much happiness your letters give me. You will be surprized, I daresay, but I shall not, at the last day, when the accounts are all settled, to find how much this counts in your favour.

Good-bye

Yours affectionately

Mary Temple

This is the only envelope I can find big enough for my photograph— the remains of some of the numerous recent weddings.

LETTER 15

Newport October *4th* 1869

Dear Mr Gray,

The Temple & Emmet Caravan have advanced as far as Newport, & now propose to retreat again to Pelham, without stopping at Boston, or anywhere else. We are all going back to-night. Mr Emmet has business in New York, & can't be away any longer. I haven't been well of late, or I should have run up to Boston for a day or two to take a sad farewell of all I love in that town & thereabouts, before I go over the Rocky Mountains. This little trip has been laid out for me by my friends, & I have determined to go, & shall probably start with Elly & her husband in about ten days, possibly not for a fortnight, to spend the winter at San Francisco. I can't be enthusiastic about it, but I suppose I might as well take all the means I can, to get well, & I daresay a winter in a warm climate might be good for me—so I am going. Now what I want you to do about it, is simply this—to come to see us before I go. This is not too much to ask, is it? & yet I do it with fear and trembling, for where the Law comes in conflict I know my claims were never of much account. Kitty is going to send you a line to add her voice—perhaps that may bring you. Just think, you may never see me again, & if I were to die in San Francisco, you'd be sorry, if you hadn't said good-bye to me, wouldn't you? And if this doesn't move you, you may come to say good-bye to Elly who is also going. But never mind *why* you come, so long as you come—I have asked Lizzie Boott to come & see me before I go. Yours,

Mary Temple.

Try, for *once* in your life not to be hard-hearted, & let the law, & stables, etc go to the — — — — — — —

Didn't you like my picter?


LETTER 16

Pelham. Oct. *24th* '69.

Dear Mr Gray,

Elly & Temple started yesterday for San Francisco and yet here I am still. But not hopelessly or irrecoverably. I did not go with them because Mr Emmet had a telegram telling him to go there at once, with no delay, as his affairs depended upon the promptness of his getting there. So it was thought safer not to take me, as they had to push through in six days, with no rest, even if we were all in a dying condition. Then he had to go at once to Oregon, on business, which I did not care about doing, & the present plan is to send me on in about three weeks, by water, under the care of one of the Emmet boys & Temple's valet (for nurse) & by the time I got there, early in December, they would be settled in San Francisco for the winter. The idea of a 21 days sea-voyage is rather appalling—but I can go if I like, at all events. I was, of course, glad of the reprieve. Elly went off in good spirits. They were both glad to go. It is odd how all ordinary considerations fade into insignificance, climate, place, etc, when people are married. What do you think of my going by water? This day is too heavenly—I have not been to church, but have been walking by myself, as happy as possible—When one sleeps well, & the sun shines, what happiness to live! I wish you were here—Wouldn't I show you Pelham at high-tide, on a day that is simply intoxicating—with a fresh breeze blowing through the red & yellow leaves, & sunshine "on field & hill, in heart and brain"—as Mr Lowell says. Perhaps you may be listening to Phillips Brooks this morning —The bipeds of this family are as you left them—nothing of importance has happened in the meantime, but among the quadrupeds there have been two excitements—I suppose you remember the pony I drove, and Pinch the little Scotch terrier, that tried to insinuate himself into your affections on the piazza the morning you left. The former has been *cutting* up, the latter *cut* up since then. You wouldn't believe me when I told you the pony was a spirited & nervous creature, but she behaved as sich one day when I took Miss Annie Crawford, who was staying near here, to drive. She shied at a dog that frightened her, & dragged the wagon into a ditch, & tried to get over a stone wall, wagon & all. I of course had to hang on to the reins, but I suggested to Miss Crawford that she should get out, as the wagon was pretty steady while the horse's forefeet were on top of the wall, which she did, into a mud-puddle, & soiled her pretty striped stockings and slippers in a horrible way. It ended by the dear little pony condescending to get back upon all four legs, & we went on our way with no further mishap. I found it very amusing & have loved the horse much more ever since—I am glad you like to drive with me better than to bring suits into chancery—(but I don't believe you really do) I like much better to have you do it too. Have you seen Ellen Mason or Lizzie Boott yet? How does Mr Holmes persevere about smoking? I pity him if he can't sleep, & wish I had a vicious habit, so that I might give it up—Don't be so awfully long about answering this, as is your habit. Tell me what you think of going to California by sea—When is Mr Higginson going to be married? Now that my departure is postponed, I feel as if I had got you here on false pretences. But I can't be penitent, really. That is quite too much to expect of me. Good-bye. Write soon—and believe me always Yours affectionately

Mary Temple

I forgot to finish my tale about the other quadruped, Pinch, who was called upon in the dead of night by five dogs of the neighborhood, and torn to pieces by them. The coachman heard him crying in the night, & in the morning we found him, that is to say we gathered him together, his dear little tail lying in one place, & his head in another etc. Well, so went out a very sweet little spirit. I wonder where his soul is now. Do you mean to tell me that he hadn't more soul than Kaufman, the fat oyster-man?

LETTER 17

[No address] Thursday evening

Nov. 1869.

Dear Mr Gray,

I am going to Boston to-morrow (D.V.) to spend a few days—I mean to Cambridge. I let you know the startling intelligence in time, so that you may come to see me, if you see fit. The California plan is in the same state it was when I wrote before. I still expect to go on the 20th, but I am waiting to hear from Elly on account of the climate. I have only time for a line. What heavenly weather we are having, I hope it will last while I am in Boston!

Good-night—

Yours affectionately

Mary Temple.

LETTER 18

Pelham Nov 21*st* 1869

Dear Mr Gray—

You say you hope I'll go to California—well—you are not destined to be disappointed, as I have decided to go—This is final—My passage is taken for the 4*th* of Dec. two weeks from yesterday. Elly & Temple have written to me to go at once—They are settled now in San Francisco for the winter. I feel quite in the mood for going since I got back from Boston, & I think I shall go very comfortably; indeed Mr McClean promises Dick that I shall be so comfortable that it will be hard to tear me from the ship when I arrive at San Francisco. The Captain is a friend of Temple's & also of my uncle, Captain Temple's—& both of them are going to write to Captain Maury about me, so that I fully expect the ship to be hung with banners and decked with flowers, in my honor—I am glad the wedding trip didn't bore you too much, but you are not very enthusiastic about your brides-maid, whose name you don't even tell me—I would like to see you, very much. I had about a thousand things I wanted to tell you about my visit in Boston, which are even now disappearing from my mind, that is becoming much less prominent than they were then. I can't write them to you, at any rate—I must have a sympathetic look now and then from you, a glance of approval—or disapproval, to feel my way by—and my impressions are not sufficiently unalterable to bear seeing them down, once for all, in black & white. In short, you comprehend, lots to talk to you about, but not to write about. Suffice it to say, I enjoyed my visit far more than I expected when it began—in fact, immensely. I would n't have missed it for anything. I feel now as if it were a necessary thing to have happened—I don't know how I should have begun the winter, & especially started off on an indefinitely long pilgrimage to the west, without the impetus that it gave me in certain directions, the settling down & shaking up—the dissipating of certain impressions that I had thought fixed, and the strengthening of others I had not been so sure of—etc, etc—an epoch, in short. I dare say you have n't had such—in which a great deal of living was done in a short time, to be turned over, & made fruitful, in days to come. I saw Mr Holmes once. I was very glad of that glimpse, short as it was. I went home by way of Newport, where I staid two days—When I got there I was surprised to hear of Fred Jones'es engagement, to a Miss Rawle of Philadelphia—Do you know her? When I got to New-York, I went to the Hows' to ask something about Fred. & his affairs, & I found that Miss Rawle was staying next door, with Mrs Willy Duncan—so I went in to see her, on the spur of the moment, just as I came from the boat, not very presentable, for a first call. However I thought if she had a soul she would n't mind it—& so I found it. She impressed me very pleasantly—is rather handsome, with the manners of a thorough woman of the world, a surprising fluency of talk, & a graceful way of posing herself, which reminds me of a French woman. She has black eyes, which she half closes when she looks at you, & pretty hands, with which she gesticulates in an enticing way that I should think would be quite delicious in a wife. She is the kind of woman I should think to keep her husband in love with her. He would n't be likely to get "all round her" as you say, at the outset. Altogether I consider Fred. a very lucky fellow. I see a lot of people coming up the path from the other house, & perhaps I shall have to go—[*sic*] talk to them. Looking down upon me, as I write, is a picture of yourself—which is quite enough like you to bring you visibly before me, though I say it that should n't, seeing that I drawed it myself. It is my first attempt with the coal, after Lizzie Boott's instructions about light & shade—& it looks unfinished to me & very faulty in many ways, but still with a glimmering of you in it that is truly delightful—I feel now as if I could see you for five minutes again, to get a fresh impression of your face, I could make a better likeness—This trusting to memory is not a *reliable* way. But beside memory I had that little outline of you I took long ago at Conway, which was a very great help—I enlarged it about four times, & made it a better likeness. I mean to draw the people on the ship—Give me some suggestions about passing my time on the voyage. You have tried it, & ought to know all about it. This letter is "patchy & scrappy"—but never mind—I like "Youth & Art" of Browning's very much. But it was just as well for them that they "missed" it, I think—and no doubt they managed sufficiently well without each other. If their souls had been exceptionally harmonious, I think matters must have infallibly have come [*sic*] to a crisis, living the kind of life they lived. I lunched with Ellen Mason the morning I came away. I saw Fanny Dixwell once—and had a good talk with her. I haven't seen her before for three years, & may not see her again for thirty—I don't know, practically how we should like each other, every day—but, it still remains clear to me, entre nous, that there is something, I know not what about her, that touches me deeply—as few people do. As hardly any other woman does. It might possibly not prove to be lasting, but my instinct tells me it would be, because it is so purely an intuition—I don't know her a bit—To analyze it—I think she impresses me with a possibility in her of abandonment, devotion to an idea, a conviction, more than most people. She has what people call *self*-reliance very strongly, which seems to my mind to be reliance upon God—trusting her own soul—more believing than doubting, in the long run. I may be all wrong about her—As I said before, I don't know her a bit—but these are my impressions about her. She gave me one of her embroideries—an extraordinary production for a young lady of the 19*th* Century—very beautiful in the workmanship & original in the design—But a truce to these prolonged dissertations about young women, which doubtless bore you frightfully—When will you write to me again? Please write soon—Just think of me alone on the ocean for three weeks, and then practically alone in Californy for three years perhaps—& please remember to write *often* to me. I was so glad to have an opportunity of seeing your sister at Lizzie Boott's—I suppose you won't mind if I say I thought her very nice & very handsome, *in spite* of *which* she didn't remind me much of you—(I consider that a delicate compliment, or rather it would have been delicate, if I had n't underscored it.) Lizzie Boott was as sweet & good to me as ever. I think she is at once the most unselfish and unegotistical girl I know—they don't always go together. But having begun on an analysis of the third girl, I will stop abruptly. Write to me before I go. And believe me

Always affectionately yours

Mary Temple—

LETTER 19

[At the top of the page is written in Alice Howe Gibbens James's hand, "Marked on cover: *No 1*." Minny was presumably indicating that this is the first of two letters in the same package: she added, an hour after finishing this letter, a second, updating Gray on the information contained in the first.]

Pelham Nov 30*th* 1869

Dear Mr Gray—

I got your letter this morning—My address in San Francisco—is simply "Care of C. Temple Emmet—" I hope you will write often to me—I am as busy as possible, making the necessary preparations—I am surely off this time, unless Heaven interposes, in a miraculous way, between now and Saturday. I have n't much courage to boast of about starting off—& yet I can't say I feel nervous about the voyage—After all, it's much the same to me, where I am—life is always full to me, of interest & mystery & happiness & three weeks of comparative solitude, between the water & the sky, will not be unattractive to me. There is one thing in your letter which I should like to have you explain to me a little, that is if you don't mind doing it. If you do, of course, I do not want to you have you [*sic*] speak about it. You say that I am at once near you, and far off, in spirit. Do you mind telling me in what way I am so far off from you?—Don't be afraid of hurting my feelings by being frank with me. It was always, to my mind, a one-sided thing, our friendship—Nothing that you can say about my being unsympathetic to you, or unsatisfactory to you in any way, will disappoint me—& I won't even allow myself to think that I am sorry, because I feel so clearly that God knows best, & we ought neither of us surely wish to distort his creatures from the use he made them for, just to serve our own purposes, such as giving us a little sympathy, to make our lives more comfortable. We must each of us, after all, live out our own lives, apart from every one else—& yet, this being once understood, as a fundamental truth, I think there is nobody's sympathy & approval which would encourage me so much as yours. I mean if our hearts and motives could be known by other people, as God knows them, without any disguise or extenuation, and then if you should tell me that *on the whole,* you *disapproved* of me, it would as much as and more than anything else could, shake my confidence in my own instincts, which must after all, forever be my guide—and yet, as I said before, I am quite prepared to hear whatever you have to say. I shall listen to it quite humbly & am very much inclined to trust your opinion before my own. And yet, after all, I don't believe, at the very bottom, that we are unsympathetic. In support of which, I have nothing to bring forward again, but my own instinct. I know that by this letter I am putting an end to that delightful immunity I have enjoyed so much with you, from sickening introspection, analysis of myself and yourself. Exhausting & nauseating subjectivity, with which most of my other friends see fit to deluge me, thereby taking much that is refreshing out of life. I have principally or at least in a good part, enjoyed my acquaintance with you because you were *not* that sort of person, and even now, I don't want you to tell me anything but that one thing, as briefly as you choose—why and in what way am I such a long way off from you— This is necessarily a frightfully egotistic letter, & I promise there shall be no more of it—You needn't tell me this if you don't want to. And if you decide to tell me (never mind how unflattering it is) it will be something for me to turn over in my mind on my solitary voyage—I may never see you again. If I don't, let me tell you that knowing you has been a source of unmixed pleasure & good to me. We have probably both a long time to live, & we must only try to make the best thing of it that we can—After this, keep on writing to me, if you care to—just as you always have—I sail on Saturday morning.

Good bye—and God bless you.

Yours affectionately

M. Temple—

[Above the address is written, presumably added by Alice Howe Gibbens James: "On cover *No 2*," indicating that this letter is to be read second.]

Pelham. Nov 30*th* 1869

An hour later—

*Sold* again, by all that is wonderful! I had almost said damnable—but not that exactly, after all, altho' I *had* one foot on the ship, so to speak. I had just sent my letter to you, to the office, when lo & behold my brother Dick walks in with a telegram from Temple "I will be home in Dec—Don't send Minny" A tremendous revulsion of feeling took place upon this announcement. There was a general sigh of relief—& it is all right, I'm sure, altho' when I wrote to you an hour ago, I thought the other place was all right. But it is so much better to have Elly back here, & if I can only manage to keep moderately well this winter, I shall be satisfied. When I heard the news I went down to the office & got out of the box the letter I had just written to you—When I found I wasn't going, I hesitated about sending you the letter that I wrote when I thought I was going—but upon second thoughts I determined to send it with this. Don't let it bother you in the least. There is certainly plenty for us to talk about without that—But at all events, write soon. I feel completely turned upside down by this change of plan, & must begin at once to organize my winter anew. Truly this is a changing world, especially when one happens to be sister-in-law to Mr Temple Emmet. But it's all right. There will be no painful parting, and as I said before, outside of that it's all one to me where I am—I have written enough, in all conscience, tonight to you. In my next I will tell you a proposal that has been made to me, not of matrimony, but better. I feel almost as if I ought to apologize for my first letter—but never mind—it had to come, sooner or later, so it must be all right. But as I said before, don't let it bore you, a bit—Do write soon—& believe me to be yours most sincerely

Mary Temple.


LETTER 20

Pelham. Dec. 12*th* 1869

Dear Mr Gray,

I understood your letter perfectly well. It was better than I feared it might be, but bad enough, better, because I knew already, all that you told me, & I had been afraid that there might be some new & horrible de-velopement in store for me, which I hadn't myself felt—but bad enough, because it is in itself, new or old, such a disquieting fact, that I am, intellectually, so unsympathetic. It is a fault that I feel profoundly conscious of, but strange to say, it is only lately that I have been conscious of it as a fault. I daresay I have always known, in a general way, that I was very unobservant about things, & took very little interest in subjects, upon which my mind did not naturally dwell, but it never occurred to me until lately, that it was a fault that ought to be corrected. Whether because I have never been given to studying myself much, but have just let myself go the way my mind was most inclined to, more interested in the subject itself, than in the fact that it interested me, or whether because one is averse to set oneself down as indolent & egotistic, I don't know, but at all events I have of late seen the thing in all its unattractiveness, & I wish I could get over it. Do you think, now that I am fully aware of the fact, that it is hopeless; or that if I tried hard for the next twenty-five years, I might succeed in modifying it? I am speaking now about a want of interest in *all* the rest of the world; of not having the desire to investigate subjects naturally uninteresting to me, just because they are interesting to some other human being, that I don't particularly owe anything to, except that he *is* a human being, and so his thoughts & feelings ought to be respected by me, & sympathized with. Not to do this is, I know, unphilosophic, & selfish, conceited & altogether inhuman. But my not sympathizing with you is quite another thing—Don't suppose I haven't wanted to—I have felt for a long time that you were a great deal to me, sympathetic & helpful, & that I was *nothing* to you; & I have wished always, & quite in vain, that I might, in some way or other, do *something* for you, by means of active sympathy in your special interests—but in the first place, you are so entirely unegotistic, & talk so little about yourself, that it is hard to know the things which really do interest you most deeply—about the middle things of life, that you speak of, Law, Politics, etc. I know how utterly ignorant I am of them, & unable to give you any practical assistance, & in the second place I have always felt that you didn't want my sympathy— Why, if I thought it would do you any good, I would gladly convert myself into a perfect Myra Blackstone, (if you understand the combination.) But it is useless to say I have *wished* to be helpful to you, when the point is that practically I have failed, & must, perhaps, always fail in being so—To be unselfish, to live for other people, to mould our lives as much as possible on the model of Christ's all-embracing humanity, seems most clearly to my mind, to be the one thing worth living for, & yet it is still the hardest thing for me to do, & I think I do it less than anybody else, who feels the necessity of it as strongly as I do. We are expecting Elly & Temple now, any day. They will have to be in Washington this winter—So we will not see much of them, I am afraid, after all. I am glad you still go to an occasional ball—I should rather like to see you there myself. That is a phase of life, that we have not seen much of together. I have been feeling so well lately, that I don't know what to make of it. I don't remember ever feeling so well & in such good spirits in my life. Not that I am not generally pretty cheerful, if there is the slightest excuse for such a frame of mind, but now everything seems bright & happy. My life is so full of interest & my time so thoroughly filled (although I get up at 6 o'clock) and such a delicious calm seems to have settled down upon my usually restless spirit, such an enjoyment of the *present,* & a grateful contentment in each new day as I see it dawn in the east, that I can only be thankful. I say to myself: "Make a note of this—you are happy—don't forget it, not to be thankful for this beautiful gift of life"—Have you ever felt so? Of course you have; but it is hardly, I should think, to be felt so strongly in the bustle and excitement of a city life—Perhaps you may have felt something like it at Conway or Switzerland? This is Sunday morning, & I wonder whether you are listening to Mr Brooks. I understand how you feel about his preaching—that it is all feeling & no reason. I felt so myself about it, last winter in Philadelphia; that he was good for those within the pale—but not good to convince outsiders that they must come in. But I am glad now, that he preaches in this way. I think his power lies in it—for it seems to me, after all, that what comfort we get in Religion, & what light we have upon it, comes to us through *feeling*—that is through trusting our *feeling,* our *instinct,* as the voice of God, the Holy Ghost, altho' it may seem to us to be directly contrary to what our Intellect teaches us. But I do not mean by this to tell you to deny the conclusions arrived at by your Intellect. On the contrary, I think we ought to trust our Intellect, to stand by it to the bitter end, wherever it may lead us. But let us fearlessly trust our whole nature, showing our faith in God, by being true to ourselves, *all through,* not dishonoring him, by ignoring what your heart says, because it is not carried out by your Intellect, or by wilfully blunting your intellectual perception, because it happens to run against some cherished wish of your heart. "But," you will say, "how can a man live, torn to pieces this way, by these contrary verdicts?" I know that it is hard to keep our faith sure that there is a stand-point where these apparent inconsistencies are all reconciled—where all this jangle & discord sounds the sweetest harmony, but I do believe it is so, from God's stand-point, and we must only try to have faith that this is so, & never mind how great the inconsistency may seem to us, how perplexing the maze it leads us into, let us never give up a single element of the problem, for the sake of coming to a comfortable solution of it in this world. I do not blame those eager minds that are always worring [*sic*], investigating, studying, to *find* the solution here below. It is a noble work, and let them follow it out, (but without a bit of compromise) to whom God has given the work. But whether we find it or not, I would have them & all of us, feel that it is to be found, if God wills— & through no other means surely than by our being *true*. Blessed are they who have not *seen*, & who have yet believed.

I am going out now to take a walk. We have had the most delightful weather for the last week, & capital sleighing. I have spent most of my time driving myself about in a little sleigh, with that same dear little pony. I went to town yesterday to a matinée of "William Tell." It was delightful, & I slept all night after it, too. What do you think of that? I am reading German a little every day, and it is beginning to go pretty well. I have written a long letter & haven't told you yet of my plan I spoke of, but it is still far ahead, so I won't say anything about it, for fear it might fall through, like my other plans. Good-bye—Please write soon. Don't tire yourself out, between studing [*sic*] and dissipating, & believe me, always,

Yours most affectionately
Mary Temple.

LETTER 21
Pelham. Dec. 30*th* 1869.
Dear Mr Gray,

I did not mean to extract from you a contradiction of what I said to you. I don't want it—for it remains a fact all the same. I only wanted to confess to you a shortcoming I have often felt, not only toward you, but toward some others, among the unselfish of my friends, a tendency to take more than I give of sympathy & interest. I did not, certainly, mean to question whether you like me more or less. What I may be, in that sense, to you or to any other person, is surely none of my business, and I should never think of apologizing for not being congenial to anybody, or taking any credit to myself for being so. You understand, don't you, that I mean a *voluntary* helpfulness, such as most friends are glad mutually to give each other. Whatever help, or the reverse, one may be to another indirectly, by force of simply *being*, is of course involuntary, & we have all a right, I suppose, to help ourselves to as much, spiritually, of our neighbor, as we can assimilate, & to call it our own. You say you hope you haven't hurt my feelings—You haven't, most decidedly—& so, let it rest in peace!

How many ideas music suggests to one—that is, perhaps it has not so much suggested ideas to my mind, as strengthened them. It is a type, to my mind, of so many spiritual truths. I can't think of one, now, that music has not made clearer. It is very interesting to me. I could give you half-a-dozen instances where a spiritual truth has been "borne in upon my mind" by means of harmony—the relation of the part to the whole, the absolute value of the individual—the absolute necessity of uncompromising & unfaltering truth, the way in which we like our likes, & our *unlikes,* etc, etc, etc,—all these ideas are made clearer by music—of course it is no *reason* to give for believing, & it may be only fancy, but I can't help feeling that all matter is but a type of the spiritual—& why not music too? At all events, whether it be wise or not to be so influenced, so long as music comes to us as it does, a glimpse of perfection, a revelation of completeness, a hint of something more beautiful & harmonious than anything we know of here, it must fill our souls with such fancies. I won't explain to you what I mean, because, as you are not a musical person, I might not make it clear to you & might bore you—but some of the most direct revelations of spiritual things that I have ever got, have been through music.

You needn't suppose you city people have a monopoly of the gayety of this winter. Probably the most brilliant affair of the season is to come off to-night, at this place. Kitty proposes to give the children a party, toward which end, Henrietta yesterday made a raid upon New York & bore off the two Murray girls, Carrie & Olivia, to spend a couple of days out here, & figure at the ball. A variety of other girls & boys are to be quartered round at the different houses, & we propose to make a night of it. The Murrays have grown to be tall girls, & very nice ones. That is, Olivia is a very sweet bright little thing. She was always my favorite. Mrs Murray has become an *old* woman, with grey hair. "Bronson" has no doubt worried her into it, with his spiritualism, etc. *Moral* Don't marry a woman who doesn't understand you, or you will make her old before her time, & she will make *you* crazy. The weather is beastly. I still keep well, & sleep like a hinnocent babe. I hope your Xmas was pleasing, if not merry. As for the New Year, you know all I wish you, without my telling you.

Good-bye

Yours—

M. Temple.

LETTER 22

Pelham January 25*th* 1870

Dear Mr Gray,

It seems a long time to me since I have written to you, and it might be still longer, if it were not that, from something that you said in your last letter, I fancy that you may possibly think that my silence comes from a flagging in my friendly feeling for you—which however, I don't believe you really think. I haven't written, & may still often fail to write to you because I couldn't write cheerfully, or in a way that would make you feel brighter for your day's work, for having heard from me. There have been times (and they will come again, no doubt,) when I could write to you about ordinary things, in a way at least not depressing—but of late, for some time, I have felt so tired out, bodily and mentally, that I could not conscientiously ask you to share the mood with me. The life that I live, here in the country, & so very much alone, is capable of being the happiest & the unhappiest of existences—as it all depends upon one's self, and is so very little interfered with by external influences. Perhaps I am more than usually subject to extremes of happiness & of depression—but I suppose everybody must have moments, even in the most varied and distracting life, when the old questioning spirit, the demon of the "Why, Whence, & Whither" stalks in, like the skeleton at the feast, and takes his seat beside him. I say everybody—but I must except those rare and happy souls, who really believe in Christianity = [*sic*] who no longer striving after even goodness, as it comes from one's own efforts, but believing in the mysterious sacrifice of Christ, his merits sufficing, in short who feel the consoling truth of the Atonement, in the Orthodox way, (to me hitherto neither comprehensible nor desirable.) These people, having completely surrendered self, having lost their lives, as it were, in Christ, must truly have found them, must have felt the rest that comes from literally casting their care of doubt and strife & thought, on the Lord—I say hitherto this doctrine of the *vicarious* suffering of Christ—has been to me not only incomprehensible but also unconsoling. I didn't want it, & I didn't understand, even intellectually the standpoint of people who did—I do not mean to say that the life & death of Christ & the example it sets for us, has not been to me always the brightest spot in history—for it has, but it has stood rather as an example that we must try to follow, that we must by constant & ceaseless effort bring our lives nearer to his life—but always I have felt that we must & *could* do it somewhat, through ourselves, that is of course with God's help, to be got by asking *him*, & with no mediation

—& when I have seen as time went by my own shortcomings all the more instead of less frequent, I have thought—Well, you don't *try* hard enough —you are not *really* in earnest in thinking that you believe in the Christian life, as the only true one. But the more I tried the less it seemed to be like the moral life—The best things I did were the more spontaneous ones— The greatest effort had the least success—until finally I could not but see that if this was Christianity, it was not the "Rest" that Christ had promised his disciples—it was nothing more than a Pagan life with a high Ideal— only the Ideal was so high that nothing but failure & unhappiness came of trying to follow it. And one night when I was awake all night it occurred to me, what if this were the need that Christianity came to fill up in our hearts? What if, after all, that old meaningless form of words that has been sounded in my unheeding ears all my life, were suddenly to become invested with spirit & truth? What if this were the "good tidings" that made so many hearts secure & happy in the most sad & trying life—For if morality, virtue, were the test of a Christian, certainly Christ would never have likened the Kingdom of Heaven to a little Child, in whose little heart is certainly no struggle, no conscious battle between right & wrong, but only unconsciousness of self, love & trust. However it may turn out, whether it shall seem true or untrue to me finally, I am at least glad to be able to put myself, intellectually, into the place of the long line of Christians who have felt the need and the comfort of this belief—& it throws a light upon Uncle Henry's talk, which has seemed to me hitherto neither reasonable nor consoling—When I was in Cambridge, it so far disgusted me, that I fear I manifested plainly unto him that that [*sic*] it seemed to me not only highly unpractical, but ignoble and shirking—I knew all the time that he disliked me what he called my *pride & conceit*—& I have felt that his views didn't touch my case a bit—didn't give me the least comfort or practical help & seemed to me wanting in earnestness & strength—Now it occurs to me, what if the good gentleman had all along got hold of the higher truth, the purer spirituality?— Verily, there are two sides to everything in this world, & one becomes more Christlike the older one grows— I am glad to think of you as so busy—I hope you find the work pleasant, & time enough to do it, without hurting yourself. So you have met Mrs Bell and heard her sing—she seems to be very charming to men. I remember Harry James was very enthusiastic about her. She struck me as interesting & very entertaining, but not I think as a woman, whom, if I were a man, I should feel a desire to "have & to hold" etc.—But I only saw her once or twice, & perhaps the fascination grows upon nearer view—I feel too seedy for *anything* today—I had a hemorrhage a week ago, which rather took the life out of me, but, as it was only one, I think I should by this time be getting strong again, if I had not got into a sleepless condition, which completely knocks me up. The old consolatory remark of "Patience, neighbor, & shuffle the cards" ought to impart a little hope to me, I suppose—but it's a long time since I've had any trumps in my hand—& you know, with the best luck, the game always tired me—This last whimpering tone you must take no notice of—It does n't mean anything. Willy James sometimes tells me to behave like a man and a gentleman, if I wish to outwit fate. What a *real* person he is. He is to me, in nearly all respects, head and shoulders above other people—When have you seen any of my friends? Lizzie Boott, Ellen Mason, etc. How is Mr Holmes? Goodbye. Write to me, if you can spare the time. I don't like to bother you when you are so busy—Elly is having a gay winter in Washington—She wants me to go on there—which I meant to do, before the reappearance of my last winter's illness—but now I feel hardly up to it. So you can always know when I don't want to write to you. If that is all you know, you don't know much; and those poor boys needn't expect to learn much from your instruction. You know the "Victim" of Tennyson, is taken from some old bit of poetry & the idea isn't Tennyson's—of course the king loved his wife better than his son—men always do, don't they? But *whom* did *she* love best?—This is the most extraordinary winter—like a damp, warm spring, all the time. The one bright spot in my existence now is the baby— he is indeed a small bit of Paradise. You will be interested to hear that he can clasp his hands now, when you tell him to, & I hope in my next to be able to tell you that he has two teeth, which are nearly through now. Goodbye again—& believe me always Affectionately yrs

Mary Temple.


January 27*th*—

Dear Mr Gray—

I kept this letter a day or two thinking I might feel in time like writing you a better one, and not sending this at all—but alas! I'll have to wait some time before I shall feel like my old self, so I may as well let this go. You see I am not in a fit condition, mentally or physically to take bright & healthy views of life. But if you really care a bit about me, you may as well see this mood as any other, for Heaven only knows when I shall get out of it—Can you understand the weariness of thinking about one thing all the time, so that when you wake up in the morning, consciousness comes back with a sigh of—"Oh yes, here it is again—another day of doubting & worrying, hoping & yearning has begun"—and if you don't get any sleep at all, which is too frequently the case with me, the strain is a "leetle" bit too hard, & I am sometimes tempted to take a little "pison" to put me to sleep in earnest. That momentary vision of Redemption from thinking and striving, of a happy Rest this side of Eternity, has vanished away again—I can't keep it—peaceful, desirable as it may be, the truth is that practically I don't believe it—It was such a sudden thing, such an entire change from anything that had ever come to my mind before, that it seemed almost like an inspiration, & I waited, almost expecting it to continue, to be permanent. But it does n't stay—and so back swings the universe to the old place—Paganism—natural Religion, or whatever you call the belief whose watchword is "God and our own Soul"—And who shall say there is not comfort in it—One at least feels that here one breathes one's native air—welcome back the old *human* feeling, with its beautiful pride, and its striving—its despair, its mystery and its faith. Write to me and tell me whether, as one goes along, one must still be tossed about more & more by these conflicting feelings, or will they finally settle themselves one way or the other, quietly—and take only their proper share, at least, of one's life? I don't even ask you to forgive my bothering you with this—but trust the instinct which lets me tell it to you—This day is like summer. If I hadn't had rather the most unpleasant night I ever spent, I should enjoy it more. I got so thoroughly tired about two o'clock last night, that I made up my mind, in despair to give the morphine an other [*sic*] trial, & as one dose had no effect, I took two, & the consequence is I feel as ill today as one would desire—I can tell you, sir, you had better prize the gift of sleep as it deserves, while you have it. If I don't never write to you no more, you'll know its [*sic*] because I really wish to treat you kindly. But some of these days you'll get another kind of a letter, brimfull perhaps with health & happiness thoroughly ashamed of this present want of Spirit. Elly & Temple are coming back next week for a few days, & want me to go back with them to Washington—I had a long letter yesterday from Harry James, from Florence—Enjoying Italy, but homesick. Did you see those verses in the North American translated from the Persian. Goodbye—

Yours affectly.

Mary Temple—

LETTER 23
Pelham. Feb. 16*th* 1870

Dear Mr Gray,

Don't be alarmed at the lead pencil. I am not in bed, & am only sitting bundled up on the piazza, by order of the Dr—& feel like writing, so excuse the appearance of the letter. Many thanks for your last letter. It was most kind, but then you always are. This letter will give you more intelligence of a cheerful nature, but this time the collapse is physical rather than mental. I hope your stern heart will be touched when you hear how immediately both of your suggestions were followed out by me—that is, I did my best. You know you said "Hadn't you better go to Washington!" [*sic*] & why didn't I consult a physician, not Homeopathic? As you see you have but to express a desire, or give a word of advice, & I hasten to obey. I packed my trunk & started for New York, feeling a good deal knocked up, but hoping to get better from the change. I was to stay over Sunday in N. Y. & see Dr Metcalfe, a physician of good standing & an old friend of my father's. I left word at his office to come & see me on Sunday eve. & in the meantime, my cousin Mrs Post with whom I was staying recommended her physician, Taylor, who came on Saturday night, just before I was going to bed, & sounded my lungs & told me very dreadful things concerning them. As his verdict was worse than Metcalfe's, I will tell you what he said first. He began in solemn tones "My dear lady, your right lung is deseased [*sic*], all your hemorrhages have come from there. It must have been deseased at least a year before they began. You must go to Europe as soon as possible—" etc. etc. This was not cheerful as I had been idiot enough to believe my former Dr. who said it was from my throat & not my lungs. But of course I wanted to hear his honest opinion, & told him I wasn't a bit nervous. He said he wasn't sure whether there were tubercles on my lungs or not—if there were it was incurable. I asked him what was the most unfavorable view he could take of the case. I didn't mean to ask him how long I should live, & was somewhat unprepared for his reply of "two or three years." I I [*sic*] however did not wish to make him repent of his honesty, so I replied, "Well Dr. if my right lung were all gone, I should still make a stand for my left," & then by way of showing how valiant a stand I proposed to make, I fainted—but that was owing a good deal to my previous used up condition from want of sleep etc.—He then told me that there was every possibility that my case was of a less grave kind, & took his departure. I was glad to have him go, he was not at all a nice man, spoke bad grammar, & made himself generally objectionable. I slept very little that night, & decided to give up my Washington trip, as I did not feel up to it. The next night my dear Dr Metcalfe came, whom I love—He is the gentlest old soul, & the kindest that I have ever seen. To start with he is a gentleman, & an excellent physician, & to end with he & my father were fond of each other at West Point, & he took a sort of paternal interest in me. He told me my right lung was decidedly weaker than my left, which was quite sound,—but that the hemorrhage had been a good thing & kept it from actual desease—& if I could keep up my general health I might get all right again. He had known a ten times worse case get entirely well. He told me not to go to Washington—but to go to Europe. So if I am not dead before June, I am to go to Europe with my cousin Mrs Post, & her four children—to stay fifteen months. In a fortnight I am going to New York to be under the Dr's. care for some time. I feel tired out, & hardly able to stir—but my spirits are good enough & I don't propose to lose them if I can help it, for I know it all depends upon myself whether I get thro' this or not. That is, if I begin to be indifferent to the result, I shall go down hill quickly—I have enough Irish blood in me to rather enjoy a good fight too. I have slept soundly every night since I saw Dr Metcalfe, which will show you that I am not at all nervous. I saw Ellen Mason several times in town. She is very sweet and one of the most gentle, sympathetic, feminine souls that I have ever known. She is coming out here to spend Sunday with us. I dreamt the other night that you were engaged to be married. I saw you and the young person together, & you seemed very happy about it. You were a sittin' in the moonlight, & the first that I knew of it, I perceived that you had hold of her hand, as if you had a right to it, whereupon you said to me, "You see how it is with us," and then I congratulated you, & kissed the other party, whom I knew, & made some pretty little speech, & woke up. She was a "dreadful nice" person. Don't you wish it was true? Kitty has just gone by & said: "Ask Mr Gray to come & make me a visit, before you go to Europe," & I replied "He won't come, because he's got his lectures at the college," & I was right wasn't I? I feel the greatest longing for summer, or spring. I think I would like it to be always spring for the rest of my life, & to have all the people I care for always with me, & never even to speak of going away—but who wouldn't like it so? Good-bye—Write soon. I hope you are successful with your lectures. I should like to hear you give them. Are respectable spinsters allowed?

Always affecty yrs,
Mary Temple.

## 1843
*April 15*

Born at Washington Place, New York City, into the wealthy family of Henry James Sr. (student of theological and social issues) and Mary Walsh James. Brother William had been born on 11 January 1842.

*October*

James family departs for England.

## 1844
*January*

Family visits France.

*May*

HJ Sr. suffers mental and spiritual crisis and is introduced to the writings of Swedenborg.

*October*

Return to New York City.

## 1845
*July 21*

Birth of Garth Wilkinson (Wilky) James.

*Fall*

Family moves to 50 North Pearl Street, Albany, New York, where they live until early summer 1847.

## 1846
*August 29*

Birth of Robertson (Bob) James.

## 1848
*April*

Purchase of 58 West Fourteenth Street, New York City, home until 1855.

*August 7*

Birth of Alice James.

HJ attends a series of private schools in New York City during these years; summer vacations spent on Staten Island and Long Island.

## 1852

Family attends numerous theatrical productions, circuses, and spectaculars in these New York years. Thackeray visits in November during his tour of America.

## 1855

*June 27*

Family leaves for Europe, stopping off at London and Paris en route for Geneva. HJ develops malaria on journey. Other boys attend school in Geneva.

*October*

Family returns to London, eventually staying in St. John's Wood. Children taught by tutor; friendship of HJ Sr. with Swedenborgian James John Garth Wilkinson. Many visits to theater.

## 1856

*June*

Family moves to Paris. HJ visits galleries and museums, having overwhelming experience in the Louvre's Galerie d'Apollon. HJ attends school, the Institution Fezandié (described as Fourierist).

## 1857

*Summer*

Family decamps to Boulogne-sur-Mer; HJ briefly attends the Collège Impériale, meeting the baker's son Benoît Constant Coquelin, who became an eminent actor. In September HJ falls seriously ill with typhoid.

*October*

Jameses return briefly to Paris, but with financial crisis in the United States, family economizes by moving back to Boulogne at end of year. HJ is tutored at home.

## 1858

*Summer*

Having returned to the United States, family settles at Newport, R.I., near Edmund Tweedy and his wife, Mary, a relative. The couple are caring for the Jameses' orphaned cousins, the Temple children, including Mary (Minny). Boys attend the Berkeley Institute; HJ forms friendship with Thomas Sergeant Perry (scholar and writer) and John La Farge (artist).

## 1859

*October*

Jameses leave Newport for Geneva. HJ attends school with inappropriately scientific curriculum, the Institution Rochette, before moving to the Academy, where WJ is also enrolled.

## 1860

*July*

WJ, HJ, and Wilky stay in Bonn to improve their German.

*September*

Jameses leave Europe, returning in October to Newport once more so that WJ can become a pupil of the artist William Morris Hunt. HJ also has lessons and furthers his friendships with Perry and La Farge.

## 1861

*April*

HJ sustains back injury in helping fight fire in Newport, referred to as his "obscure hurt." Both he and WJ are counted as unfit for military service in the Civil War, but Wilky and Bob join the Union Army in 1862 and 1863, respectively.

*Autumn*

WJ gives up study of art to attend the Lawrence Scientific School at Harvard.

## 1862

*September*

HJ enters Harvard Law School, but abandons course in summer 1863.

## 1863

*July 18*

Wilky sustains serious injuries in the attack on Fort Wagner by the 54th Massachusetts Regiment under command of Robert Gould Shaw.

## 1864

*February*

Anonymous publication of HJ's first tale, "A Tragedy of Error," in *Continental Monthly*.

*May*

Family leaves Newport for Beacon Hill, Boston. At this time HJ is encouraged in his writing by Charles Eliot Norton and, over the next few years, produces many literary reviews and stories for such journals and weeklies as the *Atlantic Monthly* and the *Nation.*

## 1865
*August*

Short holiday at North Conway, N.H., with the Temple sisters and Civil War veterans Oliver Wendell Holmes and John Chipman Gray.

## 1866
*Summer*

HJ becomes friendly with William Dean Howells, novelist, critic, and editor.

*November*

James family moves to 20 Quincy Street, Cambridge, on the east side of Harvard Yard.

## 1869
*February 17*

HJ leaves for Europe, staying in London and Malvern, where he seeks relief for chronic constipation and digestive problems. Through his connection with the Norton family he meets Leslie Stephen, William Morris, George Eliot, Ruskin, Rossetti, Burne-Jones.

*Late summer*

HJ arrives for the first time in Italy and is enchanted. He travels from Venice as far south as Naples before returning to Florence at the end of the year.

## 1870
*February*

HJ leaves Paris for London, still feeling indisposed.

*March 8*

Beloved cousin Mary Temple dies of tuberculosis; HJ is shocked and writes long letters on the subject.

*April 30*

HJ leaves Europe and returns to family home at Cambridge. Though nostalgic for Europe, continues to write prolifically.

## 1872
*May 11*

HJ Leaves for Europe, accompanying semi-invalid sister, Alice, and his aunt Kate. They tour England, Switzerland, and northern Italy, returning to London via Paris. Alice and Aunt Kate leave for America in October 1872; HJ returns to Rome via Paris; meets Fanny Kemble and mixes in American expatriate society. He is joined for a time by WJ in fall of 1873.

### 1874
*August 25*

HJ leaves Liverpool to sail for United States.

### 1875
*January*

*Roderick Hudson* begins serialization in the *Atlantic Monthly*.

*November*

HJ arrives back in London to "take possession of the old world." He then moves on to Paris, meets Ivan Turgenev and a literary circle including Flaubert, Edmond de Goncourt, Zola, Maupassant, Daudet, and Renan. For a time he writes Paris letters for the *New York Tribune*.

### 1876
*December*

HJ moves permanently to London.

### 1877

*The American* published. HJ visits Paris and Italy in the summer.

### 1878

"Daisy Miller" proves to be a great popular success. Now a part of London society, HJ meets Tennyson, Meredith, Whistler, Browning, and Gladstone, among others. *The Europeans* published in September.

This period represents the years covered by *A Small Boy and Others, Notes of a Son and Brother,* and *The Middle Years.* By 1878 HJ had established himself in Britain and visited the United States only occasionally (though for extended periods) during the rest of his life. In 1884 sister Alice also left New England for Britain and never returned; she died in 1892. HJ took an apartment in Kensington, West London, in 1883. In 1897 he first rented and then bought Lamb House, an elegant house in the Cinque port of Rye, Sussex, while maintaining his London base. In the same year, having suffered from wrist pain, HJ hired a stenographer and from this time dictated his work. He made a number of attempts to write stage plays but met with little success.

At the turn of the twentieth century HJ began to suffer increasingly from physical ailments and depressive disorders, though his work was highly respected. He enjoyed many friendships, some especially passionate with younger men. He remained close too to his brother, WJ, his wife, Alice, and their family. With the outbreak of World War I HJ involved himself in charitable work and became a British national in 1915. He was awarded the Order of Merit shortly before his death on 28 February 1916.

# GENEALOGIES

These genealogies are intended to clarify family relationships referred to in James's autobiographical writings. Not all family members are necessarily listed. The spelling of certain recurring names, such as Catharine and Jeannette, varies according to sources.

The information is derived from Rev. William Walsh, *A Record and Sketch of Hugh Walsh's Family* (Newburgh, N.Y.: Newburgh Journal Print, 1903); Katharine Hastings, "William James (1771–1832) of Albany, N.Y., and His Descendants," *New York Genealogical and Biographical Record* 55, no. 2 (April 1924): 101–19, no. 3 (July 1924): 222–36; the family genealogies provided in Alfred Habegger, *The Father: A Life of Henry James, Sr.* (New York: Farrar, Straus, and Giroux, 1994); *The Complete Letters of Henry James, 1855–1872,* ed. Pierre A. Walker and Greg W. Zacharias, 2 vols. (Lincoln: University of Nebraska Press, 2006); and *The Correspondence of William James,* ed. Ignas K. Skrupskelis and Elizabeth M. Berkeley, 12 vols. (Charlottesville: University Press of Virginia, 1992–2004)

# JAMES FAMILY

**William JAMES of Albany (1771–1832)**
**married first**
**(1) Elizabeth TILLMAN (1774–1797)**

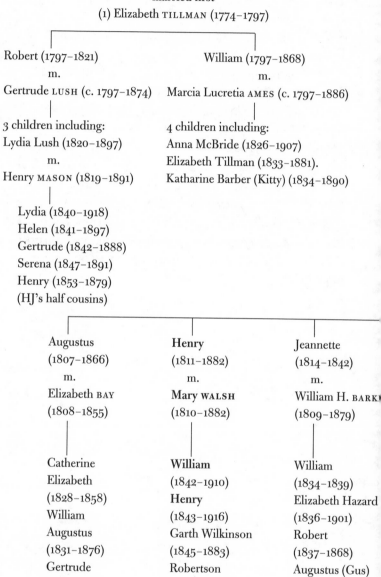

| Robert (1797–1821) | William (1797–1868) |
|---|---|
| m. | m. |
| Gertrude LUSH (c. 1797–1874) | Marcia Lucretia AMES (c. 1797–1886) |

3 children including:
Lydia Lush (1820–1897)
m.
Henry MASON (1819–1891)

 Lydia (1840–1918)
 Helen (1841–1897)
 Gertrude (1842–1888)
 Serena (1847–1891)
 Henry (1853–1879)
 (HJ's half cousins)

4 children including:
Anna McBride (1826–1907)
Elizabeth Tillman (1833–1881).
Katharine Barber (Kitty) (1834–1890)

| Augustus | Henry | Jeannette |
|---|---|---|
| (1807–1866) | (1811–1882) | (1814–1842) |
| m. | m. | m. |
| Elizabeth BAY | Mary WALSH | William H. BARK▸ |
| (1808–1855) | (1810–1882) | (1809–1879) |

| Catherine | William | William |
|---|---|---|
| Elizabeth | (1842–1910) | (1834–1839) |
| (1828–1858) | Henry | Elizabeth Hazard |
| William | (1843–1916) | (1836–1901) |
| Augustus | Garth Wilkinson | Robert |
| (1831–1876) | (1845–1883) | (1837–1868) |
| Gertrude | Robertson | Augustus (Gus) |
| (1834?–1889) | (1846–1910) | (1842–1863) |
| Marie Bay | Alice | |
| (1841–1904) | (1848–1892) | |

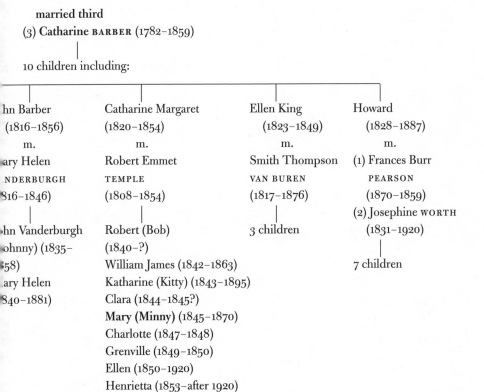

**married second**
(2) Mary Ann CONNOLLY (d. 1800 aged 21)

Ellen, or Eleanor (1800–1823) m. James KING

**married third**
(3) **Catharine BARBER** (1782–1859)

10 children including:

| hn Barber (1816–1856) | Catharine Margaret (1820–1854) | Ellen King (1823–1849) | Howard (1828–1887) |
|---|---|---|---|
| m. | m. | m. | m. |
| ary Helen NDERBURGH 16–1846) | Robert Emmet TEMPLE (1808–1854) | Smith Thompson VAN BUREN (1817–1876) | (1) Frances Burr PEARSON (1870–1859) |
| | | | (2) Josephine WORTH (1831–1920) |
| hn Vanderburgh ohnny) (1835– 58) | Robert (Bob) (1840–?) | 3 children | 7 children |
| ary Helen 840–1881) | William James (1842–1863) | | |
| | Katharine (Kitty) (1843–1895) | | |
| | Clara (1844–1845?) | | |
| | **Mary (Minny)** (1845–1870) | | |
| | Charlotte (1847–1848) | | |
| | Grenville (1849–1850) | | |
| | Ellen (1850–1920) | | |
| | Henrietta (1853–after 1920) | | |

# ROBERTSON-WALSH FAMILIES

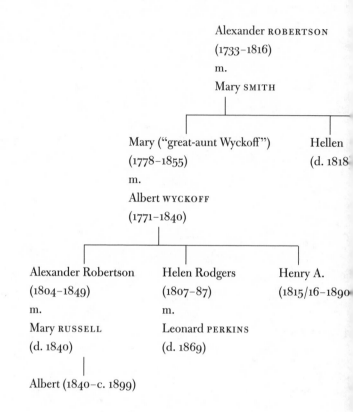

Alexander ROBERTSON
(1733–1816)
m.
Mary SMITH

Mary ("great-aunt Wyckoff")          Hellen
(1778–1855)                          (d. 1818
m.
Albert WYCKOFF
(1771–1840)

Alexander Robertson          Helen Rodgers          Henry A.
(1804–1849)                  (1807–87)              (1815/16–1890
m.                           m.
Mary RUSSELL                 Leonard PERKINS
(d. 1840)                    (d. 1869)

Albert (1840–c. 1899)

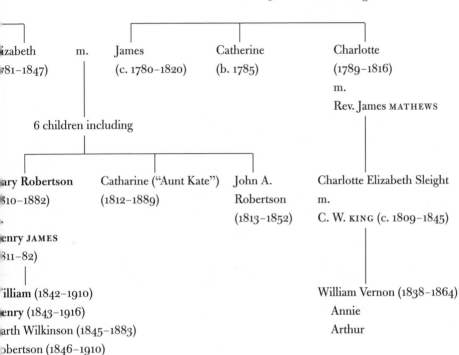

Hugh WALSH
(1745–1817)
m. Catherine ARMSTRONG
(1755–1801)
9 children including

| | | | |
|---|---|---|---|
| izabeth | m. | James | Catherine | Charlotte |
| 81–1847) | | (c. 1780–1820) | (b. 1785) | (1789–1816) |
| | | | | m. |
| | | | | Rev. James MATHEWS |

6 children including

ary Robertson    Catharine ("Aunt Kate")    John A.    Charlotte Elizabeth Sleight
10–1882)    (1812–1889)    Robertson    m.
        (1813–1852)    C. W. KING (c. 1809–1845)

enry JAMES
11–82)

illiam (1842–1910)                 William Vernon (1838–1864)
enry (1843–1916)                   Annie
arth Wilkinson (1845–1883)      Arthur
obertson (1846–1910)
ice (1848–1892)

Barker, Augustus (Gus) (1842–1863), a much admired and dynamic cousin of HJ. With the outbreak of the Civil War, he enlisted with the New York Cavalry while a student at Harvard, but was killed by guerrillas near Kelly's Ford on the Rappahannock River, Virginia.

Gray, John Chipman (1839–1915), friend of HJ in his Cambridge years, successful lawyer and Harvard professor; recipient of letters from HJ's dying cousin Mary Temple.

Grymes, Mary Helen James (1840–1881), daughter of HJ's uncle, John Barber James, who married Dr. Charles Alfred Grymes.

Holmes, Oliver Wendell, Jr. (1841–1935), one of HJ's circle of Cambridge friends of the 1860s. Holmes was a Civil War veteran who enjoyed a highly successful legal career and became a Supreme Court justice.

James, Alice (1848–1892), the youngest James child. In adolescence she began to suffer ill health manifesting itself in nervous prostration (never clearly diagnosed but probably psychosomatic in origin) and remained an invalid for virtually the rest of her life. Her Diary reveals a brilliant intellect and a trenchant manner. After the death of her parents she moved to Britain with her companion, Katharine Loring, in 1884.

James, Catharine Barber (1782–1859), third wife of William James and HJ's grandmother. She lived in Albany, caring for many of the orphaned and motherless children of the family. She successfully contested her husband's will which had unreasonably sought to limit her inheritance.

James, Garth Wilkinson (Wilky) (1845–1883), younger brother of HJ, sustained wounds fighting in the Civil War. After the war he undertook a cotton-growing enterprise in Florida with his brother Bob, but the business failed. He later moved to the Midwest and married. Suffering from chronic ill-health from his war wounds, he was declared bankrupt.

James, Henry Sr. (1811–1882), HJ's father. He suffered a severe burn to his leg in youth which resulted in amputation. He had a difficult relationship with his father, William, and early became addicted to alcohol; having dropped out for a period, he later graduated from Union College and Princeton Theological Seminary. With his mother and other family members, HJ Sr. successfully contested his father's will and gained a substantial inheritance. Much influenced by the ideas of Swedenborg, he published a number of philosophical and theological books and moved in elite intellectual circles of New England.

James, Howard (1828–1887), youngest and much admired uncle of HJ. Twice married, he suffered from bouts of alcoholism.

James, John Barber (1816–1856), HJ's uncle and father of Mary Helen and John Vanderburgh. A popular, engaging man, he led a fast life, incurring considerable gambling debts before eventually committing suicide.

James, John Vanderburgh (1835–1858), cousin to HJ, had a difficult, unsettled childhood. Prone to psychiatric disorder, he may have died by suicide.

James, Mary (1810–1882), HJ's mother, daughter of wealthy New York City merchant James Walsh. She devotedly supported her husband and was much eulogized by her children.

James, Robertson (Bob) (1846–1910), youngest brother of HJ, served in the Civil War and later became subject to severe and enduring bouts of alcoholism. After an abortive cotton-growing episode in the South, he moved to the Midwest. Because of his infidelities, his marriage failed and later years were spent in Concord, Mass.

James, William (1842–1910), the oldest James child, brilliant and talented, intended first to become a painter but went on to study science at Harvard, where he spent his entire career. Having overcome a range of enduring physical and mental ailments, he taught psychology and later philosophy. His published works placed him at the forefront of American thinkers. His relationship with HJ remained affectionate throughout their lives.

King, Vernon (1838–1864), a much admired, European-educated cousin of HJ's who, in defiance of his mother's wishes, fought and died in the Civil War.

La Farge, John (1835–1910), painter, designer, and stained-glass craftsman. He met HJ in the Newport studio of William Morris Hunt in 1858 and, with his strongly European perspective, exercised a profound influence on the younger man's conception of art and literature.

Mason, Lydia Lush James (1820–1897), daughter of HJ Sr.'s stepbrother Robert, married Henry Mason. The Masons, who lived for long periods in Europe and on Staten Island, had five children, Lydia Stringer, Helen, Gertrude, Serena, and Henry.

Norton, Charles Eliot (1827–1908), author and editor, Harvard professor of fine arts. He published much of HJ's early work and introduced him to eminent British writers in 1869.

Perkins, Helen Wyckoff (1807–1887), wife of Leonard Perkins, guardian of nephew Albert, and cousin of Mary James. The family lived close to the Jameses in New York City. A strong personality, she cared for her mother, "great-aunt Wyckoff," and governed other members of the household.

Perry, Thomas Sergeant (1845–1928), a Newport friend of HJ, had distinguished naval family connections. He later became a Harvard professor and literary scholar, and the brother-in-law of the painter John La Farge.

Robertson, Alexander (1733–1816), HJ's maternal great-grandfather. Scottish-born, he became a highly successful businessman and later philanthropist in New York City.

Russel, Cabot Jackson (1844–1863), born into a distinguished New England family, served as an officer with Wilky James in the 54th Massachusetts Infantry Regiment and died during the attack on Fort Wagner, South Carolina. His father brought the injured Wilky back to Newport.

Shaw, Robert Gould (1837–1863), born into a strongly committed abolitionist family, became the heroic leader of the 54th Massachusetts regiment in the Civil War, perishing during the abortive attack on Fort Wagner in which Wilky James was also injured.

Temple, Catharine James (1820–1854), a favorite sister of HJ Sr. She died young of tuberculosis, leaving six children, among them Mary (Minny) and William, cousins affectionately remembered by HJ.

Temple, Mary (Minny) (1845–1870), HJ's beloved cousin whose relations with other members of his family were sometimes strained. Independent and charming, on her death from tuberculosis she became the inspiration for some of HJ's later heroines.

Temple, Robert Emmet (1808–1854), army officer and lawyer. Married to Catharine, he also died prematurely of tuberculosis.

Tweedy, Edmund (c. 1812–1901), a wealthy New York City banker and a transcendentalist friend of HJ Sr., married to Mary Temple. The couple had houses in New York and Newport and also lived for periods in Europe.

Tweedy, Mary Temple (d. 1891), related by marriage to one of HJ's aunts. She was also an aunt of the Temple children, some of whom she cared for when they were orphaned in 1854.

Van Winkle, Edgar (1842–1920), New York neighbor of the James family and boyhood friend of WJ and HJ. He studied at Union College and became a civil engineer.

Walsh, Catharine (1812–1889), HJ's Aunt Kate. Though briefly married, she lived semipermanently with the James family.

# INDEX

Boott, Francis, 374, 374–75n806, 376–77, 376n810, 378–79, 379n815; with reference to *The Portrait of a Lady*, 379, 380

Boston, 153, 275–77; Athenaeum, 325, 325n685; Museum Theater 325, 325n685; Parker House Hotel, 167n347, 276n565; Park Street Church, 336, 336n706

Boswell, James, 431, 431n32

Boucicault, Dion, adaptation of *Rip Van Winkle*, 278n571

Bradford, George Partridge, 102n198

Brewster, Henry Bennet, 322–24, 322n677

Brignoli, Pasquale, 397, 397n850

Britten, Benjamin, 198n404

Brodrick, George Charles, 418–19n15

Bronson, Katherine de Kay, 333n703

Brooks, Phillips, 372–73, 372n804, 374, 380, 396

Brown, John, 100n189, 177, 198n405

Brown, Sarah, 177, 177n363

Browning, Elizabeth Barrett, 74n141, 332, 333n703

Browning, Robert, 73, 74n142, 332, 333n703, 361, 466n92, 467; "Bishop Blougram's Apology," 368n789, 386, 386n829, 457n78, 466; *Men and Women*, 73–74, 74n141, 466, 466n92; *The Ring and the Book*, 358, 359n774; "Soliloquy of the Spanish Cloister," 35n69

Brownson, Orestes Augustus, 163, 163n334

Buckle, Henry T., 231, 231n484

Bunyan, John, *Pilgrim's Progress*, 138n279

Butler, Major-General Ben, 292n600

Byron, Lord (George Gordon), 34, 34n67, 219, 219n451, 424, 425n23

Cabot, J. Eliot [Elliot], 204n423, 233, 233nn493, 494; philosophical correspondence with HJ Sr., 233

Calvin, John, 147n292

Canning, Charlotte, Lady, 467–68n94

Carlyle, Thomas, 138n279, 146n291, 147, 149, 149nn297–98, 150, 150n299, 158–59, 158n321, 162, 162n330, 162n332, 167, 167n344; *Frederick the Great*, 334n704; *Latter-Day Pamphlets*, 158n321, 159, 159n322; *Life of John Sterling*, 150n300; opinion of HJ Sr., 149n298, 150n299; *Past and Present*, 146, 146n291

Cavour, Count Camillo, 17n24, 183n377

Channing, Dr. William Ellery, 124n256, 168n348, 186n382

Channing, William Ellery (nephew), 168, 168n348, 169

Chantre, Ernest, 351, 351n747

Chaworth, Mary, 34, 34n67

Cheever, George Barrell, 163, 163n334

Cherbuliez, Victor, 13, 13n18

Chichester, Sophia, 137, 138n279, 138–39, 165n339

Child, Francis J., 102, 102n197, 124, 236n500, 256–58, 256n531, 260; *English and Scottish Ballads*, 256n531

Church, F. P., 222n458

Civil War (US), 39n77, 41n81, 53, 53n104, 193–95, 194n398, 239, 239nn505–506, 254n528, 288–316, 319; African American soldiers, 194n398, 195, 290n594; Anglo-American relations, 257–58n534; Battle of Gettysburg, 250, 250n521; Fort McAllister, 306, 306n634, 307n635; Fort Monroe, 311, 311n650; Fort Sumter, 239, 239n506, 311, 314, 314n660; Fort Wagner, 194, 194n398, 198n405, 251; looting of Darien, 303n626; and young men of Harvard, 258; retaking of Charleston, SC, 313–15, 314–15n661

Clark, Mrs., 177

Clarke, Miss, 380n817

clergy, in George Eliot and Trollope, 135–36, 136n277

Clough, Arthur H., "Blank Misgivings . . . ," 386, 386n828

Collins, Wilkie, *The Woman in White,* 352, 352n751

Collins, William, 190, 190n389

Colvin, Sidney, 429n29

Comte, Auguste, 426n27

Cooper, Fenimore, 91, 91n165; *The Last of the Mohicans,* 91n165

*Cornhill Magazine,* 18, 18n27, 20–21, 266, 266n546

Cotman, John Sell, 270n555

Couture, Thomas, 52, 52n102

Craig, Sam D., 282–84, 283n579

Cranch, Elizabeth, 182n374

Crawford, Frank Marion, 389, 389n834

Crimean War, 157–58n318

Cromwell, Oliver, 299n613

Curmer, Léon, 284n582


Danse, Augustine, 291n596

Dante Alighieri, 218n447, 231, 231n484, 332, 333n703

Darwin, Charles, 207n429, 210n436, 371, 371n797; *The Origin of Species,* 231n484, 371n797

Daudet, Alphonse, 46, 46–47n89; *Jack,* 47n89; *Numa Roumestan,* 47n89

Davis, Jefferson, 313, 313n656

Delaporte, Madame, 347, 347n731

Delmonico's Restaurant, 357, 357n767

Derby, Richard H., 348, 348n734

Desaix de Veygoux, General Louis-Charles-Antoine, 49, 49n97

Dickens, Charles, 21, 21n34, 40, 115, 118, 121, 139, 140n281, 204–5, 204n425, 246n517, 330n696, 412, 431, 439; *David Copperfield,* 205, 205n427; *Pickwick Papers,* 205

Disraeli, Benjamin, 219n451; *Coningsby,* 219, 219n451

Dodge, Mary Abigail (Gail Hamilton), 212n438, 222, 222n458

Doré, Gustave, 267n547

Drew, Anna, 191–92n393

Droz, Gustave, *Babolain,* 232n489, 233, 233n491

Dryden, John, 190, 190n389; *The Hind and the Panther,* 190n389

Dumas, Alexandre (*fils*), *Les Idées de Madame Aubray,* 347, 347n731

du Maurier, George, 23, 23n40, 265–66, 266n546

Duncan, Mrs. Willy, 392, 392–93n843

Duveneck, Elizabeth Boott, 52n102, 374–75, 374–75n806, 376, 376n810, 378, 379n815, 380, 393; with reference to *The Portrait of a Lady,* 379; relationship with father, 379

Duveneck, Francis (Frank), 132n272, 374n806


Edwards, Jonathan, 147, 147n293

Eliot, Professor Charles William, 101, 101n192, 103, 113

Eliot, George (Mary Anne Evans), 19n29, 21, 21n34, 136, 368, 368n790, 370, 370n794, 372, 372n802, 374, 380, 438n48, 440–54, 440n51, 441n53, 443n57, 444nn60–61, 447, 447n65, 453n71, 454, 454n72, 462n85; *Adam Bede,* 19, 19n29, 136n277, 432n33; *Daniel Deronda,* 368n790, 446, 446n64, 454n72; *Felix Holt,* 136n277, 341n717, 441–42, 442nn54–56; *Middlemarch,* 220n453, 222n457, 368n790, 441, 441n52, 446, 446n64; *The Mill on the Floss,* 136n277, 374, 374n805; *Scenes from Clerical Life,* 136n277; *Silas Marner,* 136n277, 440, 441n52; *The Spanish Gypsy,* 352, 352n750, 374, 374n805

Hedge, Rev. Dr. Frederic, 168, 168n350

Hegel, George Wilhelm Friedrich, 234–35, 234n495; *Phenomenology of the Spirit,* 234n495

Heine, Heinrich, 30, 31n58

Helps, Arthur, 162, 162n332

Henry VIII, 437n46

Henry, Joseph, 145n287, 214n441, 223–24, 224n462

Hill, Thomas, 344n724

Higginson, Francis Lee (Frank), 105, 105n205,

Higginson, Samuel Storrow, 100, 100n189,

Higginson, Thomas Wentworth, 45

Hoche, General Lazare, 49, 49n97

Hogarth, William, 412, 412n7, 431

Holland, Henry, 431n31

Holmes, Oliver Wendell, 346n728; *The Autocrat of the Breakfast Table,* 256n532

Holmes, Oliver Wendell, Jr., 197n404, 226n465, 262n540, 292n598, 325nn684–85, 345n726, 354, 359n776, 400

Hones family, 392, 392n843

Hood, Major-General John B., 307, 307n637

Hooper, Edward, 179, 179n370

Hooper, Ellen, 179, 179n370

Hooper, Marian (Clover), 179, 179n370

Houghton, 1st Baron (Richard Monckton Milnes), 455, 455n75, 462n85

Howe, Julia Ward, 151n301, 329, 329n693, 330, 389n834

Howe, Samuel Gridley, 330, 330n696

Howells, William Dean, 44n84, 51n101, 340–41, 340–41n716, 426, 426n26

Hugo, Victor, 419n16; *Choses Vues,* 295n605; *Les Misérables,* 304, 304n629

Humpert, Dr. [Philippus?] (landlord), 23, 24n43, 27, 28, 30, 40

Humpert, Mrs., 27, 27n51

Humpert, Theodor (son of Dr. Humpert), 30, 30n57

Hunt, Louisa Perkins, 79n148, 112, 112n225, 179, 179n369

Hunt, William Morris, 17n26, 33n62, 39n77, 51, 51n99, 53n103, 54, 58, 58n111, 63, 64n119, 65, 65n123, 66, 67n126, 77, 79n148, 112n224, 113, 266n547, 374n806; *Girl at the Fountain,* 65, 65n123

*Illustrated London News,* 422, 422n20

Ingram, Herbert, 422n20

Inness, George, 124n255

Irving, Henry, 433, 433n37

Irving, Washington, 278n571

James family, 22n39, 37–38, 103, 108–9, 110; artists in family, 39, 39n78; children lacking careers, 92n167; deaths of parents, 141, 141n282; education in Switzerland, 5–7; European education, 156n315; freedom of religious education, 132, 134–35, 137; Geneva Academy, 6, 8, 8n7; Institution Haccius, 18, 19n28; Institution Rochette, 7–8, 7n6, 12, 29; intellectual freedom of children, 126–29; leave Europe, 176; move to Boston, 316–17, 317n664; move to Cambridge, 344–45, 344n724; not New Englanders, 151; Pensionnat Maquelin, 6n4, 19, 20n32; parents' views on education, 8–9; parents' relationship, 141–43; relationship to America, 48–49; return to America, 51–52; summer in Bonn, 22; travels in Europe, 5–6n1; warmth of family relations, 142–43

James, Alice, 19n30, 37, 38, 38n75, 39, 40, 41, 55n107, 92n167, 102, 102n198, 108, 113, 114n230, 117, 129n267, 141n282, 149n298, 156n315, 173n357, 185, 202, 217, 226n465, 230, 231n485, 249n519, 312n653, 314n659, 350, 350n744,

358n770, 366n784, 371n796, 388n832, 426n27, 454n72

James, Alice Howe Gibbens, 34n64, 205n425, 355nn761–62, 392n843

James, Caroline Cary, 295n604

James, Catharine Barber (grandmother), 119n247, 214n442

James, Catharine Margaret (aunt), 95n171

James, Garth Wilkinson, 6n4, 18, 18n27, 19n28, 24, 24nn43–44, 30, 33n61, 34n64, 37, 40, 53n104, 80n150, 92n167, 100n189, 102, 102n198, 103n200, 105, 105n205, 106, 107, 108, 109n217, 110, 110n219, 123, 126, 126n263, 157n317, 175n360, 177, 177n361, 194, 194n398, 195, 198, 198n405, 199, 217, 251nn523–24, 288, 289n592, 290n593, 291, 294n603, 295, 295n604, 296nn606–7, 297n609, 298n612, 303–4n626, 305nn630–31, 306n632, 307n637, 308n640, 310, 310n646, 311nn649–50, 312nn653–54, 314n659, 315n662, 320n672, 366n784, 381, 382, 382n819, 383; "The Assault on Fort Wagner," 194n398; Civil War letters, 297–315; charm and dislike of reading, 30; and 54th Massachusetts Regiment, 251, 251n522; and 44th Massachusetts Regiment, 194n398; Florida venture, 217n445, 296, 296n606; on HJ as author, 24n44; injury in Civil War, 194–95; Kinston engagement, 302–4; leaving Boston with 54th Massachusetts Regiment, 290–91; looting in war, 303–4; recovery, 195n399; in South Carolina, 305–7

James, George Abbott, 285–86, 285n583, 415n10

James, George Payne Rainsford, 154–55, 154n309

James, Henry: at "Albany" eating-house, 431–32; at Adelphi Hotel, Liverpool, 412, 412n6; on America, 246; admiration for HJ Sr.'s intellect, 182–83; admiration for WJ, 96, 259n535; admiration for "Americanism" of fellow students, 280–81n575, 281–82; affection for HJ Sr., 45; in the Alps, 22n39; arrival in England, 410–11; aspiring artist, 287–88; Berkeley Institute, Newport, 65, 65n125; Bonn lodgings, 27–28; Boston, 152–53n307; boyhood walks around Newport, 86–87; British humor, 429; British resorts and spas, 55, 55n107; Cambridge lodgings, 243–45, 244n512; on Carlyle, 149n298; consecration to literature, 318–19; contrasted with his father, 136n278; creative-observing life, 338–41; critical of HJ Sr.'s style, 142–43; criticism of his early works, 44–45n85; on death of Mary Temple, 364n779, 385n825; desire to be "literary," 236–37n501, 238, 270–71; differing tastes from WJ, 258–60; disappointment in Tennyson and his reading, 457–58, 465–66; dislike of mathematics, 7–8; distant view of Civil War, 295–96; on Drachenfels and Rolandseck, 28, 28–29n54; early writing, 339–40; on Europe, 263; failure to appreciate father's philosophy, 129–30; failure in law exercise, 268, 268–69n551; first earnings, 318; friendship with W. D. Howells, 340–41n716; gathering of impressions, 24–25; on Geneva, 6n2; at Geneva Academy with WJ, 9; German spa towns, 46, 46n87; German woods, 29; gives up art, 76; Half Moon Street, Piccadilly, 415, 415n10, 416; Harvard campus, 243; Law School, 236–37, 236n500; ignorance of American politics, 423–24; illnesses, 37n74, 410n3, 410–11n4; interest in theater, 276–77,

James, Henry: (*continued*)
277n568; liking for Newport, 5n1; on London, 419–21; meeting with Dickens, 204–7, 204n425; misgivings about his father's writings, 132n273; nature of youth, 326; need for action, 237; on New England, 245n515, 275–76, 276n564; Newport fire, 239–40, 240–41n508; "obscure hurt," 239–42, 239n506, 240–41n508, 242n509, 255–56; observing Paris, 49–50; on periphery of art-study, 66–67; racial anxieties, 254n528; revising Mary Temple's letters, 366n782; on roles of men and women, 174–75n359; sharing room with WJ at Boulogne, 97; "sitting" for La Farge, 326; sketching with La Farge, 83–84; soldiers around Boston, 334–35; his stammer, 339n712; staying with G. A. James, 285n583; studying art with WJ, 63–64; on Swampscott, 125n260, 341–42, 345, 442; train journey from Bonn to Paris, 45–47; translation of Mérimée's *La Vénus d'Ille*, 74–75, 74–75n144; trip to Schenectady with WJ, 90–91; the Union soldier, 252–54, 248–49n519, 252–53n526, 289–90n592; Venusburg, 26, 26n47; visit to Boston surgeon, 242; visit to Portsmouth Grove, 248–50, 252–54, 248–49n519, 256n530; visit to Readville, 289–90; World War I, 253n527; writes to Maggie Mitchell, 278–79
-Fiction and Prose Works: *The Ambassadors*, 141n282, 288n586, 411n5; *The American*, 222n455, 452n70; *The American Scene*, 47n90, 54nn105–6, 74n141, 93n169, 147n294, 153n307, 245n516, 249n519, 254n528, 297n609, 310n646, 317n665, 319n670, 325n685, 326n686, 331n697, 336n706, 354n759, 411n5; *The Aspern Papers*, 34n67,

44n85; *The Bostonians*, 198n405, 270n554, 270–71n556, 452n70; *Confidence*, 46n87; "Crawford's Consistency," 223n461; "Daisy Miller," 90n163; *English Hours*, 440n51; "Eugene Pickering," 46n87; *The Europeans*, 222n455, 276n566, 452n70; *The Golden Bowl*, 58n112, 452n70; *Hawthorne*, 321n675, 323n679; *Italian Hours*, 32–33n61, 59n113, 377n813, 379n815, 417n12, 429n29; *The Ivory Tower*, 28n52, 54n105, 86n158, 238n503, 286n584; "The Jolly Corner," 120n248; "A Landscape Painter," 44n85, 71n135; "The Last of the Valerii," 75n144; "The Liar," 47n89, 76n146; *A Little Tour in France*, 417n12; "London Town," 411n5, 421n18; "Louisa Pallant," 46n87; "Madame de Mauves," 461n82; "The Middle Years," 63n117; "A Most Extraordinary Case," 44n85; "My Friend Bingham," 44n85; "Owen Wingrave," 198n404; *Partial Portraits*, 21n33, 23n40, 47n89, 136n277, 144n284; "A Passionate Pilgrim," 223n459, 430n30, 437n46; "Poor Richard," 44n85, 340n716, 359–60n776; *The Portrait of a Lady*, 44n85, 61n115, 170n354, 322n677, 354n760, 375n806, 452n70; *Portraits of Places*, 417n12; *The Princess Casamassima*, 48n93, 72n138, 277n568, 439n50, 452n70; "The Private Life," 333n703, 466n92; "The Real Right Thing," 139n280; "The Real Thing," 139n280; *Roderick Hudson*, 44n85, 120n249, 229n474; "The Romance of Certain Old Clothes," 44n85; *The Sense of the Past*, 57n110, 469n96; *The Spoils of Poynton*, 141n282; "The Story of a Year," 44n85, 195n399, 299n615,

James, Henry Sr. (*continued*)

faith in Old and New Testaments, 133–34; Boston clubs, 201n413; on his children, 231–32; on children's education, 42–43, 42n82, 89–90, 89n162, 91–92, 220; comparison of Unites States with Europe, 184; conversion to teachings of Swedenborg, 128n265; on dangers of benevolence, 189; difficulties with his father, 152; disability, 154, 213n441; dislike of "literary" men, 155; earlier years, 151n302, 151–52n303, 152–53, 153n308; in England, 149–51; on events in Europe, 183, 183–84n377; feelings about his wife, 141n282; on "free love" debate and Marx Edgeworth Lazarus's *Love vs. Marriage,* 193n397; frustration with Emerson, 148; on Horace Bushnell, *Nature and the Supernatural,* 193n396; on human independence, 192; as humane commentator on society, 170–71, 186–87n383; idealism about society, 179–81; lack of occupation, 56; *Lectures and Miscellanies,* 56; lecturing, 155n310, 159–61, 159–60n324; letters to women, 182–83n374, 199–200n407, 200–201; *Literary Remains,* 52n101, 132, 132n273, 137, 138n279; meeting with Mrs. Chichester, 137–39, 138n279, 165n339; mocked by family, 133n274; opinion of Carlyle, 146, 162–63, 167n344; pleasure in study, 126–29; plans to visit England, 147–48; public neglect of his writing, 51, 51–52n101; published works, 126n264; reading of Swedenborg, 128–29, 128n265; relationship with Emerson, 144–145, 145n288, 145–46n289, 147n294, 148n295, 161–62n329; *The Secret of Swedenborg,* 51–52n101; slavery, 191n390; "The Social Significance of Our Institutions," 19n30; spiritual crisis, 137, 137–38n279, 240n507; on spiritualism, 189, 189n386; his spirituality and moral sense, 42; as student at Union College, Schenectady, 90, 90n163; style, 200n409; thoughts of Europe, 156, 156n315; *Substance and Shadow,* 133n274; unconventionality, 130–31; visit to Ireland, 213–14, 213–14n441, 216–17; at work, 181

James, Henry (Harry, nephew), 41n81, 191n390

James, John Barber, 37n71

James, John Vanderburgh, 37n71

James, Mary (mother), 40, 105, 105n207, 116n241, 117, 177, 183n374, 202, 203, 228, 229n474, 230–31, 231n482, 264n543, 344n724, 356n766, 358n770, 391n840; HJ's feelings about, 130n269; supporting HJ Sr., 130–31; her wedding, 135n276

James, Mary Helen Vanderburgh, 37, 37n71, 38, 39

James, Mary Holton, 212n438, 294n603

James, Robertson, 6n4, 19n28, 22n39, 53n104, 56, 100n189, 102n198, 106, 177, 177n361, 212n440, 222n455, 250n521, 291n596, 292–93n601, 294–95n603, 296n607, 311n651, 314n658; in Civil War, 291–93; drawing, 33n63; and 55th Massachusetts Regiment, 194n398; Florida venture, 217n445, 296, 296n606; in Switzerland and Italy, 31–34; his serious attitude, 99, 99n182; "Three Years' Service with the 55th Massachusetts Volunteer Infantry," 194n398; troubled life, 32–34, 33n61

James, William (brother), 22n39, 27n51, 34, 34n65, 36, 63n117, 82n153, 106, 122, 122n250, 191n390, 204n425, 212n440, 229n475, 230, 230n480, 237n502, 239n504, 244n512, 260, 261–

Lee, General Stephen, 309, 309n643

Lemon, Mark, 422n20

Lessing, Gotthold Ephraim, 10, 10n11

Leverett, William C., 65; and Berkeley Institute, 65n125

Lewes, George Henry, 138n279, 370n794, 380, 440n51, 442–43, 443n57, 444, 444nn59–60, 447, 447n65, 451–53, 453n71, 462, 462n85

Lewes, Thornton, 443, 443n57, 444n59, 445

Lincoln, Abraham, 117n242, 122, 123, 124n254, 197n404, 239, 239n506, 290n594, 291n597, 298n611, 299n615, 306n634, 312–13n655, 313, 337, 337n709, 349n736; death, 320, 320n672, 335, 336nn707–8

Livy (Titus Livius), 10, 10n11

Lockhart, John Gibson, 425, 425n23; and *Blackwood's Magazine*, 425, 425n23

Lodge, David, *Author, Author,* 23n40

Logan, General John A., 309, 309n645

Longfellow, Henry Wadsworth, 57, 57n110, 166n341, 168, 218, 218n447, 333n703

Loring, Katherine, 55n107

Louvre, 49, 49n96, 50, 64, 76n146

Lowell, Anna Cabot Jackson, 301n620

Lowell Sr., Charles Russell, 301n620

Lowell, Brigadier-General Charles Russell, 300, 301, 301n620

Lowell, James Jackson, 300n617

Lowell, James Russell, 57, 57n110, 167n347, 231, 231n484, 236n500, 458–61, 458–59n79, 462n85; "Harvard Commemoration Ode," 300, 300n617; "Palinode: Autumn," 390, 390n836

Lowell, Josephine (Effie) Shaw, 300n617

Lytton, 1st Earl of (Edward Bulwer-Lytton), 219, 219n451; *Pelham,* 219, 219n451

Macaulay, 1st Baron (Thomas Babington Macaulay), 34, 34n66, 139; *Lays of Ancient Rome,* 140n281

Macdaniel, Fanny, 182n374

MacKay [MacKaye], James Morrison, 162n331

MacKaye, Steele, 124n255

Macready, William Charles, 218n448, 221n453

Manet, Édouard, 77, 79n148

Maquelin, Madame, 20

Maquelin, Monsieur (teacher), 20, 20n32

Marceau-Desgraviers, General François-Séverin, 49, 49n97

Martineau, Harriet, 161, 161n328; *Letters on the Laws of Man's Nature and Development* (with H. G. Atkinson), 161, 161n328; *Society in America,* 161, 161n328

Mason, Anne Lyman, 222, 222n457

Mason, Gertrude, 250n521

Mason, Helen, 250n521

Mason, Henry, 250n521

Mason, Herbert, 100, 100n188

Mason, Lydia, 250n521

Mason, Lydia Lush, 250n521

Mason, Serena, 250n521

May, John, 260, 260n536

Mayhew, Charles, 411n5

McClellan, Major-General George, 299, 299n615, 300n617, 349, 349n736

McLellan, H. B., 132n272

McPherson, Major-General James B., 309n645

Melville, Herman, 439n49

Mercer, Dr., and Trinity Church, Newport, 65

Meredith, George, 23, 23n40; *Evan Harrington,* 23, 23n42

Mérimée, Prosper, 74n144, 352; *La Vénus d'Ille,* 74, 74n144

Metcalfe, Dr. John T., 402–3, 402n858

Metternich, Prince Klemens Wenzel von, 267, 267n549

Michelangelo, *The Dying Captive,* 64, 64n122, 76n146

Mill, John Stuart, 138n279, 151, 151n301, 212n440, 444, 444n60

Millais, Sir John Everett, 1st Baronet, 23, 23n40

Millet, Jean François, 51n99, 64n119

Milnes, Richard Monckton. *See* Houghton, 1st Baron

Milton, John, "L'Allegro," 375n809

Mitchell, Maggie (Margaret Julia), 277, 278n569

Moleschott, Jacob, 35n68

Montgomery, Colonel James, 303n626

Moore, George, 340–41n716

Moore, Thomas, 425, 425n23

Morley of Blackburn, 1st Viscount (John Morley), 436n44

Morris, William, 370, 370–71n796; *The Earthly Paradise,* 352, 352n750

Morrison (army commander), 302

Napoleon III, 49n96, 183nn376–77

*Nation,* 131n271, 162n332, 166–67, 166–67n342, 168n351, 185n381, 205n426, 210n435, 233, 233n491, 318n667, 333, 333–34n704, 352, 352n750

National Gallery (London), 434, 434n39

Neuberg, Joseph, 158, 158n321

Newport, RI: in *The American Scene,* 54–55n106; fashionable life, 327–28; Fort Adams, 331, 331–32n700; Lawton's Valley, 329–30, 329n693; mansions, 54n105; pre–Civil War, 245, 245n516; as returning point from Europe, 54–55, 58–59; traditional character, 331–33, 331n697

Nightingale, Florence, 328, 328n691

North Conway, NH, 358, 358n772, 359, 359–60n776

Norton family, 204, 204–5n425, 368n790, 370, 370n793, 418, 418n14, 426n27

Norton, Catharine Eliot, 426n27

Norton, Charles Eliot, 168n351, 170n354, 204n425, 207–8, 207–8n429, 210n435, 318–19, 333, 333n703, 416n11, 429n29, 457n78; and *North American Review,* 318

Norton, Grace, 168n351, 204–5n425, 319n669, 370, 370n794, 440, 440n51

Norton, Jane, 208–9, 208n430, 230

Norton, Susan Sedgwick, 170n354, 204n425, 210n436, 370n794, 371, 371n798; her death, 210, 210n437

Nott, Eliphalet, 90n163

*Once a Week,* 22, 23n40, 23n42, 25, 37, 266, 266n546

Osborne, Louis, 18, 20, 20n31

Osgood, James, 223, 223n459

Page, Walter Hines, 457n78

Paget, Sir James, 444, 444n59, 445–46

Palmerston, 3rd Viscount (Henry John Temple), 183n377

Parker, Joel, 271, 272n560

Parker, Theodore, 150, 150n300

Parsons, Theophilus, 271, 272n560, 273, 274

Pasca, Madame, 347, 347n731

Pascoe, "young," 99, 99n181

Pascoe [Pasco], Mrs. (WJ's landlady), 99, 100

Pater, Walter, *Studies in the History of the Renaissance,* 58n112, 72n136, 76–77n146

Pattison, Mark, 444n61

Peabody, Andrew P., 111, 111n223

Pell-Clarke, Henrietta Temple (wife of Leslie), 62n116, 360n776, 380; at North Conway, 359n776

Pell-Clarke, Leslie, 62n116

Perkins, Charlotte, 362n778

Perkins, Helen Wyckoff, 368n787

Perkins, William E., 300, 301n619, 311

Perry, Lilla Cabot, 87n160, 358n770

Perry, Commodore Matthew Calbraith, 87n160, 111

Perry, Commodore Oliver Hazard, 87n160, 111

Perry, Thomas Sergeant, 5n1, 7n6, 13n16, 14n20, 17n24, 22n39, 28n54, 55n106, 79n149, 80n150, 87, 87n160, 107n215, 109, 110n219, 133n274, 233n491, 236n501, 248n519, 250n521, 283n579, 328n691, 332, 346, 347n730, 353, 358n770

Peters, Mr. (of Philadelphia), 32

Pfeiffer, Charlotte Birch, 278n570

Phillipps, Adelaide, 397, 397n850

Phillips, Wendell, 115, 115n232

Plumley, Miss, 177

Poe, Edgar Allan, 57, 57n110, 291; "The Gold-Bug," 292n598

Pope, Alexander, 107n215

Portsmouth Grove, RI, 248-50, 248-49n519, 252n525

Post, Mary Minturn, 224, 224n463, 402, 402n859, 403

Post, Minturn, 402n859

Potter, Brigadier-General Edward E., 293, 293n602

Probyn, Sir Dighton Macnaghten, 450, 450n68

Probyn, Letitia Maria Thellusson, 450, 450n68

*Punch,* 266, 266n546

Quincy, Henry Parker, 100, 100n187

Rabe, Annie Crawford von, 389, 389n834, 390-91

Rabe, Erich von, 389n834

Rachel [Elizabeth Félix], 10, 11n13

Racine, Jean, 10, 11n13; *Phèdre,* 11, 11n13

Rawle, Mary Cadwalader, 392, 392n842

Reade, Charles, 23, 23n40; *The Cloister and the Hearth,* 23, 23n42; *A Good Fight,* 23, 23n42

Readville, MA, 251, 251n523, 288-89, 290n592

Regnault, Henri, 342n720

Reichardt-Stromberg, Mathilde, 34-35, 35n68

Rembrandt Harmenszoon van Rijn, 435, 435n40

Renan, Ernest, 456, 456n76

Renouvier, Charles, 212, 212n440

*Revue des Deux Mondes,* 47-48, 47n90, 48n93, 60, 60n114, 68-69, 69n131, 73, 73n139, 101, 155, 201, 226, 226n466, 238, 238n503

Ristori, Adelaide, 36, 36n70

Ritchie, Anne Thackeray, 457-58n78, 463n86, 470n97

Ritter, Charles, 22n39, 351, 351n747

Robertson, Thomas William, 433, 433n36; *Society,* 433n36

Robeson, Alice, 115, 115n234

Robeson, Andrew, 103, 103n199

Robespierre, Maximilien de, 48n92

Rogers, Samuel, 425, 425n23; *Table Talk,* 425n23

Ropes, John Codman, 100, 100n187, 384n824

Rose, Charlotte (wife of Sir John), 356n765, 362n778

Rose, Sir John, 356n765, 362n778

Rossetti, Dante Gabriel, 207n429, 371, 371n801

Rossini, Gioacchino, *William Tell,* 397, 397n849

Rousseau, Jean-Jacques, *Confessions,* 268, 268n550

Rousseau, General Lovell H., 307, 307n637

Sherman, William T., 298n610, 302n624, 305n631, 306, 306n634, 307, 309, 310, 310nn646–47, 314n658

Sickles, Daniel, 125, 126n263

Simpkins, William, 251n523

Smollett, Tobias George, 412, 412n7, 431

South Kensington Museum, 436, 436–37n45

Spring, Marcus, 124n255

Stamm, Fräulein, 27, 27n51

Stanton, Edwin M., 336n708

Stearns, Mrs., 178

Stein, Gertrude, 187n384

Stephen, Sir Leslie, 438–39n48

Sterling, John, 149, 149n297, 150, 150nn299–300

Stirling, J. H., 231, 231n484

St. Mivart, George, 231, 231n484

Storrow, Samuel, 311, 311n648

Story, William Wetmore, 333n703, 359n775

Stromberg, Theodor, 24n43, 34, 34n65

Stuart de Rothesay, 1st Baron (Charles Stuart), 467n94

Stuart, Gilbert, 221, 221n454

Sturgis, Howard, 472n100

Sturgis, Russell, 472n100

Sullivan, Sir Arthur, 434, 434n38; *Patience,* 434n38; *Thespis,* 434n38

Sumner, Charles, 166, 166–67n342, 167n347

Susini, Agostino, 397, 397n850

Swedenborg, Emanuel, 128–29, 128n265, 137, 138n279, 139, 139nn280–81, 156n317, 169, 192n394, 202n416, 241n508, 295n603; *Arcana Coelestia,* 128, 128n266; *Heaven and Hell,* 128, 128n266

Sweeney [Sweeny], Charlotte Temple, 362n778

Sweetser, "Ma" (WJ's landlady), 112n224, 114, 115

Sweetser, "Old" (WJ's landlord), 112, 112n224, 115

Swift, Jonathan, 377–78n814

Swinburne, Algernon Charles, 436, 436n44, 455n75; *Atalanta in Calydon,* 436, 436n44; *Poems and Ballads,* 436, 436n44

Talleyrand-Périgord, Charles Maurice de, 267, 267n549

Tappan family, 108, 179, 191n391

Tappan, Caroline Sturgis, 108n216, 171–73, 171–72n355, 172n356, 177n361, 182, 182n374, 183n376, 185n380, 190, 190n388, 191n390, 191–92n393, 199, 200n407; and transcendentalism, 186n382

Tappan, Ellen, 108, 108n216, 113, 177n361, 185n380

Tappan, Mary Aspinwall, 108, 108n216, 113, 177n361, 185n380, 191n390

Tappan, William Aspinwall, 108n216, 176

Taylor, Bayard, 426, 426n26

Taylor, Billy, 213, 214n441, 216–17

Taylor, Dr., 402–3, 402n859

Temple, Catharine (aunt), 59n113

Temple, Clarina Hawkins, 391n839

Temple, Ellen (Ellie). See Emmet, Ellen Temple

Temple, Henrietta. See Pell-Clarke, Henrietta Temple

Temple, Katharine (Kitty). See Emmet, Katharine Temple

Temple, Mary (Minny), 61–63, 61n115, 63n117, 77n146, 95n172, 100n187, 222n457, 249n519, 325n684, 328n690, 354–56, 354–55n760, 356n763, 356n765, 358nn770–71, 359–60n776, 362n778, 364n779, 366n782, 366n784, 369n792, 375n807, 384n823, 385n825, 391–92n840, 392nn841–42, 400n854, 409n3, 410–11n4; Albany background,

Wyckoff, Helen. *See* Perkins, Helen
    Wyckoff
Wyman, Jeffries, 103, 103n203, 123, 125

*Yellow Book, The,* 72n136, 229n474,
    434n38
Young, Mrs. William, 315, 315n662

Zhukovski, Paul, 26n49
Zoffingue [Zofingue], Société de, 14,
    14n19
Zola, Émile, 340n716